M000277096

THE AMERICAN PAST

A Survey of American History

Volume II: Since 1865

NINTH EDITION

Joseph R. Conlin

WADSWORTH
CENGAGE Learning

Australia • Brazil • Japan • Korea • Mexico • Singapore • Spain • United Kingdom • United States

WADSWORTH
CENGAGE Learning

The American Past: A Survey of American History, Volume II: Since 1865, Ninth Edition

Joseph R. Conlin

Senior Publisher: Suzanne Jeans

Senior Sponsoring Editor: Ann West

Assistant Editor: Megan Chrisman

Editorial Assistant: Patrick Roach

Senior Media Editor: Lisa Ciccolo

Senior Marketing Manager: Katherine Bates

Marketing Coordinator: Lorreen Pelletier

Marketing Communications Manager: Caitlin Green

Content Project Management: PreMediaGlobal

Senior Art Director: Cate Rickard Barr

Print Buyer: Sandee Milewski

Rights Acquisition Specialist, Image: Jennifer Meyer Dare

Rights Acquisition Specialist, Text: Katie Huha

Production Service: PreMediaGlobal

Cover Designer: Gary Regaglia, Metro Design

Cover Image: © Bettmann/ CORBIS, *Women Working Lathes*

Compositor: PreMediaGlobal

For product information and technology assistance, contact us at **Cengage Learning Customer & Sales Support, 1-800-354-9706**

For permission to use material from this text or product, submit all requests online at **www.cengage.com/permissions.** Further permissions questions can be emailed to **permissionrequest@cengage.com**

Library of Congress Control Number: 2010939314

ISBN-13: 978-1-111-34340-8

ISBN-10: 1-111-34340-3

Wadsworth
20 Channel Center Street
Boston, MA, 02210
USA

Cengage Learning is a leading provider of customized learning solutions with office locations around the globe, including Singapore, the United Kingdom, Australia, Mexico, Brazil, and Japan. Locate your local office at **international.cengage.com/ region.**

Cengage Learning products are represented in Canada by Nelson Education, Ltd.

For your course and learning solutions, visit **www.cengage.com.**

Purchase any of our products at your local college store or at our preferred online store **www.cengagebrain.com.**

Instructors: Please visit **login.cengage.com** and log in to access instructor-specific resources.

Printed in the United States of America
1 2 3 4 5 6 7 14 13 12 11 10

To the memory of
J.R.C. (1917–1985)
L.V.C. (1920–2001)

Brief Contents

Contents

43

THEIR FINEST HOURS: AMERICANS IN THE SECOND WORLD WAR 1942–1945   832

44

A DIFFERENT KIND OF WORLD: ENTERING THE NUCLEAR AGE, 1946–1952   850

45

"HAPPY DAYS": POPULAR CULTURE IN THE FIFTIES 1947–1963   871

52

Only Yesterday: Politics and the Economy 1993–2009   1008

APPENDIX A

The Declaration of Independence   A-1

APPENDIX B

The Constitution of the United States of America   A-4

List of Maps

Preface

This is the eighth time I have revised *The American Past*. My take on so many of the topics I deal with in the book has undergone such heels over head changes from edition to edition that, thumbing through one of the older versions, I sometimes wonder what in the world I could possibly have been thinking when I dispatched it to the publisher.

In one matter, however, I look at *The American Past* today with precisely the same aspirations with which, almost three decades ago, I typed out the first page of the first chapter of the first edition. My ambition is that *The American Past* be enjoyable as well as educational reading. Like other professors who have taught a United States history survey course for many years, I long ago recognized that a large proportion of my students found it onerous to plow through a textbook on a subject that did not particularly interest them. A majority of survey course students are captives. They are treated better than galley slaves but they are seated at their oars only because American history is a required course or because a section of the survey was the only offering in a time slot they had to fill before their semester schedule was stamped "OK." They are accounting or botany or mathematics or physics majors for whom history has few charms, particularly if their textbook is a dry-as-dust recitation of facts, essential as they are to the course, and full of historical interpretations that only readers already well-schooled in the facts can appreciate.

So, here in the ninth edition, as in the first, I have reminded myself while revising and often writing each page from scratch that my students, with all their innumerable interests and with the tantalizing diversions that surround them on campus and beyond, have to be seduced into reading the book—*simply reading it!*—because it is a pleasant experience to do so—illuminating, interesting, and even, here and there, amusing.

I am too old and battered to worry about a 100 percent success rate. But I am gratified to be able to say that from the start until just a few months ago, I have regularly opened letters from dozens of history instructors who, in addition to criticisms of my take on various topics, added compliments to the effects that "for me, nevertheless, *The American Past* is indispensable. My students actually read it. They take me aside to tell me how much they *like* the book."

That is more than good enough for me. If students are reading *The American Past* and they like it, they must be learning some American history, which is what the survey course and textbooks are all about.

NEW TO THIS EDITION

There is a great deal of material that is brand new to this edition of *The American Past*. I have added fresh corroborative evidence in every chapter and rewritten several lengthy multichapter sections of the book to take into account historians' findings in recently published studies. For example, the wars between colonials and native populations during the eighteenth and early nineteenth centuries, especially the French and Indian War, have attracted the attention of half a dozen perceptive historians since the eighth edition was published. So, I have restructured and written anew large parts of Chapters 6 through 10 to reflect this recent scholarship. There is also a good deal that is conceptually new with this edition about Indians and Indian-settler relations in Chapters 2, 5, and 30. Several chapters have been reorganized so fundamentally that, although they deal with the same topics as the equivalent chapters of the eighth edition, they may be described as "completely re-done": Chapters 5, 6, 7, 13, 17, and, of course, the final two chapters.

I have reorganized the subjects dealt with in Chapters 13 and 14 of the eighth edition in the interests of clearer presentations. Some instructors will want to modify their syllabuses. Chapter 17 includes expanded treatment of religious beliefs and the Protestant denominations during the early nineteenth century. I have combined the material in the eighth edition Chapters 18 and 19 (slavery and the South) into a single chapter in this edition—Chapter 18. As a result, the chapter enumeration from Chapter 19 to Chapter 47 differs from that in the previous edition. The equivalent of Chapter 20 in the eighth edition (American Expansion 1920–1848) is, in this edition, Chapter 19 and so on through Chapter 46.

The accounts of the War with Mexico (Chapter 19) and of the Irish famine immigrants of the 1840s and 1850s, and the Know Nothing movement that rose in response to them have been redone. I have moved my discussion of urban political machines from Chapter 26 (late nineteenth century politics) to Chapter 29 (urban America). I have expanded the discussion of urban development in the late nineteenth century (Chapter 29), adding new anecdotal and statistical evidence as well as insights new to me. I have recast coverage of American interventionism in the Caribbean and Central America based on recent scholarship (Chapters 34 and 35). Financial booms and busts of the early twenty-first century provided the inspiration to re-do my discussions of the land speculations of the early nineteenth century and the Florida land boom and Coolidge Bull Market of the 1920s (Chapters 14, 38, and 39).

Chapter 47 is new; there was no equivalent in the eighth edition. Chapter 47 brings together the story of race in twentieth-century America and the African American struggle for equality that culminated in the civil rights movement of the 1950s and 1960s.

The eighth edition Chapter 51 (1992–present) has been divided into two topically organized chapters. The revised Chapter 51 deals with the social and cultural history of the final third of the twentieth century, including an almost entirely new discussion of late twentieth-century religion. Chapter 52 treats political and economic history from 1992 to 2009.

In addition, ten of the popular "How They Lived" features are new to this edition (Chapters 1, 12, 14, 19, 21, 23, 25, 32, 33, and 35).

Acknowledgements

I will list those persons to whom I owe thanks for the contributions they made to this book in the order that I contracted my debts to them.

One's first task in revising a textbook is to review criticisms of the previous edition. The reviewers this time around were particularly helpful. I have not agreed with every one of their criticisms. In some cases limitations of space prevented me from fully responding to some suggestions for improvement with which I was in agreement. In most instances, however, I adjusted the discussion according to their advice, and I am grateful for every suggestion provided by the professors of history who gave parts of the book a close once-over.

List of Reviewers

- Caroline Barton, *Holmes Community College*
- B. R. Burg, *Arizona State University*
- Richard A. Dobbs, *Gadsden State Community College*
- David Long, *East Carolina University*
- Karen Markoe, *SUNY Maritime College*
- James Mills, *University of Texas—Brownsville*
- Lex Renda, *University of Wisconsin—Milwaukee*
- Delilah Ryan, *West Virginia Northern Community College*
- Scott E. White, *Scottsdale Community College*
- Mark R. Wilson, *University of North Carolina—Charlotte*

Task number two, of course, was a chapter by chapter, page by page rewrite, which meant researching problems the reviewers pointed out or were obvious to me after several years away from the book.

Every day revising *The American Past* generated up to a dozen questions of fact that needed confirmation and every week the titles of up to a dozen books I needed to read or re-read. Occasionally I needed to consult hard-to-find books and for this I had the astonishingly good fortune to be acquainted with librarian Susan M. Kling of Bandon, Oregon. Ms. Kling cheerfully designed and administered a massive interlibrary loan operation that put hundreds of titles on my desk at no more inconvenience to me than typing out lists for her. I am grateful beyond graceful expression.

For the fourth time, Wadsworth/Cengage Learning assigned Margaret McAndrew Beasley as the Developmental Editor for this text. She conveyed Wadsworth's guidelines to me, selected reviewers for every chapter, provided useful wrap-ups of the reviewer comments, and—much appreciated—communicated with me, sometimes several times daily to resolve questions as they came up, thus avoiding traffic jams further on. I have long since come to think of Margaret's efficiency as just normal which, when I think about it a bit, I know is singular indeed. There cannot be many people in the business as good at her job as she is. After doing four revisions of the book under her guidance and supervision, I am still astonished by her calm and courteous demeanor as well as by her fine suggestions for improvement throughout the process.

After Margaret Beasley's review, my material was put into the hands of Lauren Wheelock, Content Project Manager. Lauren ably oversaw and coordinated the many hands responsible for milling my ruminations into a big, handsome book while keeping the entire project on schedule. Project Manager Teresa Christie of Macmillan Publishing Solutions saw *The American Past* through copyediting, proofreading, design, art, map making, composition, and indexing. Martha Williams fixed up my worst sentences; Heather Mann did the proofreading.

I worked directly with Catherine Schnurr, photo researcher with Pre-Press PMG. Catherine is a master of pictorial resources. Repeatedly she found illustrations that I did not believe existed but asked for them anyway. And in most cases, Ms. Schnurr gave me a choice of two or more illustrations of subjects I thought would be beyond graphic depiction.

Assistant Editor Megan Curry has managed the team of supplements authors to make sure that each of the ancillaries accompanying this text stays true to the approach and revised content in *The American Past.*

AND A WORD TO STUDENTS ...

This is a textbook history of the United States written for you—many of you may be women and men just setting out on your college educations.

"Textbook" means that the author is careful to stick close to the tried and true essentials—to sidestep the slippery spots on the trail where the specifics are uncertain and it is too easy for everyone to take a spill.

"History" means that our subject is the people and events of the past that have made us what we are today. Not just "the facts." They are usually easy. What happened to our country at Pearl Harbor, Hawaii, on December 7, 1941, is well known and easily documented. The facts do not change. But in retelling them, historians discover new ways in which American society was changed by the Japanese attack that day. The facts remain the same. History changes all the time.

History changes when documents believed to be lost forever turn up, sometimes in dusty corners of farmhouse attics. (It really does happen.) Or, documents we never knew existed are discovered, sometimes in the archives where they belonged, but on the wrong shelf. The diaries of important men and women that were legally sealed for thirty or forty years by the terms of their wills are opened. Governments release memoranda that had been stamped "Top Secret." With fresh sources like these, historians quite often change their own and our collective understanding of past events.

History can change when documents long in full view but indecipherable are suddenly comprehensible. Just since the first edition of *The American Past* was published, scholars who, for a century, had scratched their heads in bewilderment at the carvings on ruined Maya temples in Central America decoded what were also hieroglyphics. Almost in an instant they were able to draw a new portrait of the Maya civilization that was quite at odds with what they had previously suspected (and had been describing in textbooks like this one).

New technologies can also change history. The computer's capacity to crunch huge numbers meant that data that had been too vast for historians to do much with (for example, the handwritten reports that armies of census takers turned into the Census Bureau every ten years) became founts of a rich social history that, before the Cyber Age, was unimaginable. Moldering baptismal and marriage registries in thousands of churches became historical goldmines.

Fresh perspectives, new vantages from which to look at past events, have changed history. In the second half of the twentieth century, demands for better treatment by African Americans, Native Americans, Mexican Americans, women, and other groups with special interests led not only to political and social reforms, but also to research in African American history, American Indian history, and so on from the perspective of those groups. Environmental history, a rich and imaginative field of study today, came into being quite recently as a side effect of the recognition that our own environment has problems.

Finally, individual historians of genius change history when, poring over documents that hundreds of people had read before them, see something that none of their predecessors had noticed or thought much of. It does not happen often, but every now and then there comes along a book that, written from long familiar sources, without employing any new technology, and inspired by nothing outside the historian's mind, is so compelling in its insights that history—our understanding of the past—is radically changed.

Because American history is constantly changing, textbooks like this one must be revised every three or so years.

All of this is old hat to research historians, to history instructors, and to graduate students. I have run through it here because *The American Past* has not been revised for them, but for first- and second-year college and university students who, happily or under duress, are enrolled in a United States history survey course. *The American Past* is written for men and women who are majoring in accounting, botany, mathematics, psychology, zoology, or any of five dozen other fields. The idea that history is eternally in flux may be an idea new to them.

My goal, through nine editions now, has been to produce and improve a book that, even for reluctant readers, will be a pleasure to read. It has made my day (on quite a few days) when I open a letter or an e-mail from a history instructor that says, "my students really like your book." That is my purpose and, of course, to present the history of the United States as I have understood it at a moment in time not too long before your instructor's first lecture.

ONLINE AND INSTRUCTOR RESOURCES

Instructor's Manual with Test Bank. Prepared by Stephen Armes, this manual has many features, including chapter outlines, chapter summaries, suggested lecture topics, and discussion questions, maps, and artwork as well as the documents in the text. World Wide Web sites and resources, video collections, a Resource Integration Guide, and suggested student activities are also included. Exam questions include essays, true-false, identifications, and multiple-choice questions.

PowerLecture. This resource includes the Instructor's Manual, Resource Integration Grid, ExamView testing, and PowerPoint slides with lecture outlines and images that can be used as offered or customized by importing personal lecture slides or other material. ExamView allows instructors to create, deliver, and customize tests and study guides (both print and online) in minutes via an easy-to-use assessment and tutorial system. Instructors can build tests with as many as 250 questions using up to twelve question types. Using ExamView's complete word processing capabilities, they can enter an unlimited number of new questions or edit existing ones.

Wadsworth American History Resource Center. Organized chronologically with a user-friendly time line navigation bar, this Web site acts as a primary source e-reader with more than 350 primary source documents. It also includes time lines, photos, interactive maps, exercises, and numerous other materials you can assign in class. Contact your representative for information about providing your students with access to this resource.

Book Companion Web site. The Book Companion Web site includes learning objectives, tutorial quizzes, essay questions, Internet activities, and glossary flashcards for each text chapter to support what students read about in the book and learn in class. Students, to access these course materials, please visit www.cengagebrain.com. At the CengageBrain.com home page, search for the ISBN of your title (from the back cover of your book) using the search box at the top of the page. This will take you to the product page where these resources can be found. Instructors, please visit http://login.cengage.com.

24

AFTERMATH

The Era of Reconstruction 1863–1877

*You say you have emancipated us. You have; and I thank
you for it. But what is your emancipation?.... When you
turned us loose, you gave us no acres. You turned us loose
to the skies, to the storm, to the whirlwind, and, worst of
all, you turned us loose to the wrath of our infuriated
masters.*

—Frederick Douglass

When the guns fell silent in 1865, some southern cities were flattened. Vicksburg, Atlanta, Columbia, and Richmond were eerie wastelands of charred timbers, rubble, and freestanding chimneys. Few of the South's railroads were operating for more than a dozen miles. Bridges were gone wherever armies had passed. River commerce had dwindled to a trickle. The only new boats on the Mississippi were from the North. The South's commercial ties with Europe had been snapped. All the South's banks, having long since redeemed worthless paper money with gold and silver, were ruined.

Even the cultivation of the soil had been disrupted. By the thousands, the small farms of the men who served in the ranks were overgrown in weeds and brambles. Plantations were abandoned. An Indiana soldier, stationed in central Louisiana where there had been little fighting, wrote that "You could travel for miles and not see cotton, corn, or produce, except peaches.... A few of the inhabitants had returned from the rebel army, but the darkies were gone, and there was no one to work the farms."

THE RECONSTRUCTION CRISIS

Looking back at the desolation, *reconstruction* seems the appropriate word for the postwar era. However, as the term was used at the time, "Reconstruction" had nothing to do with laying bricks, rehabilitating railroads, or recovering fields. Reconstruction referred to the political process by which the eleven rebel states were

Reconstruction 1863–1877

1863	1865	1867	1869	1871	1873	1875	1877

1863 Lincoln's plan for reconstruction

1864 Wade-Davis Bill

1865–1869 Andrew Johnson president

1865–1866 Southern states enact "black codes"

1866 Johnson vetoes Freedman's Bill; radicals propose Fourteenth Amendment; radicals win large majority in Congress

1867 Radical Reconstruction begins

1868 Johnson impeached

Ulysses S. Grant president 1869–1877

1870–1872 Army suppresses Ku Klux Klan

1872 Liberal Republicans ally with Democrats

Disputed election 1876

Troops withdrawn from South 1877

restored to "a normal constitutional relationship" with the federal government. It was the Union, that great abstraction over which so many had died, that was rebuilt.

Blood was shed during the Reconstruction era too, but little glory was won. Few political reputations—northern, southern, white, black, Republican, Democratic—emerged from the era unstained. It may be that Abraham Lincoln is a sainted figure only because he did not survive the war. The reconstruction process Lincoln proposed in 1863 was rejected by Congress. Had he survived and pushed it, he would have had a nasty fight on his hands. His successor, Andrew Johnson, did just that, and Congress and the majority of northern voters repudiated him.

Lincoln's Plan   By December 1863, Union armies occupied large chunks of the Confederacy. Ultimate victory, while not yet in the bag, was a reasonable expectation. To provide for the rapid reconciliation of North and South—Lincoln's postwar priority—the president proclaimed that as soon as 10 percent of the eligible voters in a former Confederate state took an oath of allegiance to the Union, the people of that state could write a new state constitution, organize a state government, and elect representatives to Congress. Three southern states that were mostly occupied—Tennessee, Arkansas, and Louisiana—immediately complied.

Congressional Republicans refused to recognize them as states of the Union and restored them to military control. Many Republicans (and, of course, Democrats) had long been alarmed by Lincoln's expansion of presidential powers. Not even Andrew Jackson had effected policies by executive proclamation or played free and easy with the ancient personal protection of *habeas corpus* to the extent Lincoln did.

With the survival of the Union at stake, Republican congressmen swallowed their anxieties. But reconstruction was a postwar issue, and Lincoln's plan did not involve Congress, except to call for the election of senators and representatives in

National Archives

Richmond in ruins, more from fire than from bombardment. Atlanta looked worse. The Shenandoah Valley and northeastern Georgia were laid waste. Even areas of the South untouched by war were impoverished, dwellings and fields neglected.

reconstructed states. Congress was keenly sensitive to its right to assess the credentials of those who showed up at the capital claiming to have been duly elected. After four years when Alabama, Texas, and the other rebel states had sent no representatives to Congress, Congress had the authority to determine how and when they could do so.

The Wade-Davis Bill   Only a minority of the Republicans in Congress called themselves radicals. But the radicals were militant and persuasive with the others, and they had reasons in addition to the credentials issue to reject Lincoln's proposal. Many radicals were former abolitionists who blamed the slavocracy, the South's great planters, for causing the terrible war. They were determined that the slavocrats be punished and destroyed as a class so that the reconstructed states were free of their domination. The only way to ensure this, the radicals concluded, was to see to it that the freedmen, as the emancipated slaves were called, participated in southern state governments.

So, in July 1864, Congress enacted the Wade-Davis Bill as an alternative to Lincoln's plan. It provided that only after *50 percent* of the eligible voters of a former Confederate state swore the oath of loyalty could the reconstruction process begin. Congress—not the president—would supervise the oath taking and approve or disapprove of the state constitutions the southern states wrote. The Wade-Davis bill did not detail the reconstruction process beyond that point. Aware that Lincoln would veto it, the radicals enacted it in order to slow down things that Lincoln was trying to rush through.

Lincoln killed the Wade-Davis Bill with a pocket veto, which did not require him to explain his reasons for rejecting it in a veto message. During the final months of his life, he dropped hints that he was willing to work out a compromise with Congress. He even reached out to the radicals (whom he had never much liked) by saying that he had no objection to giving the vote to blacks who were "very intelligent and those who have fought gallantly in our ranks." He urged the military governor of Louisiana to extend the suffrage to some blacks. And there things stood when John Wilkes Booth sent events on an unforeseen course.

Lincoln's Goals Why did Lincoln dodge radical demands that the freedmen be granted civil rights equal to those of whites? Mainly because his priority was the reconciliation of northern and southern whites. He made his intention eloquently clear in his second inaugural address a few weeks before he was shot. "With malice toward none, with charity for all, ... let us strive on to finish the work we are in, to bind up the nation's wounds, ... to do all which may achieve and cherish a just and lasting peace among ourselves."

For Lincoln, the interests of African Americans were at best secondary to the interests of whites. If white southern refusal to accept the freedmen as their equals stood in the way of reconciliation—and common sense said that it would—Lincoln was willing to give way. Radical Senator Ben Wade said that Lincoln's views on black people "could only come of one who was born of poor white trash and educated in a slave state." This was as unfair as it was ugly. Lincoln's racism was passive. In finding African Americans unacceptable company and morally and intellectually inferior to whites, he was expressing the views not just of southern white trash, but of a large majority of white northerners.

There is reason to believe that Lincoln's views on race had changed during the war. He admitted being surprised and impressed by the bravery and loyalty of African American soldiers. Lincoln had always been a flexible politician, willing to bargain. "Saying that reconstruction will be accepted if presented in a specified way," he announced, "it is not said that it will never be accepted in any other way." He was telling the radicals that nothing about the reconstruction procedure and the future status of the freedmen was final.

Stubborn Andrew Johnson After April 15, 1865, it did not matter what Lincoln thought; and Andrew Johnson was not the flexible politician Lincoln had been. Nor had his "white trash" views on race undergone any changes during the war.

Johnson grew up in stultifying poverty in Tennessee. Unlike Lincoln, who taught himself to read as a boy, Johnson was an illiterate adult when he asked a schoolteacher in Greenville to teach him how to read and write. She did, then married him, and encouraged her husband to go into politics. Johnson won elective office on every level from town councilman to congressman to senator. He had owned a few slaves during his life, but he hated the secessionist cotton planters of western Tennessee. He was the only southerner to refuse to walk out of the Senate in 1861. He called for a ruthless war on the rebellion and harsh punishment of Confederate leaders, including the gallows for Jefferson Davis and other top officials. Lincoln appointed him governor of occupied Tennessee and chose him to run for vice president in 1864 in the hope of winning the votes of other southern Unionists.

Johnson's political experience was extensive, but his personality was ill-suited to Washington politics. Where Lincoln understood what he could do and what he could not accomplish, Johnson was principled, willful, and stubborn. It did him no good to have had virtually dictatorial powers as military governor of Tennessee. He got off to a bad start as vice president. Suffering from a bad cold on inauguration day, he bolted several glasses of brandy for a pick-me-up and was visibly drunk when he took the oath of office. Fortunately, only a few people were present and Lincoln told aides to keep Johnson under tight control at the public ceremony outside the Capitol.

Johnson was not, in fact, a "problem drinker." His behavior on inauguration day was a fluke and nothing was made of it at the time. The likeliest people to

President Andrew Johnson. He was a man of integrity, but inflexible and, despite his hatred of secessionists, hostile to every suggestion that the freedmen be granted civil equality.

jump on the southern vice president, the radicals, rather liked Johnson for wanting to hang Jeff Davis and because as governor of Tennessee he had approved the confiscation of some rebel estates.

But the radicals misread Johnson's anti-Confederate ardor. Emancipation pleased him not because he thought slavery wicked—the well-being of African Americans did not interest him—but because emancipation destroyed the wealth and power of the slavocrats.

Johnson: They Are Already States
Johnson adopted Lincoln's reconstruction policy with minor changes. However, the chief point of friction with Congress—presidential supervision of the process of restoring the rebel states to the Union—remained unchanged.

Johnson had sound constitutional reasons for saying that the reconstruction of the Union was an administrative matter and, therefore, the responsibility of the executive branch of the government. Constitutionally, the Union *could not* be dissolved; states *could not* secede. There had indeed been a rebellion and an entity called the Confederate States of America. However, Johnson said, individuals had rebelled; people—traitors—had taken up arms against the United States and created the Confederacy. The *states* of Virginia, Alabama, and the rest had not seceded. The contention that the states were sovereign components of a federation was Calhounism, contradicted by the Preamble of the Constitution, the Marshall Court, Andrew Jackson, Henry Clay, and the eloquence of Daniel Webster in his famous debate with Robert Hayne. During the crisis of 1861, almost every northerner, Democrats as well as Republicans, not to mention southern Unionists, had rejected secession as unconstitutional.

What had been true in 1861 was true in 1865. Virginia, Alabama, and the rest had never ceased to be states. Therefore, there was no call for congressional legislation to return them to their normal place in the Union. Indeed, for Congress to interfere in any way would be an unconstitutional violation of the southern states' legitimate rights.

An Unpopular Policy
Lincoln had worried about the reconstruction debate centering on a "pernicious abstraction." "Pernicious" and "abstract" were precisely how congressional Republicans and most Republican newspaper editors saw Johnson's justification of his policy. The nation was just emerging from four years of a terrible war forced on the North by the slavocracy in which 360,000 northern boys had died in order to defeat them. Many more were maimed for life. When, under Johnson's rules, southern voters sent four Confederate generals, six members of Jefferson Davis's cabinet, and the Confederate vice president to Congress, it was as if nothing had happened between 1861 and 1865. The same old southern leaders—traitors all—were back.

They and a great many other military officers and civil officials had been pardoned for the asking. Before the end of 1865, President Johnson signed pardons for 13,000 Confederates, restoring their civil rights. (That was a rate of 2,000 per month!) What was Johnson thinking? Lincolnian reconciliation required the goodwill of northerners too.

Southern legislatures established under the Johnson plan enacted "black codes," comprehensive laws governing the freedmen that, to some northerners seemed to return them to slavery in all but name. Indeed, Mississippi refused to ratify the Thirteenth Amendment; Alabama rejected part of it. In South Carolina, Robert Rhett frankly said that blacks should "be kept as near to the condition of slavery as possible, and as far from the condition of the white man as is practicable."

Some states made it illegal for African Americans to live in towns and cities, a backhanded way of keeping them in the fields. In no southern state were blacks permitted to own firearms. South Carolina's code said that African Americans could not sell goods! Mississippi required freedmen to sign twelve-month labor contracts before January 10 of each year. Those who failed to do so could be arrested and their labor for the year sold to the highest bidder, the slave trade in annual installments. Blacks who reneged on labor contracts were not to be paid for the work that they had already performed. Mississippi made it a crime for an African American to "insult" a white person.

Not that northern whites believed in racial equality. They did not. When the war ended, only six of the loyal states allowed African American men to vote. Between 1865 and 1867, six more states held referenda on the question of black suffrage. The voters in all six rejected it. In 1866, the same Congress that approved a constitutional amendment granting equal civil rights to blacks segregated schools in the District of Columbia by race.

The Radicals: The States Have Forfeited Their Rights   The radical Republicans feared that, despite the widespread hostility in the North to southern actions, racial prejudice would enable Johnson to have his way. They countered Johnson's compelling constitutional argument with several justifications to keeping the former rebel states out of the Union until some needed changes were made.

Thaddeus Stevens of Pennsylvania, the radical leader in the House of Representatives, said that the Confederate states had committed "state suicide" when they seceded. They were not, in 1865, alive. Therefore, it was within the purview of Congress to determine when they were satisfactorily reborn.

Charles Sumner, a prominent Senate radical, said that the former southern states were "conquered provinces." Their constitutional status was identical to that of the western territories. Congress (not the president) would admit them as states when Congress approved of the state constitutions they wrote. Another Republican, Samuel Shellabarger of Ohio, came up with language that was more agreeable to moderate Republicans who were sitting on the fence: When the rebel states seceded, they "forfeited" the rights reserved to the states by the Constitution.

Congress's Joint Committee on Reconstruction settled on a plausible formula: "The States lately in rebellion were, at the close of the war, disorganized communities, without civil government and without constitutions or other forms, by virtue of which political relations could legally exist between them and the federal government." This provided all but a few Republicans loyal to Johnson with grounds for refusing to seat the southerners who came to Washington as the elected representatives of their states.

Radical Goals
and Motives
The radicals were motivated by ideals, passions, and hard-headed politics. Many of them had been abolitionists, morally repelled by the institution of slavery. Thaddeus Stevens, Ben Wade, Charles Sumner, and others believed in racial equality and were determined that, if they could carry the day, African Americans would enjoy full civil rights. Stevens, Wade, and George W. Julian hated the slavocracy with a seething passion they did not conceal.

The planters' power had been maimed by the abolition of slavery, but they still owned the land. Julian proposed to confiscate the estates of planters who had been active Confederates, high ranking army officers, and government officials. He had a good precedent to which to point, the confiscation of Loyalist estates after the War for Independence. Not only would confiscation punish rebels and destroy their economic power, by dividing the plantations into 40-acre farms to be granted to the freedmen, the government would give southern blacks the economic independence that, in the Jeffersonian tradition, was essential to good citizenship.

The radicals had frankly partisan motives too. The Republican party was a sectional party. If the party did not establish itself in the South, it was doomed to be defeated at the polls. The party's political prospects going into the congressional elections of 1866 were worse than they had been in 1860. With slavery gone, the number of southern congressmen would actually increase. Where, formerly, slave states had counted three-fifths of the slaves in calculating the size of their congressional delegations, they were now entitled to count the entire population at face value. There would be more Democrats in Congress after 1866 than there had been in 1861, and the South would have more electoral votes, all destined to be Democratic, in the presidential election of 1868—if Johnson's reconstructed state governments were allowed to stand.

There were white southerners likely to vote Republican: old Whig nationalists who had sat out the war and farmers in the mountain counties of Kentucky, Tennessee, Virginia, and North Carolina. Many of them had fought in Union armies and they no more wanted to see the secessionist Democrats return to power than the radicals did. But white Republicans were a minority in every southern state, a tiny minority in the deep South. If the party was to compete with the Democrats in the former Confederacy, it was necessary to ensure that the freedmen voted. Thaddeus Stevens did not ask moderate Republicans to advocate African American suffrage in the North. But if southern blacks did not vote, he argued, the Republican party was a dead duck and all Republican policies, such as the protective tariff, things of the past. "I am for negro suffrage in every rebel state," he told Congress, "If it be just, it should not be denied; if it be necessary, it should be adopted; if it be a punishment to traitors, they deserve it."

1866: THE CRITICAL YEAR

Stevens and the radicals trod carefully with the moderate Republicans. The congressional radicals were a minority of the party. If they were to affect their programs, they had to win over those Republicans who hesitated about granting full citizenship to the freedmen.

President Johnson played into the radicals' hands. He pushed the Republican moderates into cooperating with the radicals when he tried to destroy a federal agency that had averted mass starvation in the South and was still, in 1866, helping to prevent social chaos there.

The Freedmen's Bureau   The former slaves responded to emancipation in different ways. Some, who were bewildered or who had been treated well by their masters, stayed where they were. Promised wages when their cash-strapped masters found money, they worked on in the fields as they always had (minus the blacksnake whip). Others took to the roads, testing their freedom by going where they pleased. They heard rumors that every freed family would be granted "40 acres and a mule," and searched for the Union officer who would give them their farm. The wanderers gathered in ramshackle camps that were often disorderly and inevitably short of food. Discharged Confederate soldiers, trudging sometimes hundreds of miles toward their homes, also had difficulty finding enough to eat.

Fortunately, Congress had foreseen both problems. In March 1865—before Appomattox and Lincoln's assassination—Congress established the Bureau of Refugees, Freedmen, and Abandoned Land. General O.O. Howard was named to head what was commonly called the Freedmen's Bureau.

Howard's most pressing task was relief: avoiding starvation. In 1865, the Freedman's Bureau distributed rations to 150,000 people each day, about a third of them whites, ex-soldiers and their families. When Congress decided against confiscating lands on a large scale, bureau employees negotiated labor contracts between destitute former slaves and land owners. Because there was little coin in the South and southern bank notes were worthless, the bureau resorted to sharecropping arrangements. In return for the use of a farm and a cabin, the sharecropper (white as well as black) gave his landlord a third of the crop at harvest time.

The Freedmen's Bureau also set up medical facilities for the inevitable health problems. (Again, whites were served as well as freedmen.) Ultimately the bureau built and staffed forty-six hospitals and treated more than 400,000 cases of illness and injury.

The most popular bureau program with the freedmen was its school system. Freedom released a craving for education among blacks, adults as well as children. Appleton and Company, a publishing house, sold a million copies annually of Noah Webster's *Elementary Spelling Book*—the "Blue-Backed Speller" from which American schoolchildren learned to read—for forty years. Except in 1866, when sales jumped to 1.5 million; the 50 percent increase was due to sales to the Freedmen's Bureau. Teachers from the North, mostly white and mostly women, opened multigrade "one-room schoolhouses" throughout the South. Many of them later reminisced that never before or after had they had such dedicated pupils.

Open Conflict   In 1865, Congress had given the Freedmen's Bureau a year to do its job. The assumption was that, by then, reconstructed state governments would take over its schools, hospitals, and other functions.

In February 1866, however, Reconstruction had not begun. Congress refused to recognize Johnson's state governments but had created none itself. The South was still occupied territory. So Congress extended the life of the Freedman's Bureau for two years.

Johnson vetoed the bill, insisting that the former rebel states had constitutional governments. A month later, he vetoed another bill that granted citizenship to the freedmen. The Constitution, he said, gave the states the power to decide on the terms of citizenship within their borders. Once again he had the better constitutional argument and he might have won the political contest had northerners not been appalled by mob attacks on freedmen in several southern cities, including New Orleans.

In June 1866, perceiving a shift in mood in their favor, radical Republicans, now joined by the moderates, drew up a constitutional amendment on which to base Congress's reconstruction plan (and to answer Johnson's point about citizenship). The long and complex Fourteenth Amendment banned from federal and state office all high-ranking Confederates unless they were pardoned *by Congress*. The amendment also established, for the first time, *national* citizenship which states could not modify. It guaranteed that all "citizens of the United States and of the State wherein they reside" were to be treated equally. If ratified, the Fourteenth Amendment would prevent the southern states from passing laws applicable only to African Americans—like the black codes.

The Republicans were taking a big chance. The Fourteenth Amendment would also cancel northern state laws that discriminated against blacks. In that, Johnson saw his opportunity. He calculated that a majority of northern voters, particularly in the Midwest, would rather have ex-Confederates in Washington than accept African American equality at home. He decided to campaign personally in the midterm elections of 1866 for congressional candidates who supported him and opposed the radicals.

The Radical Triumph   Northern Democrats supported Johnson's reconstruction policy, but the Democratic party had withered to near impotence by the end of the war; in 1866, only 42 of 191 representatives were Democratic, only 10 of 52 Senators. Johnson's hopes of success depended on the support of anti-radical Republicans like Secretary of State Seward and an uncertain number of fence-sitting senators, representatives, and governors. They persuaded friendly Democrats to join them in the "National Union party," the name under which Lincoln had been elected in 1864.

The message of the "party"—actually a makeshift coalition—was sectional reconciliation. To symbolize its ideal, the National Union convention opened with a procession of pairs, a northerner and southerner in each, marching arm in arm into the auditorium. Things went wrong from the start. The first couple in the procession was South Carolina Governor James L. Orr, a huge, fleshy man, and Massachusetts Governor, John A. Andrew, a little fellow with a way of looking intimidated. When Orr seemed to drag the mousy Andrew along, Radical newspapers had a field day: the National Union party was a front for the rebels Johnson had pardoned wholesale.

Johnson's speaking tour in the Midwest, his "swing around the circle," consummated the disaster. One after another, he delivered blistering speeches denouncing the radicals, some in halls, others where a crowd had gathered near the railroad. No president had ever politicked personally in such a manner. Republican newspapers shook their heads sadly at Johnson's lack of dignity. To make things worse, Johnson had learned his oratorical technique in the rough-and-tumble, grass-roots politics of eastern Tennessee where mountaineers liked to hear candidates scorching each other and trading gibes with hecklers. When it was the president of the United States snapping vulgarly at the bait radicals waved in front of him, the saltiest farmers were taken aback. Drunk again, radical editors surmised, rehashing the story of Johnson's inauguration as vice president.

The result was a radical landslide. Most of Johnson's candidates were defeated. The Republican party, now led by the radicals, won nearly three-fourths of the seats in the House, a dozen more than the two-thirds needed to override every veto Johnson threw at them. (Four out of five senators were Republican.)

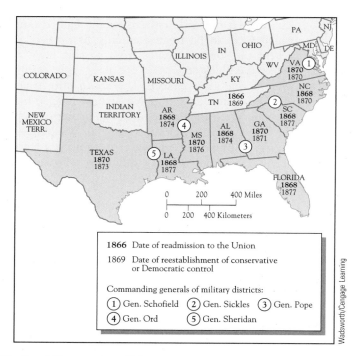

MAP 24.1 Radical Reconstruction

The radicals partitioned the Confederacy into five military districts of manageable size. The Union army supervised the establishment of state governments that guaranteed equal civil rights to freedmen whence each state was readmitted to the Union (with Republican governments). Tennessee was not included in the program. Occupied for much of the war by the Union army, Tennessee had a reconstructed state government by 1866 thanks, ironically, to its wartime governor, Andrew Johnson who, as president, opposed radical Reconstruction in the other southern states.

RADICAL RECONSTRUCTION

The lopsided Fortieth Congress dissolved the southern state governments Johnson had recognized. Except for Tennessee, which had already been readmitted to the Union (with a Republican government), the former Confederacy was divided into five military provinces, each commanded by a major general. The army would maintain order and register voters from among blacks and those whites who had not been disenfranchised. The state conventions these voters elected were required to ratify the Thirteenth and Fourteenth Amendments and to guarantee the vote to adult black males. After Congress approved their constitutions, the reconstructed states would be admitted to the Union and elect representatives to Congress.

Radicals in Control   In 1868, as a result of a large freedman vote, six more states were readmitted. Alabama, Arkansas, Florida, Louisiana, North Carolina, and South Carolina all sent Republican delegations, including some black congressmen, to Washington. In the remaining four states—Georgia, Mississippi, Texas, and Virginia—whites obstructed every attempt to set up a government in which blacks participated. The army continued to govern them until 1870.

Johnson vetoed every radical reconstruction bill, repeating his constitutional objections in every message, then watched helplessly as his veto was overridden.

Congress even took partial control of the army away from him and struck at the president's control of his own cabinet officers. The Tenure of Office Act forbade the president to remove any appointed official who had been confirmed by the Senate without the Senate's approval of his dismissal.

It was obvious what was coming. The radicals wanted Johnson to violate the Tenure of Office Act so that they could impeach him. In part because of his constitutional scruples, in part because Secretary of War Stanton had openly thrown in with the radicals—an intolerable disloyalty—he fired Stanton in February 1868. Although Johnson's term had only a year to run, the now vindictive radicals in the House of Representatives drew up articles of impeachment. As provided in the Constitution, the Senate sat as the jury in the case; Chief Justice Salmon B. Chase presided as judge. Conviction, removal of Johnson from office, required two-thirds of the senators.

The Impeachment Trial   All but two of the eleven articles of impeachment dealt with the Tenure of Office Act. Johnson's attorneys argued that even if the law was constitutional, which was dubious, it did not apply to Johnson's dismissal of Stanton because Johnson had not appointed him to office. Lincoln had. It was a good argument, quite enough to carry the day had the issue been legal rather than political.

The other two articles condemned Johnson for disrespect of Congress, which was silly. Johnson had disrespected Congress alright but, as the president's defenders pointed out, intemperate language did not constitute one of the "high crimes and misdemeanors" stipulated as grounds for impeachment.

The radicals needed thirty-six votes to oust Johnson; if more than eighteen senators voted to acquit him, the impeachment failed. The tally was 35 to 19. Johnson remained president by a single vote.

Actually, it was not that close. The radicals' case was so flimsy that at least six Republican senators who voted to convict in order to save their political careers had said that if their vote was needed to acquit the president, they would vote for him. Events proved they were prudent to vote their careers rather than their consciences. The Republican senator from Kansas who provided Johnson's margin of victory was read out of the party and defeated when he ran for reelection.

The Fifteenth Amendment

In November 1868, the Democratic presidential candidate was New York Governor Horatio Seymour, who had supported the war but been harshly critical of Lincoln. The Republican candidate was Ulysses S. Grant. Grant won easily in the electoral college, 214 to 80. However, close examination of the popular vote indicated that Grant had won several states by a hair. In fact, it appeared that a majority of white voters preferred Seymour; Grant's national plurality was 300,000; he won 500,000 black votes in the southern states.

Grant lost New York by a slender margin. Had all blacks been able to vote in New York (some could, under special circumstances), Grant would have carried the state easily. Grant won Indiana by a handful of votes; had African Americans been able to vote in Indiana (they were not), Grant would have won the state in a landslide.

Thaddeus Stevens had argued in 1865 that the Republican party's future depended on the freedmen voting in the southern states. The election of 1868 indicated that the party's edge in some northern states depended on black men voting there.

Consequently, the Republicans drafted a third "Civil War Amendment." The Fifteenth Amendment forbade states to deny the vote to any person on the basis of "race, color, or previous condition of servitude." Because Republican governments favorable to blacks still controlled most of the southern states, the amendment was easily ratified.

Grant, Race, and the South

U.S. Grant was a close-mouthed man. He was sociable; he liked company and chatting. Except on subjects in which he was expert, however, he expressed few opinions that have survived. His politics before the Civil War were Democratic, but he was clearly not very interested in them. During his interlude as a farmer in Missouri during the 1850s, he several times borrowed his father-in-law's slaves to help him. But, if no abolitionist, he was not comfortable with the institution. The single slave he briefly owned he freed rather than sold, although he was virtually penniless at the time.

His racial attitudes were undoubtedly those of his kind and times. His closest friend in the Civil War army, William Tecumseh Sherman, was an outspoken racist with whom Grant probably agreed, but with none of Sherman's passion. Now president in 1869 at 46 years of age (to that time the youngest president), he immediately understood that he owed his election and the Republican party its dominance to African American voters. Moreover, Grant was unswervingly loyal to those who were loyal to him. The radicals made him president and he turned to them when he needed advice. And his champion in the Senate and chief senatorial adviser was Roscoe Conkling of New York, who believed in African American equality as an ideal as well as an expedient.

During most of Grant's presidency, the Republican party was dominant because, when first admitted to statehood, the southern states sent mostly Republicans to Congress. In some states, where blacks were a majority of the population or nearly so—South Carolina, Mississippi, Louisiana—Republican control was likely as long as African Americans voted. In other southern states, there were enough white Republicans who, combined with a bloc African American vote, comprised a majority.

If blacks were the backbone of the southern party, providing 80 percent of Republican votes, white men ran the party. No African American was elected governor in any state. There were only two black senators, Blanche K. Bruce and Hiram Revels, both from Mississippi. There were fewer than twenty black Republican congressmen. Indeed, blacks filled only a fifth of federal jobs in the South, most in low-level positions. The tyrannical "Black Rule" of which Democrats spoke was a myth.

Corruption   Who were the white Republicans in the South? Some were former Whigs who had opposed secession. In the mountain counties, particularly in Tennessee, a majority of ordinary whites voted Republican. Some Confederates decided that their political future lay with the Republicans and joined the party. Democrats called them "scalawags"—scoundrels, reprobates—who betrayed their neighbors to ignorant, savage former slaves. Northern Republicans who moved South after the war for political purposes or to invest in the development of the shattered economy were known as "carpetbaggers." The message was that they had arrived in the South so poor they could carry everything they owned in a carpetbag, the cheapest sort of suitcase, but were soon rich from looting southern state treasuries along with their scalawag friends and their black stooges.

Lowlife carpetbaggers could be found on the lower levels of the Republican party. But the dozen or so carpetbaggers who rose to high political office were men with money the South sorely needed. The real "crime" of Reconstruction which the Democrats hammered on was the fact that African Americans had a say in government.

There was plenty of corruption, as there inevitably is when governments spend a lot of money in a short time. The Republican legislatures voted huge appropriations for legitimate, even essential programs that the prewar southern legislatures had ignored. There was not a single statewide public school system in any former Confederate state until Reconstruction. The first free schools in the South for white as well as black children were established by the Republican legislatures. Programs for the relief of the destitute and institutions for the handicapped and the insane were few in the prewar South.

The start-up costs were immense. Politicians, all the way at the top, dipped into the flow of money to fill their own purses. The Republican governor of Louisiana, Henry C. Warmoth, banked $100,000 during a year when his salary was $8,000.

Favored state contractors padded their bills and bribed state officials not to examine their invoices closely. In 1869, the state of Florida spent as much on its printing bill as had been spent on the entire state government in 1860.

There was nothing uniquely southern in the thievery. The 1860s and 1870s were an era of corruption throughout American society. Civil War contractors had cheated the government. The "Tweed Ring" that looted New York City was Democratic. And the champion crooks in the South were not Reconstruction Republicans but post-Reconstruction Democrats. After a "Black Republican" administration in Mississippi ran a largely corruption-free regime for six years, the first Democratic treasurer of the state absconded with $415,000. This paled compared to the swag E. A. Burke, the first post-Reconstruction treasurer of Louisiana, took with him to Honduras in 1890: $1,777,000.

Redeemers and the Klan Nevertheless, political corruption was an effective issue for Democrats out to defeat the Republicans at the polls. They persuaded whites who had voted Republican to switch to the Democrats as the only way to avoid ruinous taxes to pay the crooks' bills. Race was an even more effective issue. The spectacle of former slaves who had once said "yes sir" and "no sir" to every white man dressing in frock coats and cravats, making laws, and drinking in hotel bars infuriated whites. Democratic politicians called themselves "Redeemers." They would redeem the captive South from thieving carpetbaggers and scalawags and redeem the white race from the degradation the Yankees had forced on them.

In states where a more-or-less solid white vote could be mobilized to vote Democratic, the solidly Republican black vote could be overcome. Virginia was "redeemed" quickly, North Carolina and Georgia after a short campaign. Elsewhere, Redeemers brought economic pressure on blacks to stay home on election day. Most African Americans were tenants with a family to support. They were inclined to value their leased cabins and acreage more highly than the vote when their landlords told them it was one or the other.

Blacks determined to exercise their rights were met with violence. In 1866, General Nathan Bedford Forrest of Tennessee founded the Ku Klux Klan as a social club for Confederate veterans. Like other men's lodges, the Klan was replete with hocus-pocus, including the wearing of white robes and titles like Kleagle and Grand Wizard.

In 1868, the Klan turned political. The Klan and copycat organizations like the Knights of the White Camelia, masked and riding only at night to avoid Union army detachments, harassed, terrorized, whipped, and murdered carpetbaggers, scalawags, and politically active African Americans. Soon enough the night riders turned on blacks accused of being "impudent." The Klan hit the South like a tornado. The federal government estimated that the Klan murdered 700 in 1868, all but a few of them blacks. The next year was worse. Violence worked. In ever-increasing numbers, African Americans stopped voting.

In 1870 and 1871, Congress passed two Ku Klux Acts which made it a federal offense "to go in disguise upon the public highway ... with intent to ... injure, oppress, threaten, or intimidate [citizens] and to prevent them from enjoying their

Ku Klux Klan night riders shoot up the house of an African American who voted or, possibly, merely offended whites by insisting on being treated as a free man. At the peak of Klan violence in 1868 and 1869, it is estimated that Klan-like terrorists murdered an average of two people a day, almost all of them blacks.

The Granger Collection, New York

constitutional rights." The laws were effective. The Union army harassed known or suspected Klansmen and wiped out many "Klaverns." Between 1870 and 1872, Texas arrested 6,000 Klansmen. Still, the greatest Klan atrocity occurred in April 1873 when 100 blacks were killed.

By then, five of the former rebel states were in Redeemer hands and the Republicans were facing powerful Democratic opposition in the others. Just as important, northern support for radical Reconstruction was in rapid decline.

GRANT'S TROUBLED ADMINISTRATION

Grant had been lionized after Appomattox. He was showered with gifts, including cold cash. New York City's present to him of $100,000 was just the biggest. Wealthy businessmen and bankers, knowing well he would soon be president, treated him at their clubs and on their yachts. The soldier in a dusty, rumpled uniform was dumbstruck. He took zestfully to the high life, from dining on caviar and *tournedos sauce béarnaise* to wearing silk top hats and well-tailored suits of the best worsteds.

Celebrity and money came too fast to a man who had struggled to pay the bills for thirty years—and for Mrs. Julia Grant, who had struggled to keep her family together. The Grants never quite grasped the fact that their benefactors were not so much appreciating what they had done as they were paying in advance for future favors. There is no evidence that a scintilla of corruption tainted Grant personally. But his administration was shot through with crookery, and Grant's sense of loyalty was so strong that he never punished or even shunned those of his "friends" who disgraced him.

Jim Fisk and Jay Gould   Most of the corruption of the Grant administration was exposed only late in his eight years as president. But there was an odor of corruption in Washington from the start. Henry Adams, the fourth-generation scion of the distinguished Massachusetts family, smelled it in 1869 when he visited the city. Adams fairly fled Washington, writing that the capital was filled with men of shady character chasing the fast buck and, to all appearances, catching it. Another writer described the Grant years as "the great barbecue" with the government "supplying the beef."

During his first year as president, Grant made the mistake of hitching a ride on the yacht of James "Jubilee Jim" Fisk, a notorious and unabashed financial schemer. Also aboard was Jay Gould who, the previous year, along with Fisk, had bilked the railroader Cornelius Vanderbilt in a stock fraud. The final acts of the drama were played out in public, lovingly chronicled in the newspapers. Gould and Fisk were infamous when Grant accepted their hospitality.

Their purpose in entertaining Grant on a yacht was to be seen with the president. Fisk and Gould created the illusion that they had a privileged relationship with the president. Indeed, they were already scheming with Grant's brother-in-law, Abel R. Corbin. Their plan was to corner the nation's privately owned gold supply, dumping it on the market when the shortage of gold had driven its price to absurd levels. Success depended on the federal government keeping its gold holdings—the largest in the country—in its vaults, off the gold market. Corbin assured Gould and Fisk that, as a trusted relative, he would see to it that Grant would do just that. The party on the yacht was staged to fool the people Gould and Fisk planned to fleece that the president was in cahoots with them.

Black Friday   The two pirates conspicuously snapped up every gold future (a commitment to buy gold at an agreed price at a specified future date) they could. The price of gold soared because of their purchases until, in September 1869, it was selling for $162 an ounce. By taking delivery of gold futures they had purchased at $40 less per ounce, they would make a killing in an instant.

Corbin did his job persuading Grant that by selling government gold, he would cause an agricultural depression. However, Treasury officials, realizing what was happening, persuaded Grant that he would look very bad if he did not foil Fisk and Gould. On their advice, the president dumped $4 million of the government's gold on the market on Friday, September 24.

The price collapsed. New York's financial community called the day "Black Friday." Businessmen who had purchased gold at bloated prices to pay debts and wages were ruined; thousands of employees of bankrupt companies lost their jobs. And the luster of a great general's reputation was tarnished before he had been president for eight months. Jay Gould did not make as much money as he had hoped he would, but he made plenty. Without informing his partner, he had already sold most of his holdings. Nor did Jim Fisk lose; he simply refused to honor his futures commitments and hired thugs to intimidate those with whom he had signed contracts.

The Election of 1872 By 1872, some Republicans like Henry Adams's father, Charles Francis Adams; Senators Carl Schurz of Missouri, Lyman Trumbull of Illinois, and Charles Sumner of Massachusetts; and crusading editors Horace Greeley of the New York *Tribune* and E.L. Godkin of *The Nation* concluded that, with Grant's acquiescence, thieves were taking over the Republican party.

They were also disgusted by corruption in the southern state governments that, they believed, remained in power only because of Grant's support. Most of the reformers—Sumner was an exception—concluded that the whole idea of entrusting poor and ignorant blacks with the vote was a mistake. Better to allow the Redeemers, Democrats that they were, to take over and run the southern state governments. The dissidents formed the Liberal Republican party and said they would oppose Grant in the presidential election of 1872. Their convention nominated Horace Greeley to run against him.

It was an unwise choice. Greeley was a lifelong eccentric, and he looked it. During his 61 years, he had clambered at least briefly aboard every nutty fad that rolled down the road. His appearance invited ridicule. He looked like a crackpot with his round, pink face, close-set, beady eyes, and a wispy white fringe of chin whiskers. He wore an ankle-length white overcoat on the hottest days, and carried a brightly colored umbrella on the driest. Pro-Grant cartoonists had an easy time making fun of him.

Greeley also was a poor choice because, on their own, the Liberal Republicans had no chance of winning the election. They needed the support of both northern and southern Democrats. The Horace Greeley of 1872 might call for North and South to "clasp hands across the bloody chasm" and denounce carpetbaggers as "as stealing and plucking, many of them with both arms around negroes, and their hands in their rear pockets." The Horace Greeley of 1841–1869 had roasted northern Democrats daily in the *Tribune* and vilified southern Democrats for their espousal of slavery and rebellion.

Nevertheless, the Democrats nominated Greeley. If the liberal Republicans could not hope to win without the Democrats, the Democrats could not hope to win without the liberals. The ratification of the Fifteenth Amendment in 1870 had added tens of thousands of blacks—all Republicans—to the voters' lists.

In fact, the mismatched two-party coalition could not win. With half the southern states still governed by Republicans, and Grant still a hero despite the rumors of scandals, the president won 56 percent of the popular vote and a crushing 286 to 66 victory in the electoral college.

THE TWILIGHT OF RECONSTRUCTION

Poor Greeley died weeks after the election. One by one, dragging their feet, the other liberals returned to the Republican party. Grant would be gone after the election of 1876. Perhaps the party had learned its lesson and would nominate a reformer? In fact, the exposure of several scandals during Grant's second term did just that.

Except for Sumner, who was pushing for a federal civil rights law when he died in 1874 (it was enacted in 1875, thanks to the Grant Republicans in Congress), the liberals of 1872 were not unhappy when, at the end of 1874, Redeemers in Texas, Arkansas, and Mississippi wrestled those states into the Democratic party. By 1876, southern Republicans remained in power only in South Carolina, Florida, and Louisiana.

The Disputed Election   The Democratic candidate in 1876, New York Governor Samuel J. Tilden, said he would withdraw the troops from these three states, which would mean a further reduction in the numbers of black voters and the end of Reconstruction. The Republican candidate, Governor Rutherford B. Hayes of Ohio, ran on a platform pledged to protect African American rights in the South, but Hayes was well known to be skeptical of black capabilities and a personal friend of several southern Democratic politicians. Both candidates were "honest government" men. Tilden had helped destroy a corrupt political ring in New York. As governor of Ohio, Hayes had run a squeaky clean administration.

When the votes were counted, Hayes's personal opinions about the wisdom of Reconstruction seemed beside the point. Tilden won the popular vote narrowly, and he appeared to have won the electoral college 204 to 165. However, Tilden's count included the electoral votes of South Carolina, Florida, and Louisiana, where Republicans still controlled the state governments. On telegraphed instructions from Republican leaders in New York, officials in those three states declared that Hayes had carried their states. According to this set of returns, Hayes eked out a 185 to 184 electoral vote victory.

So, two sets of returns for South Carolina, Florida, and Louisiana reached Washington, one set electing Tilden, the other Hayes. The Constitution provided no guidelines for resolving such a problem. So, Congress created a commission to decide which returns were valid. Five members from each house of Congress and five members of the Supreme Court sat on the panel. Seven of them were Republicans; seven were Democrats. One, David Davis of Illinois, a Supreme Court justice, was known as an independent. No one else was interested in determining the cases on their merits. Each commissioner intended to vote for his party's candidate, no matter what documents were set before him. The burden of naming the next president of the United States fell on David Davis.

He did not like it. No matter how conscientious he was—and Davis had a good reputation—half the country would call for his scalp. Davis prevailed on friends in Illinois to get him off the hook by naming him to a Senate seat that had fallen vacant. He resigned from the court and, thereby, from the commission. His replacement was a Republican justice, and the stage was set for the Republicans to steal the election.

The Compromise of 1877   The commission voted 8 to 7 to accept the Hayes's returns from Louisiana, Florida, and South Carolina—giving Rutherford B. Hayes the presidency by a single electoral vote. Had that been all there was to it, there might well have been violence. At a series of meetings, however, prominent northern and southern politicians and businessmen came to an informal agreement with highly placed southern Republicans who had Redeemer connections.

The "Compromise of 1877" involved several commitments, not all of them honored, by northern capitalists to invest in the South. Also not honored in the end was a vague agreement by conservative southerners to build a white Republican party in the South based on the economic and social views that they shared with northern conservatives.

As to the disputed election, Hayes would move into the White House without Democratic resistance. In return, he would withdraw the remaining troops from South Carolina, Florida, and Louisiana, thus allowing the Democratic party in these states to oust the Republicans and eliminate African American political power. Those parts of the compromise were honored.

25

PATRONAGE AND PORK
National Politics 1876–1892

*That ... a man like Grant should be called—and should
actually and truly be—the highest product of the most
advanced society, made evolution ludicrous. One must be as
commonplace as Grant's own commonplaces to maintain
such an absurdity. The progress of evolution from President
Washington to President Grant, was alone evidence to
upset Darwin.*

—Henry Adams

The presidents of the late nineteenth century are not, on the face of it, an inspiring lot. Their portraits lined up on a wall—Grant, Hayes, Garfield, Arthur, Cleveland, Harrison—they might be a line of mourners at a midwestern funeral. They were dignified. They were soberly drab (except Chester A. Arthur, who was a New York dandy). They were lavishly bewhiskered. Their integrity was beyond question (save for a little slip by Garfield when he was a congressman), as were their morals (although Cleveland fathered a child out of wedlock in Buffalo). They performed their executive duties competently. But it is difficult to imagine a boy who, on looking up at the portrait gallery, would say to his mother, "I want to be president when I grow up."

HOW THE SYSTEM WORKED

Not one of them could be elected today. None could make a credible run for the office in an age when television has established the requirement that a would-be president be a personable, preferably good-looking performer. Moreover, Americans have come to prefer presidents who are vigorous leaders, who seize the initiative (or, at least, to create that impression). The presidents from Grant to McKinley believed that the initiative in government lay with Congress. The president's job was to represent the nation in his person (thus, the importance of a grave demeanor) and to enforce the laws Congress designed and enacted.

Politics 1873–1897

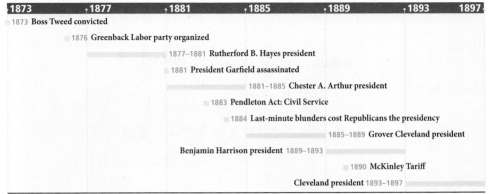

1873	1877	1881	1885	1889	1893	1897

1873 Boss Tweed convicted

1876 Greenback Labor party organized

1877–1881 Rutherford B. Hayes president

1881 President Garfield assassinated

1881–1885 Chester A. Arthur president

1883 Pendleton Act: Civil Service

1884 Last-minute blunders cost Republicans the presidency

1885–1889 Grover Cleveland president

Benjamin Harrison president 1889–1893

1890 McKinley Tariff

Cleveland president 1893–1897

And yet, Americans of the era took their politics seriously. More than 80 percent of eligible voters voted in 1876; the percentage never fell below 70 before 1900. Today, in contrast, despite the unrelenting ballyhoo, only about half those eligible to vote actually go to the polls.

Two Balanced Parties   So many voters voted because, in part, the two major parties were evenly matched nationally. Between 1875 and 1891, control of the House of Representatives changed six times. One of the parties controlled the presidency, House, and Senate only four of these years.

Almost every presidential election of the era provided evidence for the cliché that a single voter (a handful of voters, anyway) can make a difference. Between 1872, when Grant won reelection by 750,000 votes, and 1896, when William McKinley ushered in an era of Republican party dominance with an 850,000 vote victory, two of the presidential contests (1880 and 1884) saw the candidates just 40,000 votes apart in a total of 9–10 million. In two other elections (1876 and 1888), the winners in the electoral college had fewer popular votes than the losers, an outcome that would not be seen again until 2000.

Only one presidential candidate between 1876 and 1896 won more than 50 percent of the popular vote, Democrat Samuel J. Tilden in 1876, and the election was "stolen" from him by a partisan Republican commission.

Solid South and Republican Respectability   Within regions and among most identifiable social groups, the parties were not evenly matched. Except for Connecticut, where Republicans and Democrats were roughly equal in number, New England was as solidly Republican as its granite outcroppings. So was Pennsylvania, the party's crown jewel with the second largest electoral vote in the country. Democrats never considered the possibility of winning Pennsylvania. Outside of the South, the upper and middle classes were largely Republican. They thought of the GOP, the "Grand Old Party," as a bastion of morality and respectability. In the words of Senator George F. Hoar of Massachusetts, Republicans

Uncle Sam weighs the Republican and Democratic parties and finds them evenly matched. President Grant is in the background (although he was no longer the sloven depicted here). His chief ally in the Senate, Roscoe Conkling (who was mocked for having a "turkey gobbler strut") is perched at the upper right. The man at the left is holding a pathetic Liberal Republican Party bird. The Liberal Republicans joined with the Democrats in 1872.

Harcourt Picture Collection

were "the men who do the work of piety and charity in our churches; the men who administer our school systems; the men who own and till their own farms; the men who perform skilled labor in the shops."

Hoar went on to describe Democrats as (among other unattractive things) the "criminal class" and the "ballot-box stuffers" of the great cities. That was true of New York City which, with brief interludes, was run by Democrats. Philadelphia, however, was in the pocket of a Republican party machine employing the same techniques that kept the Democrats in office in New York. Indeed, Republican machines ran more of the great cities during the late nineteenth century than Democrats did.

Southern African Americans who continued to vote after Reconstruction were, of course, staunch Republicans, as were northern blacks. The GOP paid little more lip service to civil rights issues after 1877, but it was still the party of Lincoln and emancipation and historical memory played a big part in political allegiances for everyone.

Nationally, Democratic chances were based on the "Solid South." After the census of 1880, 201 electoral votes were needed to win the presidency. The states where slavery had been legal gave all 159 of their electoral votes to the Democratic party, as they did in every presidential election after 1876. On the face of it, it was a nice head start in the race.

Swing States   To win a national election, however, the Democrats had to add some northern and western states to the Solid South. Connecticut was always a possibility but added only six electoral votes to the

Democratic column. The Democrats concentrated their hopes and energies on the other swing states where the two parties were about equal in strength. Indiana and Illinois were swing states, as was Ohio, although the Republicans always managed to eke out a majority there (in 1892 by 72 votes in a total of 810,000).

The "must win" swing state was New York, with thirty-five to thirty-six electoral votes, more even than Pennsylvania. There the contest was between New York City and "upstate." New York City's Democratic machine, by hook or crook, had to roll up a larger plurality than the Republicans (with more than a little crookery involved) won in the rural and small-town counties. With the Solid South and New York, the Democrats had to win two or three swing states to elect their candidate. The Republicans had to keep them from doing so. In fact, beginning in 1880, the party that won New York's electoral votes won the presidency and would not, otherwise, have been victorious.

Consequently, a disproportionate number of national nominees were from Indiana, New York, Illinois, and Ohio, where they had demonstrated that they were personally popular. In the elections held between 1876 and 1892, the major parties filled twenty presidential and vice-presidential slots. Eighteen of the twenty were filled by men from the swing states. Eight (40 percent) were from New York; there was at least one New Yorker on one of the party tickets in every election. Five were from Indiana. Neither party was particularly interested in finding "the best man for the job." The idea was to win the election; that meant carrying the swing states.

Bosses and Conventions   Today, presidential nominations are made in primary elections. For a generation, nominations have been settled months before the party conventions. Conventions have become nothing but paid holidays for the delegates and television shows for everyone else, albeit boring ones. There were no primaries in the nineteenth century. Conventions were at the heart of national party life. The delegates (the bosses of delegations) really did make the pick.

Conventions were also vital to party life as the only occasion when state and big city political leaders could consult with one another and seal bargains face to face. There was no e-mail and, until the very end of the century, no long-distance telephone. The telegraph was too public for deal making; messages passed through the hands of any number of telegraph offices where a poorly paid employee could make a few dollars by revealing a juicy message. Congressmen and senators saw one another in Washington on a regular basis. However, governors and political bosses were the real powers in party politics. They met their counterparts elsewhere only at conventions.

There they wheeled and dealed, bargained and traded, made and broke political careers. There was no army of television reporters shoving microphones and cameras into the midst of every circle of politicos that gathered on the floor of the barnlike convention halls. There were, of course, plenty of newspaper reporters. But, with no cameras to record the action, they could be kept away from the interesting conversations by strong-arm bodyguards, a common career opportunity for washed-up prize fighters.

In the Democratic party, the most important bosses were the head of New York City's Tammany Hall, the Democratic machine, and the Bourbons of the Solid South. ("Bourbons" was the name given to the Redeemers when, by 1880, they had finished up their redemption work. They were named not after Kentucky's famous whiskey, much as most of them enjoyed a sip or two, but after the Bourbon kings of France because of their extreme don't rock the boat conservatism.)

In the Republican party, the perennial players were the bosses of Pennsylvania and the swing states, always New York's party leader when the New York party was unified. They and dozens of lesser politicos traded the support of their delegations for cabinet posts and a major say in who was appointed to federal jobs in the state and who won lucrative government contracts.

The southern states delivered no electoral votes to the Republican party. However, delegates from the South (including a few, not many, African Americans) were nonetheless courted ardently for their votes on the convention hall floor and in hotel rooms. If elective office in the South was pretty much barred to them, appointments to federal jobs were not.

The Patronage   The spoils system had come a long way since the days of Andrew Jackson. Jackson's administration had about 5,000 federal jobs to hand out to the party faithful. In 1871, 50,000 federal employees served at President Grant's pleasure. In 1881, President Garfield had it in his power to fire and hire people in 100,000 positions.

In 1870, about three federal jobs in four were with the Post Office, in 1880 about half of them. The second largest federal employer was the Treasury Department. Collecting customs duties generated tons of paperwork in every seaport and ports of entry on the Mexican and Canadian borders. Because postal and customs employees were scattered throughout the country, as were Indian agents and civilian employees of the army, local political leaders were keenly interested in them.

Low-level jobs in Washington and abroad were of little interest to them. In 1871, only about 6,000 people worked for the government in the capital. (The undesirability of clerical jobs in Washington created opportunities for women that were not abundant in the states; by the end of the century, a majority of federal employees in Washington were women.)

The government had few employees abroad. There was no professional foreign service. Wealthy benefactors were named ministers and consuls in important European countries. Ministers in London, Paris, Vienna, Rome, and Berlin had to be wealthy; their salaries did not begin to cover the huge expenditures on dwellings and the entertainment expected of them. Consulships went to less affluent party regulars. Neither embassies nor consulates employed more than a handful of staff.

Presidents did not sift through applications for postmasterships in every one-horse town. For low-level positions, job seekers made their wishes known to mayors, congressmen, and local bosses who belonged to the president's party. Paring the wish lists down to reasonable lengths, they passed their recommendations up the line to the state's senator or a senior congressman. Those worthies had direct access to the president and their picks were almost invariably appointed.

The president's automatic approval of the names given to him was known as senatorial courtesy.

When President Grant gave Senator Roscoe Conkling a blank check in filling federal positions in New York state, it made Conkling New York's most powerful politician. The sweetest plums at his disposal were at the customs house in New York City; its annual payroll was $2 million. The Collector of Customs in New York was paid a salary of $20,000 (about $400,000 in purchasing power today), and he earned bonuses when importers trying to cheat the government were caught. Conkling's choice for collector, his top political henchman and close personal friend, Chester A. Arthur, took home $40,000 a year between 1871 and 1874, more than the president made.

The big states had plenty of state employees too. Pennsylvania's Republican machine had 20,000 jobs to hand out. With so many people owing their income to the Republican party, it is small wonder that Democrats were helpless in Pennsylvania and Philadelphia.

Pork   Government contracts were another means of rewarding friends of the winning party. Usually at the end of each congressional session, when the House and Senate were tying up loose ends at top speed, Congress enacted "pork barrel" bills, so called because, like the barrel of pork in brine that once sat in the kitchens of most homes, they were not pretty to look into too closely.

Pork barrel bills were usually bipartisan because the two houses of Congress were controlled by different parties more often than not. Therefore, Republicans and Democrats had to cooperate in divvying up contracts for the construction of post offices here and there, government piers, dredging a river, and so on. The idea was not to get necessary work done, but to allow congressmen to reward their political supporters.

Thus, the River and Harbor Bill of August 1886 appropriated $15 million to begin work on more than 100 new projects; 58 federal building projects that had begun two years earlier but were not complete were abandoned. They were in the districts of congressmen who had retired or been defeated.

Memories, Memories   There was not, of course, a job or contract for every voter. In order to turn out the numbers on election day, the two parties exploited the emotional politics of memory and, for the Republicans, the decidedly unsentimental politics of soldiers' pensions.

Although the Republican party shelved its commitments to African Americans, it remembered the Civil War. Party orators "waved the bloody shirt," reminding northern voters that Democrats had started the Civil War. Lucius Fairchild, a Wisconsin politician who had lost an arm in battle, flailed the air with his empty sleeve during campaign speeches. With armless and legless veterans hobbling about every sizable town to remind voters of the bloodletting, it was an effective technique.

The GAR—the Grand Army of the Republic—was a Union veterans' association founded in 1866. Officially, it was nonpartisan. The organization was designed to remember the Union dead by strewing flours on graves on Decoration Day (now Memorial Day) and to preserve the somewhat romanticized camaraderie of the war years. The GAR had plenty of Democratic members who also donned their old uniforms (as long as they still fit) to parade on Decoration Day and to attend annual encampments—conventions under tents.

However, when the GAR became a lobby for more generous veterans' pensions during the 1880s, it functioned somewhat as an auxiliary of the Republican party. Its membership peaked in 1890 at about 450,000.

Between 1868 and 1901, every president except the Democrat Grover Cleveland was a former Union officer. (Arthur's military service was very brief, but he still liked to be addressed as "General.") When Cleveland, believing that sectional bitterness was fading, returned captured Confederate battle flags to their states for display at museums and war monuments, a protest mobilized by the GAR forced him to back down.

Vote Yourself a Pension   The Republican party converted the bloody shirt into dollars and cents in the form of pensions for veterans. Late in the war, Congress had approved federal pensions for Union soldiers who were disabled by wounds or disease contracted while in the army. The law was strictly worded, perhaps excessively so. Many handicapped veterans failed to qualify for pensions under its terms. In 1879, eligibility was liberalized, but northern congressmen also introduced "special pension" bills that provided monthly stipends to specifically named constituents who had requested them.

By the 1880s, the procedure for awarding special pensions was grossly abused. Congressmen took no interest in the worthiness of petitions for special pensions submitted to them, not even in the truthfulness of them. (One applicant was disabled, he said, because he had been thrown from a horse as he was rushing to enlist in the army.) They introduced every request made of them. When virtually all Republican congressmen and many northern Democrats had special pension bills in the hopper, the lot was rushed through by voice vote and passed on to the president. Republican presidents signed them. Instead of declining as old soldiers died off, the cost of the pension program climbed to $56 million in 1885 and $80 million in 1888.

Democrat Grover Cleveland, elected in 1884, closely scrutinized every special pension bill on his desk and vetoed those he judged undeserving. In 1888, an election year, Congress put him on the spot by enacting a revised general pension law that granted a small monthly income to every veteran who had served ninety days in the wartime army and was disabled for any reason whatsoever. An old soldier who fell from a stepladder in 1885 qualified, as did his widow when he died. Cleveland vetoed it and the Republicans ran their campaign on the slogan "Vote Yourself a Pension."

They won the election and, in 1889, the new president, Benjamin Harrison, signed an even more generous Dependent Pensions Act. Harrison appointed the head of the GAR, James "Corporal" Tanner, to oversee the distribution of pensions. "God help the surplus," Tanner said, referring to the money in the treasury. He meant it. By the end of Harrison's term, Tanner had increased the annual expenditure on Civil War pensions to $160 million. With widows qualifying for pensions too, local wags took notice of the young women of the town who promptly married doddering old Billy Yanks who had a gleam in their eyes every several months but a check in the mail every month without fail.

Northern Democrats posed as men of principle in the bloody shirt and pensions controversies. In the South, however, Democrats played the Civil War game too. They orated about the nobility of the Confederate cause and southern state governments provided some benefits for Confederate veterans.

Presidents and Personalities

In 1876, President Grant was rounding out his second term. He was only 55; he was not rich and he had given up an income from the army when he resigned to become president. Despite the two-term tradition, he wanted to run for reelection. He needed the income. Roscoe Conkling, his chief political advisor, wanted him to run too. But too many scandals had been exposed. The House of Representatives, by a vote of 233–18, crushed his hopes by endorsing the two-term tradition. The large majority included most Republican congressmen. They knew that to have a chance of electing a Republican that year, they needed a candidate with a squeaky clean reputation.

They found him in Governor Rutherford B. Hayes. *The Nation* called Hayes and his running mate "the most respectable men, in the strict sense of the word, the Republican party has ever nominated," which was scant respect for Abraham Lincoln. When Hayes was awarded the presidency in the "stolen election" of 1876, Democrats took particular delight in calling him "His Fraudulency" and "Rutherfraud" B. Hayes.

Hayes, Integrity, and Oblivion   Hayes was a brave, perhaps abnormally reckless Civil War officer. Coddled by his mother, sisters, and aunts (his father died before he was born), he found military life liberating. He served in combat units—in fifty engagements! He had four horses shot from under him and was himself wounded four times, once very seriously. He was a serious man but seems not to have been especially bright. He and his wife, "Lemonade Lucy" Hayes, were temperance people. In a dramatic change from the Grant White House, where six wines were served at formal dinners, the Hayeses banned alcohol.

As president, Hayes pleased few people. Democrats called him a fraud. Old radical Republicans were angered by the alacrity with which he abandoned southern blacks to the Redeemers, refusing to enforce the recently passed Civil Rights Act. "Stalwarts," as their leader Roscoe Conkling called Republicans who resolutely and uncompromisingly backed the party and expected to be rewarded for their loyalty with government jobs, were infuriated when Hayes appointed reformers and even southern Democrats to choice positions. He called reformers "dilletanti" and "man-milliners," as close to calling them homosexuals as was possible in the nineteenth century. When Hayes fired New York Collector of Customs Chester A. Arthur, "the prince of spoilsmen," Conkling went into opposition and began working to nominate ex-president Grant in 1880.

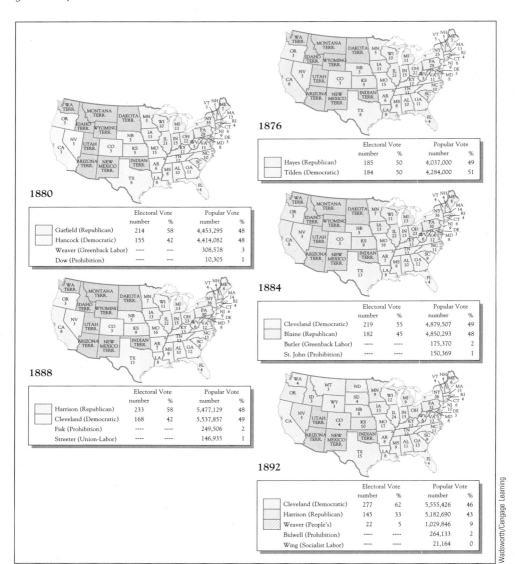

MAP 25.1 Voting the Straight Party Ticket

How most states would vote in presidential elections was predictable. Except for Connecticut, New England was dependably Republican; so was Pennsylvania which, with twenty-nine to thirty electoral votes, was critical to the success of Republican candidates. With African Americans effectively disenfranchised, the South was solidly Democratic. Only in Tennessee, where white voters from the eastern mountain counties were Republican, was the statewide popular vote something like close. Illinois and Indiana were "swing states." The two parties were approximately equal in strength; the state's electoral votes were fiercely contested. But the key to presidential elections was New York. Except in the "stolen election" of 1876, the winner in every presidential election carried New York. Except in 1892, if the winner had lost New York's electoral vote, he would not have been elected. Small wonder both parties were willing to pull out all of the stops to win in the state.

The anti-Conkling Republicans (known as Half-Breeds), who were as contemptuous of reformers as the Stalwarts were, were also unhappy with their share of the patronage. There was no difference in principle between the two factions. To a large extent, their competition was a reflection of the intense mutual personal dislike of Conkling and the leader of the Half-Breeds, Senator James G. Blaine of Maine. Early in their congressional careers, Blaine had mocked Conkling, a physical-culture nut who exercised daily and liked to show off his muscular physique, describing his "haughty disdain, his grandiloquent swell, his majestic, over-powering, turkey-gobbler strut." Conkling, who was rarely bested in a trade of insults, never forgave Blaine for humiliating him.

When Conkling announced that Grant would seek the Republican presidential nomination in 1880 and set about corralling supporters, Blaine announced that he too would seek the prize. Then Hayes's fellow Ohioan and his secretary of the treasury, John Sherman, announced his candidacy. By the last year of his presidency, poor Hayes was without political support.

Garfield: A Dark Horse

At the Republican convention of 1880, neither Grant, Blaine, nor Sherman could win a majority of the delegates and none would yield to one of the others. Nor would several "favorite son" candidates give up their votes to one of the leaders. Each hoped that the deadlocked convention would turn to them. After thirty-four ballots, several delegates broke ranks but, instead of switching to one of the favorite sons, they voted for James A. Garfield of Ohio, who was managing John Sherman's campaign on the floor. Garfield rose and protested but on the thirty-fifth ballot, more delegates named him. Because Garfield was a Half-Breed, Blaine released his delegates to Garfield and, on the thirty-sixth ballot, he was nominated.

Garfield was unprepared, but he knew he needed the support of the Stalwarts if he was to have a chance. He asked Chester A. Arthur to be his running mate. Conkling was furious and told Arthur to decline. For the only time in their long relationship, Arthur did not do as Conkling told him. The vice presidency was an honor he had never imagined possible, he said. Conkling sulked and snubbed Garfield when the candidate came to New York, hat in hand, to talk with him. But he did not fight when Arthur mobilized the Stalwart machine in New York.

Arthur's hustling won the election for Garfield as surely as Aaron Burr won it for Jefferson in 1800. Had the Democratic candidate General Winfield Scott Hancock carried New York—he lost the state to Garfield very narrowly—he would have been elected.

A Lust for Patronage

Garfield was intelligent; indeed, he was a scholar, as few presidents have been. He read both Latin and Greek; he did a parlor trick in which he wrote in Latin with one hand and Greek in the other simultaneously. He would have graced any university that had him as its president. He had succeeded in politics, however, by being a pliant, party-line regular. Blaine, whom Garfield named secretary of state, was confident he would dominate the present. He commented privately that Garfield was "a big good-natured man that doesn't appear to be oppressed by genius." The day after

Waving the Bloody Shirt

When Republican politicians assailed the Democratic party as the party of the South, the party responsible for the deaths of 360,000 Union soldiers, telling northern voters to "vote as they shot," they were said to be "waving the bloody shirt." They were cynically exploiting 360,000 personal tragedies for the sake of winning elections.

The bloody shirt was a smear, but the tactic was tough for northern Democrats to answer. They could point out that a good many of those dead young men had been Democrats. That was true and reasoned, but it was also a purely defensive response of the sort that is rarely effective against visceral, emotion-laden attacks. In the presidential election of 2004, several Vietnam veterans who had known Democratic candidate John Kerry in the war called him a coward and a fraud. In fact, Kerry had been decorated for bravery. He tried to ignore the groundless charges, but

they were sensational; Kerry's critics repeated them throughout the campaign.

Waving the bloody shirt was without substance too, but Republicans in difficult election contests inevitably resorted to it. Some were restrained, saying, for example, "Let your ballots protect the work so effectually done by your bayonets at Gettysburg." Others bordered on the hysterical.

The bloody shirt was more useful in some presidential campaigns than it was in others. With former Union generals as their candidates in 1868, 1872, and 1876, Republican orators waved it wildly. But the bloody shirt was less effective in 1880. Again the Republicans had a volunteer general as their candidate, James A. Garfield. However, his Democratic opponent, Winfield Scott Hancock, was a professional soldier who had played key roles in the battles of Fredericksburg, Antietam, Chancellorsville,

the election, Blaine's wife wrote to her daughter, "Your father and I have picked out Garfield's cabinet for him."

Garfield wanted to placate Roscoe Conkling too, but unlike the ingratiating Blaine, he was imperious and bullying with the president. He *demanded* that Garfield turn the New York patronage over to him as Grant had done. Garfield was thick-skinned, but Conkling insulted him once too often. Instead of choosing as New York's collector of customs a Republican who was neither Stalwart nor Half-Breed (his initial impulse), Garfield did Blaine's bidding and named an enemy of Conkling to the post. In protest, Conkling and his protégé, Thomas Platt, resigned their Senate seats. Their plan was to remind Garfield of their political power in New York by having the state legislature reelect them.

The lust for the patronage, from the top to the bottom, submerged the Garfield administration. "If all the reports are true," the New York *Times* editorialized sarcastically, "Pres. Garfield's Cabinet will contain about one hundred twenty-five persons." In just the first week after he was nominated, 200 people visited his home, at least half of them putting in bids for federal jobs. Between election day and his inauguration, Garfield was flooded daily with mail from office seekers. A woman he knew casually—they attended the same church—wanted a job in the Cincinnati Post Office; when Garfield politely agreed to keep her in mind, she sat in

Gettysburg, and before Richmond. Had he not been a Democrat, he would have been celebrated as a war hero in a class with Grant, Sherman, and Sheridan.

Nor was there much shirt waving in 1884. The Republican nominee, James G. Blaine, had paid a substitute to serve in the army in his place. But the bloody shirt had not been retired. In 1888, more than twenty years after the war, the Republican presidential candidate, Benjamin Harrison, assailed Grover Cleveland (who also had hired a substitute) for attempting to return captured battle flags to southern states and for vetoing veterans' pension bills he found dubious. "I would a thousand times rather march under the bloody shirt," Harrison said, "than march under the black flag of treason or the white flag of cowardly compromise."

Waving the bloody shirt has been around as long as there have been politicians and dead soldiers and it is still with us. Lyndon B. Johnson and George W. Bush, presidents who took the United States into unpopular wars, waved the bloody shirt, justifying continuing their wars by saying that the nation owed it to the soldiers who had already died in them.

The origin of the term "bloody shirt" to describe the technique is uncertain. It seems as if a Democratic party politician or journalist coined it. Despite Harrison's embrace of the phrase, it was usually used in a derogatory sense. (Perhaps a Democrat familiar with Shakespeare's Julius Caesar in which Marc Antony, in his famous "I come not to praise Caesar" speech, rouses the Roman crowd to a fury against Caesar's assassins by waving the dictator's blood-soaked toga as he spoke.) However, General James B. Weaver, a former Republican who, in 1892, ran against Benjamin Harrison as the Populist party's presidential candidate, claimed that he had coined the phrase before the Civil War. Weaver had been an abolitionist when a proslavery mob brutally whipped an abolitionist minister. Weaver said that at a protest rally, he held up the man's shirt and said, "Under this bloody shirt we propose to march to victory."

his parlor for five hours, refusing to leave until he gave in. When, in March 1881, Garfield moved into the White House, he did little but see one applicant after another morning to night. The waiting room outside his office was crowded every day with people "lying in wait for me like vultures for a wounded bison." He exclaimed to Blaine: "My God! What is there in this place that a man should ever want to get into it!"

Another Murdered President

Charles Guiteau sat in the president's waiting room several days each week. He managed to speak to the president several times, at first requesting the consulate in Vienna, then deciding he would rather be consul in Paris. When he was not waiting to pounce on the president, he was button-holing Blaine, Vice President Arthur, a vacationing Ulysses S. Grant, Senator Benjamin Harrison of Indiana, and other top Republicans, asking for their support and letters of recommendation.

Guiteau was deranged. He described himself as an important figure in the Stalwart machine. In fact, he was a penniless ne'er-do-well (he survived in Washington by jumping from one boardinghouse to another without paying) with a history of attaching himself to fringe religious groups. He believed he was entitled to a

Culver Pictures, Inc.

President Garfield did little in his short presidency but sit in his office interviewing Republicans asking for federal jobs. He had little time for any other work. Finally, on July 2, 1881, he broke away to join his wife for a mid-summer break. He was waiting to board a train in Washington when Charles Guiteau, a deranged religious fanatic who believed he was entitled to a consulate in Europe, shot him in the small of the back. The man assisting him is Secretary of State James G. Blaine, who had come to see him off. The assassin has been seized at the left. Garfield lingered for almost three months before dying in September.

consular appointment when he did not have the standing in the party to claim a post office job in the Dakotas. When he realized he was going nowhere and decided to kill Garfield, he believed that, after a few weeks in jail, he would be freed and honored by the new president, Chester Arthur. He actually scouted the accommodations at the Washington jail a week before he acted and told the jailer that they were "excellent."

Guiteau shot Garfield in the back at point-blank range in the Washington railway station on July 2, 1881, shouting, "I am a Stalwart! Arthur is president!" Had it happened today, Garfield would have recovered. But with no means of locating the bullet except by probing Garfield's wound, doctors could only guess where it was. (They were off by a full 12 inches.) Garfield lived in excruciating pain for eleven weeks, wasting away from 200 pounds to 130. He died from infection on September 19.

Guiteau should have been acquitted as insane, even under the strict definition of insanity in American law. But the country's shock was too great for that—two presidents murdered in sixteen years; he was hanged, shouting "Bound for glory! I'm bound for glory!" as the trap door opened.

**Civil Service
Reform**

The assassination wrote an end to Roscoe Conkling's political career. The New York legislature defiantly refused to send him and Platt back to the Senate. The backlash to Garfield's murder also resulted in Congress's hurried enactment of the Pendleton Act of 1883, a bill that would not have reached the floor a year earlier. The Pendleton Act established a Civil Service Commission which was instructed to draw up and administer examinations for applicants for some low-level government jobs. Once in these "civil service" positions, employees could not be fired simply because the political party to which they belonged lost power.

President Arthur put only 10 percent of 131,000 government workers on the civil service list. However, the Pendleton Act authorized future presidents to add job classifications to the civil service. Because the presidency changed hands between the two parties every four years between 1883 and 1897, each outgoing president added jobs to the list—hurried their appointees through the undemanding examination—thus protecting them from dismissal. By 1897, 41 percent of 256,000 government employees were civil service.

(The percentage peaked in 1970 at 90 percent. It has declined since to less than 50 percent largely because, in 1971, Post Office Department employees became employees of the Postal Service, which is not covered by civil service law.)

The Pendleton Act also abolished assessments. That is, the parties were forbidden to require members holding government jobs to donate a percentage of their salaries to political campaign funds. An unforeseen consequence of the reform was that both parties turned to rich businessmen and other special interests to finance them.

**1884: Blaine
versus
Cleveland**

Chester A. Arthur, his enemies said, was president illegally. They claimed that he was born not in Fairfield, Vermont, as he said, but in a cabin a few miles north—in Canada. However that may have been, the urbane and elegant Arthur, resplendent in his New York wardrobe compared to the gray look favored by Republican politicians, amazed everyone with his dignity as president and by doing a very good job. He remained personally loyal to Conkling. He twice offered him a seat on the Supreme Court, once as chief justice. He tried to woo the Half-Breeds by deferring to Secretary of State James G. Blaine's judgment in foreign affairs and appointing members of Blaine's faction to high positions. But Blaine rebuffed him as he had abandoned Hayes. He resigned from the cabinet to compete with Arthur for the Republican presidential nomination in 1884. With Conkling retired to a lucrative law practice, Blaine won it easily.

New York state was, as in 1880, the key to the election. When the Democrats nominated New York's governor, Grover Cleveland, things did not look good for the Republicans. Republican reformers, genteel and upper class, announced they would support Cleveland. He had a spotless record while Blaine had been caught in lies about a dubious railroading deal early in his career. Blaine's supporters sarcastically called them Mugwumps, supposedly an Algonkian Indian word for "big chief" or "big shot," a reference to their often pompous self-righteousness. (They described themselves as men "who need nothing and want nothing from government except the satisfaction of using their talents.")

Blaine expected to compensate for the Mugwump defection and more by cutting into New York City's large Irish Catholic vote which was usually Democratic. Blaine's mother was a Catholic; a sister was a nun. And he campaigned hard, making several hundred speeches, mostly in New York. Then Republicans broke the news that Cleveland was supporting an illegitimate child he had fathered in Buffalo. "Ma, Ma, Where's my Pa?," Republicans chanted, "Gone to the White House, Ha, ha, ha."

Little Things Decide Great Elections   Then, days before the election, Blaine blundered. Forgetting how Grant damaged himself by consorting with Jim Fisk and Jay Gould, Blaine dined with a gaggle of millionaires in Delmonico's, the most regal restaurant in New York City. It was not a good idea when he was courting the votes of working-class Irishmen. At another dinner, apparently dozing, Blaine made no comment when a Presbyterian minister, Samuel Burchard, denounced the Democrats as the party of "rum, romanism, and rebellion," that is, the party of the saloon, the Roman Catholic church, and the Confederacy.

This was garden-variety Republican sloganeering in Bangor, Maine, or Moline, Illinois. But this was New York City where Blaine was wooing Irish Catholic voters—successfully, reporters said. When Democratic newspapers plastered Burchard's insult across their front pages, Blaine rushed to express his distaste for Burchard's sentiment. But the damage was done. Irish voters trundled back into the Democratic column and blizzards upstate snowed in many Republican voters. New York state gave Cleveland a majority and its electoral votes gave him the election. (Actually, Blaine could have won anyway had he carried Indiana plus either Connecticut or New Jersey, but he did not.)

In 1888, it was Cleveland who was undone by a trivial incident. A Republican newspaperman, posing as an English-born naturalized American citizen, wrote to the British minister in Washington asking which of the two candidates, Cleveland or Benjamin Harrison of Indiana, would make the better president from the British point of view. Foolishly, the minister replied that Cleveland was better disposed toward British interests. The Republican press immediately labeled Cleveland the British candidate and thousands of Irish Democrats, reflexively hostile to anything Great Britain favored, voted Republican. Harrison won New York and the presidency.

ISSUES

There were concrete issues at stake in national politics but, with the exception of the tariff, they were not clear-cut partisan issues with Republicans lined up on one side and Democrats on the other. Even the remnants of the Reconstruction question, whether or not the federal government should protect the civil rights of African Americans in the South, ceased to be a party question as increasing numbers of Republicans abandoned the party's commitment to blacks.

The Tariff   Growers of staple crops inclined to favor a low tariff. Corn and wheat were produced so cheaply in the United States that they undersold domestically grown grain in European countries—if those countries did not levy high duties on American foodstuffs to retaliate against high

American tariffs on their manufactured products. Farmers resented the fact that the prices of just about everything they bought, from shoes to agricultural machinery, were artificially propped up by the protective tariff. The interest of agriculturalists in reducing import duties made the Democratic party, with its powerful southern agrarian contingent, the low-tariff party. Manufacturers, of course, wanted to increase their profits by taxing their foreign (mostly British) competitors out of the American market.

In the late nineteenth century, high-tariff interests had their way. After bobbing up and down from a low of 40 percent of the value of all imported goods (by no means a low tariff) to a high of 47 percent, rates were increased to 50 percent in the McKinley Tariff of 1890. That is, on average, imported shoes, cloth, iron tools, machinery were slapped with a tax equivalent to half of its value. A steel manufacturer like Andrew Carnegie, who produced rails for railroads so cheaply he won big contracts for them in free-trade Great Britain, could hike the price at which he sold rails to American railroads far higher than he needed to make a good profit.

When a depression followed quickly on the McKinley Tariff, Grover Cleveland and the Democrats campaigned against high rates. Cleveland won the election of 1892. (William McKinley lost his seat in the House of Representatives.) Congress enacted the Wilson-Gorman tariff which lowered duties to an average of 39 percent.

Money

The issue of money—the nature of money—was a divisive issue throughout the late nineteenth century, but not on party lines. There were Democrats and Republicans on both sides of the question and, briefly, a single issue third party that won the allegiance of politicians from both major parties.

The controversy had its roots in the $433 million in legal tenders greenbacks the federal government issued during the Civil War to help finance the fighting. Greenbacks were government money. They were not redeemable at face value in gold coin as bank notes were so their purchasing power fluctuated. When the war was going badly, the greenbacks were discounted. It might take $7 or $8 in greenbacks to buy what a $5 gold piece or five silver dollars bought. In 1870, the Central Pacific railroad served meals to travelers for a dollar if a diner paid with a greenback, 75¢ if he paid with coin.

Bankers wanted nothing to do with a paper currency that fluctuated. They did not want borrowers paying back loans in money that was worth less than the money they had borrowed. Their ideal was the gold standard that Great Britain had adopted in 1844, making the British pound sterling the standard in international financial transactions. Every bill issued by the Bank of England was "as good as gold" at the ratio of £1 to 7.32 grams of gold. Unlike greenbacks, the value of gold was stable. The world supply of the metal was finite and, despite the many new discoveries of the era, it increased more slowly than the economy grew.

After the war, the federal government began to retire the greenbacks. When they flowed into the treasury in payment of taxes, they were destroyed and not replaced in circulation. By the spring of 1868, $48 million of the $433 million in greenbacks had been retired. The result was deflation, a contraction of the amount of money in circulation. Wages dropped; so did prices, including the prices at which farmers sold their crops and livestock. In October, rattled by protests by their constituents, Congress ordered the Treasury Department to stop retiring the bills.

In 1875, federal policy changed again. The Grant administration announced that for each new $100 in gold notes that banks issued, the government would retire $80 in greenbacks. The result was an increased deflation. Between 1865 and 1878, the amount of all kinds of money in circulation in the United States shrank from $1.08 billion to $773 million. In 1865 there had been $31.18 in circulation for every American; in 1878 there was but $16.25.

The tightening of the money supply hit debtors hard, small manufacturers, and especially farmers. They had borrowed heavily to expand their factories and to buy land and agricultural machinery when the greenbacks were plentiful—when the currency was inflated. It was unjust, they argued, that they should have to pay off their debts in much more valuable gold. For a farmer, a $1,000 loan taken out during the 1860s represented 1,200 bushels of grain. By 1880, when many farmers were still making mortgage payments, $1,000 represented 2,300 bushels. They had to produce twice as much to repay each dollar they had borrowed.

| The Greenback Labor Party | In 1876, the Greenback Labor party was founded on the principle that the federal government should manage the supply of money in circulation by issuing enough greenbacks to ensure |

that debtors were not gouged. The party chose as its presidential candidate the 85-year-old Peter Cooper, still famous as the man who built the first American steam locomotive and, later, as an exemplary employer and as a philanthropist.

Cooper made a poor showing. However, in the congressional race of 1878, the Greenbackers elected a dozen congressmen who were joined by a good many Republicans and Democrats in their calls for government-managed inflation. But President Hayes was as conservative as Grant in his monetary policy and the retirement of the greenbacks proceeded apace. By 1880, they had practically disappeared, but the Greenback Labor party was still alive. It nominated a Civil War general from Iowa, James B. Weaver, to run for president. Weaver won 309,000 votes, a lot but not enough to affect the electoral vote count in any state. In 1884, Benjamin J. Butler of Massachusetts led the Greenback ticket. He won a third of the votes Weaver had.

The Greenback party was dead, but the demand to inflate the currency was not. Within a decade American politics would be turned upside down by inflationists who had turned to the coinage of silver in their war against the gold standard and the bankers.

26

TECHNOLOGY, INDUSTRY, AND BUSINESS

Economic Change in the Late Nineteenth Century

> *This movement was the origin of the whole system of modern economic administration. It has revolutionized the way of doing business all over the world. The time was ripe for it. It had to come, though all we saw at the moment was the need to save ourselves from wasteful conditions.... The day of the combination is here to stay. Individualism has gone, never to return.*
>
> **—John D. Rockefeller**

In 1876, Americans celebrated a hundred years of independence. The birthday party—the Centennial Exposition—was held in Philadelphia where the Declaration of Independence had been signed. It was a roaring success. It was estimated that one American in fifteen visited the fair, an extraordinary statistic when long-distance travel was a trying experience. The show was worth it. Sprawling over the hills of Fairmount Park, housed in more than 200 structures, the great show dazzled visitors with its displays of American history and American products.

The emphasis was on the products and the processes by which they were made. The heart and soul of the fair was not the hallowed Declaration of Independence, although it was there, but Machinery Hall, a building that covered 20 acres and housed the latest American inventions and technological improvements from the typewriter and telephone to new kinds of looms and lathes. And there was a dizzying variety of agricultural machines—an American specialty—bewildering to city folk but understood perfectly by the farmers who attended.

The centerpiece of Machinery Hall—it towered over everything, five times the height of a man—was the largest steam engine ever built (or that ever would be built), the "Giant Corliss." Smoking, hissing, rumbling, clanking, chugging, and gleaming in enamel, nickel plate, brass, chrome, and copper, the monster powered

Inventions and Innovations 1869–1896

1869	,1872	,1875	,1878	,1881	,1884	,1887	,1890	,1893 1896

1869 First transcontinental railroad complete; Westinghouse patents air brake

1870 United States adopts time zones

1872 Vanderbilt consolidates New York Central

1873 Carnegie begins construction of Homestead plant

1876 Bell demonstrates telephone; Edison establishes research laboratory

1877 Edison invents phonograph

1879 Edison perfects electric lightbulb; Standard Oil trust organized

1882 First electric company in New York

Great Northern completed 1893

every machine in the building through 75 miles of shafts and leather belts spinning on pulleys. When President Grant officially opened the fair by throwing the switch on the Giant Corliss, setting Machinery Hall in motion, he proclaimed without need of a speech that Americans were not just free and independent, but also that they had hitched their destiny to machines that made and moved goods quickly, cheaply, and in astonishing quantities. "It is in these things of iron and steel that the national genius most freely speaks."

A BLESSED LAND

Between 1865 and 1900, the population of the United States more than doubled from 36 million to 76 million. Wealth grew six times over. At the end of the Civil War, the nation's annual production of goods was valued at $2 billion. It increased to $13 billion by 1900.

Even in 1860, the United States ranked fourth among industrial nations with more than 100,000 factories capitalized at $1 billion. But the United States was not a fraction as industrial and urban as Great Britain, which imported much of the food to feed its population. More than 70 percent of the American people were farmers or lived in small towns that serviced farmers. In 1860, just over a million people worked in industrial jobs. Because many of them were women and children who did not vote, factory workers were an inconsequential political force. Even in 1876, it was plausible to call the United States "a farmer's country."

By 1900, however, $10 billion had been invested in factories, and 5 million people worked in industrial jobs. Early in the 1890s, American industrial production surpassed Great Britain's, making the United States the world's premier industrial power. By 1914, fully 46 percent of the world's industrial and mining economy was American, more than the combined economies of Germany and Great Britain, the world's second and third industrial countries.

An Embarrass-ment of Riches   Viewed from the twenty-first century, this success story seems to have been as predestined as John Winthrop's throne in paradise. The ingredients that went into the making of an industrial giant were heaped upon the United States in an abundance no other country has enjoyed.

The United States was rich in capital. Once the Union victory in 1865 assured foreign investors that the federal government was stable and in charge of the whole country, the pounds, guilders, and francs rolled in from abroad too. Investments were safe as well as lucrative. By 1900, more than $3.4 billion in foreign money was fueling the American economy. Americans had to divert only 11 to 14 percent of their national income into industrial growth, compared with 20 percent in Great Britain half a century earlier and in the Soviet Union half a century later. The pains of industrialization were not negligible in the United States, but they hurt less than they did in other industrializing nations. Americans sacrificed less for the sake of a more abundant future than the British, Russians, French, Belgians, Dutch, and Japanese did, and as the Chinese are doing today.

The United States drew from a labor pool that was literate and skilled at one end and unlimited in numbers at the other. The American farm had a surplus of often mechanically inclined young men to fill skilled industrial jobs. Unlike Asian or European peasants suspicious of ways of doing things differently from those that had been handed down to them, American farmers had always been quick to embrace new techniques. In 1854, an Englishman observed, "there is not a working boy of average ability in the New England states, at least, who has not an idea of some mechanical invention or improvement in manufactures." In the final decades of the nineteenth century, those boys and the children of those boys packed up in large numbers to fill "mechanical" jobs paying good wages in the towns and cities. If the older generation was more inclined to stay down home, even their heads were turned by labor-saving farm machines displayed at county fairs.

During the same half century, Europe's population underwent a spurt of growth with which European agriculture could not keep pace. Cheap American foodstuffs began to undersell peasant-grown crops all over Europe, helping to impoverish further people whose less numerous forebears had lived adequately well on the same land. Millions emigrated to the United States to fill low-paying, unskilled jobs that industrialization created in ever greater numbers.

A Land of Plenty The United States was blessed as no other country with the natural resources essential to industrialization. Its vast and productive agricultural base produced more cheap food than the population could consume, steadily reducing the cost of living. In the nineteenth century, North America's forests seemed inexhaustible. Wanderers in the mountains and deserts, first by accident, than as professional "prospectors," discovered deposits of gold, silver, semiprecious metals like copper; and—less romantic but nonetheless essential— plenty of dross ranging from phosphates to gravel. Only a few useful minerals were not found in abundance in the United States, and they could be imported from Canada and Latin America.

Iron and coal were the building blocks of nineteenth-century industrialization. The gray-green mountains of Pennsylvania, West Virginia, and Kentucky were virtually made of coal, the indispensable fuel of the age of steam. In the Marquette range of Michigan's upper peninsula, discovered in the 1840s, was a 150-foot deep vein of iron ore that was 60 percent iron and extended 100 miles. In 1890, just as Michigan iron seemed no longer up to supplying the nation's needs, the

Mesabi range of Minnesota was opened. It yielded even richer ore in greater quantity than any other iron deposit in the world.

The ever-growing American population was a huge, ready-made market for mass-produced goods. And thanks to the spirit of Alexander Hamilton and Henry Clay as preserved in the Republican party, and thanks to the Civil War triumph over southern agrarianism, industrial entrepreneurs found helpful partners in the federal and state governments.

Yankee Ingenuity   Abraham Lincoln (who himself owned a patent) observed that Americans have "a perfect rage for the new." An English visitor to the Centennial Exposition wrote, "As the Greek sculpted, as the Venetian painted, the American mechanizes." Actually, the invention that turned the most heads at the fair, the telephone, was the creation of a Scotsman who came to the United States via Canada, Alexander Graham Bell. Visitors to Bell's exhibit at the exposition picked up the odd-looking devices he had set up and, alternately amused and amazed, chatted through them with companions elsewhere in the exhibit. Young men dropped a hint of what was to come when they "rang up" young ladies standing across from them, casually striking up conversations that would have been rebuffed as improper had the young men approached the girls in person.

Bell might easily have invented the telephone in Scotland. But if he had, it was only in the United States that he could so quickly parley his idea into the gigantic enterprise it became within his lifetime, the American Telephone and Telegraph Company. Guglielmo Marconi, the Italian inventor of wireless (radio) and Nicholas Tesla, a Serbian who was perhaps the greatest inventive genius of the era, both relocated to the United States. As a writer in the *Saturday Evening Post* put it at the end of the century, "The United States is the only country in the world in which inventors form a distinct profession.... With us, inventors have grown into a large class. Laboratories ... have sprung up almost everywhere, and today there is no great manufacturing concern that has not in its employ one or more men of whom nothing is expected except the bringing out of improvements in machinery and methods."

The Telephone   Bell was a teacher of the deaf who was tinkering with a mechanical hearing aid when he realized that if he linked two of his experimental devices by wire, he could transmit voice over distance. After failing to sell his invention to Western Union (the telegraph giant), he found the capital to set up a pilot company in New York. Telephones were an immediate success in business as well as in middle-and upper-class residences. President Hayes installed a telephone in the White House in 1878. By 1880, only four years after Americans first heard of the thing, 50,000 of them were paying monthly fees to hear it jangle on their walls and jumping up to chat about—whatever. By 1890, there were 800,000 phones in the United States. By 1900, 1.5 million people in even small towns knew all about exchanges, party lines, and operators.

The first phone systems were strictly local, for communication within a city or town. The telegraph remained the medium for long-distance communication. By 1892, however, the larger eastern and midwestern cities were linked by a

Images courtesy Special Collections and University Archives, University of Oregon Libraries. #CN312.

The first telephone operators were teenaged boys. Bell fired the lot of them when, to amuse one another, a major activity of adolescent boys, they made sarcastic remarks to callers. The result was an unforeseen employment opportunity for young working-class women. They gladly obeyed instructions to be polite and deferential no matter how disagreeable customers were. They worked twelve-hour shifts but it was clean "shirtwaist work" that required no special education beyond good manners.

long-distance network. Even some rambunctious little western desert communities noted in their slim directories that "you can now talk to San Francisco with ease from our downtown office."

Instantaneous give-and-take communication was invaluable to businessmen. For getting things done, talking on the telephone was as superior to exchanging telegrams as telegrams had been better than an exchange of letters. And phone conversations were safely confidential. They generated no written records as letters did. They did not have to be put into code as was essential with sensitive telegrams, which passed through the hands of telegraphers, who (some of them) knew there might be a tidy payoff somewhere if they pocketed copies of important messages.

The Wizard of Menlo Park   Bell was lionized. Thomas Alva Edison was virtually deified. Written off in boyhood as a dunce, Edison was bewildered only by people who pursued knowledge for its own sake. He was the ultimate, practical, money-minded American tinkerer who, when he saw a need which people would pay to have filled, went to work on it. Often preoccupied and quite deaf, he was abrupt to the point of rudeness. Edison struck some businessmen as unscrupulous; in 1877, the president of Western Union remarked, "that young man has a vacuum where his conscience ought to be."

To the public, however, Edison was a great benefactor. People admired him not only because of his inventions that changed their lives, but also because of his gruff "just folks" anti-intellectual explanations of how he worked. When he was called a genius, he replied that genius was 1 percent inspiration and 99 percent perspiration. Ordinary Americans liked that. In Edison's case, it was largely true. He went to work each morning at the world's first research and development laboratory in Menlo Park, New Jersey—if he had not spent the night there—and supervised as many as twenty "mechanically-minded young men" to discover by trial and error experimentation the solution he defined for them. And he was usually by their side at the work bench.

Edison took out more than a thousand patents between 1876 and 1900. Some were seedbeds for entirely new industries: the storage battery and the motion picture projector, for example. Most were for improvements to existing machines and processes, commissioned by nuts-and-bolts manufacturers who needed to straighten out kinks in their processes. Some were improvements on the inventions of others. Alexander Graham Bell himself turned to Edison for help with a transmitter that had him stumped.

At least one invention was, despite Edison's disdain for pointless tinkering, the fruit of just fooling around: the phonograph. At first, Edison dismissed the invention as useless. However, when others began to exploit the commercial possibilities of recorded sound—music for sale—Edison set up a company to make and sell phonographs and mass-produced recordings. (They were wax-covered cylinders, not the "platters" that eventually proved to be a technology better than Edison's.)

The Light Bulb   Edison's most famous invention, the incandescent light bulb, was actually a perfection of a patent he had purchased. The goal was to convert electricity into stable, safe, controllable illumination. In the 1870s, the poor still extended the day with candles. More and more Americans were bringing light to the night with kerosene lamps. (The whale oil lamp was gone; the world's whales had been overhunted before the Civil War.) Many cities illuminated their busiest streets by pumping gas to street lamps; the well-to-do had gaslight in their homes, as did some nighttime businesses like hotels. A few cities were experimenting with electric arc lighting on streets.

But arc light was far too harsh and too noisy for use indoors and it required extremely high voltage; the lights were dangerous and had to be suspended high on buildings and poles. Gas lamps on streets had to be individually ignited each evening and extinguished each morning. Inside buildings, gas lamps, when carelessly used, caused many fires, especially in hotels. Whether because of ignorance, forgetfulness, or too much to drink, men and women blew out the flame (as they would extinguish a kerosene lamp) instead of turning off the gas valve; half an hour later, the gas having filled the room, someone decided to smoke a cigar and ....

Edison and others knew that in a vacuum within a translucent glass ball, an electrically charged filament glowed. The challenge was to find a filament that would burn brightly enough long enough that the price of the "bulb" was worth spending.

Edison's laboratory tested 6,000 different fibers before it found one (a carbonized Japanese bamboo) that glowed brightly for 40 hours. By the time he patented the incandescent light bulb, Edison had extended the lifetime of a bulb to 170 hours.

Financier J. P. Morgan (who loathed the telephone; he shouted at it angrily when he had no choice but to use it) was fascinated by electric lighting. His home and bank in New York were among the first electrically illuminated buildings in the United States. Naturally, Morgan wanted a piece of the commercial action too, and he got it.

The incandescent bulb succeeded as dramatically as the telephone. From a modest start in New York in 1882 (about eighty customers), Edison's invention spread so quickly that by 1900, more than 3,000 towns and cities were electrically illuminated. Within a few more years, gaslight in homes largely disappeared and the kerosene lantern survived only on farms or as backups when the power went out.

Westinghouse and the Air Brake

George Westinghouse was not as versatile an inventor as Edison, although he proved to be a far better businessman. His great invention was a system for bringing long trains to a safe stop: the air brake. Previously, locomotives and the cars they pulled each had brakes, mechanical friction devices that were individually operated by brakemen. It was a dangerous job, hopping from car to car on a moving train, but the brakes worked well enough when a train was making a scheduled stop. Well before arriving at a depot, the brakeman, who rode in the caboose at the end of the train, applied its brake, then the brake on the next car forward, and so on. This created a drag on the locomotive so that the train had slowed to a crawl when it reached the station.

The problem was emergency stops. When, without any preliminary braking at the rear of the train, the engineer tried to stop quickly because there was another train or a herd of cattle on the track or a bridge was washed out, the momentum of dozens of unbraked cars piled them up in catastrophic wrecks. Thousands of passengers and railroad workers were killed in emergency stops every year.

At age 22, just out of the Union army, Westinghouse solved the problem. He equipped each car on a train with brakes operated pneumatically—by compressed air forced through hoses running car to car. Even the most frantic of stops started the braking at the rear, moving forward like a brakeman, so that there was no pileup. Westinghouse patented the air brake in 1869. By 1880, all the nation's major railroads had installed them.

AC/DC

During the 1880s, Westinghouse turned his attention to a problem that Edison had shrugged off, the efficient transmission of electricity from generator to consumers. Edison used direct current (DC). DC voltage was low so it was comparatively safe. However, it could be transmitted only short distances with numerous homes drawing power through expensive copper cables several inches in diameter. In large cities, this meant building a good many generating plants—usually coal burning. That was expensive.

Alternating current (AC) could be transmitted 25 to 30 miles in the 1880s, theoretically many times that distance, making it cheaper to produce than DC. Westinghouse was introduced to its possibilities by a brilliant if somewhat unbalanced Serbian immigrant, Nikola Tesla, who had briefly worked with Edison. When Tesla and Edison quarreled about the usefulness of AC, Westinghouse hired Tesla and bought his patents.

The catch was that AC was transmitted at extremely high voltage. Edison tried to frighten the public away from it with a clever but unsuccessful campaign. He publicly electrocuted animals, including an elephant, with AC and persuaded New York State to adopt the AC electric chair to execute murderers. (New York was the first state to adopt "the chair.")

Westinghouse and Tesla countered by stringing their transmission wires on high towers and perfecting a transformer that stepped down the voltage for safe use in factories and homes. AC became the standard after Westinghouse won two high-profile contracts: electrifying the Columbian Exposition in Chicago in 1893 and, in 1896, the electrification of Buffalo, New York (then one of the country's ten largest cities) with power generated at Niagara Falls 20 miles away.

CONQUERING THE WIDE-OPEN SPACES

The single great impediment to developing a national industrial economy in the United States was the size of the country. No point in England is farther than 20 miles from a navigable river. The only significant mountains in Great Britain are on the fringes, in Scotland and Wales. In the eighteenth century, the British began to build a network of canals that crisscrossed the country. Cheaply and efficiently, manufacturers could assemble iron, coal, and the other materials needed for manufacture—and to dispatch their products to a national market and to ports for shipment abroad. Transportation costs were negligible.

The steam-powered railroad was an English invention. But the United States was the country that exploited it to the fullest. Within a few years of the first run of the *Rocket* in England, the United States had laid more miles of track than the British had. The railroad was invaluable in Great Britain; it was essential in America where vast distances and a rugged topography limited the utility of canals.

The Eastern Trunk Lines   By the end of the Civil War, there were 35,000 miles of railroad track in the United States, but only a few "systems."

In the former Confederacy, there had been 400 independent railroad companies with an average track run of 40 miles. It was possible to ship a cargo from St. Louis to Atlanta by any of twenty different routes with many interruptions because few railroad companies linked up with others. Goods shipped long distances—salt pork from Chicago to Boston, for instance—were carried in stages by lines independent of one another. At each point of transfer, the barrels had to be unloaded at one railroad's terminal (hand labor added to costs), carted across town by horse and wagon (another costly bottleneck), and reloaded on another company's cars. Six railroads ran into Richmond; no two of them shared a depot. Baltimore was a hot spot at the beginning of the Civil War because Union soldiers headed for Washington had to detrain and march across the city to another depot. A pro-Confederate mob attacked them. Chicago and New York were linked by rail on maps, but a shipment going the entire distance had to be unloaded and reloaded six times.

There were three east–west trunk lines, lines designed to haul freight and passengers long distances without such interruptions. The Baltimore and Ohio (B&O) connected Baltimore with the Ohio River (and to St. Louis in 1857). The Pennsylvania Railroad (PRR) linked Philadelphia and Pittsburgh; under J. Edgar Thompson, president between 1852 and 1874, it was the best run American railroad, managed in "sections" by superintendents Thompson picked for their business skills. The Erie Railroad linked the Hudson River just north of New York City to the Great Lakes. It was the longest railroad in the world but was hog-tied by its charter, which forbade it to build beyond the borders of New York state. During the Civil War, the Erie competed poorly with the Pennsylvania Railroad, which was better positioned to exploit federal contracts to carry supplies to the army. (The B&O was vulnerable to Confederate cavalry raids.)

Lincoln appointed the Pennsylvania's vice president, Thomas A. Scott, undersecretary of war in charge of transporting troops. By becoming, in effect, the federal government's transportation arm, the Pennsy gained political influence to the degree that, it was said, the Pennsylvania state legislature did nothing until it was cleared with the railroad. After the war, Thompson and Scott used the railroad's windfall profits to buy up other railroads in surrounding states, linking their tracks to the Pennsylvania's "main line." After he became president of the railroad in 1874, Scott extended the line to New York City and Chicago. With 30,000 miles of track in thirteen states by 1890, the Pennsy was the nation's largest and richest railroad.

The Erie War and the New York Central
The fourth great Eastern trunk line, the New York Central, was a postwar creation. It was put together from dozens of short lines in New England and New York by a crusty former ferry boat captain, "Commodore" Cornelius Vanderbilt, who never shook off his rough manners. Already rich from his ferryboats and steamship lines running to Central America and Europe, Vanderbilt was never quite respectable. To the chagrin of his children, who wanted to break into high society, Vanderbilt swore a blue streak and befriended Victoria Woodhull and Tennessee Claflin, two sisters who flaunted propriety by preaching free love and not shunning its practice. They delighted the Commodore, and he set them up as stockbrokers.

In 1867, Vanderbilt made a false start toward building his trunk line by quietly buying up stock in the 300-mile-long Erie. Unfortunately, the three scoundrels who had control of the company and were already milking it, learned of Vanderbilt's purchases.

The nominal leader of the Erie Ring was Daniel Drew, a pious Methodist who knew much of the Bible by heart but put a very liberal interpretation on the verse in Exodus that said "Thou shalt not steal." James "Jubilee Jim" Fisk, just 33 years old, had no interest in the Bible. He was a stout, jolly extrovert who sported garish clothing, tossed silver dollars to street urchins, and caroused with showgirls. The third member of the ring was Jay Gould, a quiet man smarter than Drew and Fisk put together.

As Vanderbilt bought, the Ring watered the stock; that is, they issued shares far in excess of the railroad's real assets. Gould privately told a friend that "there is no intrinsic value to it, probably." But the value of Erie stock—there was so much of it—increased from $24 million to $78 million. Vanderbilt bought and bought but was still a minority stockholder. Drew, Fisk, and Gould pocketed the profits on the watered stock and still controlled the company.

When the Commodore realized he was being swindled, he went to friendly New York judges and had the trio indicted. Drew, Fisk, and Gould fled to New Jersey where they holed up in a hotel guarded by gunmen. Eventually, a settlement was arranged. Vanderbilt got most of his money back; the Ring kept the Erie.

Bringing Order to Chaos   Drew, Gould, and Fisk took little interest in the Erie's track, locomotives, rolling stock, and the freight and passengers it hauled. They did not care if the railroad showed a profit. (It never did under their ownership.) They were pirates, manipulating Erie paper to enrich themselves. The Erie had the worst accident record of any American railroad because of neglected roadbeds and dilapidated equipment. The company did not pay a dividend to its stockholders for seventy years.

Scott and Vanderbilt were not above playing with company books for their personal benefit, but they operated railroads that were national assets. They invested profits in improvements as well as expansion. They perfected services and were open to innovation. Railroaders from the West and from Europe examined the Pennsy's roadbeds because they were "state of the art." The Pennsylvania was the first railroad to convert from wood to coal for fuel. The New York Central pioneered the use of stronger, safer steel rails and was the first major railroad to equip its trains with the life-saving Westinghouse air brake.

Time Zones   The Pennsylvania and New York Central took the lead in establishing time zones, an American innovation. In 1870, railroads set their clocks, and therefore their schedules, according to local time in city where their headquarters was located. But cities and towns along the tracks set their official times according to local astronomical calculations or the mayor's preference. In 1870, there were somewhere between 80 and 100 "official" clock settings in the United States. If one Chicago businessman arranged with another to meet at a downtown restaurant at noon, there was no problem. But when it was noon in Chicago, it was 11:27 in Omaha, 11:56 in St. Louis, 12:09 in Louisville, and 12:17 in Toledo.

When it was noon in Washington, D.C., it was 12:24 in Baltimore, 70 miles away. The Baltimorean in Washington who tried to catch a train home might discover that while his watch was correct for his hometown, he was nearly half an hour late for the train that he expected to take him there. In Buffalo's station, which served both the New York Central and the Michigan Southern, there were three clocks: one for each railroad, and one for Buffalo time. In Pittsburgh's station there were six clocks. Traveling from Maine to California on the railroad, one passed through twenty time zones. Nor was the mess just a nuisance for railroad schedules. Confusion as to what time it was caused wrecks when two trains tried to use the same track at the same "real time."

In 1870, Charles F. Dowd proposed bringing order to the chaos by establishing four official time zones in the United States. The big railroads immediately adopted Dowd's system—gladly. Many cities and towns resisted, as if Dowd were tampering with the passage of the sun across the sky. Finally, in 1883, Congress established the four zones by law. So obviously sensible was the system that, the next year, twenty-five nations met in Washington and adopted the "universal day," twenty-four worldwide time zones.

THE TRANSCONTINENTAL LINES

In the East, the creation of railroad systems was largely a matter of consolidating independent short lines. During the 1880s, the names of 540 railway companies disappeared from business registers. West of Chicago, the hub at which a dozen railroads converged, extensive and integrated railroad systems were constructed whole from scratch.

Public Finance The first four transcontinental railroads were built, owned, and managed by private corporations subsidized by the federal government. (The fifth, James J. Hill's Great Northern, was built without federal subsidies.) Without federal funding, the lines might not have been built. Railroad construction was expensive. Building just a mile of track meant excavating or building up a grade, bedding 3,000 ties in gravel, and attaching 400 iron rails to the ties by driving 12,000 spikes. And that does not count bridges and tunnels. However, between Omaha and Sacramento in the West, the terminuses of the first transcontinental, there was little population, customers who would be shipping and receiving freight.

Few paying customers meant few revenues, not a prospectus that excited investors. The impetus to the Pacific Railway Act of 1862 was the federal government's political and military interests in binding the Pacific coast to the rest of the Union.

The Railway Act gave two companies, the Union Pacific (UP) and the Central Pacific (CP); a right of way of 200 feet wide between Omaha and Sacramento. For each mile of track that the companies built, they were to be granted, on either side of the tracks, ten alternate sections (square miles) of the public domain, a belt of land 40 miles wide laid out like a checkerboard in which the UP and CP owned half the squares.

The railroads could sell the land to settlers to raise money for construction or put the real estate up as collateral with which to secure loans from banks. In addition, depending on the nature of the terrain, the government loaned the two companies between $16,000 and $48,000 per mile of track at bargain interest rates.

The Romance of the Rails These lavish terms attracted men who were less interested in operating railroads than in making money by building them. Within twenty years, this was to result in the overbuilding of railroads in the West: laying more track than was needed or than the sparsely populated country would support. The government's generosity also encouraged frauds like the Union Pacific's Crédit Mobilier, a construction company owned by the same men who owned the UP to which the UP paid grotesquely padded bills. When, during the 1870s, investigators picked their way through the accounts, they concluded that $44 million of the UP's construction expenses had been skimmed by the owners of the Crédit Mobilier. The extent of fraud in the construction of the Central Pacific was never determined because the CP burned its books.

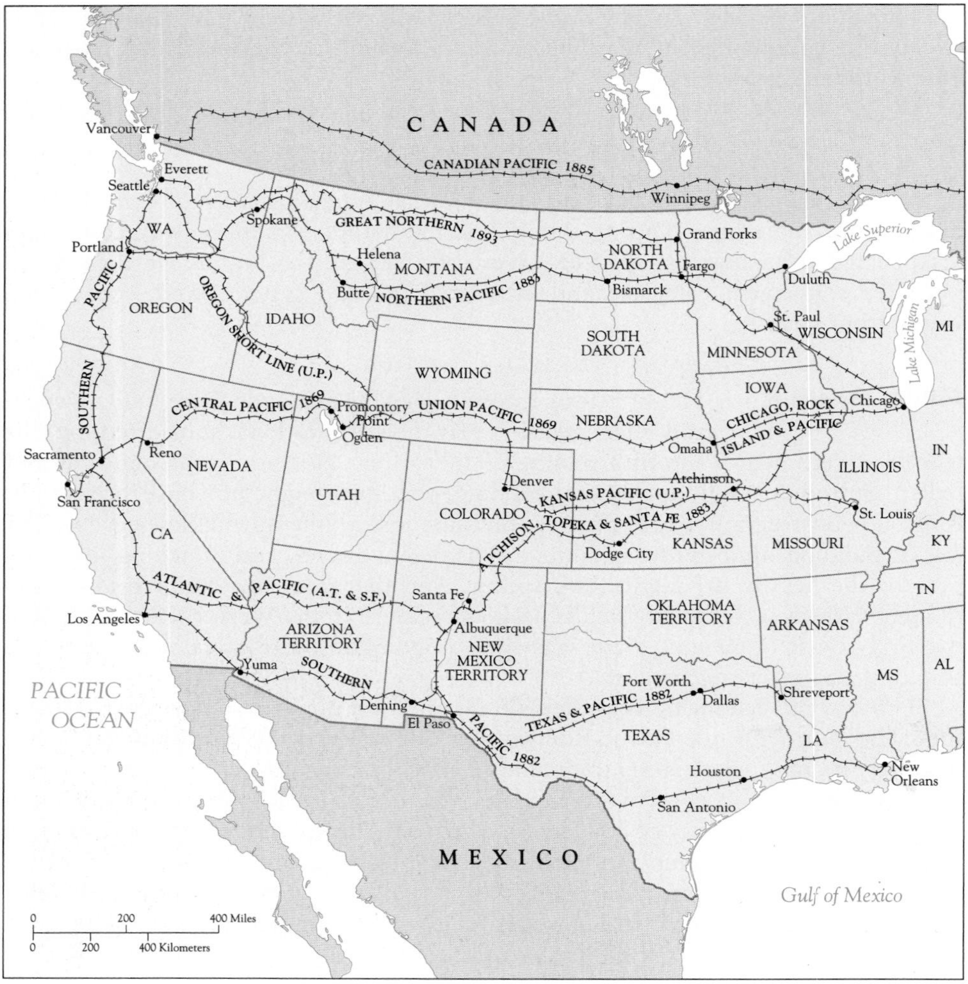

Wadsworth/Cengage Learning

MAP 26.1 Transcontinental Railroads, 1862–1900

By 1900, five transcontinental railroads spanned the United States from the Mississippi Valley to the Pacific Coast: the Great Northern, the Northern Pacific, the Union Pacific-Central Pacific, The Atchison, Topeka, and Santa Fe, and the Southern Pacific. Five was too many; the western railroad network was overbuilt. So much money was to be made from federal and state land grants and subsidies and stock manipulations that the "great railroaders" took no interest in how much the lines would be able to collect in revenue. The exception was James J. Hill who built the Great Northern piecemeal, promoting settlement along the railroad as he built.

So central was the government subsidy to construction that, when UP and CP approached one another in Utah, they raced to win every mile of land grant and loan they could. The grading crews of the two railroads actually laid out parallel grades within sight of one another for almost 100 miles. A peace meeting of the two companies' directors agreed on Promontory Point, Utah, north of Salt Lake City, as the point where they would link up. There, on May 10, 1869, the "golden spike" was driven.

Railroad Mania   Seeing the owners of the UP and CP become instant millionaires, other ambitious men descended on Washington in search of subsidies. In 1864, when the first transcontinental was hardly begun, Congress granted the Northern Pacific (NP), which proposed to build from Lake Superior to Puget Sound, an even more generous grant. In the territories, the NP received forty alternate sections of land for every mile of railway. The Atchison, Topeka, and Santa Fe—another land-grant transcontinental—ran from Kansas to Los Angeles. The Texas Pacific and Southern Pacific linked New Orleans and San Francisco at El Paso, Texas. In 1884, the Canadians (who were even more generous with government land) completed the Canadian Pacific.

The total costs were astronomical. The federal government gave railroads 131 million acres. To this, state governments added 45 million acres. An area larger than France and Belgium combined was given to a handful of capitalists. In addition, towns along the proposed routes enticed the builders to choose them over

Southern Pacific Transportation Company

Most of the laborers who built the Central Pacific Railroad from Sacramento to Utah were Chinese, hired in gangs recruited by Chinese jobbers. For the few years the railroad was under construction, they enjoyed employment opportunities denied them for racial reasons during the Gold Rush and after the age of massive construction projects was over in the West. They built trestles like this one with no "heavy equipment" and chipped shelves for the railroad out of Sierra Nevada granite. Some of them hung in baskets on thousand-foot cliffs to drill holes for explosives.

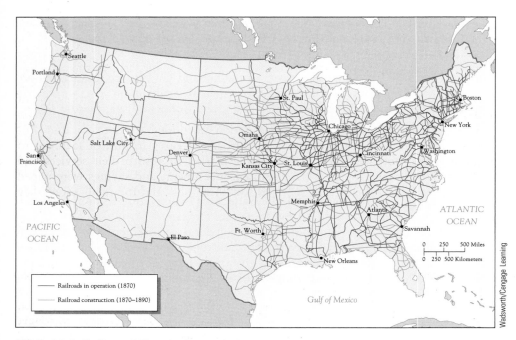

MAP 26.2 Railroad Expansion, 1870–1890

In 1870, only one railroad crossed the continent to the Pacific, the Union Pacific-Southern Pacific. During the thirty years after 1870, most railroad expansion was in the West. Four more transcontinentals were built (plus two in Canada). Perhaps more important "feeder lines" fed productive agricultural and grazing country into the east–west trunk lines.

nearby rivals as sites for depots and switching yards by offering town lots, cash bounties, and exemption from taxes.

Some of these gifts were acts of desperation. If a railroad bypassed a town, the town was likely to die. Railroad companies did not hesitate to set communities against one another like roosters in a cock fight. The UP bypassed Denver, the only city for hundreds of miles in every direction in part because the giveaways Denver offered were not up to par. The original route of the Atchison, Topeka, and Santa Fe, which was popularly known as "the Santa Fe," did not go near the city of that name. Albuquerque offered the better financial deal and got the tracks.

The Panic of 1873

Too much railroad was built too soon. When the lines were finished, high operating costs and low revenues meant that few railroad companies were profitable, only one in three in 1872. The others defaulted on their loans and, on September 18, 1873, a Friday, "Black Friday," the chickens came home to roost. Jay Cooke and Company, a bank that had loaned heavily to the NP, announced that the firm was bankrupt.

Jay Cooke was not just any old bank. It was the most prestigious financial house in the United States; Cooke had been the federal government's chief financial agent during the Civil War. Its failure led to a panic as speculators, fearing other failures, rushed to sell their stocks. The market crashed; banks failed. By the end of 1873, 5,000 businesses had declared bankruptcy and a half million workers were jobless. The depression of the 1870s was the worst in American history to that time.

It would not be the last. A by-product of fabulous economic growth was a wildly erratic business cycle, the "unprecedented disturbance and depression of trade," in the words of a contemporary. For a time the industrial capitalist economy boomed, luring investment and speculation, encouraging expansion and production. Sooner or later, the capacity of railroads to carry freight, or factories to produce goods, outpaced the capacity of the market to absorb their services and products. When that happened, banks closed, investments and savings were wiped out, factories locked their gates, workers lost their jobs, and the retail shops they frequented went broke.

THE GREAT ORGANIZERS

In a free, unregulated, market economy, the boom and bust cycle was inevitable and most Americans, then as now, regarded a free economy as sacred. Businessmen who reached the top of the economic pyramid, however, ceased to be enchanted with the idea of wide-open competition. To the entrepreneur who was no longer scrambling but in charge of a commercial or industrial empire in which millions of dollars were invested and which employed thousands of people, stability was what counted: the assurance that supplies of raw materials would be unhindered two, three, or ten years in the future, and that future revenues could be reliably projected. Competition was a threat to stability. In the late nineteenth century, the organizers of big businesses in numerous industries—from sugar refining to the manufacture of cigarettes—strove, in different ways, to minimize or eliminate the uncertainty that competitors brought to their business.

Andrew Carnegie in steel and oilman John D. Rockefeller were the two most famous big businessmen of the era. Carnegie immunized his steel manufacturing empire from the threat of competitors by cutting the costs of production in his mills so low that he could dictate the market price of steel, keep his factories running at capacity, and let other steel manufacturers pick up the business he could not handle. John D. Rockefeller faced a different kind of problem in the oil business. It was impossible to gain control of crude oil production—major new discoveries of crude oil deposits were routine news—and there were too many refineries to undersell them at a price Rockefeller and his associates needed just to stay in business. They solved their problem by persuading most of their competitors to let them take over their refineries.

Steel: The Bones of the Economy   Steel is the element iron from which all impurities have been burned out at high temperatures except for a carefully controlled amount of carbon. Its chemical composition makes steel many times stronger per unit of weight than iron. Steel has been made since antiquity but only in small quantities because the process of making it consumed huge quantities of fuel. It was practical only in making small, expensive items such as—famously—the fine swords of Japan and Toledo in Spain—and precision instruments.

During the early 1850s, working secretly in the Kentucky woods, William "Pig Iron" Kelly developed a technique for making steel cheaply in large quantities out of pig iron (iron ingots sold by iron smelters to makers of finished goods). When he emerged from the woods to patent his process, he discovered that an Englishman, Henry Bessemer, had independently developed the same process. Although it became known universally as the Bessemer process, the Patent Office acknowledged that Kelly had been first to perfect it by a couple of months.

No one grasped the possibilities created by the Bessemer process more quickly than Andrew Carnegie. He had emigrated to the United States with a destitute family when he was a child. He became a telegrapher who caught the eye of Pennsylvania Railroad vice president, Thomas A. Scott, who quickly promoted him to an executive position and recommended investments that were very good tips indeed. In 1865, Carnegie was rich enough to leave the railroad and found the Keystone Bridge Company, which built iron and steel bridges. (Keystone built the first span across the Mississippi.) When the depression of the 1870s lowered the costs of materials and labor and other businessmen nervously guarded their shrunken capital, Carnegie did the opposite. He exploited the opportunity to put all his money into constructing the world's largest steel mill on a 106-acre tract at Braddock on the Monongahela River. One of his mottos was "put all your eggs in one basket and then watch that basket."

A Head for Business
Carnegie knew apples as well as eggs—how to polish them. He named his factory after J. Edgar Thomson, the president of the Pennsylvania Railroad, his former boss. Because Carnegie would be making rails, the Pennsy would be his biggest single customer. However, Carnegie sited his great plant outside of Pittsburgh. Pittsburgh was a one-railroad city; the Pennsylvania ran the town, setting shipping rates from and to Pittsburgh at whatever levels the railroad chose. The Pennsylvania ran through Braddock too, but so did the Baltimore and Ohio. The two companies would have to bid against one another to get Carnegie's shipping business. Carnegie admired Thomson. He was willing to flatter him. But he did not trust the health of Carnegie Steel to Thomson's good will.

Carnegie knew little about the technology of steelmaking to the day he died. But he had a keen eye for men who did. He hired the industry's best supervisors and engineers and bound the cream of the professions to him by making them partners. His most important partner was Henry Clay Frick, a coal and coke magnate as well as an engineer. Frick actually ran Carnegie Steel; Carnegie was no workaholic; he spent much of each year at a castle in Scotland playing the laird.

"Vertical Integration"
Carnegie's contribution to business organization was his exploitation of "vertical integration." That is, to get a leg up on competitors, Carnegie expanded his operation from a base of steel manufacture to ownership of the raw materials from which steel was made and the means of assembling them. Bessemer furnaces were fueled by coke, which is to coal what charcoal is to wood, a hotter-burning distillation of the raw

material. It was to avoid having to buy coke from others that Carnegie made Frick a partnership offer he could not refuse. Frick brought 5,000 acres of coalfields and 1,000 coke ovens to the company. Carnegie and Frick added iron mines in Michigan, Wisconsin, and Minnesota to their holdings.

While he was independent on trunk-line railroads, Carnegie controlled as much of his own shipping as he could. He owned barges that carried iron ore from the Marquette and later the Mesabi Range to his own port facilities in Erie, Pennsylvania. He owned a short-line railroad that brought the ore from Erie to his greatest factory, Homestead. By eliminating from his final product price the profits of independent suppliers, distributors, and carriers, Carnegie was able to undersell competing companies that were not vertically integrated and had to include the profits of independent suppliers in their price. In 1870 there were 167 iron and steel firms around Pittsburgh. By the end of the century there were 47; those Carnegie did not control priced their product according to Carnegie's dictates.

Vertical integration served Andrew Carnegie very well. In 1890, his company was responsible for a quarter of the nation's steel production. His personal income rose to $25 million a year. He was able to lead an active intellectual life and spend much of his time in a castle in Scotland not far from where his father had worked as a weaver, while his company steadily assumed a more dominant role in the steel business.

In 1901, 66 years old and bored with business, Carnegie agreed to sell all his interests to a syndicate organized by investment banker, J. P. Morgan. Carnegie pocketed $500 million, then the largest personal commercial transaction ever made, and Morgan created the first billion dollar corporation, United States Steel. From birth, U.S. Steel controlled "the destinies of a population nearly as large as that of Maryland or Nebraska," and had a bigger annual budget than all but a handful of the world's nations.

The Corporation's Edge

Carnegie organized his empire of coal and iron as partnerships. In this he was untypical of the era's industrial giants. The corporation, capitalized by selling stock in the enterprise on the open market and owned in proportion to the number of their shares by stockholders, was the chief agent of industrial development and business consolidation in the United States.

The corporate structure was attractive to both entrepreneurs and investors for several reasons. A corporation's legal liability was limited to the assets of the corporation and did not extend to shareholders' other property. That is, if a business owned by an individual or partners went bust, creditors could (and did), after dividing up the assets of the business, seize the owners' other property, including, if necessary, their homes and furniture. If a corporation was bankrupted, its limited liability gave creditors access to the corporation's assets, nothing more.

Carnegie did well enough putting all his eggs in one basket and enlarging the basket during depressions when expansion was cheaper. However, the corporate structure was a better way to raise a great deal of money quickly. By selling shares in a company to anyone willing to buy them while retaining (at no cost) enough shares to determine company policy, entrepreneurs could amass capital far beyond their own resources.

**John
D. Rockefeller
and Black Gold**
The master magician of the corporation was John D.
Rockefeller, a solemn, muscular, and deeply religious young
man born in New York state who went to work as a bookkeeper
in Cleveland, Ohio. When the Civil War broke out, Rockefeller
went into business as a grocery wholesaler with the army his biggest customer.
Rockefeller dodged the draft by hiring a substitute and he correctly reckoned that
when the war ended and government contracts were canceled, the bottom would
fall out of the provisions business.

Even during the war, Rockefeller had taken an interest in Cleveland's oil refining business. Cleveland was the refining center of the new industry because of its
proximity to the world's first commercial oilfield in western Pennsylvania.

Crude oil had seeped to the surface of the earth since before there were human
beings to step into the tacky puddles. Ancient Mesopotamians wrote of it. Europeans
used it to lubricate wagon wheels. Jesuits in western New York in the seventeenth century reported of "a stagnant thick water that ignites like brandy, burning with bubbles
of flame when fire is tossed into it." The Seneca ate it for a laxative. Farmers who lived
around Titusville, Pennsylvania, hated it. It fouled the soil and polluted streams.

During the 1850s, a chemist at Yale University discovered that "cracking" crude
oil—heating it until it vaporized, then condensing it at different temperatures—broke
it down into a number of chemical compounds. Gasoline was one of them but of no
commercial value because it was so volatile. Kerosene, however, burned slowly, safely,
and brightly—an excellent illuminant. It was a timely discovery because the price of
sperm whale oil increased from $1 a gallon in 1850 to $2.55 in 1865. Indeed, by the
end of the war it was in short supply at any price. The Confederate commerce raiders,
especially the *Shenandoah*, had wreaked havoc on American whaling ships.

Kerosene was cheap. Even the poor could afford to buy it. Beginning in 1859, when
a former army officer named Edwin Drake perfected a drill-and-pump system by which
crude oil could be extracted from deep within the earth, a new industry was born.

The Pennsylvania oil rush was as wild as the gold rush of 1849. Drilling for oil,
like panning for gold, required only modest capital. Thousands of men dreaming of
instant riches descended on western Pennsylvania. The unfortunately named town of
Pithole consisted of four log cabins in 1859; it had a population of 12,000 in 1860.

Rockefeller came to the oilfields and looked. He did not like much of what he
saw. The social and moral disorder appalled him; Rockefeller was a rigorous
Baptist. And he did not like the wild swings in the price of crude oil, soaring when
refiners demanded more crude than was available, plummeting when new wells
were brought into production. In 1861, the price of crude oil swung from as high
as $10 a barrel to—briefly—10¢. Even in 1864, when the industry had settled
down some, the price of a barrel bobbed up and down between $4 tand $12.
Drilling for oil was not a bookkeeper's kind of business.

**"Horizontal
Integration"**
Oil refining was not a wildcatter's kind of work. It cost much
more to build a refinery than to sink a drill and say a prayer.
And Rockefeller liked the arithmetic. About 75 percent of a
barrel of crude oil was kerosene; a gallon of kerosene sold for twice the cost of
a barrel of crude (40–42 gallons). But refining was a fragmented, highly competitive

business too; as late as 1870, there were 250 American refiners (although most of them were paper companies). However, Rockefeller recognized that, unlike drilling, the refining end of the business was manageable. Refining was a "narrows" on the river of oil that flowed from well to consumers. Like the robber barons of medieval Europe, who built castles at narrows on the Rhine and Danube, thence charging boats to pass or be seized, a company that controlled refining would be able to determine the level of crude oil production and the selling price of kerosene. It did not matter how many wildcatters roamed the countryside with drilling rigs. If there was one great refiner, they would sell their crude at the price the refiner was willing to pay.

Controlling an entire industry by controlling the key phase of it is known as horizontal integration. Instead of dominating an industry by integrating a portion of the business from the source of raw materials to the market (as Carnegie did in steel), horizontal integration meant establishing a stranglehold on an industry at its key point.

In 1870, Rockefeller and his associates, who controlled one of twenty-six refineries in Cleveland, about 10 percent of kerosene production, formed the South Improvement Company which quickly won control of twenty-two of the city's refineries. They accomplished this by persuading their competitors that if they ceased to compete with one another, they would no longer live in fear of a price war that would destroy the losers and leave the winners with crippled enterprises.

Standard Oil   Through a complex series of reorganizations, improvised more than planned, the South Improvement Company evolved into Standard Oil, a trust. Nationwide, stockholders in refining corporations turned their shares over to the trust. In exchange, Standard issued them trust certificates equivalent to the value of their holdings. Rockefeller and his associates—notably his brother William, Henry Flagler, Samuel Andrews, and Maurice B. Clark—retained control of Standard so as to make policy without interference. They razed obsolete and inefficient refineries. Others were improved and new ones constructed. Refiners who refused to cooperate were run out of business in ruthless rate wars. Within twenty years, Standard Oil controlled 90 percent of American refining. They worked this magic by persuading cooperative competitors to throw in with them, and by driving weak and uncooperative refiners out of the business.

Former refiners who had played ball with Standard at the start became richer than they could have imagined when they were worrying about competitors, fighting fires (an omnipresent hazard at oil refineries), and slogging about in the mud and snow turning valves. Rockefeller, on the basis of a modest cash investment and a brilliant mind for business, became the world's richest man. When banking giant J. P. Morgan died in 1913, leaving an estate of $80 million, Rockefeller was stunned. He said, "and to think he wasn't even a rich man." In computations made recently that assessed personal fortunes as a percentage of gross national product, John D. Rockefeller, who left $3.7 billion when he died in 1937—this after decades of giving money away by the millions—was the richest man in the history of the world. (Bill Gates of Microsoft, the current titleholder, is only thirty-first on the list.)

27

LIVING WITH LEVIATHAN
Coping with Big Business and Great Wealth

Success is counted sweetest
By those who ne'er succeed.

—Emily Dickinson

A successful man cannot realize how hard an unsuccessful
man finds life.

—Edgar Watson Howe

The moral flabbiness of the exclusive worship of the
bitch-goddess SUCCESS.
That—with the squalid cash interpretation put on the word
success—is our national disease.

—William James

In *Democracy in America*, Alexis de Tocqueville was struck by the equity with which wealth was distributed in Andrew Jackson's America. He observed that (always excepting slaves) few households were so poor as to be without hope of improving their lot and few families were so rich that their security was invulnerable. Indeed, many of the well-fixed Americans de Tocqueville met seemed to be haunted by the anxiety that one stroke of ill-fortune would send them tumbling down into a life of hard work, sore backs, and dirty hands.

Wealth was not as equitably distributed as Tocqueville believed it was. Nevertheless, the gap between the poorest and the richest Americans was much narrower than it became after the Civil War when opportunities to amass previously unimaginable fortunes created a class of multimillionaires—think multibillionaires today—whose wealth was so great that it was impossible for them or anyone else to imagine them falling from their perches. Investment in the most conservative gilt-edge securities ensured that the largest fortunes continued to grow without attention. Cornelius Vanderbilt amassed a personal estate of $110 million (about $2 billion in today's dollars). That was $5 million more than the gold the United States government had on reserve. His son William inherited $90 million of it and doubled his

Business, Wealth, and Protest 1866–1900

1866	1870	1875	1880	1885	1890	1895	1900

1867 Horatio Alger published first "Ragged Dick" book

1877 *Munn* v. *Illinois*

1879 George's *Progress and Poverty* published

1886 *Wabash* case reverses *Munn* decision

1887 Interstate Commerce Commission

1888 Bellamy's *Looking Backward* published

1890 Sherman Antitrust Act

Bradley Martin ball 1897

Carnegie's *Gospel of Wealth* published 1900

fortune in eight years. In 1900, Andrew Carnegie pocketed $480 million ($11 billion today) in a single transaction. John D. Rockefeller, while he gave away $550 million in philanthropy, grew richer.

The emergence, within a single lifetime, of a super-rich social class antagonized some ordinary people imbued with the assumption that the United States was a land where everyone had an equal chance of prospering. Many of them supported movements aimed at reversing the concentration of wealth and power at the top of the economic pyramid—with little success. Rather more remarkable, most Americans rather quickly came to terms with grotesque concentrations of wealth in the hands of a few for the ironic reason that the wasteful, showy consumption of the moneyed classes amused them.

REGULATING RAILROADS AND TRUSTS

The railroads, America's first "big business," had enemies from the beginning. Poets, painters, philosophers, and other romantic intellectuals recoiled from them on cultural and aesthetic grounds. The ugly, dirty, noisy locomotives were "machines in the garden." They defiled the peace and moral goodness of nature and pastoral America.

In cities, railroads faced a rather different kind of critic. Ordinary people protested, even rioted, when railroads snaked deeply into city centers on streets where only pedestrians and horse-drawn vehicles had moved at a walk. Trains did not speed in cities, but even a train at a crawl could not swerve or stop instantly as a pedestrian or horse could. Trains killed an alarming 330 Chicagoans in one year. Serious injuries and dead horses were not counted.

But these were weak or passing enemies. The cultural critics did not change their minds, but they had a small audience. Cities faced up to the fact that railroads could not be tolerated on busy urban streets and required railroads to put their tracks underground or move their terminals outside the congested heart of the city. The New York Central ran underground half the length of Manhattan to its terminal at the famous Grand Central Station. The Pennsylvania moved its main station in Philadelphia from center city to west of the Schuylkill river, then the outskirts of the built-up area.

The Farmer's Grievances

The western farmers' initial enthusiasm for railroads cooled by about 1870. Railroads may have expanded the market for their crops but, as farmers in the midwestern grain belt saw it, the greed and power of the railroad companies ensured that the railroads, not farmers, were the chief beneficiaries of the new integrated national economy.

In the Northeast, where competing small feeder lines ran from cities to their hinterlands like the spokes of a wheel, and the tracks of the great trunk lines—the New York Central, the Erie, the Pennsylvania, the Reading, and the Baltimore and Ohio—roughly paralleled one another, they had to attract shippers by lowering freight charges. In the Midwest, however, there were fewer railroads. Farmers in all but a few areas had one choice when they shipped their wheat, corn, steers, or hogs to processors. The railroads had to consider nothing but their own income when they set their rates.

Moreover, the railroads owned the storage facilities at their depots: stockyards and grain elevators. Hogs and cattle needed to be fed, so they were shipped East right away. Grain, however, could be stored until it was convenient to the railroads to ship it. In the meantime, the farmers paid storage fees because of decisions in which they had no say.

The Granger Laws

In the early 1870s, a farmers' social lodge, the Patrons of Husbandry, commonly known as the Grange, organized farmer protest in the Midwest. When they turned to politics, the Grangers proved to be a formidable force in Indiana, Illinois, and Iowa. From meager beginnings—in 1869, there were only thirty-nine granges (local chapters) in the entire country—the organization grew to having 20,000 granges with 800,000 members.

The Grangers did not form a political party. In each legislative district, they endorsed the candidate—Republican, Democrat, Greenbacker, or independent—who most persuasively promised to enact laws that bridled the railroads. In Illinois, allied with small businessmen who had their own grievances against the railroads, the Grangers elected a comfortable majority in the state legislature. They enacted a series of "Granger laws" that set maximum fees railroads could charge for storing grain and—for shipments within Illinois—freight rates.

The railroads challenged the constitutionality of the Granger laws in court. They had two principal arguments. First, railroads were interstate commerce, which only Congress could regulate. Second, by dictating how much they could charge customers, the state of Illinois was depriving them of the use of their property without due process of law, a violation of the recently ratified Fourteenth Amendment. In *Munn* v. *Illinois* in 1877, the Supreme Court ruled against the railroads. By a 7 to 2 vote, the Court said that the state of Illinois had the right to regulate commerce within the state. When a corporation devoted its "property to a use in which the public has an interest," the Court said, that corporation granted the public the right to regulate that property "for the common good."

It was a big victory but it was temporary. The railroads hired high-powered and creative business lawyers with political connections like Richard B. Olney, a prominent Democrat, and Senator Roscoe Conkling, the boss of the New York Republican party. Representing the Southern Pacific Railroad in several California

The Union Pacific was the pride of the nation when it was completed in 1869. Ten years later, the railroad was denounced as an exploitative tyrant the length of the line, especially in agricultural Nebraska. In this cartoon, the thug straddling the locomotive is William Vanderbilt, son of Cornelius and notorious for replying to a reminder that the public had an interest in how he ran his railroads, "The public be damned."

cases, attorneys began to pick away at the Court's reasoning in *Munn* while looking for just the right case in which to persuade the Court to reverse itself, not something Supreme Court justices like to do.

However, five of the nine justices who ruled on *Munn* retired and were replaced by judges with pro-business records. In the *Wabash* case of 1886 (*Wabash, St. Louis, and Pacific Railway Co.* v. *Illinois*), the Court held that states could not regulate any of the operations of a railroad that crossed state lines because the Constitution reserved the regulation of interstate commerce to Congress. Even a grain elevator that stayed where it was built, if it was owned by an interstate railroad, was defined as a part of the stream of commerce. The reversal of a decision made just nine years previously was unprecedented and would never be duplicated.

The Interstate Commerce Commission   The *Wabash* case did not kill the regulatory movement. If only Congress could bridle the iron horse, anti-railroad activists demanded that Congress do so. The regulatory movement was not well organized, but anger with the arrogance of the big railroads was widespread.

In 1887, Congress passed the Interstate Commerce Act. On the face of it, the law put the railroads in reins. It required interstate railroads to publish their rates and forbade them to depart from these price lists and to pay under the table rebates such as John D. Rockefeller had collected on the kerosene Standard Oil shipped. Railroads were forbidden to charge less per mile for long hauls on routes where they faced competition than for shorter distances in areas where a company had a monopoly of shipping. (Variable costs per mile were common.) The act also forbade combinations of railroad companies to pool business in order to avoid competitive pricing. To enforce the act and to monitor rates and compliance, Congress created an independent federal commission, the Interstate Commerce Commission (ICC).

The Interstate Commerce Act calmed anti-railroad protest, but it had little effect on railroad company practices because the ICC had little power. Commissioner Charles A. Prouty complained, "If the ICC was worth buying, the railroads would try to buy it. The only reason they have not is that the body is valueless in its ability to correct railroad abuses."

The railroads did not have to buy the ICC because, for almost fifteen years, it was given to them. The Harrison, Cleveland, and McKinley administrations were sympathetic to big business and staffed the commission with railroaders and their lawyers.

Railroad Consolidation

During the early 1890s, due in part to the weakness and amenability of the ICC, most of the nation's largest railroads were linked together in five great systems. By 1900, all five were under the control, or under the influence just short of control, of two New York-based investment banks, J. P. Morgan and Company and Kuhn, Loeb, and Company—the latter in league with Union Pacific president Edward H. Harriman.

The railroaders called the bankers in because they needed capital to lay second, third, and fourth tracks; to replace aging locomotives and rolling stock; to build or purchase spur lines; or simply because they were broke. The federal government's construction subsidies were long gone. Revenues from freight charges were inadequate. Issuing new stock was out of the question. Although no railroad was as grossly overvalued as the still agonized Erie, the books of virtually all of them had been cooked to some extent. Every transcontinental line except the Great Northern was in receivership before 1900. Only the great investment banks commanded the capital the big railroads needed to get into the black.

Investment banks were not "service banks" at which working people could deposit a dollar or so a week. They did not offer checking accounts to small businesses. (Personal checking accounts were virtually unknown.) They dealt only with individuals, corporations, and institutions who did business in the tens of thousands of dollars and more. They were sales agents for the bonds big corporations and state and foreign governments issued when they needed large infusions of money. The investment banks found buyers for their bonds both privately and on the open market, collecting handsome commissions for their services. The investment banks of the 1890s and early 1900s arranged the finances of corporate mergers on commission and loaned their own money to reliable debtors.

When J. P. Morgan and Kuhn-Loeb came to the rescue, however, as they did with railroads that went bankrupt during the depression of the 1890s, they insisted that their own representatives sit on the corporations' boards of directors to ensure that their money was well used (and repaid). By 1900, either the Morgan or Kuhn-Loeb banks were coordinating the policies and practices of most big railroads. The banks called a halt to the periodic and ruinous rate wars among the New York Central, Pennsylvania, and Baltimore and Ohio in the eastern states. In 1903, J. P. Morgan engineered a merger of the Northern Pacific and the Great Northern, two systems with parallel lines between the Great Lakes and the Pacific Northwest.

Banker control of the railroads had several benefits. No more could pirates like the Erie Ring destroy transportation systems for the sake of short-term killings. The coordination of the nation's railways also resulted in a gradual lowering of freight rates and even fares for passengers. Between 1866 and 1897, the cost of shipping a hundredweight of grain from Chicago to New York dropped from 65¢ to 20¢, and the rate for shipping beef from 90¢ per hundredweight to 40¢. J. P. Morgan's self-justification was identical to John D. Rockefeller's: Competition was wasteful and destructive; consolidation better served the nation as a whole, as well as its capitalists.

J. P. Morgan In the popular mind, John Pierpont Morgan rivaled John D. Rockefeller as the personification of the consolidation of power. Where were individual freedom and opportunity, people asked, when a secretive, sinister money power could decide the fate of millions of farmers and working people in its paneled board rooms?

It never occurred to Morgan to apologize for being a powerful man. He reveled in being called a titan. He was supremely arrogant in his undisguised contempt for ordinary mortals. He liked to be feared, and held in awe. Unlike Rockefeller, he was indifferent to the fact that he was hated. He was vulnerable only to ridicule. An affliction of the skin had swollen his nose and colored it a bright red when he was angered (which was often). The people with whom he rubbed elbows—partners in his bank, industrialists seeking help, art dealers with paintings or sculptures for sale, and Episcopal bishops—did not mention his single human flaw.

The Sherman Antitrust Act The Sherman Antitrust Act's early history paralleled the ICC's. It too was enacted (in 1890) only when Congress was alarmed by popular pressure to do something about monopolies that eliminated competition in their industries. The Sherman law declared that "every contract, combination, in the form of trust or otherwise, or conspiracy, in restraint of trade or commerce among the several states ... is hereby declared to be illegal." It authorized the Attorney General to prosecute business combinations powerful enough to control the practices of an industry, and to force them to dismantle into the companies that had joined together in order to "restrain trade."

Congress was treading on ground foreign to it, and some of the wording of the Sherman Act was careless, creating loopholes and technicalities soon discovered and exploited by corporation lawyers. Its effectiveness was also undercut by the fact that both the Democratic Cleveland and the Republican McKinley administrations were friendly to big business. Neither was interested in slapping regulations on institutions they regarded as the engines of the national economy. Grover Cleveland's attorney general, Richard B. Olney, was a corporation lawyer who had won fame and wealth by fighting and usually foiling state regulatory laws. During the first ten years the Sherman Act was on the books, the government instituted only eighteen prosecutions using it; four of them were directed at labor unions which, when they went on strike, could be defined as "conspiracies in restraint of trade."

When the government did prosecute corporations, it fared poorly in the courts. The first major case under the Sherman act was brought against the most nearly perfect monopoly in the country, the American Sugar Company, which refined 95 percent of the sugar sold in the United States. Winning the case looked like a sure thing. In *U.S. v. E. C. Knight Company* (1895), however, the Supreme Court ruled that the sugar monopoly did not violate the Sherman act because its business was manufacturing which was not trade or commerce. The Court rejected the argument that because the company monopolized the manufacture of sugar, it set the prices at which sugar was sold—and that was commerce. The Court ruled that the price-fixing was an *indirect* consequence of American Sugar's monopoly and therefore not subject to the law.

The *Knight* decision effectively told business combinations to go right ahead, and they did. Big business got bigger during the 1890s. The number of state-chartered trusts grew from 251 to 290. The money invested in trusts increased from $192 million to $326 million.

SOCIAL CRITICS

The Interstate Commerce and Sherman Antitrust laws were enacted by mainstream politicians who believed that the individual pursuit of wealth was a virtue. They wished only to restore competition and the opportunity to succeed that business combinations threatened to destroy. Outside this mainstream, sometimes radical critics of the new industrial capitalism raised their voices and wielded their pens in opposition to the new order itself. At least briefly, some of them won large followings.

Henry George and the Single Tax   A lively writing style and a knack for clarifying difficult economic ideas made journalist Henry George and his "single tax" the center of a momentous political movement. In *Progress and Poverty,* published in 1879, George observed what was obvious, but also bewildering to many people. Instead of freedom from onerous labor, as the machine once seemed to promise, industrialization had put millions to work for long hours in stultifying conditions. Instead of enriching life for all, the mass production of goods had enriched the few in the "House of Have" and impoverished the millions in the "House of Want" ("want" meaning "need").

George blamed neither industrialization nor capitalism for the misery he saw around him. Like most Americans, he believed that the competition for wealth was a wellspring of the nation's energy. The trouble began only when those who were successful in the contest—and those who inherited property—were so wealthy that they ceased to be entrepreneurs. They were parasites who lived off the income their property generated. George was at his most scathing when he discussed rent, income based solely on the ownership of real estate: land and buildings.

George called income derived from ownership "unearned increment" because it required neither work nor ingenuity of its beneficiaries. Property grew more valuable and its owners richer only because other people needed access to it in order to survive. This value was spurious, George said. Government should confiscate unearned increment by levying a 100 percent tax on it. Because the revenues from this tax would be quite enough to pay the expenses of government, all other taxes could be abolished. "Single Tax" became the rallying cry of George's movement. It would destroy the idle and parasitic rich as a social class. The entrepreneurship and competition that made the country great would flourish.

George's gospel was popular enough that in 1886 he narrowly missed being elected mayor of New York, a city where unearned increment from real estate was greater than anywhere in the world.

Edward Bellamy Looks Backward Another book that became the Bible of a protest movement was Edward Bellamy's novel of 1888, *Looking Backward, 2000–1887*. Within two years of its publication, it sold 200,000 copies and led to the founding of 150 Nationalist Clubs, groups of people who shared Bellamy's vision of the future.

The story that moved them was simple, its gimmick conventional. A proper young Bostonian of the 1880s succumbs to a mysterious sleep and awakens in the United States of the twenty-first century. There he discovers that technology has produced not a world of sharp class divisions and widespread misery (as in 1887), but a utopia providing abundance for all. Like Henry George, Bellamy was not opposed to industrial development.

Capitalism no longer exists in the world of *Looking Backward*. Through a peaceful democratic revolution—won at the polls—the American people have abolished competitive greed and idle, unproductive living because they were at odds with American ideals. Instead of private ownership of land and industry, the state owns the means of production and administers them for the good of all. Everyone contributes to the common wealth. Everyone lives decently, none miserably or wastefully.

Bellamy's vision was socialistic. However, because he rooted it in American values rather than in Karl Marx's class conflict, he called it "Nationalism." The patriotic facet of his message made his gospel palatable to middle-class Americans who, while troubled by the parallel growth of fantastic fortunes and of poverty, were frightened by "foreign ideologies" and talk of class warfare.

Socialists Some Americans were attracted to the Marxist doctrine of class conflict: The interests of producers were incompatible with the interests of capitalism and must, inevitably, destroy it. But old-stock American Marxists were few. Most Marxists were immigrants and the children of immigrants, particularly Germans. Briefly after 1872, the General Council of the First International, the official administration of world socialism, made its headquarters in New York, where Karl Marx had sent it to prevent the followers of his anarchist rival, Mikhail Bakunin, from taking it over.

Most German-American Marxists were social democrats, what revolutionary Marxists called "revisionists." The revolutionaries insisted that capitalism would be destroyed in a violent and bloody upheaval. The social democrats (like Edward

Bellamy) held that, in democratic countries, socialists could come to power by winning at the polls. The social democratic program made more sense in Great Britain and Germany, where industrial workers were a majority of the population, than it did in the United States. In 1900, despite the explosive growth of industry since the Civil War, industrial workers numbered just 28 percent of the population. They were outnumbered by farmers 29 million to 21 million.

In Milwaukee, Wisconsin, the local Social Democratic party (SDP), led by an Austrian immigrant Victor Berger, grew rapidly during the 1890s. Berger's base of support was Milwaukee's Germans and German-Americans, who were more than half of the city's population. With a program that emphasized its commitment to democracy, honest government, and municipal ownership of public utilities, the SDP appealed to middle-class voters of German and other backgrounds as well as to workingmen. In the early twentieth century, "sewer socialists" like Berger won elections in a number of large and midsized cities.

Anarchists   Like the revolutionary socialists, the anarchist followers of Mikhail Bakunin thought a violent showdown with capitalism inevitable. They differed from the Marxists in two ways. First, socialists foresaw a society in which the state would own the "means of production," land and factories. Anarchists said that the state was itself responsible for oppression; the state was a creature of capitalism. Men and women would be free only when the state was destroyed. Second, whereas socialists foresaw a long campaign educating the working class before there could be a revolution, Bakuninist anarchists were skeptical that the working class could be weaned from its acquiescence in the capitalist system by rational argument. They believed that the revolution would begin when militant anarchists forced a crisis on society by the "propaganda of the deed": heroic individual acts of terrorism against capitalism and the state that resulted in violent repression and, consequently, revolution by the masses.

The 1880s and 1890s were the golden age of anarchist assassinations. Anarchists killed several heads of state including the Russian czar and the president of France. An anarchist assassinated the Empress Elizabeth of Austria who had no power but because she was popular—a celebrity. In 1901, a self-styled anarchist assassinated President William McKinley who, at best, probably had only a dim notion of what anarchists believed.

Anarchists were never very numerous in the United States. But, like Islamic terrorists today, they inspired fear and hatred because of their random acts of murder. Anarchists figured prominently in an incident in Chicago in 1886 which led to a passionate campaign to destroy them.

Haymarket   In the spring of 1886, workers at the McCormick International Harvester Company, the world's largest manufacturer of farm machinery, went on strike. The Chicago police force openly sided with the company and over several days of picketing and sporadic rioting, they killed four strikers. On May 4, a group of anarchists, mostly Germans but including a Confederate Army veteran of some social standing, Albert Parsons, called for a rally in support of the strike at Haymarket Square just south of the city center.

The oratory was red-hot, but the speakers broke no laws and the crowd was orderly. In fact, the rally was breaking up—a downpour was threatening—when a large formation of police entered the square. Someone threw a bomb into their midst, killing seven policemen and wounding sixty-seven. The police fired a volley, and four workers fell dead.

News of the incident fed an anti-anarchist hysteria in Chicago. Authorities rounded up several dozen individuals who were known to have attended anarchist meetings, and authorities brought eight men to trial for the murder of the officers. Among them was Parsons and a prominent German agitator, August Spies. The trial was a farce. No one on the prosecution team knew or even claimed to know who threw the bomb. (His or her identity remains unknown.) Nor did the prosecution present evidence that tied any of the eight accused to the bombing. There was evidence that a disturbed young German named Louis Lingg had constructed bombs, but he had a plausible alibi. Several of the defendants had not even attended the rally. Parsons had been sick in bed before the rally was called and during it. There was no evidence against any of the defendants.

All of which proved irrelevant. Chicago was determined to have scapegoats; the charge was murder but the Haymarket anarchists were in fact tried for being anarchists. Four were hanged. Lingg committed suicide in his cell. Three were sentenced to long prison terms.

DEFENDERS OF THE FAITH

Industrial capitalism had plenty of defenders. Like some of the social critics of the era, the system's apologists drew in part on well-established American values and in part on ideas new to the era.

Social Darwinism Intellectuals at peace with their times found a justification for great wealth and even dubious business ethics in a series of books, essays, and lectures by the British philosopher Herbert Spencer. Because Spencer seemed to apply Charles Darwin's celebrated theory of biological evolution to human society, his philosophy is known as social Darwinism. However, much of Spencer's writing was published before Darwin's *Origin of Species* in 1859.

According to social Darwinism, as in the world of animals and plants, where species compete and those best adapted survive, the fittest people rise to the top in the social competition for riches. Eventually, in the dog-eat-dog world, they alone will survive. "If they are sufficiently complete to live," Spencer wrote, "they do live, and it is well that they should live. If they are not sufficiently complete to live, they die and it is best they should die."

This no-nonsense tough-mindedness made Spencer—in popularized dilutions—appealing to some American businessmen. Social Darwinism justified ruthless business practices and underhanded methods; they were "natural." There was nothing pretty about a lion bringing down an antelope either. However, the frank amorality of Spencer's philosophy rendered it unpalatable to businessmen who, in their personal lives were, like the Rockefellers, deeply religious. They preferred other justifications for their success in business.

The Last Dance of the Idle Rich

In the winter of 1896–1897, the depression hit bottom. Millions were out of work. The treasuries of charitable organizations were dry; some charities had closed their doors.

Frederick Townshend Martin, an adornment of New York high society, was having breakfast at the Fifth Avenue mansion he shared with his brother, Bradley Martin and his sister-in-law Cornelia Martin. He preserved the conversation that led to the most magnificent ball ever held in the United States—and the most notorious. What could they do? Bradley Martin asked. He went on

"I think it would be a good thing if we got up something; there seems to be a great deal of depression in trade; suppose we send out invitations for a concert."

"And pray, what good will that do?" asked my sister-in-law, "the money will only benefit foreigners. No, I've a far better idea; let us give a costume ball at so short notice that our guests won't have time to get their dresses from Paris. That will give an impetus to trade that nothing else will."

And so it did, according to Townshend: "owing to the short notice, many New York shops sold out brocades and silks which had been lying in their stock-rooms for years." Indeed, a society belle, Anne Rice, hired Native Americans to make her Pocohontas costume because she had heard that Indians were particularly hard-pressed.

No sooner did the 1,200 invitations go out, however, than the ball was denounced as inappropriate when so many people were in need. The ministers at John D. Rockefeller's and J. P. Morgan's churches both condemned the ball. Neither attended; nor did the young and politically ambitious Theodore Roosevelt (although his wife did).

The ball was held on February 10, 1897, at the Waldorf-Astoria Hotel. Reporters from the New York *Times* were stunned by the scene, although not struck dumb: a full page of the paper was devoted to the affair.

The grand ballroom was quite a scene of splendor. The eye scarcely knew where to look or what to study, it was such a bewildering maze of gorgeous dames and gentlemen on the

Moreover, even outspoken social Darwinists like Andrew Carnegie, were highly selective in applying the "law of the jungle." They appealed to it when government threatened to regulate their business practices. But they had no objections to unfair competitive advantages that enriched them like high protective tariffs. And they were quick to call in the state's police power when strikers engaged them in tests of fitness.

The most important American social Darwinist was William Graham Sumner. He was not a businessman but a university professor. Having no financial stake in business, he could be consistent in applying the principle that government should in no way interfere in economic competition. He opposed government regulation of business: "The men who are competent to organize great enterprises and to handle great amounts of capital must be found by natural selection, not political election." But Sumner also opposed government policies that favored capitalists, including the protective tariff. And he objected to government intervention in strikes on behalf of employers. Strikes, to Sumner, were legitimate—"natural"—tests of fitness between employers and their employees.

floor, such a flood of light from the ceiling, paneled in terra cotta and gold, and such an entrancing picture of garlands that hung everywhere in rich festoons.

The first impression on entering the room was that some fairy god-mother, in a dream, had revived the glories of the past for one's special enjoyment, and that one was mingling with the dignitaries of ancient regimes, so perfect was the illusion.

The ballroom was decorated to resemble Louis XIV's palace at Versailles. The costumes were magnificent. If there had been a prize for the most expensive, banker August Belmont's gold-inlaid armor would have won; it cost him $10,000. Curiously, Bradley Martin did not come as Louis XIV, who built Versailles, but as his great grandson, the irresponsible hedonist, Louis XV. So did about a hundred guests. There were ten versions of Madame de Pompadour, one of Louis XIV's mistresses and eight of Madame de Maintenon, another one.

There were no incidents outside the hotel, not even hooting as guests arrived. The police were surprised; they were prepared for a riot. So were many of those who were invited. Only about half of them came and, according to the *Times*, "quite a number" looked in and immediately hurried away.

Many seemed to have put in an appearance simply out of curiosity, to witness the really superb decorations of the ballroom and the unique spectacle of a large number of persons, prominent in social circles, arrayed in the picturesque costumes of two, three, and four centuries ago.

Within half an hour after the beginning of the ball guests began to leave the place, some for their homes and others to wander about the hotel corridors. That the visitors had a set purpose in leaving early was manifest from the fact that fully half the carriages were ordered for before the time set for the cotillion.

The Bradley Martins carried on as usual, but not in New York City. The Democratic party machine that ran the city knew how to please working-class New Yorkers. City hall slapped a big property tax increase on the Martin mansion. In a huff, the Martins moved to London. Frederick Townshend Martin wrote despondently of their exile; the United States had lost two valuable citizens.

The Success Gospel

The Gospel of Success had far more influence among late nineteenth-century capitalists than social Darwinism did. The United States differed from other countries, its proponents said, in that there was no privileged aristocracy in America. Everyone had the opportunity to prosper on his own merits to get rich. If the competition for wealth was a national virtue, what was wrong with winning the contest? The fabulous fortunes of the new industrial and financial elite were indicators of their talents and energy, even of their virtue. The Carnegies and Morgans deserved their money. John D. Rockefeller was quoted as saying of his fortune, "God gave it to me."

Success manuals, books purporting to show how anyone could make good, were bought and read so avidly that publishers churned them out in quantities comparable to the numbers of "foolproof new diets" today. They were all much the same, and they were not manuals in the sense that guides to using Microsoft Office are manuals. They repeated the hallowed old saws that hard work, honesty, frugality, loyalty to employers and partners, and other bourgeois virtues would inevitably lead to material success. Having succeeded, America's millionaires deserved not resentment but admiration.

Andrew Carnegie (second from right) with other businessmen-philanthropists and educators at Tuskegee Institute in Alabama. Tuskeegee was the most famous African American college in the country. Its president between 1881 and 1915 was Booker T. Washington (front and center). In public, Washington urged blacks to be deferential to whites and content with manual labor. Among other things, his preachments made Tuskeegee a major benefactor of philanthropists like Carnegie. John D. Rockefeller was also generous with African American institutions. Spelman College in Georgia was named for his wife.

Keystone-Mast Collection UCR/California Museum of Photography, UC Riverside

A Baptist minister from Philadelphia, Russell B. Conwell, made a small fortune delivering a lecture in the same vein. In "Acres of Diamonds," which he delivered to paying audiences more than 6,000 times, Conwell said that great wealth was a great blessing. Not only could every American be rich, but also every American *should* be rich. If a man failed, the fault lay within himself, not with society. "There is not a poor person in the United States," Conwell said, "who was not made poor by his own shortcomings." Opportunities, the acres of diamonds, were everywhere, waiting to be collected. Those who already were rich were by definition virtuous. "Ninety-eight out of one hundred of the rich men of America are honest. That is why they are rich."

Horatio Alger and Ragged Dick

Another minister, Horatio Alger, conveyed the gospel of success to the next generation of businessmen in 130 novels written for boys. Unlike Conwell, who was a hypnotic lecturer, Alger was a terrible writer. His prose was leaden, his characters cardboard cutouts. Their dialogue would have put even their dull fellow characters to sleep. Alger's plots were variations on variations of a simple, straightforward theme. It was a given that the goal of male human existence was to make money. God—or America: This was not clear; Alger was neither a Bible-thumper nor a flag-waver—put wealth within the grasp of all.

The heroes of Alger's novels were lads grappling with destitution; many of them were orphans, quite on their own, although there might be an impoverished widowed mother waiting patiently back home for her boy to rescue her. The boys were honest, hardworking, loyal to their employers, and clean living. They might slip out of character here and there but their offenses were trivial. "Ragged Dick," Alger's first hero and the prototype for Tattered Tom, Lucky Luke, and dozens of others, was insufferably courteous.

Curiously, Ragged Dick and most of the others did not get rich penny by penny, putting in fourteen hours a day so as to save a dollar a week like Lowell mill girls. Such a tale would have made for even duller reading. At the beginning of the final chapter, the Alger hero was often as badly off as he had been on page one. Then, however—the Horatio Alger touch—he was presented with what amounts to a visitation of grace upon him, a reward for his virtue and pluck. The child of a factory owner falls off the Staten Island Ferry or the teenage daughter of a banker stumbles into the path of runaway Clydesdales pulling a brewery wagon or slips into the Niagara River just above the falls: Alger's boy hero reacts instantly, rescuing her, and is rewarded with a good job and, in several books, marriage to the lass whose life he saved.

So there was in the Alger books an appeal to the adolescent boy's adventure fantasies. Just as God gave John D. Rockefeller his money, God gave a less munificent life to Ragged Dick. Between 1867 and 1899, Alger's books sold 20 million copies. A battalion of imitators accounted for millions more. And yet, with pulp novels about Wild Bill Hickock and Belle Starr also on the market, and costing only a dime, it may be that the chief purchasers of the Alger books were the parents of adolescent boys.

Philanthropy   The weakness of the Success Gospel as a justification of great wealth was the obvious fact that many of the country's richest men got their money by practicing quite the opposite of the touted virtues: dishonesty, betrayal of partners and employers, and reckless speculation. And they grew richer while living lives of sumptuous luxury and leisure. Rockefeller's business methods were not nearly as unethical as his enemies said, but he cut plenty of corners. None of the great magnates of the era shied away from ruthless destruction of competitors because it occurred to them that to do so was unchristian. It would be wrong to say that the giants of American industry were all Jacob Marleys and Ebeneezer Scrooges. But there were few Mr. Fezziwigs among them.

There were, however, generous philanthropists among even the most ruthless. Horatio Alger—no multimillionaire—supported institutions that housed homeless boys in New York City. Russell B. Conwell—another man of modest riches—founded Temple University in Philadelphia where poor young men could study cheaply and improve their prospects. Leland Stanford, James Buchanan Duke (the cigarette king), and William Vanderbilt founded great universities in California, North Carolina, and Tennessee. John D. Rockefeller gave huge sums to churches, universities, medical research, and other valuable social institutions. Indeed, his son and heir, John D. Rockefeller Jr. paid little attention to business (he hardly needed to make more money); instead, he managed the Rockefeller Foundation and other family philanthropies.

Philanthropy was a better justification of huge fortunes than either social Darwinism or the Success Gospel, albeit a justification after the fact. Andrew Carnegie devised a theory that justified fabulous riches by the concept of stewardship. In a celebrated, endlessly reprinted essay entitled "Wealth," he argued that the unrestricted pursuit of riches made American society vital. However, the man who succeeded in amassing millions was merely a steward entrusted with his money. He had a social obligation to distribute his riches where they would do the most good. Carnegie said that the rich man who died rich, died a failure. Carnegie retired from business in 1901. He devoted the working hours of the rest of his life, almost twenty years, to giving money to useful social institutions, especially libraries. Despite his extraordinary generosity, he died a multimillionaire.

The trouble with justifying very rich men with their philanthropy is that only a small minority of them were philanthropists on a vast scale like Carnegie and the Rockefellers. Most of them spent their money on their own pleasures, gratifications, and whims.

How the Very Rich Lived

Indeed, philanthropists like Carnegie and Rockefeller had less to do with reconciling Americans to the existence of a permanently ensconced social class that was "filthy rich" than the shallowest and least constructive representatives of the class. The very rich who spent their millions on what sociologist Thorstein Veblen called "conspicuous consumption"—conspicuous consumption in a very big way—put on a show for the multitudes. Then, like today, most people were more than content with a good show.

Conspicuous Consumption   The very rich competed with one another in spending their money by hosting lavish parties, by building extravagant homes, by purchasing yachts and private railway cars to get from one home to another, by adorning themselves with costly jewelry and clothing which, in the case of the women, they expected to wear only once. And—the ultimate in nineteenth-century one-upmanship—they bought Europeans with aristocratic titles for their daughters.

"High society" social get-togethers lasting a few hours often cost more than $100,000. At one party hosted by Harry Lehr, who actually took pride in calling himself the "prince of spenders," a hundred dogs dined on "fricassee of bones" and gulped down shredded dog biscuits prepared by a French chef. The guests at a New York banquet ate their meal while mounted on horses (trays balanced on the withers) while the horses munched oats out of sterling silver feedbags. At a costume ball, guests boasted that they had spent $10,000 on their fancy dress to others who had just boasted they had spent $5,000.

It was a golden age for yachting or, at least, for buying yachts. Cornelius Vanderbilt's *North Star* was 250 feet long. Jay Gould's *Atlanta* had a crew of fifty-two. Albert C. Burrage's *Aztec* carried 270 tons of coal; it could steam 5,500 miles without calling at a port for more fuel. As on land, J. P. Morgan was champion at sea. He owned three successively larger, faster, and more opulent yachts called *Corsair*. (Morgan had a sense of humor; a corsair was a pirate.)

Nowhere was consumption more conspicuous than at upper-class summer resorts of which the pinnacle was Newport, Rhode Island. An ordinary summer "cottage" of thirty rooms, occupied only three months a year, cost $1 million. Coal baron E. J. Berwind spent $1.5 million to build The Elms. William K. Vanderbilt outdid everyone with Marble House. His cottage cost $2 million; to furnish it, Vanderbilt spent $9 million. There was no topping that.

A Lord in the Family

A fad of the 1880s and 1890s—almost a mania—was the competition among millionaires to marry their daughters to titled Europeans, thus ennobling the lucky girls too. It was not all that difficult to find fortune-hunting earls who were for sale. Accustomed to living well without working, their incomes were based on land that was inadequate in the age of industrial capitalism. It was a win-win marketplace. American daughter got to be introduced as "Countess" at Newport; her husband got plenty of money with which to maintain himself. A contemporary student of the phenomenon counted 100 such matches with dowries totaling $100 million.

There were, of course, personal disappointments, even personal tragedies. Heiress Alice Thaw was embarrassed on her honeymoon as Countess of Yarmouth when her husband's creditors seized their luggage. She had to wire her father for the money to get it out of hock. Helena Zimmerman, the daughter of a coal and iron millionaire from Cincinnati, married the duke of Manchester. For 20 years their substantial bills were paid by the duchess's father out of the labor of workers living on subsistence wages.

The most famous American aristocrats were the heiresses of two of the greatest robber barons, Jay Gould and Cornelius Vanderbilt. Anna Gould became the Countess Boni de Castellane. Before she divorced him in order to marry his cousin, the higher-ranking Prince de Sagan, the count extracted more than $5 million from Jay Gould's purse. No American businessman pocketed a fraction of that at Gould's expense. Consuelo Vanderbilt was forced to marry the head of one of England's proudest families, "Sunny," the ninth duke of Marlborough. Sunny was not a bad sort, but he was superficial, and Consuelo was a talented and substantial woman. After she did her social duties and produced heirs, she divorced the duke and devoted her life to social welfare projects. (His marriage and consent to divorce netted Sunny about $20 million.)

Women as Decor

The role of young heiresses in the game of conspicuous waste (another of Veblen's terms) helps to illustrate the function of the women of the gilded age super-rich. They were idler than their businessmen husbands (although not necessarily idler than their sons). With the exception of a few eccentrics like brokers Victoria Woodhull and Tennessee Claflin and investor Hetty Green, "the witch of Wall Street," there was no place for women in big business. But they had no domestic duties beyond giving instructions to servants.

They were their husband's adornments, mannequins on which to display wealth. Mrs. George Gould (Jay Gould's daughter-in-law and mother of the Countess Boni de Castellane) went through life best-known for the fact that she owned a pearl necklace that cost $500,000. Each of several portraits of her are, in fact, portraits of her necklace.

High-society fashion emphasized women's idleness. Wealthy women (and middle-class women who imitated them) were laced up tightly in crippling steel and bone corsets, which made it laborious just to move about. Their costume made the statement that there were other people to perform even the least onerous physical tasks for them—such as lacing up their corsets.

Wealthy women were often their husbands' conspicuous consumers-in-chief. While William K. Vanderbilt was not uninterested in building mansions, his wife, a southern belle named Alva Smith, was the family's big spender (and the mother who forced Consuelo Vanderbilt into a marriage she did not want).

Avid Watchers   The conspicuous consumers were interested in impressing and exciting the envy of people like them. But because it was by definition display, the lifestyle of the very rich was well known to everyone through journalists who described their yachts, mansions, marriages, balls, and dinners with as much detail as they could discover or, when necessary, invent. Some journals depicted the rich with the same awe that, today, *People* magazine and "entertainment today" television programs lavish on movie actors and popular singers.

In popular songs of the day, and in the melodramas favored by working people, the idleness and extravagance of the filthy rich were favorite themes. They were shrewdly calculated to arouse both envy and resentment but, in the end, justified great riches. New York's "Tin Pan Alley," the center of the sheet music business, turned out dozens of songs, a few of them still standards, that preached pity for the "bird in a gilded cage," the wealthy but unhappy young woman, and the moral that because poor people earned their own way by working, they were more virtuous.

Popular melodramas of the day, simple plays with little subtlety of character and predictable plots, pitted simple, right-living poor people against unscrupulous rich villains and their arrogant womenfolk. "You are only a shopgirl," said a high-society lady in a typical scene, attempting to put the heroine in her place. "An honest shopgirl," the heroine replied, "as far above a fashionable idler as heaven is above earth!" Before the final curtain fell, however, the shopgirl, like Horatio Alger's boys, was rewarded for her virtue by marriage to a rich young man.

Sensationalist working-class scandal sheets like the *Police Gazette* specialized in upper-class scandals. When the very rich divorced, court proceedings were reported in detail because, in the nineteenth century, the grounds for most divorces were adultery or lurid, sometimes sexual abuse. In 1872, the dawn of the gilded age, Jim Fisk was shot to death by a rival for the affections of his showgirl mistress Josie Mansfield. Newspaper readers could find a moral in the fact that Fisk's wealth and power could not save him from a violent death at the age of 38. The 1906 murder of high-living architect Stanford White and the trial of his killer, millionaire Harry Thaw, made for even juicier news. Thaw accused White of having seduced his beautiful fiancée, Evelyn Nesbit. Her testimony concerning White's peculiarities behind closed doors simultaneously titillated the public and served Thaw as a moral justification of his act. (He went free.)

28

WE WHO BUILT AMERICA
Working People 1860–1900

*So at last I was going to America! Really, really
going at last! The boundaries burst! The arch of
heaven soared! A million suns shone out for every star.
The winds rushed in from outer space, roaring in my ear,
"America! America!" ...*

—Mary Antin

Leland Stanford and James J. Hill thought of themselves as the men who built the railroads. Journalists referred to Andrew Carnegie as the nation's greatest steelmaker. In the popular mind, industries were associated with individuals, just as battles were identified with generals: Sherman marched across Georgia; Grant took Richmond; Vanderbilt ran the New York Central; John D. Rockefeller was Standard Oil. J. P. Morgan spoke of his hobby, yachting, in personal terms. "You can do business with anyone," he snorted, "but you can only sail a boat with a gentleman."

In reality, Morgan decided when and where his *Corsair* was to go. But it took eighty-five grimy stokers and hard-handed sailors to get the yacht out of New York harbor and safely into Newport or Venice. Stanford, Hill, Rockefeller, Carnegie, and other great entrepreneurs supervised the creation of industrial America, but it was created by anonymous millions of men and women who wielded the shovels and tended the machines that whirred, whined, pounded, and drilled in the factories and mills.

A NEW WAY OF LIFE

America's industrial workers could not be kept below decks like the crew of the *Corsair*. There were too many of them. While the population of the United States more than doubled between 1860 and 1900, the size of the working class quadrupled. In 1860, 1.5 million Americans made their living in workshops and mills, another 700,000 in mining and construction. By 1900, 6 million people worked in manufacturing, 2.3 million in mining and construction. Industrial workers, once few in numbers, came to constitute a distinct social class second in numbers only to farmers.

Labor and Immigration 1865–1900

1865	1870	1875	1880	1885	1890	1895	1900

1866 National Labor Union founded

1869 Knights of Labor founded

1877 Nationwide railroad strike

1880 Annual immigration triples

1882 First Labor Day holiday; Chinese Exclusion Act

1886 Haymarket riot

1888 American Federation of Labor founded

1892 Homestead strike

1894 Pullman strike

Factories
The size of the American workplace grew dramatically, a fact of profound significance to the quality of working-class life. In 1870, the average American workshop employed eight people. It was owned by an individual or by partners who personally supervised operations, sometimes working at the bench alongside their employees. Kind, callous, or cruel as the boss might be (*boss* was already a familiar word, adopted from the Dutch), they were personally involved in their workers' lives. Like it or not, they heard talk of births of children and deaths of parents. They discussed wages, hours, and conditions face-to-face with their employees. Even Pittsburgh's iron mills, some of the largest factories in the country at the end of the Civil War, employed on average just ninety workers. The men stoking the furnaces and pouring the molten metal were not apt to chat with the owners of the mill, although they would know them by sight.

By 1900, industrial workers labored in shops averaging 25 employees. Plants employing 1,000 men and women were common. The average payroll of Pittsburgh iron and steel plants was now 1,600, and a few companies listed 10,000 on the payroll. Carnegie Steel employed 23,000. The men who directed such mammoth concerns might never step on a factory floor; Carnegie never did. He and men in similar positions were interested in wages only in the aggregate, as costs to be factored into prices. The number of hours in a workday and safety conditions concerned them only insofar as they translated into numbers in their ledgers.

Ceaseless improvements in manufacturing machinery reduced operating costs by reducing the number of skilled craftsmen needed in factories. A few trades increased in importance: machinists, of course, the men who designed, built, and repaired specialized machine tools. In most industries, however, the machinists' machines replaced artisans, doing what they had done far more quickly, twenty-four hours a day, and often better than hand-workers.

Most machines were tended by unskilled or semiskilled men in heavy industries, women and children in textiles. They were interchangeable—that was the point of machines. Their jobs required little training. Consequently, they were poorly paid and commanded scant respect from employers, small businessmen, professionals, and skilled workers. "If I wanted boiler iron," said one industrialist, "I would go out on the market and buy it where I could get it cheapest; and if I wanted to employ men I would do the same."

Wages   The number of dollars in the average worker's pay envelope was static during the final decades of the century or it declined. Real wages, however, actual purchasing power, increased because the cost of food, clothing, and housing dropped sharply. Today, when we know only inflation—ever-rising prices and paychecks—it is difficult to appreciate that an entire generation experienced little but deflation, declining prices. Nevertheless, it happened: The working class as a whole enjoyed almost 50 percent more purchasing power in 1900 than it had in 1860.

This statistic can be misleading: the skilled "aristocracy of labor"—locomotive engineers, machinists, master carpenters, printers, and other highly trained workers—improved their economic situation much more than did the unskilled workers at the bottom of the pile. The average annual wage for all manufacturing workers in 1900 was $435, $8.37 a week. But unskilled workers were paid, on average, about 10¢ an hour, about $5.50 a week. A girl of 13, tending a loom in a South Carolina cotton mill, might take home as little as $2 a week after various fines (for being late to work, for example) were deducted from her pay. In 1904, sociologist Robert Hunter estimated that one American in eight lived in poverty.

Hours   Hours on the job varied from eight to fourteen. Most government employees worked an eight-hour day, but that was unusual. Workers in the building trades (bricklayers, carpenters, plumbers, but also the common laborers who did the heavy lifting) usually worked ten hours. Factory workers (and telephone operators) worked twelve-hour days. During the summer months, most mills ran from sunup to sundown, as long as the workers could see. Indeed, it was the success of New England's cotton mill workers in winning a ten-hour day that encouraged the mill owners to move their operations to the South. In 1880, only 5 percent of the nation's cotton cloth was manufactured in the South; by 1910, more than half was.

The average workweek was sixty-six hours long in 1860, fifty-five hours in 1910. Most employees were on the job six or five and a half days a week. In industries that had to run around the clock, such as steel making (the furnaces could not be shut down), the workforce was divided into two shifts on seven-day schedules. Each shift worked twelve hours. At the end of two weeks, the day workers switched shifts with the night workers. This meant a twenty-four hour holiday once a month. The price of that holiday was working twenty-four hours straight two weeks later.

True holidays were few. Christmas and July Fourth were almost universally observed, as were, in the northern states, Decoration Day (Memorial Day) and Thanksgiving. However, because of the swings in the business cycle, many factory workers had plenty of unwanted time off; when times were bad, employees were let go. Some industries were highly seasonal. Coal miners could expect to be without wages for weeks, sometimes months during the summer when people were not heating their homes.

Conditions   Conscientious employers were safety conscious. Nonetheless, the number of injuries and deaths on the job are chilling to us today. Between 1870 and 1910, there were 10,000 major boiler explosions in steam-powered American factories, almost one each workday. Between 1880 and 1900, 35,000 American workers were killed on the job, one every two days. Railroads were particularly dangerous. Every year, 1 railroad worker in 26 was seriously injured, and 1 in 400 was killed. In 1910, the worst year, 3,383 railway workers were killed, 95,671 injured.

In many cases, injured workers and the survivors of those who were killed on the job received no compensation whatsoever. In others, compensation amounted to little more than burial expenses. In the Pennsylvania coal fields, mine owners thought themselves generous if they allowed a dead miner's son who was younger than regulation age to take his father's job in the pit.

Employer liability law was stacked against workers. Most courts ruled that employers were not liable for an injury on the job unless the employee could prove that he in no way contributed to his accident. Short of the collapse of a factory roof or the boss's son run amok with a revolver, total lack of responsibility for a mishap was difficult to prove. Some judges ruled that if an employee was injured because the machinery he operated was malfunctioning dangerously but he had been aware of the problem and continued to operate it, his employer was not liable for the consequences.

Occupational diseases—the coal miner's "black lung," the cotton-mill worker's "white lung," and the hard-rock miner's silicosis—were not considered the employer's responsibility. Indeed, they were not entirely understood to be job related. Poisoning resulting from work with toxic substances like mercury—used in gold smelters and in the manufacture of felt—was, despite a long history (the "Mad Hatter") just beginning to be recognized as job related. Even when it was, employers' attorneys could win their cases by demonstrating that the poisoned worker was aware of the risk before he took the dangerous job.

WHO WERE THE WORKERS?

Artisans in a few highly specialized crafts had to be recruited in Europe. For example, builders of churches and public buildings adorned with carved stone had to recruit carvers in Italy; there were next to no such craftsmen in the United States. Most skilled workers in more familiar trades were native-born white males of British, Irish, or German ancestry, or immigrants from those countries.

Poorly paid unskilled jobs were, in the final decades of the century, filled by immigrants from southern and eastern Europe, a few from western Asia (Lebanon, Syria, Turkish Armenia), French Canadians in New England, and Mexicans in the Southwest. In most industrial cities, half to three-quarters of the workforce was foreign-born.

Child Labor   In 1900, the socialist writer John Spargo estimated that 1.8 million children under 16 years of age were employed full time. Children could be found doing all but the heaviest labor. Girls of 12 tended spinning machines in southern textile mills. "Bobbin boys" as young as 10 hauled boxes filled with spindles of thread from spinning rooms to weaving rooms and empty bobbins back again. Children swept filings and scraps in machine shops. Boys down to 8 worked the "breakers" at coal mines, hand picking slate from anthracite in filthy, frigid sheds.

In sweatshops in city tenements, whole families sewed button holes and finished off factory-made clothing, rolled cigars, or made small, cheap items like artificial flowers. Few employers (or working people) shared the sentiment that childhood was for play. Children were hired as soon as they were able to master the task a boss wanted done. In cities, children practically monopolized messenger work, light delivery from shops to homes, some kinds of huckstering, and, most famously, hawking newspapers on street corners.

In part, child labor was the fruit of greed. On the grounds that children had no dependents to support, employers paid them less than they paid adults doing the same jobs. In southern textile towns, the "Mill Daddy" was a familiar figure. Unable to find work because his wife and children could be hired for less money, the Mill Daddy was reduced to carrying lunches to the factory at noon and tossing them over the fence.

Child labor was also an example of cultural lag. Children had always worked. It took time for society to recognize that the nature of labor in the world of steam power and the big factory was not the same as doing chores on the family farm. Relations on a farm or in a small shop were personal. The limited capacity of children, particularly their fatigue when set to tedious, repetitive tasks, was easy to recognize and to take into account (not that it always was). Occupying a niche in a massive factory, the child laborer was just a number on the payroll, nothing more.

Women Workers   The first industrial workers were female because the first modern industry was textiles and women had been the mainstay of spinning. As factory work became dirtier and heavier, requiring greater physical strength, the workforce in manufacturing became predominantly male. Still, the difficulty of supporting a family on one income forced many working-class women to continue to labor for wages even after they married. In 1900, almost 20 percent of the total workforce was female. About half the workers in textiles were women, and the percentage in the needle trades was much higher.

With few exceptions, women were paid less than men for performing the same tasks for the same number of hours. Abysmally low pay was particularly characteristic of the largest female occupation. In 1900, 2 million women were employed for subsistence wages in domestic service: cooking, cleaning, and tending the vanities and children of the well-off. In an age before electrical household appliances, even middle-class families on a constrained budget had a live-in maid and often a combination gardener-stablehand.

No Blacks Need Apply   Blacks worked in southern logging, turpentine mills, and coal mines—all dirty, dangerous jobs—and in the most menial factory jobs such as sweeping floors. Desirable factory jobs were closed to them because of the racial prejudice of white workers North and South. Most African Americans were farmers. In 1900, more than 80 percent of the black population still lived in the former slave states, most of them on the land. In northern cities, only low-paying service occupations were routinely open to blacks. They could work as domestic servants, waiters, kitchen workers, porters, bootblacks, and the like.

Culver Pictures, Inc.

A woman and a teenage girl in a southern cotton mill. The girl would not have been the youngest employee in the factory. Younger girls and "bobbin boys" would have been kept out of sight when this posed photograph was taken. Southern mills employed only white people, and employees were well aware that African Americans would be hired to take their jobs if they were not docile.

The industrial color line was least flexible in the southern states. When the cotton industry moved south toward the end of the century, mill owners drew from the poor white population for its workforce. Implicitly and sometimes explicitly, employees were informed that if they were troublesome (that is, if they complained about wages or hours), the companies would replace them with blacks. Their own racism kept southern mill workers among the poorest factory workers in the country. Rather than lose their jobs to despised blacks, they lived with low wages with only occasional outbursts of resistance.

ORGANIZE!

The majority of workers, most of the time, tacitly accepted the wages they were paid and the hours they had to work. The alternative for the unskilled was no job at all. Nevertheless, they expressed their discontent or desperation or anger in ways as ancient as civilization. Absenteeism was high, particularly on "Blue Monday" after beery Sunday. In good times, when finding another job was not difficult, workers needing a holiday for health, sanity, or just plain relaxation quit on a minute's notice. Sabotage was a word just invented, but the practice was well understood. When the pace of work reached the breaking point, or a foreman stepped beyond the bounds of tolerable behavior, it was easy enough for a fed-up worker to jam or damage a machine so that it appeared to be an accident—and take a break while it was being fixed. An angry worker who made up his mind to quit might decide literally to throw a monkey wrench into the works or to slash the leather belts that turned the factory's machinery.

A Heritage of Industrial Violence Most worker violence was spontaneous, but not all of it. During the early 1870s, Irish coal miners in northeastern Pennsylvania formed a secret society called the Molly Maguires within a fraternal lodge, the Ancient Order of Hibernians. Knowing the risks of the terrorism they planned, they kept their numbers few and were tight-knit and secretive. The Mollies murdered supervisors they deemed exploitative and destroyed mine property.

The mine owners' efforts to identify members of the organization were stymied by the Mollies' effective organization. So, several companies hired James McParland, an employee of the Pinkerton Agency, a company that specialized in helping employers to keep their workers in line. McParland was an Irish-American, familiar with the culture of the coal miners, and he was big and strong enough to work in the mines. Although it took him months, he was able to infiltrate the Mollies. Undercover spying was dangerous; McParland would have been a dead man if his identity had been discovered. But it was not, and he gathered evidence that led to the hanging of nineteen men.

During a nationwide railroad strike in 1877, workers by the thousands stormed in mobs into railroad yards and set trains and buildings afire. In a few places they fought pitched gun battles with company guards and, toward the end of the unsuccessful strike, with troops called out to put them down.

At the Homestead works in 1892, Andrew Carnegie's partner, Henry Clay Frick, refused to talk to strikers who belonged to the Amalgamated Association of Iron and Steel Workers; he boasted to newspaper reporters that he would crush the union. Enraged steelworkers besieged the gigantic factory like an army. When Frick brought in 300 armed guards from the Pinkerton Agency on river barges, the strikers attacked them before they could get ashore. Ten Pinkertons were killed before they surrendered whence they were marched to a train that took them out of town. The Homestead strike was not an industrial dispute, it was war. Andrew Carnegie sat it out in his castle in Scotland, but his protestations of innocence when he returned to the United States were not enough to remove a stain on the humanitarian image he had cultivated.

The Pullman Boycott The Pullman Palace Car works just outside Chicago was a massive factory. Founded by George Pullman, the company made luxurious private railroad cars for millionaires but earned most of its money mass-producing sleeping cars (popularly called "Pullmans") and dining cars for long-distance passenger trains. Pullman did not sell his heavily patented sleepers and diners. He leased them to railroads, thus ensuring that the company also profited from repair and maintenance too.

George Pullman was known as a paternalistic employer. He built a town—Pullman, Illinois—adjacent to the factory. It was not a self-governing chartered city but part of the business, a "company town." Everything in it, from residences to shops to the water company, the sewers, and the land on which churches were built, was owned by Pullman company. In order to work for Pullman, employees had to reside in the town, renting their homes from the company.

Until 1894, few worker-residents objected to the arrangement. The cottages in Pullman were well built and attractive, superior to housing that a factory worker could afford outside the town. However, the depression of the 1890s hit railroads particularly hard. There were dozens of bankruptcies. Railroads defaulted on their lease payments and the bottom dropped out of new orders. Pullman cut wages by 25 percent; that was a lot, though reductions in pay during recessions was a common practice. Workers preferred wage cuts to being laid off.

However, the company did not reduce rents and utility bills in the town of Pullman. Some 4,000 employees responded by joining the American Railway Union (ARU), a newly formed organization that was rapidly enlisting lower-level railroad workers throughout the Northeast and Midwest. The ARU was headed by Eugene V. Debs, a former locomotive fireman who had been disillusioned by the refusal of the railway Brotherhoods of Engineers, Firemen, and Brakemen to take an interest in the welfare of the vast majority of railroad workers, who were unskilled. Debs founded the ARU to represent them.

When Pullman's employees went on strike, ARU members working for several of the nation's major railroads voted to support them by boycotting Pullman-owned sleepers. They refused to hook Pullmans to the trains they assembled in the switching yards. Debs did not want a conflict with the railroads. ARU members kept the trains running—except for Pullman cars.

Sensing an opportunity to destroy the ARU before it was strong enough to shut them down, the railroads arranged for nonunion employees to connect U.S. mail cars, which were usually hooked next to the locomotive for security (they carried large amounts of money), to the end of trains, behind the Pullmans. In order to cut the Pullmans out of the trains, yard workers had to disconnect the mail cars, shunt the Pullmans to a sidetrack, then reconnect the mail cars to the train.

Attorney General Richard Olney, a former corporate lawyer for railroaders, defined their actions as "obstructing" the U.S. mails, a federal offense. He took the ARU to court and won the case. The judge declared the boycott illegal and ordered the ARU to desist. Illinois Governor John Peter Altgeld protested, blaming the obstruction on the railroads, but when the workers continued to cull the Pullmans from trains, President Grover Cleveland ordered federal troops into Chicago. Railroad workers from Oakland, California, to the East Coast went on a rampage, destroying Pullmans and millions of dollars worth of railroad property. Not until mid-July did the trains begin to run again. The ARU was destroyed. Debs was imprisoned for defying the court order.

The Union Makes Us Strong   Violence, no matter who initiated it, almost always worked to the detriment of industrial workers and to the advantage of employers. Violence alienated middle-class people who might otherwise have sympathized with poorly paid workers. And violence in labor disputes meant the intervention of the police, state militia, and even federal troops ostensibly to restore order, effectively to break strikes for employers.

Almost every prominent labor leader of the era urged the members of their unions to refrain from violence for this reason. Some urged workers to improve their lot at the polls; others relied on the strike or the threat of a strike, hitting employers in the pocketbook by bringing production to a halt whence the union would negotiate wages, hours, and conditions.

Unionization was easier for skilled workers, the "aristocracy of labor." Their numbers were few and sharing the same hard-won skills gave them a sense of solidarity. If forced to strike in order to have their demands met, the fact that their employers could not easily replace them gave them immense leverage. Men in the building trades—carpenters, bricklayers, plumbers and steamfitters, plasterers— could not easily be replaced if they refused to work.

The Railway Brotherhoods rarely had to call a strike. The railroads could not run without them, and the brotherhoods cooperated. If the firemen struck, the locomotive engineers would not work. Consequently, most railroad companies recognized the brotherhoods as the bargaining agents for their members and negotiated an end to conflicts before they got started.

The National Labor Union and the Knights of Labor

However, skilled craftsmen comprised a small minority of working people in the industrial era. Recognizing this, William Sylvis, a visionary iron puddler (a man who prepared molten iron for casting in molds), founded the National Labor Union (NLU) in 1866. Sylvis hoped to enlist all industrial workers in the NLU. He devoted the final three years of his life to wandering like a mendicant friar throughout the northeastern states, addressing meetings of workers in churches and fraternal lodges.

Sylvis believed that the working-class's future depended on political action. He formed alliances with several reform groups, including the women's suffragist movement, and farmers' organizations lobbying for a cheap currency. The National Labor party put up candidates in the presidential election of 1872 but made so poor a showing that both the party and the NLU folded. From a membership of 400,000 in 1872, the NLU disappeared within two years.

A different kind of national labor union was already on the scene. Organized in 1869 by a tailors' union led by Uriah P. Stephens, the Noble and Holy Order of the Knights of Labor (Knights) spread its message quietly. Indeed, the early Knights were a secret society. Employers fired union organizers so the Knights, when they announced meetings in newspapers, did not reveal their meeting place (that was known to members) or even their name; they identified the group in advertisements as "*******". The Knights also differed from the NLU in their aversion to political action as an organization. Members were urged to vote, but Stephens believed that the interests of working people were served by solidarity in the workplace, not at the ballot box.

Some Knights believed in class conflict, irreconcilable differences between producers and parasites: workers and farmers on the one hand; capitalists on the other.

But the Knight's concept of class lines was not as clear-cut as the line that followers of Karl Marx drew. The Knights barred from membership only saloon keepers, lawyers, and gamblers. They were parasites, perhaps, but hardly the people who ran industrial America. Stephens himself disliked the idea of class conflict. He looked forward to a day when all men and women of good will would abolish the wage system and establish a cooperative commonwealth.

Women were welcome in the Knights; so were African Americans. However, the Knights had difficulties recruiting Roman Catholic Irish-Americans who, by the 1870s, constituted a large and conspicuous part of the American working class. One problem was the Knight's secrecy. The Catholic Church opposed all secret societies. A second difficulty was the Masonic rituals, secret handshakes, and other rigmarole with which Stephens, a lifelong Mason, had encrusted the Knights. The popes had long forbidden Catholics to join the Masons. Some Catholics shrugged off the ban and joined the Union anyway, but many others, obeying their priests, refused to join.

Terence Powderly

In 1879, Stephens was succeeded as Grand Master Workman by Terence V. Powderly, himself a Catholic. Powderly resolved the conflict between the Knights and the Catholic Church on two fronts. He brought the Knights into the open—no more secrecy—and toned down the Masonic flavor of union ceremonies. More important, he persuaded an influential Catholic bishop with working-class sympathies, James Gibbons, to prevail on the pope to remove his prohibition of Catholic membership in the organization.

Gibbons succeeded and the Knights grew at a dazzling rate. With 110,000 members in 1885, the organization claimed 700,000 the next year. Ironically, for Powderly disliked strikes, the major impetus of the growth was a startling victory by the Knights in a strike of Jay Gould's Missouri Pacific Railroad. Gould had vowed to destroy the union. "I can hire half the working class to kill the other half," he growled. But the Knights closed down the Missouri-Pacific, forcing Gould to meet with their leaders and agree to their terms.

The dramatic victory and explosive growth of the Knights proved to be more curse than blessing. Powderly and the union's general assembly were unable to control the new members. Instead of coordinating Knights activities nationally—the rationale of any national organization—they lost control of local leaders who called strikes, most of them ill-advised, in dozens of locations. Powderly fumed and sputtered and refused to back the rash of strikes in 1885 and 1886. But he could not stop them. Then, in 1886, the Haymarket tragedy was unfairly but effectively imputed to the Knights. Membership plummeted.

Samuel Gompers and the American Federation of Labor

In the same year as Haymarket, a national labor organization dedicated to improving the lives of *some* workers was pieced together by several existing associations of skilled workers. The American Federation of Labor's (AFL) guiding spirit was Samuel Gompers, a cigar maker born in London of Dutch-Jewish parents who emigrated to the United States as a boy. Gompers astonished his fellow cigar makers with his intelligence, learning, toughness in bargaining with bosses, and his eloquence on the soapbox. He was a homely, even ugly man, squat and thick of body with a broad, coarse-featured face. But this uncomely character had very definite ideas about how labor organizations could not only survive in the United States but also become one of the interlocking forces that governed the country.

First, Gompers believed that only skilled workers could effectively force employers to negotiate pay, hours, and conditions. He was not indifferent to the plight of unskilled laborers, but he thought their cause hopeless. With the exception of the coal miners' organization, AFL unions admitted only skilled workers to membership.

Second, the sole goal of AFL unions was "bread and butter": higher wages, shorter hours, and better working conditions. The NLU and the Knights failed, Gompers believed, because they muddied the workers' material interests by combining them with other reforms irrelevant to them: women's suffrage, for example, in the case of the NLU, the "pie in the sky" dream of a utopian society in the future in the case of the Knights. Gompers had no patience with dreamers and socialists. What counted, he said, was a better life in the here-and-now.

Third, while Gompers believed that the strike was the union's best weapon, he made it clear that AFL unions would cooperate amicably with employers who recognized them as the representatives of their employees and bargained with them. Make unions partners, he told employers, meaning AFL unions that supported the capitalist system. Industry would be peaceful and stable, radical anticapitalist unions would wither and die.

Friends of Friends

Gompers, who lived until 1924, was elected president of the AFL every year but one. With his carrot-and-stick approach to dealing with employers—striking against those who refused to deal with his unions, cooperating with those who accepted them—he saw the federation grow from 150,000 members in 1888 to more than a million shortly after the turn of the century.

Most employers, however, continued to hate him and the AFL with the same intensity with which they hated socialists and revolutionary unions. "Can't I do what I want with my own?" Cornelius Vanderbilt had said. The majority of American industrialists believed that the wages they paid and the hours their employees worked were no one's business but their own. The worker who did not like his job was free to quit. In 1893, hard-nosed antilabor employers formed the National Association of Manufacturers to fight unions wherever they appeared.

More enlightened manufacturers led by Frank Easley and Senator Mark Hanna of Ohio, a former Rockefeller associate, concluded that labor unions were here to stay, a permanent part of American industry. The choice was not between unions and no unions. The choice was (as Gompers said) between conservative, pro-capitalist unions willing to cooperate with employers and desperate, revolutionary unions determined to destroy capitalism. Easley and his associates joined with Gompers in 1900 to form the National Civic Federation. Its purpose was to work for industrial peace through employer–union cooperation.

NATION OF IMMIGRANTS

By the early 1900s, recent immigrants filled most of unskilled jobs in construction, manufacturing, and mining. Newcomers had been arriving in swarms since the end of the Civil War. In 1880, 457,000 immigrants entered the country legally. The annual total dipped below 300,000 during the depression of the 1890s, but soared to new heights when it lifted. For each of the six years after the turn of the century, more than a million people arrived in the United States. On one day in 1907, 11,747 immigrants were processed at a single point of entry, New York's Ellis Island. Always a stream, sometimes swollen, immigration was a flood.

The Flood   All the traditional European immigrant groups continued to arrive in large numbers: English, Scots, Welsh, and Irish from the British Isles, Dutch, and Germans. Swedes, Finns, and Norwegians came in increasing numbers. Beginning about 1880, however, an annually increasing proportion of immigrants came from southern Italy and the Balkan states; the Ottoman empire (Turks, Armenians, some Syrians and Lebanese); Greece; and the Austro-Hungarian empire (Hungarians, Rumanians, Serbs, Croatians, Slovenes). From the Russian empire, which included most of Poland, came both Christian and Jewish Russians, Poles, Lithuanians, Latvians, and Estonians.

Before 1880, only some 200,000 people of southern and eastern European origin resided in the United States. Between 1880 and 1910, about 8.4 million arrived. In 1896, the number of these "new immigrants" exceeded the number of "old immigrants" from northern and Western Europe. By 1907, new immigrants were almost the whole of the influx. Of 1,285,349 immigrants registered that year, a million began their long journey from somewhere in a crescent shaped belt stretching from Sicily to St. Petersburg.

Birth Pains of a   This was not a heavily industrialized region. Most southern
World Economy   and eastern Europeans were peasants, farming small plots of land using traditional tools and methods. However, the modernization of Western Europe and the United States profoundly affected their lives too. Advances in scientific health care resulted in a sharp decline in infant mortality and an increase in longevity, and, therefore, a big jump in population from Poland to Italy. Agricultural production increased too, but at a fraction of the rate in the western United States and Canada. European peasants on small properties hand seeding, harvesting, and threshing wheat could not compete with large and mechanized North American wheat growers even after the costs of trans-Atlantic shipping were factored into the price. Poles living in Warsaw, at the center of "the granary of eastern Europe," could buy American flour as cheaply as they could buy flour milled from grain grown 25 miles away.

The bottom fell out of the standard of living in these economic hinterlands. During the final decades of the nineteenth century, southern Italian and Polish farm workers made between $40 and $60 a year. When large landowners in Europe attempted to consolidate and modernize their holdings so they could mechanize American style, they pushed peasants off the land more efficiently than declining incomes were doing.

The Jews of the Russian empire felt the effects of modernization in a different way. Forbidden by law to farm, most Russian Jews lived in *shtetls*, small, crowded market towns. Most of them survived as artisans who handcrafted shoes, clothing, furniture—anything that might make a kopek—for sale to nearby peasants. Others were retailers keeping small shops selling everything from luxury goods to books to cheap sundries. Yet others were peddlers wandering the countryside selling to peasants or scavenging scrap iron or worn-out clothing and rags to sell to paper manufacturers.

The shoes and clothing they made competed no better with machine-made shoes or ready-made clothing from England and Germany. There were simply too many shopkeepers—ten times as many as the market could bear according to one source—to support more than a few of them above the poverty line.

Promoting Immigration American manufacturers and railroaders encouraged immigration. Until the Foran Act of 1885 outlawed the practice, some companies paid immigrants' steamship fares if they signed contracts agreeing to work for them when they arrived in the United States. Congress regarded these agreements as a kind of bondage and outlawed it.

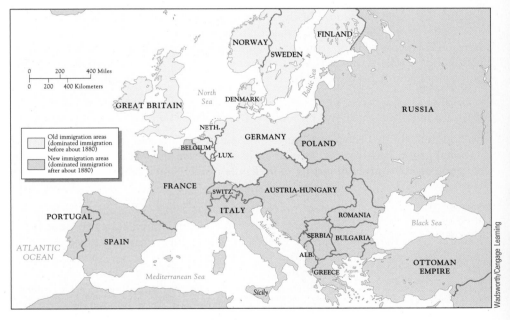

MAP 28.1 European Immigration, 1815–1914

The "old immigrants" were western and northern Europeans. After about 1880, the numbers of "new immigrants," from Italy, the Balkans, and the Russian, Austro-Hungarian, and Ottoman empires—eastern and southern Europe and the Near East—gradually overtook and then dwarfed the numbers of the earlier immigrant groups. Note that the French, who had been an important immigrant group until about 1830, were too few to be noticed as an immigrant group even before the Civil War. French men and women who emigrated usually went to one of France's colonies.

It was not against the law to advertise, however. James J. Hill plastered every sizable town in Norway and Sweden with posters describing the richness of the soil along his Great Northern Railroad. South Dakota got its strange nickname the "Sunshine State" in his promotional campaigns. (One advertisement had palm trees swaying in the balmy Dakota breezes.) One-fifth of Norway's population emigrated—mostly to the West—between the Civil War and World War I.

The American Woolens Company of Lawrence, Massachusetts, circulated handbills throughout southern Italy showing a well-dressed immigrant worker with a sleek, black handlebar moustache carrying a sack marked "$$$" from the mill where he worked to a bank.

Employers liked immigrant laborers. In general, they accepted lower wages than Americans or "old immigrants" would and they did dirty, menial jobs that others shunned. The new immigrants were more docile employees than Americans, Germans, and Irish. Many of them intended to work in America only temporarily— a few months, a year or two—then return to their homelands. Except for the Jews and Christian Poles, the new immigration was overwhelmingly male until well into the twentieth century: 78 percent of the Italians, 95 percent of the Greeks. They wanted to save, to spend as little on living expenses as they could; they had little interest in joining a union or going on strike, to sacrifice in the short run for the sake of a better life in the long run. For them, the long run was back in Italy or Greece.

Temporary immigrant labor was a pure economic asset. The "old country" had borne the expense of supporting able-bodied young males during their unproductive childhood years; it was still sustaining their women and children. In the United States, male immigrants were producers of wealth pure and simple.

THE OLD IMMIGRANTS

In addition to the economic push and pull that affected all immigrants, each national group had reasons peculiar to itself to leave their homelands and familiar rhythms of life to usually jarring experiences in the United States.

The Irish   Between the Civil War and 1900, 1.9 million Irish, Welsh, English, and Scots came to the United States. Except for the Catholic Irish, they were scarcely noticed as immigrants. They resembled Americans more than they resembled the exotic new immigrants.

Because of their religion, Irish Catholics were something of an exception. Anti-Catholicism was a powerful undercurrent in American culture. In 1887, the American Protective Association was founded as, on the face of it, a missionary movement. Members swore an oath to "strike the shackles and chains of blind obedience" to the pope from American Catholics.

Informally, the organization encouraged employers to discriminate against Irish Catholics. Some businesses attached "NINA"—No Irish Need Apply—or "Protestants Only" to their help wanted ads in newspapers. Anti-Irish prejudice was respectable among genteel northeastern Republicans because of the Irish attachment to Democratic political machines in Boston, New York, Chicago, and, to a lesser extent, Philadelphia.

Ironically, Irish-Americans took zestfully to America and exhibited a bombastic patriotism. So numerous almost everywhere that they could insulate their personal lives from prejudice, the Irish parlayed their cohesive sociability and bent for eloquence into becoming a formidable political force. By the 1880s, Irish immigrants and second-generation Irish-Americans dominated the leadership councils of the Democratic party in most big cities, including San Francisco. In fact, it was among the Irish of California that the first American anti-immigrant legislation since the Alien Acts of 1797 had its origins.

Guests of the Golden Mountain Chinese workers, mostly from the overpopulated south of China, had been coming to the United States since the California Gold Rush. This immigration too was a nearly all-male affair: young men who planned to make a bundle and return home. In 1860, the census counted 35,000 Chinese living in California; only 1,800 of them were women, most of them prostitutes.

"Americans are a very rich people," a promoter explained, and "they want the Chinaman to come and will make him welcome." The "celestials," as whites called them (China was known as the "Celestial Kingdom") were not welcome in California's rich placer mines but, in groups, they scraped out a living in diggings that Caucasians had abandoned. When they played out, the immigrants found employment in menial, low-paying work, as domestic servants, maids, nannies, cooks, gardeners, and stable-hands. The "Chinese laundry" was ubiquitous in western towns as were, soon enough, Chinese restaurants.

The Granger Collection, New York

A pro-Chinese cartoon. It shows Chinese immigrants as orderly and industrious. The fact that two of the men are minding white children indicates that this sentiment was middle and upper class, for whom many Chinese worked as domestic servants. The women scowling at the Chinese were immediately identifiable to nineteenth-century readers as Irish from their upturned noses, the usual tip-off. Indeed, Irish-American workingmen in San Francisco were the core of the anti-Chinese movement.

Race, their radically different culture and folkways, and their own contempt for "barbarians" kept the Celestials in closed, tight-knit communities. "When I got to San Francisco," wrote Lee Chew, who became a wealthy businessman, "I was half-starved because I was afraid to eat the provisions of the barbarians. But a few days living in the Chinese Quarter and I was happy again." Leaders of the Gum Shan Hok—the Guests of the Golden Mountain—encouraged the immigrants to stick to themselves. "We are accustomed to an orderly society," explained a leader of San Francisco's Chinatown, "but it seems as if the Americans are not bound by rules of conduct. It is best, if possible, to avoid any contact with them."

When the construction of the first transcontinental railroad began in 1864, Chinese immigration increased. Where 3,000 to 6,000 Chinese had entered California each year, after 1868, the annual immigration jumped to 23,000.

Keeping John Chinaman Out   As long as there was plenty of work for all in the developing West, hostility to the Chinese was restrained. In 1873, however, the depression hit California hard, bringing widespread unemployment. The Chinese were natural scapegoats. In 1877, when the Chinese were 17 percent of California's population, a San Francisco teamster named Denis Kearney began to orate on the city's "sandlots"—empty properties—blaming the joblessness among his largely Irish audiences on the willingness of the Chinese to work for less than an American needed in order to survive. From inflammatory rhetoric, Kearney moved on to leading rampages through San Francisco's Chinatown and the violence spread throughout the state. Once sizable Chinatowns in Oroville and Marysville disappeared overnight when white mobs literally drove the Chinese out. As late as 1885, an anti-Chinese pogrom in Rock Springs, Wyoming, left twenty-eight Chinese dead.

In 1882, Congress passed the Chinese Exclusion Act. Chinese diplomats, merchants, teachers, and students could still be admitted. Amendments to the act permitted close relatives of Chinese already settled in the United States to join them. Otherwise, Chinese immigration was forbidden.

The principal port of entry after the Exclusion Act was Angel Island in San Francisco Bay. Applicants for admission were detained there until they passed examinations—often hundreds of examinations—to determine their eligibility to cross the bay. Some were asked hundreds of questions to determine if they were actually related to the Chinese American whose name they gave. European immigrants passing through New York's Ellis Island were detained a few hours on average; the typical detention time on Angel Island was two weeks and some unfortunates lived there for months.

By the end of the century, would-be Chinese immigrants knew to hire San Francisco lawyers—"the very best attorneys in the city," according to the immigration service—before they left Canton. The retainer was $100, but it was worth it; about half the immigrants denied entry on Angel Island won their cases in court.

There was a small illegal immigration. A few brave souls rowed ashore from ships through the surf to thinly populated stretches of beach. Some snuck across the border from Canada, where the anti-Chinese legislation was somewhat less rigorous. The Mexican border was a better bet. Mexico encouraged Chinese immigration and an estimated 80 percent of Chinese entering Mexico continued on to the United States.

In small numbers, Japanese began to trickle into California, many via Hawai'i, an independent kingdom with close ties to America. Paradoxically, whites resented them not because they accepted substandard wages as the Chinese did, but because the Japanese were ambitious to own and farm their own land and many of them prospered in a remarkably short time.

Germans and Scandinavians

The immigration of Germans was constant for 200 years beginning in the early 1700s. Before the Civil War, a majority of German immigrants were Protestant. After the war, a majority of the 4.4 million Germans who came to the United States, an average of about 100,000 a year, were Catholic, especially after 1873 when the German chancellor, Otto von Bismark, instituted the *Kulturkampf,* a series of anti-Catholic laws.

Because many had owned land in Germany, German immigrants were generally better off than other immigrants of the period. While many of them settled in northeastern cities like other immigrants, the majority moved to the upper Midwest to buy farms. Wisconsin was heavily German in the late nineteenth century. As many Milwaukeeans spoke German as spoke English as their first language. Nationally, about 800 German language newspapers were being published in 1900.

Scandinavians also inclined to become farmers. Norwegians predominated in many counties in Wisconsin and Minnesota. Swedes and Finns (who were historically tied to Sweden) were the largest ethnic group in Minnesota. Swedes were also a conspicuous minority in the logging country of the Northwest and Finns in the iron mines of the Mesabi Range.

Ethnic groups that were numerous over large rural areas found adaptation to the New World comparatively easy because they could approximate familiar ways. They founded schools that were taught in their native languages, newspapers and other periodicals, European-style fraternal organizations—the Germans' athletically oriented *Turnverein;* the Norwegians' musical Grieg societies. They continued to eat familiar foods and to raise their children by traditional rules.

The hardships these immigrants faced were not culture and discrimination but problems common to all settlers of new lands in the West. Olë Rolvaag, a gloomy Norwegian-American writer, focused on the loneliness of life on the northern prairies; he did not write much about cultural alienation.

Sephardic and German Jews

Sephardic Jews (Jews descended from the Jews expelled from Spain and Portugal in the 1490s) were not numerous and, therefore, threatened no one. Moreover, they were generally well educated, sophisticated, and often well fixed. They eased into middle- and upper-class society before the Civil War, especially in Charleston and New Orleans. Jefferson Davis's strongest political ally in the Confederacy was Judah P. Benjamin, a Sephardic Jew. Supreme Court justice Benjamin Cardozo had Sephardic ancestry, as did the financier and presidential adviser, Bernard Baruch of South Carolina. By 1880, there were about 150,000 German Jews in the United States. Most were small businessmen; rare was the southern town without its Jewish dry goods store. In New York City, German Jews dominated the ready-made clothing industry. Of 241 garment manufacturers in the city in 1885, 234 were owned by Jews.

While preserving their Jewish identity, German Jews assimilated quickly to American ways. Led by Rabbi Isaac Mayer Wise of Cincinnati, they founded Reform Judaism. Reform communities abandoned the distinctively Jewish dress and the earlocks (hair at the temples grown long and curled) and other medieval encrustations common in European Jewry. Reform Jews rejected the ancient dietary laws of the Hebrews and the even more elaborate food rules added by medieval rabbis. They regarded them as irrelevant or, at least, as isolating Jews from gentiles. The German Jewish immigrants embraced mainstream American culture. In 1880, all but 8 of the 200 synagogues in the United States were Reform synagogues.

The New Jewish Immigration   Jews from Eastern Europe—the Russian empire and Romania—who emigrated in large numbers beginning in 1881, were altogether different. They were Orthodox in their religion—highly traditional. By 1890, the number of synagogues in America increased from 200 to 533; virtually all the news ones were Orthodox. The Eastern European Jews spoke Yiddish—"Jewish," their own language derived from medieval German and as central to their culture as their religion. The men dressed in somber clothing and wore skull caps. Married women sheared their hair and covered their heads with shawls. Like the Irish, unlike the Germans, most of them were virtually penniless when they arrived. They had been poor in Russia and spent what little they had getting to America. (On average, Ellis Island immigrants stepped ashore with $31.39.) The men were much more likely to be skilled artisans than other immigrants were, 66 percent compared to 20 percent of all new immigrants. They emigrated as families—men, women, and children—and had no intention of returning to Europe. Only 5 percent ever sailed east.

The Yiddish-speaking Jews came to the United States for good because of brutal, state-abetted persecution in Russia and Romania. In 1881, a wave of more than 200 pogroms (rampages by Christian peasants through Jewish towns) swept over Russia and the Ukraine. Even in Kiev, a large city, mobs stormed through the Jewish quarter burning shops and businesses and beating Jews. The next year, the pogroms spread into Poland, reaching as far as Warsaw. At first, authorities tried to stop the violence. More than 4,000 rioters were arrested and, in Poland, Catholic priests were ordered to condemn the violence from the pulpit.

Jews concluded they had no future in the Russian empire. They were right. There were localized pogroms almost every year of the 1880s and 1890s, and many police officers found it convenient to be out of town when they erupted. In 1903, beginning in Bessarabia (Moldavia and Romania), pogroms were bigger, more vicious, and more widespread than in 1881–1882. There were 660 just in two weeks in November. More than 300 Jews were killed just in Odessa. This time, Czar Nicholas II virtually blessed the violence. Altogether some 5 million Jews fled Russia and Romania, mostly for the United States between 1881 and 1914.

29

BIG CITY LIFE
Urban America 1865–1917

The mobs of great cities add just so much to the support of pure government as sores do to the strength of the human body.

—Thomas Jefferson

I have an affection for a great city. I feel safe in the neighborhood of man, and enjoy the sweet security of streets.

—Henry Wadsworth Longfellow

Four of five of the new immigrants settled in the Northeast, most of the rest in midwestern industrial cities. They transformed the big cities of both regions. By the first years of the twentieth century, immigrants and their children made up half the population of Philadelphia, Pittsburgh, and Seattle; 60 percent in Buffalo, Detroit, and Minneapolis; 70 percent in New York, Chicago, and Milwaukee. There were 3,000 Italians in Philadelphia in 1870, 77,000 in 1910, 155,000 in 1930. Chicago's Polish population in 1870 was 10,000; in 1910, almost 250,000 Chicagoans were Polish. New York City already had a large Jewish population in 1880: 80,000. In 1920, there were 1.25 million Jews in the "promised city."

THE FOREIGN CITY

Generous-minded Americans looked on the immigrants from southern and eastern Europe as exotics; others were contemptuous of them or feared they were destroying the country. The newcomers did not look like old-stock white Americans. Greeks, Armenians, Assyrians, Lebanese, and southern Italians were swarthy, a formidable handicap in a nation that drew a sharp color line. Christian Poles and other Slavs were "hirsute, low-browed, big-faced persons of obviously low mentality." Jews were undersized, "stunted." The immigrants' religious practices and other customs were alien to Americans. The Russian Jews disappeared from

Cities 1865–1900

1865	1870	1875	1880	1885	1890	1895	1900

1870 First elevated train (New York)

1883 Brooklyn Bridge completed

1885 Steel I-beam perfected

1887 First electric trolley line (Richmond)

1889 Jane Addams founds Hull House (Chicago)

1890 Riis's *Other Half* published

Louis Sullivan celebrates the "skyscraper" 1896

Three cities top a million in population 1900

the streets on Saturday, observing the sabbath. Then they turned Sunday—still a sabbath to some Protestants—into a raucous market day. Irish priests and bishops were scandalized by the "pagan" processions of Sicilians and Neapolitans, who carried statues of the Madonna accompanied by brass bands blaring out music that sounded anything but sacred. The rituals of the Orthodox Greeks, Ukrainians, and Balkan immigrants with their Byzantine-clad priests were equally unsettling.

In a novel of 1890, *A Hazard of New Fortunes,* William Dean Howells sent Basil March, a genteel middle-class American, on a ride on a New York city elevated train. March "found the variety of people in the car as unfailingly entertaining as ever," but he felt like a foreigner in someone else's country. Even the Irish, who ran the city, were outnumbered by

> the people of Germanic, Slavonic, of Pelagic [Mediterranean], of Mongolian stock.... The small eyes, the high cheeks, the broad noses, the puff lips, the bare, cue-filleted skulls, of Russians, Poles, Czechs, Chinese, the furtive glitter of Italians, the blonde dullness of Germans; the cold quiet of Scandinavians—fire under ice—were aspects that he identified, and that gave him abundant suggestion for the ... reveries in which he dealt with the future economy of our heterogeneous commonwealth.

A Patchwork Quilt   Immigrants clustered in their own neighborhoods, "ethnic ghettos." A map of New York, wrote journalist Jacob Riis in 1890, "colored to designate nationalities, would show more stripes than the skin of a zebra and more colors than the rainbow." The same was true of Boston, Philadelphia, Cleveland, and Chicago. A large portion of Buffalo was called Polonia. Even some smaller industrial towns were ethnic mélanges. In Lawrence, Massachusetts, a textile town, more than twenty languages and probably twice that many dialects were spoken.

There were ghettos within ghettos. In New York City's Greenwich Village, a largely Italian community in the early twentieth century, immigrants from the region of Calabria monopolized housing on some streets, immigrants from Sicily on others. On these regional blocks, investigators discovered, Italians from the same town were the sole occupants of some apartment houses; this one was the "Agrigento tenement," next door the "Catania tenement." Grocery stores, bakeries, cafés, and restaurants announced themselves not as "Italian" but as Campanian or Apulian.

Hester Street, on the Lower East Side of New York, was a major Jewish commercial center. On the ground floor of every building was a shop; stalls lined the sidewalks, pushcarts the curbs. Saturday—the Jewish sabbath—was quiet, but Sunday was a noisy, bustling market day, a fact that scandalized old-stock Americans.

Museum of the City of New York

The same held true like on New York's Jewish Lower East Side. Galician Jews (from a province of Russian Poland) looked warily on Jews from Russia proper. Each group named its own "Chief Rabbi of New York." Romanian Jews had their own community. Assimilated German Jews lived "uptown." At first, they were dismayed by the hordes of decidedly unassimilated eastern European Jews. A Jewish school teacher called the newcomers "uneducated paupers" with "stunted minds" and "warped" characters. Another German Jew said that they were "slovenly in dress, loud in manners, and vulgar in discourse." Well-to-do German Jews never did warm to the eastern Europeans socially, but they organized and financed the United Hebrew Charities to aid them.

Assimilation   The desire to assimilate, to become "American," varied in intensity from group to group and within groups. Those who came to the United States as adults generally found solace in the familiar language, customs, foods, and fellowship of "Little Italy" and "Polonia." Emigration to a society utterly unlike what they knew was psychologically jarring. The ethnic neighborhood provided a buffer between them and disdainful old-stock Americans—and rivalries with other immigrant groups. A considerable number of immigrants continued to believe that "some day" they would return to Europe. Why bother to learn American ways? In 1920, only 25 percent of Italians and Poles had taken out citizenship papers, only 17 percent of Greeks.

There was, however, a sharp generational conflict within ethnic groups. The children of immigrants, whether born in America or very young when they arrived, had no memory of an "old country." They spoke Yiddish or Slovak or Polish at home, but they learned English in school and their teachers methodically worked, in the words of one, "to break up these groups or settlements, to assimilate or amalgamate those people as part of our American race."

Many a family was divided within when the young second-generation immigrants openly disdained their parents' "greenhorn" ways. Other immigrant parents were grateful to the schools for ensuring that their children would not suffer the anxieties of being foreigners. An Italian mother chided the school her children attended because it was run according to a trendy "child-oriented" philosophy. "The program of that school is suited to the children of well-to-do homes," she said, "not to our children. We send our children to school for what we cannot give them ourselves, grammar and drill.... We do not send children to school for group activity; they get plenty of that in the street."

Except for Jews, few immigrants aspired to more than a reading, writing, and arithmetic education for their children. They had been peasants and they were still poor; they wanted to put their children to work as soon as they were old enough to contribute more than pennies to the family's finances.

Many Russian Jews, however, urged—browbeat!—their sons and daughters to learn a musical instrument or to study to be professionals, as costly as it was for parents. Musical expertise and a college diploma could not be destroyed or taken away; they were the ultimate portable properties. As early as 1916, the student bodies of New York City's public colleges were heavily Jewish: 44 percent at Hunter, the city's college for women, 73 percent at CCNY, the City College of New York. Thirteen percent of the students at elite and very expensive Columbia University was Jewish (much to the dismay of Columbia's professors). Rather more remarkable, one student in five at Fordham, a Roman Catholic college, was a Jew.

Immigrant Aid Institutions   Immigrant groups established their own institutions to assist *paesani* and *landsmen*—their countrymen—in adjusting to America while maintaining their ethnic identity. The Young Men's and Young Women's Hebrew Associations dated back to 1854. They were founded to provide Jewish counterparts to the YMCA and YWCA, which attracted young people because of the athletic facilities they provided, but which also preached Christianity to members.

Among the Catholic population, which grew from 6 million in 1880 to 10 million in 1900 (making Roman Catholicism the country's largest single denomination), traditionally charitable religious orders like the Sisters of Mercy established hospitals and houses of refuge in the slums. The St. Vincent de Paul Society functioned much like the Salvation Army without the military trappings, providing food, clothing, and shelter for the desperate.

Most Catholic parishes had elementary schools; bishops opened Catholic high schools. They were as assimilationist and patriotic as the public schools. An overwhelming majority of bishops were Irish-American and most of the rest were assimilated second-generation German-Americans. They discouraged Catholic children from attending public schools because they were Protestant in orientation. Teachers read daily from the King James version Bible and led children in Protestant prayer.

At first, Irish-American bishops resisted demands by new immigrant Catholics for churches and priests of their own nationalities. However, when the demands became more strident and the bishops began to fear that they would lose their hold on the newcomers, they gave in.

The result was two parish systems in big, multiethnic cities: a system of traditional "territorial parishes" with geographical boundaries to which assimilated Irish-Americans belonged and a hodgepodge of "national parishes," organized not geographically but by language. Religious services, church business, and schools were conducted in the old-country languages (although proper English was a major subject in the schools). In Chicago in 1915, about a hundred parishes were "territorial"; there were thirty-three Polish parishes, thirty German, ten Italian, ten Lithuanian, five Slovak, four Croatian, four French (for French Canadians), two Slovene, and one parish each for Flemish-speaking Belgians, Dutch, Czechs, Chaldeans (Assyrians), Syrians, and Hungarians. Sometimes, Catholic churches were cheek by jowl. In one square mile around the stockyards, there were two territorial parishes, two Polish churches, and a Lithuanian, Italian, German, Croatian, Czech, and Slovak church.

Settlement Houses   The settlement house was another conspicuous institution in the new immigrant ghettos. Beginning in the 1880s, middle-class Americans imbued with an evangelical impulse to help others, but no interest in challenging immigrants' religion or domestic customs, took over large buildings where they provided food to the destitute, as traditional charities had, but also child care for working mothers, public baths, recreational facilities, and courses of study in everything from English for adults to social skills and household arts necessary in the big city.

The first American settlement house was the Neighborhood Guild, set up in New York City. More famous was Hull House, established in Chicago in 1889 by Jane Addams, soon to be a national figure, and Lillian Wald's Henry Street Settlement in New York (1893). From comfortable backgrounds, educated and well-mannered, Addams, Wald and others were discomfited by the materialism of American culture. Alleviating the deprivations of poor city dwellers was a way to alleviate their own spiritual distress. The settlement houses were devoutly patriotic, but they also celebrated the cultural diversity the immigrants had brought to the city. They promoted programs at which different ethnic groups showed off their native costumes and cookery.

POLITICAL MACHINES

Big city immigrant districts had middle-class leadership from the start. Small businessmen and professionals—doctors, dentists, lawyers, teachers—and, of course, priests and rabbis accompanied the masses of peasants on the immigrant ships.

They had little choice but to do so. Emigration stripped many villages and towns of their population. Shopkeepers and professionals lost their clientele if they did not move to America too.

The "Little Italys" and "Slovak Towns" in American cities often provided better livings for professionals than they had known in Europe. There were no aristocrats or great landlords among the immigrants so the status of the ethnic middle classes bumped up a significant notch—to the very top.

There was another avenue to community leadership in the ethnic neighborhoods that had not existed in the old country, and it required neither education nor capital: the democratic politics of the United States as understood by the big-city political machine.

The Workings of the Machine   Political machines ran most big American cities during the nineteenth century, some through the twentieth. Machines worked within political parties, but they were not synonymous with them. No one who was part of a machine, from the "boss" to the street sweeper who owed his job to the fact that he voted the right way, was interested in an ideology or a principle. The political machine was a means to a very personal end: riches for those at the top; a tidy supplementary income for "middle management"—ward bosses and precinct captains; and a secure job on the city's payroll for street sweepers, firemen, and cops.

The machine was organized with a clear-cut chain of command, like an army. The supreme commander was the boss who was almost never the mayor of the city. To run for mayor, the boss picked a popular, respectable figure who would do what he was told to do for a cut of the spoils. The commander's generals were sub-bosses of large districts of the city. In Tammany Hall, New York's long-lived Democratic party machine, district leaders were called "sachems." (St. Tammany was a legendary Indian chief.) Below the district leaders were ward bosses (the urban ward was an electoral unit); below them precinct captains; and finally there were the soldiers who did the sometimes dirty work on election day.

The sole purpose of the machine was to win municipal elections by hook, crook, and understanding the material and psychic needs of the urban masses. Because ethnic groups were clustered in their own neighborhoods, it was easy to identify the "Italian vote," the "Jewish vote," and so on. The energetic Italian or Jewish hustler who could deliver majorities for the machine was rewarded proportionate to the number of voters who followed him. A Tammany sachem at the end of the nineteenth century put the machine's function among ethnic groups in laundered but not entirely distorted terms:

> Think what the people of New York are. One half, more than one half, are of foreign birth. They do not speak our language, they do not know our laws, they are the raw material with which we have to build up the state.... there is no denying the service that Tammany has rendered the Republic. There is no other organization for taking hold of untrained, friendless men and converting them into citizens. Who else in the city would do it?

Erin Go Bragh   The prototype of the machine was New York's Society of St. Tammany. Originally a patriotic and philanthropic club, Tammany Hall was converted to political uses in 1800 by Aaron Burr. By the time of the Civil War, Tammany had emerged as the single best organized political force in New York City. Between 1865 and 1934, about seventy years, Tammany was in power for sixty of them.

Tammany's first boss was William M. Tweed, a big, garrulous man of considerable charm and few scruples. His inner circle included Mayor A. Oakley Hall, "Elegant Oakley," a lightweight but colorful personality; and the city's comptroller (chief financial officer), Richard "Slippery Dick" Connolly. The core of the Tweed Ring's electoral support was New York's Irish Catholics, numerous enough that, when they voted as a bloc, they were enough to win any election.

"The natural function of the Irishman," said a wit of the period, "is to administer the affairs of the American city." Tweed himself was a Protestant Scotsman, but a list of nineteenth-century machine politicians reads like a roll call of marchers in a St. Patrick's Day parade: Connolly, Honest John Kelley, Richard Croker, George Plunkitt, Charles Murphy, and Tim Sullivan of New York; James McManes of Philadelphia; Christopher Magee and William Finn of Pittsburgh; Martin Lomasney of Boston.

The Irish were successful in politics because, unique among ethnic immigrants, almost all of them spoke English and, discriminated against by the British in their own country, they arrived admiring American institutions. In 1835, before the Catholic Irish had carved out a niche in politics, the archbishop of Charleston, John England, observed, "The Irish are largely amalgamated with the Americans, their dispositions, their politics, their notions of government; their language and their appearance become American very quickly, and they praise and prefer America to their oppressors at home." Moreover, Irish culture placed a high premium on wit and oratory—both political assets—and, in American cities, the neighborhood saloon stood in for the village pub that had been the men's social center in Ireland.

The saloon was a natural headquarters for neighborhood political organization. Most of Boss Tweed's ward bosses were saloon keepers. A joke of the time had it that the best way to break up a meeting at Tammany Hall was to open the door and shout, "your saloon's on fire."

The Tweed Ring rewarded saloon keeper–ward bosses by appointing them to city jobs paying big salaries but requiring no work. Cornelius Corson was on New York City's payroll as a court clerk at $10,000 a year, as chief of the board of elections at $5,000 a year, and he was an employee of four other municipal agencies paying $2,500 a year for each. He did not have to go to the office. His real office was his saloon where he put in long days attending to the needs of his constituents.

Winning Elections

Corson and other ward bosses did personal favors for those who came to them. They fixed up minor and sometimes major problems with the law. They found jobs for men without work, either with the city or with friendly employers whom the ward bosses helped get city contracts. Philadelphia's Boss James McManes had more than 5,000 jobs at his ward bosses' disposal. The New York machine had four times that number to hand out. It was estimated that 20 percent of New York's voters had a direct financial interest in the outcome of municipal elections. When the votes of appreciative relatives and friends were added in, the machine had a very nice political base with which to fight an election.

It was, therefore, no accident that most policemen in New York and Boston—jobs on the police force paid the best—were Irish. When the "Italian vote" became large enough to be reckoned with, jobs as firemen were found for Italian men; New York's Sanitation Department became as Italian a bailiwick as the police force was Irish.

Bosses tried not to miss a baptism, bar mitzvah, wedding, or funeral in their ward or district. They personally and conspicuously presented gifts—purchased with their own money—to the child, couple, or grieving widow. They bought tons of coal for heating the homes of the poor during severe winters. During the bitter cold winter of 1870, Boss Tweed spent $50,000 on coal. Big Tim Sullivan, a Tammany sachem at the end of the century, gave away 5,000 turkeys every Christmas. Sullivan and others held huge annual picnics on the Fourth of July. In 1871, Mike Norton treated his constituents to 100 kegs of beer, 50 cases of champagne, 20 gallons of brandy, 10 gallons of gin, 200 gallons of chowder, 50 gallons of turtle soup, 36 hams, 4,000 pounds of corned beef, and 5,000 cigars.

Some bosses were actually beloved. When handsome, generous Big Tim Sullivan died after a railroad accident, 25,000 people attended his funeral.

The Failure of the Goo-Goos
Big Tim's and others' "business expenses" brought rays of sunlight into lives lived precariously on the edge of destitution. The handouts and parties meant far more to poor immigrants than just where the Democratic and Republican parties stood on the great issues of the day. The political machine provided a kind of social safety net that official government did not.

This was why "good government" reformers never lasted long in nineteenth-century cities. The "Goo-Goos," as machine politicians called them, won elections when machine corruption reached proportions outrageous even to working-class voters. The Tweed Ring was thrown out of office as was, thirty years later, the powerful Tammany boss Richard Croker's machine. Chicago's "Gray Wolves" were ousted. In 1906, Abe Ruef's and Mayor Eugene Schmitz's corrupt machine in San Francisco was voted out.

In every case, however, reform administrations were one-term affairs. The Goo-Goos were dedicated to low taxes and honest, efficient, economical city government. Unlike reformers in the twenty-first century, they did not believe that providing social services was a function of government, let alone the distribution of city jobs on the basis of political loyalties.

The Profit Column
Where did the money for the Christmas turkeys, the Fourth of July galas, and the big bosses' fortunes come from? In the case of the Tweed Ring, most of it came from unabashed theft of cosmic magnitude. No one really knows, but estimates of how much the Tweed Ring stole from New York City in just a few years range up to $200 million.

The ring's most profitable technique was the obscenely padded contract. Anyone who wanted to do business with the city knew that the rule was to bill Slippery Dick Connolly's office for up to ten times what he needed to charge to pave a street or build a hospital and, under the table, to kick back most of the overplus to the Tweed Ring. A printing and stationery company of which Boss Tweed was a major owner supplied the city with its forms, pencils, and ink at absurd prices. The expenditures were kept secret thanks to a city charter that Tweed himself designed. Padded contracts to construct streets, hospitals, armories, reservoirs, parks, and to lay gas lines were financed not by taxes—that would have been noticed—but by borrowing, selling bonds, a debt of which the public was unaware until the Tweed Ring was thrown out of power.

New York's famous Central Park was begun by Tweed's machine; it was a gold mine of padded contracts. The most notorious swindle of all was the new New York County Courthouse, a $600,000 building that cost taxpayers $13 million. Plasterers, carpenters, and plumbers who worked on the building kicked back more than half of the padding to Tammany Hall. One of hundreds of grotesquely priced items later unearthed was a bill for forty chairs and three tables: $179,000. "Brooms, etc." cost the city $41,190.95.

Selling Influence, Abetting Vice

The Tweed Ring's great mistake was the scale of its thievery. Big-city machines continued to collect kickbacks after Tweed's downfall but they never again approached celestial levels. Bribes, sometimes open but disguised, were usually under the table. Tweed was paid off by both Jay Gould and Jim Fisk and their rival, Cornelius Vanderbilt. He arranged favorable rulings by judges who were part of the ring. In return, Gould and Fisk put him on the board of directors of the Erie Railroad at a handsome salary. Tweed was no more a lawyer than he was a railroad man, but he was on Vanderbilt's payroll as a "legal advisor." In San Francisco just after 1900, Boss Abe Ruef held office hours in the evening at elegant French restaurants. Would-be purchasers of his "influence" filed into Ruef's private dining room and, for $100,000 on one glorious occasion, bought what they wanted from the Board of Aldermen. Ruef kept a third of the swag; the mayor got a third; the rest was divided among the aldermen who would vote the favor.

During the reign of Richard Croker as boss of New York between 1886 and 1901, Tammany Hall and the police department collaborated in order to keep payoffs flowing into the coffers from after-hours saloons, illegal gambling halls, opium dens, drug dealers, and whorehouses. District leader George Washington Plunkitt denied ever taking a cent of dirty money and Big Tim Sullivan admitted only to helping out gambling halls. (He could hardly say otherwise; he was part owner of several.) If they were telling the truth, they were the exceptions.

After Croker's downfall, however, his successor as Tammany boss, Charles Murphy, concluded that protecting vice was bad politics; the money was not worth the risk of being voted out of office. Murphy eased Tammany out of its sweetheart relationship with the police. He left graft from vice and the wrath of moralistic reformers to cops on the beat in precincts in which the captains sanctioned it and kept Tammany aloft.

THE EVILS OF CITY LIFE

The social services the machines provided to the urban poor came with an exorbitant price attached: the immense corruption by which the bosses enriched themselves. Were Christmas turkeys, jobs with the city, and reservoirs that cost many times more than they should have cost worth the millions that Richard Croker took with him back to Ireland and the hundreds of thousands that saloon keeper–ward bosses banked? Most of the people who ate the turkey and drew weekly salaries for sweeping streets would have shrugged. They would have had nothing if Brahmins had run Boston, Goo-Goos New York, and patrician reformers Philadelphia.

On the other hand, machine politicians never addressed the great evils of big-city life the urban poor faced. In the late nineteenth century, city people died at a rate unknown in North America since the seventeenth century. At a time when the national death rate was 20 per 1,000 each year, the death rate in New York City was 25 per 1,000. In the slums, it was 38:1,000, and for children under five, 136! The figures were only slightly lower in every other big city except Philadelphia. In parts of Chicago mortality was worse. In one Chicago slum as late as 1900, the infant mortality rate was 200 per 1,000; 1 child in 5 died within a year of birth. By way of reference, the infant mortality rate in the United States today is less than 20 per 1,000, and the total death rate is less than 9.

| Too Many Peo-ple, Too Little Room | Big-city people died at high rates because of crowding; the poor lived in too little space. In Boston, typical working-class housing was in decaying wooden structures that had been built as homes for one family. In the late nineteenth century, |

half a dozen families plus boarders crowded into them. In Cleveland, Cincinnati, and St. Louis, the poor lived in partitioned old warehouses or in congested shanty towns on the margins of the built-up area.

In New York, the narrow confines of lower Manhattan made the crowding worse than in any other city. Narrow buildings, also former single-family residences, were carved into tenements that housed a hundred and more people. In 1866, the Board of Health found 400,000 people living in rooms with no windows and 20,000 living in cellars below the water table. An investigator said that cellar dwellers "exhibited the same lethargic habits as animals burrowing in the ground." At high tide, some cellars took on a foot of water; they all flooded during downpours too heavy for the sewers.

Jacob Riis, a reporter who exposed squalid living conditions in a book of 1890, *How the Other Half Lives,* estimated that 330,000 New Yorkers lived in 1 square mile of the city—almost 1,000 people per acre. New York was twice as congested as the London that had turned Charles Dickens's stomach; parts of the city were more densely populated than Bombay. On one tenement block in a Jewish neighborhood just a little larger than an acre, 2,800 people lived. In one apartment of two tiny rooms, Riis found a married couple, their twelve children, and six adult boarders.

A well-meaning architect, James E. Ware, designed a tenement that, he thought, would improve housing for the poor. It was called the "dumbbell tenement" because of its floor plan. At the front and rear it was wide while, in the middle, the building was indented on both sides—a reverse bay—so that every one of the thirty-two apartments had windows to admit light and provide ventilation.

Ware's design did not account for the fact that landlords would exploit their building lots to the fullest. They built the city approved dumbbells up to the lines of the 25- by 100-foot lots. When two dumbbells were built side by side, the windows of two-thirds of the apartments opened on a dark, dank shaft a few feet across. Precious little sunlight was admitted and the air became putrid as the shafts between tenements filled with garbage. Nevertheless, by 1894 there were 39,000 dumbbell tenements in Manhattan, housing almost half of New York's population.

Health

Crowding meant that it was nearly impossible to control epidemics of serious diseases such as smallpox, cholera, measles, typhus, scarlet fever, and diphtheria. Even less dangerous illnesses like chicken pox, mumps, whooping cough, croup, and various influenzas were killers in the crowded cities. Common colds were feared as a first step to pneumonia.

Jacob Riis took his readers on a tour of a tenement: "Be a little careful, please! The hall is dark and you might stumble. You can feel your way, if you cannot see it. Close? Yes! What would you have? All the fresh air that enters these stairs comes from the hall-door that is forever slamming." He paused at the entrance to a windowless apartment. "Listen! That short, hacking cough, that tiny, helpless wail.... The child is dying of measles. With half a chance it might have lived; but it had none. That dark bedroom killed it."

Philadelphia Row Houses

Philadelphia was the exception that proved the rule. A major port of entry for immigrants, it was the nation's third largest city after New York and Chicago with a population of 1.3 million in 1900. However, far fewer Philadelphians died from contagious diseases than the residents of every other large city. When the mortality rate in New York was 35 per 1,000, it was 20.9 per 1,000 in Philadelphia. When Boston's Irish immigrants were dying at a rate of 38:1,000, the mortality rate among Philadelphia's Irish was 12:1,000.

Philadelphia's difference was the fact that it was roomy. New York and Boston were both hemmed in by water; their areas were, respectively, 22 and 4 square miles. Philadelphia sprawled over 130 square miles. With so much land on which to build housing for the soaring population, developers erected not six-story walk-up tenements but "row houses" two or three stories high. A typical working-class row house built after 1870—invariably of brick—was 14 to 16 feet wide, 30 to 35 feet deep. There were three rooms on each floor and a cellar for coal. The houses were flush with the sidewalk (middle-class row houses added a front porch and a bay window upstairs) and, of course, there were no windows on the sides except for the homes at each end of the block. With windows front and back, however, there was cross ventilation such as did not exist in tenements.

During the 1880s and 1890s, newly built row houses sold for between $1,000 and $2,500. That was a lot for a working-class family to save but not an impossible amount. In the meantime, row houses could be rented for $8 a week.

In 1850, when New York and Philadelphia each had populations of about 500,000, there were only 38,000 houses in New York but more than 61,000 in Philadelphia. Twice as many New Yorkers lived in each house than in Philadelphia row houses. There were slums in Philadelphia, but the worst in the city was no more congested than New York's average population density, a figure that included middle-class neighborhoods and even the beginnings of Fifth Avenue's mansion row.

Row house living made it possible for Philadelphia's public health officials to quarantine homes with a case of a serious contagious disease. (The law required doctors to report them.) Effective quarantine was impossible in a crowded tenement.

Sanitation

Sanitation on the streets was a serious problem in big cities.

Free-roaming scavengers—chickens, hogs, dogs, and birds—could handily clean up garbage in small towns, and backyard latrines were adequate in disposing of human wastes. But neither worked when a hundred people lived in a building and shared a single privy. City governments provided for waste collection, but even when honestly run, sanitation departments could barely keep up.

Horses compounded the problem. They deposited 250,000 pounds of manure on Milwaukee's streets each day. On average, thirty horses died on Chicago's streets each day. In New York on extremely hot and cold days, old and poorly kept horses keeled over by the hundreds. Most carcasses were picked up rather quickly. Tanners paid for hides and renderers, who boiled them down for tallow. Those that had begun to decay were thrown into rivers, harbors, and lakes where, often enough, they washed ashore.

In the poorest tenements, piped water was available only in shared sinks in the hallways, which were typically filthy. To be safe, city water was so heavily dosed with chemicals that it was barely palatable. The well-to-do bought bottled spring water that was trucked into the cities. Other people depended on wells in the streets that were inevitably fouled by runoff.

Tenement apartments did not have bathrooms. Children washed by romping in the water of open fire hydrants or by taking a swim in polluted waterways. If you did not come home tinged gray or brown from the river, one survivor of New York's Lower East Side remembered, you had not washed. When adults concluded that a bath was in order, they went to public bathhouses where there was hot, clean water at a reasonable price.

Vice and Crime

Slums were breeding grounds of vice and crime. With 14,000 homeless people in New York in 1890, many of them children—"street Arabs," they were called—and work difficult to get and unsteady at the best of times, many found the temptations of sneak thievery, pocket picking, purse snatching, and even violent robbery too much to resist. As early as the 1850s, police in New York were vying with (or taking bribes from) strong-arm gangs named after the neighborhoods where they held sway: the Five Points Gang, the Mulberry Bend gang, the Hell's Kitchen gang, and so on.

Some gangs burgled warehouses and shops by night and preyed on middle-class swells slumming at brothels and illegal gambling halls. But the gangs' usual victims were other slum dwellers struggling to survive and hoping to escape. The working man who paused for a beer before he took his pay envelope home made himself a target if he drank three or four. Shop keepers were given the choice of making weekly payments of "protection" money or be burned out or beaten up.

The homicide rate declined in German and British cities as they grew larger; in American cities it tripled just during the 1880s. An Italian visitor to the United States, Cesare Lombroso, exclaimed that "lawlessness is an American phenomenon with no equal in the rest of the world." The prison population of the nation doubled in the last years of the century but plenty of thugs remained at large.

By the end of the century, more sophisticated criminals had moved into vice, themselves paying protection money to the police or local political boss in order to be left alone. In every poor neighborhood and even close to city centers, there were gambling operations, opium dens, saloons that remained open after legal hours, and brothels. Prostitution flourished at every level from swank, expensive houses for the carriage trade to 50¢-whores in dirty rooms just large enough for a bed. Immigrant communities provided an endless supply of girls and women. A majority of women arrested for prostitution were part-timers, hitting the streets when their wages from "honest work" were not enough to pay the bills.

Growing

In 1790, when the first census was taken, only 3.4 percent of Americans lived in towns of 8,000 people or more. In 1860, on the eve of the Civil War, 16 percent of the population was classified as "urban." Only New York (population 814,000) and Philadelphia (516,000) were what we would recognize as "big cities" and just nine cities had populations of more than 100,000.

By 1900, one-third of the American people were "urban." Fully twenty-six cities had populations greater than 100,000, almost three times as many as in 1860. The population of six cities topped 500,000 and three—New York, Chicago, and Philadelphia—numbered their people by the millions.

The immigrant flood accounts for the numbers in the big cities of the Northeast and Midwest. But those cities were able to fit everybody in only because of improvements in transportation within cities and their environs and innovations in construction technology.

The "Walking City" When the only way for people to move about a city was on foot or, for the well-to-do, in horse-drawn carriages, a city's extent from center to outskirts was limited to a radius of a mile or two. That was the maximum people working twelve and sixteen hour days could live from their place of employment and about the farthest teamsters driving heavy wagons loaded with everything from fine furniture to firewood, coal, ice and manure could deliver enough of their goods to make the business worthwhile. Even a light carriage drawn by the finest horses could move no faster than 3 or 4 miles an hour on streets clogged with wagons and pedestrians.

In these "walking cities," the most desirable residential neighborhood was the city center. The city's elite did not want to waste time getting from their homes to their offices, even when they were in noisy dirty factories. Domestic servants lived in the lofts of narrow three and four story townhouses. Lawyers, doctors, mechanics, and shopkeepers lived behind or above their workplaces or stores. Their

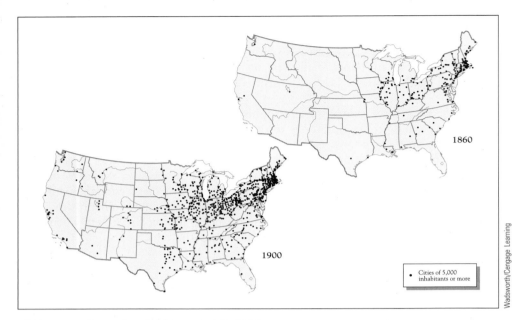

Wadsworth/Cengage Learning

MAP 29.1 Growth of Cities, 1860–1900

In 1860, few large cities were found outside of the northeastern states. By 1900, big northeastern cities had multiplied and the South and West were also heavily urbanized. In 1900, the ten largest cities were New York, Chicago, Philadelphia, St. Louis, Boston, Baltimore, Cleveland, Buffalo, San Francisco, and Cincinnati.

employees had rooms—rarely more than two—nearby. Butchers, grocers, coal, lumber, and ice dealers set up where they could find space.

People of all social classes, professions, and occupations lived cheek by jowl on narrow streets. Only a few thoroughfares, extensions of highways, were wide enough for two heavy wagons to move in the same direction side by side. The line between city and country was vividly clear. Where built-up neighborhoods, paved streets, water and gas lines, and sewers ended, farmland began. There might be a belt of ramshackle shanties where people for whom a competitive society had no place managed to survive. But that was all.

Center-city living was congested, noisy, dirty, and frantic, even for the wealthy once they stepped out of their homes. When it became possible for those who could afford to move away from the places where they worked, they fled, leaving center city to business and the poor.

The Omnibus and the Horsecar   The omnibus, an idea borrowed from France, made its appearance in the largest cities about 1840. The omnibus was a heavy, rather ugly block-shaped wagon, enclosed for shelter from the elements. (Our word *bus* derives from omnibus.) Pulled by two horses (more climbing hills) omnibuses plied fixed routes on a fixed schedule. Riding them was far from pleasant; a Philadelphian described the ride as "heavy, jolting, slow, and uncomfortable." But, for a fare of 12¢, a New York newspaper reported, the omnibus made it "particularly convenient for merchants and others doing business in the lower part of the city and living in the upper part"—away from the mess.

The licensed omnibus was "public transportation"; anyone who could pay the fare could ride one—any white person, that is; city charters permitted omnibus companies to refuse to carry African Americans, which they did. However, the fares ensured that only middle- and upper-class people rode them. Twelve cents morning and night did not work in the budget of a workingman making a dollar a day.

The horse car made it possible for people a notch or two lower on the social scale to move their homes away from the worst parts of the city and commute to work. Much lighter than omnibuses, pulled by only one horse, running smoothly and faster on rails, a horsecar ride cost only 5¢. They were constrained by their tracks, of course. If there was an obstruction, they stayed where they were. But the awkward omnibuses had never been nimble in circumventing obstacles. The horsecar lines rapidly ran most of them out of business.

The cheapness, speed, and ease of commuting by horsecar led to residential housing booms to the north on Manhattan island, west over the Schuylkill River in Philadelphia, in three directions out of Chicago, and up into the hills above Cincinnati. Horsecar lines were so cheap to build that smaller cities with fewer paying customers could afford them too.

The steam ferry filled in on rivers that were too wide to bridge. As early as 1850, fast ferryboats were shuttling across the East River between Manhattan and Brooklyn every few minutes. By 1860, 100,000 people made the six-minute crossing daily. Camden, New Jersey, was Philadelphia's ferryboat suburb across the Delaware River. San Francisco became the first western city among the top ten largest because ferryboats connected it to residential suburbs to the north and west of the great Bay.

The El and the Trolley   The "El," steam-powered passenger trains elevated above street level on hideously ugly iron scaffolds made it possible to develop residential neighborhoods even farther from city centers. Unlike horsecars, which were frequently delayed, sometimes for hours, by accidents and traffic jams, Els had their roadways to themslves.

In 1870, New York completed the first elevated railroad on Ninth Avenue. It was so successful that, by 1890, three more north-south lines were erected, on Second, Third, and Sixth Avenues, one of the east side lines all the way to Harlem, incorporating that once independent village into New York City. In 1890, there were 94 miles of elevated railway in New York, 265 miles of horsecar lines, and still 137 miles of omnibus routes. Philadelphia built an elevated and Chicago perhaps the most famous El of all. Where it made a big circle around the business district to turn around, it defined center city Chicago as "the loop."

While the El made it possible for city dwellers to enjoy roomy, airy residential neighborhoods, they were the cause of further deterioration of the quality of life for the poorer people who lived near them. They were noisy and dirty, leaving a trail of grease and sometimes still burning cinders behind them. In places, they ran at the level of third-story apartments, destroying any privacy within.

By way of contrast, the nineteenth century's final innovation in urban transportation was almost entirely positive. (The subway is a twentieth-century phenomenon.) The electric trolley was pioneered not in a big city but in Richmond, Virginia, in 1887 by inventor-businessman Frank J. Sprague. Horsecar companies embraced the conversion to electricity. Once the overhead wires to power the cars were strung, electric trolleys were faster and cleaner than horsecars, easier to stop, even a pleasant addition to the ears in their rhythmic click-clack and melodious bells. By 1895, 850 trolley lines crisscrossed dozens of American cities on 10,000 miles of track.

Because trolleys were so speedy once out of traffic, traction companies could locate their car barns and repair shops outside cities on cheap real estate, selling their old downtown stables to builders. To make the most of their distant properties—and to make money on Sundays when their charters required them to run—the trolley companies built amusement parks. For a ride costing a nickel—small children riding free—even working-class families could enjoy a day's entertainment that, before 1890, was unimaginable. New York's Coney Island is the most famous of the day-trip resorts. But Boston had Revere Beach, Philadelphia Willow Grove, Cleveland Euclid Beach, Atlanta Ponce de Leon Park, and just about every other city with a trolley line its picnic ground or amusement park.

Building Up

In transforming mixed-use city centers into all-business districts, horse cars, elevated trains, and electric trolley caused downtown property values to soar. To make the most of their real estate, landlords multiplied the square footage they could rent out by, in what Walt Whitman called the "pull-down-and-build-all-over-again spirit," erecting ever taller structures.

There were, however, limits on how high an office building could be. Businessmen were reluctant to rent office space above about the fourth floor because of the arduous and time-consuming climb to get there. But offices on otherwise desirable lower floors lost luster when a building above them grew too high. The walls of masonry structures became so much heavier with each additional story that, at the bottom, they were massive and windowless. At ground level, the weight-bearing walls of Chicago's sixteen-floor Monadnock Building (the tallest masonry office building ever erected) were 6 feet thick.

The obvious solution to the stair-climbing problem was a mechanical lift. Hoists had been used since antiquity to raise heavy loads; steam-powered elevators were being used in factories by 1835. But they were too dangerous for passengers, as countless gory accidents demonstrated. The ropes and cables that hoisted the elevators snapped without warning, the car plunging to earth.

Before the Civil War, Elisha Graves Otis devised a braking system that eliminated the risk of a free fall. His "safety elevators" were equipped with a spring-triggered catch that, if the cable broke, shot into ratchet-like teeth mounted vertically in the shaft; the elevator stopped falling instantly. Otis's sons and others developed a hydraulic system that lifted elevators faster and more smoothly. By 1878, Otis elevators could climb 600 to 800 feet per second. Offices on the upper floors of tall buildings, formerly hard to rent out, became the most desirable because (from an Otis brochure) a businessman or customer "makes the transit in half a minute of repose

The Brooklyn Bridge shortly after it was completed in 1883. It was (and is) as stunning in its beauty as in its size. The bridge made Brooklyn, then the fourth largest city in the United States, an appendage of Manhattan. In 1898, Brooklyn was amalgamated into greater New York City as one of five boroughs. In the twentieth century, engineers discovered that the Brooklyn Bridge was built six times as strong as it had to be, a great compliment to its designer.

Reproduced from the Collections of the Library of Congress, Washington, DC [LC-US262-79046]

and quiet, and arriving there, enjoys a purity and coolness of atmosphere and an exemption from noise, dust, and exhalations."

William L. Jenney made yet taller structures possible by perfecting, in 1885, the steel "I" beam girder. With girders, it was possible to raise buildings that seemed to scrape the skies without massive supporting walls. Skyscrapers were steel skeletons on which decorative nonsupporting walls of cast iron or thinly sliced stone were hung. Chicago architects pioneered in the design of the "tall office building," but New York became the classic skyscraper city. The Singer building, completed in 1906, set the record at forty-one stories. It was broken two years later by the Metropolitan Tower with fifty. In 1913, the Woolworth Building reached sixty stories.

Building Over Another technological innovation that contributed to the growth of cities was the suspension bridge, which erased broad rivers as barriers to urban expansion. The apostle of the suspension bridge was a German immigrant, John A. Roebling, who came to the United States in 1831. He set up a factory that twisted steel wire into cable, contending that if a bridge was suspended from cables instead of built atop massive pillars, unbridgeable rivers could be spanned.

Roebling built several ever longer suspension bridges, including an international bridge over the Niagara River near the falls. He planned his masterpiece for the East River that separated the nation's largest city, New York, from Brooklyn, the fourth largest American city. While working on the site in 1869, Roebling was injured, contracted tetanus, and died. His son, Washington A. Roebling, stepped in but he too suffered a serious injury, the "bends," after working too long in the caissons in which the foundations of the bridge's towers were built below the level of the river. In order to keep the work area dry, compressed air was pumped into the caisson. The pressure caused nitrogen gas to form bubbles in Roebling's and many of his employee's blood streams. When they came to the surface too quickly for the bubbles to dissolve, they were crippled.

Roebling carried on from a chair in a room overlooking the span, now called the Brooklyn Bridge. Each day, his wife carried his instructions to the construction site, acting as the project's general foreman. The Brooklyn Bridge was completed in 1883 and is still admired for its beauty as well as its engineering. P. T. Barnum herded twenty-one elephants across it in 1884. In the twentieth century, engineers determined that Roebling had built the bridge six times as strong as it had to be.

By providing easy access to Manhattan—33 million people crossed the bridge each year—the bridge ignited a residential real estate boom in Brooklyn. The bridge also spelled the end of Brooklyn's independence. Already a satellite of Manhattan, "a kind of sleeping place for New York" in Charles Dickens's words, Brooklyn was incorporated into the City of New York in 1898 along with Queens, Staten Island, and the Bronx.

The Great Symbol

The Brooklyn Bridge was dedicated with a mammoth celebration. President Chester A. Arthur proclaimed it "a monument to democracy"; sides of beef were roasted in the streets; oceans of beer and whiskey disappeared; brass bands competed in raising a din; races were run; prizes were awarded; dances were danced; and noses were punched. A fireworks display of unprecedented splendor topped off the festivities, illuminating the fantastic silhouette from both sides of the East River. The Brooklyn Bridge was America's celebration of the big city.

It was also an indictment of the city. On the morning of the gala, one dissenting newspaper editor groused that the Brooklyn Bridge had "begun in fraud" and "continued in corruption." It was no secret that much of the $15 million the project cost had gone not into concrete, stone, steel, and cable but into the pockets of machine politicians.

The glories of the finished bridge were also tarnished by its cost in lives. At least twenty workers were killed building it, and others who just vanished probably fell into the river unnoticed. Many more workers were maimed by the bends and broken bones. Then, just a few days after the dedication, a woman stumbled while descending the stairs that led from the causeway to the ground, and someone shouted, "The bridge is sinking!" In the stampede that followed, twelve people were trampled to death.

30

THE LAST FRONTIER
Winning and Losing the West 1865–1900

*The frontier! There is no word in the English language
more stirring, more intimate, or more beloved.... It means
all that America ever meant. It means the old hope of a real
personal liberty, and yet a real human advance in character
and achievement. To a genuine American it is the dearest
word in all the world.*

—Emerson Hough

*The conquest of the earth, which means the taking it away
from those who have a different complexion and slightly
flatter noses than ourselves, is not a pretty thing when you
look at it too much.*

—Joseph Conrad

After counting the American people in 1890, the Census Bureau announced that the frontier was gone. It was no longer possible to draw a line on the map to mark where settled land ended and land yet to be tamed began.

The Bureau's definition of "settled" land was not very rigorous. If 2.5 people lived on a section—a square mile—a population density that today would seem close to howling wilderness, that section was settled. Even by this liberal standard, however, just thirty years earlier, roughly half the area of the United States (not counting Alaska) lay beyond the frontier.

THE LAST FRONTIER

In 1865, the states of California and Oregon and Washington Territory were home to 440,000 people. About 40,000 lived in the Great Salt Lake basin. Santa Fe, in New Mexico Territory, was still thriving as a trading center; a few thousand *sassones* ("Saxons," Anglo-Americans) had settled among a largely Hispanic and Indian population. Except for those outposts, the vast territory west of an undulating line

The Last of the West 1860–1902

1860	1866	1872	1878	1884	1890	1896	1902

1860–1861 **Pony Express**

Sand Creek Massacre

1866 **Fetterman Massacre**

1876 **Battle of Little Big Horn**

1877 **Chief Joseph's Flight to Canada**

1884 *Century of Dishonor* **published**

1886 **Blizzard destroys "cattle kingdom"**

1887 **Dawes Severalty Act**

1890 **Wounded Knee**

1893 **Turner Thesis**

The Virginian **published** 1902

running from Brownsville, Texas, north to the Minnesota-Dakota border was still Indian country.

A Useless Land   Most Americans were content to leave it that way as long as the army protected overland emigrants and, later, the transcontinental railroad. When Americans thought land, they thought agriculture. When they thought agriculture, they thought plenty of rain during the growing season. That was what they had known from the shores of the Atlantic to eastern Kansas.

West of about 100° longitude (mid-Kansas), there were very few pockets of land where it was rainy enough and flat enough to grow grain using traditional farming methods. In the middle of this "Wild West" rose the Rocky Mountains. Their majestic peaks and dramatic scenery like the falls of the Yellowstone River were known to easterners, thanks to landscapes painted by artists who had accompanied military expeditions or ventured on their own into the wilderness, easel, oils, and canvases packed on the backs of mules. The very grandeur of the Rockies, however, told Americans that they could not support a population accustomed to living as they did.

Between the Rockies and the Sierra Nevada lay the Great Basin, quite literally a bowl from which there was no outlet for the few rivers there. Even the largest waterway of the region, the Humboldt River that emigrants followed on their final leg toward California lost heart in the Great Basin, pooled up, and evaporated in a "sink." The Great Salt Lake, vast though it was, was a sink where the creeks that tumbled down the Wasatch Range died. It was saltier than the ocean, useful for nothing but making salt. Only by diverting the mountain streams into irrigation ditches had the Mormons been able to work their agricultural miracles. However, just as Brigham Young had figured, no part of the West was less inviting to Americans than the Mormon Zion. Most of the state of Nevada was at too high an elevation for irrigation. Its gravelly soils supported sagebrush, creosote bush, tumbleweed (an accidental import from eastern Europe), and a few grasses.

East of the Rockies were the Great Plains. There was rain on the plains (and plenty of snow) but too little during the summer. Few trees grew there except for cottonwood groves along streams. Good grasses, however, carpeted the plains. They grew as tall as a man on the eastern half of the plains, shorter in the rain shadow of the Rockies. There were a few large rivers: the Arkansas, the broad shallow Platte, and two Red Rivers, one between Texas and Oklahoma, another in the Dakotas flowing into Canada.

The Native Peoples of the West

During the 1860s, an estimated 350,000 Indians lived on the plains, the desert, and in the foothills of the mountains. There were dozens of tribes speaking languages from half a dozen linguistic families. Just about every tribe was at least suspicious of all others; that is the nature of tribalism. A perpetual state of war existed between some tribes—for example, between the Sioux and the Crow—but it rarely resulted in large numbers of casualties.

Desert and Plains

Even the desolate Great Basin supported the Utes, Paiutes, and Shoshones. They survived the torrid, dry summers by dividing into small bands that moved to higher elevations where there was water and forage. Trappers and soldiers thought them the most primitive of American Indians. They were virtually nomadic, living briefly in the rudest huts and eating whatever they could find including (much to the disgust of Americans who were familiar with them) snakes and lizards.

To the south, in the marginally more hospitable environment of present-day Arizona and New Mexico, the Pima, Zuñi, and Hopi farmed intensively as they had for centuries before Francisco de Coronado discovered their pueblos (villages) in the 1530s. Most pueblos were quite compact, adobe apartment houses that could be entered only from the roof, which were reached by ladders that were pulled up when the pueblo was attacked. Several were on mesas accessible only by one or two steep, easily-defended trails. Others perched high on the sides of cliffs.

The Navajo, the most numerous people south of the Grand Canyon (and comparative newcomers there) lived in scattered family groups in substantial five-sided hogans. The Navajo were primarily sheepherders by the 1800s—the range was too sparse for cattle—and highly skilled weavers of wool.

Both the Navajo and the Pueblo Indians feared the bands of Apaches with whom they shared the southwestern desert. The Apache farmed and herded but, like the Comanche in Texas, the men preferred the raiding life. They took what they could from whomever they ran across. Before the Civil War, most Apaches were based in Mexico and only raided farther north. Between 1862 and 1867, Apaches killed 400 Mexicans and Anglos living in the borderlands and Indians no one bothered to count.

The Indians who most fascinated easterners were those who were most determined to resist the whites and their ways, the tribes of the Great Plains. From the writings of intrepid travelers like historian Francis Parkman and painters Karl Bodmer and George Catlin, Americans were already acquainted with the Comanche, Cheyenne, and Arapaho peoples of the southern plains, and the Mandan, Crow, Sioux, Cheyenne, Nez Percé, Blackfoot, and many other smaller tribes of the northern grasslands, when they began to penetrate the West.

Plains Culture   The Plains Indians' culture—their economy, social structure, religion, diet, dress—revolved around two animals: the native bison and the immigrant horse. The bison, possibly 30 million of them in North America in 1800, provided food; bones from which tools were made; horns for drinking vessels; sinew for sewing and bowstrings; and hides that became clothing, footwear, blankets, portable shelters (the conical teepees), and canvases on which artists recorded heroic legends, tribal histories, and genealogies. The Plains Indians used buffalo hair for stuffing, their brains for tanning hides, their hooves to make glue, and their tails to whisk away flies. As if that was not enough multiple use, the bison's manure, when dry, made a passable fuel for cooking and warmth in a land where trees were few and winters were harsh.

Except for the Mandan and Pawnee, who were farmers as well as hunters, the Plains tribes were nomads. They had no fixed homes. They trailed hundreds of miles annually on horseback, following the bison herds. Long-distance trekking was not an ancient practice. Before the arrival on the plains of "spirit dogs," horses, the Plains Indians hunted on foot and, necessarily, had a smaller range. By about 1700, however, horses that had escaped from Mexican herds had reached the Snake River in southern Idaho, the central plains about 1720, and the Columbia Plateau, home of the Nez Percé, about 1730.

THE FAR WEST—SHOOTING BUFFALO ON THE LINE OF THE KANSAS PACIFIC RAILROAD.

The construction of the transcontinental railroad spelled the doom of the bison that wandered the Great Plain. Herds numbering hundreds of thousands could block the line or even damage the "two streaks of rust" by trundling across them. Hunters who shot the animals to feed construction workers (most famously "Buffalo Bill" Cody) discovered that buffalo hides brought good prices in the East and began to kill the bison wholesale. Within a few years, 15 million of the beasts were reduced to 2 or 3 million. By 1890, only a few hundred survived. Miraculously, conservationists rescued them and the species.

The Indians captured and tamed the horses, developing a style of riding without stirrups, saddles, and bits. The Comanche were widely regarded as the most skilled riders. "Almost as awkward as a monkey on the ground," painter George Catlin wrote of a Comanche warrior in 1834, "the moment he lays his hand upon a horse, his face even becomes handsome, and he gracefully flies away like a different being." (Catlin's paintings show that, by 1834, some but not all Comanche warriors were using stirrups purchased from Mexicans.) Like all Plains Indians, the Comanches maintained as many horses as they could lay their hands on. One band of 2,000 Indians managed a herd of 15,000 horses.

Conflict

The wanderings of the plains tribes meant frequent contact with one another. They traded and could communicate with remarkable subtlety through a common sign language. Uncrowded as they were, however, and abundant as the bison were, the tribes were chronically fighting. Not to conquer territory; as nomads, they did not think in terms of owning land. Nor did they have as much use for slaves as the Eastern Woodlands Indians had. Plains Indians fought to steal horses and women from one another and as a way for individuals to demonstrate their courage. It was a warrior culture.

By 1865, every Plains tribe knew something about the "palefaces" or "white-eyes." They did not particularly dislike the wagon trains that traversed the plains for three decades. There were skirmishes but not that many. Of 100,000 overland emigrants to Oregon and California, only 350 were killed by Indians. As long as the white eyes kept moving, they were no problem. Indeed, they presented opportunities. The tribes traded with them, usually meat for clothing, iron tools, firearms and, of course, stole horses and cattle. Indians also scavenged the freight that the emigrants discovered they were mistaken to bring along.

The Destruction of the Bison

Everything changed after Congress authorized the construction of transcontinental railroads. The crews that laid the tracks of the Union Pacific, Kansas Pacific, and Northern Pacific across the plains were no more interested in staying than the overland emigrants. However, their needs led, in a roundabout way, to the destruction of the bison that was the heart of plains culture.

In order to feed their construction workers, the railroads hired hunters like William F. "Buffalo Bill" Cody, a sometimes army scout, sometimes stagecoach driver, to shoot bison. Using .50-caliber Springfield rifles, Buffalo Bill's crew killed 4,000 bison in just eighteen months. (Buffalo Bill did the shooting; other men reloaded his rifles; yet others skinned and butchered the carcasses.) Even that made no dent in the bison population. However, when some hides were shipped back east, they caused a sensation as fashionable "buffalo robes." An industrial slaughter of the animals began at Dodge City, Kansas, in 1872. In three months, 700 tons of hides (from 43,000 animals) were shipped east from Dodge.

As many as 2,000 men went into the business. A team could down and skin hundreds of bison in a day. Buffalo were easy targets. Living in huge herds, they were unbothered by loud noises; they stood grazing while others collapsed around them as long as they did not scent or see the hunters. By 1875, the southern herd was effectively wiped out. By 1883, the northern herd was gone. Ironically, the Sioux joined in the slaughter, selling tens of thousands of hides to buffalo robe couturiers.

Politicians encouraged the massacre because, quite correctly, they linked the "Indian problem" to the abundance of bison. "So long as there are millions of buffaloes in the West," a Texan told Congress, "so long the Indians cannot be controlled."

To apply the finishing touches, wealthy eastern and European sportsmen chartered special trains and, sometimes without stepping to the ground, they shot trophies for their mansions and clubs. Their services were not really needed and, in the case of Russian Grand Duke Alexis Alexandrovitch, they were not very efficient. Alexis fired twelve revolver shots at two bison and did not hit either. Buffalo Bill gave him a rifle and he finally killed his trophy—from a distance of about 10 feet.

In 1874, Congress tried to end the slaughter by prohibiting the shooting of bison except for food. General Philip Sheridan, then commanding troops on the plains, urged President Grant to veto the bill. Instead of saving the bison, Sheridan said, Congress should strike a medal with "a dead buffalo on one side and a discouraged Indian on the other." Grant obliged his old comrade and killed the act. In 1889, when preservationists stepped in to save the species, fewer than a thousand bison were alive. Most of the 200,000 bison alive today are descended from just 77 animals.

THE LAST INDIAN WARS

General Sheridan is usually remembered as an Indian hater. He is said to have replied to an Indian who told him, "Me good Indian" with, "The only good Indian is a dead Indian." He may have done so. If he did, he was likely speaking as a military man about his enemies, not expressing his personal feelings. He betrayed those in 1878 when he was asked why the Sioux and Cheyenne had fought for so long against impossible odds: "We took away their country and their means of support, broke up their mode of living, their habits of life, introduced disease and decay among them, and it was for this and against this that they made war."

America's final Indian wars were often brutal. Many frustrated officers in the West agreed with Commissioner of Indian Affairs Francis Walker who said in 1871, "when dealing with savage men, as with savage beasts, no question of national honor can arise. Whether to fight, to run away, or to employ a ruse, is solely a question of expediency."

But a good many others, like Sheridan, regretted that duty required them to fight an enemy whose cause was justified. General George Crook, generally considered the best Indian fighter of the era, confessed that the "hardest thing" for him was "to go out and fight against those who you know are in the right." He blamed "nine-tenths of all our Indian troubles" on "the greed and avarice of the whites." Three of the bloodiest days of the last Indian wars were the direct consequences of gold hunters who trespassed on lands granted to the tribes in treaties. Instead of ordering the army to expel the interlopers, the federal government ordered the soldiers to defend them. Gold was at stake, "the almighty dollar" in Crook's words.

The Sand Creek Massacre

There were few big battles on the plains; it was a war of many small skirmishes. During the first decade after a Sioux uprising in Minnesota in 1862, the U.S. Army counted 200 incidents. The army's total casualties were fewer than in any of several single battles with Eastern Woodlands Indians during the 1790s. Indeed, one of the bloodiest days of the wars was no battle at all but an ugly unprovoked massacre of friendly Cheyenne by Colorado militia.

In 1864, the Cheyenne were divided within the tribe. One faction wanted to fight the whites, the other to keep the peace. In May, when the war party began to prepare, Chief Black Kettle, who wanted no part of war, led about a thousand Cheyenne and a few Arapahoes to Fort Lyon in Colorado. He assured the officers there that his band was keeping the peace. He was told to make winter camp on Sand Creek about 30 miles away, raise an American flag above the village, and he would be safe. His anxieties allayed, Black Kettle sent most of his young men on a buffalo hunt to bring in the winter's provisions.

On November 29, Colonel John Chivington, who had been present at the Fort Lyon discussions, ordered Colorado militia (not regular soldiers) to charge the camp. One of his captains refused to obey the order, but the others did. They killed about 200 of the 800 people in the camp, all but a few of them women, children, and old men. Later, investigators concluded that almost all of the fifteen dead cavalrymen had been killed by the "friendly fire" of the poorly trained militiamen.

Chivington tried to pass himself off as a hero; he claimed his men had killed 200 braves about to go on the warpath. It was too big a lie to survive scrutiny. Army investigators uncovered the facts and a congressional committee denounced the Sand Creek massacre in unambivalent language:

> As to Colonel Chivington, your committee can hardly find fitting terms to describe his conduct. Wearing the uniform of the United States, which should be the emblem of justice and humanity ... he deliberately planned and executed a foul and dastardly massacre which would have disgraced the veriest savage among those who were the victims of his cruelty. Having full knowledge of their friendly character, having himself been instrumental to some extent in placing them in their position of fancied security, he took advantage of their in-apprehension and defenceless condition to gratify the worst passions that ever cursed the heart of man.
>
> (Chivington was not punished.)

The Fetterman Debacle

Two years later, an officer as foolish as Chivington was vile led seventy-nine troopers to their deaths in a well-laid trap in northern Wyoming. An army detachment commanded by Colonel Henry B. Carrington had built a stockade, Fort Phil Kearny, in Sioux country. Their assignment was to protect caravans carrying provisions to gold miners farther north. Carrington was instructed neither to attack nor provoke the Indians. One of his subordinates, Captain William Fetterman, called Carrington "timid." Fetterman had been a brave combat officer in the Civil War but he knew nothing about Indian-style warfare and did not appreciate the significance of Fort Phil Kearny's isolation. He was also a blowhard. He boasted that with eighty men he could "ride through the entire Sioux nation."

On December 21, 1866, an apparently small number of Sioux warriors harassed an army work party that was cutting firewood not far from the fort. Fetterman finagled his way into the command of a relief force of eighty men. Carrington emphatically commanded him to rescue the woodcutters and under no circumstances to pursue the Sioux.

Fetterman did exactly that only to discover that he had been decoyed into a trap by the Sioux war chief, Red Cloud. Red Cloud had hidden about 2,000 warriors who, when Fetterman pursued the decoys, surrounded and killed all eighty soldiers. The incident was called the Fetterman Massacre but it was more properly a battle in which one commander, Red Cloud, made a fool and a corpse of his army counterpart.

Custer's Last Stand   Between 1866 and 1876, the army, mostly cavalry, fought tenaciously and mostly successfully against the Sioux and their allies, the Cheyenne. But the troopers in their worn and dusty blue uniforms could not draw the Indians into a decisive battle. The Sioux and Cheyenne, led by Sitting Bull and war chief Crazy Horse, understood that they could not win a pitched battle unless, like Red Cloud, they could sucker the troopers. Instead, they exploited the vastness of the plains to evade every army sent after them.

In 1876, the army devised a plan to find and defeat the Sioux and Cheyenne by closing on them in southern Montana from three directions. Colonel George Armstrong Custer of the Seventh Cavalry, which was advancing from the south, sighted about forty warriors. He divided his command into three and led 265 troopers and Crow scouts in hot pursuit. It was a trap as perfectly choreographed as Red Cloud's at Fort Phil Kearny. Every soldier and scout, Custer included, was killed. Custer had charged into the entire Sioux nation on the banks of a stream called the Little Big Horn.

It was an ending that more than one officer had predicted for Custer. A Civil War hero, he had been reckless as an Indian fighter. He routinely neglected reconnaissance. The Seventh Cavalry had not brought its Gatling guns—the decisive weapon against Indians—because they slowed the horse soldiers down, and Custer craved glory; he wanted to get to the enemy before the other two columns. (Unbeknownst to him, one column had been fought to a standstill and delayed.) He got his glory. "Custer's Last Stand" thrilled Americans. "Yellow Hair" (as the Sioux called him) became a romantic hero in death. A brewery commissioned a painting of the Battle of the Little Big Horn and distributed 150,000 reproductions of it. One scholar has counted 967 different representations of the battle.

Senior officers who disliked Custer blamed him for the disaster, but quietly among themselves. Only in the next century would the battle be appreciated as a well-engineered tactical victory by Crazy Horse, perhaps the most brilliant Indian war chief. The Sioux and Cheyenne celebrations were short-lived, however. The other columns in the field closed in. Within a year, the Indians were under guard or had fled with Chief Sitting Bull to Canada.

Chief Joseph   Like Black Kettle, Nez Percé Chief Joseph understood that his Wallowa Band of northeastern Oregon—800 to 1,000 strong—had no chance to defeat the U.S. Army. Hinmaton Yalaktat (Chief Joseph's Nez Percé name) made concession after concession to keep the peace. But he drew the line at moving to a reservation on wasteland that would not support his people. When the army commanded by General O. O. Howard moved in on him in the summer of 1877, Chief Joseph decided to flee to Canada as Sitting Bull had done.

For three months, Chief Joseph led his tribe on a circuitous trek of almost 2,000 miles, brilliantly evading the 2,000 soldiers pursuing him. When the troopers caught up, his handful of braves fought courageous rear-guard actions while the women and children escaped. But 200 of Chief Joseph's original 800 Nez Percé were dead when, in October, Howard's troops cornered the survivors just 25 miles from the Canadian line. Chief Joseph surrendered 87 warriors (40 with wounds), 184 women, and 147 children.

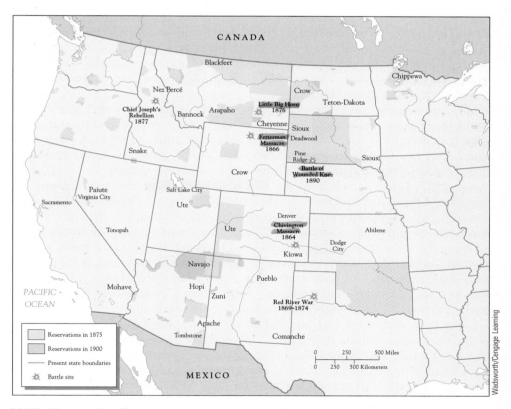

Wadsworth/Cengage Learning

MAP 30.1 Indian Reservations, 1875 and 1900

Before the destruction of the bison, the Plains Indians were impeded from ranging from Canada to northern Texas, from Minnesota and Nebraska to the Rocky Mountains, only by a healthy respect for the turf of other tribes. By 1875, they were being herded on to reservations that shrunk in size steadily and sharply in just twenty-five years. White settlers bought Indian lands that the federal government had called inviolable. The federal government opened the entire western half of "Indian Territory" (Oklahoma) to white settlers.

The heroism of his flight and the tragic eloquence of his surrender message to General Howard won the respect of many Americans:

> I am tired of fighting. Our chiefs are killed, Too-hul-hul-sote is dead.... It is cold, and we have no blankets; the little children are freezing to death. My people, some of them, have run away to the hills, and have no blankets, no food. No one knows where they are—perhaps freezing to death. I want to have time to look for my children, and see how many of them I can find. Maybe I shall find them among the dead. Hear me, my chiefs! I am tired; my heart is sick and sad. From where the sun now stands, I will fight no more forever.

Chief Joseph and the remnants of his band were forced to move to lands that no whites wanted.

Good Intentions, Tragic Results   In 1881, Helen Hunt Jackson of Colorado published *A Century of Dishonor,* a bestseller. In meticulous detail and with only minor factual errors, she traced the perfidy with which the federal government had dealt with the Indians since independence. The list of Indian treaties agreed to was a list of broken treaties. Time and again, whites had cheated "savage" Indians of their land, had herded them onto reservations, and then chipped away at those.

The government no longer made treaties with Indian "nations." Members of tribes that did not resist were defined as wards of the federal government. They were not citizens but were under Washington's protection and enjoyed a few privileges. After the publication of *A Century of Dishonor,* many easterners demanded that the government use its guardianship in a constructive manner.

In 1887, Congress approved the Dawes Severalty Act. Intentions were of the best. Assuming that the traditional Indian way of life was no longer feasible, which was obvious, the sponsors of the Dawes Act argued that the Indians must be Americanized if they were to survive. That is, they must become self-sustaining by adopting the ways of the larger culture. The Dawes Act dissolved the tribes and the reservations were distributed, homestead-style, 160 acres to each head of family, with an additional 80 acres for each adult member of the household. Lands left over were sold to whites. In order to avoid further despoliation, Congress decreed that Indian lands could not be sold or otherwise disposed of for twenty-five years.

The supporters of the Dawes Act overlooked a number of important facts. First, few western Indians were farmers. Second, the reservation lands were rarely suited to agriculture; they had been allotted to the Indians precisely because they were unattractive to white farmers. Third, tracts of 160 acres in the arid West were rarely enough to support efficient farmers, let alone novices at tillage and herding. Finally, the Plains Indians did not think in terms of individual ownership of land. The tribe, which the Dawes Act relegated to the dustheap, was their basic social unit.

Wounded Knee   The Sioux had been paramount on the northern plains in 1865. By 1890, they were living, demoralized, on a few reservations. They were ripe to be swept up by the teachings of Wovoka, also known as Jack Wilson, a religious visionary in the tradition of the Prophet.

Wovoka adapted Christian doctrines to Indian yearnings. By performing a ritual dance, he said, the Indians would prevail on the Great Spirit to make the white man disappear in a great flood. Then the buffalo herds and the Indians whom the whites had killed would be resurrected, led by "the Messiah who came once to live on earth with the white men but was killed by them." The old way of life would be restored.

In December 1890, on Wounded Knee Creek on South Dakota's Pine Ridge reservation, soldiers guarding a Sioux encampment tried to take guns from Ghost dancers. There was a shoving incident and shots were fired. The soldiers were nervous; there were not many of them, but they had four Hotchkiss guns, an early machine gun that fired 140 rounds a minute. When the battle was over, only about 50 Indians survived. An unknown number between 200 and 300 were dead. For the Indians of the Great Plains, there was no escape, not even in mysticism.

The Cattle Kingdom

In 1870, Americans were raising 23.8 million cattle. In 1900, 67.7 million head were fattening on grasslands, mostly in the West. Cattle replaced the nearly extinct bison on the great plains. The men who at first rounded up wild, scrawny long-horns of Spanish origin on public lands, and, by the 1890s, were raising more docile and meatier breeds, especially English Herefords, were motivated by the demands for cheap beef in the burgeoning cities of the East.

The First Buckaroos

The cowboys who were the knights of the cattle kingdom became central to American folklore almost as soon as they rode onto the scene. Their way of life was ruthlessly romanticized, of course, also from the very start. Rather more remarkable for literary, movie, and television characters that were salable for a century, the actual history of the real thing was quite brief, a little more than twenty years.

In the late 1850s, enterprising Texans began to round up longhorns that ranged freely between the Nueces River and the Rio Grande. They drove the cattle north over an old Indian trail to Sedalia, Missouri, a railroad town with connections to Chicago. The bosses were Anglos, but many of their employees were Mexicans who called themselves *vaqueros,* "cowboys." (*Vaquero* was anglicized as "buckaroo.")

Most buckaroos were young white men, but the Mexican origins of their trade remained obvious. The cowboy's distinctive costume was an adaptation of Mexican workclothes. The bandana, when tied over a cowboy's mouth, was a dust screen, a necessity when a thousand cattle were kicking it up. The broad-brimmed hat was not favored because it was picturesque but because it was a sun and rain shield (and held water for a rough approximation of washing up).

The pointed, high-heeled boots, awkward for walking, even painful, were designed for riding in stirrups, where a *vaquero* spent his workday. The "western saddle" was of Mexican design, providing a more comfortable seat for all-day sitting than the English saddles with which easterners were familiar. Chaps, leather leg coverings, got their name from chaparral, the woody brush from which they protected the cowboy. Spanish words adopted into English via the cowboys include *lasso, lariat, corral, cinch, bronco,* and *pronto.*

Meat for The Civil War stifled the long cattle drives from Texas before
Millions they were fairly begun. Then Missouri prohibited the importation of Texas cattle because contagious hoof and mouth disease was common among the longhorns. By 1866, however, the Kansas-Pacific railroad reached Abilene, Kansas. A wheeler-dealer from Illinois, Joseph G. McCoy, saw the possibilities of underselling beef cattle raised on expensive pasture back east with Texas steers. McCoy built holding pens on the outskirts of Abilene, arranged to ship cattle he did not yet own with the railroad, and he let it be known in Texas that if *vaqueros* drove their cattle to Kansas, he would buy them.

In 1867, McCoy shipped 35,000 "tall, bony, coarse headed, flat-sided, thin-flanked" longhorns to Chicago. In 1868, 75,000 of the beasts, next to worthless in Texas, passed through Abilene. Chicago meatpackers demanded more. In 1871, 600,000 "critters" passed through the pens of several Kansas railroad towns on their way to American dinner tables.

The profits were immense. A steer that cost about $5 to raise on the open range could be driven to Kansas for about a cent a mile ($5 to $8), and sold for $25, more in some years. That kind of profit attracted investors from back east and Great Britain. One British operation paid dividends of 28 percent its first year in business. There was nothing wild and woolly about the cattlemen. Wyoming's Cheyenne Club was as posh as a London men's club. The typical member sat on a horse only to be photographed for the folks back home. His usual mount was a plush easy chair, his range a fine carpet, and he puffed on Havana cigars when he discussed accounts with his fellow buckaroos.

As the railhead moved westward, so did the cowboys' destination. The citizens of the first cow towns like Abilene were, after two or three years, glad to see the herds and cowboys catching their trains farther west. They concluded after a few seasons that the money to be made by shipping cattle was not worth the damage the herds did to their own ranches and farms. The wild behavior of young cowboys bent on a blowout after months on the trail was not compatible with respectable civic life. As a cow town grew, its "better element" wanted churches and schools on Main Street, not saloons, casinos, and whorehouses. The stage was set for the "taming" of the town, the theme of many a movie.

Cattlemen never lacked for a place to get their herds on the trains. There were always newer towns to the west where they were still welcome. Just in Kansas, Abilene, Ellsworth, Newton, Wichita, Dodge City, and Hays had their heydays as railheads surrounded by holding pens and feedlots.

Disaster The era of the long drive and the bonanza profits came to an
end because of greed and a natural disaster. The money to be made from open range cattle was so great that the big operators ignored the damage that the herds were doing to the grasslands. Vast as the plains were, they were overstocked and overgrazed by the 1880s. Bison had migrated hundreds of miles annually in search of fresh grass, leaving the land they passed over to recover.

The cattle's wanderings were limited. They fouled clear-running springs, trampling them into mud pits. Weeds never previously noticed displaced the overgrazed grasses. Hills were scarred by cattle trails that rains turned into ravines. Some species of migratory birds that had darkened the western skies twice a year nearly disappeared; beefsteaks on the hoof had wiped out what had been their provisions on their seasonal flights.

Then, on January 1, 1886, a great blizzard buried the eastern and southern plains. Within a few days, 3 feet of snow drifted into banks 20 and 30 feet high. Between 50 and 85 percent of the livestock froze to death or died of hunger. About 300 cowboys failed to reach shelter and died; the casualties among Indians were never counted. When spring arrived, half the plains reeked of the smell of death.

A long drought that summer ruined the cattlemen who had survived the snows. Grasses that had survived summer droughts for millennia were unable to do so after being suffocated by the blizzard. Weakened cattle starved when they should have been fattening. Then, the next winter, the northern plains, which had escaped the worst of the blizzard of 1886, got 16 inches of snow in sixteen hours, followed by weeks of intermittent fall.

The cattle industry recovered, but only when more methodical businessmen took over the business. Cattle barons like Richard King of southern Texas forswore the open range. Through clever manipulation of land laws, King built a ranch that was as large as the state of Rhode Island. If no one else's empire building was quite so spectacular, King's example was imitated in Texas, Wyoming, Montana, and eastern Colorado.

The railroads built spur lines into ranch country. The long drive was no longer necessary. The cowboy became a ranch hand, a not-so-freewheeling employee of large commercial operations.

Oh, Give Me a Home

Even during the days of the long drive, the cowboy's world bore scant resemblance to the legends that permeated popular culture. Despite the white complexion of the cowboys in popular literature (and in the films of the twentieth century), a goodly proportion of cowboys were Mexican or black. In some instances, all three groups acted and mixed as equals. More often, the cowboys split along racial lines when they reached the end of the trail, frequenting different restaurants, barber shops, hotels, saloons, and brothels.

Black, white, or Hispanic, the cowboys were, in fact, little more than boys. Photographs that they had taken in cow towns like Abilene and Dodge as well as arrest records (mostly for drunk and disorderly conduct) show few men older than 25. The life was too arduous for anyone but youths—days in the saddle, nights sleeping on bare ground in all weather. Moreover, the cowboy who married could not afford to be absent from his own ranch or farm for the months the long drives consumed.

The real buckaroos were not constantly engaged in shooting scrapes such as make western novels and movies exciting. Their skills lay in horsemanship and handling a rope, not with the less-than-accurate Colt revolver that they carried chiefly as a means of signaling distant coworkers. Toting guns was forbidden in railhead towns. With a drunken binge on every cowboy's itinerary, the law officer in charge of keeping the peace could not tolerate shooting irons on every hip. Those who did not leave their revolvers in camp outside town checked them at the police station or a livery stable before they hit the saloons.

THE WILD WEST IN AMERICAN CULTURE

The legends of the West as a wild place—"no Sunday west of Bismarck and west of Miles City no God"—and of the cowboys as quick-drawing paladins of the wide-open spaces were not creations of later days. The western themes familiar to every-one today were fully formed when the cold reality was still alive on the plains.

Oddly, the myths of the "Wild West" were embraced not only by easterners, but by cowboys and other westerners too. Palisade, Nevada, a tiny town where Central Pacific trains stopped to take on water had a reputation in eastern newspapers as a den of cutthroats because there were gunfights when passengers stepped off the train for refreshments. In fact, Palisade might be considered the first theme park; locals staged the fights perhaps to tweak easterners' fantasies, perhaps because the locals were just plain bored with the Wild West as it actually was.

Dime Novels   During the 1880s, when he was a rancher in North Dakota, future president Theodore Roosevelt helped arrest two cowboys who had robbed a grocery store. In their saddlebags were found several dime novels about western outlaws driven to crime by social injustice.

Dime novels (also called "pulps" after the cheap paper on which they were printed) were short books of about 100 pages that had lots of action—fistfights and shootings—and lots of padding such as overblown description. Not all of them had western settings but those were the most popular. A former Know-Nothing who had been dishonorably discharged from the Union army, E. Z. C. Judson, using the pen name Ned Buntline, churned out more than 400 of them between 1865 and 1886. He and a host of imitators created western characters as superhuman as the heroes of Greek mythology and as chivalric as the knights of the Round Table: intrepid lawmen, fearless Indian fighters, noble bandits, and beautiful women who could shoot as straight as the sheriff.

Some dialogue was stilted. A woman pointing her revolver at a villain warned him: "Stand back! or so surely as there is a sky above us, I will send your soul unbidden before the judgement bar!" Sometimes it was rustic: "If you vally that 'ar wife of your bussum, and your little cherubims (as I allow you've got) you better be makin' tracks for safer quarters."

Some of Buntline's heros were real people whom he actually knew but whose fabulous deeds were thoroughly fictionalized. "Calamity Jane" was a real person (Martha Jane Cannary) but she was a pathetic alcoholic, not the ravishing consort of James Butler "Wild Bill" Hickock. Belle Starr, "the bandit queen," was Myra Belle Shirley, the serial mistress of several thieves and killers of no discernible nobility.

In the dime novels, train robber Jesse James was a modern-day Robin Hood who gave the money he stole to the poor. When Jesse was murdered by one of his gang, his mother Zerelda James made a tourist attraction of his grave, charging admission and explaining that her son had been a good Christian who read the Bible in his spare time. Jesse, according to Zerelda, closely examined train passengers and did not steal from those whose hands were calloused indicating that they were working men. "Wild Bill" Hickok had indeed been a lawman who killed several men in the line of duty. But his preferred and primary profession was professional gambling. He was shot down on the job in Deadwood, South Dakota, in 1876; he was playing cards.

Buffalo Bill   Hickock, Calamity Jane, and other living legends personally contributed to the mythmaking by appearing in Wild West shows that toured the eastern states. So did Sitting Bull, the chief of the Hunkpapa Sioux at the Battle of the Little Bighorn, Black Elk, and Luther Standing Bear.

The greatest of the shows was the creation of William F. "Buffalo Bill" Cody. A decent, generous man who drank too much, Cody really had been a buffalo hunter and scout for the army. Ironically, given the dozens of "merciless savages" he shot dead at every performance, Cody was famously (and unusually) fair in his dealings with Indians; he never had trouble hiring warriors to join his troupe. He may have been the only "white eyes" the embittered Sitting Bull trusted.

Deadwood, South Dakota, at the peak of its notoriety in 1876. The town is all bustle and movement, and this is a superb example of artistic photography. James Butler "Wild Bill" Hickock, a nationally known figure, was murdered in Deadwood in 1876, but the gold camp was not at all the dangerous place newspapermen and dime novelists depicted. Including Wild Bill, there were only four homicides in Deadwood in 1876, not all that many for a town of its size in Rhode Island.

His biggest star was Phoebe Ann Moses who, wisely, performed as Annie Oakley. She was a sharpshooter who defeated almost every marksman with whom she competed. But Annie was no daughter of the golden west. She was an impoverished Ohio girl who discovered her talent with guns by shooting game for restaurants in order to support her widowed mother.

Buffalo Bill's Wild West Show was impossibly popular. Four million people attended 318 performances just outside the Chicago World's Fair in 1893. In Europe a few years earlier, 2.5 million saw his show.

Not all the creators of the legendary West were sensationalists. Frederic Remington's paintings and bronze statuettes of cowboys and Indians were studiously representative. In 1902, a Philadelphia patrician, Owen Wister, published a best seller, *The Virginian*, that sold 100,000 copies in one year. Wister's hero was the prototype of the noble knight-errant of the plains who became a stock figure in movie westerns. If the cowboy gave you his word, Wister wrote, "he kept it; Wall Street would have found him behind the times. Nor did he talk lewdly to women; Newport would have thought him old-fashioned."

The Mining Frontier   The folklore of the precious-metal mining frontier is second only to the legend of the cowboy in American popular culture. Deadwood, South Dakota, where Wild Bill Hickok was shot in the back and Calamity Jane spent her final years, was no cowtown but a gold-mining center.

Gold and Silver Rushes   After the California placer mines played out, prospectors looking for "glory holes" fanned out over the mountains and deserts of the West. For more than a generation, they discovered new deposits almost annually and very rich ones every few years. In 1859, there were two great strikes. A find in the Pike's Peak area of Colorado led to a rush as frantic as that of 1849. About the same time, gold miners in northern Nevada discovered that a "blue mud" that was frustrating their operations was one of the richest silver ores ever discovered. This was the beginning of Virginia City and the Comstock Lode. Before the Comstock pinched out in the twentieth century, it yielded more than $400 million in silver (and quite a bit of gold too).

In 1862, Tombstone, Arizona (site of the famous "OK Corral") was founded on the site of a gold mine. In 1864, Helena, Montana, rose atop another. In 1876, rich placer deposits were discovered in the Black Hills of South Dakota. Whites were forbidden by a treaty with the Sioux from entering the Black Hills but they went anyway and, as usual, the government defended rather than expelled them. In 1877, silver was found at Leadville, Colorado, almost 2 miles above sea level in the Rockies.

During the 1880s, the Coeur d'Alene district in the Idaho panhandle drew thousands of miners, as did copper deposits across the mountains in Butte, Montana. In 1891, the Cripple Creek district in Colorado began to outproduce every other mining town. In 1898, miners rushed north to Canada's Klondike, Alaska's Yukon, and then to Nome, where the gold was mixed with sand on the beach. As late as 1901, there was an old-fashioned rush when Jim Butler, the classic grizzled old prospector in a slouch hat, "his view obscured by the rear end of a donkey," drove his pick into a desolate mountain in southern Nevada and found it "practically made of silver." Wandering out of the town of Tonopah, founded on the site of Butler's discovery, prospectors discovered rich gold deposits in Goldfield, a few miles away.

Mining Camps and Cities   Readers of dime novels and film fans later have reveled in the vision of boisterous, wide-open mining towns, complete with saloons rocking with the music of tinny pianos and the shouts of unkempt bearded men. The live-for-today miner, the gambler, and the prostitute with a heart of gold are fixtures of popular culture. Nor is the picture altogether imaginary. The speculative mining economy fostered a risk-all attitude toward life and work and attracted plenty of characters who can reasonably be called (among other things) colorful.

However, efficient exploitation of hard rock (underground) mining required a great deal of capital and technical expertise. Consequently, the mining camps that were home to 5,000 to 20,000 people within a few years of their founding were also modern cities with a variety of urban services and a social structure more closely resembling that of Eastern industrial towns than the railhead towns of the cattleman's frontier.

In 1877, only six years after it was founded, Leadville, Colorado, boasted several miles of paved streets, gas lighting, a modern water system, thirteen schools, five churches, and three hospitals. "Camps" like Virginia City, Deadwood, and Tombstone are best remembered as places where legendary figures like Wild Bill Hickok and Wyatt Earp discharged their revolvers, but they were also the sites of huge stamping mills (to crush the ores) and of busy stock exchanges where shares in mines were traded by agents of San Francisco, New York, and London bankers as well as by locals.

In Goldfield, the last of the wide-open mining towns, one of the most important men in the camp was the urbane Wall Street financier Bernard Baruch. The Anaconda Copper Company of Butte, Montana, was one of the nation's ranking corporate giants. The Guggenheim mining syndicate was supreme in the Colorado gold fields. Rockefeller's Standard Oil was a major owner of mines in the Coeur d'Alene. If it was sometimes wild, the mining West was no mere diversion for readers of dime novels, but an integral part of the national economy. In fact, the gold and silver that the hard-rock miners tore from the earth stood at the very center of a question that divided Americans as seriously as any other after the end of Reconstruction—just what was to serve as the nation's money.

The miners and mine owners alone could not make a national issue of the precious metals from which coins were minted, goods bought and sold, and debts incurred and paid off—or not paid off. There were too few of them. However, as the century wound to a close, the money question became of great interest to a group of people who formed a major part of the American population, and who had once been its most important segment, the farmers on the land.

31

THE NATION'S BONE AND SINEW
Agriculture and Agrarians 1865–1896

When the lawyer hangs around and the butcher cuts a pound,
Oh the farmer is the man who feeds them all.
And the preacher and the cook go a-strolling by the brook
And the farmer is the man who feeds them all.

Oh the farmer is the man, the farmer is the man,
Lives on credit 'til the fall.
Then they take him by the hand and they lead him from the land
And the middle man's the one that gets them all.

—Farmers' song of the 1890s

The census of 1790 listed 3.5 million Americans as farmers. As the area of the nation expanded, the farm population increased too. Not even the Civil War arrested the opening of new farms. In 1865, 16.5 million men, women, and children awakened each morning to the crowing of a cock, facing a day of hard labor. "Farmers don't dream," one of them said, "their sleep is too sound. Following a plough, staggering and stumbling over clods all day, is anything but poetry."

At the same time, the *proportion* of farmers in the population steadily declined. In 1790, nine-tenths of Americans were farm people. In 1865, just 55 percent were. During the 1870s, the farm population dipped to below half of the total. By 1910—after thirty years of frantic agricultural expansion—not even one person in three lived by tilling the soil and husbanding livestock.

And yet, that over declining minority fed and clothed not only the two of three Americans who worked in mines, factories, and offices, they also exported megatons of grain every year. They were the most productive agriculturalists the world had ever known.

Farmers under Stress 1870–1897

1870	1873	1876	1879	1882	1885	1888	1891	1894	1897

1873 Demonetization Act

1875 Illinois enacts "Granger Laws"

1877 *Munn v. Illinois*

1878 Bland–Allison Act

1886 *Wabash* case

Benjamin Harrison president 1889–1893

Sherman Silver Purchase Act 1890

Main Traveled Roads published 1891

Populists' "Omaha Platform" 1892

Grover Cleveland president 1893–1897

Sherman Act repealed 1893

SUCCESS STORY

Between about 1870 and 1910, American agriculture expanded explosively. Never anywhere had so much virgin land been put to the plow in so short a time. In 1870, 263 years after the founding of Jamestown, 408 million acres were cultivated in the United States, an average of 1.6 million acres of new farmland each year. Between 1870 and 1900, a single generation of Americans and immigrants put the plow to 431 million acres of forest and grassland, a 14.4-million-acre increase each year!

Productivity per farmer also increased dramatically. In 1900, Americans produced twice as much corn, wheat, and hay as they had in 1870, three times the oats. Hogs, a by-product of corn, numbered 25 million in 1870, 63 million in 1900. The number of beef cattle increased by a third; the number of milch cows and horses doubled; the mule population tripled.

A moderately well-equipped farmer in 1890 tended up to six times the land his grandfather had. Farm machinery was the difference. During the 1840s, a farmer plowed with a couple of horses or a yoke of oxen and harrowed his fields by hitching his animals to some brush. The beasts got a rest when the farmer seeded wheat, rye, or oats broadcast, just as medieval serfs had, or dropped two or three kernels of corn in holes he punched with a poke. He harvested wheat with a scythe and threshed it with a flail. Corn was picked and shucked by hand. It took fifty to sixty man-hours per acre to produce about 20 bushels of grain. Well before 1900, a farmer with a gang plow and harrow, a horse-drawn seed drill, and a mechanical reaper-thresher (drawn by steam tractors on some farms) put in as few as eight to ten hours of labor per acre to produce a larger crop.

New Farms

The fabulous expansion of farm acreage began after the Civil War. Many of the new farmers were young men mustered out of the Union and Confederate armies, and their wives. A few were able to buy going properties complete with a home and barn. Except in desolated parts of the South, however, "improved" farms were apt to be too expensive for a discharged soldier. For a year or two or more, he had been earning little more than tobacco and whiskey money.

Prime Land   There was still raw land in the Mississippi Valley states—in Arkansas, Missouri, Illinois, Wisconsin, Iowa, Minnesota. Much of the soil was prime, rainfall was plentiful, and getting produce to market was not a problem. Streams large enough to float a flatboat piled high with sacks or barrels or crammed with hogs on the hoof emptied into the Mississippi or one of its major tributaries every few miles. A geographer has estimated that there was 50,000 miles of waterway in the Mississippi system navigable by flatboats, barges, and rafts.

The Erie Canal still carried much of the produce of lands bordering the Great Lakes. By 1870, railroads crisscrossed what we call the Midwest. The Illinois Central ran the length of Illinois. The Chicago and Rock Island ran from Davenport, Iowa, to Chicago. In 1867, the Chicago and Northwestern connected Minneapolis to Chicago, providing shipping for much of Wisconsin. By 1868, the Chicago, Burlington, and Quincy had two lines across Illinois, one to Iowa, one to Missouri.

The Real Estate Market   Most unimproved lands in the Midwest were owned by the railroads or land companies. The Preemption Act of 1841 had transferred 500,000 acres of federal land to each state to be sold in order to finance railroad construction. The Swamplands Act of 1850 distributed 63 million acres of public domain ostensibly to finance reclamation. In fact, it was a landgrab: Less than half the land sold to land companies and timber

A railroad poster of the 1860s or 1870s advertising land for sale in Iowa and Nebraska. The Burlington & Missouri was the third line to cross Iowa from the Mississippi River.

Bridgeman Art Library

barons for as little as 25¢ to 50¢ an acre was swamp that needed draining. The rest was well drained, ready to be sold at a good profit. The Morrill Act of 1862 put 30,000 acres for each senator and representative (at least 90,000 acres) into the hands of each state legislature which provided similar sweetheart deals for speculators who had the right connections.

During the first years after the Civil War, railroads and land companies in Illinois, Iowa, and Wisconsin sold their land to settlers for $8–$14 per acre, as did timber companies once they had stripped it of trees. That was $640–$1,120 for an eighty-acre farm (about $10,000–$19,000 in today's dollars). It was more than most men and women willing to struggle with raw land could afford.

Homesteading   Homestead Act land was free. For a fee of $26–$34 to pay for paperwork, a citizen or an immigrant intending to become a citizen could take possession of a quarter section (160 acres) of the national domain. It became the homesteader's property after he had lived on the land for five years in a dwelling of at least 12 by 14 feet. Or, after six months' residence, homesteaders could buy their farms from the Land Office for $1.25 per acre, a terrific bargain.

There was, however, little national domain left in the older states. The federal government recorded only 29,000 homesteads in Wisconsin and a mere 9,000 in Iowa. (Somehow, 108 people found federally owned quarter sections to homestead in long-developed Ohio.)

Only after 1880 did Homestead Act land play a major part in the expansion of American agriculture, and virtually all the claims lay far to the west on the prairie and plains. Without the cheap river transportation of the midwestern states, the grasslands could be developed only when the transcontinental and other regional railroads built through them. Before 1880, the government registered about 65,000 homesteads. During the 1880s, 200,000 were proved (that is, met the government's requirements). During the 1890s, 225,000 families took up homesteads. And for every acre of public domain that passed into private ownership, the railroads sold an acre, some of it, of course, to successful homesteaders who were enlarging their farms.

Start-Up Expenses   Even homesteaders needed start-up money, often quite a lot of it. An unusually truthful sales brochure published by the Chicago, Burlington, and Quincy, Railroad (CB&Q) in 1870 advised emigrants that "it is difficult to make progress anywhere without capital and nowhere is the need for money more keenly felt than in a new settlement." Forested land needed clearing. Farm families wanting to cultivate more than an acre or two for their first-year crop needed to hire help—often an aspiring farmer saving a nest egg for the following year—to down the trees and clear brush. If the property was prairie, it was often necessary to bring in a professional plowman with a specialized 10-foot-long "breaking plow" and the half dozen yoke of oxen needed to pull it through the dense, deep sod.

How much cash did new farmers need? It varied. A man or a couple could develop a farm slowly on a shoestring. The CB&Q said that "a few hundred dollars" was "sufficient to meet the expense of putting up a low-cost house, to purchase a pair of horses, a wagon, cow, pigs, tools, etc."

Not really. A couple could erect a rude log cabin with little cash outlay, but a small carpenter-built house alone cost more than "a few hundred dollars." Basic handtools and household implements; a plow, harness; a wagon ($200 new); horses; a pregnant sow; chickens—the expenditures added up quickly. Settlers needed to buy hay and grain to keep their animals over the first winter, not to mention provisons for themselves. Come spring, seed had to be bought. (Some railroads advertised "free seed" to every purchaser of their land but the come-on seed was reputed to be half wheat and half weed.)

A reaper—a McCormick "Old Reliable" or a Hussey—sold for $150–$200, so most new farmers made do with scythe and cradle for a year or two. Sooner rather than later, however, a western farmer needed a reaper to make a decent living on his large property. A man swinging a scythe could mow 1 or 2 acres of hay or wheat in a day with his wife and children rattled and stacking. With a reaper drawn by horses (the clanking rattled oxen) a farmer could harvest 12 acres in a day.

FARMING THE GREAT PLAINS

The Union Pacific was complete to North Platte, Nebraska, by the end of 1866, to Cheyenne in Wyoming Territory by December 1867. Half of the land within 20 miles of the UP's right-of-way was open to homesteaders, and they snapped it up. More than 100,000 homesteads were filed in Nebraska. The other half of the land within a 40-mile-wide swath along tracks was railroad property. The UP's asking price for farmland varied according to its distance from a depot. Close to a town where trains stopped for water and fuel, land in Nebraska cost as much as $10 an acre, Iowa prices. UP land far from a depot could be had for $1.50 per acre.

The Kansas Pacific was across Kansas in 1870, the Atchison, Topeka, and Santa Fe by 1873. The Northern Pacific, although chartered in 1864 and given double the land the other transcontinentals received, did not break ground until 1870. By September 1873, the NP's track extended from Duluth, Minnesota, to Bismarck, North Dakota. There the bankrupt NP suspended construction for eight years. The railroad reached the Dakota-Montana line only in 1886. In the meantime, however, the eastern part of Dakota Territory had begun to fill in.

An Arid Land   The landforms, soils, climate, and agricultural techniques familiar to easterners and Europeans ended at a north–south line that ran (roughly) from International Falls, Minnesota, through Sioux Falls, North Dakota, and Grand Island, Nebraska, on to Abilene, Texas. There the forests so dense in the eastern third of the United States thinned out rapidly, and the prairies—the eastern Great Plains—began. Grassland replaced forest because, at about the hundredth meridian (100° east longitude) the land begins a steady rise in elevation from about 650 feet above sea level to, in just 200 miles, 1,600 feet. As elevation rises, rainfall declines, from 48–64 inches per year to about 32 inches.

West of a second imaginary line extending from Bismarck south along the Kansas-Colorado border to Odessa, Texas, the land tilts upward more sharply

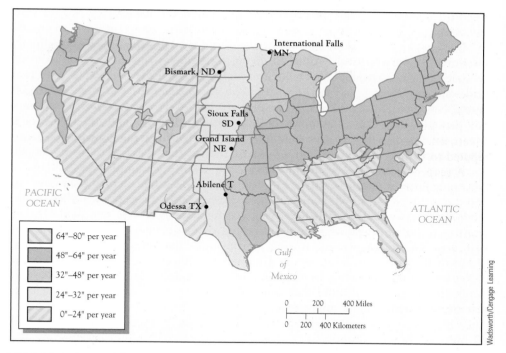

MAP 31.1 Annual Rainfall in the United States

East of the line extending south from International Falls, Minnesota, to Abilene, Texas, rainfall was sufficient to farm using traditional methods. By 1880, most good soil there was under cultivation. In the belt of territory between the International Falls–Abilene line and a second line extending from about Bismarck, North Dakota, to Odessa, Texas, only 24 to 32 inches of rain fell each year. Farmers could grow good crops of corn, wheat, oats, barley, and hay unless hit by a serious drought. West of the Bismarck-Odessa line lay the arid high plains. The land was fine for grazing but, without irrigation, not for crops. Sadly, many homesteaders were misled by exceptionally heavy rainfall during the 1880s; many were ruined, losing their land, during the 1890s.

from about 1,600 feet above sea level to an elevation of 6,500 feet at the foot of the Rocky Mountains. Annual precipitation dropped to 24 inches and was less in many years. On these semi-arid high plains—known as *steppes* in Eurasia—the winds seemed eternal and the grasses were shorter than on the prairies. The plains were treeless except for groves of cottonwoods and willows lining the creeks and rivers that flowed from the Rockies.

On the high plains, a quarter section was not enough land to support a family decently. Wheat and corn will ripen with 20 inches of precipitation a year but, as plains farmers were to learn during the late 1880s, rainfall dropped below that minimum during dry years. Few steers could be fattened to marketable size on 160 acres. On the lusher prairies of eastern Nebraska and Kansas, a steer needed no more than 5 acres on which to graze. In the western Dakotas and the plains of eastern Montana and Colorado, the ratio rose to as high as one steer per 20 acres.

Beating the | High plains settlers recognized the inadequacy of 160 acres
System | before the federal government faced up to the fact and granted
additional acreage to those who irrigated their land. In the
meantime, those who could afford to do so purchased additional acreage from the
railroads or busted neighbors. Thoughtful fiances delayed their weddings until both
bride and groom had filed for homesteads on adjoining quarter sections. With 320
acres, they could cultivate some grain and use their unplowed land for pasture and
hay. Couples built their homes on the line between their homesteads with enough
square footage on either quarter section to meet the dwelling requirement. Most Land
Office inspectors were good enough not to notice that newlyweds were actually
residing on only one of their homesteads.

Some inspectors were party to less benign frauds. Cattlemen paid their cowboys
and any drifters they could round up to homestead quarter sections in their names
whence, after six months, ranchers bought it for $1.25 per acre and paid off their
front men. Some operators beat the dwelling requirement by constructing a semblance of a cabin on wheels, towing it from one "homestead" to another a day
ahead of the inspector. Some swore affidavits that there was a 12-by-14-house on
a quarter section, neglecting to mention that it was a dollhouse 12 by 14 inches. No
doubt the suspicions of more than one Land Office official were laid to rest upon
receipt of a twenty dollar gold piece.

Sod Houses | The most urgent challenge facing a new farmer on the plains
was how to build a home. There was a lumber yard in most
railroad towns, but lumber was too expensive for settlers on a tight budget. Some
newcomers lived their first year in a "dugout," an excavation in a rise roofed with
canvas. A better solution was the sod house. A farmer mowed several acres of grassland
in the spring when the soil was moist. An itinerant with a "grasshopper plow" and
several yoke of oxen sliced the sod into strips a foot wide and 3 or 4 inches thick. These
were spaded into blocks light enough to lift and stack on a wagon.

Grass side down, the "Nebraska marble" was laid in overlapping courses like
bricks. The walls of a sod house had to be at least 2 feet thick to be stable and
strong enough to support a roof. On cottonwood rafters woven with saplings was
laid a single layer of sod grass-side up so that it would continue to grow for a
while, the roots fusing the "slates." Window and door frames were purchased or
cobbled together from packing crates.

The ceiling of a sod house dripped dirty drops of water in heavy spring rains and
dust during the summer. However, sod walls provided better insulation than the walls
of a wooden house. They were cooler in summer and more easily heated in winter.

Which was a good thing because fuel was also a problem if there was no
cottonwood nearby. The last of the buffalo chips were gone; cow flops burned but
not as well. Some settlers survived their first winter by burning tightly twisted hay or
straw and the second by burning sunflower stalks and corn cobs in a fire, they complained, it took "two men and a boy" to keep going. In time, coal was available.

Deep Plowing | The first farmers on the plains deluded themselves about how
much rainfall they could depend on. They knew little about

climatological cycles, and the summers of the 1870s and early 1880s were unusually rainy. "Experts" like Charles Dana Wilber told them that "rain follows the plow." When farmers broke the ancient sod, they altered the climate of the plains permanently by liberating moisture that had been long imprisoned in the earth. That water would recycle indefinitely. A devastating drought in 1887—the same drought that killed off so many open range cattle—pretty much put the theory to sleep.

However, farmers learned to make the most of the moisture left in the ground by each spring thaw by plowing twice as deep as they had back East. The thick layer of dirt that deep plowing left in the furrows acted as a mulch. Manufacturers of steel plowshares like Deere and Lane were quick to add plows designed for the plains to their catalogs. More than 100 plow improvements were patented between 1865 and 1880, most of them designed for plains farming.

Cool, Clear Water

In the Great Basin, which was dryer than the high plains, the Latter Day Saints had created an agricultural Eden by irrigating with surface water that tumbled down the slopes of the Wasatch Mountains. The individualistic settlers of the Great Plains lacked the Mormons' discipline. Nevertheless, many who lived within sight of the Rockies managed to organize "ditch companies" that channeled mountain streams to their fields.

Farther east, creeks and rivers were broad, shallow, and sluggish, flowing too far below ground level to be ditched. To irrigate, even to water cattle and provide for domestic use, wells were essential. Men with very strong backs actually dug wells 20 feet deep, piling the excavated dirt into levees around "cattle tanks." Too often, however, the diggers did not hit water. It was necessary to drill. (Again, wandering professionals with equipment were at the farmers' service, charging $1 to $2 a foot.) One of the world's largest underground reservoirs, the Oglala aquifer, was only 50 feet deep in parts of South Dakota, Nebraska, and Kansas (in those days).

Water was pumped into cattle tanks and irrigation ditches by mass-produced multisailed windmills mounted on wooden or steel trellises. By the late 1880s, the cheapest Climax or Eclipse windmill cost only $25. Wind was one commodity that was abundant on the plains.

Barbed Wire

Settlers who tried to keep their animals home and their neighbors' horses and cattle out discovered that wire strung on scavenged posts did not work. The animals simply pushed the fences over. The solution to the problem was obvious. The wire, had to be barbed like thorned hedges, so as to cause cattle and horses pain, while not maiming them. Between 1868 and 1873, nine inventors patented functional "bobbed wires," but they were too expensive to enclose and cross-fence properties half a mile and more on a side.

In 1874, Joseph Glidden of DeKalb, Illinois, perfected a machine that twisted two strands of wire and knotted them every 12 inches with a short length of wire clipped on both ends into a sharp point. It was an instant success. The company that manufactured it (Glidden sold his patent) produced 2.84 million pounds of it in 1876. Four years later, 80.5 million pounds had been sold. It worked so well that a starving steer would lie down and die rather than push through it to grass in plain sight.

"Bonanza Farms" measured in the thousands of acres were possible because railroad com-
panies needed cash for construction and could raise it quickly by selling 1000-acre tracts of
their government land grants for pennies per acre. In order to farm their prairie empires
profitably, investors needed agricultural machinery ten and twenty times bigger than the
harvesters, threshers and binders that family farmers employed. Thus, the age of the giant
"combines" like this one. When they were on the move, they were attended by small armies
of migrant harvest hands. It took time to harness so many horses each morning. At noon,
they had to be unhitched for water, hay, grain and rest, and another team (about 30 horses
here) needed to be standing in harness by the time the crew finished lunch.

Machines on   At annual county fairs, manufacturers of agricultural machinery
the Land   introduced farmers to their latest model reaper-harvester and an
                    ever-increasing variety of horse-drawn devices that promised to
improve productivity: disc harrows to break up clods; grain drills to plant multiple rows
at a uniform depth with each pass; twine binders that eliminated the backbreaking job
of tying sheaves of wheat together; and other ingenious machines for threshing wheat,
shucking corn, shredding fodder, and baling hay.

Even farmers who were just getting by found it hard to resist the mechanical
marvels and bought them with borrowed money. The value of farm machinery in
use increased from $271 million in 1870 to $750 million in 1900.

During the 1880s, several manufacturers introduced huge "combines" that
harvested, threshed, and cleaned grain in one operation. Families cultivating 160
or even 320 acres could not afford to buy one of the monsters let alone operate

one. They required twenty or more horses and mules to move them or a steam tractor half the size of a locomotive.

Bonanza Farms The market for the combines was on the bonanza wheat farms, well-capitalized industrial operations of 5,000 to 30,000 acres. These imperial spreads, lining the Red River of the north between Minnesota and Dakota Territory, were made possible by the depression of the 1870s. In order to recover from bankruptcy, the Northern Pacific had to dispose of its lands quickly, which meant cheaply in huge tracts. At about the same time, James J. Hill purchased the Minneapolis, St. Paul, and Manitoba less for its 565 miles of track than for the 3.8 million acres the railroad owned. Receipts from selling the land provided the capital with which Hill began to build the Great Northern, the fifth transcontinental.

Hill and the Northern Pacific sold their land in 5,000- and 10,000-acre parcels. The buyers were not farmers but syndicates of eastern and midwestern capitalists who knew little and cared less about agronomy. They hired professional managers to develop and operate their industrial farms at a profit.

By 1890, there were eighty bonanza farms just on the Dakota side of the Red River. One of the first 20,000-acre operations (about half of a bonanza farm was sown in wheat each year) had a stable of several hundred horses, 200 self-binding reapers, and 30 steam threshers. At planting time, the company hired 600 off-season loggers from Minnesota and Wisconsin and, in August and September, 800 men to harvest the wheat. Unemployed men by the thousands, many of them full-time tramps, hopped freight trains to "hiring towns" in Minnesota and the Dakotas twice each year.

HARD TIMES

The story of American agriculture after the Civil War is glorious only when looked at in the aggregate. For the people who opened the Great Plains, life was laborious, dirty, and lonely for years. Winters were marked by long stretches of subzero weather and ferocious blizzards when men and women had to find their way from house to barn via a rope they had strung between the buildings. Summers were blistering hot, and the only shade was the patch under a wagon. Winter and summer the winds blew constantly, setting nerves on edge. In Ole Rølvaag's *Giants in the Earth*, a gloomy novel about Norwegian sod busters in the Dakotas, one of the major characters freezes to death while going for a doctor; another, a woman, goes insane.

Women and the Grange Most of the era's writers about farm life dwelled on its loneliness, especially for women. In middle age (and in better times) many a farm matron told her granddaughters of the day she arrived at the new home her husband had selected in the great emptiness of the plains and sat down and wept.

Homesteaders commonly built their houses in the middle of their quarter or half sections so that every field and pasture was within equal reach. But that meant that the nearest neighbor—when there was a "next-door" neighbor—lived half a mile or more away. With work demanding attention dawn to dusk within a few yards of her kitchen and chicken coop, women saw only their husbands and children except, briefly, while marketing in town on Saturday and after church on Sunday.

Hamlin Garland's *Main-Traveled Roads*, published in 1891, described the people who worked the farms of the "middle border" with compassion. Looking back at his book later in life, Garland wrote that "even my youthful zeal" was inadequate when he tried to describe "the lives led by the women.... Before the tragic futility of their suffering, my pen refused to shed its ink."

In 1867, seven federal employees distressed by the monotony of western farm life founded the Patrons of Husbandry, organized into local granges, to serve as social and cultural centers in rural areas. The granges served as meeting places for clubs and activities of which many Protestant churches, but not necessarily all who attended them, disapproved: dances, plays, other frivolous entertainment. The national office dispatched lecturers to tour the granges; they spoke on everything from the date of creation to the customs of the people of Borneo.

By 1900, the grange had a million members. Unique among fraternal lodges, women enjoyed equality with men in decision making and other grange activities. Visitors observed that farm wives, not the men, held the lodges together. They planned and administered the activities and, of course, cleaned up after dances.

Fleeing to Cities   Hamlin Garland dedicated *Main-Traveled Roads* "to my father and mother, whose half-century pilgrimage on the main traveled road of life has brought them only toil and deprivation." He fled "the rigorous, filthy drudgery of the farmyard" to the city and a successful literary career. Tens of thousands of farm boys and girls joined him every year, choosing Chicago, St. Louis, Kansas City, and smaller industrial cities over life on the soil. They took jobs that paid enough to finance a few hours of socializing after sunset and, during the summer months, the odd Sunday at a trolley line amusement park.

Nothing better reveals the attraction cities held for farm boys and girls than the fact that rural preachers and farmers' magazines inveighed endlessly against the evils of city life, the sinful temptations that surrounded young people there and would, inevitably, corrupt them. Probably, the lubricious horror stories, like parental admonitions today, resolved many an undecided young man and woman to pack up and catch the train. A former farm girl told landscape architect Frederick Law Olmstead that "if I were offered a deed to the best farm on condition of going back to the country to live, I would not take it. I would rather face starvation in town."

Debt   From the very beginning of the great expansion of agriculture, growers of wheat and corn and raisers of hogs watched their incomes decline. After 1890, farm income collapsed. A crop that in 1872 earned a farmer $1,000 in real income (actual purchasing power) earned only $500 in 1896. A farmer 48 years of age in 1896, had to sell twice as many hogs or bushels of corn as he had produced as a young man of 24 to enjoy the same standard of living he had known in 1872.

By 1892, the selling price of corn was so low (8¢ a bushel) that farmers ceased buying coal to heat their homes and burned corn to cook and to keep from freezing.

As a boy in Kansas, Vernon L. Parrington remembered warming himself "by the kitchen stove in which the ears were burning briskly, popping and crackling in the jolliest fashion. And if while we sat around such a fire watching the year's crop go up the chimney, the talk sometimes became bitter, who will wonder?"

Farmers went under wholesale. Between 1889 and 1893, 11,000 Kansas farm families lost their homes when they were unable to meet mortgage payments. In several counties in western Kansas and Nebraska, nine of ten farms changed hands in only four years. The number of tenant farmers—those who did not own the land they worked—doubled to 2 million between 1880 and 1900, most of the increase coming after 1890. For every three farm families outside the South that owned their land, one was a tenant.

SOUTHERN FARMERS

Tenancy was even more common in the South. Below the Ohio River and in Arkansas and eastern Texas, there were as many tenant farmers as there were families working land they owned. African American sharecroppers outnumbered black landowners by almost five to one.

Sharecroppers   The Civil War freed the slaves in the South, but it left the land in the hands of those who had owned it in 1861 (or those who had bought it since). Without slaves, however, how was the land to be tilled? There was little cash in the South with which to pay the freedmen wages. Confederate paper money, perhaps a billion dollars face value, was worthless. Southern gold and silver had long since been shipped abroad to pay for arms. As late as 1880, there were more bullion and coin in the banks of Massachusetts than in the banks of the entire South. Emancipation had wiped out investments worth $50 billion. Much of the southern economy had reverted to barter, which was what sharecropping was—barter.

Landowners partitioned their acreage into farms of 10 to 40 acres, constructing a cabin on each parcel. In return for the use of the dwelling and the land, share tenants who provided their own mule, plow, and seed turned over to their landlords a quarter to a third of the cotton and corn they produced. Sharecroppers (the large majority were blacks) were tenants too poor to afford a mule, plow, and seed. The landlord provided them too in return for a half of the crop.

As a means of production, sharecropping worked well. Southern cotton production reached its 1860 level in 1870 and exceeded the prewar record a few years later. As in the West, however, increased production was accompanied by a decline in wholesale prices. In the early 1870s, a pound of cotton sold for 18¢. In the early 1890s, the going rate was 6¢. In 1894, cotton bottomed out at a nickel a pound: $30 for a 600 pound bale!

Debt Bondage   In the West, the collapse in farm income resulted in mortgage foreclosures that reduced many farmers to tenantry. In the South, where tenancy was already common, declining prices created a physically ruinous and morally debilitating poverty unknown even in Kansas—debt bondage

Agribusiness 1887

May Woodward was a widow who, during the 1880s, lived on a wheat farm in Dakota Territory. Even at 1,500 acres—1 mile wide by almost 2 ½ miles long—it was not quite a bonanza farm. But it was a commercial operation, the property of absentee owners who expected an annual return on their investment from a hired manager, Mrs. Woodward's son.

On their "small" spread, the Woodwards could have a personal, even cordial relationship with their workers. Mrs. Woodward wrote in her diary in the spring of 1885 that she was "glad that we can have the same men that were here last year." There was, however, nothing personal in employer-employee relations on bonanza farms that hired hundreds of men for 30 to 40 days each spring and fall. Frank Wilkeson, writing in the New York *Times* in August 1887, described "ragged, dirty, half-drunken men" riding freight trains into wheat belt towns and congregating "in foul-smelling crowds around the doors of saloons" waiting to be hired. "Where they come from and where they go" was of interest to no one.

There is no pretense of making a pleasant home for the workmen.... There is no eating with the farmer's family, and no love-making between handsome harvest hands and the farmer's fair daughter.... All the poetry has been knocked out of farm life on these immense farms. It is business, and the workmen are handled roughly.

Mrs. Woodward kept a diary that provides a record of the rhythm of the work year in the wheat belt, which was the same on a bonanza farm of 15,000 acres except that there were ten times as many hired hands as on the Woodward spread and almost ten times as many machines.

April 11th: They planted eighty acres yesterday which was a big day's work, as seeding is the hardest part of farming in Dakota. The men walk between eighteen and twenty miles a day besides lifting sacks, filling seeders, and managing horses; moreover it is frequently either muddy or dusty in the spring.
May 7: The grass begins to grow, and soon the whole prairie will look beautiful....

which, according to Charles Oken in 1894, "crushed out all independence and reduced its victims to a coarse species of servile labor."

It worked like this: When a 'cropper's share of the year's income was just enough to cover the costs he had incurred during the year to feed the family, he had little choice but to remain where he was. If the year's income did not cover what the sharecropper owed the general store (often owned by the landlord), he had no choice at all. Man, wife, and children were bound to the land as if they were serfs. If they fled, their landlord-creditor called on the sheriff to bring them back to pay their debt—by farming for him. In several southern states, running out on a debt was a criminal offense punishable by imprisonment on a state-owned plantation.

Debt turned landowners into tenants. The ledgers of T.G. Patrick, a general merchandiser, show that during one growing season he provided $900 worth of seed, food, and tools to a farmer named S. R. Simonton. When, in the fall, the price of cotton dropped below projections, Simonton was able to repay only $300 of his debt, leaving Patrick with a lien against his property of $600. Simonton slashed his

We have fifty acres for a dooryard [lawn and garden]. All the rest is sowed with grain and now looks like green velvet.

There was not much to do in wheat country in June and July except to watch the crop grow and worry about a hail storm or grass fire that could destroy it. On bonanza farms, the migrant workers hired for seeding were paid off at $2 a day and invited back in August (or told not to bother). Mrs. Woodward's son kept several of his best hands on the payroll to do incidental chores.

August 11: Harvest has started. Now there will be no rest for man, woman, or beast until frost which comes, thank heaven, early here. I was nearly beside myself getting dinner for thirteen men besides carpenters and tinners.... I baked seventeen loaves of bread today, making seventy-four loaves since last Sunday, not to mention twenty-one pies, and puddings, cakes, and doughnuts.

The men cut one hundred acres today. All four of our harvesters are being used as well as three which were hired to cut by the acre. Things look like business with seven self-binders at work on this home section. The twine to bind our grain will cost three hundred dollars this year.

August 13: Our family has increased until there are thirty-two. We have put the cook stove in the blacksmith shop. The men have taken all the machinery from the machine house and put in tables with bunks overhead, making a fine new living quarter. We have a man cook and he has taken sixteen at his table out there.

The yard is full of threshers. They have been running the new machine [a steam tractor] to try it.... It looks very queer indeed to see an engine running around the yard with no horses attached to it. They whistle and toot and frighten the chickens and some of the horses. At present there is about a mile square covered with buildings and machinery.

September 19: The first frost. Looking from the granary steps with the telescope I could see twenty threshing machines running. The weather is perfect and they will thresh an average of 1,500 bushels each.

During the 1880s, well-managed bonanza farms were profitable. The cost of producing a bushel of clean wheat was calculated to be between 17¢ and 21¢. Freight charges to New York added 27¢ per bushel. In New York, the wheat sold for 60¢, a profit per bushel of 12¢ to 16¢. During the 1890s, when the wholesale price of wheat collapsed, many bonanza farms, like small family operations, went out of business.

costs the following year to $400 but his accumulated debt of $1,000 was more than Patrick was willing to carry. He foreclosed, and Simonton became a tenant on farm he had owned.

THE POPULISTS

During the 1880s, disgruntled southern farmers organized the Southern Alliance and the Colored Farmers' National Alliance. In addition to serving Grange-like social functions, the alliances' leaders hoped to use the organizations to pressure public officials to take action to relieve agricultural distress.

Party Loyalties   In 1890, the Southern Alliance claimed 1.5 million members, the Colored Farmers Alliance a million. Feeling their strength, southern agrarians gathered in Ocala, Florida, in December 1890 to discuss the desirability of organizing a new national party patterned after the People's Party of

Kansas which, a month earlier, had won five seats in the House of Representatives and a majority in the state legislature, sending William A. Peffer to the Senate.

Some southern agrarians, notably Congressman Thomas Watson of Georgia, had already left the Democratic party, calling themselves Populists (from the Latin word for "the people"). Most of those at Ocala, however, resisted the third-party proposal. White agrarians had made inroads in the Democratic party in some states. They feared that if the white vote was split between the Democrats and a Populist party, the Republicans, most of whom were black, would regain the political power they had held during Reconstruction.

Members of the Colored Farmers Alliance were reluctant to sever their Republican ties because the party of Lincoln and emancipation had, however undependably, defended the civil rights of African Americans. In 1890, there were still a good many black public officials in the South, some elected, most appointed to federal jobs by Republican presidents.

Tom Watson tried to bridge the racial divide. In a widely circulated magazine article, he wrote, "You are kept apart that you may be separately fleeced of your earnings. You are made to hate each other because upon that hatred is rested the keystone of the arch of financial despotism which enslaves you both. You are deceived and blinded that you may not see how this race antagonism perpetuates a monetary system which beggars both." But he stirred up more hostility than support among white voters. In 1892, Watson was defeated in his bid for reelection to Congress.

The Omaha Convention

Old party loyalties were not quite so strong west of the Mississippi. Enough former Democrats and Republicans had given up on the old parties that they called for a Populist convention to meet in Omaha, Nebraska, in the summer of 1892. The Kansas Populists were there, of course, joined by agrarians from every state in the farm belt, some southern Populists, delegates from miners' unions in the mountain states, other union leaders from the declining but still kicking Knights of Labor, and a few Eastern reformers.

The People's Party of the United States nominated former Union General James B. Weaver to run for president against the Republican incumbent Benjamin Harrison and the Democratic former president, Grover Cleveland. For vice president—an appeal for southern votes—the Populists nominated former Confederate General James G. Field.

More important, for no one expected the new party to win its first election, was the platform the Populists adopted. In the nineteenth century, as today, party platforms were long, wordy collections of pious and patriotic sentiments that were so general as to be meaningless. There were airy generalities in the Omaha platform too, brave proclamations of the common interests of farmers and factory workers, which few took seriously. However, the bulk of the platform was a comprehensive and specific program for reforming what the Populists believed had gone askew in America. There has rarely been another party platform quite like it.

A Far-Reaching Program

The Populists believed that special interests and corrupted politicians were subverting the will of the people. Democracy had to be shored up and expanded. So, the Omaha platform called for the election of United States senators by popular vote rather than by state legislators who were too often bought by powerful railroaders and other capitalists. The Populists demanded the universal adoption of the Australian (secret) ballot so that landlords and employers could not dictate how their tenants and workers voted.

The Populists recommended that states adopt the initiative, recall, and referendum so that "the people" could bypass public officials who did not do their jobs. The initiative would allow voters to petition that a proposed law be put on the ballot to be approved or rejected independent of state legislators and governors. The recall would allow voters, again by means of a petition, to force elected officials to win voter approval before their terms expired, and to remove officials if they were voted out. The recall was designed to discourage politicians from backing down on their campaign promises. The referendum was a general election at which voters accepted or rejected initiatives and retained or removed officials who had been recalled.

The Omaha platform called for a postal savings system (savings accounts at post offices as an alternative to the banks Populists distrusted); federal ownership of the telegraph, telephone, and railroads, natural monopolies that had no competition; a graduated income tax that would soak the rich so to arrest the further growth of bloated fortunes; restriction of "undesirable emigration" and the prohibition of alien land ownership, including the confiscation of land already owned by aliens.

The two latter demands had an economic basis. Cheap immigrant labor contributed to keeping wages down; by denying farmland to noncitizens, Populists believed they could combat the overproduction of crops. But there was also an anti-foreigner bias among native-born farmers.

Finally, the Populists demanded that the government increase the "circulating medium"—the money supply—by $50 per capita. This would be accomplished by "the free and unlimited coinage of silver," its money value pegged to the money value of gold.

The Rapture   When the platform was adopted on the Fourth of July, the convention hall erupted in an uproar of religious intensity. Beloved old hymns were sung in several parts of the crowd. A brass band tried to make itself heard above the din. "Cheers and yells ... rose like a tornado ... and raged without cessation for thirty-four minutes, during which time women shrieked and wept, men embraced and kissed their neighbors, locked arms, marched back and forth, and leaped upon tables and chairs in the ecstasy of their delirium."

How to explain this near hysteria? The delegates had not just been saved at a camp meeting; they had adopted a political platform by majority vote. The pros and cons of their proposals could be debated rationally by drawing on empirical evidence; they were not religious beliefs like reincarnation or the divinity of Jesus in which one had faith or did not.

In fact, the Populist movement had a powerful religious element before the Omaha convention, a sense that evil forces were loose in the United States and the people were locked in mortal combat with them. "We meet in the midst of a nation brought to the verge of moral, political, and material ruin," Ignatius Donnelly of Minnesota wrote in the preamble to the Omaha platform. "Corruption dominates the ballot box, the legislatures, the Congress, and touches even the ermine of the bench.... We declare that this Republic can only endure as a free government while built upon the love of the whole people for each other."

Senator Peffer of Kansas, who looked like an Old Testament prophet with his white, waist-length beard, called God to aid the party on its "mission." "The people are at bay," Mary E. "Mother" Lease said, "let the bloodhounds of money beware." Hardly could two Populists converse without speaking of diabolical conspiracy, the conspiracy of the railroads to defraud shippers, the conspiracy of politicians to subvert democracy, the conspiracy of the great bankers, the "money power," to defraud farmers and workingmen like "thieves in the night."

SILVER AND GOLD

The issue that inspired the most intense religious fervor in the Populists, strange as it seems today, was the nature of American money—the dollar. In the mid-1870s, frankly self-serving western mine owners demanded that the federal government buy the silver they produced and coin it into dollars. During the 1880s, farmers suffering from the steady decline in the prices at which they sold their crops seized on the "free and unlimited coinage of silver" as, first, the solution to their economic problems and in time as a kind of salvation. When they were repeatedly frustrated, they transformed the white metal into a sacred talisman and the "Gold Bugs," proponents of a dollar based on gold, as ungodly.

A Brief History of American Coinage   The most common paper money in the nineteenth century was the bank note. Bills of $10, $50, and $100 were issued by nationally and state-chartered banks, privately owned institutions. Bank notes maintained their value in business transactions because the bank that issued them redeemed them on demand with gold and silver coins.

Coinage was the federal government's business. The United States Mint, a division of the Treasury Department—and only the mint—could strike coins so that the quantity of gold and silver in them was guaranteed. Small change, coins of five cents to a dollar, were struck in silver. (Except cents and half-cents, which were copper or bronze.) Coins worth $2.50, $5, $10, and $20 were minted in gold.

Originally, all American coins were silver. In 1792, when the Second Congress founded the U.S. Mint, the most common coin circulating in the infant United States was the Spanish *dolar*. Knowing that large numbers of the Spanish coins would continue to circulate, Congress based its dollar on them, not only adopting the name, but also providing by law that each dollar contain 371.25 grains of silver, the same as in a Spanish *dolar*.

During the 1830s, partly because of a silver shortage, partly because silver coins worth more than a dollar would be too cumbersome, Congress monetized gold. That is, the mint was directed to strike coins of denominations larger than a dollar in gold. The basic gold coin was the eagle, a $10 piece. An eagle was to contain 258 grains of gold because, at the time of the Coinage Act of 1837, the going price of 258 grams of gold was ten silver dollars. Congress thus pegged the money values of silver and gold to one another at a ratio of 16:1: 16 ounces of silver were equal in money value to 1 ounce of gold. The U.S. dollar became a "bimetal" currency, based on the two precious metals.

Bimetalism
Bimetalism had a built-in problem. Congress could link the value of gold and silver coins to each other. On the open market, however, the prices of silver and gold fluctuated independently of one another according to how much of each was available for sale and the demand of buyers for them. To resolve the problem, Great Britain, the colossus of world finance and trade, invented the "gold standard"—redeeming pound notes only in gold—in part because of Britain's trade with China. The British wanted all kinds of Chinese goods, but the Chinese had little interest in the manufactures with which the British paid for their purchases elsewhere in the world. Chinese merchants insisted on payment in silver. The China trade so seriously depleted Britain's silver reserves that demonetizing the metal seemed to be the only way to avoid money problems at home.

The China trade was a drain on silver dollars too, but not so many of them as to cause a crisis. Within the United States, bimetalism worked well enough. Each increase in the supply of one metal great enough to knock the 16:1 ratio out of kilter (such as the river of California gold that flooded the country after 1849) was soon providentially counterbalanced by discoveries of rich silver deposits like Nevada's fabulous Comstock lode.

In the early 1870s, however, the Comstock lode appeared to be playing out. Miners had tunneled so deeply that the lowest drifts filled with water faster than pumps could keep them workable. Silver was growing scarcer worldwide while the supply of gold remained steady. (American gold production increased from $49.5 million in 1869 to $56 million in 1870.) By 1873, the market price of the silver in a silver dollar was more than $1 on the open market. People actually collected silver dollars, melted them down, and sold the ingots to jewelry makers and silverware manufacturers that could pass their costs on to customers. It made little sense for the mint to continue striking dollar coins.

The Gold Standard
Congress responded with the Coinage Act of 1873. The silver dollar was dropped from the coinage (except for a small number of "trade dollars" to be used in the China trade). Silver was demonetized; that is, the metal no longer had a money value established by law. With the Coinage Act, the United States joined Britain, Portugal, the Netherlands, and Germany on the gold standard. (Within a few years, virtually every other trading nation followed.)

Silver was now a commodity. Its price, like the price of diamonds, cotton, bread, a horse, or anything else people sold and bought, was determined by how much buyers were willing to pay for it.

The Coinage Act sailed through Congress with little debate, and President Grant signed it in February 1873.

Within months, thanks to new technologies, the Comstock lode was resuscitated to record levels. Beginning at Leadville, Colorado, in 1874, prospectors unearthed new silver deposits in Colorado, Utah, Idaho, and Montana. American silver production increased from $29 million at the time of the Coinage Act to $37 million in 1874 and $45 million in 1878. The market price of the metal dropped. Silver producers worried that they could not sell the metal at prices high enough to keep their mines open.

The Kansas State Historical Society, Topeka, Kansas

Populists protesting an alleged election fraud in the chamber of the Kansas state legislature in January 1893. These rough looking men (William Allen White called them "grasy fizzles") did not seriously threaten to shoot anyone. The guns were for dramatic effect and they were ill-advised props. Photographs like this and newspaper accounts of the religious intensity of Populist meetings persuaded both Republicans and Democrats that they were facing a revolution.

They found a fiery and eloquent spokesman in Congressman Richard P. "Silver Dick" Bland of Missouri. In 1878, he introduced a bill to bail the industry out by returning the United States to "the dollar of our daddies," resuming the coinage of silver dollars at the old ratio to gold coins of 16:1.

An Unsuccess-
ful Compromise
Bland faced formidable opposition from financial conservatives in Congress and from President Hayes. Foreign capital fueled American economic development, they pointed out, and British and Dutch bankers insisted that their investments pay off in gold. It was vital to the nation's economic growth, therefore, that the dollar remain a gold standard currency.

A compromise that preserved the gold standard while placating silver interests was worked out in the Senate. The Bland-Allison Act of 1878 directed the Secretary of the Treasury to purchase between $2 million and $4 million of silver each month and mint it into silver dollars. Silver was not monetized, however. The government would continue to redeem its obligations (and banks their notes) in gold. Silver remained a commodity. The mint made its purchases at market prices.

At first, silver producers were content. Monthly silver production was within the $2–$4 million range in 1878. Silver producers had a market for their entire output—or so they thought. In fact, every Secretary of the Treasury, both Republican and Democratic, was a financial conservative. They invariably purchased the monthly minimum of $2 million that Bland-Allison mandated while silver production steadily increased. In 1884, it reached $4 million, twice what the government purchased. In 1890, fully 6,000 silver mines sent $6.6 million to smelters every month. Back in 1873, an ounce of gold had, by law, been worth 16 ounces of silver. In 1890, an ounce of gold bought 20 ounces of it.

"Silver Dick" and other silverites began to refer to the demonetization of silver as "the Crime of '73." The paranoia that would infect the Populists had germinated.

The Coinage Act was not a crime; there were no victims—in 1873! The demonetization of silver was a reasonable response to the market price of the metal. There was no conspiracy. Gold Bugs made their case for the gold standard openly and honestly: American credit abroad depended on redeeming dollars in gold. The gold standard congressmen who agreed to the Bland-Allison compromise did so in good faith. They assumed that the mint's monthly purchases of silver would be sufficient to sustain the mines, mills, and smelters. They could hardly have known that silver production was going to soar to stratospheric levels during the 1880s.

The Sherman Silver Purchase Act of 1890
Gold Bugs were, nevertheless, relieved that they had successfully resisted calls for the free and unlimited coinage of silver. If Bland-Allison had monetized silver, the utter collapse of its price would have meant runaway inflation, a collapse in the value of the dollar.

In 1890, however, the Gold Bugs lost control of the U.S. Senate. Six new states were admitted to the Union. Montana and Idaho were mining states. North and South Dakota and Washington were agricultural states where inflation was seen as the solution to the declining prices at which farmers sold their crops. Wyoming was home to a few silver mines and a farming and ranching economy. Their twelve senators gave the free silver Democrats and Republicans plus one Populist a majority in the upper house.

Not in the House of Representatives, however. It took some fancy political horse trading to enact the Sherman Silver Purchase Act of 1890, which partially remonetized silver. The Sherman Act required the Secretary of the Treasury to buy 4.5 million ounces of silver each month—which was then close to actual production in that record year. The government was to pay for its purchases with certificates—paper money—that were redeemable in gold or silver.

However, the value of silver dollars had not been pegged to the value of gold coins. That was the concession silverites had to make in order to win President

Harrison's signature on the bill. And after a brief jump to $1.50 an ounce after the passage of the Sherman Act, the market price of silver plummeted to 83¢ an ounce in 1893.

Naturally enough, when people cashed in their paper money, they insisted on gold coins rather than 83-cent silver dollars. More important, President Harrison redeemed the federal government's financial obligations in gold. Foreign lenders still worried about what Congress might do next, particularly because of the growth of the Populist party. They called in their American loans in gold and even shipped bullion they had kept in American vaults back home. In 1893, the federal government's gold reserve fell below $100 million, the figure regarded as the minimum necessary to maintain the government's credit.

"To put beyond all doubt or mistake" the commitment of the United States to the gold standard, the newly elected Democratic president, Grover Cleveland, called for the repeal of the Sherman Act. Within four days of his message, the price of silver plunged from 83¢ per ounce to 62¢. A Congress near panic hurriedly obliged the president.

A Most Unpopular President   President Cleveland blamed a stock market crash in June 1893 on the Sherman Silver Purchase Act. In fact, the stock market began to totter in February when the Reading Railroad, a major eastern line, declared bankruptcy. Whatever the cause of the crash, hundreds of banks and thousands of businesses closed their doors in its wake. Workers lost their jobs by the tens of thousands. It was the beginning of the most serious depression to that time.

Grover Cleveland had been president for less than a year but, like Herbert Hoover almost forty years later, the blame for the bad times fell on him. In 1894, Cleveland added to his unpopularity when he instructed his attorney general, Richard B. Olney, to help crush the American Railway Union's boycott of Pullman cars. Union members, mostly Democrats who had voted for the president, joined Populists and silverite Democrats in denouncing the president. When Jacob S. Coxey, an idealistic millionaire from Ohio, led an almost entirely orderly march of unemployed men to Washington to ask for government-funded make-work—"a petition with its boots on," Coxey called it—Olney ridiculed the protest by having Coxey arrested for "walking on the grass." Even genteel Easterners sympathetic to the miseries of the poor were disgusted.

Few presidents' popularity have sunk to the depths Grover Cleveland's did during his second term. His own party repudiated him. When, at the Democratic convention in 1896, a resolution was introduced thanking the retiring president for his years of public service, the delegates voted it down.

32

PIVOTAL DECADE
McKinley, Segregation, and Empire 1890–1901

*God has not been preparing the English-speaking and
Teutonic peoples for a thousand years for nothing but vain
and idle self-contemplation. No. He made us the master
organizers of the world to establish system where chaos
reigned. He has given us the spirit of progress to overwhelm
the forces of reaction throughout the earth. He has made us
adept in government that we may administer government
among savage and senile peoples. Were it not for such a
force as this the world would relapse into barbarism and
night. And of all our race, He has marked the American
people as His chosen nation to finally lead in the
redemption of the world.*

—Albert J. Beveridge

Few presidential election years have begun as anxiously as 1896 did. Politicians and pundits lamented that the country was more divided than at any time since the Civil War, not section against section this time, but class against class. The Homestead strike and an armed conflict between silver miners and company guards in Idaho four years earlier looked more like battles than "work stoppages." In 1893, Illinois governor John P. Altgeld revived memories of the Haymarket Square affair when he pardoned three anarchists imprisoned for the bombing. Agrarian protest burned white hot; Populist orators used words like "criminal" to denounce railroaders and bankers. The Democratic party split down the middle in 1894 when their once popular president Grover Cleveland used troops to break the Pullman boycott over Democratic governor Altgeld's protest. The Populists rejoiced. Where else could alienated, angry Democrats rally but under the banner of the People's Party?

Conservatives, both Northeastern Cleveland Democrats and the Republicans, who were back in control of both houses of Congress, were as worried as the Populists were optimistic.

The American Empire 1890–1904

1890	1892	1894	1896	1898	1900	1902	1904

1890 *The Influence of Sea Power upon History* published

1891 Hawaiian queen overthrown

1898 War with Spain; Hawaii annexed

1899 Philippines occupied; Open Door policy

Insurrection in Philippines 1899–1901

McKinley assassinated 1901

Panama Canal Zone acquired 1903

1896: A LANDMARK ELECTION

Early in 1896, a reporter asked the Republican Speaker of the House of Representatives, Thomas Brackett Reed of Maine, if he thought the Republicans would choose him as their presidential candidate at their convention in June. Reed thought for a second and said, "They could do worse." He added, "and they probably will."

They did. While the ever-cool Reed waited diffidently for his party to come to him, a dynamic, blustering Cleveland industrialist, Marcus Alonzo Hanna, rushed around the country lining up Republican delegates for his close friend, Ohio governor William McKinley. When the party convened, Hanna had sewn the nomination up tight. On the first ballot, Reed won only 84 votes to McKinley's 661.

Reed, Hanna, and McKinley   In their politics, Reed and McKinley were twins. Both were big business conservatives. Both were high-tariff men, the higher the better. On the money issue that was to dominate the campaign, Reed had a better record than McKinley. He was a hard line Gold Bug determined to put the United States officially on the gold standard. McKinley had waffled on the money question, trying to please both Gold Bugs and silverites in divided Ohio.

The Republican convention did not waffle on the issue. It endorsed a gold standard platform that caused the party's free silver contingent, led by Senator Henry M. Teller of Colorado, to walk out.

Personally, Reed and McKinley were of two different species. McKinley cultivated what he thought was the very image of dignity in his deportment. Others saw his public persona as merely dull and priggish. "On the whole decent, on the whole dumb," wrote Republican editor, William Allen White. McKinley "walked among men like a bronze statue looking for a pedestal."

Reed was as sharp and lively as they came, and he was unaffected, gregarious, and good-humored all the while, as Speaker, he herded Republican congressmen around as if they were sheep and shooed the minority Democrats away as if they were trespassing goats. Reporters loved Reed because he was always good for an entertaining quote. When one of his political critics died suddenly, they asked Reed if he would attend the funeral. He replied, "No, but I approve of it."

To Mark Hanna, Reed's frivolous wit was a good reason to nominate the stolid McKinley. The Populists and free silver Democrats were wild men. The Republicans

William McKinley was the personification of middle-class sobriety and respectability. But he was no match for William Jennings Bryan as a county fair orator. So his campaign manager in 1896, Mark Hanna, advised him to stay at home in Canton, Ohio, and make short, dignified speeches from his front porch (shown here) to visiting groups of faithful Republicans.

needed a statue in the park whose demeanor contrasted with their antics. Moreover, Reed was notoriously his own man. He listened to contending arguments but once he embraced the position he considered principled, he could not be budged. McKinley was a practical opportunist willing to take whatever position on an issue won the most votes.

Democrats and Populists gibed that the malleable McKinley was Mark Hanna's stooge. That did not disturb Republican bosses. Professional politicos like them dealt in front-men. Who better to be telling McKinley where he stood behind the scenes than the reliable businessman Mark Hanna?

Boy Bryan   Just a few weeks after McKinley's nomination, Hanna's arguments on his behalf turned out to look better than even Hanna could have known when the Democratic convention made a surprise nomination. Hanna knew that the Democrats would choose a free silver man. Conservative Cleveland delegates were a hapless minority at the Democratic convention. They refused even to vote a resolution of thanks to the retiring Democratic president.

Richard "Silver Dick" Bland of Missouri was the frontrunner for the nomination. He had been fighting the free silver cause for twenty years. However, with half a dozen other names in nomination and the Democrats requiring a three-quarters majority to name a candidate, the delegates were up for grabs.

The man who grabbed them was William Jennings Bryan of Nebraska. He was scarcely beyond the 35 years of age the Constitution requires a president to be. He had served two terms in Congress but had attracted no attention. He was not a national figure, but back home in the corn and hog belt, Bryan was a celebrated platform orator. For four years he had spoken at every political rally and county fair to which he was invited. He toured grange halls and spoke from the pulpits of Baptist, Methodist, and Presbyterian churches. His cause was the free coinage of silver, his villains the bankers. Like an entertainer who was aspiring to the big time, which he was, each time he delivered his single set speech, he edited and polished it a bit closer to perfection, something today's politicians, when every remark is videotaped for national telecasts, cannot do lest they be written off as bores.

Bryan's "Cross of Gold" speech was a well-organized, easily understood rehash of the arguments in favor of monetizing silver. By 1896 it was a model of phrasing, timing, and theatrical gesture. Bryan was intensely religious, as were many of the people in his rural audiences. They were not disturbed when Bryan enlisted God in a political debate about money. His speech concluded—it climaxed!—with the words:

> Having behind us the producing masses of this nation and the world, supported by the commercial interests, the laboring interests and the toilers everywhere, we will answer their demand for a gold standard by saying to them: You shall not press down upon the brow of labor this crown of thorns, you shall not crucify mankind upon a cross of gold.

Bryan landed the assignment of the closing speech in the debate of the money issue at the convention. The Cross of Gold set off so passionate and uproarious a demonstration at the convention that Bryan's supporters wanted to move on immediately to choosing a nominee. His rivals managed to postpone the balloting to the next day to allow the delegates time to cool off. They did; it took several ballots for Bryan to win the nomination, but win it he did, surprising just about everyone but himself.

"Fusion"

Republican newspapers denounced the "boy orator of the Platte" as a blasphemous, wild-eyed Populist. In fact, Bryan did not subscribe to the Populists' comprehensive reform program. Back in Nebraska and Kansas, he had debated Populists, rejecting their demands for radical reform. It was not necessary, he said. The free coinage of silver would end the depression and restore prosperity on the farm.

The Populists knew that Bryan was juggling with a single ball. But when their convention met, the delegates were divided as to how they should respond to the Democrats' embrace of free silver. Populists committed to enacting the Omaha platform in its entirety conceded that Bryan would attract many voters that the Populists had counted. The party would not win the presidency in 1896. Better, however, to concentrate on electing more congressmen and wait four years for the presidency. Let the Gold Bug Republicans discredit themselves as the Cleveland Democrats had done.

The majority of the Populists disagreed. They wanted to nominate Bryan. They were known as "fusionists" because they wanted to fuse the Democratic and Populist parties. By combining Democratic and Populist votes behind one candidate, victory was a cinch, they believed. Most Republican politicos (although not Mark Hanna) agreed with them. Bryan's charisma scared them to death.

Urban Populists like Henry Demarest Lloyd opposed fusion. So did some southern Populists like Tom Watson of Georgia. They pointed out that, in the South, the enemy was not the powerless Republican party but the Bourbon Democrats. If they fused with the Democrats, they would lose the support of those Republican black farmers with whom Watson had been trying, with some success, to form an alliance. Fusion with the Democrats would send African Americans scurrying back to the Republicans.

Midwestern Populists led by Jerry Simpson disagreed. Fusion meant victory. "I care not for party names," Simpson said, "it is substance we are after, and we have it in William J. Bryan." Delegates from the mining states, some of them Republicans a month earlier, wanted fusion. Free silver was their issue; the rest of the Populist program did not much interest them.

The fusionists had their way; the Populist party nominated Bryan. To placate the anti-fusionists, they nominated Tom Watson for vice president and asked Bryan to drop his Democratic vice presidential candidate and name Watson, an industrialist with a bad labor record who was, at best, soft on the silver issue, as his vice presidential running mate. Bryan ignored them.

The Whirlwind and the Rock Before 1896, few presidential candidates actively campaigned, none in the frenzy we know today. Some nominees made a few public appearances. Others dropped out of sight. They thought it insulting to the dignity of the presidency to chase around after it. Candidates *stood* for election; they did not *run* for it.

Not Bryan. He ran. A youthful and trim 36, he was inexhaustible. He traveled 13,000 miles by train. In fourteen weeks, he delivered 600 speeches in twenty-nine states—more than six speeches a day on average. And if he was not running late after he spoke, he mixed happily with his supporters, gossiping and gobbling up potato salad and complimenting the maker on her recipe. The enthusiasm with which he was greeted in the West and South threw a panic into already worried bankers, railroaders, and industrialists.

Panic was exactly what Mark Hanna wanted to see. He corraled wealthy Republicans and conservative Democrats as he had corraled delegates before the convention. He tapped them for contributions to McKinley's campaign in unprecedented amounts. Hanna spent more money on posters, buttons, rallies, picnics, advertisements, and a corps of Republican speakers who followed Bryan around than had been spent by both parties in every election since the Civil War. The Republicans printed five pamphlets for every American voter. Hanna was so successful a fund-raiser that, several weeks before election day, he returned contributions he did not need.

Knowing that the phlegmatic McKinley could not compete with Bryan as a stump speaker, Hanna kept him at his modest home in Canton, Ohio. Republican speakers and editors contrasted McKinley's self-respect with Bryan's vulgar huckstering. In fact, the McKinley campaign was as frantic as Bryan's, although much

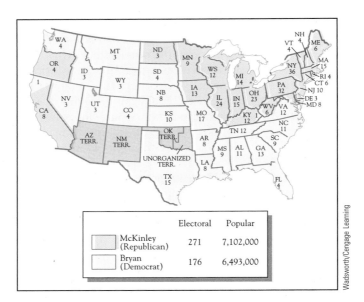

Electoral | Popular
--- | --- | ---
McKinley (Republican) | 271 | 7,102,000
Bryan (Democrat) | 176 | 6,493,000

Wadsworth/Cengage Learning

MAP 32.1 Presidential Election of 1896

McKinley won only 51 percent of the popular vote in 1896, but he ran away with the electoral college by sweeping the large northeastern and midwestern states—exactly the Republican party's goal. Rather more remarkable, the South was not "solid" for Bryan; he lost Kentucky and West Virginia. North Dakota's three electoral votes did not much matter, but by carrying the state, McKinley even cracked the Great Plains bloc that was thought solid for Bryan.

easier on the candidate. Delegations of party faithful streamed daily (except Sundays) into Canton where they marched from the depot to McKinley's home behind a marching band. McKinley emerged as if delightfully surprised to have visitors, delivered a short speech from the front porch, and invited all his friends to join him for lemonade or beer. (On the march to McKinley's house, campaign workers tactfully determined the delegation's attitude toward alcohol, a touchy matter in the 1890s.) About 750,000 people visited McKinley's home. They trampled his front lawn "as if a herd of buffalo had passed through." On one Saturday, McKinley made sixteen front porch speeches to 30,000 Republicans!

The Vote Count   More people voted for Bryan than had voted for anyone ever elected president. But he still lost. McKinley's edge in the popular vote was modest but it was the first time in a quarter century that a presidential candidate had won an absolute majority. McKinley won decisively in the electoral college, 271 to Bryan's 176. What happened? In September, most professional politicians, Republicans and Democrats, believed that Bryan was well ahead.

The pros were deceived by the numbers and noisiness of the crowds that cheered Bryan's speeches. They overlooked the fact that the crowds were large and hysterical only in the South, in the hard-pressed western farm states, and in the

Rocky Mountain mining states, each of which had only three electoral votes. McKinley swept the Northeast, including Connecticut and every one of the swing states that had decided every presidential election since the Civil War. Although he did not need their electoral votes—even Mark Hanna was surprised—McKinley won majorities in the farm belt states of North Dakota, Minnesota, and Iowa.

Bryan had little support among factory workers and city people generally. He hardly tried to win them over. Imbued with rural prejudices against big cities and the "foreigners" who populated them, he made only one visit to the thirty-six electoral vote swing state of New York. An alert Republican reporter quoted him as calling Democratic New York City "the enemy's country," as if the metropolis were inhabited solely by bankers and grain speculators. Tammany boss Richard Croker washed his hands of the "hayseed" national ticket and concentrated on state and local elections. The other fourteen biggest cities were in the hands of Republican political machines which delivered the urban vote to William McKinley.

A few industrialists tried to intimidate their employees into voting Republican. The Baldwin Piano Works posted notices on the eve of election day that if Bryan won, the plant would close its gates. But Bryan's weakness in industrial areas owed nothing to such tactics. The free silver crusade left working people cold. Much more persuasive with them was the Republican argument that the inflation Bryan advocated would hurt them by increasing prices, and by the time-tested argument that by protecting American industry, the Republicans' high tariff protected their jobs.

Finally, Mark Hanna sensed the instincts of a new element in American politics, the growing middle class of small businessmen, professionals, salaried white-collar employees, and skilled, well-paid working men: railroad engineers and firemen, factory foremen, and some workers in the building trades. They were already conscious of the social and cultural chasm between them and unskilled immigrant workers in the towns and cities. Now they were wary of Bryan's ragged, restive, marginal farmers who, before the agrarian uprising, middle-class people had thought of as comical yokels when they thought of them at all.

It was not apparent to anyone in 1896, of course, but with McKinley's election, the twenty-year equilibrium of the two major political parties was over and done with. The Republican party, the party of the decent, orderly, respectable middle class would, except for one freakish interlude, govern the United States for three and a half decades.

The End of Populism

The Populist party was dead. Fusion had killed it. When they abandoned the Omaha platform for the chance of winning the White House with William Jennings Bryan and free silver, the Populists had nothing left when Bryan lost.

In the farm belt, the party withered away as, slowly but perceptibly, the market prices of the staple crops rose. Several poor European harvests beginning in 1897 increased the demand for and therefore the prices of American grain. Gold discoveries in Canada, Alaska, South Africa, and southern Nevada gently inflated the currency—inflated it "naturally," as Gold Bugs liked to put it. "Free silver!" and all the passion invested in it as a cure-all became irrelevant to everyone but the owners of silver mines and the men who worked in them.

Populistic sentiments remained high in the South but not the Populist party. Tom Watson's vision of a party in which poor white and black farmers cooperated, if it had ever been realistic, died the day the Populists fused with the Democrats. Their place was taken by a new kind of southern politician within the Democratic party, a rabble-rousing demagogue who railed against railroads, banks, and southern Bourbons in one breath and, in the next, against the "niggers."

DRAWING THE COLOR LINE

In 1890, 90 percent of the African American population lived in the southern states. The Bourbon Redeemers had long since neutralized the blacks' Republican party as a political power to be reckoned with. However, Republican presidents continued to appoint African Americans to federal offices in the South, including some high-ranking posts in the Customs Service and Post Office. African American voters held their own in a few district elections. A few black candidates won state offices in South Carolina, Mississippi, and Louisiana to the end of the 1880s. In Tennessee and North Carolina, there were more African Americans in state offices in 1890 than there had been during Reconstruction.

The Force Bill   In 1890, in order to protect the remnants of the southern black Republican party and to provide the machinery to restore African American voting where it had been suppressed, the slim Republican majority in the House of Representatives passed the "Force Bill." If petitioners demonstrated that they were denied their right to vote because of their race, special federal officials would, on the scene, force registrars and poll watchers to observe African Americans' Fifteenth Amendment rights.

The Republican majority in the Senate was also slim, just 39 votes to the Democrats' 37, just enough to make the Force Bill law on a straight party vote. However, several southern Democratic senators informed free silver Republicans from the western mining states that unless they voted against the Force Bill, southern Democratic senators would vote against the Sherman Silver Purchase bill and kill it. The deal was struck. The silver purchase bill passed and the Force Bill failed. It was the last gasp of radical Reconstruction idealism.

A few months later, Benjamin R. Tillman was sworn in as governor of South Carolina. Although himself a prosperous farmer, Tillman won the election by arousing poor white farmers against the conservative Redeemer Democrats of Charleston who ran the state. They were flunkeys for the railroads and the bankers of New York who were fleecing poor farmers everywhere.

Tillman combined his populistic demagoguery with a call for the systematic intimidation of those South Carolina blacks who were still voting. It was not just that blacks supported the plutocratic Republican party and, in some cases, the conservative Redeemers. African Americans were inherently inferior, even depraved, a threat to decent white people: "We have never believed him to be equal to the white man," Tillman said in one of his more moderate speeches, "and we will not submit to gratifying his lust on our wives and daughters without lynching him. I would to God the last one of them was in Africa and that none of them had ever been brought to our shores."

Tillman's formula—race baiting plus legislation aiding poor whites—worked. As governor, he regulated railroad rates, raised taxes on the wealthy, and spent the revenue on improving public schools. In 1895, he led the fight for a new state constitution that virtually eliminated South Carolina's last few African American voters. Politicians in every southern state imitated him and were usually successful. Tom Watson of Geogia, who had called for biracial cooperation as a Populist, out-Tillmaned Tillman as a race baiter after 1900 whence Georgia's Democrats, his old enemies, rewarded him with a seat in the Senate.

Disenfranchise-
ment
Between 1889 and the early 1900s, every southern state adopted one or another device to ensure that few blacks voted. Several states enacted poll taxes: In order to vote, a man had to pay a tax of one or two dollars each year. On the face of it, the poll tax applied to whites as well as blacks. However, in some states, the poll tax was cumulative. Blacks who had not voted out of fear before the poll tax took effect found that they did not need a dollar on election day; they needed $20.

Alabama's, Louisiana's, North Carolina's, and Georgia's "grandfather clause" ensured that the poll tax kept blacks but not poor whites from the polls. Grandfather clauses provided that if a voter's grandfather had been eligible to vote prior to 1867, he could vote without paying the tax. Of course, no African American's grandfather had been eligible to vote before Reconstruction. Grandfather clauses worked for a decade and more. However, because they transparently discriminated on the basis of race, the Supreme Court ruled them unconstitutional in 1915.

Literacy tests were more effective in disenfranchising blacks because there was no overt racial component in them. Seven southern states required that a voter had to demonstrate that he could read. In 1900, 50 percent of southern black men were illiterate, but just 12 percent of whites. Illiterate white men—loyal supporters of the racist rabble-rousers—were able to evade the reading requirement by opting to take an "understanding" test. Registrars read them a passage from the state constitution. If they demonstrated that they understood its meaning, they could vote. With broad discretionary powers in their friendly county courthouses, registrars could and did accept all explanations of the state constitution by whites, on many occasions to the laughter of others present. They could, easily enough, find disqualifying "misunder-standings" in African American answers. The introduction of secret ballots in the 1890s and 1900s eliminated black voters in states without a literacy test because voters were required to be alone in the curtained polling booths.

In Mississippi in 1888, 29 percent of black men eligible to vote voted; in 1892 only 2 percent did; in 1895 none at all. In Louisiana in 1895, 95.6 percent of black men eligible to register as voters were in fact registered; after just two years of discriminatory legislation, only 9.1 percent were. (In 1914: 1.1 percent.) There were 180,000 black registered voters in Alabama in 1900, in 1903 there were 3,000.

Lynch Law
The conservative Redeemers made some effort to quash social instability—mob action of which the worst kind was lynching. Populistic racist politicians of the Ben Tillman stripe looked the other

Booker T. Washington, who was born a slave, was Frederick Douglass's successor as unofficial leader-spokesman of African Americans. Unlike Douglass (and W.E.B. DuBois and Martin Luther King Jr. after him), Washington urged blacks to live with social discrimination and even (in the South) exclusion from participation in politics. Their goal, Washington said, should be education, particularly in the "agricultural and mechanical arts," and economic advancement.

way. Consequently the final years of the 1890s and the early 1900s were an era of runaway lynch law in the South.

In 1890, 85 African Americans were lynched, almost all of them in the southern states, at least half of them because they were accused of raping a white woman. In 1892, with the agrarian revolt at white heat, 161 blacks were lynched. In only two of the years between 1890 and 1902, were fewer than 100 blacks mutilated, hanged, and incinerated by white mobs. No one feared prosecution. Law officers found they had duties elsewhere when they heard rumors that a lynch mob was forming. Some county sheriffs, who had been elected by the poor whites in the mobs, left jailhouses unlocked so they would not be bothered by repairs. Lynchings were often photographed; the faces of the people gathered around the hanging corpse were clearly recognizable. Few photos were used as evidence in court; lynching trials were rare. More likely, the photographs were printed on postcards and sold as souvenirs. A few lynchings were actually announced in advance. In one case in Georgia, spectators chartered a train to transport them to the hanging of a black man. In Oklahoma in 1911, a woman was lynched when she tried to protect her teenage son.

Most middle- and upper-class southern whites were disgusted by lynching. In the age of the populist demagogue, however, they no longer ran county governments. And not every genteel, progressive southerner thought of lynching as a blot on the South. Rebecca Felton of Atlanta, a feminist and anti-alcohol crusader who lobbied for compulsory public education and state-financed child care facilities said that she would be glad to see lynchings "a thousand times a week" to protect white women.

The Atlanta Compromise   Frederick Douglass, generally regarded as African Americans' most important spokesman, died in 1895. By then, another man born a slave had risen to prominence. In 1881, Booker T. Washington was hired as the first president of Tuskegee Normal School for Negroes in Alabama. (A normal school was a teacher's college.)

Tuskegee was founded with public money but, as time passed, the Alabama legislature proved stingy with appropriations. Fortunately, Washington discovered that he was a virtuoso fund raiser. Moreover, he wanted to broaden Tuskegee's curriculum beyond teacher education. He cultivated millionaires who were sympathetic to blacks—John D. Rockefeller, Andrew Carnegie, railroader Collis P. Huntington, Julius Rosenwald of Sears Roebuck among others—and Tuskegee Institute became a private institution.

By 1895, Washington recognized that the gains African Americans had made since Reconstruction were going to be wiped out by disenfranchisement, Jim Crow laws, and terrorism. At a convention in Atlanta designed to promote investment in the South, he proposed a compact between southern whites and blacks that would benefit both races. African Americans would accept segregation. "In all things ... purely social," he said, "we can be as separate as the fingers, yet as one as the hand in all things essential to mutual progress." In return for black acquiescence in Jim Crow and disenfranchisement, he asked southern state governments and wealthy whites to fund mechanical, technical, and agricultural education for African Americans.

The southern elite embraced Washington's "Atlanta Compromise." So did most southern blacks. With half of the southern black population illiterate and all but a handful impoverished, few African Americans aspired to loftier places in society than their own farms or work that paid well. An urbane northern African American who had studied in Europe, W. E. B. DuBois, condemned Washington's compromise. DuBois wanted to step up the struggle for civil and social equality. He placed his hopes for the future in the creation of a black elite educated to be professionals. Washington did not object to blacks studying medicine, law, and the liberal arts, but he was more realistic than DuBois about the plight in which southern blacks found themselves. What Washington did not anticipate was that lynch mobs did not subscribe to the Atlanta Compromise. The incidence of poor white terrorism continued to rise.

Plessy v. Ferguson   In 1890, Louisiana enacted a law requiring railroads to provide separate accomodations on trains and in depots for the two races. Within two years, nine states followed suit. The railroads did not like the law; duplicate passenger cars added to their expenses. They agreed to cooperate with a committee of African Americans in New Orleans "to test the constitutionality of the separate car law" on the grounds it violated the "equal treatment" section of the Fourteenth Amendment. Homer Plessy, a light-skinned mulatto, agreed to violate the law. He bought a train ticket, sat in a "white" car, was ordered out by the railroad, and sued.

Plessy v. *Ferguson* reached the Supreme Court in 1896. By a vote of 7 to 1, the justices ruled that the Louisiana's segregation law was constitutional. So long as state and city governments, public utilities, and schools provided separate facilities for whites and blacks that were equal in quality, they did not violate the Constitution. The doctrine of "separate but equal" legitimized the Jim Crow laws already in existence and gave the southern states the go-ahead to enact yet more, which they did, hanging "white" and "colored" signs all over the South, on toilets, water fountains, sections of movie houses and county fair grandstands, and even providing separate but equal Bibles with which to swear in witnesses at a trial.

The Court that sanctioned Jim Crow segregation was neither a southern nor a Democratic court. Six of the nine justices were Republicans; six were raised or educated in New England; only two were from former slave states and one of them, John Marshall Harlan of Kentucky, was the sole dissenter on the court. In his blistering criticism of the *Plessy* decision, he wrote that, in abolishing slavery, the Thirteenth Amendment forbade "badges of servitude" such as the denial of access to any public facility on the basis of a person's race. Separate accomodations were inherently unequal. The Constitution, Harlan wrote, "is colorblind, and neither knows nor tolerates classes among citizens." That seven northern judges approved of Jim Crow laws indicates how thoroughly northern white and southern white attitudes toward African Americans had merged.

AN AMERICAN EMPIRE

William McKinley hoped for a quiet presidency. He expected to preside over the nation's recovery from the depression and, with the return of prosperity, an end to the political turmoil that destroyed his predecessor's reputation.

McKinley got his prosperity. By the time he was inaugurated in March 1897, the "economic indicators" showed signs of improvement. Peace and quiet were more elusive. As little as the role suited him, as little as he wanted the part, William McKinley led the United States into adventures overseas and the acquisition of colonies that transformed the republic into an imperial power.

An Industrial and Commercial Giant   In 1892, Europe's great powers upgraded their representatives in Washington to the rank of ambassador. It was their recognition of America's economic power. In 1890, the United States had surpassed Great Britain as the world's leading industrial power. American agricultural production was already the greatest in the world.

American merchant ships were familiar visitors in the world's most exotic ports. As early as 1844, the United States had signed a trade treaty with China. In 1854, a naval squadron under Commodore Matthew Perry anchored off Yokohama, Japan and threatened to bombard the city unless the Japanese agreed to abandon their centuries long isolation from the West.

In 1870, American exports totaled $320 million. By 1890, $857 million in goods were sold abroad each year, and not just agricultural produce. American manufacturers competed with European nations in sale of steel and textiles and led the pack in machinery sales. Standard Oil faced stiffer competition selling kerosene in the United States than it did abroad. Standard's trademark was recognized as universally as Coca Cola's distinctive script is today. Andrew Carnegie underbid every British steel maker to land a big order supplying armor plate to the Royal Navy. By the end of the century, the British government's telephones in London were American made as were most of the typewriters. Even the Populist Jerry Simpson urged the government to pursue foreign markets more aggressively: "American factories are making more than the American people can consume; American soil is producing more than they can consume.... The trade of the world must and shall be ours."

The United States was not, however, even a third-rate military power. Since the Civil War, the men in the United States army and navy had numbered between 30,000 and 34,000. In 1880, by comparison, Italy had 216,000 men in uniform, France 543,000, and Russia 791,000.

A Distaste for Colonialism   Congress reasoned that the United States did not need much of an army. Its 30,000 soldiers had been more than adequate in suppressing the plains Indians. The border with Canada was unfortified. Mexico was weak and, since the rise of the dictator Porfirio Diaz in 1877, stable and friendly. The oceans ensured that no distant power could threaten the United States without providing plenty of time in which to mobilize a larger force. Unlike Britain, France, Germany, Italy, and Japan, the United States had no restive colonial subjects who had to be kept in line by force. The few inhabitants of Alaska were contentedly American (or unaware that they were American). The stars and stripes flew over a few pinpoint Pacific islands acquired as sources of guano—fertilizer—but they were next to uninhabited.

There had been several serious attempts to acquire overseas possessions. During slavery days, hardly a year passed that southern extremists did not demand that Cuba be bought or taken from Spain. In 1869, the Grant administration negotiated a treaty of annexation with the Dominican Republic, but the Senate rejected it, in part because many Dominicans were black or of mixed race, in part because of the American tradition of opposition to colonialism. In 1893, President Cleveland quashed a Republican scheme to annex Hawai'i when his investigators learned that a large majority of Hawai'ians wanted to remain independent.

The anti-colonial tradition was alive and apparently well in 1897. So was the Monroe Doctrine's pledge that the United States would not interfere in foreign conflicts that did not threaten American interests. Not everyone regarded these principles as sacred, however. President McKinley, who did believe in them, found it advisable in his inaugural address to admonish Americans that "we must avoid the temptation of territorial expansion."

The Frontier Thesis   Who was being tempted? Some intellectuals, not only university professors but also intellectual politicos like Senator Henry Cabot Lodge, a Harvard Ph.D. soon to be senator; Albert

J. Beveridge of Indiana; a young New Yorker McKinley appointed Undersecretary of the Navy, Theodore Roosevelt; and a good many others. They were not organized, but many were linked by friendship and all were influenced by new ideas that were in the air.

One of those ideas was the "frontier thesis" propounded in 1893 by a young historian from the University of Wisconsin, Frederick Jackson Turner. Turner said that the existence of a frontier throughout American history, a place to which discontented Easterners could go to improve their lives, had served as a "safety valve" for American society. The beckoning frontier had released social and economic pressures that otherwise might have led to unrest and even rebellion. Turner attributed the vitality of American democracy to the frontier. Freed of constraints that had grown up in the settled states, the people of the West had led the way in extending the franchise and, recently in several states, allowing women to vote.

But there were foreboding implications in the frontier thesis. Turner himself had been attracted to his subject by the Census Bureau's announcement that, as of 1890, the frontier no longer existed. There was no vast area of unsettled land to attract the ambitious and restless, no more safety valve. (Turner had forgotten about Alaska but, then, so did just about every other American.) Did that mean that the United States would stagnate and begin to suffer the social dislocations and class conflicts endemic in Europe? Some concluded that it did—unless economic, social, and moral decline was averted by creating new frontiers in colonies overseas.

That meant taking control of alien populations of different races. White Americans needed no prompting to think of black Americans and Indians as people whose wishes could be ignored. That was an American tradition. Actively seeking out other "inferior" peoples to rule, however, was another matter.

Anglo-Saxons and Battleships

In two books of 1885, historian John Fiske and Congregationalist minister Josiah Strong faced the issue head on. They posited that the "Anglo-Saxon" peoples (the English and Americans) had been more successful in creating free, stable, and progressive governments than other peoples because they were racially superior (Fiske) or "divinely commissioned" to be rulers (Strong). It was no betrayal of American ideals to undertake the governance of others. There was a racial and religious duty to do so. A political scientist, John W. Burgess, stated flatly in 1890 that the right of self-government did not apply to dark-skinned peoples: "there is no human right to the status of barbarism." The British and French were doing their part in the cause of civilization; the Americans should do theirs.

In 1890, a book by naval Captain Alfred Thayer Mahan, *The Influence of Sea Power upon History,* argued that the greatest nations had been seafaring nations, countries with a dynamic overseas trade protected by a powerful navy. That, of course, described the paramount world power of the era, the British Empire. Mahan chided Americans for allowing their own navy to lapse into obsolescence and decay. In fact, a naval construction program was already underway when, in 1880, it was revealed that the American navy ranked twelfth in the world.

Steamships burned coal. If the United States was to have a navy capable of speeding to trouble spots anywhere in the world, especially in the Pacific, it was necessary to acquire islands, however valueless in other ways, to serve as coaling stations and good harbors at which to base ships. Already in 1887, the Kingdom of Hawai'i had granted the United States a lease on Pearl Harbor, the best Pacific port not already in a naval power's possession.

THE SPANISH-AMERICAN WAR

Cuba, Puerto Rico, and the Philippines were all that remained of Spain's once magnificent empire. And that remnant was tottering. Rebellion was chronic in the Philippines and Cuba. Until 1895, Spanish troops had been able to suppress rebels in both countries, driving their leaders into exile or to remote mountain fastnesses.

Cuban rebel leaders fled to the United States where they bought arms and smuggled them from Florida into Cuba to rebels who launched a major rebellion in 1895. Cuban agents in the United States then energetically and skillfully lobbied American politicians and editors to support the uprising.

The Cuban rebellion was a classic guerrilla war. The Spanish army—100,000 strong—controlled the cities of Havana and Santiago and the large towns. By day, Spanish regiments moved untroubled amongst an apparently docile peasantry. By night, however, field workers became guerrillas and attacked Spanish patrols. In the cities, saboteurs planted bombs. As always in guerrilla wars, atrocities were common. Spanish soldiers brutalized peasants in hostile areas; rebels tortured and murdered soldiers they had captured.

The Yellow Press   American public opinion favored the rebels. They were the underdogs and while Spain was no longer an autocracy, it was a monarchy and an ancestral enemy. Cuban propagandists successfully portrayed the rebels as heirs of the American War for Independence and proposed to establish a representative democracy on the island.

Sensing a hot issue that would sell newspapers, the heads of two fiercely competitive newspaper syndicates, William Randolph Hearst and Joseph Pulitzer, adopted the rebels. Hearst and Pulitzer were sensationalists, the tabloid publishers of the day. They pioneered the abundant use of illustrations in daily newspapers, big sports sections, and the comic strip—anything that might entice buyers. Flashy reporters squeezed the most lurid publishable details out of murder trials and sex scandals. Pulitzer created the "invented" news story. In 1889, his New York *World* sent Elizabeth S. "Nellie Bly" Cochrane around the world to break the record of the fictional hero of Jules Verne's novel *Around the World in Eighty Days*. (She did it, in seventy-two days, six hours, and eleven minutes.) The cynical sensationalism was called "yellow journalism." Respectable society scorned Hearst's and Pulitzer's journalism but the newspaper sold.

Reporting on Spanish atrocities in Cuba came naturally to the yellow press. The Spanish military commander in Cuba, Valeriano Weyler, was dubbed "The Butcher" for his repressive policies, which included the establishment of concentration camps. But real suffering was not enough for Hearst and Pulitzer. They transformed innocuous and imagined incidents into horror stories. One large front-page drawing showed Spanish soldiers and customs officials leering at a naked American woman. The picture was based on a real incident except that the woman, suspected of smuggling, had been

When a War Was Popular

William Allen White remembered the excitement when war was declared on Spain: "Everywhere over this good, fair land, flags were flying ... crowds gathered to hurrah for the soldiers and to throw hats into the air." The cry was, "Remember the Maine; to hell with Spain."

When President McKinley called for 125,000 volunteers, the response was so great that 200,000 had to be turned away. Among the rejects was Buffalo Bill Cody who wrote a magazine article entitled "How I Could Drive the Spaniards out of Cuba with Thirty Thousand Indian Braves." That irked the War Department although, as things turned out, Cody could probably have made good his boast—if he could have found 30,000 braves still alive and fit. Martha A. Chute of Colorado got equally short shrift from the War Department when she offered to raise an all female regiment.

The 3rd Nebraska Volunteers commissioned William Jennings Bryan colonel, an act that probably ensured the unit would see no combat. As McKinley's likely opponent in the presidential election of 1900, Bryan could not have gotten a shot at military glory in Cuba if he had offered to pay his regiment's way there out of his own pocket.

Another Democrat who tried unsuccessfully to horn in on the war was publisher William Randolph Hearst. He offered to raise a regiment of professional boxers and baseball players. "Think of ... magnificent men of this ilk," he wrote. "They would overawe any Spanish regiment by their mere appearance." Leonard Wood (McKinley's personal physician) and Undersecretary of the Navy, Theodore Roosevelt, both good Republicans, stole Hearst's idea when they put together the 1st Volunteer Cavalry, the famous "Rough Riders" (they stole the name from Buffalo Bill). Roosevelt added cowboys from his North Dakota ranch to Hearst's mix but no Indians.

With so many comic opera elements and the easiest of victories, Secretary John Hay can be pardoned for calling the conflict a "splendid little war." The fighting in Cuba was over in three weeks. Puerto Rico was "conquered" with no resistance. Only 379 sailors and soldiers died in combat.

But the splendor of it all owed more to the ineptitude of Spanish officers and the demoralization of the men they commanded than to the performance of the American war machine. Had the United States been fighting South Africa's highly motivated Boers, as the British would be doing the very next year, John Hay would have held his tongue. American sailors and soldiers were brave, but little else about the war was glorious.

The War Department was entirely unprepared to equip and provision the 125,000 volunteers for which it called. Thousands of state militiamen and fresh searched quite properly in private by female officers. When Hearst artist Frederic Remington wired from Havana that everything was peaceful in Cuba and he wanted to come home, Hearst told him to stay: "You furnish the pictures. I'll furnish the war."

McKinley's Dark Hour McKinley wanted no part of the rebellion. He was a big business Republican, and American investors had about $50 million at stake in Cuba's railroads, mines, and sugar cane recruits were trained in subtropical Florida clothed in heavy woolen winter uniforms. There they discovered that "camp" was a hundred acres of marsh where the tents had not yet arrived and the latrines had not been dug. More troop trains arrived; crowding and sanitation became so bad that typhoid fever and dysentery incapacitated men by the tens of thousands and killed twelve of them for every one soldier killed in action.

The navy's two smashing victories owed more to surprise (Manila) and the pathetic obsolescence of Spanish warships (Santiago) than to any brilliance on the part of Commodore Dewey and Admiral Sampson. Indeed, their gunners were so inaccurate that, had their enemy been the Royal Navy, both American fleets would have been sunk.

Some junior army officers distinguished themselves. John J. Pershing, still a lieutenant at almost 40 years of age, commanded the Tenth U.S. Cavalry, one of four African American regiments in the regular army. Although Theodore Roosevelt's Rough Riders got the credit for capturing San Juan Hill, several observers said that they would have been massacred in their amateurish charge up the hill had the Tenth Cavalry not been positioned to their left. The Tenth, Pershing wrote deadpan in his official report, flanked the Spanish defenses, advancing "up the hill scarcely firing a shot and being nearest the Rough Riders opened a disastrous enfilading fire upon the Spanish right, thus relieving the Rough Riders from the volleys that were being poured into them from that part of the Spanish line."

The upper ranks of the officer corps were cluttered with deadwood, literally so in the case of the commander in Cuba, General William R. Shafter. Shafter weighed more than 300 pounds; he had not mounted a horse for years; he could not walk more than short distances without assistance. Cuba's tropical heat and humidity laid him on his back more hours than he was up and more or less around. The ossification of the army's generals was demonstrated a few years after the war when they refused the president's request to promote Pershing to major.

The "immunes," a sensible program when it was hatched, was botched by incompetent administrators. Worried about tropical diseases, the army authorized the selective recruitment of up to 10,000 young men who had grown up in low-lying parts of the South where malaria was endemic and yellow fever a regular visitor. If they had not been felled by those diseases by the ages of 18 or 20, the reasoning went, they must be immune to them.

Race did not figure in the design of the program, but the officers put in charge of it added a racial spin. They assumed that African Americans were inherently immune to tropical disease while whites were inherently vulnerable to it. So, they turned away white volunteers from the Louisiana bayous and the Florida swamps and accepted blacks from the Appalachians and even from urban New Jersey. About 4,000 of the 10,000 African Americans who served in the Spanish-American War were "immunes."

plantations. Their money was safe under Spanish rule, but who knew what would happen if the rebels were successful?

McKinley urged the Spanish to abandon the harshest of their policies and to liberalize the government of the island. With so many Americans calling for armed intervention (which McKinley said would be "criminal aggression"), a new administration in Madrid withdrew Weyler and promised Cuba autonomy within the Spanish Empire, a status comparable to Canada's within the British Empire.

That satisfied McKinley, but not the war hawks. On February 9, 1898, Hearst's New York *Journal* published a letter written by the Spanish ambassador in Washington, Enrique Dupuy de Lome, in which he said that McKinley was "weak, a bidder for the admiration of the crowd." It was by no means an inaccurate assessment of the president's personality. About the same time, Undersecretary of the Navy Theodore Roosevelt said that the president had the "backbone of a chocolate eclair."

That, and not the belief that Mark Hanna told the president what to do, was precisely the problem. McKinley trembled when he read critical headlines in the newspapers when he should have listened to Hanna. When he proposed to placate the yellow press by sending the battleship *Maine,* Hanna begged him not to do it. It was like "waving a match in an oil well," he told McKinley.

The president dispatched the ship and, on February 15, the *Maine* exploded and sank, killing 260 sailors. Who was responsible? Some believed that the Cuban rebels had planted a bomb to provoke the United States into declaring war on Spain. Some suspected that the explosion was the work of Spanish reactionaries who opposed the new liberal policies in Cuba. The yellow press, of course, bought the least credible explanation of the disaster, that a Spanish government that was bending over backwards to avoid war, had destroyed the *Maine.* (It is now known that the explosion was accidental, most likely caused by a fire in a coal bunker that spread to the powder magazine.)

McKinley continued to vacillate for a month and a half, flooding Spain with demands for a change of policy. As late as March 26, Hanna begged him on behalf of the business and banking community to keep the peace. On April 9, the Spanish government gave in to every demand McKinley had made. However, worried that preserving the peace might cost the Republicans control of Congress in the fall, McKinley caved in. On April 11, ignoring the Spanish capitulation, the president asked Congress for a declaration of war.

The "Splendid Little War"   The tiny U.S. Army was not up to launching a plausible overseas operation, but the spanking new navy was. As soon as war was official, Undersecretary of the Navy Theodore Roosevelt (the secretary was ill) ordered Commodore George Dewey, commanding a squadron of six ships in the Pacific, to attack the Spanish fleet stationed at Manila Bay in the Philippines. On May 1, with more and better guns, Dewey caught the Spanish completely unaware and destroyed all seven of their ships. The performance of Dewey's sailors was less than sparkling. Of the 6,000 rounds they fired, only 142 found their targets. But the news of the victory came as such a surprise back home that Dewey was lauded as the American Horatio Nelson.

In the Caribbean three weeks later, a small American flotilla bottled up four Spanish cruisers and three destroyers commanded by Admiral Pascual Cervera in the harbor of Santiago on Cuba's south coast. On July 3, Cervera tried to make a run for the open seas. Unfortunately for him, a major American task force including five battleships had arrived at Santiago two days earlier. In a four-hour battle, the Americans sent Cervera's entire fleet to the bottom. (Their marksmanship was worse than Dewey's; of 9,400 shells fired, just 142 were hits.)

Two days earlier—just in time—the army had gotten into the war. Some 17,000 regulars and volunteers attacked Spanish defensive positions at El Caney and on San Juan Hill west of Santiago. If many of the Americans were inadequately trained, the Spanish troops were demoralized. They were quickly defeated.

San Juan Hill gave flag-waving Americans a hero second in popularity only to Commodore Dewey. Theodore Roosevelt had resigned from the Navy Department and helped organize a volunteer cavalry regiment called the "Rough Riders." (They stole the name from Buffalo Bill.) Newspapermen loved the unit because some of its soldiers were cowboys, others boxers and professional baseball players. Colonel Roosevelt, already a favorite of New York reporters as an exuberant publicity hound, was second in command.

The Rough Riders, cowboys included, fought on foot because their horses were still in Tampa, but their charge up San Juan Hill was undeniably fearless, even reckless. Roosevelt returned quickly to the United States where (he was a superb writer), he dashed off a popular book that, amused friends observed, depicted San Juan Hill as the key event of the war and Roosevelt as the key to taking San Juan Hill. Eyewitnesses of the battle said that the Rough Riders would have been massacred had the professional Ninth and Tenth U.S. Cavalry regiments, on their left flank, not enfiladed the Spanish position with rapid rifle fire. But the Rough Riders got all the credit; the Ninth and Tenth Cavalry were African American units.

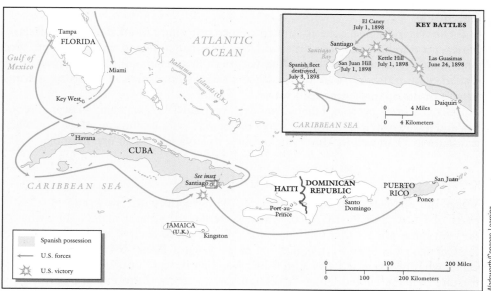

MAP 32.2 The War in Cuba

As in the Philippines, the war in Cuba was largely the navy's war. When, after San Juan Hill the army prepared to attack Santiago, Cuba's second largest city, Admiral Pascual Cervera's fleet attempted to make a run for the high seas. However, American Admiral William T. Sampson anticipated Cervera's action and destroyed the Spanish fleet outside Santiago harbor.

A few days after San Juan Hill, Congress annexed the Republic of Hawai'i by means of the same device by which Texas was annexed in 1844: a joint resolution with the Hawai'ian legislature.

Hawai'i had been a party issue since 1893 when newly elected Democratic President Grover Cleveland repudiated an agreement between the Harrison administration and a small oligarchy of the descendants of American missionaries who had overthrown the Hawai'ian queen, Liliuokalani, with the help of American marines.

The oligarchy, rich sugar planters, had happily ruled Hawai'i during the reign of Liliuokalani's brother and predecessor, the affable playboy David Kalakaua. However, they were hit hard in the pocketbook when the McKinley tariff of 1890 virtually shut their sugar out of the American market. Then, in 1891, Queen Lil came to the throne and announced that she meant to preserve Hawai'ian culture by abrogating some of the privileges the rich *haoles* (white people) enjoyed. She pronounced "Hawai'i for the Hawai'ians" the theme of her reign, and she was immensely popular with native Hawai'ians who not only resented the rich *haole* landowners but also felt threatened by the increasing numbers of Japanese plantation workers on the islands.

Aided by the American ambassador and 159 marines from the USS *Boston,* the oligarchy took control and overthrew Queen Lil. "The Hawaiian pear is now fully ripe ... for the United States to pluck it," the American minister informed Washington. A treaty of annexation was on the table when Cleveland was inaugurated, and he withdrew it.

The oligarchy had gone too far to chance restoring Liliuokalani. They declared Hawai'i a republic and bided their time as long as Cleveland was president. With McKinley's election in 1896 and the war with Spain fanning patriotic fires in the United States, Hawai'i was annexed and declared an American territory, a fringe benefit of the Spanish-American war.

Given a small pension, Liliuokalani lived on until 1917, watching Hawai'i become less and less Hawai'ian. When she wrote the islands' famous anthem, *Aloha Oe,* which translates as "Farewell to Thee," she meant it to have more than one meaning.

EMPIRE BUILDING

When the Spanish gave up in August 1898, American troops occupied Manila, parts of Cuba, and Puerto Rico, which surrendered without a fight. But what to do with these prizes? McKinley had asked Congress to declare war in April to free the Cubans from Spanish rule, nothing more. Senator Henry M. Teller of Colorado called what he suspected was a bluff by amending the resolution supporting the war to state that the United States "disclaims any ... intention to exercise sovereignty, jurisdiction, or control over said island except for pacification thereof, and asserts its determination when that is accomplished to leave the government and control of the island to its people."

So Cuba was to be independent, but what of the Philippines and Puerto Rico? Teller had not mentioned those Spanish colonies because they had not figured in the three months of discussions that led up to the war. Indeed, Americans, President McKinley included, knew less about the Philippines than they knew about life on Mars. When the president got the news of Dewey's victory at Manila Bay, he could not locate the islands on a globe. An aide had to point them out to him, tactfully.

By Jingo Imperialism
That was before the war. In August, when Spain called for a truce, jingos in Congress and the press put the heat on McKinley to annex Puerto Rico and the Philippines. A few of the "imperialists" were more or less fatalistic about the Philippines. Having shattered Spain's hold on the islands, they said, the United States could not simply pull out. There would be a civil war between *insurrectos* and Spanish loyalists, and Japan or Germany or both would move in.

A more typical and effective annexationist was Albert J. Beveridge of Indiana who, in 1898, ran for and won a seat in the Senate. In eloquent, tub-thumping rhetoric in his "March of the Flag" speech (a more significant oration than Bryan's Cross of Gold), he declared that Americans had a religious and racial duty to govern peoples who were incapable of governing themselves. Beveridge popularized the ten-year-old preachments of the intellectuals Fiske and Strong: "God has not been preparing the English-speaking and Teutonic peoples for a thousand years for nothing but vain and idle self-contemplation and self-admiration." He had made them "the master organizers of the world."

Beveridge and others like him incubated an annexation fever that infected Congress and the public. It was a repeat of the war with Spain mania that McKinley had been incapable of resisting in the spring. This time, McKinley displayed his ignorance publicly. He said that he decided to support annexation of the Philippines so that the United States could bring Christianity to the islands. Ninety percent of the Philippine population was already Christian.

The Anti-Imperialists
The treaty with Spain, signed in Paris in October 1898, transferred the Philippines to the United States, but ratification by the Senate was far from certain. Anti-imperialists, many of whom had opposed the war, mobilized quickly. They were a diverse lot. In Congress, the anti-annexationists included the ancient radical Republican George F. Hoar of Massachusetts; one time liberal Republican Carl Schurz; the ultra-conservative Speaker of the House, Thomas B. Reed; and the populistic racist Democrat, Ben Tillman of South Carolina. Free silverite Henry Teller of Colorado became a Democrat because of his disgust with McKinley's imperialism.

Outside of Congress, William Jennings Bryan asked that ratification of the treaty with Spain be put off until after the election of 1900 when the American people could express their views. Novelists Samuel L. Clemens (Mark Twain) and William Dean Howells, who had avoided political controversies throughout their careers, opposed annexation, as did popular journalists Ambrose Bierce and Finley Peter Dunne. Other members of the Anti-Imperialist League included former president Cleveland, scholars William James and John Dewey, social worker Jane Addams, steel magnate Andrew Carnegie, and labor leader Samuel Gompers.

Rarely has politics made for a stranger bunch of bedfellows. The anti-imperialists were also a distinguished lot and, on the face of it, influential.

Nevertheless, in February 1899, the Senate voted 57–27 to pay Spain $20 million for the Philippines.

The Philippine Insurrection

As usual, Thomas B. Reed was ready with a witticism although there was nothing frivolous about his message. "We have bought ten million Malays at two dollars a head unpicked," he said, "nobody knows what it will cost to pick them." Indeed, unlike the war with Spain, the pacification of the Philippines was neither easy, cheap, nor glorious. The Philippine *insurrectos,* led by Emilio Aguinaldo, a well-educated patriot as comfortable in the jungle as in the library, withdrew from Manila and other American-occupied cities and fought the troops as the Cuban rebels had fought the Spanish, guerrilla style.

The American army of occupation, 65,000 men by 1900, found itself playing the same role that Americans had called disgraceful and barbarous when Spanish soldiers were in the role in Cuba, responding to *insurrecto* atrocities with their own. The rebels frequently decapitated soldiers they captured. The Americans, frustrated by their failures, the tropical heat, insects, and diseases, retaliated by slaughtering whole villages thought to support the rebels.

The army never did defeat the *insurrectos.* The rebellion ended only when, in March 1901, Colonel Frederick C. Funston (who had fought side by side with Cuban rebels) made a prisoner of Aguinaldo by means of a daring and clever trick. Weary of the bloodshed, Aguinaldo took an oath of allegiance to the United States and ordered his followers to do the same. (He lived to see Philippine independence in 1946.) More than 5,000 Americans died in the cause of suppressing a popular revolution, a queer twist in a conflict that began, three years earlier, in support of a popular revolution.

McKinley Murdered

In 1900, the Democrats nominated William Jennings Bryan to run against McKinley. He tried to make imperialism the issue, but with the American flag flying over Hawai'i, Puerto Rico, the Philippines, and Guam (a former Spanish island in the Marianas), it was too late. Americans were either happy having overseas possessions or simply uninterested. McKinley emphasized prosperity; the Republican slogan was "Four More Years of the Full Dinner Pail." Dinner pails carried the day. Several states that had voted Democratic-Populist in 1896 went Republican in 1900, including Bryan's own state of Nebraska and once "revolutionary" Kansas.

There was a new vice president. Theodore Roosevelt had parleyed his San Juan Hill fame into the governorship of New York. There he alienated the state's Republican boss by openly chastising corrupt members of Platt's organization. Fortuitously, McKinley's vice president had died late in 1899 and Platt seized on the vacant office as his best chance of getting rid of Roosevelt before he did any more mischief.

He urged McKinley to choose Roosevelt as his running mate and bury him in the obscurity of the vice presidency. Mark Hanna vehemently opposed the idea. He begged the president to act responsibly, to put the interests of the country ahead of the interests of the New York Republican party. If McKinley died, the maniac Roosevelt would be president.

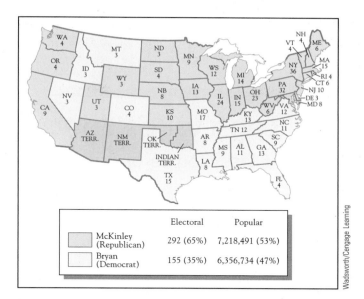

Wadsworth/Cengage Learning

		Electoral	Popular
	McKinley (Republican)	292 (65%)	7,218,491 (53%)
	Bryan (Democrat)	155 (35%)	6,356,734 (47%)

MAP 32.3 Presidential Election of 1900

By 1900, the West's long agricultural depression was finally over and McKinley was still basking in the easy defeat of Spain in 1898. Bryan won almost as many popular votes as he had four years earlier, but McKinley increased his totals and won majorities in the plains states, including once Populist Kansas and Bryan's Nebraska.

The 60-year-old president was in good health. But two presidents had been assassinated within his and Hanna's lifetime. When McKinley approved Roosevelt's nomination, Hanna told the president, "It is your duty to your country to live another four years."

As Hanna feared, McKinley's life was in another man's hands. On September 6, 1901, the president paid a ceremonial visit to the Pan-American Exposition in Buffalo. Greeting a long line of guests, he found himself faced by a man extending a bandaged hand. The gauze concealed a large bore pistol. The president was shot point-blank twice, in the chest and abdomen. Leon Czolgosz, a rather pathetic figure, told police that he was an anarchist who "didn't believe one man should have so much service and another man should have none." Eight days later, McKinley died. "Now look," Hanna shook his head at the funeral, "that damned cowboy is president."

33

TEDDY ROOSEVELT'S AMERICANS
The Middle Class Comes of Age 1890–1917

He played all his cards—if not more.
—Oliver Wendell Holmes Jr.

The universe seemed to be spinning round, and Theodore was the spinner.
—Rudyard Kipling

And never did a President before so reflect the quality of his time.
—H. G. Wells

Vice President Roosevelt was roughing it in a cabin in New York's Adirondacks when a man came hurrying toward him up a mountain trail. Roosevelt knew what it meant. He had just visited the wounded McKinley. Either because the doctors told him the president was recovering—which seemed to be so for a day—or because Roosevelt did not want to hover about like a ghoul, he left and resumed his vacation.

Just six months earlier, Roosevelt believed his political career had ended. The vice presidency was a dead-end job. New York's Republican boss, Tom Platt, had arranged his nomination as McKinley's running mate in order to bury him politically. Now it was McKinley who was being buried and Platt was facing the loss of his political pull with the "damned cowboy" at the top of the heap at just 42 years of age.

A NEW KIND OF PRESIDENT

"It is a dreadful thing to come into the presidency in this way," Roosevelt told a friend, "but it would be a far worse thing to be morbid about it." Roosevelt had been morbid only once in his life and then briefly. When his young wife died suddenly in 1884, he fled to the wilds of Dakota Territory to recover from his grief.

Entertainment 1885–1910

1885	1890	1895	1900	1905	1910

1885 Safety bicycle launches craze

1889–1890 Nelly Bly goes around the world

1891 Invention of basketball

1892 Jim Corbett beats John L. Sullivan

1893 Chicago World's Fair

1898 Steeplechase Park at Coney Island

1903 First World Series

1904 St. Louis World's Fair

Jack Johnson heavyweight champion 1908

He did. Within two years he had a new wife and was running for mayor of New York City. No Republican had a chance of winning the election, but the party compensated Roosevelt for taking the fall by naming him Civil Service Commissioner. It was not a high-profile job, but it put Roosevelt in Washington where he made the acquaintance of just about all the Republican party's national big shots.

Roosevelt next served as New York City's police commissioner, which was better than high profile. He regularly made a splash in the newspapers when he accompanied club-swinging cops on raids of brothels, gambling dens, and illegal saloons. Reporters loved it. Then, in rapid succession, the Navy Department, the war with Spain, ordering Dewey to Manila Bay, the self-celebrated heroics on San Juan Hill, New York's governorship, the unwanted vice presidency, and McKinley's assassination. It was a whirlwind career.

The Bumptious Patrician Roosevelt was a human whirlwind. He was energetic and excitable. When he quoted an African proverb—"walk softly and carry a big stick"—friends remarked that they had often seen Theodore wildly waving clubs about, but they could not recall him walking softly or even slowly. He did not walk as much as he marched, like a child who knows that everyone is watching him. The resemblance was not lost on those who knew him. "You must remember," a British diplomat told a friend to whom he was about to introduce Roosevelt, "that the president is about six." On the president's 46th birthday, the Secretary of War congratulated him on behalf of the cabinet: "You have made a very good start in life, and your friends have great hopes for you when you grow up."

The extrovert was a patrician, well bred on both sides. His mother was a plantation belle from Georgia. On his father's side, his Dutch ancestors dated to New York's New Netherlands days. His personal friends were from the same social circle: genteel Knickerbockers like himself; Boston Brahmins like Henry Cabot Lodge; proper Philadelphians like author Owen Wister; and old family Connecticut Yankees like Gifford Pinchot.

Roosevelt was rich. Not in the way that the Vanderbilts and Rockefellers were rich; his inherited income was enough that he could live luxuriously without having to think about earning money. He never held a job for its pay, and he had

Theodore Roosevelt, "the bride at every wedding and the corpse at every funeral." If any other president enjoyed being president as much as Teddy Roosevelt did, none displayed his pleasure so openly. When Iron Age magazine, a trade journal, reported that he was constantly drunk, Roosevelt sued for libel and won. In fact, he drank very little, sips only to be polite. He certainly did not need alcohol to shed his inhibitions.

little interest in making money passively. "I don't care a damn about stocks and bonds," he said and he did not; he had other things that interested him, a great many of them.

Like others listed in the *Social Register* ("one must not be 'employed'; one must make application; and one must be above reproach"), Roosevelt looked with some distaste on the ever-hustling, endlessly acquisitive, single-minded, and self-made multimillionaires of the era. As a class, they had bumped patricians like Roosevelt from the top of the pyramid of riches, but Roosevelt's people had their own gated community where residents were defined by their ancestry, their culture, and the schools and colleges they had attended. They were not averse to marrying daughters of first-generation multimillionaires; the gates to the patriciate could be opened by presentation of a substantial dowry.

Roosevelt's circle also looked disdainfully on the professional politicos who had rudely elbowed them out of the public offices that, in the Northeastern states, they had looked on as entitlements. So, when Roosevelt ran for a seat in the New York assembly in 1882, his friends were mildly scandalized. Was Theodore really going to sit down in smoky rooms with vote-chasing hacks who, when they were Republicans, were a little less vulgar and a little less corrupt than Irish Democrats but were, nonetheless, not the sort to whom one introduced one's sister?

Roosevelt was. Snob that he was in his heart, he mixed, bickered, and made deals with New York's politicos without flinching. They were less at ease around him than he was with them. So boundless was his self-assurance that, as governor and president, he did not hesitate to scold the industrial and financial titans to whom other politicians toadied. It was this spunkiness that made the privileged Roosevelt so appealing to middle-class Americans. They feared what big business's big money was doing to the country, and they delighted in Roosevelt's style.

Teddy Roosevelt's presidential style was without a precedent; and none of his successors has been so foolish as to attempt to imitate it. No president of the late nineteenth century had so priggish a public persona as William McKinley had, but all of them, even the unpretentious Ulysses S. Grant, maintained a solemnity in the way they walked, talked, and sat in a chair in public.

The frenetic Roosevelt found sitting difficult at all times, even when he was dining. He had little interest in food and drink, preferring to carry the conversation while others ate and drank. He dominated every room in which he found himself. "Father," one of his children observed, "must be the bride at every wedding and the corpse at every funeral." He stormed about the country, flashing huge smiles and waving gaily to crowds like fellow performer Lillian Russell, the most celebrated singer-actress of the era. He erupted "Bully! Bully!" when something pleased him. He threatened those he disliked with horrible retribution. He courted journalists, inviting them to watch him living what he called "the strenuous life," riding recklessly at a gallop (and he was not a very good horseman), camping, hunting, hiking, climbing mountains. When a motion-picture cameraman asked him to move, he picked up an axe and chopped down an unoffending tree.

THE NEW MIDDLE CLASS

Roosevelt could not have known it in 1901, but what came naturally to him made him the perfect president for the new century. The values and manners of the American middle class had changed gradually, but radically during the 1880s and 1890s. If William McKinley had not been murdered, his stodginess would have worn thin on the new middle class before his second term ended. But the large middle class centered in American cities and towns did not tire of Roosevelt. They loved his bumptiousness. When a toy maker named a stuffed bear doll after the president—the "teddy bear"—few parents who could afford to spend a few dollars casually failed to buy one for their children. For a year or two, it was fashionable for well-to-do women to clutch one of the dolls when they rode in their carriages or promenaded in the park. People called the president "Teddy" (he did not like the name) and "TR." He was the first president to be routinely identified by his initials.

Comfort and Respectability Then as now, the middle class was largely defined by income. Middle-class families were not rich; they did not, like TR, live luxuriously without earning. "Father" had to work, long hours often. But his "take-home" was sufficient to keep his family in a comfortable home. A large home, a "Victorian," because at a time before labor-saving home appliances—refrigerators, washing machines, vacuum cleaners, and so on—middle-class families had live-in servants to spare the lady of the house the most onerous housekeeping chores. Maids kept the place clean and tidy, did the laundry, and served tea to visitors; a handyman-gardener-stable hand might also drive the family carriage; a cook prepared meals; a nursemaid watched the younger children.

The middle class included the owners of small businesses and the well-paid managerial and technical employees of large ones. Ministers, lawyers, physicians, pharmacists, accountants, engineers, public officials, teachers, professors in college towns, newspaper editors belonged to the middle class by virtue of their educations even when their incomes were less than grand.

To an extent, "respectability" trumped income. Some white-collar employees—people who did not get their hands dirty on the job—were middle class by their own lights and they were accepted as such if they shared the "bourgeois values" and good manners of the financially more secure.

The middle class broadly defined was numerically significant, as politicians would learn after 1900. Independent businessmen and women are difficult to count accurately, but they were numerous, more so when prosperous farmers are included. In addition, there were more than 1.2 million professionals in the United States in 1900; 1.7 million managers; 1.3 million people involved in sales of one kind or another; and at least 5 million white-collar employees.

Propriety

There was a well-understood middle-class code of conduct. Men did not drop in at a saloon to have a beer. Saloons were by definition unrespectable. The cleanest and most orderly of them were the social clubs of workingmen. The saloon was intimately associated with corrupt political machines in big cities. A middle-class gent might drink a beer at a Fourth of July picnic; a middle-class lady out shopping might, by the 1890s, drink a cocktail (this a new word) in the dining room of a refined hotel, but otherwise never in public.

Middle-class men and women spoke grammatical English in modulated tones. They did not swear or raise their voices (except at baseball games). They were genteel. Middle-class men did not leave the house or even answer the door "in shirtsleeves." If a man had removed his jacket to relax and read the newspaper and there was a knock, he put his coat back on before seeing who was there. On the street he wore a hat, never a cap, which was a working man's topper. Middle-class women primped at great length before they went out, even to walk just a block to the greengrocer's. If a woman was canning peaches or busy at some other housekeeping chore when visitors arrived, she had them wait in the parlor while she washed and powdered her face, arranged her hair, and donned an appropriate gown rather than let them see her disheveled and short of breath.

Women and men, at least in mixed company, did not discuss certain subjects, notably the bodily functions. Even to mention sweating was taboo although everyone present might be soaked with perspiration. Some of the era's proprieties, such as clothing piano legs in frilly skirts because, bare, they resembled human legs, draw laughter today. Other decencies of the era are still with us although we have forgotten that they were originally delicate euphemisms. At Thanksgiving dinner, we say "pass the white meat, please" or the "dark meat." Those terms date from the later nineteenth century when one did not utter the words "breast," "leg," or "thigh" in company, even in reference to a roasted turkey. Respectable people did not mention the horse manure that was everywhere, fouling the hems of women's long skirts. They looked without comment in another direction if the dogs or ducks they had been watching decided to copulate. When children asked "what are they doing?" they were awkwardly whisked away by a blushing mother or nanny.

Many middle-class women seem not to have discussed sex among themselves. Diaries and memoirs of the era record instances of brides who had no inkling of what to expect from their husbands when they were married. When the older sister of one bride-to-be took her aside to explain what she would do on her wedding night, the bride exploded angrily at what she thought was an unspeakable joke.

Religion

Majority of middle-class people were probably church-going Protestants. They believed in the basics of Christianity, some devoutly, but they had no interest in the squabbling over doctrine that had destroyed families and friendships and divided communities in hostile camps for generations. Religion did not drive their lives as it had driven the abolitionists, and other evangelical reformers. When many middle-class Americans of the age of Teddy Roosevelt joined the movement to prohibit alcohol in the United States, they did so not because drinking was sinful but because it was social destructive and linked to political corruption.

Middle-class people were not "fundamentalist," a word coined in 1909. Their preferred churches were what today are called the "mainstream" denominations: Episcopalian, Presbyterian, Congregationalist, Unitarian. They were distinguished by the quiet refinement of their ministers who emphasized ethics in their sermons. There were middle-class Methodist churches but the ministers of them were themselves restrained; they did not think to poke aggressively into the personal lives of their flocks as their predecessors had.

Calvinism was dead. There was no place in middle-class religion for universal depravity, infant damnation, hell's fire sermons, hysterical revivals, or new enthusiasms like the speaking in tongues of the Pentecostal and Holiness movement. All those things were still going strong, but only among the uneducated lower classes, the ignorant denizens of Appalachia and "naturally emotional" Negroes. "The right kind of religion," wrote the popular author Edgar Watson Howe, tongue-in-cheek but not inaccurately, "put flowers in the yard, let sunlight in at the window, and fills the house with content and happiness."

The middle class was keenly sensitive to the fact that Jews were different and approved the fact that social clubs, neighborhoods, and hotels were "restricted"—restricted to Christians. But they were not consumed by anti-Semitism. They were leery of Catholicism but mostly on a social basis: In the United States almost all Roman Catholics were working class. Few objected when the local Catholic bishop was invited to sit on the dais at community events.

Morality

The moral code had not changed. The Ten Commandments were fully in force in middle-class America. The line between right and wrong in personal behavior was as clearly drawn as ever. Sexual morality was particularly inflexible, reinforced as it was by the importance the middle class placed on propriety and distinguishing themselves from the working class. Young people were sternly admonished to preserve their virginity until marriage, perhaps more for social than religious reasons. Adultery was worse than fornication because it struck at the family.

In practice, the sexual code was stricter for girls and women than for boys and men. Young men were discouraged from "sowing their wild oats" with prostitutes or sluttish working class girls, but those who did so were excused. Middle-class girls who slipped (and were discovered) did not get off so easily. A girl who found herself pregnant was bundled away on a long visit to "an aunt" in a distant state. Everyone knew what that euphemism meant—she was at a "home for wayward girls" where she would deliver her baby and put it up for adoption—but it was mentioned only in whispers and never to the girl's family. When an adultery was exposed—usually in a divorce suit—the gent involved might survive socially but his best friend's wife would not. The "double standard"—okay for men, forbidden to women—was emphatically the middle-class's standard.

In most matters, however, the people of the new middle class were worldly, even urbane. Diversions that had been widely considered sinful just a few decades earlier were shrugged off as "innocent pleasures": a game of cards; dancing; singing frivolous songs from Tin Pan Alley ("Ta-Ra-Ra-Boom-De-Ay," "Hot Time in the Old Town," "Take Me Out to the Ball Game"); going out to the ball game—even on Sunday; attending theaters; spending a day at the amusement park; spending a month at the seashore. Some clergymen fussed and fumed when mixed groups of teenagers bicycled off together unchaperoned, but the hordes of them in the parks in the mid-1890s tell us that their respectable parents did not.

AN EDUCATED PEOPLE

The middle class that came into its own with the sudden rise of Theodore Roosevelt was well educated. Their political pressures during the final decades of the nineteenth century not only expanded the American public school system but also reshaped the course of study. In increasing numbers, the middle class sent its sons and daughters to colleges and universities that had been preserves of the rich and young men training for the ministry before the Civil War. Book readership soared as middle-class women especially had time to read. The middle class supported a burgeoning daily press (as did the working class, albeit different newspapers). Middle-class families subscribed to genteel, well-established monthly magazines like *Harper's* and the *Atlantic Monthly* and provided the market for a slew of new general-interest periodicals that published fiction; professionally researched and written articles about exotic places and current events; and, by 1900, exposés of the malfeasances of businessmen, political corruption, and social problems.

Secondary Schools   Elementary schools—reading, writing, and arithmetic schools— were almost (not quite) universal before the Civil War. Secondary schools were not. In 1860, there had been about 300 high schools in the United States; only 100 of them were tax supported. There were actually more American colleges than high schools until about 1880.

Beginning about 1880, the number of secondary schools multiplied rapidly. In 1880 there were about 800 public high schools in the United States, by 1900 there were 6,000, by 1915 12,000. Educational expenditures per pupil increased from about $9 a year to $48. This explosion of educational opportunities was the middle class's doing. Middle-class families wanted their brighter sons prepared for university study and others prepared for vocations in business, government, or education.

Fewer middle-class girls were taken out of school once they had mastered the "three Rs." Literacy was enough for a farmer's or workingman's wife, but not for a town or city girl expected to maintain her social standing. When business replaced letters and records written longhand with more readable typewritten documents (the typewriter was first mass-produced by the Remington Firearms Company in 1874), high schools introduced typing classes to prepare young people for clean, respectable, white-collar clerical work. As early as 1880, 40 percent of employed typists were female. By 1910, typing was women's work; 81 percent of typists were female (by 1930, 96 percent were).

"Normal Schools," teacher training institutions that were beyond high schools but not quite colleges, opened doors to self-supporting respectability to single women. There were 90,000 female teachers in the United States in 1870. By 1890, 250,000 women were teachers, a figure that is all the more remarkable because, while men who married could still teach, most schools insisted that women who married resign their positions. The turnover was, of course, tremendous.

Colleges and Universities Except at a few polytechnic institutes, college courses conformed to the ancient liberal arts curriculum: Latin and Greek, classical literature and philosophy, ancient history, some mathematics. It did not prepare students for a career (except for aspiring ministers, for whom a healthy dose of true religion was added to the course load). The justification of a liberal arts education was that it was part of what made a gentleman. It was an elitist concept with which middle-class people, who lacked that other prerequisite to gentlemanhood, an inherited income, were uncomfortable.

Readily available practical education began with the Morrill Land Grant Act of 1862. Congress gave each state large tracts of the public domain which legislatures were required to use to finance universities paying particular attention to "such branches of learning as are related to agriculture and mechanic arts"—engineering. Many western state universities considered among the nation's best today originated as land grant institutions.

Gilded Age millionaires competed for esteem as patrons of learning by constructing college buildings and endowing scholarships and professorial chairs at older institutions. Some pumped so much money into struggling colleges, often on condition that they diversify their course offerings, that they were able to put their names on them: Trinity College in North Carolina became Duke after its benefactor, tobacco magnate James Buchanan Duke.

Millionaires founded completely new universities. Drew (1866), Johns Hopkins (1876), Vanderbilt (1872), Stanford (1885), and Carnegie Institute of Technology (1905) bear the names of the moguls who financed them. In Philadelphia, Success Gospel preacher Russell B. Conwell established Temple University in 1884 explicitly to educate poor boys ambitious to improve themselves. John D. Rockefeller pumped millions into the University of Chicago (1890). George Eastman, who made his fortune manufacturing the Kodak camera—a fixture in middle-class homes—gave to the University of Rochester.

Beginning with Virginia's William and Mary and Washington College (now Washington & Lee), colleges began to offer "elective" courses in addition to or in place of the traditional curriculum. Students could define their own "majors," whether Latin and Greek or business management. The elective system got its biggest boost when, beginning in 1869, Harvard permitted each student to choose most of the courses he took. At Harvard, the nation's richest and largest university, just about every "major" imaginable was available.

Universities founded postgraduate professional schools, in law, medicine, and other fields, including Ph.D. programs in traditional disciplines like history (an idea borrowed from Germany). Some professional schools grew more rapidly than undergraduate colleges. Of the first 200 degrees awarded by the territorial University of Oklahoma, founded in 1890, 86 were from the pharmacy school.

Co-Eds and Seven Sisters   Most state universities, beginning with Iowa in 1858, were open to women. The alacrity with which they matriculated at western land grant universities was pretty good evidence that young women had felt educationally deprived. The first class of the newly founded University of Oklahoma was exactly half female.

No doubt the first girls to enroll at established colleges had to endure a taunting, but the boys' fun did not last long. By the mid-1880s, women were so numerous on campus that the new word *coeducational* and its breezy abbreviation, *coed*, were part of the language. By the 1890s, about one in three college students was female.

Some of them attended all-women institutions which themselves multiplied in the final decades of the century. In 1861, when Vassar opened in Poughkeepsie, New York, there were a number of "female seminaries" with collegelike curricula; the best established were Georgia Female College (now Wesleyan) and Mount Holyoke in Massachusetts, both founded in 1837, and Mills in Oakland, California. Just in the northeastern states, Wellesley and Smith were founded in 1875 and Radcliffe in 1879 (all in Massachusetts). Bryn Mawr (Pennsylvania) set up shop in 1885 and Barnard (New York) in 1889.

Mount Holyoke, Vassar, Wellesley, Smith, Radcliffe, Bryn Mawr, and Barnard, later dubbed the "Seven Sisters," were elite institutions, founded for the daughters of the wealthy. They were valued less for the stiffness of their curricula than as "finishing schools" exposing students to "culture": French, of course, music, art, respectable literature and, most of all, the social graces expected of the future wife of a Harvard, Yale, or Princeton man. Not all of their students were filthy rich, however. Middle-class girls too were interested in the social contacts that the Seven Sisters schools were intended to expedite.

Women were few in professional schools. By the turn of the century the Unitarians were ordaining female ministers, but other denominations would not hear of such nonsense. Almost all university medical schools, on the grounds that a doctor's training involved indelicacies to which women should not be exposed, refused to admit women. In 1868, Elizabeth Blackwell, the first accredited woman doctor in the United States, established a medical school for women in New York City. By that date, the Woman's Medical College of Pennsylvania was already in operation and grudgingly recognized as providing a first-class medical education. If it was difficult for a woman to get a medical education, there was little resistance to female doctors among the middle class. With prudery at its height, many women (and many women's husbands) did not want male doctors examining them.

Commencement at Mount Holyoke College in Massachusetts. It was the oldest of the seven exclusive women's colleges in the Northeast later known as the Seven Sisters. The girls' education was not particularly rigorous but, then, plenty of wealthy sluggards found it no problem to graduate from Harvard and Yale with a "gentleman's C" average. The Seven Sisters were "finishing schools" and spoken of as such. Graduates were drilled in social graces ranging from good posture to conversational French and exposed to music, art, and literature. Perhaps most important to their parents, they lived in an upper-class cocoon and, with luck, would marry a brother of one of their friends who was better fixed than the daughter was.

The legal profession was a tougher nut to crack. In 1873, the Supreme Court approved the refusal of the law school at the University of Illinois to admit a woman on the grounds that "the paramount mission and destiny of women are to fulfill the noble and benign offices of wife and mother." Nevertheless, by the end of the century, several dozen women were practicing law, including the Populist firebrand Mary "Mother" Lease.

Minorities and Higher Education   There were, of course, middle-class African Americans, Jews, and Catholics who aspired to college educations. Blacks were admitted to most institutions in the northern and western states but not all. Pennsylvania had de facto racial segregation when two private vocational training schools for African Americans, the Institute for Colored Youth, founded in 1836, and the Ashmun Institute (1854) evolved into degree-granting colleges. Ashmun was renamed Lincoln University in 1866; the Institute for Colored Youth became Cheyney State Teacher's College, in 1913. Black applicants were admitted to other state colleges, but they were steered toward Lincoln or Cheyney where they were, in fact, more comfortable.

In the South, after the Supreme Court gave the go-ahead to racial segregation in *Plessy* v. *Ferguson*, the state legislatures founded colleges for blacks patterned after

Workers' Holiday

Working people could not afford a month or a week in the mountains or at the seashore. In the 1890s, however, very short-term commercial leisure became part of working-class life with the construction of amusement parks on the outskirts of big and even middling size cities, places like Philadelphia's Willow Grove, Boston's Paragon Park, Atlanta's Ponce de Leon Park, and Chicago's Cheltenham Beach.

Some had been leafy picnic grounds and swimming beaches for decades. Others had their origins in two financial problems urban trolley car companies faced. Street cars were profitable in built-up areas but, because of the high price of midtown real estate, they had to build their sprawling storage and repair barns outside the cities, making for long runs where there were no customers. Moreover, their charters required traction companies to operate on Sundays when, with few people commuting to and from their jobs, ridership was skimpy.

By building or encouraging the construction of "playlands" at the end of the lines, trolley companies generated business outside the city, especially on Sunday which was otherwise a dead loss. For a nickel each, parents could take their children (who rode free) on an excursion—the ride itself was exciting for housewives and kids—and spend the day breathing clean air, swimming in a lake, the ocean or a pool, picnicking on a lunch brought from home or buying cheap, tasty treats, and splurging on the cheap thrills of mechanical "rides" like the Merry-Go-Round, roller coasters, "Bounding Billows," and "Human Roulette Wheel."

Saturday afternoons and evenings were equally busy with teenagers and young people, some couples on dates, some in groups of friends, each open to making half of a couple and riding through the "tunnel of love" or walking through the "barrel of love," more accurately described as a barrel in which to fall down and land on top of a member of the opposite sex. Cocky young bucks

Alabama's Tuskegee Institute. Rarely if ever were they funded at anything like the level the states funded whites-only institutions. In Mississippi in 1915, when African Americans were 43 percent of the population, only 15 percent of the state's educational expenditures went to blacks-only institutions.

Most American Jews before 1880 were of German origin and culturally if not socially assimilated. Wealthy and middle-class families sent their sons and daughters to established institutions, both state supported and private colleges. Many of the Eastern European Jews of the "new immigration" that poured into the United States after 1880 prized education so highly that even families struggling to put food on the table scrimped and sacrificed to educate their sons to a degree unknown in any other immigrant group.

Middle-class Catholics resisted sending their children to secular colleges, whether private or public. The Church's bishops were hostile to the Protestant flavor of even state schools and especially to the "modernism" of mainstream intellectuals. A few Catholic colleges predated the Civil War, notably Georgetown in Washington (founded in 1789), Notre Dame in Indiana (1842), Villanova in Pennsylvania (1842), and Holy Cross in Massachusetts (1843).

showed off to the ladies by—for a nickel—shooting metal ducks and bears with an air rifle, trying to knock down weighted "milk bottles" with a baseball, or hitting the bull's eye three times with darts. Success won a prize costing less than a nickel. Lotharios with a pocketful of coins could win enough tickets to get a kewpie doll or a teddy bear for their companions.

The biggest playland was Coney Island on the ocean in Brooklyn, just 9 miles from Manhattan. Actually, Coney Island was by 1904 four amusement parks side by side and dozens of independent hustlers renting beach umbrellas; purveying beer, hot dogs, ice cream, and souvenirs; or, in a tent for the sporting young man without a lady friend, suggestive dances by "hootchie-kootchie girls," imitators of Turkish Fatima, who was a nationwide sensation when introduced to Americans at the Chicago World's Fair in 1893.

The most successful amusement park at Coney Island was Steeplechase Park, opened in 1897 by George C. Tilyou, a native-born Coneyite, as he said, with "sand in my shoes." A hustler since he was a teenager, Tilyou was a master of hoopla and buncombe. He tried and failed to buy the wonder of the Chicago fair, a ferris wheel 250 feet in diameter from which were suspended thirty-six "cars," each carrying sixty people. Not losing a step, he contracted with the builder to erect at Coney Island a wheel half its size which Tilyou advertised as "THE WORLD'S LARGEST FERRIS WHEEL!"

While maintaining a wholesome atmosphere to attract Sunday's families, Tilyou also provided the innocent sexual horseplay that appealed to young people. Everywhere on the boardwalks at Steeplechase were air jets that blew women's long skirts into the air to everyone's amusement.

Unlike promoters of middle-class resorts that touted "education" and even religion as justifications for idling there, Coney Island sold unadorned fun. It was the fun of Coney Island and places like it that came to mind when, twenty years later, a writer described the final decade of the nineteenth century as the "Gay Nineties." By 1910, it was not uncommon for a million people to spend a sunny summer Sunday there.

In the late nineteenth century, in a crash campaign to insulate future leaders of the Catholic community from secularism, religious orders founded an extensive network of Catholic institutions. Most of them offered an excellent liberal arts education (it was a Catholic specialty) but, like some Protestant denominational schools, they ignored or rejected the sciences that were calling some religious beliefs into question, like geology and biology. As student demands for career education mounted, however, the larger Catholic universities added engineering, business, and professional schools to keep young Catholics "in-house."

A Hunger for Words

Newspapers increased in number, size, and circulation during the late nineteenth century. Between 1870 and 1900, the number of daily newspapers in the United States increased at twice the rate as the population—and much of the population increase was due to immigrants who did not read English. The expansion of the newspaper business had less to do with new technologies than with the increasing appetite of the public for news and the discovery by businessmen with goods and services to sell that advertising really worked. Nowhere was the newspaper boom louder than where consumers were most numerous—in big cities. By 1892, ten newspapers had daily circulations of 100,000 or more; by 1914, thirty did. In 1900, Chicago had ten daily newspapers, New York fourteen.

The profits to be made from advertisers also inspired an explosion in the number of monthly general-interest magazines aimed at the middle class. In the wake of the Civil War, the two leading monthly magazines were *Harper's* and the *Atlantic Monthly*. They were "high brow" and exclusive in that they cost 35¢ a copy, not throwaway money for most people. Each had a circulation of about 50,000.

In 1883, a Philadelphian named Cyrus H. K. Curtis detected a huge market in the women of the middle class. He launched the *Ladies' Home Journal* which he sold for only 10¢, making up the costs of printing and distribution by attracting advertisers of household goods. The *Journal* explicitly honored the middle class as a steadying influence between "unrest among the lower classes and rottenness among the upper classes." In 1893, Curtis was printing a million copies each month.

Somewhat less conservative than the *Journal* was *Cosmopolitan*, founded in 1886 as a "first class family magazine." With its large circulation, it competed successfully with *Harper's* and the *Atlantic* in wooing the most popular writers of the day. *Munsey's*, with the same combination of fiction and topical articles plus serials to entice readers into subscribing so as not to miss the next issue, appeared in 1891 followed by *McClure's* in 1893. *McClure's* had a subscription list of 250,000 in 1895, *Munsey's* 500,000. At 10¢ a copy, *Munsey's* took in $50,000 in subscription payments each month, not quite enough to cover costs, but monthly revenue from advertisers was $60,000.

By 1900, the combined circulation of the four largest magazines totaled 2.5 million per month, more than all American magazines combined only twenty years earlier.

LEISURE

Vacation resorts, previously reserves of the wealthy, the only people who could afford a month or more in attractive settings, multiplied in the late nineteenth century. Railroad spur lines made it possible for middle-class people to swarm to once exclusive refuges like Saratoga Springs and Lake George in the mountains of upstate New York and to Long Branch and Cape May on the New Jersey seashore.

Some holiday destinations were middle class from the start. In 1874, a Methodist minister instituted eight-week training schools for Sunday school teachers at Lake Chautauqua in New York. The original resort never shed its religious emphasis, but many of the 200 odd copycat "Chautauquas" attracted middle-class campers and hotel guests by downplaying religion and offering a crowded schedule of evening lectures on a dizzying variety of subjects and entertainers ranging from German oom-pah bands to troupes of Italian acrobats.

Mineral springs resorts continued to lure middle-class vacationers although fewer took the claims of hydropathy as seriously as antebellum visitors had. "In the morning everyone drinks the water," a foreign visitor to Saratoga noted, "at night they make fun of it." A health resort that guests took quite seriously was the "San," for Sanitarium, in Battle Creek, Michigan. It was the creation of Dr. John

Kellogg, who denounced Americans' prodigious consumption of meat and served only vegetarian meals three times a day.

Health and Fitness

Dr. Kellogg's brother, William K. Kellogg (and a competitor, C. W. Post) created far more lucrative businesses based on the growing conviction of middle-class people that the traditional American breakfast—heaps of meats, pancakes, and eggs topped off with a slice of pie—while appropriate to farmers laboring from dawn to dusk—was the cause of the dyspepsia (indigestion) and other ailments that seemed to be epidemic among sedentary businessmen and their wives. Marketed as "health food," Post Toasties, Kellogg's Cornflakes, and other "breakfast cereals" were instantaneous successes. Within ten years they transformed the American breakfast when office workers discovered they were livelier in the morning with their bellies no longer bloated. And their wives discovered that breakfast no longer required an hour or two to prepare.

The other side of health and fitness was exercise. Even before the Civil War, foreign observers commented on the unhealthy appearance of American office workers, a "pale, pasty-faced, narrow-chested, spindle-shanked, dwarfed race." Abolitionist Thomas Wentworth Higginson wrote in the *Atlantic Monthly* in 1858, "Who in this community really takes exercise? Even the mechanic confines himself to one set of muscles; the blacksmith acquires strength in his right arm, and the dancing teacher in his left leg. But the professional or businessman, what muscles has he at all?"

The Young Men's Christian Association (the YMCA or "Y") established a presence in every major city and many smaller ones during the 1870s and 1880s to serve the "spirit, mind, and body" of single young men, perhaps attracting more members with its gymnasiums and swimming pools than its Bible classes. The young Theodore Roosevelt made a fetish of physical fitness as an essential ingredient of the "manliness" he found lacking among Americans. Puny and asthmatic as a child, he built up his body with calisthenics and sports and urged Americans to live "the strenuous life" that he did.

Upper- and middle-class people embraced all sorts of British sports: lawn tennis about 1875, archery, golf, and croquet in the 1880s. Roller skating won a huge following. Rinks like San Francisco's Olympian Club offered 5,000 pairs of skates to rent and a 69,000-square-foot floor. The biggest fitness manias of all were basketball and bicycling.

Basketball

In 1891, James Naismith, a YMCA physical education instructor in Springfield, Massachusetts, invented basketball as a rigorous team sport that young men could play during the winter between football and baseball seasons. He knocked the bottom out of two peach baskets, gave his research assistants a soccer ball, and explained his thirteen rules. Twelve, somewhat modified, are in effect today. The score of the first game would not be recognizable, however. It was 1–0, the single goal scored by one William R. Chase, who held the record for several days.

The sport spread like lightning, far faster than one could have imagined. By 1900, it was a college and high school sport throughout the United States and

Canada. In 1904, two American teams demonstrated it at the St. Louis Olympic games.

As soon as college women in New England saw their first game, they wanted to play. The men's game was somewhat rough, so Senda Berenson, a gym teacher at Smith College, modified the rules to prohibit banging into an opponent and snatching the ball, the cause of the bruising. To prevent unthreatened girls from simply standing still and holding the ball, Berenson required players to throw or bounce the ball within three seconds. Berenson limited bounces to three, but she had invented "dribbling," which was lacking in the original men's rules.

Berenson also divided the court into three zones (later two). Players were not permitted to leave the zone to which they were assigned at the beginning of play. Her purpose was to prevent a single superior player from completely dominating the game which, apparently, was more common among women than among men. Women's basketball adopted men's rules only in the second half of the twentieth century because, old style, there was too little running.

The Bicycle Craze

"Dandy horses" from France made an appearance in the United States during the 1860s. They were crude wooden proto-bicycles that exhibitionist owners straddled and propelled through crowds of pedestrians by running. In 1876, the "bone crusher," which riders mounted, was introduced. With a front wheel 5 feet in diameter, they were difficult to balance and a chore to pedal. There were no sprockets and chain; the pedal crank was fixed to the big wheel so it required one revolution of about 3 feet to move the bicycle 16 feet, a very "high gear." They were also dangerous; spills from so high off the ground broke many an arm and leg.

Because riding was so risky (and impossible for women wearing floor-length skirts), middle-class young men wishing to exhibit their manliness took to them with a passion, spending $100–$150 on their machine. In 1880, the League of American Wheelmen was founded with 44 members; by 1890, 3,500 had signed up and ten or twenty times that number were riding bikes. By 1890, twenty-seven American companies with 1,800 employees were churning them out.

By then, "safety bicycles" were displacing the bone crushers. They were essentially identical to bicycles today with two wheels of equal size, pneumatic tires, and sprockets and a chain to make pedaling them easy. It was no longer an act of bravery to ride a bicycle, but the speeds they could reach more than compensated the manly. By 1900, the American Wheelmen numbered 141,500 members; 300 companies were making a million bikes a year.

More important, women could and did ride safety bikes. Bloomers enjoyed a brief revival so that they could straddle bikes modestly, but more attractive divided skirts (*culottes*) were more popular. Temperance crusader Frances Willard learned to ride at the age of 53 and proclaimed, "She who succeeds in gaining the mastery of the bicycle will gain the mastery of life." The Founding Mother of American feminism, Susan B. Anthony, in her seventies, prudently passed on lessons. But she endorsed the bicycle: "It has done more to emancipate women than anything else. I stand up and rejoice every time I see a woman ride on a wheel. It gives women a feeling of freedom and self-reliance."

In truth, the bicycle was a godsend to women who felt repressed. On fair Saturdays and Sundays, the streets and parks of cities were crowded with bicycling young women in candy-striped blouses with billowing sleeves and sporty broad-brimmed hats. Old-fashioned moralists found the sight of female cyclists unsettling. They might start out in proper all-girl company, they said, but soon enough on secluded lanes, they were striking up conversations with young men to whom they had not been introduced. The bicycle was a step toward perdition.

The Gibson Girl No longer was the ideal young woman a shrinking violet given to fainting. She was the "Gibson Girl," named for a popular magazine illustrator, Charles Dana Gibson, whose specialty was beautiful young women, often in humorous situations but never themselves the object of amusement. The Gibson Girl was no feminist. She was uninterested in political and social questions. She was, first and foremost, an object of adoration by love-struck, often laughable young men whom she "wrapped around her little finger." She was trim and fine-featured, luxuriant hair piled atop her head. She was slyly flirtatious—sexy, we would say—but never giggly. She was her own woman and athletic. She rode a bike, played croquet, golf, and basketball.

Theodore Roosevelt's elder daughter, Alice, a national sweetheart when a popular waltz, "Alice Blue Gown," was named for her, was a Gibson Girl. Young women imitated her style as avidly as teenagers today dress to look like pop singers. Few could match her wit, however. She sometimes embarrassed her father with her outspoken "liberated" opinions and continued to be quotable until she died at age 96 in 1980.

Spectator Sports During the 1880s, spectator sports largely dependent on middle-class dollars became an important part of how Americans passed their hours of leisure. The three most important spectator sports, closely followed in newspapers by those who could not afford to attend them, were baseball, football, and prizefighting. Horse racing declined in popularity—almost disappearing—because betting was an integral part of racing and gambling did not accord with middle-class notions of propriety.

Baseball and football both had roots in centuries-old English folk games, but the two sports developed in quite different ways. In the late nineteenth century, boys everywhere of every social class, and more than a few girls, played pickup baseball. Towns had teams of young men that competed with teams from nearby towns. Games between neighboring towns were the centerpiece of community Fourth of July celebrations. The game was commercialized as a moneymaking spectator sport during the 1870s. Entrepreneurs recruited skilled town players into their "clubs" and, in the "major" leagues paid them more than a typical workingman's wages to play other clubs on a regular schedule before paying spectators. Professional baseball prospered because the game was difficult, demanding rare physical talents. It was well worth it to an enthusiast to pay 25¢ or 50¢ to see it played well. Moreover, the people of cities with "major league" teams came to invest their civic pride in the "home team."

American football, by way of contrast, evolved as a game of the elite of well-to-do students at prestigious Eastern universities. It remained a gentleman amateur's sport—on paper—until well into the twentieth century. Curiously, quite unlike professional baseball, a game of grace, speed, finesse, and little physical contact played by often rambunctious working-class men, college football was bruising and brutal. Baseball was a gentleman's game played by hooligans; football was a hooligan's game played by gentlemen.

Origins of Baseball

Americans had played English bat and ball games with varying rules since colonial times: old cat, rounders, stool ball, town ball, cricket. Cricket appeared to have eclipsed all rival games in the 1840s when a bookseller and volunteer fireman in New York, Alexander Cartwright, drew up rules to make the rounders and town ball he and his friends played more interesting. The baseball we know differs in many ways from Cartwright's, but the game played by his "New York rules" is immediately recognizable. It was Cartwright who invented baseball's unique diamond-shaped playing field.

By the time of the Civil War, baseball had displaced cricket in the affections of middle and working-class men. Cricket survived only in a few exclusive clubs. Indeed, in 1865 the wealthy members of the Merion Cricket Club outside Philadelphia distanced themselves from the vulgar masses by voting that all of the club's baseball equipment "be sold off as quickly as possible."

Winning became so important to some baseball clubs that, under the table, they began paying "ringers," highly skilled nonmembers to play for them. In 1869, the first openly all-professional team, the Cincinnati Red Stockings, toured the country playing any team that could assemble enough paying spectators to make it worth their while. Newspapers publicized the skills of the Red Stockings, which were dazzling. They won fifty-eight games, lost none, and had to settle for one tie when the sun set on the game.

And they made a pile of money; 20,000 attended the games they played in Brooklyn. Other professional teams were put together and, in 1876, clubs in six cities came together as the National League (NL) with a regular schedule and the award of a pennant to the team that won the most games. In order to attract middle-class men *and women* to games, NL teams did not sell beer or permit drinking in the grandstands and they did not play on Sunday.

The National Pastime

In 1882, the rival American Association (AA) was founded and made a play for working-class spectators by playing on Sundays (when workingmen could attend), by selling beer, and by pricing tickets at 25¢ rather than the NL's 50¢. The AA did well for a few years but folded in 1891, the Nationals absorbing the AA's best teams. Only with the founding of the well-financed American League in 1901 was the NL's monopoly of major league baseball broken. For two years, the two leagues raided each other's teams for star players. The club owners found the bidding war too costly, and both leagues agreed to respect each other's contracts—and to add a lucrative "World Series" between the two pennant winners at the end of the season.

Between 1900 and World War I, baseball became the "National Pastime." It deserved the title. Presidents William Howard Taft and Woodrow Wilson were avid fans; they inaugurated each season by throwing the game ball on the field to begin the Washington Senators' first home game. In 1912, when the Supreme Court was unable to postpone a case docketed for the week of the World Series, the Justices took turns slipping out of the courtroom to collect inning-by-inning summaries of play that had been phoned in, then passing the bulletins along the bench where every justice studied them. Beginning in 1909 with the opening of the Philadelphia Athletics' new Shibe Park, the major league teams were making enough money to replace makeshift fields, board fences, and rickety grandstands with purpose-built stadiums of steel, concrete, and brick.

Middle-class spectators paid the freight. Workingmen were fans, but they could attend games only on half-day Saturdays (games began at 3:00) and, in those cities that permitted them, on Sunday. Photographs of baseball crowds show the men wearing suits, neckties, and straw boaters, not the rough clothing of manual workers. And, in smaller numbers, nicely dressed women, for baseball courted them with promotions like "ladies' day" when women escorted by men were admitted free. The words of a hit song of 1908, "Take Me Out to the Ball Game," if heard mostly in bass, baritone, and tenor voices today, were written to be sung by a young woman to her beau.

Football! Football! Rah! Rah! Rah!
American football emerged as a distinctive sport about the same time as its British cousins, soccer and rugby. It began with pickup games of rugby among friends on the campuses of elite northeastern universities, proposed, no doubt, by students who had vacationed in England. When Princeton met Rutgers in 1869, the match traditionally recognized as the first intercollegiate football game, the two teams actually played a kind of rugby.

The rules varied from college to college; they had to be negotiated and agreed upon before each intercollegiate game until 1880 when Walter Camp, a 21-year-old Yale player and football fanatic, assembled representatives of several other schools and adopted rules for the American game: eleven players to the side, a neutral line of scrimmage separating the team in possession of the ball from its opponent before each play (instead of rugby's scrum in which both battled for possession); and no limit on the number of a team's plays as long as it maintained possession. When this rule resulted in conservative play to retain possession at all cost—progress of "six inches and a cloud of dust"—Camp revised it so that a team had three downs in which to gain 5 yards for a "first down."

At first, few professors and university presidents took an interest in football except Harvard president Charles Eliot who hated the game and campaigned endlessly to forbid it at Harvard. Eliot failed because students and alumni loved their football, identifying the honor of dear old Harvard just as Philadelphians identified their city with the Athletics and Phillies—particularly when Harvard trounced most of its opponents. Between 1883 and 1892, Harvard won ninety-two games and lost only fourteen. Princeton was even better, ninety-five–eight with two ties; and the powerhouse was Walter Camp's Yale (he became the coach after graduating). In those ten seasons Yale won 112 games (100 of them were shutouts), lost 3, and tied 2. In 1888, Yale scored 698 points to zero for the opposition.

Many professors became rabid fans, none more so than Woodrow Wilson of Princeton and, later, of the White House. Football won the attention of others because, then as now, the most absent-minded professor gave his undivided attention when the word "money" was uttered. Intercollegiate football proved, in a short time, to be a big moneymaker. In 1879, the Yale and Princeton teams each took home a mere $239 each from their Thanksgiving Day game. Two years later the take was $5,500, in 1893 $15,000, and it was all up from there.

Big Money in Academia   Football was a gold mine for Yale. The team netted $106,000 in 1903–1904, enough to pay the salaries of thirty full professors. Little of the money was applied to such purposes, however. Walter Camp controlled the athletic program with an iron fist. In 1905, a journalist claimed that he had built up a secret "slush fund" of $100,000 from ticket sales and $8 "athletic fees" collected from each student. Camp did not respond to the charge and Yale's president refused to investigate. However Camp spent the money, he did not pay either himself—he coached for free—or his players. He was religiously dedicated to the principle of amateurism. That the slush fund was considerable was confirmed in 1914 when Camp purchased the land on which Yale built the first gigantic football stadium, the 78,000-seat Yale Bowl.

As intercollegiate football spread throughout the nation, the irregularities that Camp shunned were common. "Transient athletes"—mostly big bruisers—sold their services on a week-to-week basis to the university that offered the best pay. University of Oregon footballers saw the same player on three different teams on successive Saturdays. Seven of the eleven starters on the University of Michigan's 1894 championship team were not students but paid mercenaries.

University presidents, who otherwise were pillars of integrity, promoted football in order to establish national reputations for their schools that would attract tuition-paying students. Tiny Notre Dame in Indiana and regional Stanford became national universities by developing excellent football teams. The first president of the new University of Chicago, William Rainey Harper, was entrusted with Rockefeller millions to build a first-rate undergraduate college and a major research university. He added a third goal to his program. He hired a Walter Camp protegé, Amos Alonzo Stagg, as football coach, made him a tenured full professor, and told him "I want to develop teams that we can send around the country and knock out all the colleges. We will give [the players] a palace car and a vacation." So important was football to Harper that when, in 1905, he was dying of cancer, unable to rise from his bed, he devoted his final weeks and days to fussing about ticket sales, seating arrangements, concessions, and ushers for "the big game" with Michigan.

Problems and Protest   Football was brutal and dangerous. Players did not wear helmets; padding was scanty. Coaches instructed teams to concentrate on injuring the opposition's star player so that he had to be taken out of the game early. In pileups, the players gouged and slugged one another. A *New York Times* reporter wrote of the Yale-Princeton game in 1886, "a person standing two-thirds of the length of the ground away from the players could hear the spat, spat of fists on faces."

In 1892, Harvard unveiled the "flying wedge." When a player had possession of the ball on an open field, his teammates deployed at a run in a "V" around him and charged the scattered opposition. The *New York Times* reported: "What a grand play!, a half ton of bone and muscle coming into collision with a man weighing 160 or 170 pounds." So many of them had to be carried off the field with serious injuries that the wedge was promptly outlawed. But "mass play" in other shapes continued, phalanxes of players stampeding over opponents, pushing, pulling, and even heaving the ball carrier. By the early 1900s, three or four college players were killed each season, more in high school play, and many others suffered injuries from which they would never recover.

The country was bristling with reformers on the lookout for wrongs to right. There were so many demands to prohibit football or change the rules of the game that President Roosevelt, whom the progressive reformers regarded as their leader, had no choice but to take action—or, at least, as he often did with great skill, to appear to take action. In 1905, he summoned representatives from several northeastern colleges to Washington. Walter Camp was, of course, one of them, and he was determined not to change the game he had done so much to design. Roosevelt himself was of two minds. On the one hand, he was devoted to rough and tough manliness ("Hit the line hard," he told college students.); on the other, his son was playing for Harvard and Mrs. Roosevelt was worried. In the end, Roosevelt's committee made a few cosmetic changes. Deaths in intercollegiate games actually increased from three in 1905 to ten in 1909.

A number of colleges, including first-rank Columbia and Stanford, did drop football in favor of rugby and several hundred high schools followed suit. They reinstated the sport only after the introduction of the forward pass—which Walter Camp opposed—ended mass play.

"The Fights"

There was nothing resembling respectability in prizefighting. Boxing had a well-deserved reputation for corruption, rigged bouts, and sleaziness in general and was illegal in most states. It was a carnival entertainment, tough, trained fighters offering cash prizes to locals who could knock them down or even just stay in the ring for fifteen minutes. (Few collected.) Formal, scheduled, usually illegal bouts between professionals were fought under the London Prize Ring Rules of 1743. They were bare-knuckled and ended only when one fighter was knocked down and could not get up. Rounds ended if one boxer, in need of a rest but not ready to quit, touched his knee to the canvas. Most paying customers at major bouts were "sporting men," poorly reputed bachelors who openly drank, gambled, and consorted with dubious women. Admission to illegal fights was necessarily expensive. Just to stand at the rear of a crowd 50 feet from the ring cost $10.

During the 1880s, prizefighting entered the mainstream. The Marquess of Queensbury Rules of 1873 eliminated much of the brutality of bouts. The rules forbade "attempts to inflict injury by gouging or tearing the flesh with the fingers or nails and biting"; required boxers to wear padded gloves; and specified a fixed number of short, timed rounds. Under the Queensbury rules, "pugilism" became a "manly art" acceptable to gentlemen. Theodore Roosevelt boxed at Harvard in the1870s.

Professional boxing got its first nationally celebrated hero in John L. Sullivan, the "Boston Strong Boy," who fought both bare-knuckle and Queensbury. Sullivan won the American Heavyweight Championship in 1882 and the world title in England several years later. He fought a lot of bouts, approximately 140 between 1877 and 1892 plus about 80 with impromptu challengers when he barnstormed in 1883 and 1894. He did not lose until "Gentleman Jim" Corbett took the championship from him in 1892 although a good many of his fights were stopped by police before he won them.

The *Police Gazette,* a periodical specializing in stories about showgirls, grisly murders, disasters, and sex scandals, added Sullivan and boxing in general to its repertory. Interest in prizefighting was so keen that the struggling weekly increased its modest circulation to 150,000. When distinguished men like Roscoe Conkling, William K. Vanderbilt, and the Rev. Henry Ward Beecher began to attend bouts in New York City, mainstream daily newspapers added coverage of boxing to "sports pages" where baseball and football were already being chronicled.

The nation's sporting man population could not have accounted for the 3,000 who attended Sullivan's fight with Jake Kilrain in 1889. The location of the fight was secret. Those who wished to attend were instructed to assemble in a railroad station in New Orleans on July 7. The governor of Louisiana had vowed to stop the fight so dozens of policemen mixed with the crowd that boarded a chartered train. It crossed the state line into Mississippi where the New Orleans cops had no authority. The bout was held on a remote tract of land near Hattiesburg where a ring had been built unknown to Mississippi police (or with their connivance). It was a spendy day's entertainment. The only spectators were well-heeled men including lawyers, doctors, and businessmen who were model citizens back home.

Race and Sport   Sullivan refused to fight African Americans as did the three champions who succeeded him. Finally, in 1908, after Jack Johnson of Galveston, Texas, had defeated every other heavyweight, an Australian promoter offered champion Tommy Burns too much money to be resisted, Burns fought him and was soundly defeated. Johnson aggravated the intense racial hostility to him by heaping insults on every "great white hope" that challenged him. Foolishly indiscreet, he flaunted his two white wives and numerous mistresses at a time when southern blacks were being strung up for ogling white women. Congress passed a law prohibiting the interstate shipment of a film of Johnson's victory over former champion Jim Jeffries in 1910. The San Francisco *Examiner* headlined its report of the bout, "Jeffries Mastered by Grinning Jeering Negro."

In 1912, Johnson was defeated not in the ring, but by an indictment under the newly enacted Mann Act for transporting a woman across a state line "for immoral purposes." He had taken his common-law wife from Chicago to his vacation home in Wisconsin. Sensibly, for he was facing a long prison term, Johnson fled to Europe. In 1915, he fought white American boxer Jess Willard in Havana and lost. African Americans believed that Johnson threw the match as part of a deal with the Justice Department by which he could return to the United States and receive a light sentence. But Johnson was probably beaten fair and square. It was another five years before he returned to the United States when he was arrested and imprisoned although for a short term.

Professional baseball was also whites only. The pressure to exclude blacks came not from the owners but from the players and the fans. In 1887, six of the ten clubs of the most important minor league voted not to employ African Americans. The major leagues never adopted a racial rule but excluded blacks as effectively as if they had. Southern universities were closed to blacks, of course, so their football teams were lily white. There were African Americans on some university teams in the North and West, but very few. Blacks who went to college were not apt to be thinking football. Ironically, African American Marshall Taylor won the world championship in cycling, a decidedly white middle-class sport, in 1899 and 1900. Black jockeys were common in horse racing, even in the South. Isaac Murphy won the prestigious Kentucky Derby three times. African Americans might have dominated horse racing had the sport not nearly died after 1900.

Sports and Morality   Breeding and racing thoroughbreds were the hobbies of the rich that attracted a mass following. Attendance declined somewhat in the late nineteenth century because of a well-publicized rash of doping scandals and fixed races. Nevertheless, 314 commercial racetracks were operating in 1897.

After 1900, however, state after state prohibited the sport, not so much because of the scandals but because of a growing opposition to all kinds of gambling. By 1908, only twenty-five racetracks were still in business. Within a few more years, thoroughbred racing was legal only in Kentucky, Virginia, and Maryland. Legislatures killed the few surviving state lotteries and, in 1909, the last state to permit casino gambling, Nevada, abolished it. (Casinos were revived in Nevada in 1938.) New Mexico and Arizona Territories did away with casinos as a condition of achieving statehood.

Psychologist William James observed that reformers were trying to transform the United States into a "middle-class paradise," the entire nation a replica of their orderly, moral towns and neighborhoods. His characterization of the Progressive Movement that emerged after 1900 was incomplete but, as far as it went, it was on the mark. Gambling was just one of the affronts to middle-class decency targeted by the Progressives after 1900 and their leader, many of them believed, was the young man in the White House, Theodore Roosevelt.

34

A WAVE OF REFORM

The Progressives 1890–1916

'Tis not too late to build our young land right,
Cleaner than Holland, courtlier than Japan,
Devout like early Rome with hearths like hers,
Hearths that will recreate the breed called man.

—Vachel Lindsay

A man that'd expect to thrain lobsters to fly in a year is
called a loonytic; but a man that thinks men can be tu-rrned
into angels be an illiction is called a rayformer an' remains
at large.

—Finley Peter Dunne

In 1787, Thomas Jefferson wrote that "A little rebellion, now and then, is a good thing, as necessary in the political world as storms in the physical" and again, "the tree of liberty must be refreshed from time to time with the blood of patriots and tyrants."

Such words were unbecoming of a man who was never around when rebels were rioting, breaking windows, burning houses, shedding blood, and being killed, not to say of a man who made himself scarce when there was a possibility that someone who disagreed with him might raise his voice.

Fortunately, not enough Americans, at any one time, when they were unhappy about how the nation was being run, have taken Jefferson's postures seriously enough to ravage the country and massacre one another wholesale—with the exception of the Civil War, the War of the Rebellion.

THE PROGRESSIVES

For all the injustices Americans have perpetrated and the corruption they have tolerated, the Constitution has succeeded in its stated purpose of insuring "domestic Tranquillity." During the two bloodiest centuries in world history, Americans have

Progressives 1897–1911

1897	1899	1901	1903	1905	1907	1909	1911

1897 "Golden Rule" reform mayor, Toledo

1898 Initiative, referendum, recall: South Dakota

1900 La Follette governor of Wisconsin; Carry Nation "hatchetations"

1903 "Shame of Cities" published

1905 IWW founded

1906 *Jungle* published

City manager government, Staunton, VA 1908

Promise of American Life published 1909

NAACP founded; Hiram Johnson governor of California 1910

as a whole been a cautious people in a pinch, American society exceptionally stable. Americans were never attracted to master schemes for remaking the world from scratch—at least not in numbers large enough to have a go at it. When injustices became so glaring and social evils so extreme as to be intolerable to large numbers, Americans have organized to right them politically, and they have been satisfied with piecemeal, perhaps superficial fixes of problems.

This was true of the evangelical reformers' war on sin during the Age of Jackson, and of the era of the New Deal, the 1930s. It was also the case in a wave of reform that swept over the United States about 1900 and continued for twenty years, the Progressive Era.

The progressive movement was, in fact, many movements. Some progressives were single-issue activists, little interested in other reforms. Very few progressives favored every reform that was styled progressive. People who were progressives on some issues opposed reforms proposed by others as avidly as any conservative.

In the Middle There were upper-class progressives—Theodore Roosevelt and the "blue-stocking" high-society women prominent in many movements. There were Catholic working-class progressives—Alfred E. Smith of New York who still spoke with the accent of the Lower East Side when he was governor of the state; and Jews—Lillian Wald, a pioneer of the settlement house movement and Louis D. Brandeis, a Louisville lawyer who battled monopolistic corporations. Samuel Gompers aligned the American Federation of Labor with the progressives on many issues.

But the progressive movement was overwhelmingly a middle-class movement with middle-class values. It drew its strength from Protestant and prosperous independent business people, managers, professionals, educators, and the white-collar employees who identified with them. The progressives were keenly aware that they were "in between." It was the essence of the movement that they felt that they (and what was good about America) were threatened from both above and below: by the immense wealth and power of the plutocracy industrialization had created and, from below, by the exploding numbers of impoverished immigrants from southern and eastern Europe who, in their eyes, clung to cultures utterly at odds with American values and who, at best, were indifferent to everything about the United States except that the pay was better than it had been at home. Edward Bok, longtime editor of the *Ladies Home Journal*, bemoaned lower-class "unrest" and upper-class "rottenness" to his middle-class subscribers. A progressive physician James Weir denounced the rich as "effeminate, weak" and warned of the "savage inclinations" of the working class.

Many progressive reforms were aimed at bridling and regulating great concentrations of wealth and power, others with Americanizing and uplifting the morals of the "huddled masses" and "wretched refuse" of Europe. Formidable as they believed the challenges they faced to be, progressives were optimists. They were confident they would prevail. "Our shamelessness is superficial," wrote a leading progressive journalist, Lincoln Steffens, "beneath it lies a pride which, being real, may save us yet."

Progressives could be as insufferably self-righteous as the antebellum evangelicals. Robert M. La Follette of Wisconsin, a successful reform governor and influential senator, was as humorless as an abolitionist. To "Fighting Bob," life was one long fight for what was right. California's Hiram Johnson irked his most devoted aides with his clenched-teeth sanctimony. Thomas B. Reed, a decidedly nonprogressive Speaker of the House, told Theodore Roosevelt: "If there is one thing for which I admire you more than anything else, it is your original discovery of the Ten Commandments." When, in 1912, a Democratic party delegation arrived at the home of New Jersey Governor Woodrow Wilson to inform him officially that he had been nominated to run for president, Wilson greeted them by saying, "Before we proceed, I wish it clearly understood that I owe you nothing; God ordained that I should be the next president of the United States."

A Coat of Many Colors   Almost all progressives believed that government was essential to reform. The great corporations were so wealthy and powerful—United States Steel was incorporated in 1901 with a capitalization of a billion dollars—that only a Congress and president responsive to the people could bring them to heel. Democracy and more democracy—there could not be such a thing as an excess of democracy in government—were central to progressive thought. As for the social and moral evils defiling the nation, private efforts such as settlement houses, church programs in slums, and persuasion were all very well and admirable, but most progressives believed that only government action could alleviate the miseries of poverty and the evils of child labor, prostitution, alcoholism, and other all too conspicuous immoralities.

On some specific issues of the day, progressives differed radically from one another. Most progressives believed that labor unions had the right to fight for the betterment of their members; others opposed unions on the same grounds they opposed powerful corporations. Both were organized special-interest groups at odds with the good of the whole. On one occasion, leaders of the National American Woman Suffrage Association said that women should volunteer as strikebreakers if by so doing they could win jobs from which men (and unions) excluded them.

Progressives even disagreed about the advisability of laws regulating child labor. By 1907, thanks to progressive agitation, about two-thirds of the states forbade the employment of children under 14 years of age. However, when progressives in Congress enacted a federal child labor law in 1916, the progressive President

Woodrow Wilson expressed grave doubts about it before, unhappily, for political reasons, he signed the bill. Wilson worried that to forbid children to work infringed on their rights. This was essentially the same reasoning stated by the conservative Supreme Court in *Hammer* v. *Dagenhart* (1918), which struck down the law.

Some progressives were ultranationalists. Others subscribed to a humanism that embraced all people of all countries. Some were jingo imperialists. Senator Albert J. Beveridge of Indiana saw no conflict in calling for an expansion of democracy at home while the United States ruled colonies without regard to the wishes of their inhabitants.

Race

Very few progressives took an interest in what, today, we see as the most glaring injustice of the era, the institutionalized repression of African Americans in the southern states and the informal but often violent exclusion of blacks from mainstream society everywhere in the country.

There were exceptions. A celebrated journalist, Ray Stannard Baker, wrote a scathing denunciation of racial segregation and its consequences in *Following the Color Line* (1906), which had a large readership. In 1910, active white progressives including social workers Jane Addams and Lillian Wald, journalists Baker and Lincoln Steffens, and a well-known professor, John Dewey, joined with the African American Niagara Movement, a civil rights lobby led by W.E.B. DuBois, to form the National Association for the Advancement of Colored People (NAACP). Except for his color, Du Bois was himself the progressive *par excellence*. Refined, middle-class, university-educated, he believed that a "talented tenth" of the African American population—a politically active educated elite—was the key to establishing racial equality in the United States. However, even he acquiesced in appointing whites to most of the NAACP's top offices so as better to reach the white middle class with the organization's message.

To little avail. Middle-class progressives were disgusted by lynching and northerners found Jim Crow segregation at best distasteful, but few could conceive of blacks as their social equals. Indeed, the whites who did the most to further the creation of DuBois's talented tenth were plutocrats like John D. Rockefeller who contributed millions to African American colleges. The only dependable supporters of antilynching bills in Congress were conservative northern Republicans.

Antilynching bills failed because of coalitions of northern Democrats (some of them progressives) and populistic southern demagogues who, otherwise, supported progressive reforms: Pitchfork Ben Tillman, Governor James K. Vardaman of Mississippi, and Governor Jeff Davis of Arkansas. Southern-born Woodrow Wilson lived most of his adult life in the North, and he was no populist. A gentleman and an academic, he was disgusted by "nigger-baiting." However, as president of Princeton University, he facilitated the introduction of some Jim Crowism in the town and, as president after 1913, he tolerated, perhaps encouraged, open discrimination against blacks in the Post Office and Treasury Departments.

Forebears

The great wave of reform did not spontaneously combust. Progressivism had a long, mixed genealogy. In their exaltation of democracy and more democracy, the progressives were Jeffersonian. In *The Promise of American Life*, published in 1909, Herbert Croly felt constrained to reconcile progressive statism with the Jeffersonian dogma "the less government the better" by writing that progressivism would achieve its "Jeffersonian ends"—the good of the people—by "Hamiltonian means"—the power of the state. Croly's most important disciple, then ex-president Theodore Roosevelt, said in 1910: "the betterment which we seek must be accomplished, I believe, mainly through the national government."

In their crusades against corruption in government, the progressives hearkened to the liberal Republicans of the 1870s and the Mugwumps of the 1880s. In their advocacy of expertise and efficiency in government (itself not inherently democratic), progressives drew from the preachments of the nonpolitical engineer Frederick W. Taylor, the father of "scientific management." Taylor's interest lay in the "private sector" (a term not then in use). He sought to reduce waste and increase productivity in industry by minutely analyzing procedures so as to identify points at which they could be improved. His most famous example could not have been of a more ordinary movement, that of a laborer shoveling coal or sand from one place to another. With what size shovel was a man able to move the most material in the least time with the least fatigue? When was a large shovel so heavy that tired the man wielding it so that he moved less than a man working more quickly with a small implement? What was the maximally productive size and shape of the shovel? What was the worker's most productive posture? Scientific management called for careful selection of workers for jobs and training them in a standardized procedure for performing it. The progressives believed that society could be engineered as readily by hiring expert specialists to fill the complex tasks of modern government.

In their determination to put an end to the often chaotic and wasteful economic competition of capitalism, some progressives owed a debt to forebears they would never acknowledge, business consolidators like John D. Rockefeller (a virtually satanic figure for progressives). Other progressives regarded consolidation of industries—the "trusts," monopolies—as the heart of the nation's problems. This major faultline in the movement would split the progressive vote in the 1912 presidential election between Theodore Roosevelt and Woodrow Wilson.

Some progressives had been populistic during the 1890s although they never left the Democratic party: southerners like Tillman and midwesterners like William Jennings Bryan. Most northern and western progressives were Republicans, and had been militantly anti-Populist. After 1900, however, they adopted a good many planks from the Populists' Omaha Platform: a graduated income tax to hit the wealthy harder than the middle class; the direct election of senators; returning government to the people through the initiative, referendum, and recall. William Allen White, a Kansas editor, became a national figure in 1896 with his editorial, "What's the Matter with Kansas?" in which he denounced Populist farmers as "greasy fizzles." A leading progressive after 1900, he had the good grace to admit that the progressives "caught the Populists in swimming and stole all of their clothing except the frayed underdrawers of free silver."

Some progressives wanted to nationalize the railroads and banks. Others joined the Socialist Party of America, itself a "progressive" party in its "immediate demands," calling for the public ownership of utilities: water, gas, and electric companies; elevated commuter railroads and trolley car lines.

GOOD GOVERNMENT

Progressivism originated in the cities. During the 1890s, a number of reform mayors were elected, won national reputations, and inspired imitators. They started out like the Goo-Goos of the 1870s and 1880s but went beyond honesty in government and, in smaller cities, were not so easily ousted as the Goo-Goos had been.

Progressive Mayors

The first of the new breed of mayors was Hazen S. Pingree, a shoe manufacturer who was elected mayor of Detroit in 1890. It took Pingree seven years to destroy the corrupt alliance between the city's public utilities and Detroit city councilmen. In nearby Toledo, Ohio, another small businessman, Samuel M. Jones, ran for mayor in 1897. Politicians mocked him as an eccentric because he plastered the walls of his factory with the Golden Rule and other homilies. But his employees, with whom Jones shared profits, were devoted to him, and workers elsewhere envied them. He was elected. "Golden Rule" Jones was an efficient, no-nonsense administrator and rid Toledo's city hall of graft.

Cleveland Mayor Thomas L. Johnson, elected in 1901, cleaned up a dirty municipal government, actively supported woman suffrage, reformed the juvenile courts, took over the city's public utilities, and promoted participation in government by presiding over open town meetings at which citizens could air their grievances.

Lincoln Steffens of *McClure's* magazine called Cleveland "the best-governed city in the United States." Steffens was the expert. In 1903, he wrote a sensational, well-researched series of articles for *McClure's* called "The Shame of the Cities." He named the names of grafters—it meant a libel suit if his accusations were reckless—exposed corrupt connections between elected officials and businessmen, and demonstrated how ordinary people suffered from corrupt government in the quality of their daily lives.

Steffens's exposés accelerated the movement for municipal reform. Joseph W. Folk of St. Louis, whose tips put Steffens on his city's story, was able to indict more than thirty politicians and prominent Missouri businessmen for bribery and perjury as a result of the outcry that greeted "The Shame." Hundreds of reform mayors elected after 1904 owed their success to the solemn, bearded journalist.

The Muckrakers

The medium through which the gospels of progressivism were spread was the mass-circulation magazines. Periodicals like *McClure's*, the *Arena*, *Collier's*, *Cosmopolitan*, and *Everybody's* multiplied their readership when their editors discovered the popular appetite for the journalism of exposure.

The discovery was almost accidental. Samuel S. McClure was not interested in reform. Selling magazines and advertising was his business. He hired progressives like Ida M. Tarbell and Lincoln Steffens at generous salaries because they wrote well, not because they were reformers. Indeed, Tarbell began her "History of the Standard Oil Company," which exposed dubious practices in John D. Rockefeller's career not for idealistic reasons but because of a personal grudge. Rockefeller had ruined her father, himself a pioneering oil man. Steffens was looking for a story, any story, when he stumbled upon corruption in city government.

When Tarbell's and Steffens's sensational exposés caused circulation to soar, McClure and other editors were hooked. The combined circulation of the ten leading mass-circulation magazines climbed to 3 million as they brimmed with revelations about chicanery in business, social evils like child labor and prostitution, and other subjects that lent themselves to indignant, excited treatment. In addition to his series on racial segregation, Ray Stannard Baker dissected the operations of the great railroads. John Spargo, an English-born socialist, discussed child labor in "The Bitter Cry of the Children." David Graham Phillips, later a successful novelist, described the United States Senate, then elected by state legislatures, as a "millionaires' club."

President Roosevelt did not like the journalism of exposure. He called the writers "muckrakers" after an unattractive character in the religious classic of 1678, *Pilgrim's Progress*. Tarbell, Steffens, and the rest, he said, were so busy raking muck that they failed to look up and see the glories in the stars. So long as the muck was real and deep, Roosevelt's insult fell flat. Journalists happily adopted the word "muckrakers" to describe themselves. Inevitably, however, the editors and reporters overdid it. Between 1900 and 1910, some 2,000 muckraking articles and books were published. Exposure journalism deteriorated into sloppy research and reckless accusations—anything to attract attention.

Efficiency and Democracy   In 1908, Staunton, Virginia, introduced the city manager system of government. The office of mayor was abolished. Voters elected a city council which hired a nonpolitical,

Ida M. Tarbell, one of the most conscientious researchers and best writers among the muckrakers. Her most famous work was a highly critical study of John D. Rockefeller and the Standard Oil Trust.

professionally trained administrator to manage the city's affairs. Proponents of the city manager system reasoned that democracy was protected by the people's control of the council to which the city manager answered. However, because the daily operations of the city were supervised by an executive who did not depend on votes (and the machines that delivered them), they would be carried out without corruption. By 1915, over 400 mostly medium-size cities followed Staunton's example.

The "Oregon system" was the brainchild of William S. U'ren who believed that the remedy for corruption in government was more democracy. Efficient, well-organized, and wealthy special interests were able to thwart the good intentions of the people because, once elected, officials forgot their campaign promises and did the bidding of special interests able and willing to reward them under the table.

Between 1902 and 1904, U'ren persuaded the Oregon legislature to adopt reforms pioneered in South Dakota in 1898. To these populist programs, the Oregon system added the state primary. The primary election took the nomination process away from party bosses and gave it to the voters. U'ren was also active in the national movement for a constitutional amendment providing that United States senators be elected by popular vote rather than in the state legislatures. Few people before or since have had such touching faith in the wisdom of the majority vote as William S. U'ren. He lived to the ripe old age of 90, long enough to see twenty states adopt the initiative and thirty the referendum, but none that managed to construct heaven on earth.

Fighting Bob and the Wisconsin Idea

The career of Wisconsin's Robert M. "Fighting Bob" La Follette is a capsule history of progressivism. Born in 1855, he studied law and served three terms in Congress as a Republican during the 1880s. As a young man, he showed few signs of crusader's itch. Then, a senator offered him a bribe to fix the verdict in a trial. La Follette flew into a rage at the shameless audacity of the proposition, and he never quite calmed down for the rest of his life.

In 1900, he ran for governor in defiance of the Republican organization. He attacked the railroad and lumber interests that dominated Wisconsin through the Republican party. He promised to devote the resources of the state government to the service of the people and his timing was perfect; La Follette was elected. As governor, he pushed through a comprehensive system of regulatory laws that required businesses touching the public interest to conform to clear-cut rules and submit to close inspection of their operations.

La Follette did not stop with the negative regulatory powers of government. He created agencies that provided positive services for ordinary people. La Follette's "Wisconsin idea" held that in the complex modern world, legislators needed experts to assist them. A railroad baron could not be kept on a leash unless the government could draw on the knowledge of specialists who knew as much about railroad operations as the men who owned the companies. Insurance premiums could not be held at reasonable levels unless the state was able to determine when the insurance company's profit was reasonable and when it was rapacious. The government could not determine which side was right in a labor dispute unless it had the counsel of economists.

La Follette formed a mutually beneficial relationship between the state government and the University of Wisconsin. The Wisconsin legislature funded the university better than any other state institution in the country. In return, the state government had the counsel of distinguished economists like Richard Ely, Selig Perlman, and John Rogers Commons who were attracted to Wisconsin's prestige and high salaries. The Wisconsin law school helped build up the first legislative reference library in the United States so that assemblymen did not have to rely on lobbyists for the data necessary to draft laws on complex subjects.

The university's agriculture school sent experts across the state to teach farmers up-to-date methods and solve problems they were having. La Follette even made use of the university football team when he learned that political enemies planned to break up a rally at which he was to speak. He showed up in the company of burly linemen who folded their arms and surrounded the platform.

In 1906, La Follette took his crusade to Washington as a United States senator; he held his seat until his death in 1925. He was much loved in Wisconsin and elsewhere. He was "Fighting Bob," incorruptible and unyielding in what he regarded as right.

Leaders   In New York State, Charles Evans Hughes came to prominence as a result of his investigation into public utilities and insurance companies. Tall, erect, dignified, with a smartly trimmed beard that was going out of fashion, he lacked the charisma of La Follette and Teddy Roosevelt, who called him "a cold-blooded creature" and later "the bearded lady." Nevertheless, he had a large following in New York.

George Norris of Nebraska, a Republican, was elected to Congress in 1902 and in 1912 to the Senate. He was a relentless critic of big business, one of a few progressives who continued to win reelection during the conservative 1920s. Another was Hiram Johnson of California. He came to progressivism by much the same path as La Follette, drawn to reform by revelations of the colossally corrupt Abe Ruef machine that ran San Francisco. After the great earthquake and fire of 1906, Ruef set up a system by which those who wished to profit from rebuilding cleared their plans and licenses with him (in private rooms in fashionable restaurants). Scarcely a street could be paved or a cable car line laid out until money changed hands. On just one occasion, Ruef collected $250,000 of which he kept one-quarter, gave one-quarter to Mayor Eugene Schmitz, and distributed the remainder among the aldermen.

What galvanized Johnson was the discovery that Ruef's network extended beyond San Francisco contractors to the Southern Pacific Railroad: The state's most distinguished businessmen were linked not only to petty grafters but also to the sleaziest vice, which the Ruef machine also protected. Johnson turned into "a volcano in perpetual eruption, belching fire and smoke." In 1910, he was elected governor on the slogan, "Kick the Southern Pacific out of politics."

William E. Borah of Idaho could spout rectitude as eloquently as La Follette and Johnson, and his supporters were equally devoted to him; he held his Senate seat from 1907 until 1940. He did not, however, come to Washington as a progressive. He had a long, cozy relationship with Idaho's mining and ranching interests and it was revealed, decades after his death, that he accepted cash gifts from special interests throughout his career.

MAKING PEOPLE BETTER

Progressives were as concerned with the masses below them as they were with powerful business interests. Monopoly and corporation control of politics mocked democracy. The industrial working class was susceptible to revolutionary socialism, a threat equal to plutocracy. The urban hordes of immigrants from southern and eastern Europe seemed to resist becoming good Americans. The immigrants could at least be educated. Progressives increased the funding of public schools in industrial states, creating what remained, for more than half a century, the best public educational system in the world. Teachers in schools in which most pupils were children of immigrants were commissioned to teach American values—middle-class values!—as well as the three Rs, biology, and typing.

Sexual Morality   The crusade against sexual immorality began decades before reformers called themselves progressives. In the 1870s, supported by a New York state law he had sponsored, an employee of the YMCA, Anthony Comstock, began a single-minded crusade against obscenity. Comstock's first target was pornography, which photography has made more readily available, but he was soon calling for the prohibition of advertisements with sexual allusions and books that so much as mentioned sexual activity.

In 1873, Congress enacted a law empowering postmasters to examine the mail for obscene material and to destroy it. Comstock doubled as a postal inspector and head of the New York Society for the Prosecution of Vice. Although the courts occasionally rejected his definition of obscenity, politicians feared crossing him and gave him his head. In his final report in 1914 (he died the next year) Comstock boasted that he had been responsible for 3,697 arraignments under the obscenity laws with 2,740 defendants pleading guilty or convicted. Some prosecuted books are now considered literary classics and routinely assigned to high school students because Comstock cast so large a net. Publishers took to printing "banned in Boston" on the dust covers of their books in order to boost sales. Boston's "Watch and Ward" society, another of Comstock's organizations, was the nation's most industrious.

The American Society of Sanitary and Moral Prophylaxis aimed its betterment campaign at men, Protestant middleclass more than working-class men, who were not likely to read its pamphlets or attend its lectures. The society's message was traditional sexual morality, its target the double standard. The "purity movement"—any number of organizations—reached out to young women. It was the first respectable mainstream effort to discuss sex openly and frankly with middle class girls.

Prostitution   Some purity movement organizations actively rescued prostitutes, feeding and housing women who wanted out of the profession, and finding "honest employment" for them. But the war against prostitution was one of the campaigns that, progressives recognized early on, was too big for private voluntary action.

No one believed that prostitution was a positive good, but many people accepted it as an inevitable evil. At best, they thought, it could be kept out of the sight of decent people by restricting it to the fringes of towns and cities. Although most states had laws criminalizing prostitution before 1900, they were enforced (spasmodically) only against streetwalking "hookers" who were a public nuisance. Discreetly operated "houses of ill repute" were tolerated in most cities with or without payoffs to police. Even small towns had their woman on the wrong side of the tracks who would entertain gentlemen callers (or teenage boys) for a dollar or two.

In cities, prostitution ran the gamut from lushly furnished and expensive brothels for high-society swells such as Sally Stanford's house in San Francisco to "the cribs," tiny cubicles rented by whores who serviced workingmen for a dollar. Because pay was so low for unskilled work, many working women moonlighted as prostitutes part time.

The progressives, spearheaded by women's organizations, determined to wipe out the institution because it corrupted young women simply because they were poor, because it spread "social diseases," and because patronization of prostitutes destroyed the sanctity of marriage. During the first decade of the century, most states enacted stricter antiprostitution laws and police, prodded by progressive organizations, enforced them rigorously. In 1917, at the behest of the army which, previously, had encouraged prostitution near bases, even New Orleans's wide-open Storyville, the birthplace of jazz, was closed down. By 1920, all but a few states had antiprostitution laws on the books. Only Nevada, with its mining camp heritage and few progressive politicians, continued to tolerate the institution legally.

Crusade Against Alcohol   The anti-alcohol crusade that began with the evangelicals never died. The Methodist and Baptist churches, with uneven success, forbade drinking as a condition of membership. At one time or another during the nineteenth century, dozens of states enacted some kind of restrictions on the manufacture and sale of alcohol. As a rule, however, prohibition laws were soon repealed or were not enforced.

The Prohibition party began running presidential candidates in 1872. In 1879, the Women's Christian Temperance Union (WCTU) elected the able and energetic Frances E. Willard president. She crisscrossed the country espousing at a minimum individual abstinence. But the WCTU also introduced the idea, by constitutional amendment, of the national prohibition of the manufacture and sale of intoxicating beverages.

WCTU women publicized their cause by entering both fancy hotel bars and sleazy saloons to kneel and pray. In 1900, an avid anti-alcohol crusader, Carry Nation, took direct action a step further. She entered a saloon in Wichita, Kansas, with a hatchet. While the bartender and tipplers looked on dumbfounded, hid under tables, or fled, she smashed bottles and glasses, the mirror behind the bar, and much of the furniture. For six months she repeated her forays across Kansas and was arrested thirty times.

Middle-class progressives disapproved of Carry Nation's "hatchetations," but the one woman demolition squad energized them. Unlike the evangelicals, they emphasized social and political arguments against alcohol. They pointed out that, in big cities, saloons were the local headquarters of political machines. Close the saloons and the bosses would be crippled. Progressive prohibitionists argued that much of the misery of the working classes was the consequence of husbands and fathers spending their wages on demon rum and John Barleycorn. Because the public bar was an all-male institution, the temperance movement formed a close alliance with suffragists.

The prohibition movement was not an exclusively progressive phenomenon. Religious leaders interested in no other reforms supported it. Except in big cities in the Northeast and Midwest, however, progressive politicians, even those who enjoyed a beer or a drop of the creature, became sympathizers for the sake of the prohibitionists' votes.

Feminism and Progressivism The woman suffrage movement dated to 1848 but, in 1900, it seemed as far from its goal—a constitutional amendment guaranteeing women the vote—as ever. Fifty years of labor by the now ancient leaders of the suffragists, Elizabeth Cady Stanton and Susan B. Anthony, had few victories. In their twilight years at the beginning of the progressive era, Stanton and Anthony could look back on liberalized divorce laws, women voters in six western states, and a unified movement in the National American Woman Suffrage Association.

But opposition to "votes for women" was as strong as ever, especially in the South and the big cities of the Northeast and Midwest. Most Americans, women quite as much as men, continued to believe that women's finer moral sense made

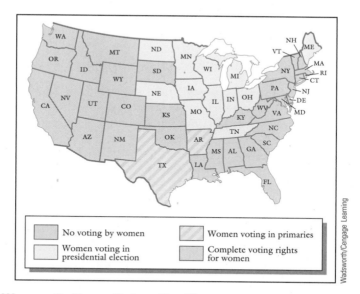

MAP 34.1 **Woman Suffrage Before the Nineteenth Amendment**

Votes for women were guaranteed in every state by the Nineteenth Amendment, ratified in 1919. The impact of the amendment is, however, often overstated. By 1919, women were voting in at least some elections in thirty of forty-eight states. Hard-core opposition to female suffrage was stubbornest among white men in the South and New England, strange bedfellows.

it best that they remain in a domestic sphere insulated from public life. In fact, when Anthony died in 1906, success was less than fifteen years away. The democratic inclinations of the progressives made it increasingly difficult for them to deny the franchise to half the population on any grounds.

Changing
Strategies
The key to the victory of the women's suffrage movement was a fundamental shift in its strategy. Under the leadership of Carrie Chapman Catt, the National American Woman Suffrage Association came to terms with popular prejudices as Stanton and Anthony never quite could. Catt's movement quietly shelved the comprehensive critique of women's status in society that earlier feminists developed. The new suffragists downplayed, even jettisoned, the argument that women should have the right to vote because they were equal to men—like men—in every way.

"Social feminists" clung to the old verities. Charlotte Perkins Gilman, an independently minded New Englander, argued in *Women and Economics* (1898) that marriage was itself the cause of women's inequality. Alice Paul insisted that the suffrage alone was not enough to resolve "the woman question."

But most middle-class suffragists argued that women should have the right to vote precisely because they were not like men; they were indeed more moral by nature. Their votes would purge society of its evils. Not only did the suffragists thus turn the most compelling antisuffrage argument in their favor—the belief that women were the morally superior sex—but they told progressives that in allowing women to vote they would be gaining huge numbers of supporters. Middle-class women voters would counterbalance the ignorant, easily corrupted new immigrants.

THE PROGESSIVE PRESIDENT

In a personal note to Chauncey Depew, then senator from New York, President Roosevelt made an intriguing remark. He wrote, as if with a weary sigh, "How I wish I wasn't a reformer, Oh Senator! But I suppose I must live up to my part, like the Negro minstrel who blackened himself all over!"

Was TR mocking his own sincerity as the national leader of the progressive movement? Was he reassuring Depew that there was nothing personal when, in speeches, he denounced "malefactors of great wealth," one of whom railroader Depew certainly was? Probably. Roosevelt was not an introspective man, but he did not miss the irony in the fact that he headed a movement of middle-class reformers zealously bent on putting Roosevelt's social equals in their place.

The mock weariness of his note, however, was pure affectation. Roosevelt loved the adulation the crowds lavished on him and the hubbub his policies caused in the boardrooms of the Depews and J. P. Morgans.

Busting Trusts
Roosevelt moved cautiously during his first months in the presidency. The nation was mourning McKinley, and the president knew that the Republican party's old guard was already discussing the necessity of replacing him on the party ticket in 1904. Mark Hanna himself was ready to challenge TR for the nomination.

Time was on TR's side, of course. He had three and a half years to entrench himself. Quietly and gradually, he replaced the party hacks in the cabinet he inherited with his own men and, by giving them more autonomy than McKinley had, he won the loyalty of those he retained: Secretary of State John Hay; Secretary of War Elihu Root (who succeeded Hay in the State Department in 1905); and Attorney General Philander C. Knox. Quite noisily and suddenly in April 1902, he directed Knox to institute the action that made him the leader of the Republican party's progressive wing.

Knox, himself a former corporation lawyer, prosecuted the Northern Securities Company for violating the Sherman Antitrust Act. Northern Securities was designed by J. P. Morgan and railroaders Edward H. Harriman and James J. Hill to put an end to costly railroad competition in the northwestern quarter of the country. Funded by the nation's two largest investment banks, Morgan's and Kuhn Loeb and Company, Northern Securities was a holding company patterned after the United States Steel Corporation, another Morgan creation.

Morgan was stunned. That the Northern Securities Company was very likely in "restraint of trade" as defined by the Sherman Act was obvious. The idea of the combination was to end competition between the Northern Pacific and Great Northern Railroads. But the ten-year-old Sherman Antitrust Act was practically forgotten. It has fallen into disuse because, in part, of adverse court decisions and, in part, because Grover Cleveland and McKinley had been big business presidents, happy to ignore company consolidations if they were drawn up so as to slip plausibly through legal loopholes.

Morgan wrote to Roosevelt: "If we have done anything wrong, send your man to my man and we can fix it up." That was how things had been done. And that was why Roosevelt chose to act differently. He remembered the newspaper cartoons showing a frightened President Cleveland waiting hat in hand in Morgan's waiting room and McKinley as a ventriloquist's dummy on Mark Hanna's knee.

Knox won the case in 1904. The Supreme Court ordered the Northern Securities Company dissolved. Delighted with the praise heaped on him, TR instituted forty more antitrust suits, winning twenty-five of them. Progressive newspapers dubbed him the "trustbuster."

Later in his presidency, Roosevelt became uncomfortable with his title. He had demonstrated that he was no one's flunkey. He had no more elections to win, and he had begun to wonder if bigness in corporations was always undesirable. In 1907, he allowed United States Steel to gobble up a regional competitor, Tennessee Coal and Iron, without comment.

The Great Coal Strike
Roosevelt earned a second perhaps dubious title in 1902: "friend of the workingman." The occasion was a coal miners' strike, on the face of it just one of an epidemic of work stoppages. There had been 1,098 strikes in 1898, 1,839 in 1900, and 3,012 in 1901—almost 60 a week on average. Since Grover Cleveland had destroyed what was left of his popularity by intervening on behalf of the railroads in the Pullman boycott, he and McKinley had steered clear of labor disputes.

The miners' strike that began in May 1902 was hard to ignore. About 140,000 anthracite miners and helpers in Pennsylvania walked off the job, demanding an eight-hour day, a 20 percent pay hike, guarantees against dishonest weighing (miners were paid by the ton), and the mine owners' recognition of the United Mineworkers Union (UMW) as their bargaining agent. (That is, when there were problems, the employers would resolve them by negotiating with the UMW.)

Demand for their coal was minimal in May so the several dozen mine owners involved (coal mining was not a consolidated industry) resolved to sit tight and wait for the ethnically fragmented miners to feel the pinch and return to work. To universal surprise, the workers stayed out. And by fall, orders for coal began to pour in. In the Northeast, the retail price of a ton of anthracite climbed from $5–$6 to $15–$20. Coal-burning factories began to shut down, unable to absorb such a jump in expenses. Worse, winter was coming. In 1902, most homes in both city and country burned coal for warmth.

Public opinion was pro-miner. They had been well disciplined; there had been practically no violence. Muckraking journalists publicized the dangers coal miners faced daily for pay that barely paid for wretched housing and just enough food to survive. The president of the UMW, John Mitchell, was an attractive and reasonable man while the spokesman for the mine operators, George Baer, was a public relations disaster.

Had more been known about Mitchell, he would not have been so popular. He was a drunk; he took bribes from mine owners to settle local disputes; and he was contemptuous of immigrant miners. "They remind me very much of a drove of cattle, ready to stampede," he said in private. But all this leaked out only later, and Baer was an arrogant fool who defended the mine owners with his unique reading of the Bible. "Strikes began with Genesis," he said. "Cain was the first striker and he killed Abel because Abel was the more prosperous fellow." Even more disastrous was his remark that the welfare of the miners would be looked after "by the Christian men to whom God in His infinite wisdom has given the control of the property interests of this country."

The Working-man's Friend A politician with half Roosevelt's savvy would have known whose side to take—or appear to take. He could coerce the mine owners in only one way. He announced that if the strike continued into winter, he would declare a national emergency (which it would have been) and order the army to take over and work the mines. That was for public consumption. Quietly, he asked J. P. Morgan to pressure Baer and the other operators to sit down and talk. The likes of George Baer did not defy J. P. Morgan. He and his colleagues went angrily to Washington. They sulked and refused to meet with the UMW. Roosevelt's men had to shuttle between two rooms as messengers and mediators.

The strike was ended with a compromise. Pay was increased by 10, not 20 percent as demanded. The workday was reduced to nine hours, not eight. The mine owners did not recognize the UMW as an official bargaining agent. Baer and his colleagues could legitimately claim that they won more than half of "splitting the difference." But, in an industry with a long history of bitter conflict and violence, with more truculent and exploitative employers than any other, the miners won too. People by the millions did not freeze to death that winter, and everyone but the mine operators lauded Theodore Roosevelt.

THE REFORMER RIDING HIGH

The Republicans (conservatives gritting their teeth) unanimously nominated TR for a second term in 1904. The Democrats, hoping to capitalize on the grumbling of big-business Republicans, did an about-face from the party's embrace of populist agrarianism in 1896 and 1900 and nominated a Wall Street lawyer and judge, Alton B. Parker.

Parker was able but colorless, and the second most colorful politician in the country would have looked like a cardboard cutout next to TR. Even Parker's Wall Street friends deserted for him. J. P. Morgan personally donated $150,000 to Roosevelt's campaign. He had not reached the pinnacle of American finance by nursing personal grudges.

Roosevelt won a lopsided 57.4 percent of the vote. His 336–140 electoral sweep was the largest since Grant's in 1872. The only unpleasant election news was the fact that Eugene V. Debs, the Socialist party candidate, won 400,000 votes. It was only 3 percent of the total. Nevertheless, it represented a fourfold increase over Debs's vote in 1904.

Regulating the Railroads   Theodore Roosevelt lost few opportunities to denounce socialism. In 1905, when three leaders of the socialist Western Federation of Miners were arrested in Colorado for the murder of a former governor of Idaho and perhaps illegally transported to Idaho for trial, Roosevelt shrugged the incident off because, he said, the two men were "undesirable citizens." Their lawyer for the defense, Clarence Darrow, then at the outset of a distinguished career as "attorney for the damned," complained with some justice that the president had rendered a fair trial difficult. Sensational as the Idaho trial was—both men were acquitted—it was sideshow news compared to the series of reforms the increasingly aggressive president proposed and an increasingly progressive Congress enacted.

As they had been for thirty years, the railroads were a focus of popular resentment. The vital role of transportation in the economy preoccupied progressives at every level of government. Roosevelt's prosecution of the Northern Securities case encouraged progressives in Congress, led by Senator Follette, to introduce and pass the Hepburn Act in 1906. It authorized the Interstate Commerce Commission (ICC) to set maximum rates that railroads could charge their customers and forbade them to pay rebates to big shippers.

Rebates were already illegal, but the prohibition had been difficult to enforce. The Hepburn Act gave the ICC some teeth. Even more than the Northern Securities prosecution, the Hepburn Act represented a reversal of the federal government's deferential treatment of the railroads. Also in 1906, Congress passed a law holding railroad companies liable to employees who suffered injuries on the job. By Western European standards, it was a mild compensation law, but in the United States, it marked a sharp break with precedent, which held employees responsible for most of their injuries.

Labeled Drugs, Healthier Meat   Also in 1906, Roosevelt promoted and signed the Pure Food and Drug Act and the Meat Inspection Act. The first forbade adulteration of foods by processors engaged in interstate commerce and regulated the patent medicine business, a freewheeling industry of

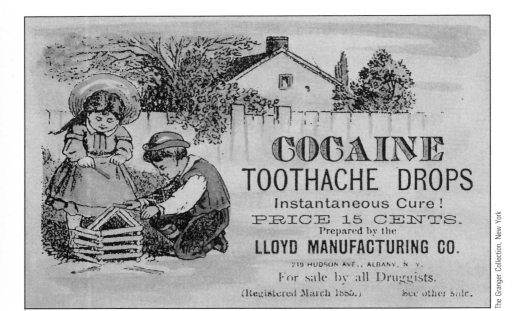

The label of one of hundreds of tonics and nostrums that were laced with cocaine (and opium) in the late 19th century. Opiates were slipping into disrepute, but cocaine was a miracle ingredient of which manufacturers boasted. They worked, of course. Nobody was likely to be hooked by the occasional toothache drop, but many "feel good" syrups created unknowing addicts.

hucksters who marketed nostrums of mostly alcohol infused with addictive drugs, opium derivatives for the nervous, cocaine for people who needed a lift.

Mrs. Winslow's Soothing Syrup and Lydia Pinkham's Vegetable Compound, touted as relief for "female complaints," worked well enough and—good for profits—after downing a few quarts, users were hooked. Any number of "feel good" elixirs were laced with cocaine. The act did not outlaw cocaine—the extent of its risks was not yet known—but manufacturers were required to list it as an ingredient.

The Meat Inspection Act provided for federal inspection of meatpacking plants to eliminate the abuses in slaughterhouses that muckraker Upton Sinclair detailed gruesomely in his novel *The Jungle:* rats ground up into sausage, workers with tuberculosis coughing on the meat they packed, and worse. It was a sensation, read widely in serial form in a popular socialist newspaper, *The Appeal to Reason,* and in 100,000 copies in book form.

None of the seventy-five other books Sinclair published in his ninety-year lifetime sold nearly as well, but *The Jungle*'s reception disappointed him. The packing house scenes were incidental to his story about a Lithuanian immigrant with dreams of improving himself in America who was crushed by ethnic discrimination, greedy landlords, and exploitative employers. The novel concluded with the protagonist vowing to fight to bring socialism to the United States. "I aimed at the nation's heart," Sinclair said, "and hit it in the stomach."

Big companies like Armour, Swift, Wilson, and Cudahy grumbled about the federal inspectors, notebooks in hand, puttering about their plants. However, the Meat Inspection Act actually worked in their favor in their competition with smaller, local slaughterhouses. With their greater resources, the big packers found compliance with federal standards no more than a nuisance. Small companies had been able to stay in business only by slashing costs at every turn, which usually meant neglecting sanitation. The big packers made advertising hay of the inspection stamps on their half-beefs and legs of pork: The government endorsed them. Small companies unable to meet federal standards closed their doors or restricted their sales to the states in which they were located. Like all other federal programs, meat inspection applied only to firms involved in interstate commerce.

Preserving Nature Theodore Roosevelt and the progressives were not always far seeing. However, the president's affection for outdoor life and his commitment to conserving natural resources, resulted in monuments to him that he richly deserves.

TR, the first president born in a big city, was a passionate outdoorsman long before camping, hiking, and climbing were fashionable. As a historian, he was more sensitive than most of his contemporaries to the role of the wilderness in forging the American character. He actively courted and gained the friendship of John Muir, a mystical Californian who founded the Sierra Club in 1892. Muir's interest in nature was aesthetic, cultural, and spiritual. "God has cared for these trees"—California's redwoods—Muir said, "saved them from drought, disease, avalanches and a thousand straining, leveling tempests and floods; but He cannot save them from fools." Muir lobbied effectively to protect natural wonders like the redwoods and Yosemite Valley, which he helped to establish as a national park in 1890, from exploitation.

Roosevelt shared Muir's sentiments—to a degree. He helped create a number of national parks and national monuments. But Muir was a preservationist, uninterested in the economics of natural resources. His proposals met powerful opposition in Congress. "Not a cent for scenery," the reactionary Speaker of the House, Joseph G. Cannon of Illinois, snapped.

Conservation But Roosevelt is more accurately described as a conservationist like his friend and tennis partner, America's first professionally trained forester, Gifford Pinchot. Pinchot had no gut sympathy for Muir's work to preserve unblemished nature for its own sake. Indeed, Pinchot said that "wilderness is a waste." His concern was the protection of forests and other resources from rapacious exploiters bent on short-term profits. He wanted to ensure that future generations would have access to enough timber and nonrenewable natural resources to maintain a decent life. Echoing him, TR told Congress in December 1907, that "to waste, to destroy, our natural resources, to skin and exhaust the land instead of using it so as to increase its usefulness, will result in undermining in the days of our children the very prosperity which we ought by right to hand down to them amplified and developed."

Pinchot and Roosevelt had good reason to be concerned. Lumbermen in the Great Lakes states had already mowed down forests that had been thought inexhaustible, leaving behind worthless scrub. For the sake of their own bank accounts, western ranchers put too many cattle on grasslands, transforming them into weedlots. Coal and phosphate mining companies and drillers for oil thought in terms of next year's profits. The fact that, a century hence, Americans might run out of these resources was the business of Americans a century hence.

The National Forests   The National Forest reserves had been established in 1891 when Congress authorized presidents to withhold forests in the public domain from private ownership. Unlike National Parks (there was just one in 1891), the Forest Reserves were open to developers, but the Interior Department was entrusted with licensing and monitoring loggers. Presidents Harrison, Cleveland, and McKinley reserved 46 million acres of forestland. But Roosevelt discovered that, with Interior Department connivance, cut-and-run loggers and cattlemen had had their own way on many reserves.

In 1905, Roosevelt renamed the reserves the National Forests and named Pinchot to head the Forest Service. He transferred authority over national forests to the Agriculture Department, partly because Pinchot did not trust the Interior Department, partly because the philosophy of forestry is agricultural: Trees were a crop that, because the growing cycle was so long, harvesting had to be regulated so as to sustain the yields of the "fields."

In just two years, Roosevelt added 125 million acres to the National Forests, tripling their size. He also reserved for future use 68 million acres of coal deposits, almost 5 million acres of phosphate beds (vital to production of munitions), several known oil fields, and 2,565 sites suitable for the construction of dams for irrigation and generation of electrical power.

Roosevelt's national forests represented the best kind of the progressives' hopes for government. The system promised an indefinite supply of forest products for the nation, put the government in the business of flood control and development of hydroelectric power. The national forests also provided recreational opportunities by constructing cabins, campgrounds, and trails.

Most of the big logging companies were happy with the system. It took them out of the land-owning business—a big savings—and Pinchot was no John Muir; he wanted timber cut, if it was cut responsibly.

In the western states, however, there was angry opposition to Roosevelt's policies. Cattlemen, clear-cut loggers, and private power companies banded together to fight the conservationists. In 1907, with support from reactionaries like Joseph Cannon, western congressmen attached a rider to the Agriculture Department's annual appropriation that forbade the creation of national forests in six western states. Roosevelt had no choice but to sign the bill. But he took one last swipe at what he called the "predatory interests." Before he signed the bill, he reserved 17 million acres of forest land in the interdicted states.

35

A TIME OF FERMENT
Imperialism and Politics 1901–1916

Big business is not dangerous because it is big, but because its bigness is an unwholesome inflation created by privileges and exemptions which it ought not to enjoy.

—Woodrow Wilson

We demand that big business give the people a square deal; in return we must insist that when anyone engaged in big business endeavors to do right he shall himself be given a square deal.

—Theodore Roosevelt

By taking possession of Spain's Philippines, Puerto Rico, and Guam in 1898 (and, in 1899, annexing half of Samoa), the United States joined the small club of colonial powers: Britain, France, the Netherlands, Germany, Portugal, Italy, Belgium, Japan, Denmark, and (with two colonies in Africa) Spain.

AMERICA'S COLONIES

The acquisition of overseas colonies was not merely a new turn for the United States. It marked a departure from first principles to which the nation had been fairly true. The United States had been born in a revolt against Americans' inferior status as colonial subjects of the first British empire, especially the strict limits on their political power. Official American policy and popular opinion remained anti-colonialist throughout the nineteenth century. It was a point of national pride that when, by purchase or by war, the United States expanded, the residents of those acquisitions (excepting Indians) were accorded U.S. citizenship and populated areas were organized as territories as the first step toward statehood.

That was not so in the case of the Philippines, Puerto Rico, Guam, and Samoa. They were colonies, dependencies governed from Washington as surely as Algeria was governed from Paris and Korea from Tokyo. The historical record of the United States

National Reforms 1900–1914

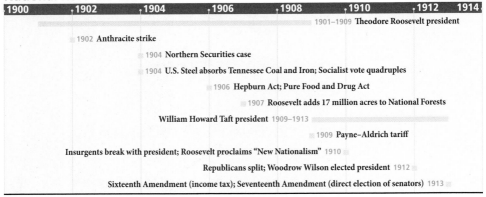

1900	1902	1904	1906	1908	1910	1912	1914

1901–1909 Theodore Roosevelt president

1902 Anthracite strike

1904 Northern Securities case

1904 U.S. Steel absorbs Tennessee Coal and Iron; Socialist vote quadruples

1906 Hepburn Act; Pure Food and Drug Act

1907 Roosevelt adds 17 million acres to National Forests

William Howard Taft president 1909–1913

1909 Payne–Aldrich tariff

Insurgents break with president; Roosevelt proclaims "New Nationalism" 1910

Republicans split; Woodrow Wilson elected president 1912

Sixteenth Amendment (income tax); Seventeenth Amendment (direct election of senators) 1913

as a colonial power is better—less exploitative, more constructive—than the record of any other member of the imperialist club. After 1898, however, Americans could no longer take pride in not telling other peoples what they could and could not do.

Annexing the Philippines   President McKinley asked Congress to declare war on Spain for the purpose of helping the Cuban people win their independence. However, enough congressmen, mostly Democrats and Populists in the Senate, suspected that the administration intended to make a colony of Cuba that they attached the Teller Amendment to the resolution supporting the president. It committed the United States, once Spain was driven out of Cuba, "to leave the government and control of the island to its people."

Like the Cubans, indigenous people in the Philippines had long been waging a rebellion against Spanish rule. But few Americans, in Congress or out, gave a thought to the Philippines before April 1898. President McKinley, famously, could not find the archipelago on a globe when he was told of George Dewey's victory over the Spanish fleet in Manila Bay.

Without a Teller Amendment tying his hands, President McKinley came out in favor of buying the Philippines from Spain and annexing them. His reasons were the same as those other imperial powers had given for seizing colonies for half a century: It was the duty of the United States to bring civilization and Christianity to the benighted people of the islands. Many annexationists (including Theodore Roosevelt) were embarrassed by the president. They called for making a colony of the Philippines because, if the United States pulled its troops out of the country, instability was inevitable whence Japan or Germany (which had made colonialist noises about the island) would move in. The United States would then be shut out of the Philippine trade and its strategic position in the Pacific gravely weakened.

The hard, brutal, and demoralizing war the United States had to fight to suppress the Philippine *insurrectos* who had been allies in the easy war with the Spanish was a rude lesson to Americans of the price a colonial power had to pay when its subjects resisted them.

William Howard Taft was never more popular or successful than when he served as Governor General of the Philippines. He was most comfortable with the elite of Manila, greeting him here, but thanks to Mrs. Nellie Taft's active sponsorship of social programs for the poor, he was well-liked by ordinary Filipinos too.

A Paternal Governor

Roosevelt proclaimed the insurrection ended in July 1902 and named William Howard Taft, a former judge from Ohio, to be the colony's governor-general. Roosevelt and Taft had met only recently, but they hit it off royally from the start, which was odd because they had little in common. The president was an athletic bundle of energy, an unabashed and aggressive colonialist, often a bully, and an extroverted politician to the marrow of his bones. Taft was easy-going, phlegmatic; he weighed 300 pounds; the only exercise he enjoyed was golf, then widely regarded as a sissies' game. Taft had opposed annexing the Philippines, and he loathed politics, both the back-room horse trading and the modern political campaign, storming about giving self-praising speeches and, most disgusting of all, asking people for their votes. Taft was an administrator, and as good as they got. He was a man of the office, a desktop covered with reports, doing what his superiors asked and expecting his subordinates to follow his instruction. His life's ambition was to be appointed a justice on the Supreme Court.

Nevertheless, as so many other people were, Taft was smitten by Roosevelt, and the president recognized in Taft a competent self-effacing man who got things done.

He could not have made a better choice for the job of reconciling the people of the Philippines to American over-lordship. Taft was popular within months, not only with the cultured and sophisticated elite of Manila (that Americans, fed on newspaper accounts of half-naked savages swinging bolo knives in the jungle, hardly knew existed), but also with the Filipino masses.

Perhaps because he personally disliked colonialism, Taft instituted a paternalistic government in which he made partners of well-to-do and influential Filipinos. He created an efficient "Philippine Constabulary" to replace American soldiers in putting down local rebellions that continued to break out in remote corners of the country. He established a public school system and publicly financed health services that were not available in many parts of the United States. He persuaded the Roman Catholic Church to sell the United States its many plantations and factories and resold them at bargain-basement prices to the Philippine elite. (Most turned out to be at least as exploitative as the Church had been.) When, in 1903, Roosevelt offered Taft the Supreme Court seat he longed for, Filipinos, both the wealthy and ordinary people, begged him to stay on with such fervor that he did.

No subsequent governor-general was as popular as Taft. Because of the precedents he set, American rule continued to be light-handed. In 1916, a Democratic Congress passed the Philippine Autonomy Act that, except for retaining the appointed governor, put domestic matters in Philippine hands. Nothing better illustrated Philippine appreciation of the relatively benign character of American rule than the fact that, when the Japanese invaded the islands in 1942, the Philippine masses sided with the Americans. Nothing of the sort happened in the European colonies in Asia the Japanese occupied.

Puerto Rico   American rule in Puerto Rico was constructive compared to the island's experience as a Spanish colony. Even under military control between 1898 and 1901, the foundations of a public school and public health system were laid and freedom of speech, press, assembly, and religion were guaranteed, unique concessions in an occupied country. The army's prohibition of cockfighting was unpopular, but it was too easily evaded to cause much resentment.

If Puerto Rican independence had ever been an option in Washington, it was no longer so by 1900. Although the route had yet to be decided, the United States was committed to digging an isthmian canal connecting the Atlantic and Pacific oceans. Puerto Rico's location between two main channels into the Caribbean made the island vital as a naval base. The Foraker Act of 1900 created a civil government in which Puerto Rican participation was checked by federal power. The people of the island elected the lower house of a legislature; an appointed "executive council"—half Puerto Ricans, half Americans—served as an upper house. The appointed governor held veto power over legislation although the assembly could override his veto by a two-thirds vote, that possibility was precluded by the Americans on the executive council.

The U.S. dollar replaced the peso; Puerto Rican products were exempted from the protective tariff; the Post Office Department took over the mails; and the work day for government employees, as in the United States, was limited to eight hours. Less popular (and unsuccessful) was the decision that English be the language of instruction in the public schools. Where Filipinos readily abandoned the Spanish language in favor of English, Puerto Ricans clung to Spanish. American hopes of cultural assimilation of Puerto Ricans were quickly dashed.

Nevertheless, in 1917, at the same time the Democratic Congress pledged the United States to Philippine independence, it granted United States citizenship to Puerto Ricans. They had the same access to the states and the same rights there as a Kentuckian moving to California. This and the fact that Puerto Ricans living in the "organized but unincorporated" territory were not required to pay federal taxes accounted for the fact that independence never appealed to more than a small minority of the people.

Guam and Samoa had populations of less than 10,000 each. They and several dot on the map American islands in the Pacific were administered by the U.S. Navy as if they were naval bases—which, indeed, was what they were.

THE AMERICAN EMPIRE

In the twenty-first century, *imperialism* has become a dirty word. Calling a nation or a policy "imperialist" is the equivalent of a sixteenth-century German peasant pointing to an old woman boiling a pot of herbs and saying "witch." But that has not always been the case, and it is important that we not think that we have everything right and the people of the past were always wrong.

Therefore, it is important to use a value-neutral definition of the word *imperialism,* such as, one country exercising hegemony—preponderant influence—over the political and economic affairs of other countries. There is no implication in this that imperialism is by nature a good thing or a bad thing nor as to whether the hegemonic relationship was forced by one country on another (like the annexation of the Philippines) or was the consequence of circumstances and events not particularly shaped by anyone.

So, while William McKinley is entitled to be called America's first imperialist president, it is difficult to believe he began to understand the consequences of what his thoughtful and energetic secretary of state, John Hay, was up to in his imperialistic foreign policy. As was the president's political habit, McKinley fell in behind the parade with the loudest bands and the most flags. Theodore Roosevelt, who kept Hay on in the State Department, knew exactly what he was doing when he transformed the Caribbean into an American lake and developed naval bases in Hawaii, Samoa, and the Philippines that gave the United States a presence in the Pacific second to no other power.

In 1907, Roosevelt sent sixteen battleships and various smaller vessels on a 43,000 mile voyage around the world. Painted white for the occasion, the flotilla made a mind-boggling sight and was a great public relations success. However, naval experts knew that the ships of the Great White Fleet were somewhat obsolete. Japan, Britain, and Germany already had several larger, more powerful super-battleships called "dreadnoughts." (The first American dreadnought was then nearing completion.)

The "Open Door" The commercial prize in Asia was the Chinese Empire with a market of 160 million customers for Western manufactures and a backward economy ready for investment and profiteering. By 1899, China's Qing (or Manchu) dynasty was tottering. Through a series of "unequal treaties" forced on the emperors, Britain, France, Russia, Japan, and Germany had carved out "spheres of influence" in different parts of the country where their citizens enjoyed commercial and political privileges.

For good reason—it had happened in southern Asia and Africa—John Hay feared that, on some small pretext, one or more of those nations would convert their spheres of influence into full-fledged colonies. In that case, American manufacturers would be shut out of the markets there and American investors restricted in their activities.

In 1899 and 1900, in an attempt to forestall the partition of China into colonies, John Hay dispatched what came to be called the Open Door Notes to all the countries involved. The notes called on the imperialist powers to guarantee equal trading and investment rights to all nations within their spheres of interest and to guarantee China's territorial integrity and political independence.

The Boxer Rebellion

Only Great Britain was genuinely friendly to the Open Door policy. The British had learned that the cost of governing a colony could be higher than the money to be made from it. The other imperial powers shilly-shallied around, each conceding that it might accept the Open Door if the other nations with spheres of influence did so first. In July 1900, Hay outfoxed them by declaring that the Open Door had been accepted "in principle" by all concerned parties.

It was in the nick of time. In June, members of the Society of Righteous Harmonious Fists, or Boxers, an antiforeigner, anti-Christian movement, killed more than 200 foreigners and trapped 900 others and some Chinese Christians in the British legation. Eight nations, the five sphere of influence countries plus Italy, Austria-Hungary, and the United States, sent armies that eventually numbered more than 50,000 soldiers to rescue the besieged foreigners and suppress the rebellion.

Japan and Russia, two of the three chief targets of the Open Door Notes, provided the biggest contingents, 21,000 soldiers from Japan, 13,000 from Russia. It is difficult to believe that, but for the Open Door policy (and the presence of troops from other nations), they would have left without cutting slices of the Chinese pie for their empero. Indeed, Russia and Japan went to war in 1904–1905 as to which nation would be paramount in Chinese Manchuria.

Yanqui Imperialismo

In March 1901, with American soldiers and marines still occupying parts of Cuba, Congress added several conditions to its three-year-old pledge of Cuban independence. The Platt Amendment (added to an army appropriations bill) stated that the United States would withdraw its troops from the island only when the Cuban government agreed to American supervision of its finances and foreign relations; to provide land suitable as an American naval base (what became Guantanamo Bay); and agreed that "the United States may exercise the right to intervene [in the country] for the preservation of Cuban independence [and] the maintenance of a government adequate for the protection of life, property, and individual liberty."

The uproar among Cuban nationalists was furious but, as they knew, futile. The American warships anchored in the harbors of Havana and Santiago were capable of leveling both cities. The United States had 120,000 troops in the Philippines that, with the insurrection dying, were ready for service in Cuba. The young Cuban government had two options: rebellion, probable defeat, and likely annexation of Cuba as a colony; or accepting the status of a protectorate—not a colony, but not a sovereign state either. The Cubans caved in and wrote the Platt Amendment into the nation's constitution.

The American humiliation of Cuba marked the beginning of Latin American resentment of *yanqui imperialismo*, a resentment that is far from dead today. Not that every American interference in the affairs of the nations of the Caribbean was without its benefits. The governments of Cuba, Haiti, the Dominican Republic, and Nicaragua were ineffective and unstable, the playthings of rival and often corrupt *caudillos*—"strongmen."

Much as ordinary people resented the arrogance and bullying of American troops (usually marines), as long as they were present, there was domestic peace, no small thing for a helpless peasant or day laborer.

There was, however, no semblance of a justification for Theodore Roosevelt's encouragement of and collaboration in what he regarded as the greatest achievement of his presidency, the taking of the Panama Canal Zone and the construction of "the path between the seas."

The Path Between the Seas   No sooner had Vasco Nuñez de Balboa discovered that Panama was a narrow isthmus than visionaries began to propose digging a ship canal across it to link the Atlantic and Pacific. Such an undertaking was a pipe dream until the nineteenth-century when steam-powered excavators and railroads to remove the dirt and rock made it conceivable. In 1880, a French company won a concession from Colombia, of which Panama was a province, to construct a canal.

The French project was probably doomed from the start. Its designer, Ferdinand de Lesseps, insisted on a sea level canal (no locks) like the canal he had built across Suez. That soon proved impossible in mountainous Panama, and tropical diseases savaged supervisors and laborers in Panama. Three of five Frenchmen and women on the scene—high-level employees who lived well—died of malaria or yellow fever. Mortality among West Indian pick and shovel workers was worse. As many as 22,000 died. By 1893, the construction company was bankrupt and work slowed nearly to a halt.

A long-standing American interest in a Central American canal was intensified during the war with Spain. The battleship *Oregon,* based in San Francisco, was ordered to join the fleet assembling to attack the Spanish in Cuba. The *Oregon* was sixty-seven days steaming the 12,000 miles around Cape Horn. Had there been a "path between the seas," the voyage would have been but 4,000 miles and taken the *Oregon* less than three weeks.

Most American engineers disliked the Panama route. The terrain was rugged. The Chagres River, that crossed the canal route fourteen times, flooded violently every year. And the world was horrified by the death toll of workers on the French project.

The engineers and, it seemed, Congress, favored digging the canal across Nicaragua. The crossing was longer, but ships would steam 50 miles on the Lake of Nicaragua and 50 on navigable rivers. The terrain was gentler; in fact, the lowest pass across the Americas from Alaska to the Straits of Magellan was in Nicaragua. Malaria and yellow fever were a problem but not the scourges they were in

Panama. In a straw vote in January 1902, the House of Representatives endorsed the Nicaragua route.

Enter Bunau-Varilla Already, however, one of the era's greatest diplomatic manipulators was at work. Philippe Jean Bunau-Varilla represented the New Panama Canal Company that had inherited the assets of the failed French company. The French had excavated 60 million cubic meters, but that ditch would still be there when the Colombian concession expired. The buildings the French had constructed were next to worthless, having decayed after a decade of neglect. French equipment, largely obsolete anyway, had rusted into uselessness in the tropical humidity.

Bunau-Varilla kept his distance from President Roosevelt. He was already flirting with scandal with his relentless courtship of congressmen and influential businessmen. His attorney, William Nelson Cromwell, scored a propaganda coup against the Nicaragua route by distributing Nicaraguan postage stamps showing a smoking Mount Momotombo. What was a little high water on the Chagres River compared to the damage a volcano could do a canal?

In fact, Momotombo was dormant and, in any case, was some miles from the proposed canal. Nevertheless, days after the stamps were distributed to senators, they voted in favor of paying Bunau-Varilla's company $40 million for its assets (Cromwell's fee was $600,000) and building in Panama.

There is no evidence of bribery, and Roosevelt was both incorruptible and too knowledgeable to be panicked by a picture on a postage stamp. Nevertheless, he enthusiastically backed the Panama route and hurriedly negotiated the HayHerran Treaty, which paid Colombia $10 million and annual payments of $250,000 for control of a 10-mile-wide American "zone" across the isthmus.

"I Took the Canal Zone" The project stalled when Colombia rejected the treaty, demanding a $25 million payment. No doubt, corrupt Colombian politicians were dreaming of a bonanza in graft, but the higher price tag was not unreasonable. Bunau-Varilla's company collected $40 million for its virtually worthless assets.

But Roosevelt's hackles were up. Instead of paying the $25 million or turning to Nicaragua, he conspired through intermediaries with the resourceful and never-give-up BunauVarilla to collaborate in a parody of a Panamanian war for independence. On November 2, 1903, Roosevelt dispatched warships to Panamanian waters to warn the Colombians off. The next day, two Panamanian towns erupted in riots and Bunau-Varilla's local associates declared Panama's independence. Four days later, the United States recognized the Republic of Panama. (It had taken the United States fifty years to recognize Haiti's independence.) On November 18, the Panamanian foreign minister, none other than Phillippe Bunau-Varilla, signed a treaty that granted the United States perpetual use of a 10-mile-wide zone through the middle of the new nation.

Roosevelt's high-handed intervention in Panama was only the first of numerous presidential interventions in Latin American affairs. Ironically, they based their imperialism—including the Platt Amendment—on the nation's great anti-imperialist statement, the Monroe Doctrine.

**The Monroe
Doctrine**

In 1823, President James Monroe responded to a French and Russian threat to restore Spain's former colonies to her by declaring that the Americas were closed to further colonization by European powers: "We should consider any attempt on their part to extend their system to any portion of this hemisphere as dangerous to our peace and safety." In diplomatic language, he stated that if any Old World power attempted to establish or restore colonial authority over any American republic, the United States would consider it an act of war

In 1864, with the United States preoccupied with its Civil War, French Emperor Napoleon III defied the Monroe Doctrine when he sent an army to Mexico to install an Austrian archduke on a throne. In 1865 President Andrew Johnson demanded the withdrawal of the French army. In 1867, Napoleon did so although more because he feared war with Prussia back home than because he expected the United States, so soon after its terrible bloodletting, to mobilize a large army to march on Mexico.

In 1895, President Grover Cleveland cited the Monroe Doctrine when he pressured Great Britain to submit a dispute with Venezuela over unpaid loans to an

© Bettmann/UP/Corbis

Tawdry as the acquisition of the Canal Zone was, constructing it was one of the most glorious feats of engineering and organization of all time. This photograph indicates how much rock and earth had to be excavated. Gigantic 95-ton Bucyrus steam shovels picked up 5 cubic yards (about 8 tons) with each scoop. The organizational problem was getting the spoil out of the way so that the shovels—sixty-eight at one point—could work continuously. In one "cut," twelve parallel railways on terraces as here removed the rock and dirt twenty-four hours a day.

independent arbitrator rather than invade the country. In 1902, Venezuela was in money trouble again, with German and Italian as well as British creditors. Ships from the three nations blockaded the coast; the next year, a German warship bombarded a Venezuelan port. Roosevelt protested and informed the German ambassador that the American Caribbean fleet would respond to further violence.

That crisis passed, but Roosevelt worried that his diplomatic success in Venezuela was encouraging other governments in the region to neglect repayment of their debts in the belief that the United States Navy would protect them from European warships. If a Caribbean republic defaulted, he feared, a multinational European operation would be too much for the United States to handle.

The Roosevelt Corollary

The most worrisome case was the Dominican Republic, the Spanish-speaking country that shared the island of Hispaniola with Haiti. General Ulises Heureaux, dictator between 1882 and 1899, had brought political stability, in part, by borrowing heavily in France, the Netherlands, Italy, Germany, and from an American firm with friends in Washington. The Dominican foreign debt was $32 million, a whopping sum for a nation of just 650,000 people.

In 1904, with the Dominican Republic uppermost in mind, the president proclaimed what came to be called the "Roosevelt Corollary" to the Monroe Doctrine. His object was to assure European creditors that military action was not necessary to guarantee repayment of their loans. He placated—so he pretended—Latin American countries governed "with reasonable efficiency and decency in social and political matters" by saying that they "need fear no interference from the United States." However, in countries guilty of "chronic wrongdoing"—failure to repay loans on time and political disorder—the United States would be forced, "however reluctantly, in flagrant cases of such wrongdoing or impotence, to the exercise of an international police power."

The Roosevelt Corollary was insulting. Roosevelt was telling the "dagos" (as, in private, he called Latin Americans) that they were children in need of stern supervision by their Anglo-Saxon big brother from the north. Roosevelt's defenders point out that he had little wiggle room in the matter. The alternative to preemptive American intervention was intervention by European powers that could lead easily to permanent occupation.

Interventions

Roosevelt's first application of his corollary was not military. In 1905, the Dominican president agreed to put the collection of the country's customs duties in American hands, ensuring that the repayment of foreign debts was a high priority. The arrangement had its benefits for the Dominicans. It reduced corrupt diversions of government funds and freed the government for other tasks. The United States insurance policy also encouraged a surge of badly needed American investment in the Dominican Republic but that too had its downside. A disproportionate number of the country's ranches and sugar plantations fell into the hands of American speculators who were interested in profits, not the welfare of Dominicans. And the fact that the interveners were not soldiers but coat-and-necktie bureaucrats did little to alleviate the insult to Domincan patriotism.

Also in 1905, several hundred marines were sent into Honduras. They departed within a few months, but it was only the first of five times the United States responded to internal problems in that country with uninvited invasions. In 1908, troops crossed the line from the Canal Zone into Panama to put down riots (the first of four interventions in that country).

In 1910, Roosevelt's successor, William Howard Taft, who had hoped not to employ "gunboat diplomacy," intervened in Nicaragua and, in 1912, he sent troops into Cuba to help crush an uprising of sugar plantation workers.

These were small operations, as most American interventions of the 1910s and 1920s were. The marines numbered only in the hundreds, with specific objectives, and departed quickly. They were also so frequent, however, as to arouse increasing Latin American resentment of American arrogance.

Occupations   In several instances, interventions became extended occupations by marines numbering in the thousands. In 1906, citing the Platt Amendment, Roosevelt responded to threats of civil war in Cuba by "sending in the marines." They stayed for three years. (The Marine Corps, not the army, did most of the dirty work in the Caribbean because they were the navy's ground troops, aboard ship and always ready for action.) In 1912, President Taft intervened in Nicaragua and the troops stayed until 1925; they were gone less than a year when they returned for six more years.

The two longest occupations were in Haiti (1915–1934) and the Dominican Republic (1916–1924). They were launched by a Democratic president, Woodrow Wilson, who was on record as opposing colonialism, imperialism, and gunboat diplomacy. It was Wilson who signed the bill giving Puerto Ricans citizenship and promising independence to the Philippines.

His reason for abandoning his own principles was the great war that broke out in Europe in August 1914—World War I—and which was to become Wilson's obsession. Wilson learned that German diplomats had made overtures to political groups in both countries to exploit the endemic instability in both to put pro-German governments in power. Haiti and the Domican Republic would have provided submarine bases superbly located for raiding British and—a real possibility by 1916—American shipping. Once there, the American troops stayed.

It is a mistake to imagine that all Cubans, Nicaraguans, Dominicans, and Haitians seethed with anger over the American occupations. Some political factions in each country maneuvered to curry American favor for their own benefit. As a rule, the marines did not brutalize ordinary people as indigenous armies and police often did. The common people enjoyed social stability, a rare commodity in the region. Nevertheless, as the American government was to recognize in 1930, what Theodore Roosevelt started earned the United States an unfortunately deserved reputation for bullying the weak.

THE UNHAPPY PRESIDENCY OF WILLIAM HOWARD TAFT

In 1908, Roosevelt was unable to persuade Congress to act on any of his legislative proposals. The Republicans had big majorities in both houses but most of them were "Old Guard" conservatives who had obliged the president only when they were afraid of him. But Roosevelt was a "lame duck." Four years earlier, celebrating the victory of 1904—Roosevelt had declared that "a wise custom which limits the President to two terms regards the substance and not the form, and under no circumstances will I be a candidate for or accept another nomination." Having served three and a half years of McKinley's term, he considered himself a two-term president in "substance."

Picking a Successor   Did he regret his decision come 1908? He was only 50 and as energetic and healthy as he had ever been. (Which was not all that healthy. TR had had heart problems since boyhood. He discreetly carried nitroglycerin pills to pop when suddenly hit by attacks of *angina pectoris*.) His personal popularity was undiminished. Had he announced he had changed his mind about running, he would have won a third term easily.

There is no evidence he had second thoughts. Roosevelt had interests other than politics or, at least, he thought he did. He had been mulling over a trip to East Africa to massacre lions, elephants, rhinoceroses, and other creatures that could not be bagged in the United States. (It was the golden age of the "great white hunter.") He was content to be the only president since Andrew Jackson in a position to hand-pick his successor.

His first choice was Secretary of War William Howard Taft who would have prefered to decline the honor and wait for the next vacancy on the Supreme Court. But his ambitious brother and his wife were dazzled by Roosevelt's offer. They browbeat the always obliging Taft to accept the nomination. He would regret his decision.

But not in November. Taft easily defeated a now shopworn William Jennings Bryan, running for a third time with no cause like free silver or anti-imperialism to preach. The silver issue was a dead letter, even among farmers. Prosperity had returned to American farms as food exports to Europe soared. Thanks in no small part to Taft's successful governorship of the Philippines, anti-imperialism, once a powerful movement, had become the cause of a ragged fringe.

"I think that it is very rare," Roosevelt said in endorsing Taft, "that two public men have ever been so much as one in all the essentials of their public beliefs." This was hyperbolic, but Taft had been loyal to Roosevelt and his policies. The difficulty of the succession was the radical difference in style between the bombastic, aggressive Roosevelt and the phlegmatic, accommodating Taft. Roosevelt was aware of the difficulties Taft faced following his act on stage. He departed on his African safari immediately after Taft's inauguration so that the new president would have the spotlight to himself.

The Tariff   Taft continued antitrust prosecutions throughout his term. His administration initiated ninety suits in four years, twice as many as the trustbusters in almost eight. But Taft won no plaudits from progressives for his efforts because, almost immediately after taking office, he stumbled over an issue that Roosevelt had danced around—the tariff.

In 1909, the Dingley Tariff had been in effect for twelve years. Enacted by a Republican Congress in 1897, it taxed imports at, on average, 46.5 percent. That is, an English-made pair of boots that could have been sold profitably in Chicago for $10 had to be priced, because of the tariff, at almost $15.

Yellow Fever

One benign consequence of American imperialism was the confirmation by an army doctor in Cuba, Major Walter Reed, that yellow fever was transmitted by mosquitoes and his development of a procedure to control and even eliminate the disease.

Yellow fever (called *vomito negro* in Spanish-speaking countries) originated in Africa and was brought to the Americas in slave ships. Most people who contracted it recovered, but the mortality rate was high and the disease was especially terrifying because it came to an area mysteriously in epidemics and then mysteriously disappeared. There were serious outbreaks in the cities of the Northeast between 1793 and 1798, in Virginia in 1855, and in Memphis in 1878. It was a more frequent visitor in the Caribbean. Yellow fever more than any other single cause was the undoing of the large French army sent to defeat rebels in Haiti in 1802. It was particularly lethal in Cuba. It is estimated that during the nineteenth century, 10 percent of the island's population died of it.

Doctors were mystified by the cause of the disease and assumed that it was contracted by coming into direct contact with an infected person. In 1881, a Cuban physician, Carlos Finlay, observed that epidemics in Havana coincided with mosquito seasons and conducted experiments that indicated all but conclusively that *vomito negro* was transmitted from person to person not by direct contact but by mosquito bites. Finlay's findings were ignored until 1900 when Major Reed confirmed his theory.

Reed put hundreds of soldiers to work patrolling every street in Havana. They forcibly removed infected people to quarantine in hospitals where they died or survived but, because the windows of the buildings were tightly screened, mosquitoes could not bite them and move on to others with the virus. On Reed's orders, the soldiers dumped or smashed every receptacle where water collected (mosquitoes reproduce in still water) and poured kerosene on ponds. The soldiers being the roughnecks they were and many *habaneros* resisting the removal of ailing family members and furious when their pottery was broken, incidents of Cubans left bleeding and bruised (and furiously anti-American) were numerous. But Reed's program could not have been carried out except by soldiers carrying rifles with bayonets fixed and acting arbitrarily.

The program's success astonished even the army. Yellow fever disappeared from Havana within three months. Reed's methods were then employed in Panama where the disease had killed between 10,000 and 20,000 employees of the defunct French canal company. The disease was virtually eradicated on the isthmus. Reed and the Panama Canal authority had a stroke of luck that was understood only later. In the Western Hemisphere, only one genus of mosquito, *Haemagogus*, transmitted the yellow fever virus. Unless *Haemagogus* was widely dispersed by powerful winds, the insects passed their entire life spans within a very small area. By killing the larvae and quarantining infected people in a locality, the disease could be controlled in that locality with comparative ease.

Today, there is an effective vaccine for the disease. Nevertheless, the World Health Organization estimates that 200,000 people in tropical areas die of it every year.

Only a few American industries needed "protection" from foreign competition to survive by 1909. In the "infant industries" of the era—electrical equipment, telephones, typewriters—American manufacturers undersold Europeans with superior products throughout the world market, charging less abroad than, thanks to the Dingley Tariff, they charged Americans at home. Half the streetcars in British cities were American made. American steelmakers regularly won big contracts for naval armor in Britain by underbidding British mills. The United States navy, thanks to the tariff, paid a big premium for its ships.

The Democrats had never ceased to call for lower duties. During Roosevelt's presidency, they were joined in Congress by progressive midwestern Republicans. Roosevelt sidestepped the issue because, if he defended the Dingley tariff, he would lose his progressive supporters; if he advocated a reduction of rates, he would alienate conservative Republicans, the majority of the party.

Taft was a better progressive on the issue than TR but, unsurprisingly, a woefully worse politician. As one of his first presidential acts in 1909, he called Congress into special session for the purpose of lowering duties. The House of Representatives wrote a moderate reduction of the tariff. In the Senate, however, a master of political manipulation and high-tariff man, Nelson Aldrich of Rhode Island, arranged to have 800 amendments attached to the bill. Because tariff legislation was so complex, full of highly technical language and long tables of numbers, it was not clear to many before the bill was law that the Payne-Aldrich Tariff actually raised duties on more than 200 of the items. Aldrich feigned innocence, pointing out that Payne-Aldrich lowered duties in 650 categories. This was rubbing it in (another Aldrich specialty) for the significant reductions were on agricultural products and gewgaws.

To rub it in a bit more, Aldrich removed all duties and other restrictions on imports of fine art, a savings of interest only to millionaire art collectors like J. P. Morgan, Henry Clay Frick, Andrew Mellon, and Aldrich himself.

Taft's Blunders   Taft could have vetoed Payne-Aldrich, sending the tariff back to Congress with specific instructions for changes. But that act called for a hard-nosed president who liked a good fight, an Andrew Jackson or a Theodore Roosevelt. Taft was nothing of the kind. He was a political regular who was more comfortable with other regulars like Aldrich and uneasy with Republican progressive crusaders like LaFollette and Jonathan Dolliver of Iowa. Five members of his cabinet were corporation lawyers who were, of course, high-tariff men who understood the political risks of approving Payne-Aldrich less than Taft did.

He concocted what he hoped was a split-the-difference compromise. He signed the Payne-Aldrich bill while announcing his support for a progressive project, a constitutional amendment to permit the enactment of a graduated income tax. (It was ratified in 1913 as the Sixteenth Amendment.) But then Taft blundered. In Minnesota, a progressive stronghold, he described the Payne-Aldrich Act as "the best tariff that the Republican party ever passed."

In March 1910, Taft blundered again when he backed Speaker of the House Joseph Cannon when progressive Republicans and Democrats introduced a resolution to destroy the Speaker's dictatorial control of the powerful House Rules

Gifford Pinchot of Pennsylvania. A patrician, America's first professional forester, and Theodore Roosevelt's intimate friend, Pinchot's battle with President Taft led directly to Theodore Roosevelt's break with his successor and his decision to run as the Progressive Party presidential candidate in 1912.

Committee. There was nothing to be gained in taking Cannon's side. The dispute was, as the constitutional lawyer Taft knew very well, a congressional matter in which the president had no business meddling. Nor was there anything to be gained politically. Congressmen feared Cannon but did not like him. He was arrogant, foul-mouthed, and frequently drunk. Indeed, enough Republican moderates supported the resolution to adopt it. The progressives announced their opposition to the administration, calling themselves "Insurgents."

| Return the Conquering Hero | In the spring of 1910, former president Roosevelt was still in Europe. In Norway, he delivered the Nobel Peace Prize speech he had been unable to deliver in 1906. He was preparing to return home when the king of England, Edward VII, died. At |

Taft's behest, he represented the United States at the funeral.

To all appearances, president and vice president were on the best of terms. Roosevelt had not commented on Taft's problems with the tariff and the Cannon affair. He may well have sympathized with Taft's mistakes had it not been for the president's dismissal of his close friend Gifford Pinchot as head of the Forest Service.

The Pinchot-Ballinger Affair began when, with Taft's approval, Secretary of the Interior Richard Ballinger released to private developers several hydroelectric sites that Roosevelt and Pinchot had declared off limits. Ballinger's stated grounds for the action were some irregularities in the reservation procedure. In a memorandum to Taft, Pinchot accused Ballinger of selling out to the kind of greedy exploiters that conservationism was designed to foil. When Taft sided with Ballinger, Pinchot "leaked" the story, complete with documents, to *Collier's* magazine, which was still in the muckraking business. Taft fired him, and Pinchot caught the first steamer to Europe to vent his fury to Roosevelt.

When TR returned to the United States in June, he exchanged only the curtest greetings with the president. In his first speeches on behalf of Republican congressional candidates, he ignored or played down the split between Old Guard and Insurgent

Republicans. Then, at Ossawatomie, Kansas, in September, Roosevelt outlined a comprehensive program of progressive reform that he called the "New Nationalism."

Roosevelt endorsed woman suffrage, a federal minimum wage for female workers, national abolition of child labor, strict limitations on the power of courts to issue injunctions in labor disputes, and a national social insurance scheme much like today's Social Security system. Proposing a legislative program as if he were a president addressing Congress was an insult to Taft. Roosevelt made the split explicit when he demanded that a commission set tariff rates "scientifically." Several of Roosevelt's associates spoke of nominating him in opposition to Taft at the Republican convention in 1912.

Challenging Taft

The gossip angered Taft; it depressed Robert La Follette. The senator had stated his own intentions to seek the Republican nomination. He sent mutual friends to ask Roosevelt of his plans, implying (none too happily) that he would drop out if TR wanted to run. Roosevelt responded that he was not interested in returning to the White House. Relieved, in January 1912, La Follette organized the Progressive Republican League to promote his candidacy.

In fact, Roosevelt was itching to run. When, in March, La Follette collapsed while making a speech, Roosevelt announced almost immediately, "my hat is in the ring."

La Follette was not ill; he had been exhausted from overwork; and he never forgave TR for using him as a stalkinghorse. Fighting Bob was no match for the old master when it came to stirring up progressive activists, and his campaign fell apart. Roosevelt swept most of the thirteen state primary elections, winning 278 convention delegates to Taft's 48 and La Follette's 36.

If La Follette was beaten, Taft was not. He had a powerful weapon in his arsenal, control of the party organization. As president, he had appointed Republicans to lucrative government jobs, wedding their careers to his own success. Most important were convention delegates from the southern states. Republicans won few elections in the South; for many southern Republicans, the only point of the party was the federal appointments at the president's disposal: to jobs as postmasters, customs collectors, agricultural agents, and the like. Southern delegates to the Republican convention were, therefore, Taft delegates. Along with northeastern conservatives, they outnumbered the delegates Roosevelt won in the primaries.

The Taft forces demonstrated their control of the convention when they awarded 235 of 254 disputed seats to Taft. Roosevelt's supporters shouted "Fraud!" and walked out to organize the Progressive party, or, as it was nicknamed for the battle with the Republican elephant and the Democratic donkey, the Bull Moose party. (In a backhanded reference to Taft's obesity, Roosevelt said that he was "as strong as a bull moose.")

WOODROW WILSON'S PROGRESSIVISM

In one piece, the Republican party was the nation's majority party. Split into two, it was vulnerable, and the Democrats smelled victory. When they assembled in Baltimore in 1912, there was an abundance of would-be nominees.

Southern states played a special role in Democratic conventions too. Because the South usually delivered all its electoral votes to the Democratic candidate, the southern states were given a virtual veto on the nomination. A candidate needed to win not a simply majority but two-thirds of the delegates. No one solidly opposed by southern Democrats could be nominated.

In 1912, several Democratic hopefuls were southerners so the southern delegates were divided. For forty-five ballots, none of half a dozen candidates approached the two-thirds mark. William Jennings Bryan, rather pathetically, hoped that the party would turn to him as a compromise candidate. As a three-time loser, however, Bryan was not very attractive. When he faced up to that fact, he used what influence he had left to turn the convention to the southern-born governor of New Jersey, Woodrow Wilson.

A Moral,
Unbending Man

Woodrow Wilson's rise in politics really was meteoric. He was a college professor who, in 1902, became president of Princeton University, the first non-minister to hold that post.

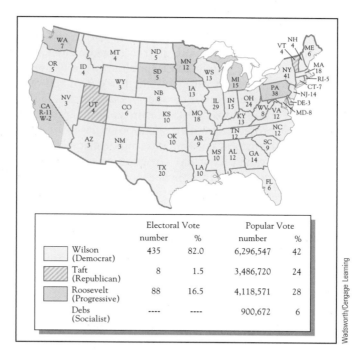

	Electoral Vote		Popular Vote	
	number	%	number	%
Wilson (Democrat)	435	82.0	6,296,547	42
Taft (Republican)	8	1.5	3,486,720	24
Roosevelt (Progressive)	88	16.5	4,118,571	28
Debs (Socialist)	----	----	900,672	6

Wadsworth/Cengage Learning

MAP 35.1 Presidential Election, 1912

Woodrow Wilson won only 42 percent of the popular vote in 1912. Only in the elections of 1824 and 1860 (also four-candidate contests) was a president elected with a smaller share of the vote. However, with Republicans split down the middle, Wilson won a landslide in the electoral college. President Taft won only two states, Vermont and Utah, and was less humiliated than relieved. He hated being president. The Socialist party's highwater mark was 1912; Eugene V. Debs won 6 percent of the popular vote, one vote for every four cast for Taft.

Actually, Wilson had a lot of the Presbyterian clergyman in him. His father and both grandfathers had been ministers. So was his wife's father. He was raised to observe an unbending Calvinist morality, and to be acutely sensitive to the struggle between good and evil in the world. Wilson had his light side. He was an affectionate father, an avid football and baseball fan, and—unusual; the movies were still largely a working-class entertainment—a film buff. In public, however, Wilson was formal, sometimes icy.

As late as 1910, Wilson was still an educator, albeit an honored one. When he clashed with Princeton alumni, his academic career looked to be over. So it was a godsend when New Jersey's Democratic party, under attack for corruption, asked him, because of his upright public image, to run for governor. To everyone's surprise except Wilson's, who attributed the outcome of elections to God's will, he won. His upset victory made him a national figure overnight—a Democratic progressive.

The Election of 1912   In fact, Wilson was less a social reformer than a good government progressive. He set about cleaning up New Jersey's state bureaucracy and the Democratic party. Like Teddy Roosevelt in New York a decade earlier, Wilson was soon at odds with the party bosses. They were pleased when he decided to seek the presidency and delighted when he won the nomination. They were glad to be rid of him.

With Taft and Roosevelt dividing the Republican vote between them, Wilson won easily in the electoral college with only 42 percent of the popular vote. His campaign program (called the "New Freedom") was just on the progressive side of middle of the road. He called for a lower tariff, as Democratic candidates always did, and for intensified prosecution of trusts. Roosevelt, in his four years out of office, had concluded that business consolidation was inevitable in modern industrial society so that trustbusting was reactionary. The point was that the federal government had the power to regulate corporate operations—even direct them—in the public interest. Wilson called this a dangerous concentration of government power; there was still a good deal of the states rights southerner in him.

Tariffs, Taxes, and Trusts   President Wilson was an Anglophile. Before he became a politician, he vacationed in Great Britain most summers. He admired the British and Canadian parliamentary system in which the head of government, the prime minister, is himself a member of Parliament. There was no altering the constitutional separation of powers, but Wilson addressed Congress in person, which no president had done for a century.

Wilson's brief speech was aimed less at persuading congressmen than at inspiring their constituents to put the heat on them, and it worked. A number of Democratic senators who were dragging their feet on tariff revision fell into line. The Underwood-Simmons Tariff reduced Payne-Aldrich rates by 15 percent and put iron, steel, woolens, and farm machinery on the free list.

That meant reduced government revenue. To make up the loss, Wilson called for a corporate and a personal income tax. The personal tax was not high by present standards. People who earned less than $4,000 a year paid nothing. On annual incomes between $4,000 and $20,000, a tidy sum in 1913, the rate was only 1 percent. People in the highest bracket, $500,000 and up, paid only 7 percent.

In 1914, Congress enacted new antitrust legislation. The Clayton Antitrust Act fined corporations for business practices that stifled competition. It forbade interlocking directorates (the same men sitting on the boards of competing companies and coordinating policies), and declared that officers of corporations would be held personally responsible for offenses committed by their companies. Congress also created the Federal Trade Commission to supervise the activities of the trusts, more a New Nationalism than a New Freedom innovation.

The Federal Reserve System   The Federal Reserve Act of 1913 was designed to hobble the power of Wall Street by giving the federal government a say in banking. The law established 12 regional Federal Reserve Banks which dealt not directly with people but with other banks. The Federal Reserve System was owned by private bankers who were required to deposit 6 percent of their capital in it. However, the president appointed the majority of the directors, who sat in Washington, theoretically putting the government in control of the money supply.

The greatest power of the Federal Reserve System was its control of the discount rate, the level of interest at which money is loaned to other banks for lending to private investors and buyers. By lowering the discount rate, the Federal Reserve board could stimulate investment and economic expansion in slow times. By raising the rate, the Federal Reserve could cool down an overactive economy that threatened to blow up in inflation and financial panic.

The Federal Reserve System did more systematically and openly what the notorious J. P. Morgan had done in several dramatic incidents. (Morgan died in 1913.) But it did not hobble powerful banks like the House of Morgan. Representatives of the big private New York banks sat on the Federal Reserve Board. Nevertheless, the system, still in place today, held the great banks accountable. There would never again be a J. P. Morgan, a single man with such immense financial power that the government had to go to him to put the lid on crises.

Wilson Changes Direction   The Democrats retained majorities in House and Senate after the congressional elections of 1914, but many Bull Moosers who had lost their seats in the House in the Republican party split in 1912 regained them—as Republicans. It was obvious to the president and Democratic strategists that if the president were to survive the election of 1916 against a reunited Republican party, the Democrats had to woo progressives who had voted for Teddy Roosevelt in 1912.

In order to do so, Wilson agreed to back New Nationalist social legislation that he had warned against in 1912 and as late as 1914. He did not like laws that favored any special interest group, farmers any more than bankers. However, in order to win support in the Midwest, where progressive Republicans were strongest, he agreed to the Federal Farm Loan Act of 1916, which provided low-cost credit to farmers. Early in his administration, Wilson had opposed a child-labor law on constitutional grounds. In 1916, he signed the Keating-Owen Act, which severely restricted the employment of children in most jobs.

The Adamson Act required that railroads put their workers on an eight-hour day with no reduction in pay. Wilson even moderated his approval of Jim Crow legislation although, during his first years as president, Washington took on the racial character of a southern city that it had not had during the long era of Republican supremacy. Despite his lifelong opposition to woman suffrage, the president began to encourage the states to enfranchise women; he hinted that he would support a constitutional amendment that would guarantee the right nationwide.

Wilson, anticipating that Theodore Roosevelt might well win the 1916 Republican nomination with no Republican incumbent able to use the patronage against him, had co-opted much of TR's New Nationalism. It is impossible to say how effective his change of direction would have been in 1916 because, by the summer of that year, domestic reform was no longer the issue on voters' minds. Simultaneous with the enactment of Wilson's New Freedom and much of TR's New Nationalism, the great powers of Europe had tumbled into the bloodiest war in history. Theodore Roosevelt was still Wilson's great rival—the two men despised one another personally—but was a war hawk while Wilson, reluctantly in 1916, was the candidate pledged to keeping the United States out of the conflict.

36

OVER THERE
The United States and World War I 1914–1918

*Good Lord! You're not going to send soldiers over there,
are you?*
—Senator Thomas S. Martin

*The world must be made safe for democracy. Its peace must
be planted upon the tested foundations of political liberty.
We have no selfish ends to serve. We desire no conquest, no
dominion. We seek no indemnities for ourselves, no material
compensation for the sacrifices we shall freely make.*
—President Woodrow Wilson

A few days before Wilson's inauguration in 1913, an aide reminded him of difficulties in American relations with Mexico. Wilson remarked, "It would be the irony of fate if my administration had to deal chiefly with foreign affairs."

Wilson did not fear such a challenge. His self-confidence—his belief that God guided him—was sturdy enough to encompass more than foreign policy. He once said: "I am sorry for those who disagree with me, because I know they are wrong."

However, except for his dislike Theodore Roosevelt's bullying in Latin America, Wilson had never paid much attention to the snarls of international relations. That he appointed as Secretary of State William Jennings Bryan, for whose intellect he had no respect, indicates how little he expected to be troubled by other nations.

WILSON, THE WORLD, AND MEXICO

The president took pride in the fact that American population, industrial might, and wealth ranked the United States at the pinnacle of nations. He believed that the United States was uniquely blessed by the two oceans that insulated the country from other great powers. The Atlantic and Pacific meant that the United States needed no large standing army such as, by 1912, every country in Europe

Neutrality and War 1910–1919

1910	1911	1912	1913	1914	1915	1916	1917	1918 1919

1911 Mexican Revolution

1914 War in Europe

1915 *Lusitania* sunk by U-boat

Pancho Villa raids New Mexico; Sussex Pledge; Wilson reelected 1916

Wilson tries to mediate war Jan 1917
Germany resumes submarine campaign; Zimmerman note revealed Feb 1917
United States declares war April 1917

Final German offensive May 1918
Second battle of Marne July 1918
St.-Mihiel Salient Sept 1918
Armistice Nov 1918

maintained. Founded on ideals rather than on tribalism and territory, the United States could and should act in accordance with high principles, Wilson believed, not narrow self-interest.

Moral Assump-
tions   Wilson intended to depart from the foreign policies of his three Republican predecessors: McKinley, Roosevelt, and Taft. He disliked McKinley's colonialism and pushed for Puerto Rican citizenship and a firm commitment to Philippine independence. In 1919, he unsuccessfully asked Congress to liberate the Philippines immediately.

Wilson criticized Roosevelt's bullying in the Caribbean by stating that his administration would deal with all countries "upon terms of equality and honor." As a progressive Democrat who looked on Wall Street with a jaundiced eye (he appointed no corporation lawyers to his first cabinet), he rejected Taft's "dollar diplomacy." Shortly after taking office, Wilson pointedly withdrew the government's encouragement of an investment scheme in China because endorsement implied the United States would be obliged to intervene if the investors' money was threatened. To Wilson, high-rolling speculators were welcome to gamble on making big profits in Chinese railroads, Guatemalan bananas, or real estate in Timbuctoo. But the risks were theirs. The United States government would not write them an insurance policy against losses.

Secretary of State William Jennings Bryan leaned toward pacifism. He believed that only defensive wars could be justified and that nations on the brink of war could work out their differences peacefully if they "cooled off." Wilson's views were much the same. He approved Bryan's negotiation of conciliation treaties with thirty nations. The signatories pledged that in the event of a dispute, they would delay declaring war for one year. Bryan believed that, in that time, a peaceful resolution of the conflict would be found. (All of the nations of Europe except Germany and Austria-Hungary signed Bryan's treaties.)

Wilson's good intentions were complicated by personal assumptions and prejudices he shared with most Americans, most notably the hated Roosevelt. Wilson was a racist. He was not a redneck apt to join a lynch mob. Wilson was of the southern social class that abhorred the violence of "white trash." He was kindly and generous toward the few African Americans with whom he came into contact and minded his manners very well when receiving mixed-race ambassadors from

Latin American nations. But he did not believe that non-Caucasians were the equals of whites. The academic world from which he came regarded race as a fundamental determinant of a people's intelligence, character, moral sense, and energy.

And Wilson had more than a little of the missionary in him, the kind of missionary who, when he could not persuade others to do things the right way by setting a good example, forced them—"for their own good"—to do so. "We are chosen, and prominently chosen," he said, "to show the way to the nations of the world how they shall walk in the paths of liberty." And so, while he had criticized Taft for sending marines into Nicaragua in 1912, he did not withdraw them. In 1915, he applied the Roosevelt Corollary (never using the name) when he ordered American troops into Haiti and the Dominican Republic. And twice, with no cooling-off period, intervened in Mexico's civil war in ways bearing little resemblance to equality and honor.

¡Viva Madero!
¡Viva Huerta!
¡Viva Carranza!

In 1911, the Mexican dictator of thirty-five years, Porfirio Díaz, was overthrown. British and American investors, whom Díaz had favored, were worried. The leader of the revolution, Francisco Madero, spoke of returning control of Mexican resources to Mexicans. Americans owned $2 billion worth of property in Mexico: most of the country's railroads, 60 percent of the oil wells, and more mines than Mexicans owned.

Madero and Wilson might have gotten along. Both were educated nineteenth-century liberals. Madero was not about to expropriate any foreign property without compensation. But they never had the chance. Shortly before Wilson took office, a junta of generals led by hard-drinking, no-nonsense Victoriano Huerta, quietly encouraged by British and American diplomats, staged a coup and murdered Madero.

Wilson was appalled. With little reflection, he announced that the United States would not recognize "a government of butchers," and he persuaded Britain to withdraw its suspiciously hasty recognition of the Huerta regime. When peasants in several parts of Mexico rebelled against Huerta, a Constitutionalist army took shape behind somber, bearded Venustiano Carranza from Coahuila on the Texas border. Wilson openly approved, a triumph of moral rectitude over prudence when a neighboring country was descending into a civil war.

In April 1914, seven American sailors on shore leave in Tampico were arrested by one of Huerta's colonels. They were released almost immediately; Huerta wanted no more trouble with the gringos than he already had. But authorities in Tampico refused Admiral Henry T. Mayo's demand that they apologize for the affront to American honor with a twenty-one-gun salute. Mayo was blowing a trivial incident out of proportion. Sailors on shore leave did, after all, commit arrest-worthy offenses all the time.

Wilson might have let the incident pass after a bit of diplomatic huffing and puffing. However, when he was informed that a German ship bringing arms for Huerta was nearing Vera Cruz, he ordered marines to occupy the port. To his surprise, Mexican civilians joined with Huerta's soldiers to resist. Before things calmed down, 400 people were dead. Wilson failed to understand that while Huerta was less than beloved in Mexico, the United States was less popular yet. Even Carranza, whom Wilson thought he was trying to help, condemned the intervention. Wilson recognized that he had gotten himself into a fix that could only get worse. He accepted an offer by Argentina, Brazil, and Chile to mediate the crisis and withdrew the troops within six months.

¡Viva Villa!   Huerta did not last. Carranza's forces soon ousted him. However, there was no breather for the Mexican people. Carranza quarreled with one of his best generals, a charismatic character who was born Doroteo Arango but was universally known as Pancho Villa. Villa was both a shrewd military tactician who confounded his enemies with his skill with using railroads to move his Army of the North at lightning speed, and a bandit who paid his *"villistas"* by seizing the property of (mostly wealthy) Mexican ranchers. He was well known in the United States because of a series of magazine articles romanticizing, even idolizing him as "The Robin Hood of Mexico." Villa enjoyed the celebrity and played for American approval.

For a short time, Wilson was convinced that Villa represented democracy in Mexico, but he opted for the stability represented by the more predictable Carranza. When Carranza's army marched into Mexico City in October 1915, Wilson recognized his regime as the official government of Mexico. In fact, Carranza's army controlled as little of the country as Huerta's had. In the south, forces led by Emiliano Zapata

© Bettmann/Corbis

Pancho Villa (center) was a charismatic revolutionary leader and military commander. Although he spoke for the common people and social justice, his villistas sometimes preyed on the poorest and weakest as well as the wealthy. Villa's murder of American engineers traveling on a train and a villista raid on Columbus, New Mexico, led to an American intervention in Mexico. That was Villa's purpose; he hoped to cause a conflict between the United States and his enemy, Venustiano Carranza.

repelled every attempt to defeat him. Much of Chihuahua, the richest and most populous northern state, was governed as if it were an independent country by Pancho Villa.

Stung by what he considered Wilson's betrayal, Villa stopped a train carrying American engineers invited by Carranza to reopen abandoned mines, and summarily shot all but one of them. Early in 1916, he dispatched something between 800 and 1,500 *villistas* (witnesses differed) to raid the dusty desert town of Columbus, New Mexico, where, in a chaotic shoot-'em-up, they killed seventeen people.

Instead of giving Carranza a chance to run Villa down, Wilson ordered General John J. Pershing and 6,000 soldiers, including the African American Tenth Cavalry, to pursue and capture the bandit general. The expedition was more humiliating than Vera Cruz had been. Villa and his men were at home in every arid canyon in northern Mexico. Pershing did not have a reliable map. Ordinary Mexicans who adored (or feared) Villa shrugged dumbly when Pershing's officers asked them for information. Without catching a glimpse of Villa's main force, the Americans penetrated 300 miles into the country. On several occasions, however, they exchanged fire with Carranza's troops, who were also looking for Pancho. In one skirmish, forty men were killed. Thanks to ignorance and arrogance, Wilson did not have a friend in Mexico. In January 1917, he called Pershing home, not because of the debacle south of the border, but because Wilson was approaching a showdown with a more formidable enemy than Pancho Villa.

THE GREAT WAR

Most of Europe went to war in August 1914. The immediate cause was the assassination of Archduke Franz Ferdinand of Austria-Hungary by a Serbian nationalist. At first it appeared that the incident would pass with the usual expressions of grief and anger. It was the golden age of high-profile assassinations; within twenty years, an empress, a czar, a king, and two presidents had been murdered. At worst, diplomats feared, there would be another localized Balkans war, the third within two years, between Serbia and Austria-Hungary.

German Emperor Wilhelm II advised his Austrian ally not to go too far but carelessly wrote Austria a "blank check," saying that Germany would go to war if Russia defended Serbia. France was involved because of a partly secret agreement with Russia. Great Britain had no treaty obligations to the "Allies," but the British had been so unnerved by Germany's construction of a navy challenging her own that she sent her small army to France. Italy was one of the "Central Powers," but was required to fight only if Germany or Austria was attacked. Claiming that Austria was the aggressor, Italy stayed out. The smaller countries of southeastern Europe lined up with one side or the other. By August 1914, much of Europe was at war. Eventually, thirty-three nations would be part of the war.

Americans React   Americans reacted to the sudden explosion with a mixture of disbelief and disgust. "This dreadful conflict of the nations came to most of us as lightning out of a clear day," a congressman said. Threatening talk was nothing new. For a generation, Europeans had been rattling their sabers. Every politician in France was on record calling for "*revanche!*", revenge for Germany's humiliation of France in 1871. Kaiser Wilhelm II was as military crazy as a child; he owned 300 dress uniforms, donning an admiral's insignia to visit an aquarium, a British uniform to eat a plum pudding.

For forty years, however, even the Kaiser had pulled back at the brink of war. No one comprehended just how terrible twentieth-century warfare would be, but they had a notion on the subject. Americans were not unreasonable to assume that Europeans would threaten war without going to war indefinitely. When, in August, Germany launched a massive attack on France through neutral Belgium, they were stunned. Politicians and editors praised the wisdom of George Washington's warning against entangling the United States in Europe's quarrels by joining alliances. They blamed Europe's tragedy on Old World corruptions of which their country was free: hereditary kings and princes and the stockpiling of armaments that were a superfluous waste if they were not used and murderous on a massive scale if they were.

Never did America's moat, the Atlantic Ocean, look better. No one lodged an objection when President Wilson proclaimed the neutrality of the United States. However, when the president also called on Americans to be "neutral in fact as well as in name, ... impartial in thought as well as in action," he was, as he did all too often, ignoring the realities of human nature, even the human nature of what Wilson called "this great peaceful people."

Sympathy for the Allies

A majority of Americans were inclined to favor Great Britain. Britain was the ancestral motherland of the majority. The nation's linguistic, legal, and political legacy was English. President Wilson was an unreserved Anglophile; before becoming president, he vacationed most summers in Great Britain and he had written a book praising the British parliamentary form of government as, in some ways, superior to America's system of checks and balances. In his first year as president, he resolved the last points of conflict between the two countries, a minor border dispute in British Columbia, a quarrel between Canadian and American fishermen, and British objections to discriminatory tolls on the Panama Canal.

There had been at least 300 marriages between American heiresses and British aristocrats in the generation before 1914. Wealthy families not tied by wedlock to Great Britain had been indulging in an orgy of Francomania for decades. More important, most big American investment banks—Wall Street—had long-standing ties to British finance, none more intimate than the most powerful investment bank of all, the House of Morgan. The Morgan bank acted as the agent for British war bond sales in United States. By mid-1915, Edward Stettinius, a Morgan partner, was purchasing up to $10 million worth of American goods ranging from weapons to wheat for the British government each day. By 1917, Great Britain owed Americans $2.3 billion. By comparison, the Germans had managed to borrow a meager $27 million in the United States. Wall Street had good reason to want a British victory or, at least, to shudder at the thought of a British defeat.

Sympathy for the Central Powers

There was, however, a reservoir of sympathy for the Central Powers in the country. One American in three was foreign-born or the child of immigrants. Millions traced their roots to Germany; many still spoke German at home and in their churches. Millions of new immigrants had begun their lives in the Austro-Hungarian Empire. They had left for economic reasons, not because they were oppressed by the old emperor, Franz Joseph, on the throne for sixty-four years in 1914. Indeed, he was looked on as a benign grandfather by Hungarians and many Czechs, Slovaks, Slovenes, and Jews from the empire. They knew that the United States, with its English attachments, would never side with the Central Powers, but they hoped to preserve American neutrality. The National German League, with 3 million members, sponsored lectures and distributed pamphlets touting the virtues of German culture and responding to Allied anti-German propaganda.

Then there were Irish-Americans, numbering about 5 million. Many—by no means all—nursed an ancestral hatred of Great Britain. The most militant Irish Anglophobes joined with German-American groups in the German-Irish Legislative Committee for the Furtherance of United States Neutrality. When, in the spring of 1916, the British crushed a rebellion in Ireland (ineffectively supported by Germany), some prominent Irish-American politicians declared for the German cause.

Similarly, Russian and Polish Jews had been driven out of their homelands to America by discriminatory laws and mob violence sometimes abetted by the authorities. To them, the "old country" was not a place to daydream about with wistful nostalgia. They hated the Czarist regime. Indeed, many Jews from the Russian empire looked positively on Germany and Austria where Jews had been granted near civil equality with Christians. In order to emigrate to the United States, they had first to cross into Germany where, in an instant, treatment of them had improved. Socialists, a large minority in the German-American community and among eastern european Jews, hated Russia above all other countries because of the power and brutality of the Czar's secret police in suppressing them. In Germany, by way of contrast, the Social Democratic party was one of the country's largest.

With such a tangle of conflicting loyalties, Wilson's insistence on neutrality not only reflected America's geographical apartness from Europe, but it also made sense politically in the industrial states and the large cities where the Democratic party depended on the support of ethnic voters.

Stalemate

Both the Allies and the Central Powers expected a short war. German military strategists, facing powerful enemies to both the East and the West, believed that Germany had to strike first and quickly in order to win. Their "Schlieffen Plan," first adopted in 1905 and updated almost annually, was designed to address the challenge of a war on two fronts. It called for an overwhelming assault on the modern and well-trained French army through neutral Belgium so as to circumvent powerful French fortifications on the French-German border. Once France was defeated, Count Alfred von Schlieffen proposed, Germany would transport its army to the Eastern Front and dispose of the Russians. The Russian army was the largest in the world. However, because of the size of the country, the Russians needed many more weeks than France or German to mobilize it—to call up the reserves and move them to the front. The German railroad system was designed for the rapid movement of troops from west to east. Stations in tiny rural villages on the Belgian border had platforms a mile long so that a Russia-bound train could be loaded in a few minutes and another immediately pull in behind it.

MAP 36.1 The Central Powers and the Allies

Italy was tied to the Central Powers in 1914, but its obligations applied only to defensive wars. The Italian government said that Austria-Hungary and Germany were the aggressors and remained neutral. Later, Italy entered the war on the Allied side but was completely neutralized by Austria on its front west of Switzerland.

Count von Schlieffen died in 1913. After making his final revision of his plan, he wrote, "we must conclude that the enterprise is one for which we are not strong enough." In order to capture or surround Paris within the 40 days Schlieffen said was the maximum, seven-eighths of the German army had to be concentrated on the far right of the front. Because the Kaiser decided against invading Holland as well as Belgium, the German right had to squeeze through a strip of Belgium just 12 miles wide, attacking rather than bypassing the fortress city of Liège.

It could not be done, von Schlieffen concluded before he died. Nevertheless, in August 1914, the German generals had nothing else. The commander, Helmut von Moltke, unnerved by Russian advances in Poland, dispatched several divisions from the army in Belgium at a critical moment. And the tiny Belgian army proved more effective than even the cautious von Schlieffen had thought possible. Subduing Liège took twelve days, longer than the plan had allowed for the conquest of all of Belgium.

By the time the German right flank was in a position to threaten Paris, the soldiers were exhausted. Fearing they would be cut off from the rest of the German force, they swung to the south exposing their flank to the British Expeditionary Force and to the French army defending Paris. Thanks to aerial reconnaissance, the Allies saw a chance to break through the German line. *Poilus* (French soldiers) in Paris were ferried to the River Marne where they failed to divide the German forces but did force a retreat of 40 miles.

There both sides dug in, fighting only smaller actions as they raced to extend their trenches to the North Sea. There the front would remain, moving very little for three years, despite savage battles that would kill several million men.

The Eastern Front also bogged down into trench warfare after one great German victory at Tannenburg in which more than a million Russian soldiers were captured. Never had a war racked up such numbers.

New! Improved!   In the forty years since the last war between major powers, technology had changed the face of warfare, profoundly in some cases. The automobile made its impact immediately when several hundred Parisian taxicabs were conscripted to ferry soldiers to the Marne in August 1914. Each year of the war, more and more gasoline and diesel-powered trucks were used to transport men and supplies from railroads to the front lines. However, the horse (and mule) remained the chief motive power of overland transport throughout the war. The sheer size of the armies fighting in Belgium and France (and in Russia) soon churned rural roads into quagmires through which horse-drawn wagons could struggle but not trucks. Each infantry division of 10,000 men had 5,000–7,000 animals assigned to it. Field guns were moved by horses. The German army conscripted 715,000 horses during the first months of the war. By war's end, Britain ran through a million horses; five died of exposure or privation to each one killed in battle.

The telephone and wireless (radio) improved communications between the generals and officers at the front but unevenly. The French and British line had far better telephone and telegraph connections than the Germans because, in retreating in August 1914, they destroyed every wire in Belgium and France. This forced the Germans to rely more heavily on wireless. Because the other side could listen in on messages, they were coded. However, French intelligence was very good at cracking the German codes.

The airplane made reconnaissance deep behind enemy lines possible. The French learned of a 50-mile gap between two German armies in 1914 from a pilot. The "dogfights" between biplanes that captured the popular imagination were not fought because there was anything to be gained by risking an expensive airplane to destroy another, but in order to protect reconnaissance missions or to destroy the enemy's planes before they could return to their bases with valuable information. Foot soldiers slogging in mud resented the "flyboys" who finished each day with fine food and drink and slept in a warm bed. But there was no job in the war with a higher mortality rate than flying a plane. The average life expectancy of British pilots at the front was two weeks. To the generals, crippling the enemy's knowledge was worth the horrendous losses. By 1916, the British Royal Flying Corps had built 10,000 aircraft and trained the pilots to fly them.

Poison gas was terrifying when used on soldiers unprepared for it. The Germans bombarded a 3-mile long British front at Ypres with chlorine gas in April 1915. At least 5,000 men were killed and 15,000 suffered permanent lung damage. But the very effectiveness of the gas prevented the Germans from exploiting the attack. Heavier than air, the gas clung to the ground so that German troops could not advance to the abandoned trenches. On several occasions, shifting winds blew the gas from a bombardment back on the army that launched it. Every belligerent quickly equipped its soldiers with gas masks and set its chemists to work developing new gases. German "sneeze gas" could penetrate the filters on the gas masks that protected against chlorine. American chemists at the University of Notre Dame developed "Lewisite," but the war ended before it could be deployed and the entire stock was dumped into the ocean.

Machine Guns and Tanks   Poison gas was responsible for 1.3 million casualties over four years, but at the expense of manufacturing, transporting, and firing 66 million shells. The Maxim Gun, which employed recoil to expel spent shells while loading another, had been used in colonial wars for thirty years. In 1893, some 700 South Africans with Maxim Guns killed at least half of 3,000 charging Matabele tribesmen at the battle of Shangani River.

Nonetheless, pig-headed British generals like Douglas Haig (who said a machine gun could never stop charging cavalry) did not see the effectiveness of the machine gun when it was demonstrated before their eyes. The Germans did. By August 1914, the German army had paid Maxim's company royalties on 1,259 machine guns.

The machine gun made the cavalry, the glamorous arm of the nineteenth-century army, obsolete. It made the infantry advance over open country an exercise in mass slaughter. When soldiers went "over the top" toward enemy trenches, they were mowed down by hurricanes of iron and lead from enemy machine guns that fired 500 rounds a minute effective at up to 4,000 yards. On the first day of the Battle of the Somme in July 1916, 60,000 British soldiers were killed or wounded, most of them during the battle's first half hour. By the time the Somme campaign sputtered to an end, with nothing gained, British losses were 400,000, French losses 200,000, and the Germans had lost 500,000 men. Many were victims of artillery barrages, but machine gunners claimed their share.

The Vickers Heavy Machine gun required a crew of six men. The gun weighed 40 pounds, the tripod 50. Four men were needed to carry the ammunition that the gun consumed like popcorn and several extra barrels. (They burned out quickly.) Once set up, the gun needed two men to fire it, the other four to keep it loaded.

Late in 1916, the British introduced the tank as a means of neutralizing German machine guns. They were heavily armored so as to be invulnerable to bullets and driven not by wheels but by treads so that they could cross the mud and bomb craters of No Man's Land. Armed with a small cannon, tanks could be driven directly at machine gun emplacements and destroy them. However, British generals failed to exploit their speed. They attached individual tanks to small infantry units, slowing the vehicles to a walk. Until the tank did its job, the men walking with it suffered the usual horrendous losses from enemy machine guns. Only late in the war was it recognized that tanks were most effective when they advanced rapidly in groups ahead of foot soldiers.

War at Sea   The sheer numbers the war generated sickened Americans: a million prisoners at Tannenberg, a million casualties at Verdun, a million dead on the Somme. American ambassador to Britain, Walter Hines Page, had it right when he described Europe as "a bankrupt slaughterhouse of unmarried women." And yet, Page and President Wilson and Secretary of State Lansing moved closer to intervening on the side of the Allies in 1916. The reason was yet another innovation in the technology of war, the *Unterseeboot*—the U-boat—the German submarine.

Naval warfare was economic warfare, aimed at destroying the enemy's commerce. The British, with naval superiority, immediately proclaimed a blockade of Germany. According to the rules of war, enemy merchant ships were fair game, although tradition required that the crews of sunken ships be rescued. The ships of neutral nations had the right to trade with any nation as long as they did not carry contraband—defined as war materiel. However, the British played fast with the rules. They mined parts of the North Sea. Neutral nations were informed of the location of the mine fields but, if one of their ships struck one and went down, there was no warship there to rescue the crew. The British then redefined contraband to include most trade goods, including some foodstuffs. When neutral Holland, Denmark, and Sweden began to import goods for secret resale to Germany (pastoral Denmark, which had never purchased American lard, imported 11,000 tons of it in the first months of the war), the British slapped strict regulations on trade with those countries.

American objections were mild. Neither the German nor the Danish market had ever been important to American exporters, when wartime sales to Britain and France rose so sharply, American trade with the Allies climbed from $825 million in 1914 to $3.2 billion in 1916, a fourfold increase in two years.

As long as a quick victory on land was on the table, Germany was indifferent to the British blockade. Its agricultural base was adequate to the country's basic needs. When the war stalemated, however, the General Staff concluded that the British import economy, particularly the island's dependence on American and Canadian foodstuffs, was the weak link in the Allied chain. The Imperial Navy believed that submarines might be able to snap that link and force Britain to withdraw from the war.

Submarine Warfare   When the war began, there were only twenty-five submarines in the German navy. By February 1915, however, a crash construction program had resulted in a flotilla of U-boats, each armed with ninteen torpedoes, large enough to proclaim the waters surrounding the British Isles a war zone. The subs would sink all enemy merchant ships within those waters and, because British vessels were likely to run up neutral flags, the safety of neutral ships could not be guaranteed. Within days, several British vessels went to the bottom. President Wilson warned the Kaiser that he would hold Germany to "strict accountability" for American lives and property lost to U-boats.

Some Americans considered submarine warfare peculiarly inhumane because U-boats usually struck without warning, giving merchant seamen little time to abandon ship. Moreover, unlike surface ships, submarines did not rescue crewmen in the water. Both accusations were true. On the surface, the fragile submarines were helpless. A light gun mounted on the bow of a freighter was enough to sink one. The first-generation submarines were very slow diving. If a U-boat surfaced to warn an unarmed merchant vessel of its presence, it could be rammed. Since submarines were tiny, their small crews cramped, there was no room to take aboard survivors of a sinking.

On May 7, 1915, antisubmarine feelings in the United States burst into fury when the English luxury liner *Lusitania* was torpedoed off the coast of Ireland; 1,198 of the 1,959 passengers and crew aboard were killed, including 139 Americans. What kind of war was this that killed innocent travelers? The *New York Times* described the Germans as "savages drenched with blood."

Wilson Wins a Victory   The German Embassy in Washington replied that it had specifically warned Americans against traveling on the *Lusitania* in advertisements in New York and Washington newspapers, including the *Times*. The ambassador pointed out that the liner was also a freighter carrying contraband: 4,200 cases of small arms purchased in the United States and some high explosives. So many lives were lost because the *Lusitania* went down in a mere eighteen minutes. Its hull was blown wide open not by a torpedo, but by a secondary explosion. The British were the savages, shielding war materiel behind innocent passengers.

The Germans had a point, but Wilson aimed his two most aggressive notes at them. The second was so antagonistic that the pacifistic Bryan feared it meant war. He resigned rather than sign it. Wilson replaced him in the State Department with Robert Lansing, an international lawyer.

While making no apologies or formal promises, the Germans attacked no more passenger vessels. Then, early in 1916, when the Allies announced that they were arming all merchant ships, Germany responded with a declaration of "unrestricted submarine warfare." The U-boats would sink all enemy vessels without warning. On March 24, 1916, a sitting duck, the *Sussex,* a French channel steamer on a scheduled run between Dieppe and Folkestone, went down with an American among the casualties. Wilson threatened to break diplomatic relations with Germany—considered a prelude to a declaration of war—if unrestricted submarine warfare were continued.

The German General Staff did not want the United States in the war. Plans for a major offensive were afoot. In any case, the navy did not have enough U-boats to carry out a full-scale assault on British shipping. In the Sussex Pledge of May 4, 1916, the Germans promised Wilson to observe the rules of visit and search before attacking enemy ships. This meant abandoning the submarine's effectiveness, but it kept the United States at home which, at the time, was what Germany wanted.

© Bettmann-UPI/Corbis

Unterseeboot 15, an early German submarine. U-boat design was improved throughout the war. By the end of 1916, after a period of inactivity in response to Woodrow Wilson's threat to enter the war if submarine warfare was not restricted, Germany's U-boats numbered more than a hundred. The German General Staff calculated that an all-out attack on British shipping could starve Britain into suing for peace before the United States could send enough soldiers to Europe to make a difference and resumed "unrestricted submarine warfare."

AMERICA GOES TO WAR

Wilson had won a spectacular diplomatic victory at the beginning of his campaign for reelection. He was enthusiastically renominated at the Democratic convention, and his campaign was given a motto he did not much like. The keynote speaker at the convention, New York Governor Martin Glynn, built his speech around the slogan "He Kept Us out of War."

Wilson disliked it because, as he told an aide, "I can't keep the country out of war. Any little German lieutenant can put us into war at any time by some calculated outrage." He meant that a submarine commander, perhaps acting without orders, could torpedo the Sussex Pledge. Like many other national leaders before and since (like the Kaiser in 1914!) Wilson had put himself into a position in which control of a momentous decision was out of his hands.

Preparedness   Wilson had begun to prepare for the possibility of war as early as November 1915, when he asked Congress to beef up the army to 400,000 men and to fund a huge expansion of the navy. To some extent, he was pushed into "preparedness" by Theodore Roosevelt. The Nobel

Peace Prize laureate had become the nation's most bellicose warmonger. In speech after speech he called for war against Germany. He jabbed and poked at the fact that the U.S. army totaled 108,000 men, ranking it seventeenth in the world; that the Quartermaster Corps (supply) had only recently begun using trucks; and that at one point in 1915 American artillery had enough ammunition for only two days' fighting—with guns that were obsolete.

Wilson could not ignore him. On the other side, he had to contend with pacifists. Automobile manufacturer Henry Ford chartered a ship to steam him and other celebrities to Europe where, Ford thought, they would pummel the belligerents into peace with their prestige. Feminists Jane Addams, Carrie Chapman Catt, and Charlotte Perkins Gilman formed the Women's Peace Party and attended a pacifist conference in the neutral Netherlands. There were dozens of similar groups plus the politically important German and Irish nationalist lobbies. The Socialist Party, strong enough in some cities to deny the Democrats votes they needed, opposed intervention.

Most worrying was an antipreparedness faction in Congress led by Representative Claude Kitchin of North Carolina. With widespread backing among western progressives, on whom Wilson generally depended for support, Kitchin argued that it was Europe's "preparedness"—the great arms race of the 1890s and 1900s—that had plunged the continent into war in the first place. If the United States had the means to fight, it was all the more likely that the United States would enter the war. Kitchin regarded nonpreparedness as the best way to keep the country neutral.

Wilson had to settle for a compromise, less of a military buildup than the interventionists wanted, more than Kitchin and his supporters liked.

The Election of 1916   The Progressive party expected Teddy Roosevelt to be its candidate for president in 1916. Roosevelt wanted to run, but he knew he needed the Republican nomination to oust Wilson. When Republican conservatives, still steaming over 1912, made it clear they would not have Roosevelt, he declined the Bull Moose nomination. Indeed, he insulted the Progressives by suggesting that they the Republicans jointly nominate his personal friend, Senator Henry Cabot Lodge of Massachusetts.

This was absurd. Lodge was not merely conservative on the economic and social issues the Progressives advocated, he was downright reactionary. Personally, he was unpopular even with Republican conservatives with whom he agreed. The Republicans had a much better alternative in Supreme Court Justice Charles Evans Hughes. Hughes had been a progressive governor of New York, but he was as dignified in his bearing as Woodrow Wilson. Roosevelt sneered at Hughes's low-key moderation by calling him "the bearded lady."

Hughes's weakness as a candidate was the fact that his views on the war differed little from Wilson's. Like the president, he wanted to keep the United States out, but not at any price. Like Wilson, he recognized that the president, whoever he was, would have little choice about declaring war on Germany if the Germans abandoned the Sussex Pledge, which everyone knew was a shaky proposition.

Roosevelt's tireless campaigning on Hughes's behalf created a perception that the Republican was the war candidate and "He Kept Us Out of War" Wilson the peace candidate. But was such a perception decisive? The election was very close.

Hughes carried every northeastern state except New Hampshire, which he lost by just fifty-six votes. Every midwestern state except Ohio voted for the "war candidate," including antiwar Bob LaFollete's Wisconsin. Almost every western state voted Democratic until the election came down to California's thirteen electoral votes. California was then a Republican state, and Hughes assumed he would win there. When the votes were toted up, however, Wilson had a paper-thin majority of fewer than 4,000 votes, three-tenths of a percentage point. He won the electoral college by 277 votes to Hughes's 254. In 1916, California made the difference.

Failing to Keep the Peace Heartened by his surprising reelection, Wilson threw himself into an attempt to mediate a peace in Europe. The winter of 1916–1917 seemed like a good time for mediation. After more than two years of war, the Western Front was pretty much where it had been in August 1914. In a few sectors, troops were huddled in the first line of trenches they had dug. Italy, which had joined the Allies in 1915, was stalemated with Austria-Hungary in what is now Slovenia. The Eastern Front had been more fluid, but the Germans and Austrians could not advance and the Russian army was mutinous.

Wilson concluded in a message to Congress in January 1917 that both sides had to face up to a "peace without victory," a negotiated "peace among equals" simply to put an end to the slaughter. The differences that had led to the war—and the rules of war at sea in the age of the U-boat—would be worked out after the armistice by some sort of international congress that, as a permanent body, would prevent future wars.

Wilson's hopes were high when, a week after he addressed Congress, the German ambassador informed Secretary of State Lansing that, as of February 1, Germany would resume unrestricted submarine warfare. The German General Staff had, like Wilson, concluded that the German army could not alone win the war. However, the navy had crunched numbers and concluded that an all-out assault on British commerce by the submarine fleet, more than a hundred strong and growing by up to ten a month, could literally starve Great Britain into suing for peace within six months.

Abandoning the Sussex guarantees meant the United States would intervene, of course. However, the navy argued, the United States was far from ready for action. The admiral's figures said that the war would be over before more than a token American army could be landed in Europe. "They will not even come," the Navy Minister boasted, "because our submarines will sink them. Thus, America from a military point of view means nothing, and again nothing, and for a third time nothing."

Wilson severed diplomatic relations with Germany and asked Congress for authority to arm American merchant ships. When progressive Republicans La Follette, Norris, and Borah filibustered against the bill, the president denounced them as "a little group of willful men, representing no opinion but their own." On the evening of April 2, after submarines sent three American freighters to the bottom, a solemn Wilson asked Congress for a formal declaration of war. "The right is more precious than peace," he said, "and we shall fight for the things which we have always carried nearest our hearts."

For four days, the Capitol shook with angry debate. Six senators and fifty representatives held out against declaring war. They accused Wilson of failing to be truly neutral. Some claimed that the United States was going to spill its young men's blood in order to bail out Wall Street's loans to England and to enrich the munitions manufacturers, the "merchants of death." In the most eloquent antiwar speech, Senator George Norris of Nebraska said, "We are going into war upon the command of gold ... We are about to put the dollar sign on the American flag."

The Hun and His Kultur   Wilson was no Wall Street flunkey. He was driven to war by his determination to defend the rights of neutral ships— "freedom of the seas." However, it is difficult to believe that the issue aroused the public to such a furor that, suddenly, in April 1917, an overwhelming majority of Americans wanted war. In fact, public opinion had been drifting slowly but steadily from "a plague on both of your houses" toward support for the Allies—or, more accurately, hostility to Germany—since August 1914. It is probably a mistake to think of Wilson's election victory in November 1916 as an antiwar vote. He won by the skin of his teeth. The South was, as usual, solidly Democratic because the Democratic party protected white supremacy not because Wilson was the antiwar candidate. The South was the most fiercely prowar section of the country. If two or three southern states had voted for Hughes, he would have won the election without California's help.

The American people's turn in favor of war was a result of heavy-handed German military brutality and brilliant British propaganda. In August 1914, frustrated by unexpected Belgian resistance, including civilian attacks of German troops, the army executed as many as 6,000 Belgian villagers. No doubt, some had violated the rules of war by taking up arms. But the Germans also shot peasants being held not for guerrilla actions but as hostages. The army deliberately destroyed the ancient University of Louvain (Leuven) as retaliation for Belgian resistance. About 230,000 priceless manuscripts and books went up in smoke.

When British propagandists successfully depicted Germans, as a people, as barbaric, destructive "Huns" driven by an evil *Kultur,* in the United States and other neutral countries, describing the occupation of the small country as the "rape of Belgium," the German army cleaned up its act. German rule was militaristic and harsh; the Belgian people depended on food from abroad to avoid starvation. But the effectiveness of the chilling word *rape* was not lost on anti-German propagandists. Wall posters and newspaper cartoons depicted the broken body of an adolescent girl being dragged away by a bloated, beastlike German soldier in a spiked helmet and soldiers bayoneting babies. The idea was to dehumanize the Germans, and it was effective. Ham-handed German officers helped the campaign along when, in October 1915, they executed Edith Cavell, a British nurse at a hospital in Brussels, for helping British prisoners of war to escape. Cavell was guilty and what she did was a capital offense under British as well as German law. However, hanging a nurse for a humanitarian act in an era when women were rarely executed for murder was a public relations disaster.

Propagandists made the most of German acts of sabotage that were documented and some that were probably accidents. In 1915, several German diplomats

In modern warfare, when it is necessary to win popular support, it is common for nations to dehumanize the enemy. With the exception of American depictions of the Japanese during World War II, no propaganda campaign has been so extreme as the portrayal of Germans as bestial "Huns" during World War I.

were caught red-handed when a bumbling agent left incriminating papers on a train! In July 1916, 2 million pounds of explosives being readied for shipment to England blew up at the Black Tom munitions depot outside Jersey City, New Jersey. The explosion, felt in Philadelphia 100 miles away, was traced to German agents.

The anti-German propaganda blockbuster was a cable sent in February 1917 by the German foreign minister, Arthur Zimmerman, to the Mexican government. Intercepted and decoded by British intelligence it said that in the event that the United States declared war on Germany, Germany would finance a Mexican attack on the United States in order to keep American troops at home. When Germany won the war, Mexico would be rewarded with the return of the "lost provinces" of New Mexico and Arizona.

It was a foolish proposition. Mexico was still torn by civil turmoil, in no condition to make war on Guatemala, let alone the United States. With American danders up, however, the Zimmerman telegram persuaded many people that the Hun was indeed a threat to them as well as to Britain and France.

The American Contribution

German's resumption of unrestricted submarine warfare was a gamble. The navy calculated that a massive U-boat assault on shipping bound for Britain starve the island out of the war before American troops could affect the outcome. For three months, it appeared the Germans would win the bet. In February 1917, submarines sunk 250 vessels, in March 330, a total of 570,000 tons of shipping, about as much as the navy projected. In April, U-boats destroyed 430 ships, bringing the total losses to 900,000 tons. At one point in April, Britain had enough food on hand to feed the nation for only three weeks.

By summer, however, sinkings tailed off and the destruction of German subs increased. The credit for the turnabout belonged to American Admiral William S. Sims, who finally won his argument with the anticonvoy British navy when he convinced Prime Minister David Lloyd George to support him. The British argued that freighters traveling alone had a better chance of getting through than fifty and more vessels in formation, a target that a submarine could hardly miss. Sims responded that, one ship or fifty, a U-boat got one shot. With convoys escorted by speedy destroyers, ships designed for antisubmarine warfare, a U-boat had to flee as soon as it betrayed its location by its torpedo trail.

Sims was right. By July 1917, submarine kills were far below the German navy's projections of the number necessary to starve Britain out. In 1918, of 1,133 Britain-bound ships the subs sank, only 134 had been in a convoy. Of 2 million American soldiers sent to France in 1917 and 1918, only 200 were drowned because of submarines. Of the eighty seven new submarines the Germans commissioned in 1917, seventy-eight were sunk by destroyers.

President Wilson, who continued to think of himself as a mediator, insisted that the United States was not one of the Allies; it was an associated power.

Fighting Over There

When the British asked him to send them 500,000 recruits fresh out of the induction centers whom they would train and incorporate into the British Expeditionary Force, Wilson refused. Americans would go "over there," in the words of a popular song, under an independent American command. General Pershing arrived in Paris in July 1917 with the first units of the American Expeditionary Force, the First Infantry Division. It was a symbolic gesture, for Pershing refused to send his men to the front until there were enough of them in France to take over an entire sector. (A few Americans saw action near Verdun in October when Pershing consented to using them temporarily to beef up decimated French, British, and Canadian units.)

Except for the American intervention, 1917 went poorly for the Allies. The Germans and Austrians defeated the Italian army in Italy and knocked Russia out of the war. A liberal democratic government that deposed Czar Nicholas II in March 1917 was unable to restore morale in the mutinous army. Revolutionary Communists, "Bolsheviks" led by Vladimir Ilyich Lenin, seized power promising "peace and bread." The Treaty of Brest-Litovsk, which the Germans forced on Russia, was so vindictive and harsh that Americans were further convinced that Imperial Germany was beyond the pale of civilization. By shutting down the Eastern front, however, the Germans were able to reinforce their army in France.

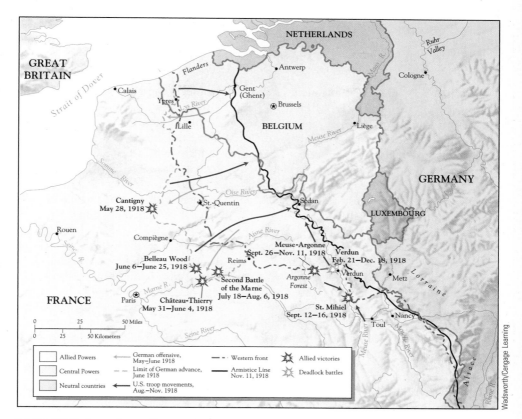

MAP 36.2 American Operations 1918

A few Americans saw action attached to French units in 1917: not many; they were not yet adequately trained for the new kind of war. In May 1918, the American Expeditionary Force took over the Allied center for the five-month push that ended the war on November 11. On Armistice Day, most of Belgium was still occupied by Germany. Only on the right flank did French troops penetrate into Germany and that was in Alsace, which had been French before 1871. When the war ended, there was one soldier for every 4 inches of the front.

In May 1918, Germany had 192 divisions on the Western front to 178 French, British, and American divisions. The new commander in the West, Erich Ludendorff, launched a do-or-die offensive coordinated with the submarine campaign. The Allies fell back to the Marne River, close enough to Paris that the shelling could be heard on the Champs Elysées. But the American "doughboys" were arriving by the hundred thousand. About 27,000 fought at Château-Thierry near the hottest part of the fighting. By the middle of July, when the Germans attempted one last drive toward Paris, about 85,000 Americans helped hurl them back at Belleau Wood.

Ludendorff went to pieces, attributing the collapse of German morale to "the sheer number of Americans arriving daily at the front." In July, Americans took on the attack on a bulge in the German lines called the St.-Mihiel Salient and succeeded in clearing it out. The final American battle was along a 24-mile line in the

Argonne Forest, rugged country near the intersection of the borders of France, Belgium, and Germany. It was in that position that a million doughboys were sitting when, on November 11, 1918, the Germans capitulated.

Armistice   In the trenches and back home, Americans celebrated deliriously. Millions of people gathered in city centers throughout the country, dancing and whooping it up. The Yanks had won the war! Had not the Germans stalemated the French and British until our boys went "over there"? Less than a year after the Americans began to fight, it was all over. General Pershing was a hero. An even more celebrated hero was "Sergeant York," Alvin C. York, a Tennessee mountaineer who, a few weeks before the Armistice, attacked a German machine gun nest alone, killed seventeen men with seventeen bullets and, single-handed, marched 132 prisoners and thirty five machine guns back to American lines.

In fact, the infusion of American troops was the key to the Allied advance to victory in 1918. But the joyous celebration in the United States was possible only because the American blood sacrifice was so small. 114,000 American soldiers died in the war, more than half of them, as always, from disease. Romania, with a population of 8 million, not much more than New York City, lost twice as many. About 1.4 million Frenchmen and almost a million British soldiers died. Three-quarters of all the Frenchmen who served in the war were casualties. France and Britain were maimed. Germany and Russia were maimed and defeated. If it was going too far to say that the United States "won the war," it was quite true that the United States was the only belligerent nation where people could feel like victors.

37

OVER HERE
The Home Front 1917–1920

*Once lead this people into war, and they'll forget there ever
was such a thing as tolerance. To fight you must be ruthless
and brutal, and the spirit of ruthless brutality will enter into
the very fiber of our national life.*

—Woodrow Wilson

*When I think of the many voices that were heard before the
war and are still heard, interpreting America from a class or
sectional or selfish standpoint, I am not sure that, if the war
had to come, it did not come at the right time for the
preservation and reinterpretation of American ideals.*

—George Creel

Woodrow Wilson called it "a war to make the world safe for democracy." He
sent the doughboys to Europe and he threw the industrial might of the
United States behind the Allies in the belief there would be no victors in
the traditional sense of the word—no conquerors on the take. Instead, the peace-
makers (led by him) would create a new world order dedicated to settling disputes
between nations justly and peaceably. Wilson also called the war "a war to end all
wars."

THE PROGRESSIVE WAR

The First World War was simultaneously the apogee of progressivism, when reformers turned ideas into policies, and the undoing of the progressive movement. For
two years, progressive moralists and social planners had free rein in Washington.
Within a few years of the armistice, however, there was no progressive movement
left, only a few voices crying in the wilderness in Congress and the states hearing only
echoes.

The Home Front 1916–1920

1916	1917	1918	1919	1920
1916 Shipping board established				
	1917 Railway Administration; War Industries Board; Food Administration; Selective Service Act; Race riots in Houston and East St. Louis			
		1918 Fourteen Points; Debs imprisoned; Wilson sails to Europe		
	Schenk v. U.S.; Fight for the League; Eighteenth Amendment (Prohibition) 1919			
		Nineteenth Amendment (woman suffrage); Harding elected 1920		

Split

The question of intervention split the progressives. A few itched to fight from the start, most notably Theodore Roosevelt. When the United States declared war, he asked for a command in Europe. Wilson ignored him. Other Republican progressives, mostly westerners like Robert La Follette of Wisconsin, George Norris of Nebraska, William E. Borah of Idaho, and Hiram Johnson of California, voted against the declaration of war. When they lost, they moderated their antiwar rhetoric but not their opinion that intervention was foisted on the country by munitions makers and bankers. The "willful men" prolonged the debate on the Conscription Act of 1917 for six weeks until Congress exempted boys under 21 from the draft. Any affinity the isolationist progressives felt with Wilson before April 1917 dissipated thereafter.

Democratic party progressives wholeheartedly supported the war. Like Wilson, they came to believe that Germany was a serious threat to free institutions everywhere. Moreover, in the task of mobilizing resources in order to fight the war, and in the wave of patriotic commitment that swept the country, progressives saw a golden opportunity to put their ideas for economic and social reform to work.

They were right on one count. It was impossible to wage a modern war while clinging to the idea of a free, unregulated economy. Armies numbering millions of men could not be supplied with food, clothing, shelter, medicine, and arms by private companies entirely free to do as their owners chose. France and Britain had clamped tight controls on factories and farms in 1914. Germany already had them. When America went to war, progressives knew that their government had to do the same and they were delighted. At the core of their beliefs was the assumption that the power of the state, in the right hands, was a force for good. Now the whole country, caught up by patriotism, would be behind them.

They were not disappointed—for the duration. Proposals for regulation of business that were rejected as "radical" in peacetime proved, in the urgency of wartime, to be less than was necessary. The federal government took over the direction of much of the economy.

Planned Economy

Government grew like a mushroom. Federal spending increased tenfold. The bureaucracy doubled in size. Employees of the executive branch, 400,000 in 1916, numbered 950,000 in 1918.

All kinds of new agencies were set up during the twenty months that the United States was at war. Some were useless and wasteful, established without thought; they served little purpose beyond providing desks, chairs, inkwells, and salaries for the functionaries who ran them. A few agencies were plain failures. The Aircraft

Production Board was commissioned to construct 22,000 airplanes in a year. The figure was unrealistic, but the 1,200 craft that the board actually delivered were far fewer than a hustler with a bank loan could have supplied.

Some agencies were quite successful. The Shipping Board, founded in 1916 before the declaration of war, produced vessels twice as fast as German submarines could sink them. Privately run shipbuilding companies, loaded with deadwood in management, were not up to that achievement.

The United States Railway Administration, headed by Wilson's son-in-law and secretary of the treasury, William G. McAdoo, was created early in 1918 when moving the volume of freight the war created proved to be beyond the capabilities of the men who ran the nation's railroads. The government paid the stockholders a rent equal to their earnings in the prewar years and simply took over. McAdoo untangled a colossal snafu in management within a few weeks; he reorganized the railroads into an efficient system such as the nation had never known. About 150,000 freight cars short of the number needed to do the job in 1917, American railroads had a surplus of 300,000 cars by the end of the war.

The war production boards were coordinated by a super agency, the War Industries Board, headed by Wall Street financier Bernard Baruch. His presence at the top of the planning pyramid indicated that the progressives had not won their campaign for a directed economy without paying a price. American industry and agriculture were regulated as never before. But elected officials and public-spirited experts with no stake in the profits were not always in the driver's seat.

Herbert Hoover

Food Administrator Herbert C. Hoover's task was as challenging as McAdoo's, and it kept him in the public eye. Hoover's job was to organize food production, distribution, and consumption so that America's farms fed the army, the American people, met some of the needs of the Allied armies, and made up Great Britain's shortfall.

Only 43 years old when he took the job, Hoover was known as the "boy wonder." An orphan, Hoover grew up in California with relatives. He worked his way through Stanford University, graduated as a mining engineer, and decided to work abroad on new strikes, where he could share in the profits, rather than for a salary in the United States. He had his adventures; Hoover and his wife were besieged in China during the Boxer Rebellion. Mostly, however, he developed mines, made shrewd personal investments, and was so soon a millionaire that he was bored with money making when still a young man.

Hoover's ambitions were in public service. He believed that able, wealthy men like himself had responsibilities to society. He got his chance to start out in a high-profile position when he happened to be in London at the outbreak of the war. He was asked to take over the problem of getting food to the people of devastated Belgium and he jumped at the challenge. Hoover liquidated his business interests, mastered the complex and ticklish task of feeding people in a war zone, and undoubtedly saved hundreds of thousands of lives.

He did it without charm or personal flash. Hoover was serious, intense, and humorless. He shared the progressive faith in the application of scientific principles—engineering—to social problems. Hoover became a war hero in almost the same rank as General Pershing, Sergeant York, and America's ace airplane pilot, Captain Eddie Rickenbacker.

In one important way, Hoover differed from other progressives (and it helps to explain his popularity). Even undertakings as massive as organizing food production, distribution, and consumption, Hoover believed, did not require the state's coercive powers. It could be done by voluntary cooperation.

Unlike the Railway Administration, which took control of the nation's railroads on its own terms, Hoover did not force anything on anyone. Food was not rationed in the United States as it was in every other country in the war. Instead, Hoover engineered colorful publicity campaigns urging Americans, in the spirit of patriotism and "pulling together," to observe Wheatless Mondays, Meatless Tuesdays, Porkless Thursdays, and so on. The program worked because compliance was easy, yet psychologically gratifying. Making do without a commodity vital to the war effort one day a week (most weeks) was painless, but it allowed civilians to feel that they were part of the fighting machine. It was shrewd psychology and it worked. When tens of millions of people observed a Meatless Tuesday, the additional tonnage of meat available for export in just one week was enormous.

Hoover increased farm production through a combination of patriotic boosting and cash incentives. Acreage planted in wheat increased from 45 million in 1917 to 75 million in 1919. American shipments of foodstuffs to the Allies tripled over pre-war levels that were already high. Hoover added "Miracle Man" to his list of flattering nicknames. Another young Washington administrator, Undersecretary of the Navy Franklin D. Roosevelt, wanted the Democratic party to nominate Hoover for president in 1920.

Managing People
People were mobilized along with railway cars and potatoes, workers and housewives as well as soldiers. In May 1917, Congress passed the Selective Service Act, the first draft law since the Civil War. Registration was compulsory for all men between the ages of 21 and 45. (In 1918, the minimum age was lowered to 18.) From the 10 million who registered within a month of passage (24 million by the end of the war), local draft boards selected able-bodied recruits according to quotas assigned by the federal government.

Some occupational groups were deferred as vital to the war effort, but no one was allowed to buy his way out, as was possible during the Civil War (and had been bitterly resented). Indeed, authority to make final selections was given to local draft boards in order to silence critics who said that conscription had no place in a democracy. The draft contributed about 3 million young men to the armed forces in addition to 2 million who volunteered.

About 21,000 draftees claimed to be conscientious objectors on religious grounds. (In the end, only 4,000 insisted on assignment to noncombatant duty, usually as medics or in the Quartermaster Corps.) Approximately 500 men refused to cooperate with the military in any way, some for political rather than religious reasons. They were imprisoned and, in general, treated poorly. Camp Leonard Wood in Missouri had an especially bad reputation. In Washington State, a man who claimed that Jesus had forbidden him to take up arms was sentenced to death. He was not executed, but the last conscientious objector was not freed from prison until 1933, long after a majority of Americans had come to agree with him that the war had been a mistake.

SOCIAL CHANGES

War is a revolutionary or, at least, it is an agitator. The changes impressed on American society from the top in the interests of victory inevitably affected social relationships. Some groups consciously took advantage of the government's wants, needs, and preoccupations to achieve old goals. Others were merely caught up by the different rhythms of a society at war.

Labor Takes a Seat In order to keep the factories humming, Wilson made concessions to the labor movement that had been unthinkable a few years earlier. He appointed Samuel Gompers, the patriotic president of the American Federation of Labor, to Baruch's War Industries Board. The Postmaster General refused to deliver an issue of a socialist magazine in which Gompers was criticized. In return for recognition and favors, Gompers pledged the AFL unions to a no-strike policy for the duration of the conflict.

Because most wages rose during the war, there were comparatively few work stoppages. Business boomed, and employers dizzy with bonanza profits did not jeopardize them by resisting moderate demands by their employees. Most important, the National War Labor Board, on which five AFL men sat, mediated many industrial disputes before they disrupted production.

The quiet incorporation of organized labor into the federal decision-making process made the AFL respectable as it never had been before, Samuel Gompers's dream come true. From 2.7 million members in 1914, the union movement (including independent unions) grew to 4.2 million in 1919.

Blacks in Wartime Booker T. Washington died in 1915. When America went to war two years later, there was no African American of his stature to act as a "spokesman for the race." The president of the National Association for the Advancement of Colored People was white. Moreover, most of its members were middle-class northerners. Founded only in 1910, the organization had little prestige among the masses of African Americans, who were poor and, overwhelmingly, lived in the South. Many blacks had, no doubt, never heard of it.

W.E.B. DuBois, the scholar-editor of the NAACP journal, the *Crisis,* said, as Frederick Douglass had during the Civil War, that the willingness of young black men to serve in the army should be rewarded by the government's support of African American civil rights. DuBois was not naive about the possibilities. He was well aware that President Wilson was a southerner who approved (if quietly) of the South's Jim Crow laws. In an open letter to Wilson, he was content to pressure the president on the lynching epidemic in the South. He pointed out the irony of fighting against the savagery of "the Hun" in Europe while ignoring the savagery of American lynch mobs. Wilson issued a stronger anti-lynching statement than he

The National Archives

Members of the 369th Infantry. The army was racially segregated; the 369th was entirely African American except for senior officers. While General Pershing refused British demands that American soldiers be merged into depleted British units, he "loaned" the 369th to the French. They were so effective, the entire unit was awarded the French Croix de Guerre. Note the medal each soldier is wearing.

ever had previously, but said nothing about the federal anti-lynching act that was one of the NAACP's goals. Lynching incidents declined to 38 in 1917; the annual average for the five prewar years was 59. But 1917 was a fluke. There were 64 lynchings in 1918 and 83 in 1919, the highest total since the bloody 1890s.

About 400,000 African Americans served in the armed forces. They were strictly segregated in "Negro Units." All but a few black sailors were assigned to the galleys as cooks, dishwashers, cafeteria line workers, and waiters at officers' messes. Few enlisted in the interests of their race. Black doughboys joined up for the same reasons whites did: the chance for adventure (they were young men), a clean, warm bed and three good meals a day (like white enlistees, most blacks had dirt-poor backgrounds), or because they were drafted. Except for the three well-trained black units in the regular army, few African American enlistees and draftees were in combat units. Most dug trenches or loaded trucks behind the lines. Only a few were taught skills that would be useful to them after the war.

Segregation in the military paid one dividend to educated blacks. Unlike in the Civil War, when black soldiers were commanded entirely by whites, the army trained and commissioned 1,200 African American officers. Only a handful of them rose higher in rank than captain, but the fact that black officers existed was a point of pride in African American communities.

Migration: From Jim Crow to Race Riot

World War I was a landmark in African American history because the war years were the beginning of the massive emigration of blacks from the rural South to the industrial cities of the North. Each year before 1914, about 10,000 blacks drifted from the South to Philadelphia, New York, Detroit, Chicago. After 1914, just when American factories needed new workers to fill orders from Europe, the risks of ocean travel choked off immigration. More than 1.2 million immigrants entered the United States in 1914, 326,000 in 1915. In 1918, only 111,000 immigrants were recorded, the fewest in a year since the Civil War and, except for two Civil War years, the fewest since 1844.

Industry could not afford to observe the informal color line that had kept African Americans out of factory jobs that paid decent wages. Lured by the abundant jobs and the chance to escape rigid racial segregation, 100,000 blacks moved north each year, usually by train. It was not as great a leap in miles as European immigrants made, but it was just as wrenching socially and culturally. Plowing the Mississippi delta one week and working on an assembly line in Detroit the next, moving from an isolated sharecropper's cabin to an apartment in a congested city meant elemental psychological upheaval.

Most of the African Americans who moved north were young, less conditioned than their parents to tolerate the daily humiliations of Jim Crow. This was particularly true of veterans who had found in France not a colorblind culture, as is sometimes said, but one in which race counted for little. However, the epidemic of race riots that began during the war owed not to the insolence of the odd "uppity Negro," as newspapers often reported, but to the rapid growth of the black population in northern cities and, consequently, the expansion of African American communities into neighborhoods white people thought of as their own.

Between 1910 and 1920, Detroit's African American population rose from 5,700 to 41,000, Cleveland's from 8,400 to 34,000. Chicago's black population, already substantial in 1910 at 44,000, more than doubled to 109,000. Philadelphia, with the nation's largest black population in 1910 (84,000) was home to 134,000 African Americans in 1920.

There was a frightening race riot in industrial East St. Louis, Illinois, in 1917. At least forty, possibly three times that many people were killed. In 1918, there were race riots in Philadelphia and nearby Chester, Pennsylvania. The first postwar year, 1919, was worse, possibly because demobilized white veterans were competing with blacks for jobs as well as streets. More than twenty cities experienced race-based violence. Chicago was a racial battleground for five days; thirty-eight deaths were recorded. At least forty people were killed in a riot in Washington. The war was not a window of opportunity such as DuBois thought or, at least, hoped it would be.

Voting at Last

Personally, President Wilson did not like the idea of women, voting (although his only children were daughters). But the suffrage movement was too long in the field and, by 1917, too large to be denied.

A woman welding in a wartime factory. Women in such industrial jobs were not as common as they would be during the Second World War. But World War I women filled a good many jobs outside factories from which they were barred before the war.

The National Archives

Wilson announced his support of a constitutional amendment guaranteeing the vote to women, and Congress sent the Nineteenth Amendment to the states in June 1919, six months after the Armistice. In August 1920, ratification by Tennessee put it into the Constitution. The right of citizens to vote, it read, "shall not be denied or abridged by the United States or by any State on account of sex." Carrie Chapman Catt, head of the National American Woman Suffrage Association, had no doubt about what put the long-sought reform over. It was the war, the one-time pacifist said, that enfranchised American women.

Catt was a progressive on social and economic issues, but a conservative feminist; the suffrage was her goal. She sold woman suffrage to progressive politicians by assuring them that responsible middle-class white women would provide the votes to counterbalance the political power of immigrant radicals and corrupt political machines.

Alice Paul was the leader of the radical wing of the suffrage movement. She and her followers had employed showy, militant tactics in the campaign to win the vote. They chained themselves to the fence around the White House, and Paul burned a copy of Wilson's Fourteen Points to dramatize what she saw as his hypocrisy. (Carrie Chapman Catt shuddered.) The radical feminists—they adopted the name after the Nineteenth Amendment was enacted—believed that the woman vote, because women thought differently than men did, would change American society, particularly women's social and economic status, in far more fundamental ways than the progressive movement proposed.

During the wartime labor shortage, women took jobs that had been considered entirely unsuitable for them. Working-class women took factory jobs. Women operated trolley cars, drove delivery trucks, cleaned streets, and directed traffic. But it was a temporary phenomenon. The belief that men and women had different "spheres" was still powerful. When the veterans returned home, most women in untraditional occupations quit and made way for the menfolk.

The Moral War   One of the reforms that suffragists said women voters would push over the top was in place before the Nineteenth Amendment. The prohibition movement appeared to be stalled before the war. In 1914, only one state in four had some sort of anti-alcohol law on the books, and many of those were casually enforced. By the end of 1917, when a constitutional amendment providing for nationwide prohibition was proposed, only thirteen states were completely "dry." And yet, within a year and a half, prohibition was the law of the land.

The war added several new arguments to the anti-alcohol armory. Distilleries consumed a great deal of grain that the Food Administration was urging Americans to conserve. It was hard to defend whiskey when people were urged to eat less bread. Shortly after declaring war, Congress passed the Lever Act forbidding the sale of grain to distilleries.

Brewers, who had distanced themselves from distillers, contrasting the wholesome beer garden with the disreputable saloon, found themselves vulnerable because most breweries were run by German Americans, their teutonic names proudly emblazoned on bottle, keg, and delivery wagon. They were easy targets for prohibitionists who took to waving flags: Beer was the product of the hated Hun. Congress approved the Eighteenth Amendment, prohibiting "the manufacture, sale, or transportation of intoxicating liquors"—wine as well as beer and spirits—in 1917. The war was over before it was ratified.

The Campaign Against Prostitution   Modern wars have usually meant a relaxation of sexual morality because military service removes young men from the social restraints of family and community. So it was in World War I. Doughboys in France discovered that, with the war two years old, brothels were everywhere, even in tiny French villages.

Moral progressives in the Wilson administration joined forces with army doctors to try to control the inclinations of the recruits. They were warned of the dangers of venereal disease—"A German bullet is cleaner than a French whore"— with unpleasant photographs of syphilitic chancres and victims of the disease whose faces had been disfigured. Physicians drummed the symptoms of gonorrhea into soldiers' heads. In France, the army obliged both doctors and moral progressives by forbidding soldiers on leave to take their holiday in wide-open Paris. (The order was ineffective; soldiers on leave took their chances on getting caught rather than miss the chance to see "Gay Paree." Deserters invariably headed for Paris where they could lose themselves in the city's seamier quarters.)

Josephus Daniels, the deeply religious secretary of the navy, actually believed that having authority over so many young men was a God-given opportunity to *improve* their morals. He called navy ships "floating universities" of moral reform.

Daniels gave orders to the navy to clear out the red-light districts that had been a fixture near every base. The army did the same in towns near its training camps, most famously Storyville, across the river from New Orleans.

Prostitution no more disappeared than people stopped drinking alcohol. But the flush of excitement in the reformers' short-term victories confirmed their belief that, among its horrors, the war had transformed society into a laboratory where it could be reshaped for the better.

CONFORMITY AND REPRESSION

As Wilson had predicted, the white-hot patriotism of wartime scorched political expression. "Free speech" was not defined a fraction as broadly as it is today, but it was generally accepted that political opinion short of advocating violence was protected by the First Amendment. Once the United States was at war, however, federal, state, and local governments harassed and even jailed those who vociferously criticized the war and winked at vigilante actions against people who did not conform to the standards of the super-patriots.

The Campaign Against the Socialists   The Socialist party of America was the most important national organization to oppose the declaration of war. In April 1917, as Congress was debating Wilson's request, the party called an emergency convention in St. Louis and proclaimed "unalterable opposition" to a conflict that killed working people while paying dividends to capitalists. The party's stance did not hurt it at the polls. The Socialist vote increased during the war; voting Socialist was one of the few ways non-Socialists who opposed the war could register their disapproval.

Governments moved promptly to squelch the possibility of a Socialist-led antiwar bandwagon. The legislature of New York expelled seven Socialist assemblymen simply because they opposed the war. Not until after the war did courts rule the expulsion unconstitutional. Socialist Victor Berger was elected to Congress from Milwaukee but denied his seat by the House. When, in the special election to fill the vacancy, he defeated an opponent supported by both the Democratic and Republican parties, Congress again refused to seat him. Berger's district remained unrepresented until 1923 when, finally, he was allowed the place he had been elected to fill five years earlier. In the meantime, Postmaster General Albert S. Burleson denied the Milwaukee *Social Democratic Herald* and other Socialist newspapers cheap mailing privileges. Most of them never recovered from the blow.

The most celebrated attack on the Socialists was the indictment and trial of the party's longtime and much beloved leader Eugene V. Debs for a speech in which he advocated resisting the draft. In sending Debs to Atlanta penitentiary, the Wilson administration was taking a chance. The four-time presidential candidate was admired by many non-Socialists. At his trial in September 1918, Debs was at his most eloquent. "While there is a lower class I am in it; while there is a criminal element I am of it; while there is a soul in prison, I am not free," he told the jury. But in jailing him and a few other prominent Socialists such as Kate Richards O'Hare, the government made it clear that dissent on the issue would not be tolerated.

The Destruction of the IWW

The suppression of the IWW, the Industrial Workers of the World, was heavier-handed than the harassment of the socialists. There was a bitter irony in this for, while the IWW, like the Socialist party, officially opposed the war, the head of the union, William D. "Big Bill" Haywood, tried to soft-pedal the issue. The IWW was enrolling new members by the thousands every month. Haywood, a union man first, hoped to ride out the patriotic hysteria and emerge from the war with the IWW a powerful labor organization.

In fact, the federal government set out to destroy the IWW less because of its official opposition to the war than because it was an increasingly large and effective labor organization. By 1917, the IWW's membership was concentrated in three sectors of the economy that were vital to the war effort: among the migrant harvest hands who brought in the nation's wheat; among loggers in the Pacific Northwest (Sitka spruce lumber was essential to aircraft manufacture); and among copper miners in Globe and Bisbee, Arizona, and Butte, Montana. Unlike American Federation of Labor unions, IWW unions refused to pledge not to strike during the war.

The IWW was also a tempting target for repression because, representing workers on the very bottom and preaching revolution, most respectable middle-class people disapproved, even feared the union. In contrast, most Socialist party leaders were themselves middle class and moderate; and the party's program was no more radical than the programs espoused by many progressives. The socialists had friends, the IWW not many.

The IWW was crushed by a combination of vigilante terrorism and government prosecution. In July 1917, 1,000 "deputies" wearing white arm bands so as to recognize one another rounded up 1,200 Wobbly strikers in Bisbee, put them aboard a chartered train, and dumped them in the Hermanas desert of New Mexico, where they were without food for thirty-six hours. The next month, IWW organizer Frank Little was lynched in Butte, possibly by police officers in disguise. In neither case was there any serious attempt to identify the vigilantes.

In the grain belt, sheriffs and farmers had a free hand in dealing with suspected Wobblies. In the Sitka spruce forests of Washington and Oregon, the army organized the Loyal Legion of Loggers and Lumbermen to counter the popularity of the IWW. There, at least, working conditions were improved, but "5L" attacks on the IWW were frequently vicious. Local police and federal agents ignored the obvious violations of civil rights and violence.

Civil Liberties Suspended

The fatal blow on the IWW fell in the fall of 1917. The Justice Department raided IWW headquarters in several cities, rounded up the union's leaders, and indicted about 200 under the Espionage Act of 1917. Later enhanced by the Sedition Act of 1918, the Espionage Act outlawed not only overt treasonable acts but also made it a crime to "utter, print, write, or publish any disloyal, profane, scurrilous, or abusive language" about the government, the flag, or the uniform of a soldier or sailor. A casual snide remark was enough to warrant bringing charges; a few cases were based on little more than wisecracks.

In *Schenck* v. *the United States* (1919), the Supreme Court unanimously upheld this broad, vague legislation. As if to leave no doubt as to the Court's resolve, Oliver Wendell Holmes Jr., the most liberal-minded justice at the time, wrote the opinion which established the principle that when "a clear and present danger" existed, such as the war, Congress had the power to pass laws that would not be acceptable in normal times.

Even at that, the prosecutors never proved that either the IWW leaders or the organization itself was guilty of sedition. In effect, the individuals who were sentenced to up to 20 years in prison were punished because of their membership in an organization the government wanted to crush. Liberals who had no taste for IWW doctrine were shocked at the government's cynicism and fought the prosecutions. In 1920, led by Roger Baldwin, they organized the American Civil Liberties Union to guard against a repetition of the repressions.

Molding Public Opinion   The attack on the Socialists and the Wobblies was not the only reflection of the spirit of intolerance that Wilson feared the war would loose. Many otherwise reasonable people were stirred by patriotism to believe that they were part of a holy crusade against a foe with the wiles and dark powers of the devil.

There were many violent acts against individual German Americans. Most incidents were spontaneous; for example, a Midwestern mob dragged a German-American shopkeeper from his home, threw him to his knees, forced him to kiss the American flag, and made him spend his savings on war bonds. But intolerance and even vigilante activity were also abetted and even instigated by the national government.

The Committee on Public Information (CPI) was entrusted with the task of mobilizing public opinion behind the government. Headed by George Creel, a progressive news-paperman who had fought against the very sort of intolerance he now encouraged, Creel's job was twofold. First, in order to avoid demoralization, the CPI censored the news from Europe. CPI dispatches emphasized victories and suppressed or played down stories of setbacks and accounts of the misery of life in the trenches. With most editors and publishers solidly behind the war, Creel had no difficulty persuading them to censor their own correspondents.

Second, the CPI attempted to mold public opinion so that even minor deviations from full support of the war were branded as disloyal. Obviously, all German Americans could not be condemned as disloyal. (Only 6,300 Germans were actually interned compared with 45,000 of Great Britain's much smaller German-born community.) However, the CPI could and did launch a massive propaganda campaign that depicted German *Kultur* as intrinsically evil.

The CPI issued 60 million pamphlets, sent prewritten editorials to pliant (or lazy) newspaper editors, and subsidized the design and printing of posters conveying the impression that a network of German spies was ubiquitous in the United States. With money to be made in exploiting the theme, the infant film industry centered in Hollywood, California, rushed to oblige. A typical title of 1917 was *The Barbarous Hun*. In May 1917, a movie producer, Robert Goldstein, was arrested and convicted under the Espionage Act for making a film about the American Revolution, *The Spirit of '76*. One scene showed a redcoat impaling an American baby on his bayonet. Goldstein's crime was to have aided the enemy by disparaging America's British ally.

At movie theaters during intermission, some 75,000 "Four-Minute Men," all volunteers, delivered patriotic speeches of that duration, 7.5 million messages in all. Film stars like action hero Douglas Fairbanks, comedian Charlie Chaplin, and

"America's Sweetheart," Mary Pickford, appeared at Liberty Bond rallies and spoke anti-German lines written by the CPI.

Liberty Hounds and Boy Spies The anti-German hysteria sometimes took laughable form. Restaurants revised their menus so that sauerkraut became "liberty cabbage," hamburgers "Salisbury steak" (after a British lord), and frankfurters and wiener sausages, named after German and Austrian cities, became universally known as "hot dogs."

The real dog, the dachshund, had to be rebred into a "liberty hound." Towns with names of German origin voted to choose more patriotic designations. Berlin, Iowa became Lincoln; Germantown, Nebraska became Garland; East Germantown, Indiana, became Pershing. German measles, a common childhood disease, was "patriotic measles." Hundreds of schools and some colleges dropped the German language from the curriculum. Dozens of symphony orchestras refused to play the works of German composers, leaving conspicuous holes in the repertoire. Prominent German Americans who wished to save their careers found it advisable to imitate opera singer Ernestine Schumann-Heinck. She was a fixture at patriotic rallies, her ample Wagnerian figure draped with a large American flag and her magnificent voice singing "The Star-Spangled Banner" and "America the Beautiful."

But the firing of Germans from their jobs, discriminating against German farmers, burning of German books, and beating up German Americans were not so humorous. Nor was the treatment of other people designated as less than fully patriotic by organizations of self-appointed guardians of the national interest with names like "Sedition Slammers," "Terrible Threateners," and "Boy Spies of America." Members stopped young men on the streets and demanded to see their draft cards. It was not an atrocity, just an obnoxious annoyance comparable to the "thank you for not smoking" mania of the 1990s. But the assumption that one citizen had the right to police another was indicative of an unhealthy social mood. The largest of the self-anointed enforcers of patriotism was the American Protective League. At one time it numbered 250,000 members, although many people probably signed up merely to avoid being themselves harassed.

WILSON AND THE LEAGUE OF NATIONS

Why did Woodrow Wilson tolerate and even tacitly encourage these activities? Because his dream of creating a new world order became an obsession that virtually destroyed his interests in anything else. Before the war, there was an easy-going quality to Wilson. He worked only three or four hours a day and not at all on Saturday and Sunday. (He had, after all, been a college professor.) He had been a regular at Washington Senators baseball games. When the war came, however, he hardly ever stopped toiling.

Like no president before him (but like several since), Wilson lost interest in domestic affairs except insofar as they affected his all-consuming foreign concerns. The one-time enemy of big government presided over its extraordinary expansion. Repression of dissenters, even unjust and illegal repression, appeared to hasten the defeat of the Kaiser, so Wilson abandoned liberal values that had guided his life.

The Fourteen Points

In January 1918, Wilson presented Congress with his blueprint for the postwar world. It consisted of fourteen guidelines that were (he said) to shape the treaty that ended the war. Most of Wilson's points dealt with specific European territorial problems; five general principles wove through the plan.

First, defeated Germany must be treated fairly and generously in order to avoid festering resentments that would lead to another war. Wilson was well aware that, for forty years before the Great War, French politicians had demanded revenge for Germany's annexation of Alsace and Lorraine in 1871. In practical terms, Wilson meant that Germany must not be stripped of territory populated by Germans and the nation must not be saddled with huge reparations payments such as Germany had forced on France in 1871.

Second, Wilson said, the boundaries of all European countries must conform to nationality as defined by language. Wilson believed that the aspirations of people to govern themselves was a major cause of the war. He avoided mention of the non-white peoples in Britain's and France's colonies, although he did say that Germany's colonies were to be disposed of on some basis other than as spoils of war.

Third, Wilson demanded "absolute freedom upon the seas, … alike in peace and in war." This was a reference to the German submarine campaign that Wilson blamed for American involvement, but it also had to do with Britain's historical in-clination to use her primacy on the ocean to interfere with American shipping.

Fourth, Wilson demanded disarmament. It was obvious to all parties that the arms race of the two decades preceding the war had been a major cause of the tragedy.

Finally and most important to Wilson, he called for the establishment of "a general assembly of nations," a congress of countries, to replace the alliances and secret treaties that contributed to the debacle of 1914. More than any other aspect of his program, the League of Nations came to obsess the president.

Wilson Fools Himself

When an Allied breakthrough in the summer of 1918 put victory within view, Wilson turned nearly all his energies to planning for the peace conference to be held in Paris. He announced that he would personally head the American delegation.

The enormity of World War I justified his decision, but Wilson paid too little at-tention to a clear shift in the mood of the electorate. In the midterm election of 1918, just a week before the Armistice, the voters returned Republican majorities of 240–190 to the House of Representatives and of 49–47 to the Senate. Not only was Congress Republican, but it also had a decidedly unidealistic tinge. The machine bosses and pro-fessional politicians who had resisted progressive reform for a decade were back.

Not all the freshmen were reactionaries, nor were they Wilson-haters; they were politicians who were willing to deal, to settle for less than they really wanted. It was Wilson who was uncooperative. He seemed not to recognize that the election of so many Republican regulars might reflect a weariness with his endless idealistic ex-hortations. The president failed to include a single prominent Republican in the party he took with him to Europe on December 4, an almost unprecedented and inexplicable stupidity. Any treaty he brought back with him had to be ratified by the Republican Senate.

Wilson also misinterpreted his reception in England, France, and Italy. Everywhere he went he was cheered and buried in flowers by crowds of hundreds of thousands. It had to have been a heady experience for a man who, ten years earlier, was content to be a university president hosting garden parties. Wilson believed that the people of Europe had risen to greatness along with him. He believed they were cheering the author of the Fourteen Points.

The Peace Conference

He was dead wrong. The hysterical crowds were cheering Wilson the conqueror, the man who had won the war for them after four years of fruitless slaughter. The leaders of the Allies, the men with whom Wilson sat down in Paris, understood this very well. They knew that after four years of savagery and sacrifice on an unprecedented scale, the peoples of the victorious nations wanted to be rewarded. Georges Clemenceau of France, David Lloyd George of Great Britain, and Vittorio Orlando of Italy paid lip service to Wilson's idealism, but just to be polite. Once behind the closed doors of the conference room, they made it clear to Wilson that their nations had interests that had to be served.

Georges Clemenceau, a hard-bitten, cynical, no nonsense French nationalist, was the most candid. "God gave us the Ten Commandments and we broke them," he said, "Wilson gives us the Fourteen Points. We shall see." Clemenceau blamed Germany for the war. (It was true enough that France had not wanted to fight in 1914.) And he meant that Germany would pay for the death and destruction it had caused. France had legitimate grievances that Wilson had rather cavalierly waved off when he called for a "peace without victors." Belgium and France had been the battlefields for four years, not Germany. Germany was physically untouched. The Allies had crossed the German border at only one point at the time of the Armistice. The entire northeast of France, the country's industrial heartland, was one big ruin. No reparations?

British Prime Minister David Lloyd George admired Wilson and had no ravaged counties to restore. But he too was a political realist and his constituents had suffered the loss of almost a million sons, husbands, and fathers with a million more men permanently maimed and deserving of government support. There were billions in pensions to be paid to them and to the widows of the dead soldiers. But the British economy was shattered. Lloyd George could not help but hold Germany liable.

Italy had been soundly trounced by the Austrians on the "southern front." Prime Minister Vittorio Orlando went to Versailles to save face. He insisted that Austria cede the South Tyrol and the Dalmatian port of Fiume to Italy. The Tyrol's 200,000 people were German-speaking Austrians; Fiume's population was mostly Croatian. That Italy should incorporate them was as blatant a violation of Wilson's principle of "national self-determination" as was imaginable.

The Japanese delegate Count Nobuaki Makino meant to retain the German colonies in the Pacific that Japan had seized. So much for Point Five.

So Much for the Fourteen Points

Line by line, the Versailles Conference redrew Wilson's blueprint until the president's chaste Greek temple looked like an old farm house to which rooms, dormers, and lean-tos had been added over a century. Three of the Fourteen Points survived intact; six were completely scuttled; five were compromised almost beyond recognition.

Wilson had little choice but to give in. He had no answer when Clemenceau pointed out that Germany had extracted large reparations from France after the Franco-Prussian war although that war too had been fought in France, not in Germany. In creating the new nations of Poland and Czechoslovakia, large regions populated almost exclusively by Germans were included within their borders. Otherwise, Poland would have no seaport (which Wilson himself had, in fact, promised) and Czechoslovakia, without the mountains of the German Sudetenland, would be defenseless. Indeed, if all Germans living contiguous to Germany had been incorporated into the nation, its German population would have been greater than it had been in 1914. Victors do not write treaties that enlarge the power of the vanquished. Wilson wilted.

In the Balkans, national self-determination—ethnically homogeneous nations— was impossible. The region was a crazy quilt of Hungarian, Romanian, German, Croatian, Serbian, Slovenian, Bulgarian, and Albanian counties, towns, and villages. Romanian communities sat cheek by jowl with Hungarian communities. Every city was home to several ethnic groups. The only alternative to Balkan nations with large ethnic minorities nursing ancient resentments was a forced relocation of millions of people. Italy's demand of the South Tyrol was without justification. Even the Italian army said that the province was not essential to Italian defense. But Orlando wanted it and Wilson gave in.

Cruel realities exposed the Fourteen Points as the ivory tower doodling of a fuzzy-minded idealist who did not reflect on his first draft. Wilson had no choice but to give in, but he was incapable of facing up to his illusions (or the fact that the American people might conclude that he had been snookered). He accepted the Treaty of Versailles by staking all on the League of Nations. He persuaded himself that the League would correct the mistakes in the Treaty of Versailles, as if, in a few years, human nature would undergo a transformation.

Article 10   Shelving the Fourteen Points did not much bother the sena-tors who would ratify or reject the treaty, particularly the twelve of the forty-nine Republican senators, mostly westerners, who announced that they were "irreconcilable" in their opposition to ratifying it. To them, entering the war had been a mistake. They meant to isolate the United States from Europe's corruptions and squabbles once again, not to involve the United States in them eternally in a League of Nations.

In March 1919, the other thirty-seven Republican senators signed a round robin stating they would vote to ratify the treaty with certain reservations, which varied from senator to senator. The reservations that counted revolved about Article 10 of the Covenant of the League of Nations. It pledged all member states to "preserve against external aggression the territorial integrity and ... political in-dependence of all members." Article 10, the reservationists said, committed the United States to go to war if any other League member were attacked. Bulgaria? Uruguay? Article 10 unmodified was a surrender of national sovereignty, the reser-vationists said; they would have none of it.

Wilson replied that Article 10 was nothing more than a moral obligation; the United States was not surrendering its independence of action. This was cant. If the obligation was merely moral, it was meaningless, which Wilson, who wrote it, did not believe. Nevertheless, although he had given in to the Allies on dozens of questions, he refused to change a word of Article 10 in order to win the backing of enough Republican senators—not many were needed—to get the treaty ratified. In his righteous recalcitrance, he created an opening for the chairman of the Senate Foreign Relations Committee, Henry Cabot Lodge of Massachusetts, who openly admitted he "hated" Wilson.

The Fight for the League

Lodge was an unlikely giant killer. He was not especially popular with his colleagues in the Senate. As determined to have his way as Wilson was, he lacked the greatness to which Wilson could rise. In the battle over the League, however, Lodge proved an infinitely better politician. Perceiving that Wilson grew less flexible as the debate developed, Lodge became uncharacteristically open and cooperative with the "mild reservationists," Republicans who wanted to vote for the League—with a few reservations. Understanding that the longer the debate dragged on, the less the American people were interested in it, a realism of which Wilson was incapable, Lodge played for time. He read the entire 264 pages of the treaty into the record of his committee's hearings, even though it had been published and sat on every senator's desk.

Lodge's calculations were dead right. While a majority of Americans probably favored American participation in the League during the first months of 1919, their interest waned slowly but perceptibly during the summer.

The climax came in September. With the treaty about to come before the Senate, Wilson announced an exhausting 8,000-mile speaking tour that his doctors, knowing of his extremely high blood pressure, begged him not to undertake. He believed that he could rally the people behind him—he had done it before—and bring pressure in that way on the reservationist senators to vote for the treaty as it stood. By September 25, when his train moved into Colorado, the crowds seemed to be with him. At Pueblo, however, his speech was slurred, and he openly wept. Wilson had suffered a mild stroke or was on the verge of a nervous breakdown due to exhaustion or both. His physician canceled the tour and rushed him back to Washington. A few days later, Wilson crumpled to the floor of his bedroom, felled by a cerebral thrombosis, a blood clot in the brain.

The Invisible President

No one knows to this day just how seriously Wilson was disabled. For six weeks, his protective, strong-willed wife isolated him from everyone but physicians. She screened every document brought to him and returned them with a shaky signature at the bottom. When suspicious and concerned officials insisted on seeing the president, they discovered that his left side was paralyzed and his speech was halting. However, he was in complete control of his wits. To a Republican senator who said, "We've all been praying for you," he replied, "Which way, Senator?"

Wilson did not meet officially with his cabinet for six months, and photographs of that occasion show a haggard old man with an anxiety in his eyes that cannot be seen in any earlier picture. Even if the clarity of his thinking was not affected, his removal from the scene probably had little effect on the outcome of the battle. In the pink of health, Wilson had refused to entertain a compromise.

The inevitable outcome was defeat. In November, on Wilson's instructions, the Democratic senators voted with the irreconcilables to kill the treaty with Lodge's reservations by a vote of 55 to 39. When the treaty was introduced without the reservations, the reservationists and the irreconcilables defeated it against the Democrats. In March, over Wilson's protest, twenty-one Democrats worked out a compromise with the reservationist Republicans and again voted on the treaty. But twenty-three Democrats continued to go along with Wilson's insistence that he get the original treaty or no treaty at all. They and the irreconcilables defeated it.

The Election of 1920

Incredibly, Wilson believed that he could win the League of Nations by running for a third term in the presidential election of 1920 and winning. That was too much for even the most loyal Wilsonians. They ignored Wilson's hints and chose Governor James M. Cox of Ohio, a party regular who looked like a traveling salesman. For vice president the Democrats nominated a staunch young Wilsonian with a magical name, the undersecretary of the navy, Franklin D. Roosevelt. The Democrats were pessimistic but

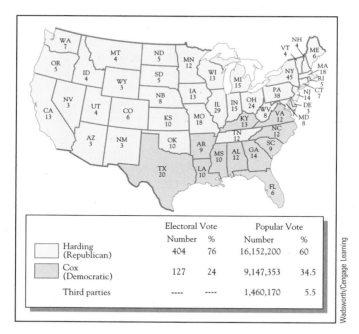

	Electoral Vote		Popular Vote	
	Number	%	Number	%
Harding (Republican)	404	76	16,152,200	60
Cox (Democratic)	127	24	9,147,353	34.5
Third parties	----	----	1,460,170	5.5

MAP 37.1 Presidential Election, 1920

Harding's election restored the Republican party's "natural" supremacy in national elections. Indeed, he enhanced it. Harding swept the West which had elected Wilson in 1916. He even cracked the "Solid South," winning majorities in West Virginia and Tennessee.

hoped that the Roosevelt name on the Democratic ticket would win enough former Progressive party voters to put Cox across.

The Republicans had better reason to expect victory. Their party was still the majority party. Wilson's victory in 1912 was possible because the Republican vote had split in two. He won reelection in 1916 by a hair because—they concluded—western isolationists believed that Wilson would keep the country out of the war. The Republican victory in the congressional elections of 1918 confirmed their belief that the bad times were past and gone.

As usually happens when a party's candidate, whoever he is, looks like a shoo-in, there was a cat fight for the nomination. The two leading candidates were General Leonard Wood, an old comrade of Theodore Roosevelt (but no progressive), and Illinois Governor Frank O. Lowden. Senator Hiram Johnson of California was the candidate of the party's shrinking progressive wing. On the first ballot, Wood had 287 votes, Lowden 211, Johnson 133. With a herd of favorite sons and minor candidates, none was close to the 492 needed to win.

Which is exactly what a small-time but very clever politician supporting Warren G. Harding expected to happen. Harding was seventh on the first ballot with just 65 votes. Nevertheless, when reporters cornered a wheeler-dealer from Ohio named Harry M. Daugherty and asked him whom he thought would be nominated, Daugherty replied genially: "Well boys, I'll tell you what I think. The convention will be deadlocked. After the other candidates have failed, we'll get together in some hotel room, oh, about 2:11 in the morning, and some 15 men, bleary-eyed with lack of sleep, will sit down around a big table and when that time comes Senator Harding will be selected."

His prediction was eerily correct, right down to the details. After the eighth deadlocked ballot, Daugherty, Lodge, and other Republican bigwigs met in a hotel room. The next morning, on the ninth ballot, Harding led Wood and Lowden. On the tenth, he was nominated.

The Great Bloviator   Harding was the owner and editor of a newspaper in Marion, Ohio, whom the Republicans sent to the senate in 1915 as a reward for long years as an easy-going, affable party regular who did as the bosses asked. He was handsome, sociable, and honest but unconcerned about the ethics of his friends. He had not distinguished himself as a senator; he was content to be a follower. He had been a reservationist in the votes on the Treaty of Versailles. He was "the available man," the first choice of few Republicans but acceptable to all.

Harding waffled on the treaty issue during the campaign. His theme was the country's need to calm down after so many years of experimental reforms, crusading, and war. This strategy allowed Harding to make use of his technique of "bloviation." Bloviating, as Harding liked to explain, was "the art of speaking for as long as the occasion warrants, and saying nothing." In a speech in Boston, Harding declared that "America's need is not heroism but healing, not nostrums but normalcy, not agitation but adjustment, not surgery but serenity, not the dramatic but the dispassionate, not experiment but equipoise, not submergence in internationality but sustainment in triumphant nationality."

A Democratic politician remarked that the normalcy speech "left the impression of an army of pompous phrases moving over the landscape in search of an

Warren G. Harding speaking from his front porch in Marion, Ohio. (The Republican National Committee added the porch to Harding's home in order to remind voters of the "normalcy" of the days when McKinley was president.) Harding did not run the pure "front porch campaign" in 1920 that McKinley did. He delivered speeches all over the country.

Brown Brothers

idea." The iconoclastic journalist H. L. Mencken did him one better. He said that Harding's speech reminded him of "stale bean soup, of college yells, of dogs barking idiotically through endless nights." But Mencken added perceptively that "it is so bad that a sort of grandeur creeps through it."

Harding won 61 percent of the popular vote, more than any candidate who preceded him in the White House since popular votes were recorded.

Wilson lived quietly in Washington until 1924. His wit returning after his retirement, he said, "I am going to try to teach ex-presidents how to behave." He set a good example. A semi-invalid specter out of the past, he took drives almost daily in the elegant Pierce-Arrow automobile that was his pride and joy. He attended vaudeville performances and baseball games and watched movies, of which he was an avid fan, at home.

Unlike Harding (whose funeral he lived to attend), Wilson was a giant who loomed over an age. His intelligence, dignity, steadfastness, and sense of rectitude overshadowed even the boisterous Theodore Roosevelt, something TR himself must have sensed: Like Lodge, he hated Wilson. Wilson's end was therefore more tragic than that of any other president, including those who were assassinated. For Wilson, like the tragic heroes of great drama, was murdered not by his enemies or by his weaknesses, but by his virtues.

38

TROUBLED YEARS
America After the Great War 1919–1923

I have no trouble with my enemies but my goddam friends,... they are the ones who keep me walking the floor nights.

—Warren G. Harding

Harding was not a bad man. He was just a slob.

—Alice Roosevelt Longworth

The decade between Armistice Day and the Great Depression of the 1930s is (and always will be) known as the "Roaring Twenties." In literature and film, even in the novels and movies of the period, the 1920s are a time of unprecedented prosperity when Americans, worn out by the reforming fervor of the progressives and disillusioned by the war for democracy that only killed off millions, decided to have a little fun and ended up having a lot.

Our historical memories of the Roaring Twenties are set in swanky speakeasies run by bootleggers who blasted their competitors with "tommy guns" (but never their customers) and in stadiums shaking with the cheers of 50,000 sports-mad fans cheering Harold "Red" Grange on to touchdowns, Jack Dempsey on to knockouts, and Babe Ruth on to another home run. They are set in dark movie houses where the only sound is a piano and the stars are Charlie Chaplin, Rudolph Valentino, Mary Pickford, and Clara Bow.

It is the age of cocky college boys with slicked-down hair, big capital letters on their sweaters, and, in their pockets, "hip flasks" full of illegal "bath-tub gin"; of "flappers" wildly dancing the Charleston and, between numbers, talking flippantly about sex; of sweating, ever-smiling black musicians who know their place—playing "Dixieland" jazz. One crazy fad follows another. And there are the automobiles. Every other car on American roads during the Twenties was a cheap, homely Model T Ford, but the prosperous decade is better remembered for elegant Pierce Arrows, sporty Stutz Bearcats, roaring Hispano-Suizas, and sleek Packards.

Postwar Instability 1919–1929

1919	1920	1921	1922	1923	1924	1925	1926	1927	1928–1929

1919 Major strikes; Red Scare; "Black Sox" scandal

1921–1923 Warren G. Harding president

1921 Race riot in Tulsa

1922 Antilynching bill fails in Senate

Calvin Coolidge president 1923–1929

1924 Immigration restriction; KKK at peak of power

Scopes "Monkey Trial"; Marcus Garvey imprisoned 1925

Sacco and Vanzetti executed 1927

POSTWAR TENSIONS: LABOR, REDS, IMMIGRANTS

There is nothing *false* in this picture. However, it is a mistake to assume, as the phrase "Roaring Twenties" implies, that the free and easy good times were enjoyed by everyone for a decade before the stock market crashed in 1929. For 60 percent of the population, the Twenties were less rewarding than the 1910s; they saw their share of the nation's income shrink by 13 percent. For the upper 40 percent, who did prosper, the carefree, easy money years numbered not ten but about five. From 1919, the first postwar year, to 1923 when President Harding unexpectedly died and even into the presidency of his successor, Calvin Coolidge, American society was characterized more by labor unrest, racial conflict, tensions between city and country and between religion and modernism, and by bigotry and anxiety rather than by hedonism and glitter.

1919: Year of Strikes
During the war, unions belonging to the American Federation of Labor pledged not to strike as their contribution to the war effort. Wages rose during 1917 and 1918 but not as quickly as the prices of consumer goods, which soared during a runaway postwar inflation in 1919. The war's end also meant the cancellation of huge government contracts. Tens of thousands of men and women in war-related jobs were thrown out of work, leading to the inevitable: 3,600 strikes in 1919 involving 4 million workers.

The grievances of almost all the strikers were legitimate by any measure. Nevertheless, few middle-class Americans, themselves hit hard by inflation, were sympathetic. When employers described strikers as revolutionaries bent on destroying the country, or the tools of revolutionaries, a lot of people nodded agreement, and more than nodded. In Seattle, a dispute that began on the docks of the busy port turned into a general strike involving most of the city's 60,000 working people with most of the others staying home out of fear. Most of the strikers were interested in nothing more than better pay. However, the concept of the general strike was associated with revolution—toppling government by paralyzing the economy. Mayor Ole Hansen said that the strike was instigated by dangerous foreign Bolsheviks. That was nonsense, but it worked. With the help of U.S. Marines, Hansen crushed the strikers to general applause.

The magnates of the steel industry employed similar devices to combat a walkout in September 1919 by 350,000 workers, mostly in the Great Lakes states. Steelworkers had good reasons for striking. Many of them worked a twelve-hour day and a seven-day week. It was not unknown for an unlucky individual to put in thirty-six hours at a stretch to keep his job. If a man's relief failed to show when his shift ended, he might be told to stay on for another twelve-hour shift or lose his job. When that shift ended, his own began again.

Steelworkers took home subsistence wages. For some unmarried immigrants—mostly slavic—home was not even a bed to themselves. They contracted with a boarding-house to rent a bed for half the day. After their shift and a quick meal, they rolled under blankets still warm and damp from the body of a worker who had just trudged off to the mill.

These inhuman conditions were well known. And yet, the heads of the industry, Elbert Gary of United States Steel and Charles Schwab of Bethlehem Steel, were able to persuade public opinion that the strike was the work of revolutionary agitators like William Z. Foster. In fact, Foster's leadership was in the AFL's bread-and-butter tradition but he had been an IWW in the past, so the bosses' line was plausible. The strike failed and the union disintegrated.

The Boston police strike was the most frightening work stoppage of 1919. Boston's patrolmen, mostly conservative Roman Catholic Irishmen, were grossly underpaid. Their wages had been set in 1916, before the wartime inflation. They were not able to support their families in a city where rents and the prices of food and clothing had, in many cases, tripled during the war.

Nevertheless, they commanded little public support when they walked out. With no cops on the streets, people feared, by no means irrationally, there would be a crime wave as hoodlums and lowlifes took advantage of the chance to snatch purses and mug men who looked as if they might be carrying a fat wallet with no fear of arrest. When Massachusetts Governor Calvin Coolidge ordered the National Guard into Boston to take over police functions and break the strike, the public applauded and the strike collapsed. Samuel Gompers asked—virtually begged—Coolidge to restore the defeated patrolmen to their jobs. Coolidge refused, replying, "there is no right to strike against the public safety by anybody, anywhere, anytime." The phrase made him a national hero. He was awarded the vice-presidential nomination on Warren G. Harding's ticket in 1920.

Red Scare	Some of the popular reaction to the strikes of 1919 revealed a widespread hostility toward immigrants—foreigners. The

xenophobia took its most virulent form in the "Red Scare." Even before the Armistice in November 1918, a new stereotype was replacing the Hun as the villain Americans most loved to hate: the seedy, lousy, bearded, wild-eyed Eastern European Bolshevik—the "red."

The atrocities during the Russian Revolution were real and numerous. Nevertheless, they were not enough for sensationalist American newspapers, few of which had correspondents on the scene. Anti-communist editors exaggerated reports that were bad enough straight and even invented tales of mass executions, torture, children turned against their parents, and women proclaimed the common sexual property of all workingmen. Americans were ready to believe the worst about a part of the world from which so many recent immigrants had come.

Many were convinced that foreign-born communists threatened the security of the United States. In March 1919, the Soviets organized the Third International, or Comintern, an organization dedicated to fomenting revolution worldwide. So it seemed to be no coincidence when, the next month, the Post Office discovered 38 bombs in packages addressed to prominent capitalists and government officials. In June, a few bombs reached their targets. One bomber who was identified—he blew himself up—was an Italian. When, in September, two American communist parties were founded in Chicago, the press emphasized the large immigrant element in the membership.

One of the two rival parties was a mostly immigrant organization. The other, however, was led by Americans who boasted (or belittled) a white Anglo-Saxon Protestant ancestry as impeccable as Henry Cabot Lodge's. Max Eastman, the editor of the radical magazine *The Masses,* was of old New England stock. John Reed, whose *Ten Days That Shook the World* was a sympathetic account of the Bolshevik Revolution, was a bushy-tailed Harvard boy from Portland, Oregon. William D. Haywood, who fled to the Soviet Union rather than go to prison, said he traced his ancestry "to the Puritan bigots."

But the dread of a ghost can be as compelling as the fear of a grizzly bear. Americans were uneasy in 1919. The temptation to exploit the anxiety for political gain was irresistible for Woodrow Wilson's Attorney General, A. Mitchell Palmer. Sensing he might be able to ride the "Red Scare" into the Democratic presidential nomination in 1920, he ordered a series of well-publicized raids on communist offices. Only 39 of the hundreds Palmer arrested were foreigners who could be deported legally. Nevertheless, crying "foreign menace," the attorney general put 249 arrestees on a Russia-bound steamship that was dubbed "the Soviet Ark."

On New Year's Day 1920, Palmer's agents again swooped down on several hundred locations, arresting 6,000 people. Many of them, like a Western Union boy delivering a telegram, were guilty of nothing but being in the wrong place at the wrong time. Others were arrested while peering into the windows of storefront offices. All were jailed at least briefly.

Palmer's presidential hopes fizzled when he predicted massive demonstrations on May Day 1920 (the socialist and communist holiday) and nothing happened. By midsummer, the great Red Scare was over. Antiforeign sentiment, however, continued to shape government policy and public opinion.

Sacco and Vanzetti   The marriage of antiradicalism and xenophobia was focused for much of the Twenties on two Italians, Nicola Sacco and Bartolomeo Vanzetti. In 1920, they were arrested for an armed robbery in South Braintree, Massachusetts, during which a guard and a paymaster were killed. They were found guilty of murder and sentenced to die in the electric chair.

Before they were executed, however, the American Civil Liberties Union learned that the hard evidence against the two was scanty and some evidence appeared to have been invented by the prosecution. (It was.) The judge at the trial, Webster Thayer, was openly prejudiced; he referred to Sacco and Vanzetti as "those damned dagos." To the ACLU and several Italian-American associations that joined the fight to save the two, and a distinguished law professor at Harvard University, Felix Frankfurter, the men had been found guilty not on the basis of the facts but because prosecutor, judge, jury, and the press despised them as sinister-looking Italians who spoke no English and, worse, they were both anarchists.

Sacco and Vanzetti won admiration in many quarters by the quiet dignity with which they carried themselves in prison. They insisted on their innocence of the crimes while refusing to compromise their political beliefs and their right to have them. "I am suffering," Vanzetti said, "because I am a radical and indeed I am a radical; I have suffered because I was an Italian, and indeed I am an Italian ... but I am so convinced to be right that if you could execute me two times, and if I could be reborn two other times, I would live again to do what I have done already."

The movement to save Sacco and Vanzetti was international. Even the fascist dictator of Italy, who had disposed of a few anarchists himself, joined the protest. They were granted several stays of execution while lawyers attempted to find evidence to prove their innocence and petitioned the governor of Massachusetts to commute their sentences for, if nothing else, public relations. But the governor was under far more pressure from people determined to see them dead. In 1927, they were electrocuted. The question of their guilt or innocence had ceased to be relevant to either side in the controversy.

Immigration Restriction

At the turn of the century, "new immigrants"—from southern and eastern Europe—poured into the United States in numbers that exceeded a million in several years. Old stock Americans, some of them quite distinguished, organized in groups like the Immigration Restriction League to stop the flood of people that some saw as too alien ever to be assimilated as Americans, and others saw as genetically inferior.

Before the world war, the anti-immigration movement's device to limit the influx of "undesirables" was the literacy test. Three times, Congress enacted legislation that required would-be immigrants to demonstrate that they could read. Three different presidents vetoed the bills on constitutional grounds: Cleveland, Taft, and Wilson.

The war reduced European immigration to just 110,000 in 1918. With peace, however, the numbers again increased rapidly to 800,000 in 1921. So Congress tried again, avoiding the constitutional difficulties of literacy tests by restricting immigration on the basis of nationality. The Immigration Restriction Act of 1921, as amended in 1924, limited admissions to 150,000 people each year. (Latin Americans were freely admitted; Asians were completely excluded.) Immigrants from each European nation were admitted until their numbers reached 2 percent of the number of people of their nationality who were residents of the United States in 1890.

This convoluted system ensured that few southern and eastern Europeans would come to the United States. Very few Poles, Czechs, Slovaks, Hungarians, Romanians, Yugoslavians, Bulgarians, Russians, Greeks, and Italians had come to the United States before 1890. Under the Restriction Act, only 5,802 Italians were admitted each year, 6,524 Poles, 2,784 Russians. The quotas for southern and eastern Europe were filled by the end of January every year. The quotas for the prosperous countries of northern and Western Europe were generous and rarely filled. The annual quota for Great Britain under the 1924 law was 75,000. It was never filled. During the 1930s, only 2,500 Britons emigrated to the United States each year.

RACIAL TENSIONS

If Caucasian immigrants faced serious hostility during the 1920s, the decade was not, of course, kind toward African Americans. This was a major blow to black civil rights leaders like W. E. B. DuBois, the editor of the National Association of Colored People's newspaper *The Crisis*. Like Frederick Douglass during the Civil War, DuBois had urged young African Americans to enlist in the army during the war rather than wait to be drafted. He hoped that by emphatically demonstrating their patriotism, blacks' claims to social equality—or at least, justice—would be heard more cordially after the Armistice. His hopes did not survive New Year's Day 1920.

Race Riots and Lynchings   In late 1918, there was a race riot in little Elaine, Arkansas. Several hundred blacks and whites were arrested. Twelve were sentenced to death. (The Supreme Court later freed them.) In 1919, much of Chicago exploded in a racial fury. A black teenager swimming in Lake Michigan drifted into "whites-only" waters. He was battered by rocks thrown from the beach and drowned. The ugliness of the attack infuriated African Americans all over the city. White and black men and boys (and women and girls!) battled in the streets, sometimes with guns, for five days and nights. Thirty-eight were killed; 500 people were injured seriously enough to seek medical attention. The death toll in other race riots that summer was 120. In 1921, a

Five young African American men lynched in Texas at the height of the lynching tragedy. It was the largest single incident. Authorities were unable (or unwilling) to explain the reasons for the murders.

The Granger Collection, New York

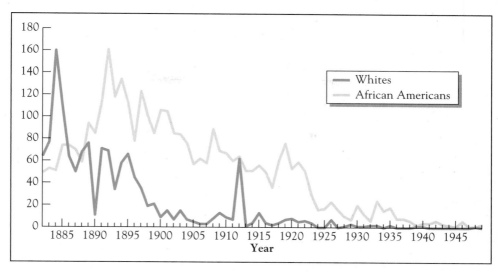

CHART 38.1 Lynchings in the United States, 1875–1950

Before the rise of southern populism during the 1890s, lynching was common in the United States, but blacks were not singled out as victims. After 1900 (except in 1912), lynchings of whites virtually ceased. By the 1920s, middle-class social pressures on southern sheriffs (who had often been active accomplices to lynchings) resulted in a steady decline in the crime. Not until World War II, however, were the numbers of lynching victims reduced to two or three per year.

citywide race riot in Tulsa left at least 100 dead; 1,000 homes and shops in the once prosperous African American business district were destroyed.

In the first year after the war, seventy-six blacks were lynched, more than in any year since 1904. Ten of the victims were veterans, several still in their uniforms. In both 1920 and 1921, lynchings exceeded fifty, and the House of Representatives enacted the Dyer Bill, which provided for federal prosecution of sheriffs and other police officials who cooperated with or ignored lynch mobs. The bill died in the Senate when southerners filibustered against it with support from several northern Democrats.

Nevertheless, lynchings dropped sharply in 1923 and never again reached 1919 levels. To some extent, southern politicians got the message of the Dyer Bill and passed it on back home. If police authorities did not act to prevent lynchings, sooner or later Congress would enact a federal antilynching bill that would overcome obstruction in the Senate. More important, middle-class white southerners and southern newspapers had had their fill of the savagery and what it meant for the South's reputation. Provincial southern sheriffs who could shrug off Yankee contempt for them were not willing to risk the opposition of influential southern whites.

The Ku Klux Klan
The increase in lynchings in the early 1920s reflected the rise of the new Ku Klux Klan (KKK), itself inspired by the sensationally successful film *The Birth of a Nation* that romanticized the Ku Klux Klan of the Reconstruction Era. The revived Klan was founded in 1915 by a

The Tin Lizzie

The "horseless carriage"—the automobile— was proved workable in Germany and France. During the 1890s, however, the tinkerers, mechanics, and venture capitalists who went crazy were American. By 1900, thirty American companies were competing for the automobilist dollar. It was a small, luxury market. Their cars were quite expensive, affordable only by the wealthy and of interest, for the most part, only to wealthy faddists who made nuisances of themselves racing around, running down dogs, and frightening horses. In 1900, carmakers sold only 8,000 vehicles.

Henry Ford was a farmboy who hated farming and a self-taught engineer who worked for an Edison-owned electric company in Detroit. Ford was a mechanical genius—he had "wheels in his head"—but no more so than many others in the business. However, where other car makers competed for the luxury dollar, ever improving their designs and ever increasing

their selling prices, Ford wanted to "build a car for the great multitude." As other cars grew larger, faster, more comfortable, and more attractive, Ford designed an ever more basic automobile that could be mass produced in quantities so large and a profit margin so slim that its selling price would be within the reach of everyone but the poor.

After several flawed designs and constant tinkering with the manufacturing process, Ford came up with the Model T, which made its debut in 1908. It had a tiny 4-cylinder 20-horsepower engine, a two-speed (plus reverse) planetary transmission operated by pedals (no gear grinding), and it sat high off the ground on wheels 3 feet in diameter. The Model T cleared obstacles and putted along in ruts in country roads that brought other cars to a halt.

The first Model T Ford cost $825. That was not peanuts in 1908, but it was considerably less than every other car maker charged. Ford sold 10,000 Model Ts the

Methodist minister, William Simmons, after he saw the movie. Under Hiram Wesley Evans, a dentist who succeeded Simmons as "Imperial Wizard" in 1922, the Klan grew rapidly. Evans gave local units and officials exotic names such as Klavern, Kleagle, Grand Dragon, and Exalted Cyclops. More important, he expanded the Klan's enemies list to tap all the anxieties of the postwar period. Evans's Klan was anti-black, anti-immigrant, anti-Catholic, anti-Semitic, anti-communist, anti-labor, anti-big city, anti-modern morality, and pro-prohibition and pro-Protestant fundamentalism.

With so large a net, Evans snared members not only in the South, but also in the Northwest, Midwest, and California. By 1924, Klan membership may have reached the 4.5 million the Imperial Wizard claimed. Numerous state legislators and congressmen, a few senators, and the governors of Oregon, Ohio, Tennessee, and Texas were klansmen or openly sympathetic with it. In Indiana, Grand Dragon David Stephenson was the state's political boss. At the Democratic national convention in 1924, the Klan was influential enough to prevent the party from adopting a plank critical of its bigotry and to veto the nomination of a Roman Catholic, Governor Alfred E. Smith of New York, as the party's candidate for president.

That, however, proved to be the KKK's last hurrah. In 1925, David Stephenson was found guilty of second-degree murder in the death of a young woman whom he first year. The car was dubbed the "tin lizzie" and the "flivver" because it looked flimsy. In fact, the Model T was tougher than any other American or imported car. Not only could it be driven on all but impassable roads, its body was made of a vanadium steel alloy with a tensile strength of 170,000 pounds compared to the 60,000-pound strength of the steel in other cars. In a New York to Seattle endurance race in 1909, only two cars finished, both Model T.

Ford made few changes in the Model T each year. He devoted his time and the brilliant engineers and business organizers he hired to improving the manufacturing process, increasing production, and lowering the price of his car. Ford and his associates perfected the assembly line, decreasing the time it took to produce the T by breaking the hundreds of complex operations required to assemble so complex a machine into simple tasks that unskilled workers standing in one place could learn how to perform in an hour. The parts each man attached were brought to them by finely orchestrated conveyors. In 1910, Ford made and sold 19,000 Model T's, in 1912 78,440. In 1914, 260,720 Model T's rolled off the assembly line, half of all the cars made in the United States that year. There was a new Model T Ford ready to be loaded on trains every couple of minutes. The price of the car dropped almost annually, bottoming out at $290, which was peanuts. When, after nineteen years, the Model T was discontinued (only the Volkswagen Beetle has had a longer run), 15 million had been built and most of them were still on the road, especially on rural roads.

In part, the Model T lost favor with the prospering middle classes of town and city during the 1920s because it was associated with country hicks in overalls. In part, it declined in popularity because Ford resisted the obvious, that in the 1920s, more and more people were able and willing to spend more for a car with more powerful engines, more sophisticated technology like electric starters, good looks, and "status"—all the things he had repudiated when he designed the Model T.

had taken to Chicago for a tryst. In an attempt to win a light sentence, Stephenson turned over evidence showing that virtually the whole administration of the Klan was involved in thievery and that Indiana's Klan politicians were thoroughly corrupt. In 1930, the first year of the Great Depression, membership dwindled to 10,000.

Marcus Garvey and the Call of Africa At its peak, the Klan was endorsed from an unlikely quarter, by the founder of the United Negro Improvement Association (UNIA). Marcus Garvey, born in Jamaica, was based in New York's Harlem but had followers in every city with a large African American population. Like the Klan, Garvey preached separation of the races. In his widely circulated newspaper *Negro World*, he hammered on the theme that Africans had once had a civilization far superior to that of the whites. "When Europe was inhabited by a race of cannibals, a race of savages, naked men, heathens, and pagans," Garvey told cheering crowds, "Africa was peopled by a race of cultured black men who were masters in art, science, and literature." That such a people should seek the acceptance of whites was humiliating and self-destructive. African Americans (and black West Indians) should, among themselves, pool resources, and work toward the day when they would return to Africa and build a great nation.

How seriously Garvey took his ultimate goal is impossible to say. After the disillusionments of 1919, however, tens of thousands of blacks living in northern cities joined the UNIA. Many who did not join admired Garvey. On one occasion, he claimed a million followers, on another 4 million. The *Negro World* had a circulation of 200,000, more than the NAACP's *The Crisis*.

Like Hiram Wesley Evans, Garvey was a showman. He founded paramilitary orders with exotic names like "The Dukes of the Niger" and the "Black Eagle Flying Corps," which he dressed in gaudy costumes. In parades in Harlem, Philadelphia, Detroit, and other cities, he rode in a limousine dressed in a ceremonial uniform as the president of Africa.

Garvey was not all show. He encouraged blacks to found businesses in Harlem and other cities' African American neighborhoods and urged his followers to patronize them and not white-owned businesses. He himself owned or was a partner in a number of enterprises. The most ambitious, the Black Star steamship line (which would carry black Americans to Africa), was his undoing. Black Star was capitalized at $750,000 raised by sales of stock to 35,000 investors. With classic 1920s hoopla, Garvey touted shares in the company as an "opportunity to climb the great ladder of industrial and commercial progress."

Black Star was a disaster, soon bankrupt with virtually no assets. Ignorant of the rudiments of the shipping business, Garvey purchased three old ships that needed expensive repairs before they could be moved. A fourth ship on the books did not exist. When the federal government prosecuted Garvey for mail fraud—he sold Black Star shares by mail—he claimed that he had paid for the fourth ship but it had not been delivered. The papers submitted to prove that he had been the victim, not the perpetrator, of a fraud were not convincing. Insisting to the end that he was innocent, Garvey was convicted and sentenced to five years imprisonment. After two years, his sentence was commuted whence he was immediately deported to Jamaica.

By that time, without Garvey on the scene, the UNIA had collapsed. However, the attraction of Africa did not die among African Americans disillusioned by the fruitless battle for equal rights. Fraternal lodges took African names. Baptist and Methodist churches added "Abyssinian" or "Ethiopian" to their names. (Except for Liberia, Ethiopia was the only African nation governed by Africans.) In Detroit, a mysterious figure named W. D. Fard (or Wali Farad) founded the Nation of Islam, claiming that Christianity was the white man's religion; Islam was for blacks. Even W. E. B. Du Bois wrote that "the spell of Africa is upon me. The ancient witchery of her medicine is burning in my drowsy, dreamy blood."

PROHIBITION AND FUNDAMENTALISM

The Eighteenth Amendment to the Constitution, forbidding the manufacture or sale of "intoxicating liquors," went into effect in 1920. Although only Rhode Island refused to ratify it, Prohibition had critics in the Northeast, Midwest, and other states with large cities from the beginning. Known as "wets," they regarded Prohibition as an intolerable abridgement of individual freedom, and prominent wets were not necessarily tipplers. Alfred E. Smith, the popular governor of New York for four terms, drank very little. But he was an outspoken wet and, semipublicly, violated the law. He kept liquor in the governor's mansion in Albany and offered guests a drink.

"Drys," politicians, businessmen, and community leaders who favored prohibition, were not necessarily teetotalers. As a politician in Ohio, President Harding had spoken in favor of Prohibition and, as a senator in 1917, he had voted in favor of the Eighteenth Amendment. But he enjoyed a jigger or two of bourbon when he was out with the boys—all of them Republican drys—and probably kept whiskey in the White House.

Moonshiners, Bath-Tub Gin, and Bootleggers   The wet versus dry debate reflected a serious cleavage in American society that predated the 1920s and survived the decade. It was in part a country versus city cleavage, in part a reflection of the conflict between "Old Time Religion" and an evolving, looser modern morality, in part an aspect of the old-stock American suspicion of ethnic Americans and the latter's resentment of the former.

Most big city people were wet and, within a few years, they were probably a majority in states with large urban populations. New York's legislature ratified the Eighteenth Amendment in 1919 only after it was part of the Constitution. In 1923, the legislature repealed the law it had enacted to enforce the Eighteenth Amendment. The rural South and rural counties in the Midwest were solidly dry.

Catholics and Jews, for whom wine played a part in religious observance, were, for the most part, wets. Rhode Island, the state with the highest proportion of Catholics in its population, was the only state to refuse to ratify Prohibition. Other states and parts of states that were heavily Catholic—Massachusetts, Connecticut, northern Illinois, French and Cajun Louisiana—were wet. Protestants who, by the 1920s, called themselves "fundamentalists"—believers in the literal truth of the Bible—were dry. The "Bible Belt," extending from upland South Carolina to Oklahoma and Kansas, was the citadel of Prohibition's defenders. On the West Coast, cosmopolitan Seattle and San Francisco were wet; Oregon and southern California, settled largely by Protestant midwesterners, were dry.

Violation of Prohibition, even in dry regions, was widespread. Southern mountaineers had a long tradition of moonshining (illegal distilling) and, no matter that fundamentalist Pentecostalism had swept the area, moonshining continued, probably on an increased scale with the new markets for "white lightning" in southern and midwestern cities.

There were "speakeasies"—illegal drinking places ranging from quite plush (and expensive) "clubs" for the well-to-do to back rooms of groceries and drug stores—in every city. In Boston, New York, Philadelphia, and Chicago, hotel clerks kept stacks of cards advertising speakeasies under the registration desk. Jimmy Walker, Democratic mayor of New York from 1926 to 1932, openly frequented the town's best. Republican William "Big Bill" Thompson ran for mayor of Chicago in 1927 on a "wide-open-town" platform and won. Illinois governor Len Small pardoned bootleggers as quickly as they were convicted. Modest restaurants in "Little Italies" that had previously catered to locals, attracted plenty of new customers from elsewhere in town because, Prohibition or no Prohibition, no self-respecting Italian caterer was going to serve a meal unaccompanied by a glass of "dago red."

"Prohibition," commented Will Rogers, the nation's favorite humorist, "is better than no liquor at all." Alcohol in one form or another was accessible just about everywhere. Appalachian moonshiners trucked their raw whiskey to cities to sell to wholesalers. Shops sold kits for making wine or "bathtub gin" at home quite legally as long as the instructions solemnly warned buyers that this is what they absolutely must not do lest they unwittingly manufacture an alcoholic beverage. Small breweries managed to stay in business (with the cooperation of police) making soda pop as a front. Small California wineries continued operating making sacramental wines (which were legal), disguising the fact that they were bottling enough to fill the storerooms of every church and synagogue in the Western world.

For connoisseurs, bootleggers imported the best Scotches, rums, English gins, and French wines in fast boats shuttling between Bermuda, the Bahamas, the West Indies, and even ships anchored beyond the 3-mile limit to American ports. Canada, which had its own anti-alcohol laws, amended them so that huge new distilleries—Seagram's and Canadian Club being the most famous—could serve the American market via bootleggers' speedboats on the Great Lakes.

Businessman Gangsters

Large-scale evasion of the Volstead Act (the federal law providing for the enforcement of Prohibition) was probably inevitable. Attempting to abolish by law so widespread a practice as drinking was a fool's errand. But evasion was made easier by the fact that having approved abstinence with self-congratulatory hurrahs, the frugal Congresses of the 1920s never appropriated nearly enough money for effective enforcement. When state and municipal authorities refused to help out—as many did—the result was big time bootlegging.

The most famous provider of "intoxicating liquors" was Alphonse "Al" Capone. He inherited a going concern on the south side of Chicago from Johnny Torrio and "Big Jim" Colosimo and built it into a huge organization as structured and as finely tuned as any business in the country. At its peak, the Capone organization supplied 10,000 speakeasies, employed 700, and grossed $60 million in one year. Capone had to have the administrative acumen of a corporation executive. Indeed, he diversified his company into other illegal businesses: "protection," gambling, prostitution, and drugs.

Capone bristled when he was called a gangster. "What's Al Capone done?" he told a reporter. "He's supplied a legitimate demand.... Some call it racketeering. I call it a business. They say I violate the Prohibition law. Who doesn't?" He had a point although those who called him a gangster did too. Some of Capone's business methods were unorthodox. With so much money at stake, he had plenty of competition; he never did monopolize the beer and liquor supply in Chicago. Capone preferred to absorb competing bootleggers into his organization. When they resisted, he responded with violence; between 1920 and 1929, gunmen shot down somewhere between 450 and 550 other gangsters in their homes, in restaurants and speakeasies, and on the streets.

Few innocent bystanders were killed in these frays, almost none by Capone's hit men. As sensitive to public opinion as other businessmen who catered to a consumer market, Capone and bootleg bosses in other cities kept the use of violence on a professional level. They were, for the most part, successful. Capone was not unpopular in Chicago. A good many people admired him and envied his wardrobe, his luxurious Hot Springs vacations, and his winter retreat in Florida.

Alphonse "Al" Capone, the richest, most-powerful and most publicity hungry bootlegger-gangster of 1920s. Capone openly boasted that he was a patriotic Coolidge Era business-man, filling the public's demand for beer and liquor in an orderly fash-ion at a reasonable price. He was a popular public figure until the "St. Valentine's Day Massacre" when his gunmen murdered thugs from a rival gang.

AP Photos

Largely because of Capone's national prominence, Prohibition gangsterism became associated in the popular mind—and in history—almost exclusively with Italians. In fact, if a census of big-time bootleggers could have been taken, it would probably have revealed as many Jews as Italians at the top. Maxie Hoff of Philadelphia, Solly Weissman of Kansas City, Hyman "Little Hymie" Weiss, and the bosses of Detroit's "Purple Gang" (major importers of fine Canadian spir-its and notoriously violent) were Jews. Meyer Lansky and Benjamin "Bugsy" Siegel, who would become gambling kingpins, got started in the illegal liquor business. There were Irishmen in the trade: Dion O'Bannion on the north side of Chicago and Owney Madden of New York. Arthur "Dutch Schultz" Flegensheimer of New York was of German extraction. Joseph Saltis, another Chicagoan was Polish, "Polack Joe."

Illegal business attracted members of ethnic groups on the bottom of the social ladder because success in it required no social status or family connections, no edu-cation, and, to get started, little money. With less to lose than the respectable and socially established people who looked down on them (but patronized their speak-easies), immigrants and ethnics with a crooked bent were less likely to be discour-aged by the high risks involved. But the majority of Americans were not inclined to take a sociological view of the matter. To them, organized crime was violent, and "foreigners," especially Italians, were the source of it.

The Zenith of Anti-Semitism

Upper-class New York's resentment of the success of German Jewish businessmen among New York's elite had never died. J. P. Morgan and his son, Jack Morgan, did business with Kuhn, Loeb and Company, a Jewish-owned investment bank, but never without private grousing about "the Jews." Except for a few firms, Wall Street was pretty much closed to Jews.

Nevertheless, the old Populist demonology that banking was in the hands of Jews remained resilient in rural areas. Henry Ford's anti-Semitism was a holdover from his boyhood on a Michigan farm. Like his idol Thomas Edison, Ford hated banks, borrowed from them as little as possible, and thought of banking as a Jewish business. During the war, Ford was taken in by the *Protocols of the Elders of Zion,* a turn of the century Russian forgery that was passed off as the manifesto of a sinister, international conspiracy of powerful (un-named) Jews sworn to destroy Christian civilization. (Ford was vulnerable to all kinds of quackery. For a time he urged Americans to adopt a diet consisting largely of carrots; he hired chefs to dream up dozens or recipes for the orange root.) Ford founded a newspaper, the *Dearborn Independent,* that was printed and editorialized on the *Protocols* but, after a few years of very bad publicity, he shelved his campaign, perhaps where he had shelved his left-over carrots.

Hooray for Hollywood

The anti-Semitism of the Klan and rural religious fundamentalists focused not on the Elders of Zion but on Hollywood, California, the production capital of the movie industry. Filmmaking was dominated by Jewish immigrants or the sons of immigrants. Seven of the eight major studios had been founded by Jewish businessmen who had started out as exhibitors—owners of nickelodeons—moved into distribution to keep their theaters supplied, and from there into moviemaking. A former scrap iron dealer, Louis B. Mayer of Metro-Goldwyn Mayer, had been a scrap-iron dealer in New England who branched out into theaters. Adolph Zukor of Paramount Studios had been a furrier in New York who noticed the constant stream of workingmen and women going into a nickelodeon near his shop and put two and two together. Movies were a perfect business for what the sociologist Max Weber called "pariah capitalists," people with money to invest but without the background, education, and connections to get into most respectable businesses.

Moviemaking, although not respectable in its early years, quickly transformed a little money into a great deal of it. The movies were immensely popular. By 1919, Hollywood was churning out 700 feature films a year and innumerable "shorts." Many movies had sexy themes and aroused the ire of both Protestant ministers and Catholic priests. Jewish movie moguls were corrupting American youth.

In 1922, three sensational Hollywood sex scandals involving two deaths, one of them a murder, threw the studios into a panic. Several city and state governments had already set up censorship boards and others were considering doing so. The moviemakers were businessmen who budgeted every film to the penny. If they had to edit every film to accommodate the very different standards of each state's censors, the added expense would be disastrous. Sensitive that anti-Semitism underlay much of the hostility to Hollywood, the big studios hired President Harding's Postmaster General, Will Hays, an epitome of the Midwestern Protestant, to be the industry's spokesman and to "clean up" the movies.

The "Hays Code," adopted in 1930, forbade sympathetic treatment of crime, indecorous treatment of sex, nudity, vulgarity, profane language (including "hell" and "damn"), indecent dancing, and—bait for the ministers and priests who were in the forefront of the movement for censorship—disrespectful treatment of religion and clergymen. Independent film-makers sometimes ignored the code, but the major studios observed it. When a Hays Office censor told Walt Disney to remove the udders from the cows in his cartoons, he did.

Evolution

The clash between fundamentalist Protestantism and the increasingly secular values of educated urban Americans reached a climax in a controversy over Charles Darwin's theory of the evolution of species. (The word *fundamentalist* was coined just before World War I by a religious journal condemning Darwinism because it denied the biblical account of creation.) Revivalists like Billy Sunday and even William Jennings Bryan, who was a militant fundamentalist, urged people to prohibit the teaching of evolution in public schools. Tennessee enacted a law to that effect, which set the scene for a dramatic confrontation of country versus city, dry versus wet, old fashioned Protestant America versus cosmopolitan America.

In the Appalachian town of Dayton, Tennessee, in the spring of 1925, several friends who had been arguing about evolution over coffee decided to test the new state law in the courts. One of them, the high school biology teacher, John Scopes, agreed to violate the law in front of adult witnesses. Scopes would explain Darwin's theory to his pupils. The witnesses would have him arrested, and the law would be tested in a trial.

The men's motives were mixed. The earnest young Scopes hoped that the law would be struck down by the courts as unconstitutional. Some of his friends wanted to see it confirmed. Others, businessmen, did not particularly care either way. They looked on a sensational trial as a way to put their town on the map—and as a way to make money when curiosity-seekers, cause-pleaders, and newspaper reporters—the more the merrier—flocked to Dayton and needed lodging and meals.

The "Monkey Trial"

The town boosters succeeded beyond their dreams. The "Monkey Trial," so called because evolution was popularly interpreted as meaning that human beings were descended from apes, attracted reporters by the dozen. First among them was the nation's most famous iconoclast and debunker, Henry L. Mencken of the Baltimore *Sun*, who came to poke fun at the "rubes" of the Bible belt.

Number-one rube was Bryan, weak and aged now (he died shortly after the trial) who agreed to come to Dayton to advise the prosecutors. Bryan was a fundamentalist, but he was still the man of the people he had been in 1896. He urged the prosecution to avoid a squabble on the rightness of wrongness of Darwinism. Prosecute the case, he said, on the principle that, in a democracy, the people of a community

Famous defense attorney and free thinker Clarence Darrow (left) and three times presidential candidate William Jennings Bryan (right) were personally hostile as well as opponents on principles by the end of the Scopes "Monkey Trial" in Dayton, Tennessee. Darrow set out to make a fool of Bryan by putting him on the witness stand and Bryan, after trying to argue the case on strictly legal grounds, foolishly played into his hands. The two adversaries nevertheless agreed, obviously not happy about it, to pose together for a photographer. The Monkey Trial was, after all and above all, a "media event."

had the right to decide what might and what might not be taught in their public schools. His excellent advice was ignored. Their heads spinning from the carnival atmosphere in the town, the prosecuting attorneys wanted no dull, legalistic trial. They wanted a debate between religion and science.

Which was also what the defense, funded by the American Civil Liberties Union (ACLU), wanted because they knew the case was unwinnable on its legal merits. Scopes freely admitted be had violated state law. The ACLU's intention, articulated by a distinguished libertarian lawyer Arthur Garfield Hays, was to argue that the biblical account of creation was a religious doctrine and, therefore, could not take precedence over science in schools because of the constitutional separation of church and state. Scopes's defense also maintained that freedom of intellectual inquiry, including a teacher's right to speak his or her mind in the classroom, was essential to the health of a democracy.

Hays was assisted by the era's most famous criminal lawyer, Clarence Darrow, who loved publicity and drama more than he loved legal niceties. Darrow looked on the trial as an opportunity to discredit fundamentalism by making Bryan look like a superstitious old fool. Bryan played into Darrrow's hands. He consented to take the stand as an expert witness on the Bible. Under the trees—the judge feared that the tiny courthouse would collapse under the weight of the crowd—Darrow and Bryan talked religion and science. Was the world created in six days of twenty-four hours each? Was Jonah literally swallowed by a whale?

Darrow's supporters were delighted that, to them, Bryan ended up looking like a monkey. Hays and the ACLU were disappointed because the points they had hoped to make—no religion in the schools; the importance of free enquiry—were lost in the uproar surrounding the Darrow–Bryan bout. Fundamentalists were crestfallen when Bryan admitted that some parts of the Bible may have been meant figuratively. John Scopes was found guilty and had to pay a fine. The only winners in the Monkey Trial were Dayton's businessmen who raked in outside dollars for almost a month; and H. L. Mencken, who wrote a dozen rollicking articles mocking Bryan and the hicks of the Bible Belt.

"THE WORST PRESIDENT"?

Warren Gamaliel Harding presided over the troubled first years of the 1920s. There is no evidence that before his presidency or during it that he was personally corrupt. But the cronies he appointed to high office were so rapacious that Harding's administration has been regarded as the most corrupt in American history, and Harding, at least until 2001–2009, as "the worst president," presiding over policies that did more harm to the United States than any other.

A Decent Man But was he so bad? The voters of 1920 gave Harding the biggest majority any presidential candidate had won. When he died in 1923, more people, heads bowed, lined the track of the funeral train taking his remains back to Ohio than had mourned the assassinated McKinley and Garfield. Harding was a very likable man, at the podium as well as among friends. He was a handsome, smiling figure who conveyed a sincere modesty. He had no illusions about his intelligence. "I am a man of limited talents from a small town," he said privately.

He freely admitted that he could not hope to be "the best president," but that he would try to be "the best liked." He was a decent, obliging man, and not only to cynical cronies who used him. At Christmas 1921, he pardoned Eugene V. Debs and other socialists who had been jailed for their opposition to the war. (He received Debs at the White House.) After the steel strike of 1919, he urged the directors of the United States Steel Corporation to reduce the workday in the mills to eight hours, not to win votes but because he was appalled to learned that anyone should have to put in twelve hour days seven days a week. He shrugged it off when a mentally unbalanced professor at the College of Wooster published the worst smear on him imaginable in 1920, saying that Harding had African American ancestors. How did he know, he told a friend, if one of his forebears "had jumped the fence"?

After his death, journalistic gossips tsk-tsked about the president's poker parties, drinking bourbon with his cronies. In 1927, Nan Britton, a woman Harding had watched grow up in Marion, added a shovelful of soil to his reputation's grave when she published *The President's Daughter,* a lascivious (for the day) and probably richly embroidered account of her love affair with the president through his years in the senate and the presidency.

Whatever the extent of Harding's after-hours recreation, he worked longer days at his desk than Wilson, Taft, or Roosevelt had. He probably worked harder than any president but James K. Polk. Four of his cabinet appointees—Secretary of State Charles Evans Hughes; Secretary of the Treasury Andrew Mellon; Secretary of Commerce Herbert Hoover; and Secretary of Agriculture Henry C. Wallace. The same can not be said for those George W. Bush appointed to his cabinet.

The Smart Geek   When Wilson's popular food administrator Herbert Hoover announced he was a Republican, he was a shoo-in for a cabinet post. Harding made him Secretary of Commerce although, personally, the easy-going president soon regretted his choice. The no-nonsense, all-business, all-efficiency Hoover made the president uncomfortable. He admitted that Hoover was "the smartest geek I know" but he was still a geek. Harding told friends that his day always improved when the Commerce Secretary walked away.

As he had been his entire life, Hoover was tireless. He sorely wanted to be president, but he knew better than to promote himself conspicuously. He would let his achievements take care of his career. Conservative Republicans were as uneasy with Hoover's pro-activism as Harding was with his intensity. Big business wanted the Commerce Department to revert to being a research service, not the regulatory agency it had been under Wilson. Hoover mollified conservatives by saying that he opposed government coercion of business. His programs to eliminate waste, develop uniform standards of production, and end "destructive competition" in various industries were voluntary.

In fact, Hoover would have liked to employ more coercion in dealing with businessmen than, as a Republican, he possibly could. For example, as Secretary of Commerce he had authority over the young radio broadcasting industry. But "authority" was hardly the right word. The Radio Act of 1912—adopted long before broadcasting—forbade the secretary to deny anyone who applied for a license to open a radio station. The result, when broadcasting mushroomed during the 1920s, was a free enterprise chaos of the sort Hoover loathed. In many parts of the country, commercial stations broadcast on frequencies so close to the frequencies of nearby stations that neither could be heard clearly.

Hoover helped design the Radio Act of 1927 that defined broadcast radio as a special kind of public utility requiring close government supervision because it intruded into people's homes. The Federal Radio Commission (precursor of our Federal Communications Commission) was empowered to deny licenses and revoke them as well as the authority to assign frequencies in the public interest. Obscenity and profanity were forbidden. If Hoover had had his way, the act would have kept cynical profiteers out of broadcasting by severely restricting advertising on the airwaves. He was disgusted that radio's potential as an educational and uplifting force was already being destroyed by the seemingly nonstop blathering of hucksters selling toothpaste, dishwashing soap, coffee, and patent medicines.

Naval Disarmament   The Senate had not ratified the Treaty of Versailles when Harding became president and Charles Evans Hughes Secretary of State. Legally, the United States was still at war with Germany, which made for all sorts of difficulties in trade and financial relations. Hughes remedied the problem without reviving the League of Nations issue by having Congress "-resolve" that the war was over, whence he recognized Germany's "Weimar Republic."

Hughes then pulled off a stunning disarmament coup that caught the world completely by surprise. He invited representatives of the major naval powers to Washington to discuss disarmament. Expecting the usual drone of platitudes and round of dinners and receptions (alcohol-free, alas), the delegates were shocked when Hughes opened the Washington Conference with a detailed, fully formed "agreement," ready for signing, to reduce the size of the world's navies. Hughes's plan required the five nations with the largest navies—the United States, Britain, Japan, France, and Italy—to destroy some of their capital ships (battleships and battle cruisers) and to cancel construction of others already underway or planned.

By 1921, everyone agreed that the arms race had been instrumental in causing the World War, so the delegates at the Washington Conference had little choice but to listen. His Treaty of Washington would set the size of the fleets the five naval nations were permitted at a ratio to one another that reflected their existing fleets and their respective interests and defensive needs. For each 5 tons of capital ships that Great Britain and the United States kept afloat, Japan was allotted 3 tons, and France and Italy 1.67 tons each.

There was something in it for all five powers. They saved millions of dollars by scuttling ships and canceling construction. Maintaining capital ships was expensive. The construction of one was a major line item in a national budget. Slashing government expenditures was especially important to the United States where the Harding administration was committed to reducing the national debt. Economizing was almost a matter of national life and death in financially devastated Britain while the treaty ensured Britain equality with the United States on the high seas. (British primacy would have been destroyed had the United States not agreed to scrap thirty battleships and cruisers and cancel new construction.)

France and Italy were naval powers only in the Mediterranean so their allowances were reasonable; and the treaty averted a nascent naval arms race between them. Japan needed only a one-ocean navy so that, at an allowance of three-fifths the size of the American and British navies, it got a rough equality with—even superiority to—the British and American fleets in the Pacific.

But not with the British and American Pacific fleets combined, which was why the Japanese alone left the Washington Conference disgruntled.

39

THE NEW ERA
When America Was a Business 1923–1929

Civilization and profits go hand in hand…. The business of America is business.

—Calvin Coolidge

Perhaps the most revolting character that the United States ever produced was the Christian businessman.

—H. L. Mencken

In the summer of 1923, President Harding and his wife left Washington on a long anticipated vacation. They traveled by rail to San Francisco where they boarded a steamship to Alaska. After they had seen the sights, they steamed back to Seattle. Physicians examined Harding every day; few knew it, but the president suffered from dangerously high blood pressure and was under tight medical supervision. The holiday did not improve his condition and, after a public appearance in Seattle, he took to his bed. His train skipped several scheduled stops, and Harding was taken into his San Francisco hotel through a rear door. On August 2 he died.

THE COOLIDGE YEARS

Harding had more than medical problems. Shortly before his vacation, he discovered that Charles R. Forbes, whom he had made head of the Veterans' Bureau because he was "my friend," had been stealing Bureau equipment and supplies from bedsheets to pajamas and selling them. Harding was seen in the White House shaking Forbes by the shoulders and calling him "a double crossing rat." He fired him but allowed him to flee to Europe. Harding never learned that Forbes's grafting was even worse than cadging supplies. He had been getting kickbacks of one-third of the money the Veterans Bureau spent on hospital construction. He and his confederates may have looted the government of $200 million. One of Forbes's confederates was the Attorney General Harry Daugherty, who quashed information about

The Roaring Twenties 1920–1930

1920	1922	1924	1926	1928	1930

1922 Hollywood scandals; studios hire Will Hays for public relations

1923 Harding dies in office

1925 *The Man Nobody Knows* published

1925 Florida boom

1926 NBC radio network

Lindbergh hysteria; Babe Ruth hits sixty home runs; Model T Ford discontinued 1927

Democrats nominate Al Smith; Hoover elected 1928

Stock market crash 1929

the thievery in return for payoffs. It was eventually discovered that Daugherty also took payoffs from big-time violators of Prohibition laws.

Harding was spared knowledge of Daugherty's betrayal but, before his Alaskan trip, the president suspected that Secretary of the Interior Albert Fall had duped him into being an accessory of Fall's transfer of federal oil reserves at Elk Hills, Calfornia, and Teapot Dome, Wyoming, to two swashbuckling oil millionaires, Harry Sinclair and Edward Doheny. Fall told Harding that both deposits of crude were "leaking"; experts had recommended that they be tapped immediately. In fact, the commission of geologists that had surveyed Elk Hills and Teapot Dome reported that the reserves were stable. Fall's reward from Sinclair and Doheny was at least $300,000 in "personal loans" that he wanted in order to expand his New Mexico ranch. Harding's reward for giving the transfer "my entire approval" was a posthumous disgrace that he did not deserve.

Changing of the Guard

Calvin Coolidge liked being vice president. The pay was good, $12,000 a year—almost $150,000 in today's money. As a retired Massachusetts governor, he could probably have earned more with a prestigious Boston law firm, but that would have involved some work. The vice president's constitutional duties were nil, which suited Coolidge fine. Had there been a trophy to honor "America's Laziest Man," Coolidge would have been a contender.

One of the vice presidency's fringe benefits—several dinner invitations every week—also appealed to him. Not because he enjoyed socializing; he often sat at the dinner table for more than two hours uttering nothing but peremptory answers to questions from other guests. But Coolidge was also a tightwad of championship stature. He pitched into a free meal with the gusto of a mountain climber rescued after a week in an ice cave.

The vice president was visiting his father in tiny Plymouth Notch, Vermont, when, in the middle of the night, the news of Harding's death was brought to him. Instead of rushing by train to Washington, Coolidge changed out of his pajamas and walked downstairs to the farmhouse parlor where his father, a justice of the peace, administered the presidential oath by the light of a kerosene lamp. At the pinnacle of his political career—he was making $20,000 a year now—Coolidge was the picture of homely rectitude. Or, some suggested, he had an unerring eye for showmanship.

Calvin Coolidge enjoyed angling, but this photograph is just one of dozens of the costume poses photographers were constantly asking him to strike. Anglers of the 1920s did not wear boaters or high, stiff collars, neckties, and three-piece suits.

Brown Brothers

A Singular Man   Both Harding and Coolidge had been "don't rock the boat" party regulars, initiating nothing, dissenting from nothing on which the party's bosses pronounced. Beyond that, they had little in common. Harding was as handsome as an aging movie star and unfailingly charming. Coolidge's features were bony and pinched; he may never in his life have attempted to win someone over by making himself pleasant. When he smiled, he seemed to say that he would rather be somewhere else. Alice Roosevelt Longworth, TR's daughter, said that Coolidge looked as if he had been weaned on a pickle.

Harding's private life was tawdry, Coolidge's impeccably proper. Indeed, his personal habits were dreary; his idea of a good time was to take a nap. He spent twelve hours in bed each night and, on slow days, snuck in a few winks in the afternoon. He spent so much time sleeping that when, in 1933, writer Dorothy Parker was told that Coolidge had died, she asked, "How could they tell?"

Coolidge might have cracked a smile had he heard her. He was known as "Silent Cal," but when he did speak he was often witty. Attempting to break the ice at a banquet, a woman seated next to the president told him playfully that a friend had bet her Coolidge would not say three words to her all evening. "You lose," Coolidge replied, and returned to his plate. "I found out early in life," this very successful politician observed, "that you don't have to explain something you haven't said."

A Master of the Occasion

And he was clever. At the 1928 Pan American Conference in Havana, Coolidge was sitting in a semicircle of his fellow presidents when waiters began to walk down the line serving drinks. The American reporters and photographers present, who were consuming as many daiquiris as they could hold in their brief respite from Prohibition, held their breath in anticipation. If Coolidge accepted a drink, it would make for a juicy front-page story. If he waved the waiter off a hair too righteously, his Latin American colleagues would take it as yet another of "big brother's" insults. The dilemma did not faze Coolidge. A second before the waiter would have presented his tray, the president bent over to tie his shoe and fussed at the task until the waiter moved on.

Coolidge was "silent" only when it came to conversation. He made plenty of speeches. In 1925, a less busy year for the president than usual, Coolidge gave twenty-eight speeches; in 1917, the year the United States went to war, Woodrow Wilson spoke publicly only seventeen times.

Oddly, Coolidge enjoyed deadpan clowning. He posed for photographers in ludicrous costumes: in a 10-gallon hat, in a Sioux war bonnet. On request, he strapped on skis on the White House lawn and posed as a farmer in a smock working at the hay—in patent leather shoes with his Pierce Arrow waiting in the background. Perhaps the photos were Coolidge's way of telling the American people he was at one with them in loving novelties and pranks. When he was asked about one of the costumes, he said that "the American public wants a solemn ass as president and I think I'll go along with them."

Keeping Cool in 1924

Coolidge, quietly forewarned of the scandals about to go public, began immediately to get rid of the hacks from Ohio who had come to Washington with Harding. He kept most of Harding's cabinet on (although he was as uncomfortable around Hoover as his predecessor had been).

Any plans other prominent Republicans might have had to challenge Coolidge for the 1924 presidential nomination were shelved. Before New Year's Day 1924, it was clear that the erratic postwar economic slump had run its course. Even before the party renominated Coolidge by acclamation, Republicans were able to drown out the Democrats by crowing about "Coolidge Prosperity." After the Democratic nominating convention, they added the slogan, "Keep Cool with Coolidge."

The Democratic convention in New York was a hellish chaos; the party tore itself into pieces. The packed gallery raucously demanded the nomination of New York's popular governor Alfred E. Smith. A machine politician (although an honest one), Smith had the support of delegates from several urban industrial states but trailed well behind the first ballot leader, former Treasury Secretary William G. McAdoo, whose support came mostly from the South and the West. However, the 431 votes for McAdoo were far fewer than the 731 (two-thirds of the total) required by Democratic party rules. No fewer than seventeen favorite son candidates divided almost that many votes among them. And few of them had dropped out after 100 ballots. The convention was obviously deadlocked. Lightning had to strike one of the minor candidates.

It did. On the hundredth ballot, John W. Davis of West Virginia, who had started out with thirty-one votes, displaced McAdoo in second place. The other minor candidates released their delegates to him, and he was nominated on the 103rd ballot, by far the record.

In one way, it was an odd choice. Both Smith and McAdoo had progressive credentials (increasingly called "liberal" by 1924). Davis was a hidebound conservative, a big business lawyer. He would have been more comfortable in Coolidge's cabinet than rubbing elbows with Smith's ethnic working-class supporters or McAdoo's farmers in overalls. He was anti-Prohibition which made him acceptable to the Smith faction but anathema to McAdoo's forces. However, he was also (and would remain) a strong supporter of Jim Crow segregation in the South, which made him acceptable to the Ku Klux Klan element among McAdoo supporters.

Coolidge crushed Davis in the general election. Davis won only 29 percent of the popular vote. The remnants of the once vital reform movement cast their ballots (17 percent of the total) for aged Robert LaFollette, running as a Progressive. For four more years, Calvin Coolidge presided over "Coolidge Prosperity" and what businessmen called the "New Era."

Andrew Mellon   The keystone of the New Era was the financial program of Secretary of the Treasury Andrew Mellon. Mellon was an extremely wealthy Pittsburgh banker although he looked no more like a political cartoonist's pot-bellied moneybags than he looked like the seedy Ohio hustlers who had come to Washington with Harding. Mellon looked like a sporting duke; he was rail thin with finely chiseled aristocratic features and an exquisite mustache that he must have groomed several times a day. No suits were ever tailored better than those Mellon wore nor tiny pointed shoes shined to a higher luster. He was as close-mouthed as Coolidge. One of his friends said that if Mellon "had got religion, he would not have told it to God."

Unlike Coolidge, however, Mellon had a well-planned program that he had only begun to put into effect when Harding died. He meant to slash government spending, reduce the national debt, and cut income taxes, especially the taxes the very rich paid.

Mellon pressed other cabinet members to reduce their departments' expenditures. The cancellation of naval construction engineered by Secretary of State Hughes was a massive savings. The budget reduction enabled Mellon to cut income taxes sharply for individuals with annual incomes larger than $60,000 ($700,000 today) and corporations with annual profits topping $60,000. By 1929, Mellon was actually shoveling their tax payments back to them. United States Steel received a refund check for $15 million.

Mellon compensated for the loss of income tax revenues by supporting an increase in the tax the wealthy loved, import duties (except duties on luxuries like the old masters' paintings Mellon among others collected). The Fordney-McCumber Tariff of 1922 increased import duties to levels not seen for twenty years. Mellon also increased regressive taxes, that is, taxes that fell disproportionately on the middle and working class. The costs of some kinds of postal services increased. The excise tax was raised and Congress levied a new tax on new automobiles, both taxes on all consumers.

To those who complained that his tax policies penalized the middle classes while further enriching the rich, Mellon replied that the burden of consumer taxes on individuals was small and that his reduction of taxes on the rich benefited everyone. The wealthy invested their tax windfalls, creating jobs, the means to better lives for working people. Coolidge Prosperity would "trickle down" to everyone.

For six years, it appeared that everything Mellon did was right. He halved government expenditures and reduced the national debt by $6 billion. In 1929, the federal budget surplus topped $600 million. Mellon was toasted as "the greatest secretary of the treasury since Alexander Hamilton."

Short-Sighted Creditor   Seventy years later, after the attention of hundreds of historians and economists, there is nothing close to a consensus as to the causes of the Great Depression of the 1930s. Would policies other than those of the New Era Republicans have avoided the catastrophe? It is clear, however, that the sky-high Fordney-McCumber tariff—a vital part of Coolidge-Mellon financial policy—played a big part in the economic problems in Germany that nurtured the rise of the Nazi party and, inevitably. a second world war.

The Treaty of Versailles required Germany to pay France and Great Britain $33 billion in reparations. Almost at once, Germany's shaky democratic government fell behind in making payments. Germany's wartime expenditures—more in four years than the government had spent in the preceding forty years—had crippled the country's economy. France and Britain refused German requests to reduce the level of reparations, and Germany's condition was worsened when the French army occupied the Ruhr valley, Germany's most concentrated industrial region.

With Germany so far in arrears, it was obvious that some adjustments were necessary. The British and French reluctantly agreed to discuss a reduction in reparations if the Coolidge administration persuaded American bankers to forgive some of the massive debt they owed in the United States. Coolidge bluntly refused. When asked why, he replied, "they hired the money, didn't they?"; it was as simple as if he had loaned a visitor a dollar with which to buy his lunch.

A commission headed by soon-to-be vice president, Charles G. Dawes, brokered an agreement to get the French out of the Ruhr and reschedule reparations payments by pledging American loans to Germany. Unfortunately, the Dawes Plan resulted in a circular international flow of money that benefited only American bankers. British and French payments of their debts flowed into the United States. American banks loaned money to Germany. Germany paid its reparations. American banks collected interest. It worked for a few years. In 1929, the Young Plan did reduce Germany's obligations somewhat but, after the stock market crash in the fall of 1929, American banks called in the loans they had made in Germany.

Reducing the Fordney-McCumber rates would have indirectly ameliorated Europe's economic woes by making it possible for Germany, Britain, and France to sell more of their products in the United States. But the Republican Congress refused to budge.

PROSPERITY AND BUSINESS CULTURE

Coolidge was immensely popular to the end of his presidency and the pro-business Republican party retained comfortable majorities in the House of Representatives (and narrower majorities in the Senate). Only in the South, in some lightly populated western states, and in big cities could the Democrats count on winning elections.

The Predestined Election of 1928

In 1928, Coolidge faced the same question that Theodore Roosevelt had confronted in 1908. Should he run for reelection? He had been elected president only once, but he had served a good part of his predecessor's term. Coolidge answered the question with a strange phrasing. "I do not *choose* to run for president," he said. Politicians at the time and many historians think that he was telling the party that he could be drafted. Other evidence indicates that, no, Coolidge wanted to retire and was just playing one of his pranks.

Herbert Hoover took Coolidge at his word. He resigned from the Commerce Department and rushed about the country buttonholing prominent Republicans. He was nominated on the first ballot. His opponent was Al Smith who had spent four years mending fences with southern and western Democrats. In the election, however, Smith was unable to win over western and southern voters among whom anti-Catholicism was rife. Prominent southerners led by Texas governor Dan Moody and Methodist Bishop James Cannon urged voters to go Republican rather than support a Roman Catholic.

Smith also aroused the dislike of southern and western voters because of his nasal New York City accent. Heard over the radio—or "raddio" as Smith called it—his voice conjured up all the unsavory images country people associated with New York City for thirty years. Smith was vocal in his opposition to Prohibition. That did not hurt him in the Northeast or in cities in the industrial Midwest. But it was a major handicap among western and southern fundamentalists who were still militantly dry.

Hoover would have nothing to do with anti-Catholicism. Personally (in private) he was dubious about Prohibition. Playing politics on that issue, however, he called Prohibition "a great social and economic experiment, noble in motive and far-reaching in purpose."

Had Al Smith been a Kansas Baptist who drank nothing stronger than Dr. Pepper, he would have lost the election. It is a mystery why he wanted so badly to run for president when he did not have a chance. When the country is as prosperous as the United States was in 1928, the party in power does not lose elections.

Buy Now, Pay Later

Industrial and agricultural productivity soared during the 1920s, even though there was not much increase in the size of the industrial workforce and the number of agriculturalists. Wages did not keep up with the contribution that more efficient workers were making to the economy. While dividends on stocks rose 65 percent between 1920 and 1929, wages increased only 24 percent.

Nevertheless, the increase in wages was enough to satisfy most of the working people who enjoyed them. Consumer goods were cheap, and retailers promoted an irresistible new way for people to live beyond their means—consumer credit.

Before the 1920s, it was common for ordinary people to buy their groceries on account and settle up on payday. Borrowing large sums was something businessmen did in order to expand and farmers did to get a crop in the ground. Banks loaned money for productive enterprises that would provide the means of repayment. Some banks—not all—loaned money to home buyers. Homes did not generate income, but they were there to seize if payments were not forthcoming. During the 1920s, Americans began to borrow in order to have pleasanter lives. They went into debt not to produce income or to shelter their families but so they could consume.

The chief agency of consumer borrowing was the installment plan. A refrigerator that sold for $87.50 could be ensconced in a corner of the kitchen for a down payment of $5 and monthly payments of $10. Even a low-cost item like a vacuum cleaner ($28.95) could be taken home for $2 down and "E-Z payments" of $4 a month. During the New Era, 60 percent of automobiles were bought on time; 70 percent of household furniture; 80 percent of refrigerators, radios, and vacuum cleaners; and 90 percent of pianos, sewing machines, and washing machines. With 13.8 million people owning radios by 1930 (up from next to none in 1920), the Americans who were basking in the glow of Coolidge prosperity were also up to their necks in hock.

Traditional moralists warned that borrowing to consume was a sharp break with American ideals of frugality. But others spoke more attractively and in more congenial tones. They were the advertisers, members of a new profession dedicated to creating desires in people—advertising men called them "needs"—which people had never particularly felt before.

Buy, Buy, Buy   Traditionally, advertisements were announcements, nothing more. Eighteenth- and nineteenth-century merchants placed tiny notices in newspapers—like "classifieds" today—listing what they had for sale. During the 1870s, Robert Bonner, the editor of the *Ledger,* a literary magazine, accidentally learned the curious effect on the human brain of repetition. He placed his usual one-line ad in a daily newspaper—"Read Mrs. Southworth's New Story in the Ledger." The compositor misread his specification of "one line" as "one page." The line ran over and over, down every column of the paper. To Bonner's amazement, the blunder did not bankrupt him; his magazine sold out in an afternoon.

The lesson was unmistakable. During the 1890s, C. W. Post, with scarcely a cent to his name, borrowed money to plaster a city with the name of his new breakfast cereal, Post Toasties. He was a millionaire within a month. Bombarded by the name in newspapers, painted on the sides of buildings, and slipped under doors on leaflets, people bought the stuff as if commanded to do so. By the 1920s, advertisers had moved on to making preposterous claims and telling outright lies in newspapers and magazines, on billboards along highways (a new medium, thanks to the automobile), and on the radio. They discovered the selling power of sly sexual titillation, no matter what the product was. Pictures of young ladies in suggestive clothes and poses were the centerpieces of ads for soda pop, train tickets, razor blades, and Buicks.

Advertising professionals considered themselves practical psychologists, and they were. They sold goods by exploiting anxieties and, in the words of Thorstein Veblen, "administering shock effects" and "trading on the range of human infirmities which blossom in devout observances, and bear fruit in the psychopathic wards." In the Coolidge era, the makers of Listerine Antiseptic, a mouthwash, invented the disease "halitosis," of which the symptoms included nothing more than a curter than usual greeting from a friend: "Even your best friend won't tell you" (that you have "BAD BREATH"). Listerine made millions. A picture of a wealthy fop on a yacht conversing with a beautiful young woman was captioned: "You'd like to be in this man's shoes … yet he has 'ATHLETE'S FOOT'!" Fleischmann's yeast, losing its market because fewer people were baking bread, advertised their product as just the thing to cure constipation and eradicate adolescent pimples. The success of anxiety advertising made underarm deodorants, without which humanity had functioned for millennia, a necessity.

Consumerism

Manufacturers of low-priced commodities like mouthwash advertised nationally. If they succeeded in creating a demand for their brand, they were able to charge a premium to "Mom and Pop" grocery stores and sundries shops that could stock only a few cans of Chef Boy-Ar-Dee Spaghetti or tubes of Ipana toothpaste. Wholesalers charged them a premium because their orders were small. A centrally managed chain of stores bought the same goods by the hundreds of cases and, therefore, paid a lower per-unit price. The 1920s marked the beginning of the steady decline of the small, locally owned retail shop.

By 1928, 860 chain stores competed for the dollars of a population that was eating more expensively. Among the biggest success stories between 1920 and 1929 were the first supermarkets: Piggly-Wiggly (from 515 to 2,500 stores), Safeway (from 766 to 2,660 stores), and A & P (Atlantic and Pacific Tea Company, from 4,621 to 15,418 stores). Chains dominated the sundries and clothing trades (F. W. Woolworth expanded from 1,111 outlets in 1920 to 1,825 in 1929 and J. C. Penney from 312 to 1,395); and then there was the gas station. Standard Oil of New Jersey owned 12 gas stations in 1920, a thousand in 1929.

Some economists pointed out problems built into the consumer economy. The day would dawn when everyone who could afford a car, a washing machine, and other consumer durables would have them. They would no longer be buying those items and industries producing them would be in serious trouble.

Another weakness of Coolidge Prosperity was the fact that significant numbers of Americans were not sharing in the good times and were, therefore, not part of the buying spree. Coal and textiles were depressed throughout the decade. The 700,000 to 800,000 miners and their dependents and the 400,000 cotton mill workers were buying few cars and vacuum cleaners. Wheat, corn, and cotton farmers were struggling after the good years of 1900–1920. Dairy and truck farmers who were doing well enough financially to own appliances that had to be plugged in could do so because they had electricity. Not many electric companies extended their lines very far into the countryside. The southern states lagged far behind the rest of the country in income and every category of the standard of living that depended on income. It goes without saying that African Americans, Indians, and Hispanics in the Southwest tasted the Coolidge good times only in the odd bite.

**Business
Culture**

The plight of the deprived gets little attention when a large majority of people is doing well and enjoying the goods and diversions society offers, especially when those goods and diversions are novel, diverse, and continually changing. When businessmen took credit for Coolidge prosperity, as if they were harbingers of a new religion, their critics were few and opposition to them nil.

"Service clubs" flourished in towns and small cities: the Shriners, Rotary International, Kiwanis, the Optimists, Lions Clubs of America, Jaycees, all except the Shriners, a Masonic organization, founded on the eve of the 1920s (and the Shriners first began building children's hospitals in 1919). The clubs promoted a chummy fraternalism among small businessmen; shunned political involvement and religious associations because they were divisive; sponsored community events such as Fourth of July parades and picnics, providing volunteers to make them work; preached a cheery boosterism—"If you can't boost, don't knock"—and financed hospitals, scholarships for promising high school graduates, and programs for poor children; and honored acts of heroism and service to the community.

On the national level, from the president on down, politicians, newspaper and magazine editors, writers, and, of course, prominent businessmen preached a business cult. "The business of America is business," Calvin Coolidge said, and "the man who builds a factory builds a temple."

In 1925, Bruce Barton published *The Man Nobody Knows*. He depicted Jesus not as the son of God (although the possibility was allowed) nor even primarily as a teacher of morality, but as an unmistakably American businessman of the era, a smiling hale fellow well-met, "the most popular dinner guest in Jerusalem," a gladhander who had something to sell and sold, perhaps a Rotarian or Kiwanian or even both, and an advertising genius. Instead of finding Barton's book blasphemous, Americans bought hundreds of thousands of copies. It was on the best-seller list for two years.

Lincoln Steffens, who had excoriated business as a muckraker and flirted with both Soviet communism and Italian fascism, wrote that "Big business in America is producing what the socialists held up as their goal: food, shelter, and clothing for all."

John Jakob Raskob of General Motors told readers of the *Ladies Home Journal* that every American could be and should be a successful businessman. The value of all kinds of property was rising, Raskob wrote. If working men invested a mere $15 a week in stocks, bonds, real estate, whatever, they would find themselves well-off within just a few years. Raskob overlooked the fact, if he ever knew it, that the working man who earned $25 a week was at the top of the wage scale and spending every cent. But middle-class readers had nest eggs and they were, rather than "investing," plunging their savings into one get-rich-quick scheme after another.

**Getting Rich
Quick**

The most colorful get-rich-quick craze of the decade centered on Florida. The "Sunshine State" had been an agricultural backwater until in the 1880s, Henry M. Flagler, one of the

Fads, Sensations, and Ballyhoo

The Roaring Twenties were a golden age of fads (fashions wildly popular for a short period), sensations (events or people of intense popular interest), and ballyhoo (a deliberate clamor promoting a fad, a sensation, or a revolutionary new toilet disinfectant). The immunities that enable some of us to survive fads, fashions, and ballyhoo without emotional scars had not yet fully evolved.

Some fads were commercial, briefly paying bonanza profits for those who jumped into them before the mania crested. A new publishing company, Simon and Schuster, gambled with its first book, a collection of crossword puzzles, and hit the jackpot. Yo-yos, an import from the Philippines, made of lot of money for their manufacturers for a year or two. Mah-Jongg, a Chinese gambling game with inscrutable rules, was introduced in 1922. The next year sets of Chinese-made Mah-Jongg tiles, although expensive, outsold radios. Briefly, the game obsessed many middle- and upper-class women; some played all day every day for months, like addicts. When the Chinese ran out of the shin bones of calves from which the tiles were made, Chicago slaughterhouses filled ships with their extras to be rushed across the Pacific.

Other fads, like contract bridge, made little money for anyone. Nor did college boys who swallowed live goldfish. Exhibitionists reaped no reward beyond seeing their names and photographs in newspapers:

"Clarence Tillman, 17, local high school student, put forty sticks of chewing gum in his mouth at one time, sang 'Home, Sweet Home,' and between verses of the song, drank a gallon of milk." Barnstorming daredevils who walked on or hung from a plane's wing were paid—very little—by county fairs. One of them said that the greatest personal danger he faced was starvation. Flagpole sitting—balancing for days atop a flagpole—was equally unremunerative. For reasons yet to be discovered, Baltimore was the storm center of the fad with as many as twenty flagpole sitters on exhibit in the city at one time.

Newspapers ballyhooed innocuous events to increase sales: the visits of the Prince of Wales in 1924 and Queen Marie of Romania in 1926; the death of movie sex symbol Rudolph Valentino at age 31; the 655-mile trek across Alaska by the dog Balto to bring diphtheria serum to a sick Eskimo in Nome. The prince, the queen, and Valentino's remains were mobbed by thousands of people who were not asked to reflect on why they were there. Statues of Balto were erected.

The publishing industry was swept by sensationalism. Newspapers nationwide covered in detail stories like the eighteen-day entrapment in a Kentucky cave of Floyd Collins as he died slowly of exposure. Floyd's neighbors sold hamburgers to the crowds that gathered at the entrance to the cave.

creators of Standard Oil, traveled to St. Augustine on his doctor's advice. Flagler was enchanted. He built the luxurious Ponce de Leon Hotel where millionaires could enjoy a midwinter vacation and a more modest hotel for the less richly endowed.

Finding even more captivating locations to the south on Florida's Atlantic coast, then thinly populated because it was inaccessible, he began constructing the Florida East Coast Railway. He developed, in succession, the resort towns of Daytona Beach, Palm Beach, and Miami Beach. That would have been overbuilding

When Evangelist Aimee Semple McPherson disappeared for thirty-seven days in 1926, then emerged in the Arizona desert claiming she had been kidnapped, she re-created her abduction for photographers. Reporters prolonged the life of the story by claiming that Aimee had actually been holed up in a "love nest" with an employee.

Sex sold. Movie comedian Roscoe "Fatty" Arbuckle was tried for the death of a young woman at a orgiastic party; the small tragedy was national news. When a Hollywood director was murdered, the story took on added zest because he was said to have been "involved" with actresses Mabel Normand and Mary Miles Minter.

Fortuitously, a murder case with a sexual angle came along about annually. The greatest of them was the trial of two rich Chicago boys, Nathan Leopold and Richard Loeb, for the "thrill killing" of a 14-year-old neighbor. The New York *Mirror* successfully pressured the police to reopen a murder case on which they had given up. A minister, Edward Hall and his lover, Mrs. James Mills, had been found shot on an isolated farm. The *Mirror* produced an eccentric neighbor who raised hogs, immediately dubbed "the pig woman," who claimed that Rev. Hall's widow and several of her relatives had killed the paramours. (They were acquitted and successfully sued the *Mirror*.)

The *Mirror* was a tabloid. These new dailies (the first, in 1919, was the *New York Daily News*) were half the size of traditional newspapers and opened like a book. The format was a brilliant idea. The size and the ease of turning pages appealed to people who rode crowded subways and trolley cars.

The tabloids were more than convenient: They lavishly plastered their pages with large photographs and specialized in reporting sex scandals and violent crimes in breathless, suggestive prose. In just five years, the *Daily News* had the largest circulation of any newspaper in the nation. Its biggest scoop was a front-page photograph of the electrocution of murderess Ruth Snyder. The picture was taken illegally with a hidden camera.

Even tabloid aficionados were appalled by the *Evening Graphic*, which they called the "Pornographic." It was published by Bernarr MacFadden, the "father of physical culture" who had been having trouble with obscenity laws for decades. MacFadden solved the problem of how to illustrate a story when there were no photographs. The "composograph" was put together by pasting photos of the celebrities of the moment on cartoons of titillating scenes. One showed Enrico Caruso welcoming Valentino to Italian heaven.

MacFadden also published the immensely popular women's magazine *True Story*, tear-jerking love stories as sexy as the law allowed "told by" ordinary women "just like" the readers. Founded in 1926, it was soon selling 2 million copies of each issue. MacFadden followed with *True Romances* and *True Detective*, all of them actually written by employees in cubicles in MacFadden's offices.

for the millionaire market, but improved rail connections from eastern and midwestern population centers to Flagler's railway made it possible for middle-class people to escape winter's snows for a month or so.

The Florida Land Boom

By the 1920s, a good many northerners had built their own vacation and retirement homes in the beach towns. The financial potential of speculating in desirable land—buying orange groves and sandy wasteland at bargain prices, then waiting for developers of hotels, homes, and businesses to show up willing to pay more for it—was obvious.

Until about 1923, Florida land speculators were few, mostly local, and patient. However, a spurt in the state's population from 950,000 to 1.2 million within two years resulted in newspaper accounts of speculators whose land tripled in value overnight. Florida attracted the attention of masters of ballyhoo like the colorful playwright Wilson Mizner, and perhaps the most successful promoter of the era, Carl G. Fisher.

Fisher made the first of his fortune selling bicycles during the 1890s, then became a puffer and dealer of automobiles, which led to a few years as a lobbyist for highway construction. Mizner and Fisher and other boomers took options on huge tracts of Florida real estate and advertised it nationally. During the winter of 1923–1924, Fisher erected a massive electrically illuminated billboard in New York's Times Square that read "It's June in Florida!" He knew how to get the most out of his advertising dollar. It was the exceptional daily newspaper that did not run a photograph of the monstrosity.

People who had no intention of moving to Florida rushed down to get in on the bonanza that could not miss. Others bought land sight unseen from real estate brokers (there were 2,000 of them just in Miami). At the height of the boom in 1924, a Miami newspaper printed 500 pages of advertisements of land for sale.

It was a bubble. People bought acreage not to sell to the Piggly Wiggly supermarket chain five years down the line, but to sell at a profit in a month or a week to another speculator who was betting the price would go higher yet. Purchases involving very little outlay were made by buying "binders" on a parcel, putting down a nonrefundable deposit with the balance due in thirty days. The seller could not lose; either he got his price in a month or he got his property back and pocketed the deposit. The buyer risked only his deposit in the expectation that before the binder expired, he would sell the land to someone else.

Frauds were inevitable. Snowbound dreamers in Chicago and Minneapolis purchased alligator-infested swamps from fast-talking salesmen. People bought beach front lots that were a bit closer to the ocean than was desirable—underneath 6 feet of salt water at high tide. But the mania was fueled not by fraud but by the foolishness of human beings when their greed has been aroused.

The Florida Land Bust

As with all financial bubbles—irrational speculations—the day arrived when there were no more buyers willing to bet that land values would go even higher. After a few months of making mortgage payments on land that no one wanted to buy, speculators tried to cut their losses by reducing the asking price. And reducing it again. In 1925, speculators stuck with Florida land saw their paper fortunes evaporate. Banks that had loaned too much money to too many of them failed.

The final blow was a 1925 hurricane that demonstrated, as one observer memorably phrased it, what a soothing tropical breeze could do when it got a running start from the West Indies. Citrus growers who had kicked themselves in the parts for selling their groves too cheaply at the beginning of the boom discovered that, thanks to a chain of defaults, they owned their orchards again, only a little worse for the wear of speculators tromping through them. Wilson Mizner, who lost more than a million dollars in one month, was good humored about it all. "Always be pleasant to the people you meet on the way up," he said, "because they are the very same people you'll meet on the way down."

The Coolidge
Bull Market

Neither Fisher nor Mizner learned the lesson of the Florida land mania; both lost everything they had in a much larger speculative mania, already underway when the Florida bubble burst. That was the Coolidge bull market on the New York Stock Exchange.

Before the 1920s, speculating in stocks, as opposed to long-term investing in companies in order to collect dividends on their profits every three months, was a game for the rich. (And not for all of the rich. John D. Rockefeller did not "play the market" until he retired from Standard Oil and needed a hobby; he looked on speculation as a game.) Buying stock in order to sell it when its market price rose a few points was not something that small-timers with a few thousand or a few hundred dollars in the bank did because of the risk of losing their capital in frequent market downturns.

Then, beginning in 1927, the few downturns worth noticing lasted only a few days. In what was called the "Coolidge Bull Market," the prices of shares—shares of companies ranging from trusty old New York Central and Standard Oil of Ohio to firms of which no one had ever heard—went up almost every day, often in giant leaps. The increases had nothing to do with the profits of the companies being traded. Everything on the market went up, up, up. The shares of companies that never paid a quarterly dividend went up.

Stock prices were rising because, just as in Florida a few years earlier, the "greater fool" principle was operating. Fools bringing new money bought stocks at the asking prices and more in the expectation that a greater fool willing to pay even more was just around the corner. For more than two years, there was an abundant supply of greater fools. It was difficult for the most cautious dentists and successful hardware store owners to leave their nest eggs in bank accounts paying interest of a few percent a year when, at the Rotary, the country club, or on the porch of the church after services, neighbors boasted of making 20 and 30 percent within a few months.

Buying on
Margin

Stock brokers and banks made speculation even more inviting to small-timers Brokerage houses, previously few in number and concentrated on New York's Wall Street, multiplied in number and opened offices complete with "stock tickers" connected by telephone lines with the New York Stock Exchange all over the country. In 1928 and 1929, 600 local brokerages were opened, an 80 percent increase in access to the market.

They urged their customers to buy "on margin" and multiply their winnings as much as tenfold. A dentist with $1,000 to play was advised not to be satisfied with buying ten shares of a $100 stock. He could buy a hundred of the same shares on margin. That is, his $1,000 was a down payment of 10 percent on $10,000 worth of the stock. A "broker's loan" covered the $9,000 he owed with the stock serving as his collateral. When the value of each share rose to $120 (which was inevitable!; look at the record!), instead of realizing a profit of $200 on ten shares, his gain on 100 shares was $2,000. He owed the bank $9,000 plus a little interest, but he had doubled his money—in a very short time.

In an extremely short time in March 1928, shares of General Motors rose in value by $28 one day, $31 the next, and two days later, by $91. Radio Corporation of America went up 123 points in one day. Some obscure issues enjoyed even more dizzying rises.

The Inevitable   Joseph P. Kennedy, a Boston millionaire (and father of President John F. Kennedy), said in later years that he sold all his stocks during the summer of 1929 when the man who shined his shoes told him that he was playing the market. Kennedy reasoned that if a man who worked for peanuts and tips was buying stock, there was no one left out there to bid prices higher. The crash was coming soon. John Jakob Raskob of General Motors was just lucky. In 1929, after he had been named national chairman of the Democratic party, GM's directors insisted that, because of a possible conflict of interest, he sell

Wall Street on Black Thursday, October 24, 1929. Many of the people milling about were speculators stunned by the money they had lost within a few hours. Others in the crowd were, no doubt, spectators, some of whom, human nature being what it is, were quietly enjoying the comeuppance the others had sustained.

© UPI/Bettmann/Corbis

the $29 million of the company's stock that he owned. He did, at just about the peak of the Coolidge bull market. Had he held on to it for another year, 90 percent of his investment would have vaporized.

On September 3, 1929, the average price of shares on the New York Stock Exchange peaked in the morning and then dipped sharply. For a month, prices spurted up and down, a sign that some people recognized the fluctuations as a signal to cash in and get out of the market. Margin buyers received unpleasant phone calls from their brokers when the value of their stocks—their collateral—dropped to less than the amount they owed on their brokers' loans. If they did not "cover the margin" within a day—repay enough of the loan so that their stock was worth more than they owed—they lost everything. For most margin buyers, the only way to cover the margin on some of their stock was to sell other shares at a loss. And so, yet more stock was dumped on the market, depressing its value further.

On "Black Thursday," October 24, a record 13 million shares changed hands; values collapsed. General Electric fell 471/2 points in one day; other major issues dropped almost as much.

On Tuesday, October 29, the wreckage was worse. In a panic now, speculators dumped 16 million shares. Clerical workers on Wall Street worked through the night to sort out the avalanche of paperwork. When the dust settled, more than $30 billion in paper value had been wiped out.

The Crash and the Depression   The Great Crash of 1929 did not *cause* the Great Depression of the 1930s, but it contributed to it. Middle-class families that had played the market on margin lost their savings. Banks that were deep in brokers' loans went belly up. When they closed their doors, they wiped out the savings accounts of simple, frugal people who thought that a bank was a vault where their money was kept safe from thieves and fires.

Corporations whose cash assets were wiped out curtailed production or shut down completely, throwing people out of work or—for the lucky ones—cutting their wages. Unemployed workers who had taken out mortgages were unable to meet payments and lost their homes. Farmers, debtors by the nature of their work, lost the means by which they made a living. Every wave of defaults caused additional bank failures.

Virtually everyone but the very rich had to reduce consumer purchases. There were not enough very rich people to sustain Five and Dime stores, beauty parlors, and manufacturers of vacuum cleaners. More and more businesses and factories closed their doors. And so it went, from buy, buy, buy to down, down, down.

40

HARD TIMES

The Great Depression 1930–1933

What our country needs is a good big laugh. If someone could get off a good joke every ten days, I think our troubles would be over.

—Herbert Hoover

Prosperity is just around the corner

—Herbert Hoover

The stock market crash was a bolt of lightning on a sunny day. It seemed (to most people) to come out of nowhere and was front page news for a month. The Great Depression descended quietly, like a fog. Americans experienced the collapse on Wall Street collectively or, more accurately, they watched it collectively, for only a small proportion of the population "experienced" its consequences. The depression affected all but a wealthy few, much of the population profoundly. But individuals felt it singly, in different ways at different times.

By the end of 1930, the depression engulfed the nation. There had been depressions before, severe ones in the 1870s and 1890s, a brief one after World War I. What made the depression of the 1930s the "Great Depression" was not that it affected more people than the others but, for most of Herbert Hoover's four years as president, it grew progressively worse each month. When Hoover tried cheerleading—"Prosperity is just around the corner"—he only soured most people on his administration. Six in ten voters supported Hoover in 1928; in less than two years, just about everyone except the president himself knew that he had no chance of being reelected.

Except for the Civil War, the Great Depression shook Americans morally more than any other shared experience. Those who were adults during the 1930s would be haunted by the dread of economic collapse until they died. Their children, too young to have noticed much out of the ordinary, were shaped by what they were told. Not until the 1960s did a generation come of age for which the Great Depression was "ancient history" and not very interesting.

The Great Depression 1929–1945

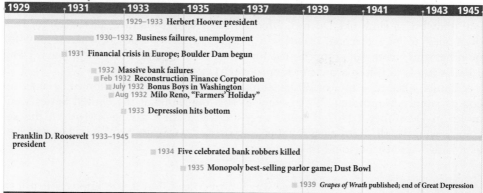

| 1929 | 1931 | 1933 | 1935 | 1937 | 1939 | 1941 | 1943 | 1945 |

1929–1933 Herbert Hoover president

1930–1932 Business failures, unemployment

1931 Financial crisis in Europe; Boulder Dam begun

1932 Massive bank failures
Feb 1932 Reconstruction Finance Corporation
July 1932 Bonus Boys in Washington
Aug 1932 Milo Reno, "Farmers' Holiday"

1933 Depression hits bottom

Franklin D. Roosevelt 1933–1945
president

1934 Five celebrated bank robbers killed

1935 Monopoly best-selling parlor game; Dust Bowl

1939 *Grapes of Wrath* published; end of Great Depression

THE FACE OF THE BEAST

Not every depression story was a tale of woe. People took pride in the fact that when times were toughest, family and neighbors stuck together and carried on with vitality or, at least, made do. Whether the memories were sweet or sour, however, the depression generation was, to date, the last generation of Americans whose values and political behavior were forged by economic insecurity and often serious deprivation.

Numbers During the first year after the crash, 4 million people lost their jobs. In 1931, the second year of the depression, 100,000 people were laid off each week. By 1932, fully a quarter of the work-force was unemployed: 13 million people with 30 million dependents. In heavily industrialized areas the figures were worse. In Chicago, 40 percent of people who wanted work could not find any. For a year in Toledo, Ohio, 80 percent of workers were unemployed. In some coal-mining towns like Donora, Pennsylvania, virtually no one had a job. African Americans, "the last hired and the first fired," had it worse than whites: *Nationally*, 35 percent were unemployed.

Those who held on to their jobs took paycuts—gladly, given the alternative. Between 1929 and 1933, the average weekly earnings of manufacturing employees fell from $25 to less than $17. Farmers' income, already low in 1929, plummeted. By the winter of 1932–1933, some corn growers were burning their crop to heat their homes—shades of the 1890s!—because they could not sell it. Wheat farmers had to sell 5 bushels to earn enough to buy a pair of shoes. The wholesale price of cotton dropped to 5¢ a pound: $30 for a 600-pound bale!

With no money coming in, hundreds of thousands could not pay rent or the monthly mortgage. They lost their homes. One farm family in four was pushed off the land by 1933, mainly in the cotton, grain, and pork belts of the South and Midwest. In one day, a quarter of the farms in Mississippi went on the auction block.

People who could not pay the rent did not go shopping. More than 100,000 small businesses went bankrupt, 32,000 just in 1932 (88 a day). Doctors and lawyers reported big drops in income. When counties' and cities' property tax collections dwindled, even schools—pretty much everyone's first priority—were hit. In several midwestern cities like Dayton, Ohio, children went on a three-day week for lack of money to pay teachers' salaries. Chicago's teachers worked without pay for months; some were not compensated for years; others never were. In January 1933, 1,000 schools in Georgia did not reopen after Christmas vacation.

Banks failed at a rate of 200 a month during 1932; $3.2 billion in savings accounts simply evaporated. When New York's big Bank of the United States went under in December 1930, 400,000 depositers lost their savings. Most of the accounts were small, hard-earned money squirreled away by working-class families as a hedge against personal misfortune.

What Depression Looked Like   Not everyone was hit, of course, but it was impossible not to be reminded of the suffering of others at the turning of a corner or the delivery of a newspaper. Each week, more than 5,000 men lined up at a New York employment agency to apply for 500 low-level jobs. When the city of Birmingham, Alabama, called for 800 workers to put in an eleven-hour day for $2, there were 12,000 applicants. In 1931, a Soviet agency, Amtorg, announced openings in Russia for 6,000 skilled technicians; 100,000 Americans said they would go. Once-prosperous skilled workers and small businessmen sold apples or set up shoeshine stands on street corners.

Charitable organizations were paralyzed by the scope of the demands made on them. Philadelphia's social workers managed to reach only one-fifth of the city's unemployed and could provide each of those families only $4.23 for a week, not enough to buy the cheapest food. "Soup kitchens"—free meals—mostly set up by churches, offered little more than a slice of bread and a bowl of stew, but for three years many ran at capacity. A journalist described the crowd at the Municipal Lodging House in New York City in 1930: "There is a line of men, three or sometimes four abreast, a block long, and wedged tightly together—so tightly that no passer-by can break through. For this compactness there is a reason: those at the head of the grey-black human snake will eat tonight; those farther back probably won't."

On the outskirts of cities (and smack in the middle of New York's Central Park), homeless men and women built shantytowns out of scavenged lumber, scraps of sheet metal, and cardboard boxes. The number of people who wandered the country—a new generation of tramps, this one including women—brought the scale of the catastrophe to rural America. Railroads gave up trying to keep tramps off freights; there were too many of them. The Missouri Pacific had counted 14,000 hopping its freights in 1928; in 1931 they estimated they had 186,000 passengers. In 1931, some 1.5 million people were moving about the country in search of work.

In a broad belt running north and south from the Dakotas into Texas, a severe annual drought beginning in 1931 piled natural catastrophe on top of man-made distress. Only farmers with deep artesian wells could produce crops until rainfall levels rose in 1939. By 1935, fields plowed for a generation were so powdery that the topsoil literally blew away. Hardest and most dramatically hit was the "Dust Bowl": northern Texas, southern Kansas, southeastern Colorado, and the epicenter, western Oklahoma. Dust storms blew dirt through pencil-line crevices in homes and blacked out the sun for days at a time. In some Oklahoma counties, 90 percent of the population went on the dole; then, beginning in 1935, lost half their population. The "Okies" (originally a derogatory term) gave up, abandoned even farms they owned, and—most of them— headed west on Route 66, which bisected the state, to California.

THE FAILURE OF THE OLD ORDER

Will Rogers, the nation's most popular humorist, quipped that the United States would be the first country to drive to the poorhouse in an automobile. He was trying to infuse a sense of proportion into the way some people thought about the depression. President Hoover made the same point more awkwardly. "No one is starving," he said.

They were right. The depression was not a pandemic or plague laying the continent waste. The United States was as rich in material blessings as ever. There was plenty of food. The capacity of American factories to produce goods ranging from pins and pleated trousers through vacuum cleaners to airplanes was the same in 1932 as it had been in 1929.

The fact that so many were deprived while living in the mouth of a cornucopia was what bewildered many and embittered others. An elderly, mild-mannered California physician, Francis E. Townshend, was transformed into an angry crusader when, one morning, he looked out his window to see old women picking through the garbage pails of a grocery store that was heaped high with foodstuffs. "Ten men in our country could buy the whole world," Will Rogers cracked, not humorously this time, "and ten million can't buy enough to eat."

In fact, it was abundance—super-abundance—too much food, too many goods— combined with the greed of New Era businessmen and the Coolidge administration's blindness that caused the disaster.

Not Enough Customers   During the 1920s, the American economy churned out things to sell in ever-increasing plenty, but the people who ran the coun-try did not spread around the money to enough of the population so that they could be sold. The president and Congress, partly because of principles they believed were eternal, partly in obeisance to big business, ignored indications that the combination of overproduction and underconsumption was a dangerous mix. The signs were obvious by 1929; a few economists tried to draw attention to them, but the government clung to policies that worsened the situation.

Andrew Mellon's tax policies favoring the wealthy were intended to pump money into constructive investment. But much (most?) of the tax windfalls the wealthy enjoyed went into speculation, doing nothing but inflating the already high price of stocks to the inevitable bursting point.

Wages in general lagged far behind the growth of wealth concentrated at the top of the economic pyramid. The masses of consumers were never able to consume the nation's agricultural produce at a price high enough to make farmers into consumers too. By 1928, it was obvious to the few economists who studied the figures that consumers were no longer buying all the pins and toasters that manufacturers were churning out. Too many "big-ticket" commodities like cars and refrigerators that were sold were purchased on the installment plan, with money, in other words, that the buyers did not have.

Large and visible sectors of the population were so impoverished that they were unable to buy much of anything, even on credit. Coal miners, not a very large or important occupational group today, were just that during the 1920s: More than 600,000 men were mine workers. Their low wages—frozen since 1920; just enough to pay the rent and feed the family—meant that miners and their wives did not buy many of the consumer goods on which Coolidge Prosperity was based.

For farmers who produced the staples—corn, wheat, pork, cotton—the hard times began not in 1930, but in the aftermath of World War I. American farms were so productive that the prices at which they sold their crops dropped steadily. During the 1920s, a good year down home was a year that farmers broke even. Thanks to Prohibition, there were no breweries and distilleries buying grain. The booze that most city people drank was distilled from Canadian grain. Electricity reached only one American farm in ten. The other nine were buying nothing that had to be plugged in, including lamps and light bulbs.

The entire South was a glaringly obvious "pocket" of underconsumers. Per capita income in the Deep South—rural Georgia, Alabama, Mississippi, and Louisiana—was about half the per capita income of the rest of the country. Sharecroppers might not see $20 in cash in a year. They bought their seed and food on credit and hoped that their share, when the crop was sold, would cover the previous year's expenditures. Nothing was trickling down to them.

African Americans who fled the South to northern and midwestern cities were part of the money economy but—as a group—not buying much more than necessities. The black middle class was growing, but most urban African Americans had low-paying menial jobs. They were not very helpful consumers.

American foreign policy contributed to the problem of an inadequate market by making it difficult for Europeans to buy American products. Foreign policy was designed to serve American finance virtually to the point of ignoring other American economic interests. Banks were encouraged to make huge loans to Germany on the assumption that the Germans would use much of the money to make reparations payments to the British and French who would then pay their debts in the United States. Bankers made lots of money from the transactions, but they did no one else any good.

The Republican party's high tariffs—when American industry needed no "protection"—made it difficult for Europeans to sell their product in the United States in order to pay for American goods ranging from big-profit American machinery (which was coveted) to dirt-cheap American foodstuffs. Congress was so obstinately blind to the obvious that, in 1930, in the depths of the depression, a new tariff, the Hawley-Smoot Tariff, actually raised the average duty on European imports from 40 percent to 60 percent!

Herbert Hoover, Scapegoat   Herbert Hoover had long aspired to be president, and he had a right to be proud when he was elected. He had earned the office by his achievements, not by hustling dimwitted voters. Except for military heroes—Washington, Taylor, Grant, Eisenhower—he remains the only president who was not a professional politician. Unfortunately for him, the singular nature of the American presidency is such that, if things go badly during a president's watch, he takes the fall, no matter how innocent of blame he may be.

Hoover was not responsible for the depression. He never subscribed to Harding's and Coolidge's unqualified obeisance to big business; he was the one member of Coolidge's cabinet who was not a flunkey. It was, in part, his "progressive" suggestions that the federal government govern more that made Coolidge nervous.

No matter: He got the blame for the depression, and from the start. The shantytowns that people evicted from their homes built in empty lots were dubbed "Hoovervilles." Men sleeping on park benches called the newspapers they wrapped around themselves for warmth "Hoover blankets." An empty pocket turned inside out was a "Hoover flag"; a boxcar was a "Hoover Pullman."

When the president visited hard-hit Detroit, riding in a motorcade, people on the sidewalk stared at him silently. Wisely, he cut personal appearances to a minimum, but his disappearance from view only contributed to a popular belief that he was unconcerned, doing nothing, paralyzed by the crisis. He could not take a brief vacation without arousing scorn. "Look here, Mr. Hoover, see what you've

One of the many "Hoovervilles"—shanty towns—erected in parks or other empty spaces by people who had lost their homes. This one, in New York's Central Park, has a look of semipermanence with its orderly straight "streets" and tidiness. Keeping it free of trash and garbage was a condition set by authorities if they were to tolerate the trespassing. Some Hoovervilles were squalid, unhealthy, and nests of drunkenness, altercations, and crime, but most, populated by decent people impoverished by the depression, were not.

done," an Appalachian song had it, "You went a-fishing, let the country go to ruin." The "Great Humanitarian" who had saved the Belgian people from famine during the war was now seen as callously indifferent to the sufferings of his fellow Americans.

Hoover's Program

Hoover was depressed, subdued, and withdrawn. An aide later said that speaking with him in his office was like sitting in a bath of ink. But he was not callous to the suffering in the country. He gave a big chunk of his salary to charities helping the stricken. No other president has been half as generous.

Nor was Hoover paralyzed into inaction. He had a program to fight the depression that would have been beyond Coolidge's ken. Hoover recognized the role that Mellon's regressive taxes had played in causing the depression and abandoned some of them. He persuaded Congress to commit $500 million a year to public works, building or improving government properties not primarily because the work was needed but so as to put people to work. The greatest of his projects, the Hoover Dam, was a 700-foot high, 1,200-foot wide wall of concrete spanning the Colorado River southeast of Las Vegas that, seventy years after its completion, is still among the world's greatest feats of engineering. Hoover's Reconstruction Finance Corporation (RFC), established in 1932, was a federal agency that funneled money to banks, railroads, and other vital corporations that were teetering on the edge of collapse.

Spendy federal projects and policies intended to manipulate the economy—kick-start it in the case of the RFC, had been anathema to the Republican party establishment since Teddy Roosevelt had rattled party conservatives with his New Nationalism.

But everything Hoover did was too little, too late, or misunderstood. Reducing taxes on consumers did nothing for the millions who were unemployed, earning nothing, spending nothing. Public works projects like Boulder Dam helped only the few who were employed on them. Boulder City, Nevada, a town thrown up overnight to house workers on the dam, was a hive of working-class prosperity. It was also a speck in the desert. The RFC shored up several important banks and railroads that might otherwise have gone under. But with one in four workers without a job, it looked like a welfare program for millionaires.

Hoover's Limitations

What was most urgently needed was relief for the massive numbers of people who had been earning decent livings one day and through no fault of their own were struggling the next. Hoover believed in helping the stricken; he was no "let the unfit perish" social Darwinist. But charity was the province of well-off individuals like himself and relief programs the job of municipal and state governments. Hoover would not hear of proposals that the federal government assume such responsibilities even when, after just a year of depression, charities' resources everywhere had been reduced to little more than operating expenses, and city and state government treasuries were empty.

Hoover's distinction between the social responsibilities of federal and state governments was obsolete. His assignment of relief to state and local governments was inconsistent with his belief in "rugged individualism," the individual's responsibility for his own welfare, to which he occasionally gave voice. If federal relief sapped the American character of self-reliance, state-sponsored relief programs could hardly fail to do so.

Hoover was a "self-made man." He did not rise from the dregs of society. His father was a blacksmith; the uncle who took him in when he was orphaned at age 9 was a doctor. But he paid his own way through Stanford University by working. As a salaried mining engineer in Australia and China, he invested his savings in failing mines that he recognized as potentially rich but mismanaged. Before he was 40, he was a millionaire.

He had a right to be pleased with himself and to attribute his success to his own efforts. But he discounted the luck of his birthdate. Had he been a just-graduated mining engineer in 1930 instead of at a time when metal mining was booming in Australia, he would have faced a bleaker future than he had as a young man. All the "rugged individualism" he could muster would not have gotten him a job that did not exist.

Hoover was far from alone in believing that individuals were largely responsible for their success or failure. During the first years of the depression, psychologists marveled that the most common initial response to joblessness and homelessness was self-blame. They reported on homeless hitchhikers who apologized because their clothing was shabby. A stroller through a big-city park in 1930 and 1931 saw scores of unsuccessful job seekers slumped on benches, heads in hands, elbows on knees, collars drawn up, wondering where they had failed.

Gillette, a manufacturer of razor blades, exploited the widespread sense of personal failure with an advertisement showing a husband shamefully telling his wife that he still had work. He had a heavy beard, a "five o'clock shadow." The message was that employers had turned him down because he needed a shave, not because they had no jobs to offer. A maker of underwear put the responsibility for the unemployment of a bedridden man squarely on his own shoulders. He was out of work not because 13 million others were but because he had worn an inferior brand of undershirt and had caught a bad cold.

Hoover was reduced to other incantations. "Prosperity," he said too often given his crumbling popularity, was "just around the corner." In 1931, briefly, Hoover's prediction seemed to be coming true. What we call the economic indicators made modest gains. Hoover brightened; the country was turning the corner. Then, in May, one of Europe's biggest banks failed. The Kreditanstalt of Vienna had been shaky for years; other European banks had been propping it up. So, when the Kreditanstalt collapsed, other major banks followed. In September, in order to save the Bank of England, Great Britain abandoned the gold standard. Worried that the American dollar was in danger, foreign and American depositors withdrew $1.5 billion in gold from American banks, launching a new wave of business failures.

THE NOT-SO-RED DECADE

Many Americans blamed Hoover and the Republican party for the hard times; in the midterm election of 1930, the Democrats picked up fifty-three seats in the House of Representatives and eight in the Senate. But few faulted the American political system and only a few more faulted capitalism. This was not for a lack of trying by the Socialist party of America and the Communist party. Leaders of both concluded that if ever there was an opportunity to move from the political fringe and become authentic political alternatives to the capitalist parties, the depression had provided it. There was something basically wrong, socialist and communist newspapers and recruiters argued, when people were willing and able to work and produce plenty of everything for everyone, yet millions had lost their jobs and millions of farmers had been forced off the land. The enemy was not the hapless Hoover; the enemy was the system.

The Communist Party

In the presidential election in prosperous 1928, Communist party leader William Z. Foster polled 49,000 votes. After three depression years during which the Communists campaigned hard, especially in industrial cities, Foster expected a big increase in the election of 1932. The Communist vote more than doubled to 103,000, but party leaders were gravely disappointed. With the failure of capitalism so obvious to them, how did the voters miss this?

And the year 1932 marked the high-water mark of American communism's popularity. Americans blamed greedy, corrupt capitalists for their misfortunes, not capitalism itself. And the example of the Soviet Union, the first "workers' state," was not inspiring. The stomach-turning crimes of Joseph Stalin's dictatorship were not yet widely known, but Americans knew enough about the dreariness of life in Russia and Stalin's suppression of political and religious freedoms to imagine preferring living under communism over living in American society with the depression at its worst. The dean of American investigative journalists, Lincoln Steffens, visited the U.S.S.R. and returned home to write, "I have seen the future and it works." He blamed the shortcomings of the Soviet system on Russia's deep-rooted poverty and the government's fear of invasion. He was not convincing.

The American Communist party made some high-profile converts among literary figures and intellectuals. Writers Theodore Dreiser, Mary McCarthy, Sherwood Anderson, John Dos Passos, Dashiell Hammett, Lillian Hellman, and critics Edmund Wilson and Granville Hicks either joined "the party" or openly espoused communism as a desirable alternative to the system that, they believed, had brought economic disaster upon the United States. Absurd as it seemed even to his friends, the immortalizer of flappers and "flaming youth," F. Scott Fitzgerald, said that he was studying Marxism.

The intellectuals' entrance into the party was a revolving door. Few carried membership cards for more than a year or two. Party meetings were secretive and conspiratorial. Free discussion was acceptable only on issues on which the Comintern in Moscow (the "Communist International") had not defined an official "party line." Free-thinking writers and university intellectuals were not apt to react favorably to being told what they were to think.

Communists and Unions

The party was more successful penetrating the leadership of some labor unions. Communists headed the United Electrical Workers, the Mine Mill and Smelter Workers, and a number of smaller unions. Wyndham Mortimer of the United Automobile Workers, journalist Len De Caux, and lawyer Lee Pressman were communists in influential positions in the Congress of Industrial Organizations (CIO). Selfless, hard-working party members dedicated themselves to union organization. Indeed, CIO organizers who were secret communists were probably the key to the rapid growth during the depression of the steelworkers, automobile workers, and longshoremen unions.

But communist influence among the rank and file was negligible. Most party members in leadership positions in unions obscured, concealed, and even denied their communist affiliations. They were Leninists. They did not believe ordinary workers were capable of making a revolution (or of much else). For their own good, they had to be manipulated by the "militant minority" organized in secret, small cells.

Similarly, the communists had little success in enlisting African Americans despite the fact that party activists, often courageously, led successful rent strikes in the black neighborhoods in northern cities. Others spearheaded attempts to organize sharecroppers in the South (whites as well as blacks) and, with only belated support from liberals, communists led a campaign to save the lives of the "Scottsboro Boys," nine young black men convicted of rape in Alabama in 1931 on tainted evidence. Had the party not made that fight, the hapless Scottsboro Boys would have been executed.

Norman Thomas and the Socialists The Socialist party of America was not saddled with the Leninist baggage and Soviet party line that hampered the communists. The party was, in fact, militantly anticommunist. Norman Thomas, the socialist candidate for president six times, beginning in 1928, was more hostile to communism because of its opposition to political democracy and individual liberties than he was to capitalism.

Thomas was a former Presbyterian minister and a pacifist who had opposed American entrance into World War I. He did much better at the polls than communist candidates did. He won 267,000 votes in 1928 and 882,000 in 1932. But even that total was less than his predecessor as head of the party, Eugene V. Debs, won in the prosperous election years 1912 and 1920. Where the communists offered an unattractive and alien alternative to the "American way of life," Thomas's all-American democratic socialism was not much different from what politicians in the liberal wing of the Democratic party offered. It made little sense to vote for Thomas and the Socialists when a vote for the Democrats promised to have results. In 1936, with the liberal Democrats in power, Thomas's vote in the presidential election dropped to 187,000.

Thomas understood this. He knew that the Socialists would never exercise political power. He regarded his and the party's role as being the nation's conscience, pushing and pulling the Democrats toward, not socialism, but more humane social policies.

POPULAR RESPONSES

There was some violence, most of it spontaneous: food riots in St. Paul and other cities, people storming grocery stores and clearing the shelves. Wisconsin dairy farmers stopped trucks picking up milk and dumped it into ditches, partly in anger at the low prices processors were paying them, partly to dramatize their need for government help. In Iowa, the National Farmers' Holiday Association urged hog raisers to withhold their products from the market—to take a holiday—and attracted attention by blockading highways. Eat your own products, Holiday Association leader Milo Reno told Iowans, and let the money men eat their gold.

But incidents of violence were few and quickly over with. Americans coped with hard times peacefully. The most violent episode of the Hoover years was the work not of stricken people, but by the authorities or, rather, one politically ambitious and slightly unbalanced general, General Douglas MacArthur, who attacked the "Bonus Expeditionary Force" in Washington in the summer of 1932.

The Bonus Boys   In 1924, Congress voted to reward World War I veterans with a "bonus" of $1,000 to be paid in 1945. When the depression threw thousands of not-so-old soldiers out of work, veterans asked for payment of half the bonus immediately. Congress obliged, but Hoover vetoed the bill because it was federal relief, which, indeed, it was, and which Hoover opposed on principle.

Congress passed the bill over his veto and Democrats, taking the popular side of an issue in a presidential election year, called for paying veterans the entire bonus immediately. In support, 20,000 veterans (and some wives) massed in Washington. When Congress adjourned in July without taking action, all but about 2,000 of the demonstrators left the capital. Some entered vacant government office buildings and squatted. Others moved to a "Bonus Expeditionary Force" Hooverville on Anacostia Flats, wasteland on the outskirts of the city. There was some drunkenness and fistfights, but the camp was, on the whole, remarkably peaceful. The Bonus Boys policed themselves and cooperated with authorities.

Hoover persuaded himself that the Bonus Boys were led by communist agitators. (They were not; the most influential organization among them was the anticommunist American Legion.) The president sent General Douglas MacArthur with troops to clear out the Bonus Boys who were trespassing in government buildings. He said nothing about Anacostia Flats. MacArthur, a brave and talented soldier who already had a reputation for making up his own orders, assembled armored vehicles and tear gas. They were not needed to clear the federal buildings. The squatters departed when asked.

After a short delay, while MacArthur waited for a full-dress uniform to be brought to him, he moved his soldiers to Anacostia Flats, forced the Bonus Boys out at bayonet point, and burned the camp. Most Republican editors congratulated him; MacArthur was the Republicans' favorite general. Hoover was angry; he still had hopes of winning the election in November and he knew the Bonus Boys enjoyed widespread report. MacArthur was probably guilty of insubordination, but Hoover let it pass and took the blame for the spectacle of young soldiers driving off unarmed old soldiers.

Midwestern Robin Hoods   Americans expressed their anger toward values of the New Era they now thought had been foisted on them in several indirect ways. Businessmen, lionized just a few years earlier, became objects of ridicule in films, on radio programs, and in the columns and comic strips of daily newspapers. Ordinary people, especially in the heartland between the Mississippi and the Rockies, lavished tacit approval on a new kind of criminal: the heavily armed midwestern bank robber who exploited automobiles and the sleepiness of small towns to make "getaways" on little-traveled rural roads.

Bank robbers like John Dillinger, Charles "Pretty Boy" Floyd, Lester "Baby Face Nelson" Gillis, Clyde Barrow and Bonnie Parker ("Bonnie and Clyde"), George Barnes ("Machine Gun Kelly"), and Kate "Ma" Barker, her four sons, and Alvin "Creepy" Karpis Kelly all enjoyed a brief spell of celebrity. Some newspapers depicted them as romantic heroes, driven reluctantly to a "life of crime" by the depression, who only robbed banks which had robbed the people, and were, like Robin Hood, kind and generous with the poor.

Some of them reveled in the publicity. Bonnie and Clyde photographed themselves with their guns and getaway cars in theatrical poses. Bonnie Parker wrote a rhyming account of their adventures more or less in the form of a chivalric ballad with an inevitably tragic conclusion: "it's curtains for Bonnie and Clyde." It was printed in hundreds of papers. On one of the occasions he was in custody (he escaped from the police several times), John Dillinger was charming in a filmed interview, convincingly claiming he had never injured an ordinary, unoffending citizen. The police who were holding him flocked around him, shaking his hand. "Pretty Boy" Floyd was immortalized in a song written by Woody Guthrie, the author of popular songs with social and patriotic themes in the 1930s and 1940s. When Clyde Barrow wrote in a letter that the 1934 Ford V-8 was his favorite getaway car, the Ford Company used it as a valued endorsement.

The robbers' celebrity was also promoted by the head of the Federal Bureau of Investigation, J. Edgar Hoover, as part of an effort to promote himself as the country's number one "G-man" ("government man"). Several arrested gangsters said that Kate "Ma" Barker's reputation as the middle-aged brains of the Barker-Karpis gang was a fiction created by Hoover after Ma was shot and killed in 1935. Alvin Karpis said that she had nothing to do with the gang's heists. Another member of the gang said that "Ma couldn't plan breakfast."

Unlike the businessman-gangsters of the 1920s, the bank robbers enjoyed no luxurious living and their careers were short. Their faces were well known because of the publicity; they could spend the money they stole only by holing up in dingy hide-outs and dining on canned soup and beans until the treasury was depleted. Within a few months in 1934, Bonnie and Clyde, Pretty Boy Floyd, John Dillinger, and Baby Face Nelson were gunned down. When Floyd was buried in Salisaw, Oklahoma, 20,000 people attended the funeral. Creepy Karpis and Machine Gun Kelly survived to serve long prison terms, taking what satisfaction they could out of the many reporters who came to visit them.

The Movies: The Depression-Proof Business   Hollywood, particularly Warner Brothers studios, exploited the celebrity-gangster phenomenon by making movies slyly glamorizing lawbreakers while always taking care to end the films with a moral law and order message. Like the adulterous woman in nineteenth-century novels, who had to be killed off no matter how she had been the victim of others, movie gangsters paid for their crimes "in a hail of bullets" or strapped into an electric chair. But the message was clear: Criminals played by George Raft, Edward G. Robinson, Humphrey Bogart, and James Cagney had been pushed into their careers by poverty and social injustice, and most of them had redeeming personal qualities.

At first the depression hit the movie business hard. Between 1929 and 1932, the number of theaters in the country declined from 22,000 to 12,000. But the industry recovered rapidly even as the depression dragged on. By the mid-thirties there were 28,000 movie houses in the United States compared to 8,000 in France and Germany with a combined population about the same as in the United States. Nineteen of the twenty-five highest salaries in the United States, and forty of the highest sixty-three, were paid to motion picture company executives.

Why was the movie business, almost alone, so successful in hard times? First, tickets were cheap, 25¢ to 38¢ (10¢ for children) at neighborhood "second run" theaters. Theater owners changed their programs three times a week, offering "double features," one film fresh from the midtown "first run" movie palaces and a cheaply made "B" movie, a formula comedy or western. Each neighborhood movie house rented 300 films from distributors each year. Exhibitors added a newsreel and a travelogue to each program and, to keep the kids coming back every Saturday afternoon, cliff-hanger serials. Early in the depression, the Carrier company developed a movie house air-conditioning system that neighborhood theaters could afford. Many a "fan" spent a quarter just to sit in refrigerated air for a few hours on a sweltering evening. And a night out at the movies was a social occasion. After the show, people sat down with neighbors to share a banana split or milkshake at a nearby drugstore or, after 1933, a glass of beer.

Each week, 85 million people watched Marie Dressler, Janet Gaynor, Shirley Temple, Mickey Rooney, Jean Harlow, and Clark Gable in a dizzying array of adventures and fantasies. The favorite themes were escapist. During the mid-1930s, Shirley Temple, an angelic little blonde girl who sang and danced, led the list of moneymakers. Her annual salary was $300,000, and her films made $5 million a year for Fox Pictures. Royalties from Shirley Temple dolls and other paraphernalia made her a multimillionaire before she reached puberty—which pretty much ended her career. Choreographer Busby Berkeley made millions for Warner Brothers by staging plotless dance tableaux featuring dozens of beautiful starlets transformed by mirrors and camera tricks into hundreds. The movies were a depression-proof business.

Music, Music, Music   Radio, even cheaper entertainment than the movies, also flourished, even during the rock-bottom years of 1930–1932. There were 8.5 million radio receivers in the country in 1929, 18 million in 1932. By 1936 there were 33 million. Advertising revenues quadrupled. (Newspaper advertising declined by 30 percent.)

Networks broadcast dance bands "live" from famous big city ballrooms like the Waldorf-Astoria, transforming thousands of living rooms into dance floors. Daily fifteen minute serials for adults in the evenings (mostly comedies) hooked adults as effectively as afternoon adventure serials hooked children. By far the best and the most popular radio program was *Amos 'n' Andy* on NBC. It dramatized the continuing adventures of a group of African Americans who were part of the "Great Migration" of black people north to New York's Harlem. Amos was a hard-working guy just trying to get by, Andy a hustling would-be 1920s-type capitalist and a bumbling fool. The networks increased news coverage, also a success. In 1928, 8.5 million people listened to the presidential election returns, in 1932 18 million, and in 1936 33 million.

The recorded music business, by way of contrast, did not recover from the depression until the 1940s. Sales of 78-rpm records, usually priced at 35¢, had risen to $50 million a year during the 1920s. In 1932, sales had collapsed to $2.5 million, a disaster as bad as the worst performances on the New York Stock Exchange. The chief casualties were "hillbilly" groups and African American blues and jazz musicians whose markets were among two of the hardest hit social groups in the country. Columbia, Decca, and RCA discontinued their "race record" division, which had targeted an African American market. Only a few black performers like blues singer Bessie Smith and cornetist Louis Armstrong continued to sell enough records to stay in the business.

The introduction of the jukebox, playing a record for a nickel in bars and teen-ager hangouts, helped recovery. There were 25,000 jukeboxes in use in 1930, 330,000 by 1940. Record sales were 33 million in 1938, still well below predepression levels. (Sales soared again in the 1940s with the return of prosperity—to 127 million in 1941.)

"Big bands" that won national reputations on the radio toured the country. For 50¢ to a dollar, young and not-so-young people could dress up and dance for three hours to the music of Benny Goodman, Harry James, and other groups. It was not an every-evening diversion. The big bands had to rush from city to city from one one-night-stand to another in order to draw full audiences. Even the most popular orchestras might play in thirty different ballrooms in as many nights. But they were very popular. At the Palladium in Hollywood, Harry James drew 8,000 dancers in a single night, 35,000 in a week.

THE ELECTION OF 1932

Nostalgia for the Thirties, by people who were young then—memories of a favorite radio program, of going to a ballroom or to a movie palace decorated like a Turkish seraglio—fixed on the middle and later years of the depression decade. In the summer of 1932, when the economy hit bottom, the country's mood was somber; 1932 was, of course, a presidential election year.

The Democrats' Roosevelt Senator Joseph I. France of Maryland challenged Hoover for the Republican presidential nomination. He won primaries in New Jersey, Pennsylvania, Illinois, and Oregon. Had presidential nominations been determined by primaries as they are today, Hoover would have been rejected by his own party. But primary elections were few in 1932; in most states, professional politicians allied to big business still made decisions, and the Republican bosses could not abandon an incumbent president, no matter that they knew that Hoover was doomed to defeat in November.

The Democratic presidential nominee in 1932, New York governor Franklin D. Roosevelt, said nothing in his campaign to indicate that he intended to sponsor a massive and comprehensive federal program of relief and reform. He knew he was going to win and that any specific proposals he made would alienate some people who planned to vote for him. He waged the campaign as a cheerful, outgoing, supremely confident leader in contrast to Hoover, who was glum and almost a recluse by 1932.

Democratic hopefuls, knowing that their party's nomination was a ticket to the White House, had a catfight. The chief contenders were John Nance Garner of Texas, who had inherited the McAdoo Democrats of the South and West; Al Smith, the party's standard-bearer in 1928, who believed he deserved a second go; and Smith's successor as governor of New York, Franklin Delano Roosevelt (FDR).

When the beginnings of a convention deadlock brought back memories of the bitterly divided party of 1924, some Garner delegates switched to Roosevelt and gave him the nomination. FDR—newspapers already called him by his initials in headlines—then presented the nation with the first indication of his flair for the dramatic and his willingness to break with tradition. Rather than wait quietly at home to be officially notified of his nomination, Roosevelt rushed to a plane prepared for flight, flew to the Chicago convention despite nasty weather, and personally told the cheering Democrats that he meant to provide a "New Deal" for the American people. Roosevelt simultaneously slapped at the discredited Republican "New Era" and reminded voters of both parties—the older ones, anyway—that he was a distant cousin of the energetic president of the Square Deal, Theodore Roosevelt.

The Campaign   Hoover's campaign was dispirited; it could not have been otherwise. He was in the impossible position of having to defend policies that had failed. Roosevelt, like any other candidate for whom victory is a cinch, avoided taking any stand likely to be controversial. He knew that a good many

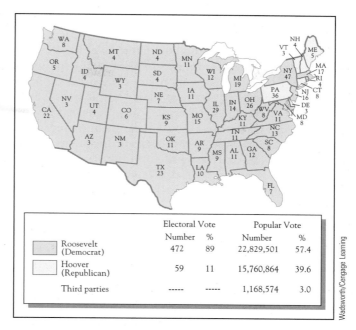

	Electoral Vote		Popular Vote	
	Number	%	Number	%
Roosevelt (Democrat)	472	89	22,829,501	57.4
Hoover (Republican)	59	11	15,760,864	39.6
Third parties	-----	-----	1,168,574	3.0

MAP 40.1 Presidential Election, 1932

Never had an electoral college map looked like this map of Roosevelt's victory in 1932. Only four New England states and Pennsylvania, still under the thumb of a 60-year-old Republican machine, gave Hoover majorities. In 1936, Roosevelt improved on the 1932 count; he carried every state except Maine and Vermont. Not until 1972, when Republican Richard Nixon carried every state except Massachusetts, would that record be broken.

people were voting *against* Hoover; a strong statement by him on any subject could only cost him votes. Roosevelt even spoke of balancing the budget although he well knew that, with tax revenues way down, the new programs to which he vaguely alluded would make a balanced budget impossible.

The big difference between FDR and Hoover was their personalities. No small thing with American voters. Roosevelt's buoyant charm, good humor, and bursting self-confidence—they all came naturally to him—made for a sharp contrast with Hoover's tight-lipped gloominess. The campaign was all image. Roosevelt smiled constantly. He conveyed to his audiences that he was a man who knew how to take charge. His theme song, blared by brass bands at every rally, was the up-beat "Happy Days Are Here Again." It was enough. FDR's victory was lopsided: 472 electoral votes to Hoover's 59.

In 1933, Inauguration Day was a full four months after the election, a vestige of an age when the fastest a person (or news) could travel was at a horse's pace. The interregnum was six weeks longer than it is today (which many political scientists think is too long). At a critical time like 1933, the four-month interregnum seemed to drag on as if it were four years. It meant a long winter of Hoover who, soundly defeated, was powerless. Concerned about what Roosevelt had in mind, he wrote the president-elect, asking him in the interests of national morale, to endorse several of his policies.

Roosevelt did not bite. He made no commitments either in support of Hoover or criticizing him. He disappeared from the public eye on what was, in fact, a very hard-working retreat. Roosevelt met long hours several days a week with experts on agriculture, industry, banking, and relief. His "brains trust," as reporters called it (people decided they preferred "brain trust") was organized by Raymond Moley, a professor at Columbia University. Most of the men invited to FDR's estate at Hyde Park to present their ideas were professors at Ivy League universities. Whatever Roosevelt had in mind—and he relished the suspense he was creating—there was going to be an entirely new crowd in Washington. The businessmen who had set the capital's tone under Coolidge and Hoover turned over their D.C. apartments and sold their suburban homes in Virginia and Maryland to intellectuals, men (and—this was quite new—a few women) from universities and state social agencies.

41

REARRANGING AMERICA
FDR and the New Deal 1933–1938

*This generation of Americans has a rendezvous
with destiny.*

—Franklin D. Roosevelt

A few days before his inauguration in 1933, Franklin D. Roosevelt visited Miami. From the crowd surging around him, a jobless worker named Joe Zangara, later found to be mentally unbalanced, emptied a revolver at Roosevelt's party. Anton Cermak, the mayor of Chicago, who was sitting next to the president-elect, died from his wounds. Roosevelt escaped without a scratch.

There was a lesson in the incident. Roosevelt was cool in a crisis. He barely flinched during the chaos. Just what he intended to do about the depression, however, remained a mystery. Roosevelt knew what legislation he would call for as soon as he took office. But he had no idea as to whether or not it would work. He was not a man with an ideology but was a quintessential pragmatist, like the legendary American mechanic who said: "Well, let's start her up and see why she doesn't run."

THE PLEASANT MAN WHO CHANGED AMERICA

Henry Cabot Lodge had called Roosevelt "a well-meaning, nice young fellow, but light." Edith Galt Wilson said that he was "more charming than able." In 1932, Walter Lippmann, dean of political columnists, called Roosevelt "a pleasant man who, without any important qualifications, would very much like to be president." Many people wondered if someone who had enjoyed so pampered and sheltered a life as Roosevelt had was capable of appreciating the hardship that had befallen millions of Americans.

Silver Spoon   The new president was born into an old and rich, but somewhat decayed, New York family. Boyhood vacations were spent in Europe and at yachting resorts in Maine and Nova Scotia. He attended the

The New Deal 1933–1945

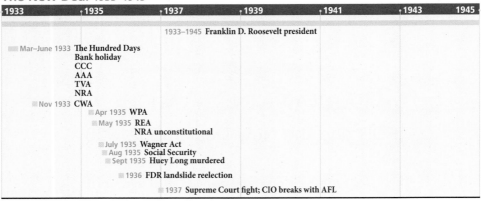

1933	1935	1937	1939	1941	1943	1945

1933–1945 **Franklin D. Roosevelt president**

Mar–June 1933 **The Hundred Days**
Bank holiday
CCC
AAA
TVA
NRA
Nov 1933 **CWA**
Apr 1935 **WPA**
May 1935 **REA**
NRA unconstitutional
July 1935 **Wagner Act**
Aug 1935 **Social Security**
Sept 1935 **Huey Long murdered**
1936 **FDR landslide reelection**
1937 **Supreme Court fight; CIO breaks with AFL**

most exclusive private schools and was adored and sheltered to the point of suffocation by his mother. When Roosevelt went to Harvard, Sara Roosevelt packed up and rented a house near the university so that she could keep an eye on her boy. FDR's wife, Eleanor Roosevelt, was from the same tiny, exclusive social set; she, like Theodore Roosevelt, was the president's distant cousin. Even the immense charm with which Roosevelt ran his campaign—a jaunty air, toothy smile, and cheery small talk that came easily—was the charm of a socialite.

And yet, from the moment FDR delivered his eloquent inaugural address—the clouds over Washington parting on cue to let the sun through—it was obvious that he was a natural leader. From his first day as president, Roosevelt dominated center stage as his cousin Theodore had done thirty years earlier, and without the bluster. He held eighty-three press conferences in 1933, ninety-six in 1940. (Recent presidents have four or five a year.)

Where Teddy had been liked and hated, Franklin Roosevelt was loved and hated. Poor sharecroppers, white and black, and African Americans living in big cities tacked his photograph to the wall next to prints of Christ in Gethsemane and named their children for him. Few other presidents, however, have been so passionately hated as FDR was. It was said that some of the nation's wealthiest people could not bear to pronounce his name. They referred to him through clenched teeth as "that man in the White House" and as a "traitor to his class."

Roosevelt's Contribution   Roosevelt's self-confidence reflected a less-attractive aspect of his personality. Probably due in part to the adoration of his mother, he was the center of the universe in which he lived. "He was the coldest man I ever met," his successor Harry S. Truman said years later. "He didn't give a damn personally for me or you or anyone else in the world." There is plenty of evidence confirm to Truman's characterization. But FDR's public persona was bubbling, buoyant, and ingratiating. His optimism was infectious. The mood in Washington changed overnight in March 1933.

Roosevelt was more than a charmer, more than an amoral manipulator. He was not afraid to make decisions. And, while he preferred to blame his enemies when his decisions went wrong, or let his aides take the blame for them—if he had to accept responsibility for his mistakes, he did.

He was decisive. A day after he was sworn in, he called Congress into special session for the purpose of enacting crisis legislation, and he declared a bank holiday. Calling on emergency presidential powers, he ordered all banks to close their doors temporarily in order to forestall additional failures. Although the bank holiday tied up people's savings, the drama of his action won wide approval.

In 1933, Justice Oliver Wendell Holmes Jr. said privately that the president had "a second-class intellect." That was true. Roosevelt never understood many of the complex economic and social processes with which his administration had to grapple. He did not think it necessary that he should. He had professors at his command, the "brain trust," and he was open to suggestions from every quarter.

No one cowed him. No one in his administration was so foolish as to try. He was the boss of a stable of headstrong, bickering intellectuals. He stroked their vanities when it suited his purposes, played one brain-truster against another as only a supreme egotist would, and yet, for a while, he retained the loyalty of all, including those whose suggestions he ignored. Roosevelt never lacked talented advisers because he did not fear talent.

In the end, Roosevelt's greatest strength was his flexibility. "The country needs bold, persistent experimentation," he said. "It is common sense to take a method and try it. If it fails, admit it frankly and try another." Roosevelt's pragmatism suited the American temperament far better than Hoover's insistence on clinging to a tattered ideology did.

A Very Active First Lady   One of FDR's greatest political assets was his remarkable wife Eleanor, the first First Lady to lead an active public life of her own. Decades later, in the age of anything-goes journalism, it was revealed that her marriage to FDR had been shattered years earlier when she learned that her husband was having an affair with her friend and social secretary Lucy Mercer. Eleanor offered Franklin a divorce. He begged off; a divorced man had no political future in New York's Democratic party, which depended on a big Catholic vote to win elections. Eleanor agreed to stay on the condition that Lucy had to go and she did, or so Eleanor believed until after Franklin died.

Eleanor's upbringing was as privileged as FDR's but, unlike his, her life was emotionally painful. She was unattractive and awkward with an unpleasant shrill voice. She was aware that she was an "ugly duckling," merely tolerated in her exclusive social set. It caused something of a sensation among the New York gentility when the handsome, outgoing Franklin married her in 1905. He could have done so very much better! FDR's mother tried so stridently to quash the match that she and Eleanor were never more than proper with one another.

Perhaps in part because her personal life was unhappy, Eleanor (who bore five children) threw herself into the social and political causes that, with the twentieth century, were acceptable avocations for well-to-do women. Her political interests were a godsend to Franklin when, in 1921, a year after running for the vice presidency, he was paralyzed from the waist down by polio. He never walked again, except for a few steps he could manage for the sake of appearances by wearing heavy, painful leg braces, and one of his sons at his side poised to save him from falling.

Eleanor urged the stricken Roosevelt not to give up his political ambitions. She became his legs, his locomotive rather, tirelessly traveling, schmoozing with politicians, and filling in for her husband at less important political functions. She kept her political campaigning low key when FDR ran for governor of New York in 1928 and president for 1932. Not everyone was as tolerant of activist women as upper-class New Yorkers were. Indeed, FDR's political enemies were as nasty in vilifying her as they were in their often ugly personal attacks on the president.

Eleanor provided FDR with more than a mobile alter ego. Where the president was indeed detached, Eleanor was compassionate, genuinely moved by the misery and injustices suffered by the "forgotten" men and women on the bottom of society. She interceded with her husband—nagged him—to appoint women to high government positions. She supported organized labor when FDR was trying to straddle the sensitive issue of unions. She made the grievances of African Americans a particular interest, persuading FDR to name blacks like educator Mary McLeod Bethune to government posts. Much of the devotion of African Americans to FDR was earned not by his actions or sentiments—FDR was much more concerned with placating white racist southern Democrats—but by "that woman in the White House." In 1932, 70 percent of black voters voted against Roosevelt; in 1936, 75 percent voted for him.

Eleanor Roosevelt was in her thirties before she thought much about poor or struggling people other than as servants or charity cases. As First Lady, she sat down, unaffected and unpatronizing, as an equal with grimy coal miners, illiterate African American sharecroppers, and—in this photo—with a destitute woman collecting a basket of free food for her family.

AP Photos

THE HUNDRED DAYS

Never before or since has the United States experienced such an avalanche of legis-lation as Congress enacted in the spring of 1933. By nature deliberate, Congress had been jolted by the economic crisis and by Roosevelt's landslide election victory, which brought in big Democratic majorities in both Senate and House. Roosevelt's legislative demands, new ones delivered to the Capitol almost daily, were enacted without serious debate. Some bills were passed without being read. During what be-came known as the Hundred Days, FDR might as well have been a dictator and Con-gress a gaggle of sycophants. Conservative congressmen simply shut up and slunk back into their chairs, unmanned by their own failure and the decisiveness of the Democrats.

Saving Banks and Farms   The most pressing problems in March 1933 were the immi-nent collapse of the nation's financial system, foreclosures on farm and home mortgages, and the distress of the millions of unemployed workers.

Enacted during the "bank holiday," the Emergency Banking Act eliminated the weakest banks merely by identifying them and letting them die. Responsibly man-aged banks in danger of folding were saved when the Federal Reserve System issued loans to them. When the government permitted banks to reopen, depositors con-cluded that they were safe, ceased to withdraw their money, and returned money they had taken home and hidden in the cellar. Roosevelt halted the drain on the nation's gold reserve by forbidding the export of gold and, in April 1933, by taking the nation off the gold standard. No longer could paper dollars be redeemed in gold coin which was then hoarded. Instead, the value of money was based on the gov-ernment's word, and the price of gold frozen by law at $35 an ounce. ("Well, that's the end of western civilization," a Wall Street financier said.) Private ownership of gold coins was forbidden although that law was impossible to enforce totally.

The New Deal attempted to halt the dispossession of farmers by establishing the Farm Credit Administration (FCA). The FCA refinanced mortgages for farmers who had missed payments. Another agency, the Home Owners' Loan Corporation, pro-vided money for town and city dwellers who were in danger of losing their homes.

Helping the Helpless   Nothing better illustrated the contrast between Hoover's paralysis and Roosevelt's flexibility than the establishment of the Federal Emergency Relief Administration (FERA). Whereas Hoover had resisted federal relief measures on ideological grounds, the FERA quickly distributed $500 million to states so that they could save or revive their exhausted programs for helping the desperately poor. The agency was headed by Harry Hopkins, an Iowan become New York social worker with a cigarette ever dangling from his lip and a fedora pushed back on his head.

Hopkins disliked handouts. He believed that people who were capable of work-ing should be required to work in return for government assistance. It did not mat-ter to him that the jobs they did were not particularly useful. His point was that government-funded jobs should not only get money into the hands of those who needed it to get by but also provide relief in a way that workers knew they had earned it. The aversion to taking charity permeated American society up to the level of big businessmen looting the treasury down to the level of wretched who could not eat without a handout.

Hopkins soon discovered that the depression had progressed so far that money had to be gotten out into the country more quickly than jobs earning something could be invented. Putting his belief in work for pay into a desk drawer, he and FERA put up with extensive boondoggling and bureaucratic waste. FDR was pleased. He worried less about moral principles than he did about politics. FERA created hope where there had been despair and increased the popularity of the president and the New Deal. Hopkins was so efficient Roosevelt soon made him one of his closest advisors. In time, he would pick the one-time social worker tramping New York sidewalks to be his point man in secret discussions with Winston Churchill and Joseph Stalin.

Alphabet Soup: CCC, CWA, WPA New federal bureaucracies (and speaking in initials) were the order of the day. With an initial appropriation of $500 million, the Civilian Conservation Corps (CCC) employed 274,375 young men between the ages of 17 and 25 in 1,300 camps. By 1935, CCC workers numbered 502,000 in 2,514 camps. Before the corps was phased out, 2.9 million people served in it. About 10 percent of them were African American, almost equal to the proportion of blacks in the population.

Signed on for six-month enlistments and organized into crews, CCC workers reforested land that had been raped by cut-and-run lumbermen and undertook other conservation projects in national parks and forests. The CCC built 46,854 bridges, 318,076 small check dams, 3,116 fire lookouts, 87,500 miles of fence, and 33,087 miles of terracing to reduce soil erosion.

Workers were paid $30 a month of which they were required to send $22–$25 home to their families. The CCC provided bed and board and the satisfaction of earning their keep and helping their families: The CCC was one of the New Deal's most popular programs both because of its achievements—visitors to National Forests and National Parks today still hike on CCC-built trails and sleep in CCC shelters—and because it provided city boys an opportunity to breathe fresh air in the woods and mountains. Some critics sniped at its quasimilitary discipline (the army ran the program), but few paid attention to them.

The Civil Works Administration (CWA), which Harry Hopkins took over in November 1933, put 4 million unemployed to work within a few months. The CWA built roads, constructed public buildings—many post offices, city halls, and recreational facilities still in use today—and taught in bankrupt school systems. When the CWA spent more than $1 billion in five months, FDR shuddered and called a halt to the program. But private investors would not or could not take up the slack, and the unemployment rate threatened to rise again. In May 1935, the president returned to Congress to establish the Works Progress Administration (WPA) and called on Harry Hopkins to run it.

The WPA broadened the CWA's program. In addition to construction, the agency hired artists to paint murals in public buildings and organized actors into troupes that brought theater to people who never had seen a play. WPA photographers created a treasury of Americana, taking 77,000 pictures. The Writer's Program, with John Cheever as editor and other soon to be distinguished contributors such as Saul Bellow, Ralph Ellison, and Richard Wright, as well as hundreds of writers of no fame who, nevertheless, liked to eat, wrote guidebooks to each of the 48 states. Several of them are still regarded as models of the genre. In the South, the WPA dispatched workers to collect the reminiscences of old folks who remembered having been slaves. There were not many still alive, but ten years down the line there would have been none. The "Slave Narratives" were and are a precious historical treasure. By 1943, when the WPA was liquidated, it had spent more than $11 billion and employed 8.5 million people. The National Youth Administration, part of the WPA, provided jobs for 2 million high school and college students.

The NRA

The New Deal's relief programs were successful. Direct benefits reached only a fraction of the country's hardship cases, but they were usually the worst off. Moreover, the government's mere willingness to act was a morale booster. To many New Dealers, however, relief was just a stopgap. Fermenting with ideas, dozens of men—only two women, Eleanor Roosevelt and Secretary of Labor Frances Perkins, had access to FDR—wanted to put the government to work stimulating and shaping economic recovery. In this, they were less effective.

The National Recovery Administration (NRA) was a bold and controversial attempt to bring order and prosperity to the shattered economy. It was headed by General Hugh Johnson, something of a blowhard but also an inexhaustible organizer and cheerleader. A one-time Bull Moose Progressive, he believed zealously, like Theodore Roosevelt, that the economy should be *ordered*.

Johnson supervised the preparation of codes for each basic industry and, before long, some less-than-basic industries, too. NRA codes set minimum standards of quality for products and services, fair prices at which they were to be sold, and the wages, hours, and conditions under which employees worked. Section 7(a) of the act creating the NRA was pathbreaking in the area of labor relations: It required companies that signed the codes that benefited them in numerous ways to bargain collectively with their workers through labor unions when a majority of their employees selected a union.

The NRA was designed to eliminate waste, inefficiency, and, most of all, destructive competition—the goal of industrial consolidators since John D. Rockefeller. In making the federal government the referee among competing companies and between employers and employees, the NRA was the legatee of Theodore Roosevelt's New Nationalism and the policies of the Wilson administration during World War I. The differences were that it was peacetime; the NRA codes were compulsory; and they were intended to be permanent. A business was bound to its industry's code not by Herbert Hoover's moral suasion, but by the force of law.

Critics of the NRA, including some within the New Deal, likened it to the fascist system that had been created in Italy by Benito Mussolini after 1922. The criticism was not out in left field, but it was unfair. Mussolini suppressed free labor unions; the NRA gave them a role in making industrial policy.

More to the point was the criticism that Blue Eagle functionaries (the NRA's symbol was a stylized blue eagle) sometimes went ridiculously far in their codes. Hugh Johnson was code crazy; he wanted to regiment peripheral and even trivial businesses. There was a code for the burlesque "industry" that specified how many strippers were to undress per performance, what vestments they were to discard, and the quality of the tassels and G-strings. They still had most at the end of the night. Had prostitution been legal in the United States, Johnson would have risen to even greater heights.

Such extremes were made possible by the enthusiasm, almost a frenzy, with which, at first, Americans took to the NRA. Rooted on by the bombastic Johnson, 200,000 people marched in an NRA parade in New York carrying banners emblazoned with the NRA motto, "We Do Our Part." The Blue Eagle was painted on factory walls, pasted on shop windows, and adopted as a motif by university marching bands.

Briefly, Hugh Johnson seemed as popular as Roosevelt himself. He was certainly more conspicuous. Johnson stormed noisily about the country, publicly

© Bettmann/Corbis

For a year, popular enthusiasm for the NRA bordered on the hysterical. NRA "happenings" like this one—"bathing beauties" submitting to being stenciled with the NRA logo, the "Blue Eagle" so that when they tanned in the sun, they would have a pale eagle to show off— were staged by NRA propagandists, but the popular enthusiasm for the program was genuine. NRA head Hugh Johnson was a promoter without equal—an evangelist. For a year, the NRA seemed to many a panacea that would put an end to "Old Man Depression." Then, however, Johnson's excesses, the president's second thoughts, and— most important—the Supreme Court's ruling it was unconstitutional, killed the NRA and left few mourners.

castigating as "chiselers" businessmen who did not meekly fall into line. Apparently, he inherited his style from his feisty mother. At an NRA rally in Tulsa, she said that "people had better obey the NRA because my son will enforce it like lightning, and you can never tell when lightning will strike."

FAILURES AND SUCCESSES

The New Deal suffered serious setbacks in the Supreme Court. The justices were quite conservative: Seven of the nine justices had been appointed by the Republican presidents Taft, Harding, Coolidge, and Hoover. The "nine old men," as FDR was to denounce them, had no sympathy for the New Deal's fundamental reforms of the relationship between government and the economy. They declared a law regulating railroad finances and the NRA unconstitutional in 1935 and the Agricultural Adjustment Act—the foundation of FDR's farm policy—invalid in 1936.

Death of the Blue Eagle   The NRA was killed by a suit brought by a small company that slaughtered chickens for the kosher kitchens of observant Jews. The Schechter brothers, owners of the company, argued that the sanitary standards mandated by the NRA were incompatible with the ritual requirements of kosher slaughter and that the code represented unjustifiable federal interference in intrastate commerce. (Their business was almost entirely within New York state.) In 1935, the Supreme Court ruled unanimously that the Schechters were right: The NRA was unconstitutional.

There was little fuss. Popular enthusiasm for the NRA had cooled. Although he did not say so publicly, FDR was not displeased to see the Blue Eagle (and Hugh Johnson!) go. Congress moved promptly after the Court's decision to salvage the one provision of the NRA that still commanded widespread support, Section 7(a). In the Wagner Labor Relations Act of 1935, Congress reinstated the requirement that employers recognize and negotiate with labor unions that had the support of a majority of the company's employees. The Wagner Act went further than the NRA by setting up the National Labor Relations Board to investigate unfair labor practices and to issue cease and desist orders to employers found guilty of them.

Farm Policy   Another salvage operation preserved parts of the Agricultural Adjustment Act. Enacted during the Hundred Days, the Agricultural Adjustment Act established the Agricultural Adjustment Administration (AAA) to enforce the principle of parity, for which farmers' organizations had agitated throughout the 1920s.

In effect, parity meant increasing farm income so that it provided farm families the same standard of living they had enjoyed during the prosperous years of 1909 to 1914. This meant raising the prices at which farmers sold the crops and the livestock they raised. The AAA accomplished this by restricting farm production. Growers of wheat, corn, cotton, tobacco, rice, and hogs were paid government subsidies to take some of their land out of production. The costs of this expensive program ($100 million was paid to cotton farmers in one year) were borne by a tax on

Café Society

Very rich Americans lost plenty of paper wealth in the stock market crash, but they were still plenty rich. During the first years of the New Deal, however, with popular opinion hostile to rather than awed by "high society," the day of old-style conspicuous consumption seemed to be gone forever. By 1935, a new kind of social whirl had emerged.

"Café society" centered around posh former speakeasies that had come above ground as restaurants and nightclubs. There one sat, dined on mediocre over-priced food, chatted, and danced, seeing and being seen. In New York City, the capital of café society, the chic clubs were El Morocco, the Stork Club, and "21."

Before long, ordinary Americans were as dazzled by the "rich, young, and beautiful" café set as they had been by yachts, fifty-room Newport "cottages," and private railroad cars. Whom Alfred Gwynne Vanderbilt was dating was breathlessly reported in nationally syndicated "society columns" by hangers-on like Walter Winchell and "Cholly Knickerbocker." Lowly as their origins were, they were welcome in café society because they were publicists. It was now *news* if the heiress to a coal and iron fortune dropped in at El Morocco and danced the rhumba with her "agile husband." It was even better news when agile hubbies danced the rhumba with willowy Brazilian beauties who were not their wives.

Debutantes (or debs), young women who were "coming out" when in fact they had been lounging around night clubs since they were 15, were the queens of café society. The leading deb of 1937 was Gloria "Mimi" Baker, whose mother replied to someone who called her a decadent aristocrat: "Why Mimi is the most democratic person, bar none, I've ever

processors—millers, refiners, butchers, and packagers—which were, of course, passed on to consumers in higher food, clothing, and tobacco prices.

Because the 1933 crop was already in the ground when the AAA was enacted, some of it was ordered destroyed. "Kill every third pig and plow every third row under," Secretary of Agriculture Henry A. Wallace said. People were repelled by the slaughter of 6 million hogs and 220,000 pregnant sows. Others wondered why food was being destroyed when millions were hungry. (Actually, 100 million pounds of the prematurely harvested pork was diverted to relief agencies and charities.) Economically, however, the AAA worked; the income of hog growers began to rise immediately.

Fully a quarter of the 1933 cotton crop was plowed under and the fields left fallow. Unfortunately, because cotton farmers tended those fields still under cultivation more intensely, production actually rose in 1933. It took two years for cotton (and wheat and corn) prices to rise by 50 percent.

A less desirable consequence of the AAA was to throw people off the land. Landlords dispossessed tenant farmers in order to collect the subsidies fallow land would earn without the headaches of actual farming. Between 1932 and 1935, 3 million American farmers lost their livelihood. Most of them were dirt-poor black and white tenants in the South.

known." Café society actually was democratic in ways that the rich of the Roaring
Twenties or Gilded Age could not have
imagined. Because status was based on
beauty, on what passed for wit (there
was little of it), and simply on being well
known, the café set freely admitted movie
stars, athletes, and celebrated musicians.
International "playboys" jumped at the
opportunity to do more than be photographed at night clubs they could not afford, and therein lay the great morality
play of the 1930s.

Barbara Hutton, who had to endure
torturous diets to keep her weight down,
was sole heiress to $45 million made in
very small increments in the five-and-tens
of F. W. Woolworth. In 1933, she married
Alexis Mdivani, who claimed to be a
Russian prince dispossessed of his ancestral holdings by the communists. Immediately after the couple exchanged vows,
Mdivani began to make Barbara miserable, railing day and night at her weight
problem. Drawing on the $1 million that

Barbara's father had given him as a wedding present, the prince spent much of his
time with other women. In 1935, Barbara
won Mdivani's consent to a divorce by
paying him $2 million more.

She then married a Danish count, Kurt
von Haugwitz-Reventlow. Hutton showered the playboy with gifts, including a
$4.5 million mansion in London. They
were divorced in 1937. The same photographers who snapped pictures of laugh-
ing, dancing debutantes at the Stork Club
rushed to get shots of tearful Barbara
Hutton, the "poor little rich girl."

Some who pored over the pathetic pictures pretended sympathy. "She's made
mistakes," wrote columnist Adela Rogers
St. Johns, "been a silly, wild, foolish girl,
given in to temptations—but she's still our
own ... an American girl fighting alone
across the sea." Others did not disguise
the pleasure they took in her self-inflicted
misery. "Why do they hate me?" Barbara
asked. "There are other girls as rich, richer,
almost as rich."

Electricity: REA and TVA

New Dealers were devoted to the AAA. Its rejection by the
Supreme Court was a far more serious blow than the death
of the Blue Eagle. The Democrats in Congress salvaged what
they could. In the Soil Conservation and Domestic Allotment Act (1936), parity
and limitation of production were restored under the guise of conserving soil.

More worrying was the fear that, piece by piece, the Supreme Court would dismantle the entire New Deal. Roosevelt's supporters were particularly worried about
the Tennessee Valley Authority (TVA), created in 1933, and the Rural Electrification
Administration (REA) of 1935. Old Bull Moose Progressives, now New Dealers, had
long dreamed—they could do little but dream during the conservative 1920s—of
such exercises in government planning that would bring benefits to impoverished
people whom private enterprise ignored.

Cities and towns were electrified by 1933, but not much of the countryside.
Power companies could reach tens of thousands of paying customers by stringing
a mile of wire in urban areas, but they could not afford to incur the same fixed
costs in rural areas where there might be a dozen houses (or none at all) on a mile
of road. The REA loaned the entire cost of electrifying the countryside to power
companies (favoring publicly owned companies over private companies when there

was a choice) at just 3 percent interest payable over twenty years. At such rates, even twelve households on a mile of wire paying electric bills returned a profit.

The REA was a nationwide program. Farms in rural New England were no more likely to be electrified in 1933 than ranches in Wyoming. (When Calvin Coolidge was sworn in as president at his father's home in Vermont in 1923, it was by the light of a kerosene lantern.) The TVA was regional, limited to the banks of the Tennessee River that rises in Virginia, loops through Tennessee and northern Alabama, and flows north through Kentucky to the Ohio River. The project encompassed much more than electric lights and toasters. It promised a systematic, comprehensive, far-reaching economic reconstruction of one of the poorest regions in America: jobs in a massive construction project, electrification, flood control (the Tennessee was a killer river), manufacturing where there was none, and social planning.

The TVA was the longtime darling of George Norris, a Republican senator from Nebraska (an Independent in 1936). Norris had fastened on southern Appalachia as a laboratory for an unprecedented experiment in economic and social planning. The Tennessee River Valley was so poor much of its length that it would be impossible for the government to make things worse than they were.

The TVA was to construct a series of dams both to control the annual floods and to generate electricity. Appalachia's "hillbillies," plagued by poor health and ignorance, would enjoy the comforts of the twentieth century. The electricity would power factories, especially for the manufacture of fertilizers, which would provide jobs for people who literally lived hand to mouth. Although not much was made of it during the 1930s, the lakes behind the dams on the river would be recreational centers.

Norris also argued that by generating electricity itself, the government would be able to determine the fairness of the prices private companies elsewhere charged their customers. Until the 1930s, the actual cost of generating electrical power was a mystery outside of the industry.

During the 1920s, Henry Ford had tried to buy key sites on the Tennessee River from the government, notably Muscle Shoals, a tumultuous rapids, in order to build a privately owned power plant. Norris fought Ford off in Congress, arguing that the Tennessee Valley provided too good a testing ground for regional planning to give it to one of the country's richest men so that he could get richer. Had the corrupt government giveaway of its oil reserves at Teapot Dome not been exposed during the debate over the Tennessee Valley, Ford would likely have gotten Muscle Shoals. However, Norris and his allies were unable to implement government development of the region until Roosevelt's election.

"Creeping Socialism"   Fiscal conservatives were appalled by the astronomical expenditures of the New Deal. With a good-humored wit he should have exhibited when he was president, Herbert Hoover spoke of the decimal point in the government's debts "wandering around among the regimented ciphers trying to find some of the old places it used to know."

Republicans and some southern Democrats assailed REA and the TVA as socialistic. Big business, which had been happy enough with FDR's banking reforms and the NRA, funded a political offensive against New Deal programs that put the government into the production and distribution of electrical power. As early as

1934, bankers and big businessmen founded the American Liberty League, accusing Roosevelt of trying to destroy free enterprise and set up a socialist dictatorship.

Most Liberty Leaguers were Coolidge-Mellon Republicans, but they were joined by a few prominent Democrats, including two of the party's presidential nominees, John W. Davis and Alfred E. Smith. Davis was a corporation lawyer; he found the Liberty League Company familiar. Smith, however, who had tapped FDR to be his successor as governor of New York, had been a reformer during the 1910s and 1920s. Bitter that Roosevelt's nomination in 1932 ended his political career before he was 60, he had fallen in with bankers and businessmen of whom he had once been critical.

Combating the Liberty Leaguers was like swatting flies for Roosevelt. Ordinary Americans generally remained wary of big businessmen throughout the 1930s. FDR labeled the Leaguers "economic royalists." They never had a popular following.

The Supreme Court was another matter, a serious threat to the New Deal. Making one of his rare political miscalculations, Roosevelt proposed saving the New Deal by adding to the Court new justices who would endorse his reforms. The reaction to the "court packing" plan was almost universally hostile. The New Deal remained popular, but Roosevelt's scheme smelled of tampering with the Constitution to win a political contest. Roosevelt quickly retreated. The crisis passed when the Court approved several New Deal reforms that had been thought vulnerable. Then Father Time lent a hand; beginning in 1937, retirements and deaths enabled FDR to create a pro-New Deal majority on the Court without tampering with it size. When Roosevelt died in 1945, eight of the nine justices were his appointees.

POPULIST SPELLBINDERS

FDR made his court-packing proposal in 1937. He may have been overconfident because he had won reelection so easily in 1936, carrying every state except Maine and Vermont. Oddly enough, none of his political strategists, including the canny Postmaster General James A. Farley, anticipated a landslide until well along in the campaign. They were seriously worried that FDR was going to lose.

The problem was a trio of charismatic critics of the president who built up large personal followings among the people on whose votes FDR counted. If the three joined forces—and the possibility was discussed—the third party they formed would not itself win the election, but it might well hand the presidency back to the Republicans.

Father Coughlin   Charles E. Coughlin, a Catholic priest in suburban Detroit, had broadcast a weekly religious program on the radio since 1926. With a mellow baritone voice and a hint of Scots in his accent (he was born and raised in Canada) Coughlin had a large Catholic audience even before the depression turned his interests toward politics. He condemned Hoover and endorsed FDR in 1932. The next year, he told his listeners that "the New Deal is Christ's deal."

Within a year, however, Coughlin had soured on Roosevelt's financial policy. Like many populists before and since, Father Coughlin believed that the manipulation of the money supply by sinister "international bankers" underlay the economic suffering of the common people and a good deal more that was wrong with the world. The argument has always been so technical that it can attract a mass following only because, implicitly or explicitly, it has drawn on a deeply rooted prejudice: anti-Semitism. *International bankers* meant the Rothschild family, which was code for "the Jews." By the end of 1934, inveighing against the Federal Reserve System, Coughlin had an estimated weekly audience of 10 million.

What worried the Democratic party's vote counter, Jim Farley, himself Catholic, was that most of Coughlin's devotees were big city Roman Catholics in the northeastern and midwestern industrial states with big blocs of electoral votes. The Democrats needed to win those states.

Dr. Townsend

Dr. Francis E. Townsend of California stumbled on a panacea—a cure-all—that attracted millions of people. Townsend had been a rather mild retired physician, a different type than the high-voltage Coughlin, and his following was drawn from entirely different social groups. The core of Townsend's support—1.5 million members of 7,000 Townsend Clubs by 1936—were elderly people, mostly Protestant, and mostly middle class, or formerly middle class.

The Townsend plan, which the doctor expounded tirelessly at rallies and on radio, was an old age pension plan that, Townsend argued, would quickly end the depression and then sustain prosperity. Unlike Coughlin's convoluted vision of reality, the Townsend plan was stunningly simple. The federal government would pay a monthly pension of $200—a great deal of money in the 1930s—to every person over 60 years of age, with two conditions attached.

First, the pensioners would be forbidden to hold jobs. Second, they were obligated to spend every cent of their $200 within the month they received it. Thus, Townsend said, his plan would not only provide security for the elderly, it would also reinvigorate the economy, creating jobs for young men and women making the things and performing the services that the old folks were buying.

Economists shook their heads. The Townsend plan was not financially plausible; it could not be funded and it would not work anyway. When FDR ignored Townsend, the doctor retaliated. He condemned the president and began discussing the possibility of a third party with disciples of Father Coughlin and agents of a third spellbinder who was already a political power among yet another social group: poor and modestly fixed white southerners.

The Kingfish

Huey P. Long grew up among struggling white farmers in northern Louisiana. He educated himself as a lawyer and clawed his way up in state politics as a colorful populistic sweating stump orator baiting the railroad and oil industry elites who ran the state. Unlike most southern demagogues, Long avoided race baiting. He never questioned segregation laws—to have done so in the South was political death—but he refused to fall back on "nigger baiting" to win votes. Indeed, Long won the votes of many of the Louisiana blacks (mostly in New Orleans) who had held onto the franchise. Unlike other southern populists, Long improved social services for African Americans as well as for white people.

As governor of Louisiana between 1928 and 1932, Long built roads and hospitals, provided free textbooks and lunches for schoolchildren, benefits almost unknown elsewhere in the South and not universal in the North. He was a clown; he called himself "the Kingfish" after a character on the popular radio program *Amos 'n' Andy*. Picking up a megaphone, he led cheers at Louisiana State University football games (and personally fired the football coach when LSU lost a game Huey thought should have been won).

He was also ruthless. He bribed and even strong-armed state legislators who threatened to vote against him. He was boorish, a drunk who ate off other people's plates at restaurants and summoned his aides at four o'clock in the morning. He was neurotic: He recoiled violently when people touched him without warning, and he spent most nights in hotels well guarded by the state police, changing his address often and suddenly. (It would be going too far to call him paranoid: Some of his enemies called openly for his assassination and organized a kind of SWAT team complete with machine guns and spoke of storming the state capital.)

He was popular not only in Louisiana but also throughout the South and Midwest, and he intended to run against FDR in 1936 on a platform called "Share the Wealth" or "Every Man a King." Long said he would confiscate, through taxation, every dollar of individual annual incomes in excess of $1 million. To people buying food on credit, it was an appealing program.

FDR had good reason to fear Long's presidential candidacy. He would likely carry at least some of the southern states that the Democrats assumed were in their column. If Townsend and Coughlin supported him, which they were likely to do, he might win over enough Democratic voters outside the South to give other electoral votes to the Republicans.

Co-optation and Murder   Roosevelt's response to the threat of the three spellbinders was to co-opt them. He undercut Coughlin's monetary monomania by making moderate reforms. To steal Townsend's thunder, he sponsored the Social Security Act of 1935. The pensions it paid the elderly were peanuts compared to the $200 per month the Townsendites wanted. But the monthly social security checks that were in the mail before the election were real and, when all but the most zealous Townsendites calmed down, the doctor's promises seemed as unlikely as the promise of winning a lottery. Thanks to FDR and the New Deal, for the first time the United States government assumed responsibility for helping people too old to work.

In 1935, to co-opt Huey Long's Share the Wealth program, Roosevelt and Congress revised the income tax law. The rates paid by the well-to-do were radically increased, up to a much publicized 90 percent for those with the highest incomes. The 90 percent rate was largely show: Loopholes in the complex tax law meant that only a handful of people ever paid anything approaching that percentage, but it sounded as if it were as confiscatory as Long's proposals.

In the end, it was a historical accident that ensured FDR's landslide victory in 1936. In September 1935, Huey Long was shot down in the Louisiana Capitol by a young man who hated him, not for political but for personal reasons. Long had ruined the career of a member of his family. (The assassin died immediately; half a dozen Long bodyguards emptied their revolvers into his body.)

The Republican candidate in 1936 was Governor Alf Landon of Kansas. He was no Liberty Leaguer but a personally likable and moderately progressive midwesterner. His assignment, to defeat FDR, was impossible. Straining to come up with an issue on which to differ with the president, Landon unwisely settled on social security pensions, calling them an "unjust, unworkable, and a cruel hoax." Social security was popular. Support for the Townsend plan evaporated. Father Coughlin continued to have a following, although it declined in size. The "radio priest" became increasingly and more openly anti-Semitic, praising Adolf Hitler and the Nazis. When World War II began, his bishop (who had previously encouraged Coughlin) took him off the radio.

THE LEGACY OF THE NEW DEAL

Even before the 1936 election, the character of the New Deal underwent a significant change. In 1933, FDR thought of his program as a new deal for everyone. He believed, with some justification, that the Hundred Days legislation saved American capitalism. He felt betrayed when big business, instead of recognizing his services, vilified him.

In 1935, threatened by the populist spellbinders and encouraged by Eleanor, FDR accepted his role as the president of the people on the bottom. In his break with "the classes" and embrace of "the masses," FDR made the New Deal era a period of American history ranking in significance with the age of the War for Independence and the era of the Civil War.

Black Democrats   If Roosevelt emphasized the problems of the disadvantaged after 1936, he deftly avoided taking up the unique disadvantages African Americans suffered because of the color line. This was a conscious political decision. FDR was a lifelong Democrat. In national elections, the Democratic party depended on the Solid South, the former slave states that, with rare exception, sent solidly Democratic delegations to Congress and delivered all their electoral votes to the Democratic party.

The southern Democratic party was racist, unabashedly committed to white supremacy and Jim Crow segregation. Even after many southern congressmen abandoned the New Deal after 1936, Roosevelt concluded that he dare not attack racial discrimination in any significant way. He refused even to endorse a federal anti-lynching bill that a majority of southerners supported; and he accepted segregation by race in work gangs on federal building projects like the TVA. Roosevelt did, however, resist Southern Democratic demands that African Americans working for the government be paid less than whites doing the same jobs.

Nevertheless, New Deal programs benefited African Americans simply because a large majority of them were poor. Black people moved into more than a third of new housing units constructed by the federal government and they shared proportionately in relief and public works projects. As a result, there was a revolution in African American voting patterns. In 1932, about 75 percent of black voters were loyal Republicans. They still thought of the GOP as the party of Lincoln and emancipation and of Republican congressmen as the chief supporters of anti-lynching bills. The only African American congressman in 1932 was a Republican, Oscar De Priest of Chicago.

African Americans who migrated from the South to northern states found there were no legal obstacles to exercising the right to vote. Just as significant, where the Democratic party had been the party of white supremacy in the South (and remained so until late in the twentieth century), to northern blacks the Democratic party as the party of the New Deal and Democratic politicians, not Republicans, courted them. Within a few years, the black vote converted from, overwhelmingly, the "party of Lincoln" to, overwhelmingly, the "party of FDR."

© UPI-Bettmann/Corbis

By 1936, more than 75 percent of African American voters were Democrats. Even De Priest was defeated by a black New Dealer—and the trend continued for 40 years until blacks were more than 90 percent Democratic.

The Growth of the Unions

During the first years of the New Deal, Roosevelt was wary of organized labor. Left to his personal predilections, he would have stayed neutral in labor disputes. However, when militant unionists like John L. Lewis of the coal miners (a lifelong Republican) and Sidney Hillman and David Dubinsky of the large needle-trades unions made it clear they would throw their influence behind the president only in return for administration support, Roosevelt gave in. Lewis raised $1 million for the president's 1936 election campaign, insisting that Roosevelt be photographed accepting the check from him. Within a month, the photograph was reproduced on thousands of posters with the message: "The President Wants You to Join the Union."

FDR disliked Lewis—a lot of people did—but he gave Sidney Hillman unlimited access to him. He valued Hillman's advice and counted on him to keep organized labor friendly. FDR's stock answer to questions of policy in which the unions had an interest was: "Clear it with Sidney."

Lewis, Dubinsky, and Hillman were leaders of the Committee on Industrial Organization which, after the Wagner Act of 1935, guaranteed employees the right to be represented by unions and launched massive organizing campaigns in basic industries: coal, steel, rubber, electricity, automobiles. At first a faction within the American Federation of Labor, the CIO, left the AFL in 1937 renaming itself the Congress of Industrial Organizations (CIO).

The CIO's organizational campaigns won members in astonishing numbers. The parent organization of the United Steel Workers was founded in 1936. By May 1937, it had 325,000 members. The United States Steel Corporation, the nerve center of anti-unionism in the industry, recognized the union as bargaining agent without a strike.

The United Automobile Workers enlisted 370,000 members in a little more than a year. The story was similar among workers in the rubber, glass, lumber, aluminum, electrical products, coal mining, the needle trades, and even textiles. "The union" came to have a mystical significance in the lives of many workers. Workers fought for the right to wear union buttons on the job. The union card became a certificate of honor. Old hymns were reworded to promote the cause. Professional singers like Woody Guthrie, Pete Seeger, and Burl Ives lent their talents to organizing campaigns. In 1933, fewer than 3 million American workers belonged to a union. In 1940, 8.5 million did; in 1941, 10.5 million.

Labor Wars   Not every employer responded so sensibly to its unionized employees as United States Steel did. Tom Girdler of Republic Steel called the CIO "irresponsible, racketeering, violent, communistic" and threatened to crush the union with armed force. In this heated atmosphere occurred the "Memorial Day Massacre" of 1937, so called because Chicago police attacked a crowd of union members, killing ten and injuring about a hundred.

Although there was no personal violence and little destruction of property, labor's "sit down" strikes worried even pro-union politicians because they involved the seizure of property. The first took place in January 1937 during a strike by 150,000 General Motors (GM) employees. Most of the United Automobile Workers walked out as usual. At GM's plant in Flint, Michigan, however, they stayed in the factory; they "sat down." Family members and sympathizers brought food and clothing. The workers policed themselves. No doubt recalling what the attack on the Bonus Boys did to Herbert Hoover's reputation, FDR, through Michigan governor Frank Murphy, mediated the dispute. After forty-four days, the sit-down strikers emerged from the factory happy with the settlement Murphy brokered.

Henry Ford eventually came to terms with the United Automobile Workers (UAW) but, at first, he vowed, like Girdler, to fight unionization with force. He employed a small army of toughs from the Detroit underworld and fortified his factories with tear gas, machine guns, and grenades. At the "Battle of the Overpass" in Detroit, Ford "goons" (as anti-union strong-arms were called) beat organizer Walter Reuther and other UAW officials until they were insensible. Violence, including numerous murders, was so common in the coal fields of Harlan County, Kentucky, that the area became known in the press as "Bloody Harlan."

The Bottom Line   The greatest achievement of the New Deal was to ease the economic hardships suffered by millions of Americans and, in doing so, to preserve their confidence in American institutions.

In its relief measures, particularly those agencies that put jobless people to work, Roosevelt's administration was a resounding success.

As a formula for economic recovery, the New Deal failed. When unemployment dropped to 7.5 million early in 1937 and other economic indicators looked bright, Roosevelt began to dismantle many New Deal programs. The result was renewed collapse, a depression within a depression. Conditions in 1937 never sunk to the levels of 1930–1933. But the recession of 1937 was painful evidence that for all their flexibility, experimentation, and spending, the New Dealers had not unlocked the secret of maintaining prosperity during peacetime. Only when preparations for another world war led to massive purchases of American goods from abroad (and to rearmament at home) did the Great Depression end. By 1939, the economy was on the upswing. By 1940, with Europe at war, the Great Depression was history.

Through such programs as support for agricultural prices, rural electrification, Social Security, insurance of bank deposits, protection of labor unions, and strict controls over the economy, the federal government came to play a part in people's daily lives such as had been inconceivable before 1933. In the TVA, the government became an actual producer of electrical power and commodities such as fertilizers. It was not socialism, as conservative critics of the New Deal cried, but in an American context it was something of a revolution.

Although unavoidable, the most dubious side effect of the new system was the extraordinary growth in the size of government. Extensive government programs required huge bureaucracies to carry them out. The number of federal employees rose from 600,000 in 1930 to a million in 1940. In that bureaucracies are ultimately concerned with their own well-being above all else and inevitably divert funds meant for their mission to pay benefits to bureaucrats (not to mention the aggravations of dealing with bureaucracies), the New Deal contributed to American life, along with its many blessings, a phenomenon that has, at one time or another, driven every American to near distraction.

A Political Revolution

Between 1896 and 1933, the Republican party was the nation's majority party. The Great Depression and New Deal changed that. FDR and Jim Farley forged a new majority, an alliance of southern whites, northern and western liberals, blue-collar workers (particularly union members and urban white ethnics), and African Americans, with substantial support from western farmers. The New Deal alliance was not without problems. Beginning in 1937, some southern Democrats who disapproved of even the New Deal's minimal concessions to blacks and the prominence in Washington of "Yankee liberals," often voted with Republicans against New Deal measures.

Still, grass-roots support for the New Deal among southern whites prevented the crack from becoming a split during FDR's presidency. The Democratic majority forged during the 1930s lasted for half a century. During the fifty years between 1930 and 1980, a Republican lived in the White House only eighteen years. During the same fifty years, Republicans had a majority in the Senate only six years and in the House of Representatives only four. Between 1930 and 1997, two-thirds of a century, the Republican party simultaneously controlled the presidency, Senate, and House for just two years, 1953 to 1955.

42

GOING TO WAR AGAIN
America and the World 1933–1942

*I ask that the Congress declare that since the unprovoked
and dastardly attack by Japan on Sunday, December
seventh, a state of war has existed between the United
States and the Japanese Empire.*

—Franklin D. Roosevelt

In 1933, the year Franklin D. Roosevelt became president, Adolf Hitler of the
extreme right National Socialist or Nazi party was named chancellor in Germany.
The character and political values of the two men could hardly have differed
more. The cultivated patrician Roosevelt was a liberal, dedicated to democracy,
personally tolerant. He kept his emotions to himself, even in the company of longtime aides. Hitler had risen from the lower middle class. He was socially awkward,
his manners crude. He was contemptuous of tradition but allowed followers to surround him with lunatic ancient teutonic symbolism. He despised democracy and the
"bourgeois freedoms." He was a vicious anti-Semite and occasionally flew into
frightening rages.

Both men were virtuosos in their use of modern mass communication. Roosevelt
was at his best as a voice on the radio. In what he called his "Fireside Chats," evening radio broadcasts from the White House, he spoke as if he was indeed a respected
old uncle seated in an easy chair in front of a fireplace conversing with the family.
Hitler's medium was the massive rally of tens of thousands of roaring devotees listening to their *Führer,* their leader, through loudspeakers which, in fact, the Nazis hung
from buildings in city centers.

Hitler knew that, in time, his Germany would clash with the United States. In
his rise to power, he had excoriated America as a partner of Britain, France, and
Jewish German socialists in forcing the humiliating Treaty of Versailles on
Germany. But there was a lot to be done before that time, just as Roosevelt had
little time for foreign policy in the critical depression years.

Threats from Abroad 1931–1941

1931	1932	1933	1934	1935	1936	1937	1938	1939	1940	1941

1931 Japan seizes Manchuria; Stimson Doctrine

1932 Japan attacks Shanghai

1933 Nazis in power in Germany; Recognition of USSR

1934–1936 Nye Committee investigations

1935 Italy invades Ethiopia; *Road to War* published

1935–1937 Neutrality Acts

1937 Japanese offensive in China

1938 Anschluss; Munich Agreement

War in Europe; Lend–lease 1939

Fall of France; Battle of Britain; FDR elected to third term 1940

Germany invades Russia; Pearl Harbor 1941

NEW DEAL FOREIGN POLICY

Like Woodrow Wilson, Roosevelt passed over professional diplomats in picking a secretary of state. He appointed Tennessee Senator Cordell Hull, whose courtly bearing belied his log cabin origins. Hull and Roosevelt were generally content to follow the foreign policy guidelines charted by Hoover and his distinguished secretary of state, Henry L. Stimson. Where they departed from them, their purpose was to further the New Deal's program for economic recovery at home.

The Good Neighbor Policy   Roosevelt and Hull even adopted Hoover's phrase, "good neighbor," to describe the changed role of the United States in Latin America Hoover and Stimson inaugurated. No longer would big brother intervene militarily in the Caribbean and Central America or even strongarm Latin American republics to further American financial interests. The Colossus of the North was now a good neighbor. Roosevelt withdrew U.S. marines from Nicaragua, the Dominican Republic, and Haiti. Like Hoover, he refused to intervene in Cuba despite the chronic civil conflict in the island and the Platt Amendment's open invitation to send in troops.

When a military coup led by Fulgencio Batista stabilized Cuba in 1934, Hull formally renounced the Platt Amendment. Although concerned about the safety of considerable American investments in the "banana republics" of Central America and in the West Indies, Roosevelt never seriously considered resuming the interventionist policy his cousin Theodore had inaugurated and even Wilson adopted. The biggest test for the good neighbor was in 1938 when Mexico nationalized the properties of American oil companies and offered little compensation, Roosevelt was conciliatory and, a few years later, American diplomats worked out a settlement that was acceptable to all but the greediest of the dispossessed oilmen.

The Good Neighbor policy paid dividends that Roosevelt could not have imagined in 1933. When Europe lurched toward war again later in the decade, Nazi Germany made strenuous efforts to secure footholds in the Western Hemisphere. The Germans had no success in the countries ringing the Caribbean. Even the South

The Nazi party's Führer, Adolf Hitler, shortly after he was named chancellor of Germany, with President Paul von Hindenburg at the monument to the great German victory at World War I's battle of Tannenberg. The 86-year-old president held Hitler in contempt, but conservatives like him convinced him that they would keep the Führer and the Nazis on a short leash.

American countries that were cordial toward the Nazis were cautious. During World War II, every nation in the Western Hemisphere except Argentina joined the United States in declaring war on Germany. Only Brazil actually sent troops to Europe, but the point was that if even one South American country, even distant Argentina, had permitted Germany to establish naval and air bases on its soil, it would have inhibited the American contribution to the war effort.

The Stimson Doctrine   Roosevelt's Asian policy also followed paths staked out during the Hoover administration. The challenge in East Asia was to maintain Chinese independence and territorial integrity and free access to the China trade—the Open Door Policy. The obstacle was an increasingly aggressive and expansion-minded Japan. Complicating the problem was the fact that China's Nationalist government, headed by Generalissimo Chiang Kai-shek, was inefficient, riddled with corruption, and controlled only parts of China.

Late in 1931, exploiting Chinese weakness, the Japanese detached the province of Manchuria from China and set up a puppet state called Manchukuo. They dug up the dissolute last emperor of China, then called Henry Pu-yi, and set him up as

Manchukuo's emperor. Hoover's secretary of state, Henry L. Stimson, proposed that the United States retaliate by imposing severe economic sanctions on Japan, refusing to sell to Japan raw materials, particularly oil and iron, that were vital to Japanese industry. That was too aggressive for Hoover. Instead, he announced that the United States would not recognize the legality of any territorial changes resulting from the use of force. Curiously, this toothless policy became known as the Stimson Doctrine.

It was a rap on the knuckles, shrugged off or laughed at by Japanese militarists who were driven by a fanatical sense of national destiny and combated Japanese politicians who opposed them by assassinating them. In 1932, the Japanese army attacked Shanghai, the center of Chinese commerce. In 1937, the Japanese bombed the city, the first massive aerial attack on a civilian population. Roosevelt was disgusted but, preoccupied with an unexpected economic downturn at home, he went no further than Hoover had in 1932. He responded with a scolding.

Promoting Foreign Trade

Where Roosevelt parted ways with Hoover's foreign policy, the impetus was his determination to end the depression. Thus, in May 1933 he scuttled an international conference in London that Hoover had endorsed for the purpose of stabilizing world currencies. Delegates of sixty-four nations had just found their seats when Roosevelt announced that he would not agree to any decisions that ran contrary to his domestic recovery program. He reaffirmed his decision to take the United States off the gold standard, which the conference hoped to restore. The conference collapsed.

In November 1933, Roosevelt formally recognized the Communist regime in the Soviet Union, which four presidents had refused to do. In part, he was facing up to realities. When, ten years earlier, the permanence of Communist party rule in Russia was highly questionable, nonrecognition made sense. By 1933, Joseph Stalin and his henchmen were firmly in control of the country. Every other major power had diplomatic relations with the USSR. Roosevelt also had economic reasons to exchange ambassadors and other diplomats with Moscow. He was persuaded that the backward Soviet Union would be a large market for ailing American manufacturers and agricultural exports.

Promoting foreign trade was also the motive behind Secretary of State Hull's efforts to lower tariff barriers through reciprocity agreements. With a southern Democrat's distaste for high tariffs, Hull negotiated reciprocal trade agreements with twenty-nine countries. He was able to slash the high Republican import duties of the 1920s by as much as half on the products of countries that agreed to reduce their duties on American goods.

Isolationism

Roosevelt and Hull were Wilsonian internationalists. Both had favored American membership in the League of Nations, which was still extant in 1933 although rather a joke. Both believed in preserving peace by collective international cooperation. However, FDR was a politician who counted votes before they were cast. He was not, like Wilson, willing to destroy himself because a cause was righteous. In his public statements, he never wandered far from what he read—almost always accurately—as the mood of the populace.

During the 1930s, the mood of most Americans concerning the rest of the world was isolationist, staying out of Europe's messes. A public opinion poll in 1935 showed that 95 percent of Americans believed that the United States had no vital interests in either Europe or Asia and that they were dead set against a repetition of what they regarded as the big mistake of intervening in the Great War.

Suspicion of Europeans was reinforced in the 1930s by the belief, encouraged by President Hoover, that a European financial crisis was to blame for America's depression or at least, for its severity. Isolationist feelings intensified after 1934 when Senator Gerald Nye, a La Follette Progressive Republican from South Dakota, sponsored an investigation into the role of banks and the munitions industry in involving the United States in World War I. During the hearings of the Munitions Investigating Committee, popularly called the Nye Committee, he claimed that the United States had been manipulated into the war by "merchants of death" led by the giant Du Pont Corporation.

The Nye Committee actually proved little more than the fact that munitions makers made a great deal of money during the war. But journalists, as ever, focused on Nye's more extravagant claims. In 1935, a respected writer on military matters, Walter Millis, published *The Road to War,* which popularized the "merchants of death" explanation of World War I.

Neutrality Policy   Isolationism took on legislative form in several Neutrality Acts passed by Congress between 1935 and 1937. They warned American citizens against taking passage on ships flying the flags of nations at war (no *Lusitanias* this time); required that belligerents pay cash for all American products they bought and carry their purchases home in their own ships. Finally, nations at war were forbidden to buy arms in the United States and to borrow money from American banks: Congress's rebuke of munitions makers and Wall Street bankers. There would be no powerful lobbies in Washington representing parties with a vested interest in the victory of one side or another as, isolationists said, had been the case in 1917.

Critics of the Neutrality Acts argued that they favored aggressor nations and penalized their victims. The victims would be unprepared for war while the nations that attacked them would arm themselves in advance of war—even from American factories. This was the message, they said, of Fascist Italy's invasion of Ethiopia in 1935 and the Spanish civil war that began in 1936. With its stockpile of modern weaponry, Benito Mussolini's army was able to overrun Ethiopians sometimes armed with century-old muskets. When Spain's Generalissimo Francisco Franco rose up against the constitutional republican government of Spain, he was swamped with armaments and even troops from Italy and Germany. America's neutrality policy denied the legitimate republican government of Spain access to armaments in the United States.

THE WORLD GOES TO WAR

Almost every year of Roosevelt's presidency presented new evidence that the world was drifting into another bloodbath. In 1934, Hitler began to rearm Germany in defiance of the Versailles Treaty. In 1935, he introduced universal military training, and Italy invaded Ethiopia. In 1936, Francisco Franco launched the Spanish civil war that Italy and Germany used as a proving ground to test their weapons and military tactics.

In July 1937, Japan sent land forces from Manchukuo into China proper and occupied Beijing, then called Peiping, and most of the coastal provinces. In March 1938, Hitler forced the political union of Austria to Germany (the *Anschluss*), increasing the resources of what he called the Third Reich, or "third empire." In September, claiming that he wanted only to unite all Germans under one flag, Hitler demanded that Czechoslovakia hand over its Sudetenland.

The Sudetenland had never been a part of Germany. Before World War I, it was a province of the kingdom of Bohemia, a possession of the Austrian Hapsburgs. It was populated largely by people of German language and culture, but it was also Czechoslovakia's mountainous natural defense line in the west. France and Britain had guaranteed the borders of Czechoslovakia, the only democratic state in central Europe, including the Sudetenland. So, Hitler's ultimatum involved them.

Germany's generals begged Hitler to be cautious; the *Wehrmacht* (armed forces) was not prepared for war with Britain and France. Hitler dismissed them. France and Britain would back down. When the British prime minister, Neville Chamberlain, gave into every one of Hitler's demands, the *Führer* rolled up a diplomatic and strategic victory so stunning it silenced dissent among his generals. In March 1939, he seized what was left of the Czech half of Czechoslovakia and set up a puppet regime in Slovakia.

The Aggressor Nations: Japan   The three aggressor nations of the 1930s were very different. Germany and Italy were modern totalitarian dictatorships based on mass support. Japan was an authoritarian state dominated by a military that nurtured ancient traditions but was also highly political. Of fourteen Japanese prime ministers between 1932 and 1945, only four were civilians (and the army assassinated two of them). Nevertheless, the government operated within a constitutional framework—there were elections to the Diet in 1942—and it was not the bloody tyrant over its own people as the German and Italian regimes were. Only fifty-seven Japanese were executed for political reasons during the war compared to thousands in Italy and tens of thousands in Nazi Germany.

Japan invaded China (and started the Pacific War with the United States in 1941) for economic reasons. A modern industrial nation, Japan was poor in the natural resources essential to industry: coal, iron, other minerals, petroleum, rubber, everything but hydroelectric power. China had plenty of coal and iron. Japan could have traded for them, selling manufactures in exchange. But China's political instability made aggression a more inviting alternative to twentieth-century samurai.

High-ranking Japanese naval officers still fumed with anger against the United States because the Treaty of Washington limited the Japanese navy to three-fifths the size of the American fleet. Cooler temperaments tried to point out that in an unregulated naval arms race, the United States could build not five battleships to every three the Japanese built, but fifty. Such common sense was waved off by militarists in 1930s Japan. Until 1940, the aggressive militarists in the army and navy were restrained by the fact that the United States was providing much of the oil Japan imported as well as copper, cotton, and cheap scrap iron.

In July 1941, however, attempting to pressure Japan to end its aggression in China, the Roosevelt administration forbade further sales to the Japanese of some strategic minerals and chemicals, airplane parts, and aviation fuel. In September, Roosevelt embargoed scrap iron. In July 1941, after Japan took control of French Indochina, Roosevelt ended oil sales, wiping out 80 percent of Japan's oil supply in one stroke.

The Aggressor Nations: Italy and Germany   Unlike Japan, Fascist Italy under dictator Benito Mussolini directly threatened no American interests. Locked into poverty, its industrial complex inefficient despite *il duce's* efforts, Italy was a threat to no nations except primitive countries like Ethiopia. Aside from a few elite units, the Italian military commanded little respect. The army suffered significant setbacks even in its war in Ethiopia against often barefoot Ethiopian irregulars. American sympathies were with the Ethiopians and their exiled Christian emperor, Haile Selassie, who toured Europe and the United States begging for help. But there was no sentiment for action beyond nonrecognition.

Hitler's Germany was another matter. By 1935, Nazi control of the richest and most populous and industrialized nation in Europe was absolute and Germany was an openly—proudly!—criminal regime. Opposition parties had been dissolved. Tens of thousands of socialists and communists were in concentration camps. Others had been murdered. The Nuremberg Laws of 1935 stripped Jews of their citizenship and forbade marriage between Jews and "Aryans." Jews had already been expelled from schools and universities. "Jews Forbidden" signs were everywhere. Jews trying to escape Germany were forced to sell their property at a fraction of its value.

German military power grew greater by the month, and Hitler had not been secretive about his ambitions abroad. In his autobiography, *Mein Kampf* (*My Struggle*), he made it clear that Germany must extend its sway over Poland, the Ukraine, and western Russia in order to provide *Lebensraum* ("living space") for the German people. He did not detail exactly what was in store for the displaced Poles, Ukrainians, and Russians, but in Nazi cosmology, they were considered *Untermenschen,* subhumans, only a notch above Jews.

And the War Came   Because of Hitler's fierce anti-communism and his announced designs on eastern Europe, some British and French statesmen quietly hoped that, in time, Nazi Germany and the Soviet Union would go to war and destroy one another. They were, therefore, stunned when, in 1939, out of the blue, Germany and Russia announced that they had signed a nonaggression treaty. Hitler's interest in Russian neutrality was obvious. He had been pressuring Poland to turn over to Germany a region known as the "Polish Corridor" (it provided the country with its only access to the sea).

Britain and France guaranteed Poland's borders. After the lesson of Czechoslovakia, they made it clear that German aggression in Poland meant war with them too. Hitler wanted war, but not a war on two fronts. The Nazi-Soviet Pact guaranteed that Russia would not contest the German conquest of Poland. In fact, secret provisions of the treaty gave eastern Poland to the Soviets.

MAP 42.1 German and Italian Aggression, 1934–1939

Italy's invasion of Ethiopia in 1935 was the first of a series of the territorial aggressions by Italy and Germany that culminated in World War II. Only Britain and France would have been justified in responding with force to any one of them, but they pulled back because of guilt over the excessive terms of the Treaty of Versailles, hopes that war with Hitler could be avoided by making concessions to him, and the fear that a weakened Germany would provide an opportunity for the Soviet Union to expand the sway of Communism.

Stalin's motives in agreeing to the treaty are more difficult to fathom. He knew that Hitler was sworn to destroy Bolshevism. Stalin had discussed an anti-German alliance with Britain and France, but when they dragged their feet, Stalin concluded that they were counting on a Soviet-German bloodletting. He preferred a scenario in which Germany fought a long, mutually destructive war with Britain and France.

On September 1, 1939, the Germans invaded Poland. The Poles resisted heroically. But their army was no match for the German *Blitzkrieg,* "lightning warfare," massive air attack and ground advances of unprecedented speed spearheaded by tanks and infantrymen moving not at a walk but as fast as trucks could move them.

The Fall of France, The Battle of Britain   So rapid was the German (and Russian) conquest of Poland that Britain and France were unable to move troops there. They massed their armies behind the Maginot Line, an awesome network of modern fortifications the French had built on the German border to stop a German advance dead. But they did not advance during the winter of 1939–1940 even with the bulk of the *Wehrmacht* still busy in Poland. Journalists wrote of the "phony war": Two great armies faced one another on a long static front, resumption of World War I.

Behind the "impregnable" Maginot Line, sitting tight made sense for the French and British. Hitler had other plans: a *Blitzkrieg* that had worked in Poland on a much larger scale. In April and May 1940, the Germans unleashed massive, rapid, coordinated land, sea, and air attacks on Denmark, Norway, the Netherlands, Belgium, and Luxembourg, where the Maginot line was weakest. Every targeted country buckled under within weeks, and the *Wehrmacht* poured through Holland and Belgium into France around the Maginot Line, intending to attack it from the rear.

That was not necessary. France surrendered. In the meantime, however, the British were able to evacuate 340,000 of their men and some French and Polish units from the port of Dunkirk by mobilizing every ship and boat capable of crossing the English Channel in, luckily, perfect weather. Great Britain hunkered down, preparing for a German invasion that few believed could be resisted.

THE UNITED STATES AND THE EUROPEAN WAR

In March 1940, during the "phony war," only 43 percent of Americans told pollsters that a German military victory in France would threaten the interests of United States. When France fell so quickly, however, and the German *Luftwaffe* (air force) commenced bombing British bases, factories, and cities, the mood changed. In June, 80 percent of Americans admitted to being, at least, "worried." They were inspired by the new British prime minister, Winston Churchill, who told the nation, Germany, and the world, "We shall fight on the beaches, we shall fight on the landing grounds, we shall fight in the fields and in the streets, we shall fight in the hills; we shall never surrender."

Churchill's eloquence and the phlegmatic but stubborn defiance of the English people under nightly German bombing raids inspired a sympathy for Great Britain greater even than during World War I. Pro-British feelings were deftly encouraged by an Anglophile radio news reporter based in London, Edward R. Murrow. In nightly broadcasts, heard "live" in the evening in the United States, Murrow brought the sounds of the "Blitz" into American living rooms and tacitly encouraged American support for Britain with low-key but shrewdly composed descriptions of British resistance: "You will have no dawn raids, as we shall probably have if the weather is right. You may walk the night in the light. Your families are not scattered by the winds of war. You may drive your high-powered car as far as time and money will permit ...."

Roosevelt Leads the Way   President Roosevelt played no small part in nudging public opinion in favor of aiding Britain. As early as 1938, when France and Britain were still appeasing Hitler and American neutrality policy was intact, Roosevelt had privately concluded that only force would stop Hitler. He hoped that, with American aid, the French and British could do the job so that American troops did not have to be sent over there again. Still, he knew not to get too far ahead of public opinion in the matter of material assistance. FDR's technique was to float trial balloons such as delivering a militant anti-Nazi speech. If the popular reaction was hostile, he backed off; if it was supportive, he pushed a bit further.

In 1939, at FDR's behest, Congress amended the Neutrality Acts so that Britain and France could buy war materiel cash-and-carry. (No paying for it with loans from American banks; no hiring American ships to transport it.) In 1940, with the Battle of Britain underway, and a majority of Americans worried about how a Nazi victory would affect them, FDR announced that he was trading Britain fifty old destroyers the Navy had in mothballs for British permission to establish eight naval bases in British possessions in Newfoundland, Bermuda, and the West Indies. He presented it at home as a purely defensive measure. In fact, the British were delighted to have the United States take over the protection of sea lanes in the western Atlantic so that they could concentrate their warships in European waters.

Defense was also the justification for the Burke-Wadsworth Act of September 1940. Congress appropriated $37 billion to build up the navy and army air corps, instituting the first peacetime draft in American history. The draft was run like a lottery to avoid accusations of favoritism as in World War I. More than 16 million young men registered; each was assigned a number between 1 and 8,500, about 2,000 men per number. Henry L. Stimson (now FDR's Secretary of War) picked the first number (#158); the remaining 8,499 were drawn and the order in which they were picked was published. A potential draftee knew whether he was likely to be called up soon, later, or (if his number was near the end) probably never. The first draftees were in uniform in November 1940; 900,000 would be called up for one-year terms of service.

FDR had little difficulty winning support for these measures. Even the draft had the approval of two-thirds of the population. Nevertheless, when the president decided to flaunt tradition and run for a third term in 1940, he found it advisable to assure the electorate that "your boys are not going to be sent into any foreign wars."

The Third Term   Why did FDR run for reelection in 1940? First—and there was truth in his vanity—he believed that he alone was capable of leading the country through very difficult times. None of the Democrats likely to be nominated if he retired were inspiring or sure winners. Vice president John Nance Garner was a tobacco-chewing provincial with little appeal outside the South. Postmaster General James Farley had an aura of the machine politician about him and he was a Catholic. (It was only twelve years since Al Smith had lost half the South because of the religion issue.) Another Catholic who made noises about running was Joseph P. Kennedy, a rich businessman who was ambassador to Britain and had a dubious past. Worst of all, Kennedy was a defeatist, convinced that Great Britain was doomed.

Several Republican hopefuls seemed to have a good chance of beating any of the Democrats. The front-runner, anti-New Dealer Senator Robert A. Taft of Ohio was an isolationist. Thomas A. Dewey of New York, only 38 years old, was not burdened with Taft's Stone Age conservatism, and he was extremely popular as a crime-busting district attorney. If Taft and Dewey deadlocked at the Republican convention, the likely compromise candidate was Senator Arthur Vandenberg of Michigan, who was also an isolationist. Most worrisome was Wendell Willkie, a utilities magnate who had come out of nowhere to be a serious contender for the nomination. Of all the Republicans and Democrats, he had the best claim to be FDR's successor. He had been a New Deal Democrat until 1938. He alone of the candidates fully supported FDR's policy of fighting Naziism by aiding Great Britain. He was personable, likable, and a tireless campaigner. He very likely would have defeated any Democratic nominee except Roosevelt.

Willkie won the Republican nomination after several ballots but, with FDR his opponent, he never had a chance. Differing with the president on so little, he was a "me too" candidate. He offered nothing that the tried and true and effective FDR did not. The president was easily reelected.

The Undeclared War   His victory emboldened Roosevelt to step up aid to Great Britain. In asking Congress to enact "Lend-Lease," he stated boldly that the United States would be the "arsenal of democracy," manufacturing arms of all sorts to be "loaned" to Britain. To help defend British shipping against "wolf packs" of German submarines, Roosevelt proclaimed a neutral zone in the Atlantic extending from North America to Iceland, assigning destroyers to patrol the sea lanes, warning British merchant ships of German submarines. He sent troops to Greenland, a possession of Nazi-occupied Denmark, to keep it out of German hands.

This put the United States at war with Germany in everything but name. In August 1941, Roosevelt and Churchill met on two ships off the coast of Newfoundland and adopted what amounted to war aims redolent of the Fourteen Points. The Atlantic Charter called for the self-determination of nations after the war; free trade and freedom of the seas; the disarmament of aggressor nations; and the creation of some new means of collective world security.

It was only a matter of time before German guns were fired on an American warship. In October 1941, a destroyer, the USS *Reuben James* was sunk by a submarine with a loss of 100 sailors. Roosevelt did not, however, ask Congress for a formal declaration of war. His hopes that Germany could be defeated without sending American troops to Europe were up because Britain was not standing alone. In June 1941, Germany blitzed the Soviet Union. Astonishingly, Stalin was utterly unprepared despite the fact that Churchill had warned him of the exact date of the attack and one of Stalin's top spies had twice reported that a German onslaught was imminent. (Stalin really did *trust* Hitler!) The unprepared Red Army was pushed back to the city limits of Leningrad (St. Petersburg) and Moscow before winter halted the Germans.

The America First Committee   In 1941, Roosevelt faced formidable opposition at home to his policy of all-out aid to Britain and, after June, the USSR. Robert Wood, the executive head of Sears Roebuck, had organized and generously funded the America First Committee. It called for the buildup of an impregnable defense of the Western Hemisphere against the Nazis but opposed further aid to Great Britain. America First claimed 600,000 supporters, but it was less a membership than a propaganda organization, sponsoring publications, speaking tours by prominent members, and rallies.

Its list of prestigious sponsors gave the committee considerable clout. The editors of the Chicago *Tribune,* the New York *Daily News,* and many other newspapers pushed its message. Senators Gerald Nye, Robert M. LaFollette Jr., and Burton Wheeler; former president Herbert Hoover; former New Dealer Hugh Johnson; Socialist party leader Norman Thomas; and (like today) celebrities including movie star Lillian Gish, Teddy Roosevelt's daughter Alice Roosevelt Longworth, and aviators Eddie Rickenbacker and Charles Lindbergh.

The America Firsters' motives for opposing aid to Britain varied. The midwestern Republican Progressives were dyed-in-the-wool isolationists. Most Firsters believed that the aid was a waste, that Britain was already doomed to defeat. Some were Anglophobes who looked forward to the break-up of the British empire. Others feared that a German defeat would make the Communist Soviet Union the paramount power in Europe. Some members, like Norman Thomas, were pacifists.

The committee tried to dodge Father Coughlin's endorsement because of his pro-Nazi and anti-Semitic leanings. However, America First's most effective spokesman, Charles Lindbergh, also slipped in his speeches and betrayed hostility toward American Jewish organizations that were, of course, pro-intervention.

Ironically, the America Firsters and Roosevelt's support group, the Committee to Defend America by Aiding the Allies, were so preoccupied by the war in Europe that they (and, for that matter, the Roosevelt administration) overlooked the possibility that the United States might be drawn into the war by Japan, halfway around the world.

AMERICA GOES TO WAR

When France surrendered, a Japanese army moved into the French colonies of Indochina. The "peace party" in the Japanese cabinet, headed by Prince Fumimaro Konoye, continued to negotiate with the United States, hoping for American concessions that would enable Japan to break the stalemate in its war. By October 1941, it was clear that an agreement was impossible, and General Hideki Tojo, head of the "war party," succeeded Konoye as premier.

Pearl Harbor   Oddly, the Japanese and American governments concluded within hours of one another that their differences were unresolvable. Although talks continued—empty formalities on both sides—Secretary of State Hull handed responsibility for Japanese affairs over to the War Department on the same day that, halfway around the world, Admiral Isoroku Yamamoto was ordered to prepare a surprise attack on Pearl Harbor, the American naval base in Hawaii, that he had designed.

Yamamoto had opposed war with the United States. He told the cabinet, "If I am told to fight regardless of the consequences, I shall run wild for the first six

AP Photos

The wreckage at Pearl Harbor after the unopposed aerial assault on Hawaii by carrier-borne Japanese planes on December 7, 1941. But the Japanese victory was far less than that for which its commander Admiral Isoroku Yamamoto hoped. None of the Pacific fleet's aircraft carriers were docked in Pearl the day of the attack. Moreover, as critics of Yamamoto's strategy had warned, by launching the war by attacking the United States directly instead of the British in Malaya and the Dutch West Indies, Japan ensured that the United States military would retaliate with the entire American people behind it.

months or a year, but I have utterly no confidence for the second or third year." Because of several years' residence in United States, Yamamoto was personally familiar with America's vast resources. Other "peace party" officers made the same point. In August 1941, Col. Hideo Iwakuro presented the cabinet with the numbers of the American edge: In steel resources, the United States could produce 20 tons to every ton Japan made; its coal supply was ten times Japan's; its edge in shipping two to one, in oil 100 to 1.

If there must be war, however, Yamamoto insisted that it was essential to destroy the American Pacific fleet at Pearl Harbor. Other Japanese strategists disagreed. Admiral Takijiro Onishi wanted to invade the oil-rich Dutch East Indies (Indonesia) and British Singapore and Malaya. A war with the British and Dutch, he pointed out, could be concluded—perhaps quickly—with a negotiated peace guaranteeing Japan the oil that the American embargo had cut off. An attack on Pearl Harbor, however, no matter how successful it was tactically, would only unite Americans to fight a war to the finish with Japan.

Yamamoto's prestige carried the debate. In December 1941, his fleet of six aircraft carriers, two battleships, two heavy cruisers, a light cruiser, nine destroyers, three submarines, and 432 planes disappeared in the Pacific with not so much as a radio signal. On December 7, he launched a perfectly executed air attack on Hawaii that sank or badly damaged eight battleships, seven other vessels, and 188 airplanes, killing or wounding 3,435 servicemen at minimal costs to the Japanese. Yamamoto celebrated with his officers just long enough to be polite, however. His primary target had been the three aircraft carriers stationed at Pearl. He knew that carrier-borne aircraft were the key to a war he had just begun. But the American carriers were at sea on maneuvers when the Japanese struck. "I fear we have only

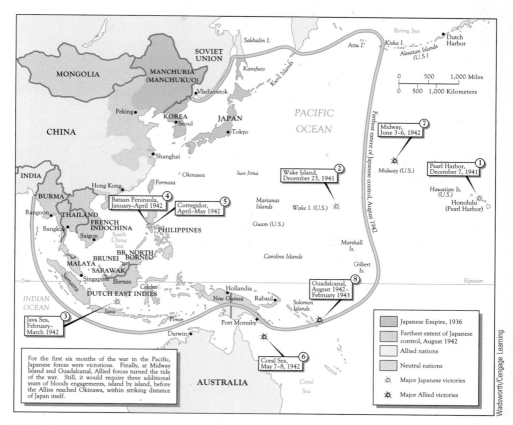

MAP 42.2 Japanese Empire, 1931–1942

As distant from Japan as the outer defensive perimeter of August 1942 was, it was not as far as Admiral Yamamoto and other strategists believed necessary to force the United States to negotiate a peace rather than fight costly war. The Japanese military had hoped to occupy and fortify Midway Island (for regular air strikes against Hawaii), all of New Guinea, the Solomon Islands, and at least northern Australia—and to control the sea lanes to Australia—in order to deny the United States a base from which to launch a counterattack.

awakened a sleeping giant," he told his officers, "and his reaction will be terrible," exactly what Admiral Onishi had warned against.

The Reaction   The giant awakened with a start. Pearl Harbor was attacked on Sunday. The next day, Roosevelt went before Congress and immortalized December 7, 1941 as "a day that will live in infamy." Except for Representative Jeannette Rankin of Montana, a pacifist who had also voted against entry into the First World War, Congress voted unanimously to declare war.

In every city in the nation for weeks, the army's and navy's recruitment offices were jammed with young men. Pearl Harbor was so traumatic an event in the lives of Americans that practically every individual who lived through it would remember exactly what he or she was doing when news of the attack was announced.

Very quietly at the time, openly later, Roosevelt's enemies accused him and other top officials of knowing in advance of what was coming and ensuring that Pearl Harbor and nearby Hickham Field, an air base, were unprepared for the attack and therefore destroyed. It was said that Washington withheld vital intelligence from Hawaii, sacrificing American lives for the political purpose of getting the United States into the war.

In fact, the lack of preparation at Pearl Harbor was shameful but not at all unusual in a bureaucracy in which every individual's chief goal is his own security. As early as 1924, air-power advocate General Billy Mitchell pointed out that Pearl was vulnerable to air attack. In 1932, Admiral Harry Yarnell snuck two aircraft carriers and four cruisers to within bombing range of Oahu before his presence was detected. In the first days of December 1941, indications that something was brewing were either ignored or reached the appropriate desks only after unjustifiable delays. At Hickham Field, fighter planes were drawn up wing tip to wing tip so that they could be protected against sabotage on the ground. This made their destruction from the air all the simpler. When the attack began, few fighters were able to get into the air.

But there was no conspiracy to set Pearl Harbor up for a devastating defeat. The blunders of officials in Washington and of the military in Hawaii were just examples of the incompetence with which all large bureaucracies are shot through. The key to the Japanese victory was the planning behind it, its execution, and more than a little luck in pulling off total surprise. Nevertheless, there is little doubt that President Roosevelt was relieved to be officially into the war with the entire country behind him.

Getting the Job Done   Of all the people at war in 1942, only the Japanese celebrated the outbreak. Europeans, including Germans before the *Blitzkrieg* victories, turned their collars up upon hearing the news and walked on. In the United States, the popular attitude was and remained: There's a job to be done; let's get it over with.

Popular songs of the era, "I'll Be Seeing You" and "I'll Never Smile Again," were melancholy, about the separation of lovers and their longing to be together again. There was little of the cocky, exuberant patriotism of George M. Cohan's anthem of World War I, "Over There." Seven times during the war, popular illustrator Norman Rockwell painted covers for the *Saturday Evening Post* showing an American soldier coming home.

Organizing for Victory
Military mobilization was underway before Pearl Harbor. By 1942, more than 1.5 million Americans were in uniform. By the end of the war, the total number of soldiers, sailors, airmen, and women in auxiliary corps climbed to 15 million.

The draft provided the majority of "GIs," the soldiers' self-adopted name for themselves. (It referred to the "government issue" designation of uniforms and other equipment.) Draft boards made up of local civic leaders worked efficiently and with remarkably few irregularities to fill the demands. The "Friends and Neighbors" who informed young men of their fate with the salutation—"Greetings"—exempted only the physically disabled and those with jobs designated as essential to the war effort: farmers and workers in defense plants. (One draftee in three was classified "4F," rejected for physical reasons.)

With time, another exemption was added: "Sole surviving sons," men of draft age all of whose brothers had been killed in action, were not asked to serve. In the windows of homes that lost a soldier were hung small banners, a gold star signifying a lost son or husband.

Money was mobilized. When the war began, the government was spending $2 billion a month on the military. During the first half of 1942, the expenditure rose to $15 billion monthly. By the time Japan surrendered in August 1945, the costs of the war totaled more than $300 billion. In less than four years, the American government spent more money than it had spent during the previous 150 years of the nation's existence. The national debt, already high in 1941 at $48 billion, doubled and redoubled to $247 billion.

Big Business
A few businessmen resisted wartime restrictions on their operations, particularly labor laws designed to avoid strikes. The least graceful was Sewell L. Avery, head of the retail chain Montgomery Ward. New Deal relief measures had saved his company from bankruptcy and full employment during the war meant bonanza profits for Ward's. But Avery had to be carried bodily to jail for refusing to obey a law that guaranteed his employees the right to join a union.

He was not typical. Most big businessmen, including former critics of the Roosevelt administration, accepted unionization and, when asked, rushed to Washington to join the government. Corporation executives recognized that the government's astronomical expenditures meant prosperity. General Motors was paid 8 percent of all federal expenditures between 1941 and 1945, $1 of every $12.50 that the government spent.

General Motors president, William S. Knudsen, was, therefore, delighted to be a "dollar-a-year man," a business executive who worked for Roosevelt for that sum. Knudsen headed the War Resources Board (WRB), established in August 1939 to oversee the conversion of factories to military production.

New Alphabet Agencies
After the congressional elections of 1942, which brought many conservative Republicans to Washington, Roosevelt announced that "Dr. New Deal" had been dismissed from the country's case and "Dr. Win-the-War" was now engaged. He explained that

since there was now full employment, the government's social programs were no longer necessary.

The creation of new government agencies continued apace. In addition to Knudsen's WRB, the Supplies Priorities and Allocation Board (SPAB) under dollar-a-year man Donald M. Nelson of Sears Roebuck was commissioned to ensure that raw materials, particularly the scarce and critical ones, were reserved for military production. The Office of Price Administration (OPA) had the task of controlling consumer prices so that the combination of high wages and scarce goods did not cause a runaway inflation.

After Pearl Harbor, a National War Labor Board (NWLB) was set up to mediate industrial disputes. Its purpose was to guarantee that production was uninterrupted and that wage increases remained within government-defined limits. This irked many of Roosevelt's former supporters in the labor movement, none of them more powerful than John L. Lewis of the United Mine Workers, who returned to the Republican party. But the NWLB also worked to ensure that employees were not gouged by avaricious employers. The board was reasonably successful. There were strikes, including a serious one led by Lewis in 1943, but labor relations were generally good, and union membership continued to rise.

The Office of War Mobilization (OWM) was the most important of the new alphabet agencies. Theoretically, it oversaw all aspects of the mobilized economy, as Bernard Baruch had done during the First World War. It was considered important enough that James F. Byrnes of South Carolina resigned from the Supreme Court to head it. He was widely considered an "assistant president."

Success   The size of the federal government swelled from 1.1 million civilian employees in 1940 to 3.3 million in 1945. (State governments grew at almost the same rate.) Inevitably there was waste (agencies doing the same thing), inefficiency (agencies fighting at cross-purposes with one another), and corruption (lots of people doing nothing but collecting paychecks). But with national unity and military victory constantly touted as essential, the few critics of the problems, such as Republican Senator Robert A. Taft of Ohio, were unable to have much effect. Taft was a thoughtful man but also a knee-jerk carper. The most effective check on waste, inefficiency, and corruption was the Senate War Investigating Committee, which was headed by a New Deal Democrat from Missouri, Senator Harry S. Truman.

Lessons learned during the First World War and the administrative skills of the dollar-a-year businessmen worked wonders in production. New factories and factories formerly given to the manufacture of America's automobiles canceled civilian production for the duration and churned out trucks, tanks, the famous jeeps, and amphibious vehicles in incredible numbers. In 1944 alone, 96,000 airplanes (260 per day) rolled out of American factories. Industrialist Henry J. Kaiser perfected an assembly line for producing simple and cheap but serviceable freighters, the Liberty ships. American shipbuilders sent 10 million tons of shipping down the ways between 1941 and 1945. The Ford Motor Company alone produced more war materiel than all of Italy.

The Workers   Anyone unemployed either could not work or was a congenital loafer. Factories running at capacity had difficulty finding enough people to fill the jobs that needed doing. There was a significant shift of population to the West Coast as the demands of the Pacific war led to the growth of defense industries in Seattle, Oakland, San Diego, and Long Beach. Among the new Californians (the population of the Golden State rose from 6.9 million in 1940 to 10.5 million in 1950) were hundreds of thousands of African Americans. Finding well-paid factory jobs previously closed to them, blacks also won a sense of security unknown to earlier generations because of the colorblind policies of CIO unions and FDR's executive order in 1941 that war contractors observe fair practices in employing blacks.

Women, including many of middle age who had never worked for wages, entered the labor force in large numbers. The symbol of the lady working in an unladylike job was "Rosie the Riveter." Rosie might have forearms like a boxer from wielding a heavy riveting gun, but she was reassuringly feminine, made up and lipsticked. Women performed just about every kind of job in the industrial economy. By the end of the war, 16.5 million women were working; they made up more than a third of the civilian labor force.

Few of these genuinely independent women were feminists. Rosie after Rosie told newspaper reporters that they looked forward to the end of the war when they could quit their factory jobs and return to the home as wives and mothers. They were the perfect wartime workforce: intelligent, educated, energetic, patriotic, and, most of them, uninterested in competing with the soldiers who eventually would come back and take their jobs.

Prosperity

The Office of Price Administration was remarkably successful in its very difficult assignment. Coveted consumer goods—coffee, butter, sugar, some canned foods, meat, shoes, liquor, silk, rayon, and nylon—were scarce because of rationing, but high wages meant that workers had plenty of money to spend. (Real wages rose 50 percent during the war.) The black market, the illegal sale of rationed goods, never got out of control and prices rose only moderately between 1942 and 1945. Unable to consume wholesale, Americans pumped their wages into savings accounts, including $15 billion in loans to the government in the form of war bonds. It became a point of patriotic pride with some women to paint the seam of a nylon stocking on their calves.

There was an element of good-humored innocence in the way Americans fought the Second World War. If they did not believe that a problem-free world would follow victory (no one doubted that the Allies would win), Americans were confident that they were in the right. By the time the fighting was over, 290,000 Americans were dead. Shocking as that figure is, American losses were negligible compared to the losses of other belligerents. Winston Churchill had described the year 1940, when the British stood alone against Nazism, as "their finest hour." The years Americans were at war were their finest hours.

43

THEIR FINEST HOURS

Americans in the Second World War 1942–1945

*We are now in this war. We are all in it—all the way. Every
single man, woman, and child is a partner in the most
tremendous undertaking of our American history.*

—Franklin D. Roosevelt

Nazi Germany was defeated by British pluck, Russian blood, and American industrial might. By holding out alone against Hitler in 1940 and 1941, Britain
prevented the Nazis from establishing an impregnable "Fortress Europe." In
saving their island, the British saved the base that made an invasion of continental
Europe possible. The Soviet Union sapped the might of the German *Wehrmacht,*
killing 4.9 million German soldiers and wounding 5.8 million, four times as many
casualties as the Americans and British together suffered.

The United States, with an economy double the size of Germany's and Japan's
combined, kept both Britain and Russia afloat with its incredible industrial output.
Without the American army and navy, Britain and the Soviet Union might have
fought Germany to exhaustion and toppled Hitler, but it is highly unlikely they
could have won the total victory with which the war ended had the United States
not been an ally.

Against Japan, the Chinese tied down a million Japanese soldiers on the Asian mainland (without fighting them much). British, Dutch, Australians, and New Zealanders
bore the brunt of Japanese power in the South Asian theater of operations. But the
two-front Pacific war against Japan that proved decisive was largely an American
show. World War II was America's "Great War," the victory of 1945 perhaps America's
greatest contribution to Western civilization.

STOPPING JAPAN

Americans knew that they were in a fight between December 1941 and August
1945. Adults remembered the day Pearl Harbor was attacked, D-Day when the
invasion of Europe began, the day Franklin D. Roosevelt died, and V-E Day and

World War II 1942–1945

1942	1943	1944	1945

May 1942 **Surrender of Corregidor; Battle of Coral Sea; fighting in New Guinea**
June 1942 **Midway; tide turns**
■ Nov 1942 **Americans in North Africa**

■ Feb 1943 **German surrender at Stalingrad; tide turns**
■ July 1943 **Invasion of Sicily**
Nov 1943 **Tarawa**

■ June 1944 **D-Day**
Oct 1944 **Landing in Philippines**
■ Dec 1944 **Battle of the Bulge**

Iwo Jima falls; kamikaze attacks begin Mar 1945
April 1945 **Okinawa**

Pacific Theater ■ European Theater

Germany surrenders; FDR dies in office April 1945 ■
Hiroshima and Nagasaki; Japan surrenders Aug 1945

V-J Day, when Germany and Japan surrendered. The memories ended up sweet, sustaining a generation with the knowledge that their lives had had some meaning.

Humiliation and Anger

The first months after Pearl Harbor brought nothing but more bad news. After Admiral Yamamoto shattered the American Pacific Fleet, the Japanese army advanced easily into Malaya, Hong Kong, the Philippines, Java, and Guam. Within a few weeks, the dramatic Japanese battle flag, rays emanating from the rising sun, snapped in the breezes of British Singapore and Burma, and the Dutch East Indies, present-day Indonesia.

There was heroism in the sequence of disasters. On Wake Island in the central Pacific, a mere 450 marines held off a Japanese onslaught for two weeks, killing 3,000 before they surrendered. On Luzon in the Philippines, 20,000 GIs under General Douglas MacArthur and a larger force of Filipinos fought valiantly to hold back far greater numbers of Japanese on the Bataan Peninsula and, at the end, the rocky fortress island of Corregidor in Manila Bay. At first the men thought relief was on the way. Slowly the sickening truth sank in: They were the "battling bastards of Bataan," quite alone and expendable, an ocean away from a crippled navy. Nevertheless, they grimly carried out the hopeless task of delaying and punishing the Japanese.

General MacArthur was prepared to stay and surrender. However, Roosevelt ordered the nation's best-known general to flee to Australia in a submarine. FDR must have been tempted to let MacArthur fall into Japanese hands. With good reason, he disliked and distrusted the general. Indeed, aside from a coterie of devoted aides, MacArthur had alienated much of the military's top brass. He was an egomaniac and an insufferable posturer in Mussolini's league. He had cultivated a stage persona complete with props—sunglasses and a deep-bowled corncob pipe. "I studied dramatics under MacArthur," General Dwight D. Eisenhower waspishly remarked. MacArthur also had a history of ignoring orders or interpreting them to suit himself and he was openly political, a taboo in the American military.

For all that, his personal bravery and flashes of military genius were undeniable. FDR believed that MacArthur was, if not essential to winning the war with Japan, vital. The general's connection with the Philippines was lifelong and mutually affectionate. When MacArthur left the islands, he promoted his mystique and inspired the Philippine resistance (the most effective resistance in Asia or Europe) with a radio message that concluded, "I shall return."

On May 6, 1942, the last ragged, starving, and sick defenders of Corregidor surrendered. American dismay at their defeat gave way to livid anger when reports trickled back to the United States of Japanese cruelty toward their prisoners on the infamous Bataan Death March. Of 10,000 men forced to walk to a prison camp in the interior, 1,000 died on the way. (Another 5,000 died in the camp.)

Japanese Strategy

During the siege of Corregidor, the Japanese piled up victories in South Asia and Oceania. British and empire forces and Dutch soldiers who escaped from Indonesia—there were not many of them after two years of war in Europe—retreated to India. Japanese strategy was to establish a defensive perimeter beginning at the Burmese-Indian border, extending south and east between the Dutch East Indies and New Guinea and Australia and then far enough into the Pacific that the United States, the only offensive threat, could not bomb Japan.

Had further advances been possible—into India, Australia, the Central Pacific—the Japanese were prepared to venture them. But the outer defensive perimeter was the only essential. With an impregnable defensive position, the Japanese believed they could force Britain and the United States to negotiate a peace that would leave the Japanese empire supreme in East Asia.

By early May 1942, the outer perimeter was complete except for southern New Guinea around Port Moresby where Australian and recently arrived American troops stubbornly held on. Admiral Yamamoto moved his yet unbloodied fleet to the Coral Sea off Australia's northeastern coast to cut the supply line between Hawaii and Australia, thus choking off the resistance in New Guinea.

Coral Sea and Midway

On May 6 and 7, 1942, the Japanese and American fleets fought to a standoff. The battle of the Coral Sea was a new kind of naval encounter in that the ships of the opposing forces never caught sight of one another. Carrier-based aircraft did the fighting, attacking enemy vessels and one another. Japanese losses were lighter than those the Americans suffered. Early in the war, Japanese pilots were better trained and more experienced than American pilots, having flown combat missions in China. The Japanese fighters, the "Zeros," were superior to every other plane in Asia. When the Zero was introduced in China in September 1940, 13 of them downed 27 Chinese planes within ten minutes. They had their weaknesses, however; powered by small engines, they were not well armored. Their fuel tanks were vulnerable, and they were clumsy in a dive. The Hellcat and the Corsair were developed specifically to defeat Zeros, and they did.

Coral Sea was a tactical victory for the Japanese, but a strategic setback. Admiral Yamamoto had to abandon his plan to cut the southern shipping lanes. He had "run wild" not for a year, as he expected to do, but for only five months.

Yamamoto turned immediately to the central Pacific where Japanese supply lines were more secure. His object was the American naval and air base on the

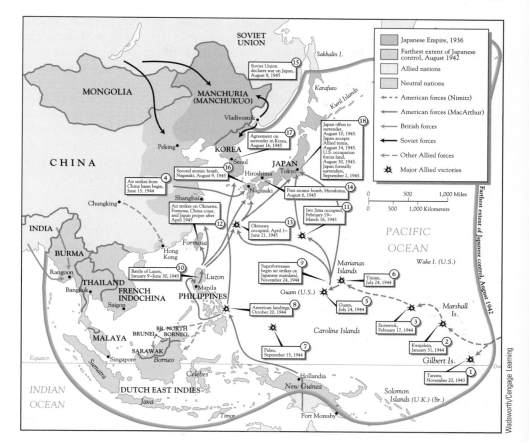

MAP 43.1 The Pacific Theater

Japan faced enemies on four fronts: British, Dutch, and colonial troops attacked Burma from India; Chinese Nationalists and Communists faced the Japanese in China; General MacArthur's soldiers and marines, with naval support, drove through New Guinea to the Philippines; Admiral Chester Nimitz's forces "island-hopped" through the Central Pacific to Iwo Jima and Okinawa, dearly won positions from which land-based American planes could bomb Japan. By the summer of 1945, Japanese defenses consisted of little more than Kamikaze—suicide bomb-planes that wreaked havoc on American ships but did not stop American bombers.

island of Midway, about a thousand miles northwest of Hawaii. There, between June 3 and June 6, 1942, the Japanese suffered a major defeat. U.S. intelligence had broken the Japanese naval code, knew Yamamoto's object, and a fleet under Admirals Raymond A. Spruance and Frank Fletcher was waiting for him. They lost the carrier *Yorktown* to Japanese dive bombers and torpedoes, but American planes destroyed four Japanese carriers.

It was worse than a one-for-four trade. Japan lacked the resources to replace fabulously expensive aircraft carriers as easily as the United States could. During the war, Japan would commission 14 new carriers of various sizes, the United

States 104. The loss of 4 carriers six months into the war was a more serious setback than even the pessimistic Yamamoto anticipated. The defeat at Midway put an end to Japan's offensive capacity. Much earlier than he had planned, Yamamoto had to shift to defending what the Japanese had won, the Japanese army to fortifying the islands on the outer perimeter.

Yamamoto did not live to see the catastrophic end to Japan's war. By 1943, the Americans were reading Japanese naval communiques only minutes after the officers to whom they were radioed. They learned that Yamamoto would be flying over Bougainville in the Solomon Islands and shot down his plane, killing the admiral. By remaining silent until the Japanese announced Yamamoto's death, they nurtured the Japanese illusion that the American attack had been routine and just lucky in killing Yamamoto. The Japanese never discovered that their code had been deciphered.

Hysteria

About 200,000 Japanese immigrants (called *Issei*) and their children (*Nisei*) lived in Hawaii, more than a third of the islands' population. About 120,000 Japanese and Japanese-Americans lived in the continental United States, almost all in the Pacific States. For fifty years, California politicians had aggravated racist feelings by railing against them as the "yellow peril." Newspapers owned by William Randolph Hearst had been particularly ugly. (Hearst, convinced he personally was Japan's Number One Target after Pearl Harbor, hurriedly moved out of his palace, San Simeon, which overlooked the Pacific and could, indeed, had the Japanese taken him seriously, have been shelled from a submarine.)

Hearst was not the only hysteric in the weeks after Pearl Harbor. For a few days, parts of Los Angeles were near panic because of a rumor the Japanese were invading. Coastal communities in California organized networks of civilian lookouts, hundreds of volunteers training binoculars on the horizon. In Hawaii, several high-ranking officers called on Washington to evacuate the *Issei* and *Nisei*. They were tactfully diverted to other concerns when it was pointed out that Japanese Hawaiians were the backbone of the islands' labor force, 90 percent of the carpenters and transportation workers. Evacuate them, and the Hawaiian economy would cease to exist. Moreover, there was no evidence that more than a handful of Japanese-Americans harbored sympathies for Japan. A mere 1,400 of the 200,000 Hawaiian Japanese were interned as suspects.

In California, Japanese-Americans were only 1 percent of the population. There, however, popular hysteria threatened to develop into social disorder. Chinese and Koreans wore buttons reading "I am not Japanese" to avoid being roughed up. The Justice Department announced that very few Japanese, all known to the Federal Bureau of Investigation, were disloyal (2,000 suspects were arrested; most were quickly exonerated of subversive activities). Indeed, Japan's consul in Los Angeles had advised Tokyo that, in the event of war, no help whatsoever would be forthcoming from the Japanese-American community. He never bothered to institute a program to recruit saboteurs.

Internment Camps

But California's attorney general, Earl Warren, and the commanding general at San Francisco's Presidio, John W. DeWitt, joined the anti-Japanese clamor. DeWitt argued, in a triumph of logic, that "the very fact that no sabotage has taken place to date is a disturbing and confirming indication that such action will be taken." FDR gave in. Executive Order 9066 forbade "Japanese," including American-born citizens, to reside in a broad "coastal zone." About 9,000 *Nisei* responded by heading east by train and automobile. Service stations would not sell them gasoline; others were turned back, quite illegally, at the Nevada line. So, early in 1942, the federal government forcibly removed 110,000 Japanese-Americans from their homes and interned them in hurriedly constructed camps in seven states, from inland California to Arkansas.

Some federal officials were appalled by the idea of American internment camps. Because the criteria for relocation were ancestry and race, and many internees were native-born citizens, the federal government itself was flaunting the Fourteenth Amendment. The protests were usually ignored; when it was not, the government's response was, "don't you know there's a war on?" In June 1943, now governor Earl Warren said that if the internment camps were closed, "no one will be able to tell a saboteur from any other Jap." In *Korematsu* v. *the United States* (1944), the Supreme Court voted 6 to 3 to uphold an action that cost 110,000 people their freedom for several years and about $350 million in lost property. Earl Warren would soon be known as the leading liberal on the Supreme Court. In 1944, eight of the nine justices were New Deal liberals appointed to the Court by FDR.

The internment of Japanese-Americans was the most massive federal violation of civil liberties in the history of the United States. However, the internment camps should not be equated with Nazi, Japanese, and Soviet concentration camps as has sometimes been done. Life in the camps was humiliating, but there was no cruelty, brutality, or forced labor, let alone murder. On the contrary, most camp supervisors were disgusted by the internment. They helped internees find employment outside the fences, provided recreational and educational programs in the camps, helped internees protect property they had been forced to abandon, and nagged Washington to close the camps. Some 17,000 *Nisei,* the majority from Hawaii, enlisted in the army. Some served as translators and interrogators in the Pacific; most were combat soldiers in Europe.

About 1,700 pro-Nazis were arrested, members of the German-American Bund and the Silver Shirts, a copycat of the Nazi's elite Storm Troopers. Altogether, 10,000 German alien residents and a few Italians were interned. Most Japanese internees were home or, at least, released in 1944, the last early in 1945. By then, high government officials, ashamed by their actions, refused to discuss the internment openly. Interestingly, former internees did not like to discuss their experiences. They regarded internment as a personal humiliation they pretended never happened.

DEFEATING GERMANY FIRST

Within a month after Pearl Harbor, President Roosevelt and his advisers concluded that, in the words of George Marshall, the head of the Joint Chiefs of Staff, "Germany is still the prime enemy and her defeat is the key to victory. Once Germany is defeated, the collapse of Italy and the defeat of Japan must follow." Their reasoning was sound. Japan could not conceivably win its war. Nazi Germany, however, if entrenched in Fortress Europe, could. Japan did not threaten the Western Hemisphere. The Nazis had friends, albeit cautious friends, in several South American dictators, and there were large, sympathetic German populations in Brazil, Uruguay, and Argentina. Except for a few months early in 1942 when it was vital to maintain a foothold in New Guinea, the bulk of resources was devoted to the European theater of operations; just 15 percent, later 30 percent of men and materiel went to the Pacific.

Friction among the Allies   Roosevelt and British Prime Minister Churchill often disagreed, but, until late in the war, the two men were bound together by affection, admiration, and trust. Their relations with Soviet Premier Stalin, on the other hand, were distorted by suspicions on Stalin's part that could brim over into paranoia. Churchill had been an aggressive anticommunist throughout his long career. He did not pretend that the alliance with the Soviet Union was anything other than a matter of expediency. He said that if hell declared war on Germany, he would manage to say a kind word about the devil in the House of Commons.

Roosevelt had never thought of Communist rule in Russia an American concern. Personally, he soon discovered he had a soft spot for Stalin personally; he referred to him privately as "Uncle Joe." FDR believed that he could allay the Russian's suspicions that he and Churchill wanted to sit out the ground war while Germany and the Soviet Union destroyed one another.

So, in an attempt to hinder Hitler's onslaught in Russia, the United States Army Air Corps (the forerunner of the Air Force) joined the British in nearly constant day and night bombing raids over German industrial areas. Eventually, 2.7 million tons of bombs would level German cities. On an impulse explicable only by Roosevelt's sensitivity to Stalin's fears—for it was utterly out of the question—FDR told Stalin that, before 1942 was out, the British and Americans would open a second front in the west, easing the pressure on the Soviets. The best the western Allies could do to honor his ill-advised pledge was to attack on German and Italian forces in North Africa. It was not a front that meant enough to Hitler to weaken his army on the Eastern front.

The African Campaign and Stalingrad   The British and Anzacs (Australians and New Zealanders) had been fighting a seesaw stalemate in Libya and Egypt against Italian troops and German Field Marshal Erwin Rommel's *Afrika Korps* since the beginning of the war. In mid-1942, the Germans and Italians had the upper hand, having advanced to a line not far from Alexandria, thus threatening the Suez Canal, Britain's link with India.

In October, under the command of British General Bernard Montgomery, their arsenal beefed up by Sherman tanks from the United States, the British launched a counterattack at El Alamein. Montgomery sent the Germans reeling. In November 1942, as the British advanced from the east, Americans commanded by General Dwight D. Eisenhower landed far to the west in French North Africa.

It was Eisenhower's first experience in combat, and it did not go well. After winning over French generals in Morocco bound to Hitler by treaty, Eisenhower led raw American tank forces east to Kasserine Pass where, in February 1943, they were soundly defeated by the *Afrika Korps*. It might have been the end of Eisenhower's rapid rise in command except for two facts. First, at the same time as Kasserine Pass, deep within the Soviet Union, the Russians won one of the war's pivotal Allied victories. The Red Army had been slugging it out with a German army of almost 200,000 men within the city of Stalingrad (now Volgograd) for six months. By February, Field Marshall Friedrich von Paulus's command was reduced to 110,000 in two small pockets with no airfields. Von Paulus surrendered in February. (Only 5,000 of the 110,000 German prisoners taken at Stalingrad survived Russian prisoner of war camps.) Eisenhower's defeat in North Africa was little noticed.

General Dwight D. Eisenhower, supreme commander of the Allied Armies in Europe, with two of his ablest subordinates, Omar Bradley and George Patton. Bradley detested the flamboyant Patton and the feeling was mutual. Eisenhower's ability to keep such rivals (and British Field Marshall Bernard Montgomery) in harness was why he was by far the best choice for overall command.

Second, Roosevelt's Chief of Staff, General George C. Marshall, had taken note of Eisenhower's considerable organizational abilities and, even more important with British and American generals jealous of one another and rarely in agreement on strategy, Eisenhower's political skills. Cool and modest in manner, he was a magician in persuading headstrong prima donnas to work together. Marshall jumped Eisenhower over 366 officers senior to him to make him commander of all Allied forces in Europe with the assignment of planning and preparing the invasion of Hitler's "Fortress Europe."

The Invasion of Italy   Stalin had been demanding a second front in Europe since 1942. Marshall had persuaded Roosevelt that an invasion in 1942 was predestined to be a failure. When Stalin increased pressure in 1943, the British proposed that after clearing the Germans out of North Africa, the Allies open a second front in Italy. Marshall regarded such an advance as a waste; it would be impossible to defeat the Germans in the mountainous peninsula. Persuaded that, for the sake of the Soviet alliance, it had to be done, Marshall backed down.

In July 1943, American, British, and Anzac forces invaded and, in six weeks, overran Sicily. Americans got their first colorful war hero in the commander of the Third Army, General George Patton. Patton was a throwback, a warrior. He was a spit-and-polish general with a gleaming helmet and two pearl-handled revolvers. He ordered his men at the front to shave daily, to wear neckties, and to wash their jeeps. Oddly, his soldiers liked him because of his personal bravery and the coarse "blood and guts" language with which he rallied them. And because he was a winner, a superb commander of tanks.

Unfortunately, before the Allies moved from Sicily into Italy proper, Patton was relieved of his command. While visiting hospitals, he had rebuked two soldiers as cowards, slapping one of them in front of reporters. Eisenhower had no intention of losing the services of his best combat commander, but he had to silence Patton's many critics by getting him out of the news. He assigned "Old Blood and Guts" to a desk job in England.

To take Patton's place in Italy, Eisenhower made his worst assignment in the war. He named Mark Clark commander of the Fifth Army. Clark was as vain as Douglas MacArthur without MacArthur's military talents. His Italian campaign was a series of blunders. Clark ordered the leveling, by bombardment, of an ancient mountain monastery, Monte Cassino, where German forces were holed up. The rubble the American guns created improved the German defenses. After a risky amphibious landing at Anzio north of Monte Cassino, one of Clark's subordinates, with Clark's backing, failed to advance. The astonished Germans counterattacked and came close to capturing the entire American army. When, in June 1944, the Germans abandoned Rome, Clark ignored orders to bypass the city and surround the German army while it was in light. Instead, he staged a glorious victory parade into undefended Rome. The Germans regrouped on the "Gothic Line" north of the city and held it to the end of the war, grinding up the men unfortunate enough to be commanded by Clark.

Ike   Headquartered in England, General Eisenhower—"Ike" was his nickname—supervised the mobilization of the greatest amphibious invasion the world had seen or ever will. His job involved assembling and maintaining 4,000 vessels, 11,000 aircraft, tens of thousands of motor vehicles, and the same number of weapons of all sorts. Two million American, British, French, and Polish soldiers and small detachments of half a dozen other countries had to be trained and coordinated. He presided over constantly evolving complex plans. And through it all, he maintained cordial relations with British generals unhappy with an American commander and even had a working relationship with General Charles De Gaulle of the Free French Forces. The French contingent was not numerous but, in De Gaulle's eyes, the war was all about France, and he intensely disliked Americans.

Eisenhower made use of the suspended Patton to deceive the Germans as to where the Allies would invade France. He named Patton commander of a new army stationed in southeastern England far from the real jumping-off points of the D-Day forces. Patton's army did not exist except for mock-ups visible from the air of barracks, tanks, trucks, planes, and the other components of an invasion force. The ruse worked; the Germans were better prepared for invaders around Calais, where the English Channel is narrowest, than they were in Normandy where the landing was made. Once the fighting began, Patton was given command of the Third Army, which was real.

Politics and Strategy   There were uneasy hours, but D-Day was a colossal success. In one day, 175,000 soldiers were put ashore. By the end of June, there were 450,000 American, British, Canadian, Free French, and Polish troops in France, and 71,000 vehicles. The army charged across France and into Paris on August 25. By September, they were in Belgium and across the German border. In three months, the Allies had taken more territory than the Allies of World War I had taken in more than three years.

The British and Americans disagreed about how to finish off the Germans. Field Marshall Montgomery wanted to concentrate Allied forces in a single mighty thrust into the heart of Germany. The plan had much to recommend it. However, Eisenhower tactfully rejected it for both military and diplomatic reasons. He feared that a rapid advance on a narrow front would expose the Allies' flank and long supply line to a German counteroffensive that might surround the army. Ike preferred to exploit the Allies' overwhelming superiority in men and armaments by advancing slowly on a broad front extending from the North Sea to the border of Switzerland.

Also arguing against a rapid thrust into Germany was the fact that, now that he had a second front, Stalin was worried that the Allies intended to negotiate a separate peace with Germany from deep within the country and join German troops in attacking the Red Army. A broad, slow advance would put Stalin's suspicions to rest. Eisenhower was himself concerned that unless an orderly rendezvous of Allied and Russian troops was arranged—which could be done only when German resistance had ended—there might be spontaneous fighting between the two armies.

As always, however, Eisenhower aimed to please everyone. He consented to Montgomery's proposal that he command a miniversion of his plan by making a dash into the Netherlands to capture the mouth of the Rhine River. Montgomery was defeated, less because his plan was faulty than because, untypical for him, he executed it poorly.

The Battle of the Bulge and the End

Some historians suggest that Eisenhower gave Montgomery the go-ahead because he hoped the British general would fall on his face. (Neither man much liked the other.) If so, Eisenhower sustained a comeuppance of his own in December 1944. Paused in their broad, slow advance and expecting no action until spring, the American army in Belgium was hit with a German offensive far more powerful than Eisenhower believed the Germans capable.

The German goal was to split the broad front in two, pin the troops in the north against the North Sea, and capture the port of Antwerp, through which the Allies were receiving most of their supplies. The Battle of the Bulge (so-called because of the huge bulge the Germans pushed into Allied lines) came disturbingly close to succeeding. Snow and overcast prevented the Allies from bringing their air superiority into play. An entire division under General Anthony McAuliffe was surrounded at Bastogne. McAuliffe won his place in the quotations books by replying "Nuts!" when the Germans demanded he surrender. (An anonymous medic was the author of a cleverer remark: "they've got us surrounded, the poor bastards.")

During two anxious weeks, Patton led the Third Army in a race from the south whence he attacked the German flank. Then the weather cleared, permitting Allied planes to fly, and one by one, German defenses collapsed.

The Soviets closed in on Berlin, and a Hitler close to a mental breakdown withdrew to a bunker under the Chancery in Berlin where he presided over the disintegration of his "Thousand-Year Empire." To the end, he clung to the perverse Nazi romanticism. It was *Götterdämmerung,* the final battle of the Norse gods. The German people deserved their misery, he said, for letting their Führer down. On April 30, 1945, Hitler committed suicide after naming Admiral Karl Doenitz his successor. A few days later, Doenitz surrendered.

The Yalta Conference

Eisenhower's sensitivity to Russian suspicions reflected President Roosevelt's policy. He had insisted on "unconditional surrender" because, he thought, it would assure Stalin the United States would fight to the end. At a meeting with Stalin at Teheran in Iran late in 1943, and again at Yalta in the Crimea in February 1945, FDR did his best to assuage the Russian dictator's fears.

A few years later, when the Soviet Union was the Cold War enemy and Americans lamented Russian domination of Eastern Europe, Yalta became a byword for diplomatic blunder or, to many, for a sellout to Communism. It was at Yalta that Roosevelt did not press Stalin for specifics when Stalin said that the Soviet Union had "special interests" in eastern Europe.

Right-wing Republicans said that FDR handed the Poles, Czechs, Hungarians, Romanians, and Bulgarians over to Stalin's mercies because he was himself a Communist sympathizer. Rational critics of American diplomacy said that the president's weariness and illness, obvious in his haggard face and sagging jaw, affected his mental powers when he dealt with the calculating Stalin. At the Yalta

MAP 43.2 Allied Advances in Europe and Africa

The costly German failure to take Moscow and the Red Army's destruction of a 500,000-man German force at Stalingrad, and the successful American, British, and Canadian invasion of Normandy were the battles that ensured Nazi Germany's defeat. Except for a setback at the Battle of the Bulge late in 1944, which was brief, the war after D-Day was a war of slow but steady Allied advance on both fronts.

conference, quite privately, a British Air Marshall had remarked "his brain is obviously not what it was, ... [he] is completely unable to think hard about anything."

Plausible as that may have been, Roosevelt at his best could not have done much at Yalta to shape Stalin's intentions. He did not give Stalin anything that he did not already have. By February 1945, the Red Army occupied the Eastern

Amphibious Landing

"Tarawa was not a very big battle, as battles go," wrote G. D. Lillibridge, who was a second lieutenant there in November 1943, "and it was all over in seventy-two hours." The casualties were only 3,300 Marines, about the same number of Japanese soldiers plus 2,000 dead Japanese and Korean laborers who doubled as soldiers.

"Bloody Tarawa" was, nevertheless, a pivotal battle. If the totals were small by World War II standards, the incidence of casualties was shocking. Lillibridge's 39-man platoon lost 26; 323 of 500 drivers of landing craft died; overall, more than a third of the Americans involved were killed or wounded. The figures stunned the admirals who planned the battle. Tarawa was their introduction to the fanaticism of the Japanese soldier. Only seventeen Japanese on the tiny atoll of Betio were captured, those few because they were too seriously wounded to commit suicide.

This willingness to die for a code of honor incomprehensible to Americans was not something that could be taught in a training film. It was bred into Japan's young men from infancy. In his reflections on the battle, Lillibridge remembered a Japanese his platoon had trapped. Another Japanese Marine was moaning in agony from his wounds. The defender would reassure his dying friend, then hurl challenges and insults at Lillibridge's platoon, then comfort his buddy again.

Betio was 2 miles long and 800 yards wide—half the size of New York's Central Park. The Japanese airstrip there was the objective of the American assault. Japanese planes based in Tarawa had been harassing American supply lines between Hawaii and Australia. Tarawa was also an experiment. Admirals Chester W. Nimitz and Raymond Spruance wanted to test their theories of amphibious assault on a small, lightly manned island before what they knew would be far more difficult fighting in the Marshall Islands. "There had to be a Tarawa, a first assault on a strongly defended coral atoll," an American officer explained.

Amphibious assault against an entrenched enemy was a new kind of fighting for the American military. Still, they thought that Tarawa would be easy. They had no illusions about the fierceness of Japanese soldiers, but they had not had much time to dig in. The American assault force was overwhelming, covering 8 square miles of the Pacific. The naval bombardment itself would "obliterate the defenses." Lieutenant Lillibridge told his platoon that "there was no need to worry, no necessity for anyone to get killed, although possibly someone might get slightly wounded."

The predawn bombardment knocked out Rear Admiral Keiji Shibasaki's communications. However, the network of concrete blockhouses, coconut-log pillboxes, and underwater barricades was hardly touched by the big guns and bombs. Nature was a Japanese ally. The tide was lower than expected so the larger American landing craft could not clear the reef that fringed Betio. All but the first

European countries that Stalin insisted must have governments "friendly" to the Soviet Union. No doubt Churchill and FDR expected Poland and other Eastern Europe countries to have greater independence than they were to have. Historians disagree as to whether Stalin was set on domination of the region in 1945 or made the decision to eliminate all opposition to Russian rule only two years later, when the Cold War was underway.

wave of marines had to wade, breast deep, 800 yards to shore.

This was an element of amphibious attack in the Pacific that was painfully tested at Tarawa. Could men with no more armor than "a khaki shirt" and no way to defend themselves even get to the beach, let alone establish a base from which to displace an enemy which, during this same critical minutes, freely wreaked havoc among them?

Wading to the beach was the first horror that would haunt the survivors of Tarawa and subsequent Pacific landings for the rest of their lives. Men remembered it as a "nightmarish turtle race," run in slow-motion. It was "like being completely suspended, like being under a strong anesthetic." "I could have sworn that I could have reached out and touched a hundred bullets." "The water never seemed clear of tiny men." They had to push through the floating corpses of their comrades and hundreds of thousands of fish dead from the bombardment. The lagoon was red with blood all day.

The second nightmare waited on the beach. Shibasaki had constructed a sea wall of coconut logs, 3 to 5 feet high. To the Americans, it looked like shelter. In fact, Japanese mortars had been registered to batter the long thin line precisely. To peek above the log palisades was to draw the fire of 200 well-positioned Japanese machine guns. Marines remembered that they were capable of moving beyond the sea wall only because to remain there meant certain death. About half the American casualties were suffered in the water, most of the rest on the beach.

One by one, almost always at close quarters, the blockhouses and pillboxes were destroyed, but it took three days to secure the tiny island. The aftermath was almost as devastating to morale as the unexpected difficulties of the battle. The vegetation that had covered the island was gone. Thousands of corpses floating in the surf and festering in the blockhouses bloated and rotted in the intense heat. The triumphant marines looked like anything but victors. They sat staring, exhausted. "I passed boys who ... looked older than their fathers," General Holland Smith said, "it had chilled their souls. They found it hard to believe they were actually alive."

Smith and the other commanders learned from Tarawa that one did not gamble on tides over coral reefs. Not until the last months of the Pacific War, when the close approach to the Japanese homeland made much larger forces of Japanese defenders even fiercer in their resistance, would the extremity of Tarawa's terror be repeated.

The Pacific commanders also learned that while the vast American superiority of armament and firepower was essential and ultimately decisive, taking a Pacific island was a much more personal and human effort than twentieth-century military men had assumed. With a grace rare in a modern officer, General Julian Smith frankly asserted, "There was one thing that won this battle ... and that was the supreme courage of the Marines. The [Japanese] prisoners tell us that what broke their morale was not the bombing, not the naval gunfire, but the sight of Marines who kept coming ashore."

THE TWILIGHT OF JAPAN, THE NUCLEAR DAWN

Also on Roosevelt's mind at Yalta was his determination to bring the Soviet Union into the war against Japan so to save American lives in the final battles. Stalin agreed that the Red Army would attack Japanese forces in China, in August 1945.

The Strategy   After the battle of Midway in June 1942, the United States aided the Chinese by flying supplies from British India "over the hump" of the Himalayas. The Kuomintang troops under Chiang Kai-shek and Communist soldiers commanded by Mao Zedong were tying down a million-strong Japanese army. Unfortunately, they were more hostile toward one another than toward their common enemy. The Japanese, Chiang Kai-shek said, were "a disease of the skin," the Chinese Communists were a "disease of the heart."

American forces in the Pacific were divided into two distinct commands. After the conquest of the Solomon Islands, which were vital to Australia's security, troops under Douglas MacArthur pushed toward Japan via New Guinea and the Philippines. MacArthur was a bizarre man who often acted as if he were the immortal he posed as being. He exposed himself to Japanese fire until his aides physically restrained him. He commanded his soldiers to take antimalaria drugs but refused to take them himself. He was not the demigod he thought he was; he was a superb commander. He planned and executed eighty-seven amphibious landings, all successful. He worked hard to minimize his soldiers' casualties. He also took all the credit for his operations. Some of his field commanders were superb soldiers, but their names are forgotten today because, in MacArthur's telling, he was the only general in the hemisphere.

The second American advance on Japan, through the Central Pacific, was commanded by Admiral Chester W. Nimitz. MacArthur's goal was highly personal; he wanted to liberate the Philippines to redeem his promise of 1942 despite the fact that his superiors in Washington concluded that the Philippines be bypassed in favor of an assault on Japan itself. Nimitz's mission was to island-hop across the Pacific near enough to Japan that big American land-based bombers could bomb the country into submission. By its nature, Nimitz's war involved passing by Japanese-occupied islands that could not threaten his fleet from the rear. He let the Japanese garrisons there wither.

Island Warfare   To soldiers slogging through the mud and cold of Europe, the troops in the Pacific were on a holiday. They were basking in a balmy climate, meeting the enemy in battle only after long intervals of relaxation. Life between battles in Hawaii and Australia was very pleasant, but elsewhere it was miserable. "Our war was waiting," novelist James Michener wrote, "You rotted on New Caledonia waiting for Guadalcanal. Then you sweated twenty pounds away in Guadal waiting for Bougainville. ... And pretty soon you hated the man next to you, and you dreaded the look of a coconut tree."

Capturing islands that were specks on an all-blue map meant battles more vicious than any Americans experienced in Europe: "a blinding flash ... a day of horror ... an evening of terror." Japanese soldiers were more frightening enemies than Germans. They were indoctrinated with the belief that it was a betrayal of national and personal honor to surrender under any circumstances.

A Terrifying Enemy   To an astonishing extent, Japanese soldiers did fight to the death, taking American marines and soldiers with them long after it was obvious the battle was over. It took the Americans six months to win control of microscopic Guadalcanal in the Solomons, even though the defenders had not had time to complete their fortifications. At Tarawa in the Gilbert Islands, defended by 5,000 Japanese troops, only 17 were taken prisoner. In the Marshall Islands, 79 Japanese survived. Of 35,000 Japanese on Saipan, including civilians, all but 1,000 fought to the death or committed suicide. On the Alaskan island of Attu, which the Japanese occupied much of the war, only 27 soldiers were captured; 2,700 committed suicide when they could no longer fight.

The deadliness of fighting Japanese led to American brutalities that were rare in Italy and France where opposing officers observed rules of war and, with some exceptions, German soldiers surrendered when their position was hopeless. In the Pacific, after numerous incidents of Japanese soldiers surrendering and then blowing themselves and their captors up with concealed hand grenades, shooting Japanese with their hands raised was commonplace.

When escapees from Japanese prisoner of war camps in the Philippines and Burma revealed the viciousness with which prisoners were treated, American atrocities increased. Marines cut off the ears of dead Japanese as gifts for their girlfriends. Newspaper editors applauded reports of American sailors machine-gunning Japanese sailors treading water after their ship had been sunk.

Fighting to the Last Man   By the spring of 1945, Japan's situation was hopeless. America's war with Germany was over. When the fall of Saipan in November 1944 provided a base from which bombers could reach Japan with ease, the country's wooden cities went up like tinder. A single incendiary bomb raid on Tokyo on March 9, 1945, killed 85,000 people and destroyed 250,000 buildings.

After the huge Battle of Leyte Gulf in October 1944 (it involved 282 warships), the Japanese navy, for practical purposes, ceased to exist while the Americans cruised the seas with 4,000 vessels, shelling the Japanese coast at will. United States submarines destroyed half of Japan's merchant fleet within a few months.

When the United States invaded Okinawa in April 1945, Japanese air power was reduced to little more than Kamikaze suicide pilots flying slapped together planes packed with high explosives. They did terrific damage. At Okinawa, kamikazes sunk 36 ships (more than were lost at Pearl Harbor) and damaged 300. The Japanese turned the biggest battleship in the world, the *Yamato*, into a Kamikaze. With 2,300 sailors aboard, the *Yamato* steamed for Okinawa on April 6, 1945, with just enough fuel for a one-way trip. It never even burned that. Attacked by 400 carrier-based planes, the great ship was hit by at least ten torpedoes and twenty-one bombs and sank.

And yet, the closer the Americans got to the Japanese homeland, the more fanatically the Japanese fought. Taking Iwo Jima, a wretched volcanic island wanted as a landing strip, cost 28,000 American lives. In almost three months on Okinawa, 80,000 Americans were killed or wounded. More than 100,000 Japanese were killed; only 8,000 surrendered (100,000 civilians may have committed suicide).

The military estimated that the invasion of Japan, scheduled for November 1, 1945, would cost a million casualties, as many as the United States had suffered in more than three years in both Europe and the Pacific. The Japanese still had 5 million men under arms.

Hiroshima: What a single bomb did.

A Death and a Birth

This chilling prospect put the atomic bomb, conceived as a weapon to be used against now defeated Nazi Germany, on the table in the Pacific theater. The Manhattan Project, code name for the program that secretly developed the first nuclear weapon, dated to 1939 when physicist Albert Einstein, a refugee from Naziism, wrote in longhand to President Roosevelt that it was possible to unleash inconceivable amounts of energy by nuclear fission—by splitting an atom. Einstein was a pacifist, but he was aware that German scientists were interested in and capable of producing an "atomic bomb." Such a device in Hitler's hands was terrifying.

Einstein was too prestigious to ignore. The government secretly allotted $2 billion to the Manhattan Project. Under the direction of J. Robert Oppenheimer, scientists worked on Long Island, underneath a football stadium in Chicago, and at isolated Los Alamos, New Mexico. At one point, the Manhattan Project was consuming one-seventh of the electricity generated in the United States. In April 1945, Oppenheimer told Washington that the project was four months away from testing a bomb.

The decision whether or not to use the bomb against Japan did not fall to President Roosevelt. Reelected to a fourth term in 1944 over Governor Thomas E. Dewey of New York, Roosevelt died of a stroke on April 12, 1945. He was at Warm Springs, Georgia, sitting for a portrait painter when he said, "I have a terrific headache" and slumped in his chair.

The outpouring of grief that swept the nation at the loss of the man who was president longer than any other was real and profound. Silent crowds lined the tracks to watch the train that brought FDR back to Washington for the last time. People wept in the streets. In Washington, however, sorrow was overshadowed by apprehensions that his successor, Harry S. Truman, was not up to the job.

Truman, "Little Boy," and "Fat Man" Truman was an honest politico who rose as a dependable, hard worker in the Kansas City Democratic machine. He proved his abilities as chairman of an important Senate committee during the war but impressed few as the caliber of person to head a nation. Unprepossessing in appearance, bespectacled, a dandy (he once operated a haberdashery), and given to salty language, Truman was nominated as vice president in 1944 as a compromise candidate. Democratic conservatives wanted the left-liberal vice president, Henry A. Wallace, out of office, but they could not force southerner James J. Byrnes on the party's liberal wing. Harry Truman was acceptable to both sides.

Although FDR was obviously in bad health, Truman was stunned to learn he was president. "I don't know whether you fellows ever had a load of hay or a bull fall on you," he told reporters on his first day in office, "but last night the moon, the stars, and all the planets fell on me." If he too was himself unsure of his abilities, Truman did not shy from difficult decisions and never doubted his responsibility. A plaque on his desk read "The Buck Stops Here." As president, the president could not "pass the buck" to anyone else.

When advisors informed him that the alternative to using the atomic bomb was a million American casualties, he did not hesitate to give the order to use it. On August 6, a bomb nicknamed "Little Boy," was dropped on Hiroshima, killing 100,000 people in an instant and dooming another 100,000 to death from injury and radiation poisoning. Two days later, a bomb of different design, "Fat Man," was exploded over Nagasaki with the same results.

Incredibly, some in the Japanese high command still wanted to fight on. (It is impossible to overstate Japanese military fanaticism.) Had they known that the Americans had no more atomic bombs in their arsenal, they might have carried the debate in Emperor Hirohito's cabinet. After some hesitation, Hirohito agreed to surrender on August 15, 1945, if he were allowed to remain emperor. The United States agreed. The war ended officially on the decks of the battleship *Missouri* on September 2.

44

A DIFFERENT KIND OF WORLD
Entering the Nuclear Age, 1946–1952

The release of atomic energy constitutes a new force too revolutionary to consider in the framework of old ideas.

—Harry S. Truman

Science has brought forth this danger, but the real problem is in the minds and hearts of men.

—Albert Einstein

The world has achieved brilliance without wisdom, power without conscience. Ours is a world of nuclear giants and ethical infants.

—Omar Bradley

Few wars have ended so abruptly as the war with Japan. Even after Hiroshima and Nagasaki, some American strategists feared that Japanese fanatics, who were numerous even in high government positions, would continue to resist, whence it would be necessary to invade the country and sustain a predicted million casualties. As late as August 5 (although this was not then known), Emperor Hirohito was prepared to order his ministers to exhort the Japanese to fight the Americans village to village to extermination, if necessary. On August 10, after the destruction of Hiroshima and Nagasaki, Hirohito was still considering going on. Only on August 14, did he decide on surrender and even then some of his officers launched a plot to silence him and continue the suicidal war.

THE SHADOW OF COLD WAR

The fireballs and mushroom clouds over Japan announced the beginning of a new era in world history—the nuclear age—when going to war meant not merely the risk of defeat, but also the risk of total destruction. For the victorious Allies, the first legacy of World War II was not a triumph so total that the world was theirs for the shaping. It was the stewardship of an uncertain place with a dubious future.

Cold War 1945–1953

1945	1946	1947	1948	1949	1950	1951	1952	1953

1945 Yalta Conference

1945–1953 Harry S. Truman president

1946 Churchill's "Iron Curtain" speech

1947 Kennan defines "containment"; aid to Greece and Turkey; Marshall Plan

1948 Truman wins upset victory

1948–1949 Berlin blockade and airlift

1949 NATO and Warsaw Pact; Communists win in China

1950 Korean War begins; Hiss guilty of perjury

1951 Truman fires MacArthur

Eisenhower elected president 1952

Korean War concluded 1953

Legacies   A second legacy of the Second World War was the recognition that human beings were morally quite capable of "pushing the button," of loosing the power of nuclear weapons, and risking worldwide desolation to achieve goals that could not possibly justify the gamble. Indeed, World War II demonstrated human depravity on so colossal a scale as to end, for all but fools, the millennia old debate over the goodness of human nature. Reliable evidence that the Nazis were systematically murdering Jews had been in Allied hands for two years when the war ended. But no one was prepared to learn that the Nazis had killed 6 million people, disposing of their bodies in purpose-built crematoria. Nor were Soviet, British, and American soldiers prepared for the sights that greeted them when they liberated the death camps and the more numerous slave labor camps—living skeletons, sometimes still able to walk, but not really quite human; the human garbage dumps, arms and legs protruding obscenely from hillocks of corpses. These spectacles, recorded in hundreds of photographs and films, mocked every delusion before and since that, at heart, people are good as poor Anne Frank, who almost survived, wrote in her diary.

The third legacy of the war was that only two nations emerged genuine victors—the United States and the Soviet Union—and that, once the Nazis were defeated, they had little in common. For two years after the war, Russian and American leaders seemed to be trying to preserve the cooperation that had brought Germany down. Sixty years later, no one has convincingly proved the sincerity or the deviousness of the motives and acts of the key leaders in either country in 1945, 1946, and 1947. No one—and many have claimed they did—has persuasively apportioned *blame* for starting the "Cold War." Almost the only thing about the postwar whirl of events that can be stated as historical fact is that, by the end of 1947, the world's only two great military powers glowered at one another belligerently, stopping short only of World War III.

The great majority of Americans, but not all, believed that the ungrateful, treacherous, atheistic Russian Communists, bent on ruling the world, started the Cold War. Until September 1949, it was enough to be angry. The United States held the trump card—"the bomb." Then, in September 1949, years before

Margaret Bourke-White. LIFE Magazine © Time, Inc./Getty Images.

Nazi concentration camp inmates awaiting processing and release in 1945. This was not an extermination camp or even a labor camp in Poland forgotten by the Nazis when it was no longer able to produce war material. These men, mostly young and healthy, were lucky enough to be fed adequately until the end of the war.

American scientists believed it within the competence of Soviet science, Russia tested an atomic bomb. The catastrophe for which the species had demonstrated its capacity was no longer an American monopoly. In a nuclear war, Americans would be victims as well as executioners.

Roots of Animosity   A good many words have been written about the origins of the Cold War between the United States and the Soviet Union that began about 1947 and ended in 1989. Why did the allies of World War II have a falling out that poised them opposite one another as enemies for forty years, refraining from "hot war" only because of fear of the consequences for their own people? Which side was to blame?

The final question is the one least worth asking. American principles and Soviet ideology were incompatible and always had been. The United States was dedicated to preserving capitalism as the bulwark of individual freedoms and material prosperity. Internationally, that meant a world open to free trade and economic development. The Soviets, to the year of Stalin's death and beyond, remained committed to state ownership of the means of production for the enrichment not of a small class of capitalists but of the entire society.

During World War II, propagandists on both sides downplayed the incompatibility of their principles—ignored it, actually, and for good reason. The Soviet Union was fighting for its very survival, and the Roosevelt administration believed that if Russia fell to the Nazis, the United States too would be facing destruction. When the war was over, the differences between the "free world" and the "Communist system" resurfaced quickly, focusing on the future status of the nations of Eastern Europe: Poland, Czechoslovakia, Hungary, Romania, Yugoslavia, Albania, and Bulgaria. Would they be self-determining liberal democracies perhaps hostile to the Soviet Union? Or Soviet "satellite states," Russia's broad buffer zone against another invasion like Hitler's in 1941.

It Started in Eastern Europe Exactly what Stalin had in mind in 1945 for postwar Europe cannot be known. He had, in the interests of the alliance, proclaimed an end to fomenting international revolution. His public statements and diplomatic demands late in the war (and after) were often uncongenial to the United States but, taken at face value, not beyond negotiation. President Roosevelt was confident he could continue to "work with" Stalin.

Exactly what Roosevelt believed was to be the status of the nations of eastern Europe liberated from the Nazis is also unknowable. As a Wilsonian, he was committed to national self-determination and democratic governments in Poland, Czechoslovakia, Hungary, Romania, Bulgaria, and Yugoslavia—nations World War I had revived or created. He was also aware that, except in Czechoslovakia, democracy had failed in every one of those countries. Did he appreciate that democracy and individual liberties as defined in the Atlantic Charter had only the weakest of roots in Eastern European history and culture? There is reason to believe that, like other later American policy makers, these things did not much matter to him.

Then there were Soviet interests, the fact that Hitler had come within an ace of destroying the country. Did Roosevelt understand that when, at the Yalta Conference, Stalin said that the nations bordering the Soviet Union must be "friendly," a buffer zone providing some security in case of another attack from the West, that Stalin was not mouthing platitudes?

How could a democratic Poland be "friendly" to Russia? The Nazis ruled Poland for 5 years; Russia had ruled the country, and not gently, for almost 150 years. Historically, Poles looked on Russia more than on Germany as the national enemy. The notion that the war against the Nazis had ushered in a new era in Russo-Polish relations was resoundingly discredited in 1940 when the Red Army massacred 5,000 Polish army officers at Katyn, proof of which was released by the Germans in 1943. Then, late in the war, with Russian troops advancing rapidly toward Warsaw, the Polish government-in-exile in London called for an uprising behind German lines. As soon as it started, Stalin abruptly halted the Russian advance and the Germans were able to butcher the Polish partisans.

A democratic Poland would not be "friendly" to Russia. A Poland "friendly" to the Soviet Union would not be fully democratic. To a lesser degree, the same was true of Romania, Hungary, and Czechoslovakia. And their destinies was not a matter of table talk. In 1945, the whole of Eastern Europe was occupied by the Red Army.

Truman Draws a Line

If Roosevelt had a workable solution to the dilemma, it died with him. And Harry Truman was not the sly prevaricator FDR had been. As a man and as president, in Dean Acheson's words, he was "straightforward, decisive, simple, entirely honest." He neither liked nor trusted the Soviets and did not hide his feelings. Even before he met Stalin at Potsdam, he summoned Soviet Ambassador V. M. Molotov to the White House and scolded him so harshly for laying the foundations of puppet governments in Eastern Europe that Molotov exclaimed, "I have never been talked to like that in my life!" For a man who was so close to the bullying Stalin for so long, this was surely not the truth, but that Molotov said it indicates how hard-nosed Truman had been.

By 1946, it seemed clear that the Russians were not going to permit free elections in Poland. Truman was restrained in his official pronouncements, but he applauded a speech by Winston Churchill in Fulton, Missouri, in March that Truman had read in advance. An "iron curtain" as descending across Europe, the former prime minister said, a fortified frontier; it was time for the Western democracies to confront the Soviet Union about it. In September 1946, Truman himself signaled that, if a cold war had not begun, the wartime alliance was dead. He dismissed secretary of commerce and former vice president, Henry A. Wallace, the only member of his cabinet who openly argued that the United States should be more accommodating with the Soviets.

Containment and the Truman Doctrine

In 1947, Truman's policy moved beyond "getting tough with the Russians." In a long memorandum later published anonymously in the influential journal *Foreign Affairs,* a Soviet expert in the State Department, George F. Kennan, argued that Russian actions in Eastern Europe should not be understood in terms of Communist revolutionary zeal alone. Long before Communism and its missionary impulse, Russia had been pushing its frontiers—or trying to push them—to the West. Stalin's expansionism was new only in the Soviet conviction that the capitalist states of Western Europe (and the United States) were determined to destroy communism in Russia.

Kennan said that it was impossible to come to a satisfactory accommodation with the Soviet Union as long as its leaders feared for the survival of their revolution. Only time, probably quite a long time, would alter the premises of Soviet foreign policy.

Until that time, Kennan argued, Soviet territorial expansion must be halted. The United States must make it unmistakably clear that further Soviet expansion would not be tolerated: Where the iron curtain hung in 1947 was where it would stay. The Russians, he predicted, would repeatedly test American resolve to hold the line with limited aggressions that were not sufficient to merit all-out war. The object of American policy should be to respond to such Soviet probes at just high enough a level to stop them, but not so aggressively as to threaten Soviet security. From his knowledge of Russian history, Kennan predicted that the Soviet leaders would back off. By *containing* Russian expansion without threatening the security of the Soviet Union and the satellite states, nuclear war could be avoided until such time as the Soviets were willing to make agreements that reduced the intensity of the Cold War.

"Containment Policy" did not yet have its name when Truman put it to work. Stalin had stepped up Soviet support of Communist guerrillas in Greece and Turkey. On March 12, Truman asked Congress to appropriate $400 million in military assistance to the pro-Western governments of Greece and Turkey. That was more than enough for them to suppress the rebels. When they did, more or less as Kennan predicted, Stalin did not raise the ante and the risk of direct Soviet-American confrontation; he abandoned the guerrillas. He accepted the line the United States had drawn. Truman's policy of decisively supporting governments threatened by communist rebels came to be known as the Truman Doctrine.

The Marshall Plan The United States feared that France and Italy were also vulnerable to a Communist takeover, not from armed rebels but because Communist political parties in both countries had considerable popular support. In parliamentary elections, the Italian Communist party dependably won about 25 percent of the vote, the French party slightly less.

Truman's advisors persuaded him that the French and Italian Communists were flourishing because only they offered a plausible response to the widespread unemployment and poverty due to the war's destruction of the economy in both countries. The remedy was to redistribute the disproportionate share of the world's wealth in American hands to the nations of Europe so that they could construct prosperous economies.

On June 5, 1947, Secretary of State George C. Marshall proposed that the United States spend huge sums to reconstruct the European economy. Not only were Allies and the victims of German aggression invited to apply for assistance, but also Germany (then divided into British, French, American, and Soviet occupation zones), and nations neutral during the war such as Sweden and Switzerland. So as to disguise the fact that the Marshall Plan was a Cold War measure, Marshall even invited the Soviet Union and the nations behind the Iron Curtain to participate in the program.

This was a gamble. Had Russia's satellite states agreed, they could easily have sabotaged the Marshall Plan. Marshall and Truman calculated that Russia and the iron curtain countries would reject American aid as a plot to destroy socialism. Stalin had made it clear as early as mid-1946 that the Soviet Union would tolerate no western interference in its internal affairs which, by mid-1947, meant the affairs of the nations of Eastern Europe too. Even before the Soviet Union had an atomic bomb, Stalin rejected an international proposal by Bernard Baruch to outlaw nuclear weapons because Baruch's plan involved enforcement on the scene by the United Nations.

As expected, the Soviets condemned the Marshall Plan. The Communist regimes in Eastern Europe, now including Czechoslovakia, did the same. The massive American financial and technical aid went to sixteen nations, both those with strong Communist political parties like France and Italy, and countries where Communism was weak: Switzerland, the Netherlands, Ireland, Norway. Winston Churchill called the Marshall Plan "the most unsordid act in history." British Foreign Minister Ernest Bevin was even more effusive: "It was like a lifeline to sinking men. It seemed to bring hope where there was none. The generosity of it was beyond my belief."

Freezing the   Containment was successful. The United States managed to
Lines   freeze the extent of the Russian sphere of influence where it
                      had been when Churchill delivered his "iron curtain" speech.
In June 1948, the Soviets did as Kennan had predicted they would do—tested American resolve—when Stalin blockaded West Berlin, the allied-occupied half of the German capital deep within Communist East Germany. Unable to provision the city of 2 million by train and truck, the United States seemed to have two options: give up West Berlin or invade East Germany.

Instead, President Truman ordered a massive airlift that no one entirely believed could succeed. For a year, huge C-47s and C-54s flew in the necessities of life and a few of luxuries that the West Berliners needed in order to hold out. Day and night, planes flew into West Berlin, unloaded, and returned for a new load. More than 250,000 flights carried 2 million tons of everything from candy bars to coal. The immensity of the operation and American tenacity in maintaining it made it clear to the Soviets that the United States did not want war but the Soviets had overstepped the limits. The Soviets responded as Kennan said they would. Instead of shooting down the planes—an act of war—they watched. In May 1949, they lifted the blockade.

By then, the Cold War had entered a new phase. In April 1949, the United States, Canada, and nine western European nations formed NATO, the North Atlantic Treaty Organization, a military alliance—the first, during peacetime, in American history. In September, the Soviet Union responded with the Warsaw Pact, an alliance of the nations of Eastern Europe. In September 1949, the Soviet Union exploded its first atomic bomb, and soon thereafter the United States perfected the hydrogen bomb, a much more destructive weapon. A nuclear arms race was under way.

DOMESTIC POLITICS UNDER TRUMAN

President Truman's foreign policy was decisive and, in Europe, successful. At home, he struggled with common postwar problems: rapid inflation, a serious housing shortage, and bitter industrial disputes. At first he seemed to founder. He could not "command" Congress as FDR had been able to do. In 1946, the Republicans won majorities in both the House and Senate for the first time in sixteen years. Their leader, Senator Robert A. Taft of Ohio (son of President Taft) had opposed just about everything Truman's predecessors, Dr. New Deal and Dr. Win-the-War, had ever done.

The Taft-Hartley   The Republicans ran their congressional election campaign
Act   of 1946 on an effective two-word slogan, "Had Enough?"
                       The results seemed to say that voters had. They picked up
fifty-five seats in the House, an astonishing nineteen in the Senate. One of the few

Democratic senators to win in 1946, J. William Fulbright of Arkansas, was so crestfallen he suggested that in the interests of a functional government, Truman resign in favor of a Republican successor. Truman did not take the proposal well, and the Republicans did not take it seriously. It was enough that such a turnaround guaranteed that they would win the presidency in 1948—Taft was justified in thinking he would be the candidate. However, they were understandably confident they would elect their nominee in 1948; in the meantime, they set out to dismantle as much of the New Deal as Congress could.

Their biggest success was the Taft-Hartley Labor-Management Relations Act of 1947. Enacted over Truman's veto, it reversed the government's active backing of the labor movement. Taft-Hartley emphasized the workers' rights to refuse to join a union by forbidding the "closed shop." That is, under the Wagner Act of 1935, when a majority of a company's employees chose a union as their bargaining agent, all of the company's employees were required to belong to that union as a condition of employment. Taft-Hartley made it illegal to dismiss an employee who refused to join the union or to pay the union a fee equivalent to union dues.

Truman called the Taft-Hartley Act a "slave labor" law. It was not that. Indeed, by emphasizing individual rights, it won the approval of all but pro-union zealots. Taft-Hartley did not, as the Republicans hoped, cripple the organized labor movement, now more than 10 million strong. Workers in former closed-shop companies did not quit their unions wholesale, hoping to avoid the benefits the unions had won without paying dues. Gratitude for what unions had done for them was still a powerful force. Social pressures to support the union were strong (and, no doubt, some workers not delighted with their union were afraid of getting beat up).

The major consequence of Taft-Hartley was to rally organized labor and its political muscle behind President Truman who, as a senator, had not been particularly prolabor. Encouraged by this unexpected support, he took the offensive against a Congress out to embarrass him. He vetoed eighty anti-New Deal bills, converting himself into a crusading liberal. When Republican critics mocked his homey manners and common appearance, he denounced his enemies in Congress as stooges of the rich and privileged.

Truman coined his own two word slogan, the "Fair Deal." He sent proposal after proposal expanding social services to Capitol Hill. Among them was a national health insurance plan such as most European nations had adopted. All his proposals were rejected, but Truman harvested a bumper crop of political hay. He stole the initiative from a somewhat bewildered Taft, denouncing the "no-good do-nothing Congress" that denied Americans sensible programs designed to improve their lives.

Civil Rights   Truman was a southerner by conviction. However, when conservative southern Democratic segregationists voted with Taft's Republicans as often as they voted with northern and western Democrats, the president sent Congress an antilynching bill that sorely embarrassed Taft who, in his rhetoric, had never abandoned the Republican tradition of sympathy for African Americans. Truman forced the Taft Republicans into voting against it in order to placate their southern Democratic allies. He also asked Congress to declare the poll tax illegal and to enact legislation to protect blacks who had gotten good factory jobs during the war. The Republican-Southern Democrat coalition defeated both. To show he meant business—and that he, unlike Congress, was doing his job—he issued an executive order banning racial discrimination in the armed forces, the civil service, and in companies that did business with the government.

Truman did not assail Jim Crow segregation laws in the southern states. (Personally, he approved of them.) But he went much further in attacking the civil inequality of African Americans than Roosevelt had considered doing.

Four Candidates   In the spring of 1948, Truman's popularity was on the upswing. His attacks on the "do nothing" Congress swung many people to his side. Americans were getting accustomed to the president's hard-hitting style. Still, not a single journalistic political expert, including devoted Democrats, gave Truman a chance to win the presidential election in November. The Democrats had been in power for sixteen years, longer than any party since the Virginia dynasty of Jefferson, Madison, and Monroe. Many New Deal bureaucracies were inefficient; and rumors of corruption wafted about the capital and in Republican newspapers.

One of the most famous photographs in American political history: President Harry S. Truman displays a prematurely headlined edition of the Republican Chicago Tribune announcing the results of the 1948 presidential election. The Tribune was wrong even about Illinois ("G.O.P. Sweep Indicated in State") which, when all the votes were counted, gave its electoral votes to Truman.

In the summer, Truman's prospects went from poor to impossible. The Democratic party split three ways. Former vice president and Secretary of Commerce Henry A. Wallace agreed to be the candidate of the newly formed Progressive party. Except for adopting the name, the Progressives of 1948 were unrelated to the Progressive party of 1912–1916. That had been a Republican party. Henry Wallace's Progressives were left wing Democratic party liberals and socialists supported—somewhat to Wallace's chagrin—by Communists and "fellow travelers," non-members who sympathized with the Communist party. Wallace claimed that he, not Truman, was FDR's heir. He would further New Deal reforms and restore FDR's wartime policy of cooperation with the Soviet Union. Implicitly, explicitly on occasion, Wallace blamed the Truman administration for the Cold War.

Southern Democrats, angry at Truman's civil rights proposals and criticism of racial discrimination in the party platform written by the liberal mayor of Minneapolis, Hubert H. Humphrey, formed the States' Rights party, or "Dixiecrats" as they were generally known. They nominated 46-year-old Governor Strom Thurmond of South Carolina as their candidate. Thurmond was an aggressive proponent of Jim Crow segregation, but he was by no means the racist extremist many other southern politicians were. He took a strong stand against lynching in South Carolina, threatening to prosecute and convict whites who participated in lynch mobs. He opposed the poll tax, not so that African Americans could vote but because it prevented poor whites from voting.

The Dixiecrats had no illusions about winning the election. (Wallace, who had a mystical streak, entertained them from time to time.) The Dixiecrat goal was to take enough electoral votes away from Truman to remind the national Democratic party that acquiescence in racial segregation in the South was a prerequisite of winning presidential elections.

Presented with a sure victory, the Republicans backed away from Senator Taft and his dogmatic views and, once again, nominated Thomas E. Dewey, a moderate and proven vote getter; he was the first Republican governor of New York since 1922.

Give 'Em Hell, Harry Dewey's campaign strategy was a tried and true one. With every poll showing him winning the election easily, he avoided taking a strong stand on any issue just as Franklin D. Roosevelt had done in 1932. People were voting *against* Truman. Any strong position Dewey took could only cost him votes. Unlike FDR, who was a superb public speaker, Dewey's platform manner was bland and uninspiring. So he made only sixteen speeches during the entire campaign.

That was a mistake. President Truman, facing defeat, with nothing to lose, pulled out the stops. He campaigned hard, as if he were the challenger, hoping that one or another of his Fair Deal proposals would touch a nerve or, at least, that his earthy, aggressive style would convince voters that he was the leader that Dewey was not. "Give 'em hell, Harry," a supporter shouted at a rally, and Truman made it his motto. In the spring he traveled 9,500 miles by train, delivering 73 speeches in eighteen states. During the summer of 1948, he called Congress into

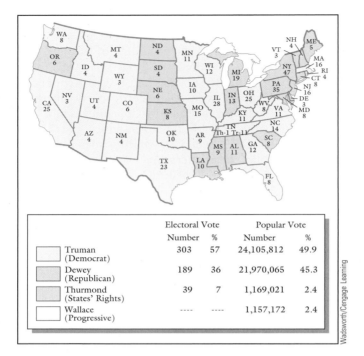

	Electoral Vote		Popular Vote	
	Number	%	Number	%
Truman (Democrat)	303	57	24,105,812	49.9
Dewey (Republican)	189	36	21,970,065	45.3
Thurmond (States' Rights)	39	7	1,169,021	2.4
Wallace (Progressive)	----	----	1,157,172	2.4

MAP 44.1 Presidential Election, 1948

Dewey's sweep of the Northeast and favorable early returns from the Midwest are why Republicans went to bed on election day night believing they had won. By noon the next day, the final count in Ohio and Illinois that had looked to be Dewey states went to Truman, a swing of 100 electoral votes. And the late-reporting West was solidly Democratic. The election of 1948 was one of the greatest surprise upsets in the history of American presidential elections.

special session and a corps of assistants led by Clark Clifford sent bill after bill to the Republican Congress. As the Republicans voted down his proposals, Truman went back on tour, totaling up 32,000 miles and 356 speeches. Did Americans want four years of Republican negativism under Thomas E. Dewey?

On election night, when returns from states in the Eastern time zone were nearly complete, Dewey had swept the Northeast and seemed to be winning in the Midwest. The editor of the passionately anti-Democratic Chicago *Tribune* decided to scoop the competition by declaring Dewey elected in a banner headline. The next day, Truman took uncontained delight in posing for photographers with a copy of the newspaper. He had won. He squeaked out majorities in Illinois and Ohio, big states thought to be in Dewey's pocket, and swept the western states. The Republicans were stunned. Dewey said he felt as if he'd awakened in a coffin "but if I'm dead, why do I have to go to the bathroom?" The Dixiecrats were stunned. Thurmond carried only four southern states. Truman's upset victory demonstrated that the Democratic party did not necessarily need a solid South in order to win a national election.

SUCCESS IN JAPAN, FAILURE IN CHINA

The Democrats won majorities in both houses of Congress too, but little more was heard of the Fair Deal. Like Wilson and FDR, Truman was diverted from domestic concerns by a crisis abroad—in Asia.

The Japanese conquest of East and parts of South Asia left most of the region's colonies and nations on the brink of chaos. The French returned to Indo-China (Vietnam, Laos, Cambodia) which President Roosevelt had determined to prevent. The British reasserted colonial authority in Malaya and Singapore (which FDR disliked but did not openly oppose). The Dutch were unable to regain control of the East Indies (Indonesia). The Indonesians had welcomed the Japanese as fellow Asians and did not want the Dutch back. When Dutch civilians were freed from Japanese internment camps after more than three years of suffering, they were pelted with stones. The Filipinos, by way of contrast, had resisted the Japanese and were granted independence in 1946.

MacArthur in Japan
The only other firmly pro-American nation in East Asia was defeated Japan. Marshall-Plan-like financial aid nurtured a slow but steady recovery of the Japanese economy and an enlightened military occupation won the support and even the friendship of the Japanese people.

American soldiers, sailors, and marines had come to think of the Japanese as fanatics who fought to the death or committed suicide rather than surrender. When they occupied the country they were astonished to discover that the Japanese, including former soldiers, were submissive, polite, deferential, and even cordial. The first occupation troops off the boats were greeted by women calling "yoo-hoo."

The Japanese economy was devastated. Some 2.7 million soldiers and civilians were dead. A fourth of the nation's wealth had been destroyed. Forty percent of the 66 largest cities had been leveled, 65 percent of Tokyo, 89 percent of industrial Nagoya. Nine million people were homeless. But somehow, within months, a barter economy had emerged and recovery had begun.

Douglas MacArthur, commanding the occupation forces, must be credited for the democratization of Japanese government. MacArthur understood the importance of continuity in Japanese culture. He assumed the role of *shogun,* a familiar figure in Japanese history. *Shoguns* were military strongmen who, while never molesting the sacred person of the emperors, actually ruled the country without regard for the emperor's wishes. He virtually disappeared from sight, which added to his mystique. He did not travel except for a speedy commute each day between his residence and his office. He did not socialize with Japanese as he had socialized with the Philippine elite in Manila. He passed his evenings watching Hollywood movies. During almost five years in Tokyo he spoke to only sixteen high Japanese officials more than once. He gave his orders through his American subordinates.

He was more mysterious a figure to ordinary Japanese than the emperor was. When he decided it was advisable that he meet Hirohito, Hirohito came to him; he did not call at the imperial palace. The Japanese constitution he virtually dictated established a democratic parliamentary democracy closed to the military that had taken Japan into war. The Constitution minimized the influence of the *zaibatsu,* the huge corporate conglomerates that had dominated the Japanese economy. Few conquerors have been as successful in winning the friendship of those they conquered as the United States in Japan.

An Opportunity Missed?   The story in China was altogether different. The United States never had a military presence on the mainland. When the Japanese army in China was evacuated, Chiang Kai Shek's Nationalists controlled half the country, Mao Zedong's Communist forces the rest. The United States recognized Chiang's Nationalist government but, since the beginning of the war, many high-ranking American "old China hands" had denounced the regime. At best Chiang was an ineffective ruler; at worst his supporters were hopelessly corrupt, exploiting the peasantry and driving them into Mao's camp. General Joseph "Vinegar Joe" Stilwell had peppered Washington with denunciations of Chiang's refusal to launch a meaningful attack on the Japanese. He urged Roosevelt to cultivate relations with Mao's army which was, unlike the Nationalists, willing to fight the Japanese.

After the war, Truman sent General Marshall as a special envoy to China to assess the political and military situation there. Marshall reported that Mao was as much agrarian reformer as he was a Communist or, at least, he was not a Soviet stooge. He was a nationalist hostile to all foreign interference in Chinese affairs, Russian as well as Japanese and, of course, American. By opening relations with Mao and providing economic aid, a China under Mao could be cajoled into pursuing an independent course.

The China Lobby   The intensification of the Cold War in Europe killed the possibility of establishing workable relations with the Chinese Communists. George Kennan had defined the conflict with the Soviet Union as more a power than an ideological struggle. However, most American politicians, including President Truman, saw the Cold War with Communism as, first of all, a contest between incompatible ideologies and ways of life. Even when the Communist dictator of Yugoslavia, Josef Broz Tito, broke free of Soviet influence, American policy makers were unable to see the possibility of encouraging a similar independence among the Chinese Communists.

Nor, thanks to the effective propaganda of the "China Lobby," influential friends of Chiang Kai-Shek in the United States led by his brilliant and articulate wife, "Madame Chiang," the American people were misled into believing that the Nationalists had more support in China than they actually had. Through 1949, the China Lobby bombarded the United States with the message that the Chinese loved Chiang and that the Nationalists were defeating Mao's forces on the battlefield. The campaign was so effective that Americans were literally stunned at the end of the year when newspapers reported out of the blue that Chiang and his army had fled to the island of Taiwan (then better known as Formosa).

How could it have happened? Instead of deducing that they had been misled, Americans accepted the China Lobby's explanation that Chiang and the Chinese people had been betrayed by inadequate American support. The Roman Catholic archbishop of New York, Francis Cardinal Spellman; publisher of *Time* and *Life* magazines, Henry Luce; and a majority of Republican senators and congressmen demanded that aid to Chiang be increased and that he be "unleashed" for an assault on the mainland.

Truman and his new secretary of state, Dean Acheson, knew better. For twenty years, Chiang had demonstrated his ineptitude as a general and political leader. He needed American aid just to hold on to Taiwan. To allow him to attack China proper would involve the United States in a war on the Asian mainland that every American military strategist, including General MacArthur, had said would be catastrophic.

An Unexpected
War
Truman and Acheson applied containment policy to Red China despite the fact that Kennan derived his strategy from his study of Russian history and said so publicly when China policy was on the table. What were the tolerable limits of Chinese expansion? Taiwan had been part of China since antiquity and never, as Chiang's Nationalists would soon say, an independent nation. And what of Quemoy and Matsu, two tiny islands a few miles off the coast of China still occupied by the Nationalists? Was the United States to risk war to "contain" Chinese expansion over two worthless rocks? And what of the Republic of Korea, set up by the United States in the southern half of the Korean peninsula? Or, for that matter, North Korea, where the Russians had set up a Communist regime dependent on the Soviet Union?

The Korean question ceased to be academic in June 1950 when a Soviet-trained North Korean army poured across the 38th parallel, the line dividing the Russian and American occupation zones after the war and now the border between the South and North Korean republics. The Russians were gone from North Korea, but the American Eighth Army was still based on the toe of the peninsula.

The Korean
Conflict
There was an American fleet in Korean waters so Truman was able to respond immediately. Because the Soviet delegate to the United Nations Security Council was absent, he was able to win UN approval of a "police action" to expel the North Korean aggressors from the South. With the United States providing almost all of the police, General MacArthur took command.

The old soldier was to have one last day of glory. With the Eighth Army barely holding on in the far south, MacArthur engineered a daring amphibious landing at Inchon, far behind North Korean lines. American troops cut off and captured 100,000 North Korean soldiers. MacArthur took back all of South Korea in just two weeks. The Americans and ROKs (soldiers of the Republic of Korea) surged northward, crossing the thirty-eighth parallel in September 1950. By October 26, they occupied the entire peninsula except a narrow band along the border of Chinese Manchuria. One forward unit actually reached the banks of the Yalu River, the boundary.

MacArthur had been ordered not to approach the Yalu so that the Chinese would not feel threatened. But the American advance was so rapid that Truman had no time to reflect on MacArthur's assurance that the Chinese would not

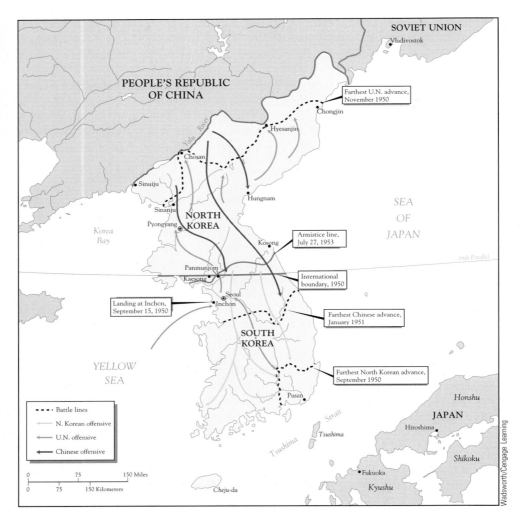

MAP 44.2 The Korean War

During the frantic last half of 1950 until 1953, newspapers regularly, sometimes daily, ran front-page maps of Korea to show the rapidly changing front line. Then the war bogged down in a stalemate.

intervene. He was dead wrong. Perhaps confusing China Lobby propaganda with official American policy, the Chinese feared an attack on Manchuria, the avenue through which China had been invaded twice before. Mao Zedong threw 200,000 "volunteers"—battle-tested soldiers, actually—into Korea. By the end of 1950, they had pushed MacArthur's forces back to a line that zigzagged across the 38th parallel.

There, whether because the Chinese were willing to settle for a draw—a containment policy of their own—or because American troops found their footing and dug in, the war bogged down into a stalemate. For two years, the Americans,

Going Underground

The fear of nuclear war and the widespread assumption that it was inevitable took many forms during the 1950s and early 1960s. On the federal government's urging, virtually every school in the United States inaugurated atomic bomb drills that look foolish today and struck many people at the time as ridiculous: On the teacher's command, students hunkered in the fetal position under their desks.

In the early 1960s, basement rooms in schools, government buildings, and large businesses were designated as "fallout shelters" and stocked with nonperishable foods (World War II soldiers' C and K rations), first aid kits, toilet paper, and the like.

There was spawned a building boom in family fallout shelters in backyards all over the country. They were covered pits to which the owners, upon hearing the sirens announcing the approach of Soviet bombers, would repair and survive the bomb that the Soviets had earmarked for their community. *Popular Science* and *Popular Mechanics,* then popular magazines, published plans for do-it-yourself models. Professionally built shelters, carpeted and painted beige, the signature wall color of the period, cost $3,000—more than the price of all but luxury automobiles. Some had air conditioning with as little as possible said about where the electricity to run them would come from. The recommended

cache of food and water was a two-week supply. A Stanford University professor recommended that poor people take shelter in a junked car they could bury.

A Los Angeles woman told a newspaper that even if her family was not bombed, their backyard shelter "will make a wonderful place for the children to play in." Others observed that fallout shelters were useful storage areas. In religious journals, ministers and priests argued whether, when the bombs fell, a person was morally justified in shooting neighbors who tried to horn in on them.

One manufacturer in Texas was called, "The Peace O' Mind Shelter Company." Another firm, in a pamphlet called, "How to Survive an Atomic Bomb," advised: "Things are probably going to look different when you get outside. If the bomb hit within a mile and a half of where you are, things are going to look very different."

The federal government promoted the mania. Congress had a huge fallout shelter underneath the Capitol. Navy Seabees built one for President John F. Kennedy at his winter vacation home in Palm Beach, Florida. In 1961, Kennedy asked Assistant Secretary of the Navy Paul Fay if he had built his shelter yet. When Fay replied, "No, I built a swimming pool instead," Kennedy replied, "You made a mistake." Fay commented, "He was dead serious."

ROKs, and token delegations of troops from other United Nations countries fought the North Koreans and Chinese over forlorn hills and ridges that did not even have names, only numbers given them by the military. Even after armistice talks began in a truce zone at Panmunjom, the war dragged on, meaninglessly chewing up lives.

The Chinese had protected their borders, and the Americans had ensured the independence of the Republic of Korea. But, in the Cold War, with "ideology" taking on sacred significance on both sides, neither party knew quite how to end the fighting. Some days at Panmunjom, the negotiators simply sat at the table all day, saying nothing.

MacArthur's Comeuppance
Americans were frustrated. Not five years after the Second World War, the Korean Conflict put 5.7 million young men in uniform, killed 37,000 of them, and wounded 100,000. Defense expenditures soared from $40 billion in 1950 to $71 billion in 1952. Truman and Acheson said that the goal was containment, but having contained, they were unable to conclude hostilities. What was wrong?

Early in 1951, General MacArthur gave his explanation. Forgetting his own warning against a war with the Chinese on the Asian mainland, he told reporters that the only reason he had not won the war was that Truman would not permit him to bomb the enemy's supply depots in Manchuria. Later, MacArthur went further; he sent a letter to Republican Congressman Joseph W. Martin in which he wrote that "there is no substitute for victory" and assailed the commander-in-chief for accepting the stalemate. In April, Martin went public with the letter.

Not even George McClellan had so blatantly challenged the president's constitutional authority as commander-in-chief. Truman's military advisors were appalled and, on April 11, with their support, the president fired MacArthur. Americans— what seemed to be a large majority of them—were shocked. They knew MacArthur as the successful commander of the war against Japan. They knew little of MacArthur's previous acts of insubordination because his superiors, from Herbert Hoover through George C. Marshall, had let them pass. They did not know that twice between 1945 and 1951, Truman had ordered MacArthur to come to the United States for discussions and MacArthur refused. It was easy to reckon that the great general knew better how to fight the Chinese than Harry Truman did. Returning home after his dismissal, the general was feted with ticker tape parades and cheered by Congress (a Democratic Congress!) after a speech heard on the radio by more people than had tuned in to Truman's inaugural address in 1949.

MacArthur concluded his speech to Congress by quoting a line from an old barracks song: "old soldiers never die; they just fade away." He had no intention of fading away. Establishing his residence and a kind of command center at New York's Waldorf-Astoria Hotel, MacArthur issued a series of political proclamations aimed at winning him the Republican presidential nomination in 1952.

But MacArthur was no politician; he believed he was a man of destiny, in the hands of fate. He assumed that the people would come to him. They did not. As the savvy politician Harry S. Truman calculated, the enthusiasm for MacArthur dissipated within a few months. Meanwhile, the Korean Conflict dragged on, dissipating Truman's popularity too.

YEARS OF TENSION

Periodically in American history, during times of great political or social stress, many people have turned to conspiracy theories to account for their frustrations. The era of the Korean War was such a time. Large numbers of Americans came to believe that their failure to enjoy a sense of security after the great victory in the

Second World War was the work of sinister forces at work within the United States.

"Twenty Years of Treason" The view that, at Yalta, President Roosevelt sold out Eastern Europe to Stalin was an early expression of the belief that betrayal explained the Communist menace. In March 1947, President Truman inadvertently fueled anxieties by ordering all government employees to sign loyalty oaths, statements that they did not belong to the Communist party or to other disloyal groups. Thirty states followed the federal example, requiring solemn loyalty oaths even of employees who waxed the floors of the state university's basketball courts.

Truman also contributed to the belief that there was widespread treason within the federal government by allowing his supporters to "red bait" Henry Wallace in the 1948 presidential campaign. Wallace was eccentric, even wacky; his analysis of Soviet intentions in 1948 and the possibility of reviving good relations was mistaken. The tiny American Communist party supported his candidacy in 1948, but he was no Communist. In calling him one, as many Truman Democrats did, they created a political tactic that, in the end, could only work against their party. If there were traitors in high places, the Democratic party was responsible; as of 1952, Democrats had been running the country for 20 years.

Before 1952, frustrated right-wing Republicans like John Bricker of Ohio and William F. Knowland of California raised the specter of "twenty years of treason." But the two chief beneficiaries of the second red scare were Richard M. Nixon, a first-term congressman from southern California and Joseph McCarthy, the junior senator from Wisconsin.

Alger Hiss and Richard Nixon Richard M. Nixon built his career on the ashes of the career of a New Deal bureaucrat named Alger Hiss. A bright young Ivy Leaguer in the 1930s when he went to Washington to work in the Agriculture Department, Hiss had risen to be a middle-level aide to Roosevelt at the Yalta Conference. He was aloof and fastidious in manner, a bit of a snob, and he was a militant liberal.

In 1948, a journalist, Whittaker Chambers, admitted to having been a Communist during the 1930s and accused Hiss of helping him funnel classified American documents to the Soviets. At first Chambers aroused little fuss. He had a reputation for making wild claims. His accusations of the distinguished Hiss looked like a smear designed to put him in the spotlight. Because of the statute of limitations, none of the crimes of which he accused Hiss (and himself) could be prosecuted.

Hiss could have ignored Chambers. Instead, he forced the issue for what seemed at the time his honor but which, in retrospect, probably reflects his arrogance and snobbery. Who would take the seedy Chambers's word rather than his? Indignantly, he swore under oath that Chambers's claims were lies. He said he did not even know Chambers.

To Democratic party liberals, Hiss, with his exemplary record of public service, was telling the truth. The right-wing Chambers was a liar. But many ordinary Americans, especially working-class ethnics and citizens of western farming states, were not so sure. With his aristocratic accent and expensive tailored clothing, Hiss, to them, represented the Eastern upper-class establishment, traditionally an object of their distrust.

Congressman Nixon shared these feelings. On little more than a hunch, he pursued the Hiss case when other Republicans had lost interest. Nixon persuaded Chambers to produce microfilms that seemed to show that Hiss had indeed retyped classified documents on his own typewriter, which was in Nixon's possession. Questioning Hiss at a congressional hearing, he poked hole after hole in Hiss's testimony. Largely because of Nixon's doggedness, Hiss was convicted of perjury—lying under oath. With his conviction, it was plausible to wonder how many other New Dealers had been spies. Republicans pointed out that Hiss was a personal friend of Secretary of State Dean Acheson.

Senator Joe McCarthy

Joseph McCarthy of Wisconsin was an unlikely character to play a major role in the governing of a nation. Socially awkward and furtive, he was also a bully who had won election to the Senate in 1944 by posing as a combat marine, which he was not. McCarthy was facing an election in 1952 that he seemed likely to lose; his record in the Senate was terrible. He needed a big issue but turned down several proposals by friends as dull. Almost by accident, he decided to try out the question of Communist subversion of the government, a subject in which he had previously taken little interest.

In 1950, McCarthy told a Republican audience in Wheeling, West Virginia, that he had a list of 205 Communists who were then working in the State Department with the full knowledge of Secretary Acheson. McCarthy had no list. Only two days later, he could not remember if he had said the names on it totaled 205 or 57. He never released the name of a single State Department Communist or, indeed, of a Communist anywhere in the federal bureaucracy. It was all bluff. But in his reckless quest for publicity, McCarthy had stumbled on the effectiveness of the "big lie"—making fabulous accusations so forcefully and repetitively that people concluded that they must be true.

When a few senators denounced his irresponsibility, McCarthy discovered just how sensitive was the nerve he had touched. Senator Millard Tydings of Maryland was a conservative whose distinguished family name gave him practically a proprietary interest in a Senate seat in his state. In 1950, after Tydings denounced him, McCarthy threw his support behind Tydings's opponent. He fabricated a photograph—like a tabloid composograph without the jokes—showing Tydings shaking hands with American Communist leader Earl Browder. Tydings was defeated.

McCarthyism

Other Senators who were disturbed by McCarthy got the point. If McCarthy could retire a senator with as safe as seat as Tydings had, why risk their own careers by alienating him. By 1952, McCarthy was so powerful that when Republican presidential candidate Dwight D. Eisenhower was campaigning with McCarthy in Wisconsin, McCarthy denounced George Marshall as disloyal and Eisenhower said nothing. He betrayed the man who had lifted him from obscurity to command the war in Europe because of his fear of a lying bully.

Even liberal Democrats in Congress rushed to escape McCarthy's wrath by voting for dubious laws like the McCarran Internal Security Act, which defined dozens of liberal lobby groups as "Communist fronts." The McCarran Act also provided for the establishment of concentration camps for disloyal citizens in the event of a national emergency. The Supreme Court fell into line with its decision in *Dennis et al. v. United States* (1951). By a vote of 6 to 2, the Court agreed that membership in the Communist party was sufficient evidence in itself to convict a person of advocating the forcible overthrow of the United States government. Nothing had to be proved about the accused individual's views.

At the peak of McCarthy's power, only a very few universities (including the University of Wisconsin) and journalists like cartoonist Herbert Block and television commentator Edward R. Murrow refused to be intimidated. Only in 1954 did McCarthy's meteoric career crash to earth. When he was unable to secure preferential treatment from the army for a friend of his aide, Roy Cohn, McCarthy accused the army of fostering infiltration by Communists. He had stepped over the line. The Senate was emboldened to move against him, and he was censured in December 1954 by a vote of 72 to 22. It was only the third time in American history that the nation's most exclusive club rebuked one of its members so strongly.

The Making of a Politician   Nixon and McCarthy built their careers on exploiting anxieties. Less directly, the leader of the conservative Republicans, Senator Taft, did the same. Taft encouraged the party's hell-raisers as a way of chipping away at the hated Democrats. But the Republican Party turned neither to Taft nor another mover and shaker to guide them through the 1950s. Instead, they chose a man with no background in party politics, whose strength was a warm personality and whose talent was a knack for smoothing over conflict.

After World War II, General Dwight David Eisenhower wrote his memoirs of the conflict, *Crusade in Europe,* and, early in 1948, accepted the presidency of Columbia University. Leaders of both parties approached him with offers to nominate him as president. Truman told Ike that if he would accept the Democratic nomination, Truman would gladly step aside.

In 1948, Eisenhower was not interested. He was a career military man who, unlike MacArthur, believed that soldiers should stay out of politics. It is not certain that Eisenhower ever bothered to vote in an election before 1948. But academic life did not suit him either. Ike's intellectual interests ran to pulp western novels. And, after a lifetime accustomed to having his instructions carried out, he found the chaos of shepherding academics he could not fire to be intolerable.

As one of New York City's most eminent citizens, however, Eisenhower associated and socialized with the wealthy businessmen who dominated the moderate wing of the Republican party. They showered him with gifts such as those that had turned General Grant's head and investment advice that was inevitably sound. As an administrator himself, something of a businessman in uniform, Eisenhower found it easy to assimilate their politics.

In 1950, Ike took a leave of absence from Columbia to command NATO troops in Europe. There, because the Korean War dragged on and because of MacArthur's insubordination (which disgusted him), Ike grew more receptive to the blandishments of his Republican friends that he seek the presidential nomination. Eisenhower had no illusions, as Taft did, that the New Deal could be dismantled, nor much interest in doing so. He was convinced to run by evidence of corruption in the Truman administration and the belief that it was unhealthy for one party to be in power as long as the Democrats had.

Landslide 1952   Eisenhower easily won the nomination. His opponent was the governor of Illinois, Adlai E. Stevenson, a New Deal liberal but not associated with the unpopular Truman administration. Stevenson was an effective campaigner; he was personable, witty, and as attractively modest as Eisenhower. For a few weeks late in the summer of 1952, there were hints that Stevenson was catching up with Ike.

But Eisenhower had too much going for him, and Eisenhower's campaign managers shrewdly turned Stevenson's intelligence and glibness against him. They pointed out that "eggheads" like him (intellectuals) were the people who were responsible for "the mess in Washington." Despite Eisenhower's resistance, they applied the techniques of television commercials to "selling" Eisenhower. The party filmed a series of short TV "spots" in which an ordinary person asked a simple question and Eisenhower answered in a few "hard-hitting" words. Ike administered the *coup de grace* to the Stevenson campaign when he promised that, when he was elected, he would personally go to Korea and end the aimless war. Stevenson had no choice but to defend the principles of limited conflict on which the frustrating conflict was based.

Stevenson won nine southern states. Although he supported civil rights for African Americans, he brought the Dixiecrats back into the Democratic party by naming as his running mate a southern moderate, Senator John Sparkman of Alabama. Otherwise, Eisenhower swept the country winning 56 percent of the popular vote.

In December, before he was inaugurated, Eisenhower kept his promise to go to Korea. He donned military gear and was filmed sipping coffee with soldiers on the front lines. He had long recognized that prolonging the stalemate was senseless while the all-out war MacArthur had proposed meant disaster. Without bluster, which would have defeated his purpose, he suggested that using the atomic bomb might be the only way to end the war. It was a bluff; Eisenhower had said in private that it had not been necessary to use the bomb to defeat Japan. But it worked: Whether or not the new "collective leadership" in the Soviet Union applied pressure to the Chinese (Stalin died in March 1953), the Chinese agreed to end the hostilities in July 1953. It was an auspicious beginning for President Dwight David Eisenhower.

45

"HAPPY DAYS"
Popular Culture in the Fifties 1947–1963

A multitude of uniform, unidentifiable houses, lined up inflexibly, at uniform distances on uniform roads in a treeless waste, inhabited by people of the same class, the same incomes, the same age group, witnessing the same television performances, eating the same tasteless prefabricated foods, from the same freezers, conforming in every outward and inward respect to a common mold manufactured in the same central metropolis.

—Lewis Mumford

The voters of 1952 chose a Republican president for the first time in twenty-four years, but no one spoke of the election as a political "revolution." Americans wanted a change of pace, not radical change. They had learned to live with the Cold War; they had no choice. They wanted out of Korea, where soldiers were dying daily for reasons the Democrats could not persuasively explain. But most Americans remained grateful for the New Deal reforms that had improved their lives. They wanted no returning to the days of Calvin Coolidge such as Robert Taft had called for since the 1930s. But Harry S. Truman's proposals to revive the spirit of the New Deal and expand New Deal programs found no mass support. Ordinary people were weary of reformers' moral demands—and the sacrifices the war had required. They wanted to kick back and taste the fruits of living in the world's richest nation.

In fact, they were already enjoying them when they elected Dwight David Eisenhower to the White House. As a decade with a personality, "the Fifties" lasted about fifteen years, beginning in 1947 or 1948, when the armed forces had been demobilized and people were beginning to spend freely on new homes, cars, and consumer goods, and the era ended in November 1963 when President John F. Kennedy was assassinated and the good times did not feel quite as good any longer.

Fifties Culture 1946–1960

1946	1948	1950	1952	1954	1956	1958	1960

1947 "New Look" in women's fashions

1948 "Kinsey Report" published

1949 Levittown, New York

1950 4 million TV sets in use; 6 million cars sold

1954 Davy Crockett mania

The Man in the Gray Flannel Suit published 1955

Interstate Highway System; Mickey Spillane best-selling author of all time 1956

Peyton Place published 1957

TV quiz show scandal; Barbie doll introduced 1959

LET THE GOOD TIMES ROLL

The amiable Ike with his favorite uncle grin was reassuring. He promised peace in Korea. He replaced the political pros, do-gooder intellectuals, and *apparatchik* liberal planners of the Roosevelt-Truman era with professional administrators like himself and with the stolid businessmen who had swarmed around him since 1945.

Ike's advisors were not a colorful lot. "Eight millionaires and a plumber," a Democrat sniffed when Eisenhower announced his cabinet. (The plumber, the secretary of labor, resigned within a year to be replaced by another millionaire.) When Congress created the new Department of Health, Education, and Welfare, Eisenhower's pick to head it was not a social worker, briefcase bulging with new programs, but a military bureaucrat like himself, Oveta Culp Hobby, the head of the Women's Army Corps.

Ike's Style and Its Critics Eisenhower's style was soothing. He did not leap into political cat fights with claws flashing as Truman had. He calmly sidled away when the caterwauling started, leaving the dirty work to his subordinates. Vice President Richard Nixon (whom Eisenhower never liked) was one of his hatchet men. More important was Eisenhower's special assistant, former New Hampshire governor Sherman Adams. Adams screened everyone who wanted to see the president, turning away those who might ruffle Ike, entangle him in a controversy, or trick him into making an embarrassing statement. Adams vetted every document that was to cross the president's desk. He weeded out those he found trivial and summarized the others, which was what Eisenhower wanted, no more than a page or two on any subject—"briefs" such as he had dealt with as a general in charge of a profoundly complex operation involving millions of soldiers and many millions more civilians. Operation Overlord was a pretty good lesson in how to delegate authority and responsibility.

Democratic party critics claimed that Adams was too powerful, that he made many presidential-level decisions himself. He did. Eisenhower was no micromanager. He appreciated the flinty New Englander's services. In 1958, when it was revealed that Adams had rigged some government decisions to benefit an old friend and then accepted a gift from him—a rather petty one, a vicuna wool overcoat—he was forced to resign. Eisenhower let Adams go, but he bitterly resented losing him and those who had made hay out of Adams's indiscretion.

The president also allowed the members of his cabinet loose reins. They were told to study the issues before their departments, report their findings—briefly. If they disagreed among themselves on a decision to be made, they debated—briefly— while Ike listened. Eisenhower never shirked ultimate responsibility for his decisions. He preferred finding a compromise to flat out backing one advisor against another. That was how he had handled subordinates as headstrong and feisty as Bernard Montgomery and Charles DeGaulle and generals as mutually hostile as Omar Bradley and George Patton during the war. The members of his homogenous cabinet were pussycats compared to them.

Intellectuals poked fun at what seemed to be Eisenhower's losing battle with the English language. Ike was never been comfortable speaking to large audiences. His preferred playing field was the closed conference room and the morale-boosting "public appearance" when he could beam, wave, lead cheers, shake the hands of sixty people a minute, and exit stage right.

At presidential press conferences, when faced with a contentious reporter, he sometimes lapsed into gobbledygook. When asked what he was doing about an economic downturn, he replied

> this economy of ours is not so simple that it obeys to the opinion or bias or pro-
> nouncements of any particular individual, even to the president. This is an economy
> that is made up of 173 million people and it reflects their desires: they're ready to buy,
> they're ready to spend, it is a thing that is too complex and too big to be affected ad-
> versely or advantageously just by a few words or any particular—say a little this and
> that, or even a panacea so alleged.

In some cases, at least, Eisenhower knew exactly what he was doing when he spoke like this. When an aide warned him reporters would ask him a question better not answered, he said, "Don't worry. I'll just confuse them." Eisenhower was quite a good writer. The prose in his *Crusade in Europe* was simple, direct, economical, and clear.

We're in the Money

Critics mocked Eisenhower's undisguised enjoyment of leisure. The nation was drifting, they said, while Ike relaxed on his gentleman's farm on the battlefield at Gettysburg (a gift of wealthy businessmen) and took too many vacations in places where the golf courses were always green, the sun warm, the clubhouses air-conditioned, and the martinis dry. But Ike's mockers found an audience only among themselves. The majority of Americans did not object to a president who liked to take it easy. In 1956, when Ike ran for reelection shortly after suffering a serious heart attack and undergoing major surgery, voters reelected him by a greater margin than in 1952. Better Ike recuperating on a fairway than a healthy Adlai Stevenson telling them to roll up their sleeves and get to work making America better.

For a large majority of white Americans, the 1950s were good times. This was not just because the New Deal and the World War had spread the nation's wealth around more equitably. Those people defined as living in poverty were about as numerous proportionally as they had been in the 1920s. The lowest paid fifth of the population earned the same 3 to 4 percent of national income that they had earned during the Coolidge era. The wealthiest fifth of the population continued to enjoy 44 to 45 percent of earnings. The remaining 60 percent, therefore—the American middle class (households with an annual income of $3,000–$10,000, $24,000–$78,000 in today's money)—was proportionately no better off than it had been before the New Deal.

The difference in the 1950s was the size of the pie from which the slices were cut. Never in history had the world's richest nation been so very much richer than all the others. Two-thirds of the world's gold reserves were in the United States, half the world's manufacturing. Each year, Americans consumed a third of the world's goods. Energy, notably gasoline, was dirt cheap thanks to the wartime increase in refining capacity. In 1950, discretionary income—income not needed to pay for necessities—totaled $100 billion compared with $40 billion in 1940, a quantum jump.

Traditional values—thrift and frugality—dictated that such money be saved against a rainy day or invested; it was capital. After the Great Depression, however, when so many had pinched pennies just to get by, and after the rationing and scarcities of the war years, middle-class Americans, blue collar and white collar, itched to spend on goods and services that made life more comfortable, varied, and stimulating. Consumer-oriented businesses obliged them and then, just as in the Roaring Twenties, there were the amusing fads.

Fads

In late 1954 and early 1955, Hollywood's Walt Disney telecast three programs about a half-forgotten nineteenth-century frontiersman and politician, Davy Crockett of Tennessee. Disney's Davy wore a coonskin cap, hooped tail hanging down his neck, headgear, historians rushed to point out, the real Crockett never did. Who cared? The cap was eye-catching and Disney, anticipating a mania, licensed a hat manufacturer to make the "official" Davy topper. The price of coonskins soared from $.25 to $6 per pound and many more of the 10 million Crockett hats sold were made from rabbit or cat skins or synthetic fur than from the real thing.

And it was not just hats. Schoolchildren's lunch boxes decorated with pictures of Davy shooting bears, also licensed by Disney, were must-haves. After the bell, children played with plastic long rifles and Bowie knives reasonably safe for use in backyard Alamos. (Crockett was killed in the Mexican army's assault on the Alamo in 1836.) Within a year, Americans spent $100 million on some 3,000 different Crockett items, from fringed pseudo-buckskin shirts to wading pools on which the magic name and image were embossed. In the summer of 1955, several large department stores reported that 10 percent of their sales were in Davy Crockett paraphernalia.

In 1958, Wham-O, a toy manufacturer, brought out a plastic version of an Australian exercise device, a simple hoop that one twirled about the hips by means of hulalike gyrations. Almost overnight, 30 million "hula hoops" were sold for $1.98, 100 million within six months. Simple as the toy was to make, four Wham-O factories could not keep up with demand. Like the Crockett mania, the hula hoop craze lasted less than a year; then one could be had for 50¢. But who wanted one?

Chlorophyll, a long-known chemical compound found in most plants, became a rage when manufacturers of more than ninety products, ranging from chewing gum to dog food, proclaimed that the green stuff improved the odor of those who chewed it, shampooed with it, and rubbed it into their armpits. Americans spent $135 million on chlorophyll products. That boom may have busted when scientists pointed out that goats, famously hard on the nose, consumed chlorophyll all day every day.

Some investors who dreamed up surefire fads did not fare so well. Trampolines, for example, extensively promoted, were too big, too expensive, and broke too many kids' bones. Some fads profited only the newspapers and magazines that reported them: College students competing to see how many of them could squeeze into a telephone booth or a Volkswagen Beetle, for example.

The Boob Tube The most significant new consumer bauble of the decade was the home television receiver. TV was introduced as a broadcast medium in 1939. However, "radio with a picture" remained a toy of electronics hobbyists until after the war. In 1946, there were just six commercial TV stations in the U.S. and 8,000 privately owned receivers, one per 18,000 people.

Gambling that middle-class Americans would spend money on yet another kind of entertainment, the radio networks sidled into television, at first offering only a few hours of programming each evening. Furniture stores left TV sets in their display windows turned on and, sure enough, in the evening knots of people gathered to watch the flickering screen. Manufacturers of sets like Dumont peddled their product as a healthy social innovation: "There is great happiness in the home where the family is held together by this new common bond!" The American Television Dealers and Manufacturers Association asked parents, "How can a little girl describe the bruise deep inside?—the hurt that her friends' parents have a TV—Can you deny television to your children any longer?"

Parents could not. By the end of 1950 almost 4 million sets had been sold, by 1952 18 million. In 1956 some 442 stations (now called channels) were on the air. By 1970, more households would be equipped with a TV set than with refrigerators, bathtubs, or indoor toilets.

A few high-minded network executives hoped that television would be an agent of education and cultural uplift. They telecast serious plays, both classics and original dramas, on the "small screen." But no one deluded himself as Herbert Hoover had during the 1920s when he said that radio should be free of commercial advertising. From TV's first days, "sponsors" peddling consumer goods interrupted programs every fifteen minutes with their spiels. The first commercial blockbusters were variety shows, one hosted by Milton Berle, a manic burlesque clown. Another, *Toast of the Town* on Sunday evenings, was rather more remarkable in that its host, Ed Sullivan, was homely, stiff, and awkward on stage with a less than sterling reputation as a New York gossip columnist.

Cowboys and Quiz Shows In 1955, the networks found another moneymaker in a venerable American genre, the western. Within two years they launched more than forty programs set in the "Wild

West." By 1957, one-third of "prime time" (the evening hours between supper and bedtime) was given over to horses, rustlers, sheriffs, federal marshalls, badmen aplenty, and the occasional "saloon girl" with a heart of gold. In Los Angeles a hopeless addict could watch sixty-fours hours of westerns each week.

One of the first westerns, *Gunsmoke*, ran through 635 episodes. A quarter of the world's population saw at least one episode in which Marshall Matt Dillon made Dodge City, Kansas, safe for decent law-abiding citizens. *Death Valley Days* revived the career of actor Ronald Reagan. As the host who introduced stories with different characters each week, he was able to "play himself" before millions of viewers. His self was very likable. *Death Valley Days* set Reagan off on a trail of celebrity that eventually led to the White House.

Quiz shows offering huge prizes caught the popular imagination. The first was *The $64,000 Question*. (The name was a play on an old radio quiz show on which the ultimate challenge was "the $64 question.") Millions sat entranced as secretaries, postal clerks, and idiot savants rattled off the names of Medieval Polish kings, flyweight boxers of the 1920s, and lines from Shakespeare's plays. Then, in 1959, an investigator discovered that a popular contestant on a show called *21*, a young university instructor named Charles Van Doren, had been fed answers. So had others who had telegenic personalities while less attractive contestants (like the one who fingered Van Doren) were helped until they were no longer wanted and then, just in case they actually knew the right answers, were paid to take a dive.

The exposé was sensational because Van Doren had grimaced with agony when he pretended to struggle to retrieve some obscure morsel of knowledge from deep within his mind and gasped for air to avoid fainting with relief when he came up with the answer he had memorized. Academics said they were shocked, simply shocked by Van Doren's betrayal of their profession's integrity. The producers of the quiz shows said that they were entertainers, not intelligence testers: It was a show, for goodness sake.

Ordinary folks just changed the channel. There was always *I Love Lucy* which, on one evening in 1953, 44 million people tuned in, 15 million more than watched President Eisenhower's inauguration the next day. And *Gunsmoke* was still going strong, although its writers admitted stress trying to come up with fresh stories. "We've used up De Maupassant," said one, referring to a prolific author of short stories, "and we're halfway through Maugham" (another).

Economic and Cultural Fallout   Television's expropriation of so many leisure hours virtually destroyed social dancing and transformed radio and movies. The "big bands" that had toured the country playing at ballrooms could not compete with TV. The high costs of moving thirty or more musicians and several tons of equipment from one "one night stand" to another meant that bands needed to play to full houses in order to survive. The competition of free entertainment at home was too much for them.

The major radio networks—NBC, CBS, and ABC (and, for a few years, Dumont)—became the major TV networks. They retooled their most popular radio serials for television and, in the Sixties, abandoned radio comedies and dramas in the evening hours. Who listened to *Gunsmoke* or *Amos 'n' Andy* when they could watch them? In the evenings, the radio networks provided little more to affiliated stations than hourly news and sports reports, the odd fifteen minutes of "commentary," and special events. Local stations filled the empty hours with their "disk jockeys" who played recorded music and prattled moronically between "numbers." Local radio reported the weather and traffic conditions, broadcast local sporting events, and reminded listeners who were working or driving of the time. The medium was utterly changed in just a few years from a centerpiece of popular culture into white noise.

In 1946, 82 million Americans had gone to the movies each week. Ten years later, that figure was cut in half. The biggest Hollywood studios (MGM, Paramount, Warner Brothers, RKO, 20th Century Fox, Columbia) responded by experimenting with themes taboo on TV, particularly sex (what else?) and with spectacular films "with a cast of thousands!" that could not be "experienced" on TV's small screen: in 1952, for example, *Quo Vadis?* (ancient Rome) and *The Greatest Show on Earth* (the circus).

Indeed, Hollywood made its "big screen" bigger—wider, actually—with technological innovations such as Cinemascope. There were experiments with "3-D"— three-dimensional movies. Wearing special cardboard spectacles smudged with greasy thumbprints (buttered popcorn), moviegoers shrieked as they dodged spears and anything else that an actor could hurl at the camera. That novelty wore off quickly.

Neighborhood theaters, especially in cities, did not fare as well as the Hollywood studios. They depended on repeat patronage, locals who could walk to the movies for the sake of an evening out. Small theaters could not afford the high rental fees charged for new films, let alone install Cinemascope at a cost of $12,000–$25,000. Instead, they ran three different programs each week, at least one of them a double feature. Their staples were old films and "B" movies, cheaply made formula films that rented at a small fixed price.

By 1950, "B" movies were supplied by studios on Hollywood's "poverty row" such as Republic, Grand National, and Monogram. The trouble was that, in effect, TV was showing several half-hour "B" movies each evening for free. Theaters that had been neighborhood social centers closed, 55 in New York City just in 1951, 134 in Los Angeles. By 1963, half the movie houses in business in 1947 were boarded up or pulverized by the wrecking ball.

TV and Reading The "one-eyed monster" did not much affect the circulation of "high-brow" magazines like the *Atlantic* and *Harper's*, an indication that more educated people were less likely to be hooked on TV. However, general-interest magazines that had been "middle-brow" stalwarts like the *Saturday Evening Post, Collier's, Look,* even *Life,* a picture magazine, saw their readership drop. In time, they all folded. By way of contrast, new sex and scandal "low-brow" magazines such as *Confidential* and *Hush Hush,* which trafficked in material TV would not touch, boomed. In 1955, *Confidential* sold more than 4 million copies a month.

Sales of new hardcover books remained steady. Cheap paperback editions of classics and last year's best sellers boomed—another sign that serious readers were less smitten with television. Once again, however, less educated people were reading too. They made a publishing phenomenon of Mickey Spillane, who created a crude, even sadistic detective, Mike Hammer, for whom, every twenty or thirty pages, women discarded their clothing. Hammer shot one such loose lady in the belly. Spillane's first book, *I, the Jury*, sold 3 million copies in a 25¢-paperback. By 1956, Spillane had published seven books; every one was on a list of the ten best-selling books of fiction in American history.

What Americans cut out in order to watch TV was socializing. Instead of chatting with neighbors or with relatives by phone, or "getting together" in the evening to play cards, for a dance or at a club, families barricaded themselves in their homes, resenting interruptions. Food processing companies invented the "TV dinner," a complete meal in an aluminum foil tray that could be put in and taken out of the oven during commercials and eaten in silence from a "TV table," a metal tray on folding legs, one for each member of the family. Not even suppertime conversation, the central moment of American family life, need get between viewers and their favorite shows.

SUBURBIA

Social critics said that the TV-addicted family, staring slack-jawed at the flickering tube during the few hours all were together, had abandoned the personal interactions that alone gave the modern nuclear family meaning. If so, television provided substitutes. In 1954, a group of psychologists described the most popular morning program—housewives were the audience—*The Arthur Godfrey Show,* as shrewdly creating an "illusion of the family structure" but without conflicts. Godfrey was the most "amiable" of husbands and fathers but there was on his program no "wife" or "mother" figure. Viewers vicariously filled those roles.

In the evenings, television provided affectionate happy families to watch. In *Ozzie and Harriet* (first aired in 1952), *Make Room for Daddy* (1953), *Father Knows Best* (1954), and *Leave it to Beaver* (1957), the adults were young, healthy, handsome, even-tempered, middle class, and, of course, white. Father, the bread-winner, might be wise or a lovable bumbler. Mother, a homemaker, worshiped him or, at least, was formally submissive even when she, the kids, and viewers knew that she was the one who held everything together. The children—two or three, usually—were great friends with one another, often mischievous but never nasty, and ultimately obedient and respectful. TV families were utterly without ethnic identification; they were vaguely mainstream Protestant but never dealt with religion or anything else controversial. They did not watch TV at dinnertime; they interacted with one another.

TV's idealized families (except *Make Room for Daddy*) lived in the suburbs (and *Daddy* moved his family there after a year or two) because the suburbs were where the white middle class of the Fifties watched its TV.

White Flight   One TV family had an African American maid who functioned— almost—as one of the family. However, hers was just about the only black face ever seen in television's portrait of suburban America. In fact, the massive movement of population from cities to suburbs after World War II owed in part to white people's racial anxieties. During the war, African American neighbor-hoods in big cities expanded rapidly as southern blacks migrated north and west to take factory jobs open to them for the first time. When African Americans pushed into white neighborhoods, the result was "white flight."

Another cause of the flight to suburbia was a severe urban housing shortage. Construction of new homes had been virtually suspended during the war. Suddenly, in 1945 and 1946, millions of returning veterans and their wives, and often an infant—a four years' backlog of young families—needed places in which to live. The demand for apartments and houses in the cities pushed prices and rents far be-yond the means of most newlyweds.

Municipal housing authorities financed with federal money began to demolish old neighborhoods to build multistoried apartment buildings. In the short run, such "clearance" projects aggravated the housing shortage. In cities with "fair housing" laws that opened public housing to African Americans, whites shunned the new "developments." Young white couples squeezed into single rooms in white neigh-borhoods or, even less comfortable for many, moved in with parents. What was to be done?

Assembly Line Homes   The answer was entirely new "bedroom communities" built on cheap land outside cities but easily accessible to the fac-tories and offices where the family provider worked. Such land was plentiful because, before universal automobile ownership, American cities had clear boundaries; they ended where the trolley lines ended and there the countryside began. About 10,000 acres *within* the city limits of Philadelphia were still being farmed at the end of World War II. Most of the million housing starts in 1946 (compared with 142,000 in 1944) were in the suburbs.

Most new homes were built by small contractors, five a year each on average. There were not enough skilled carpenters, plumbers, electricians, and plasterers to do much more. William Levitt, who had mass-produced barracks for the army early in the war and then served in the Seabees, the navy's construction unit that turned captured Pacific islands into airfields and bases in days, saw that the crying demand for housing could be met profitably by producing affordable homes quickly using assembly-line methods and a minimum of skilled craftsmen.

Levitt bought 1,000 acres of potato farmland on Long Island. It was 25 miles from New York City but close to a commuter railroad. He unleashed a panzer divi-sion of excavating machines that graded a hundred acres a day while, in the cloud of dust they raised, surveyors drove color-coded stakes into the ground laying out gently curving streets. With the earth movers advancing to the next tract, ditchers opened trenches that were instantly occupied by water, gas, sewer, and electrical lines. Every 60 feet, semiskilled men with hammers and nails built forms and, by the time they stood up to move to the next lot, cement trucks poured slabs (no cellars and founda-tions—a kind of construction new in the East). When the slabs were dry, framers erected partially prebuilt walls of identical one-story "Cape Cods," two-bedroom homes. Next, closely coordinated, one crew on the heels of another, came roofers, floor layers, plumbers, electricians, painters. Several men did nothing eight hours a day but bolt washing machines to floors, trotting from one house to another.

The photographer has captured (or carefully posed) several of the suburban idylls of the 1950s: the happy house-wife impeccably dressed even to water the grass, the weedless lawn, chil-dren playing on a safe street on which dad, when he comes home from work, will not drive faster than 20 miles per hour as he waves to all the neighbors.

AP Photos

There were missteps, each one teaching a lesson. When cement trucks bogged down in mud, Levitt learned that streets had to be paved before house construction began. Eventually, he reduced his operation to twenty-seven steps and had thirty-six homes ready for occupancy each day.

In March 1949, he set the date when sales would begin at Levittown, New York. Buyers lined up at the sales office a week in advance, camping outside the door. On the first day open, Levitt turned over deeds (to whites only) for 1,400 houses at $7,900 each. His profit on each was $1,000. Within two years, Levittown, New York, was a community of 17,000 homes. Fixed-rate mortgages payable over twenty years, hard to get before World War II, put a Levitt home within reach of any young white family with a steady income. Factory workers were making $2,500 to $3,500 a year, enough to make the monthly payment with ease.

Construction of Levittown, Pennsylvania, outside Philadelphia began in the fall of 1951. There, crews finished somewhat larger and fancier houses every sixteen minutes. There were also Levittowns in New Jersey and Florida; Levitt built 140,000 homes. Developments constructed by others using Levitt's methods fringed every large American city. By 1960, as many Americans lived in suburbs as in cities. It was a demographic revolution.

Conformists or Innovators?

The new suburbanites were as homogenous as what critics called their "cookie-cutter" houses. The adult population of the new communities was 95 percent Caucasian, between 20 and

35 years of age, recently married couples with young children, most families living on roughly the same income from skilled occupations and white-collar jobs.

Suburbanites were staunch supporters of the Eisenhower equilibrium; they swelled the membership of churches and synagogues to well above prewar levels. However, they also tacitly insisted that their clergymen not disturb them with hard-hitting moral prescriptions, let alone fire and brimstone. Rabbi Joshua Liebman, Catholic Bishop Fulton J. Sheen, and Protestant Reverend Norman Vincent Peale became national figures by solacing people. Even that most unnerving of American religious phenomena, revivalism, was gussied up by a slick Baptist preacher from North Carolina, Billy Graham. The conversion hysteria of "Decisions for Christ" at his revivals was restricted to a little gentle sobbing.

A survey of Christians showed that while 80 percent said that the Bible was the revealed word of God, only 35 percent could name the authors of the four gospels (50 percent could not name one of them). Jewish suburbanites organized Reform congregations that, unlike Orthodox and Conservative communities, did not observe the dietary laws and the strict observance of the Saturday Sabbath that set them apart from their Christian neighbors.

Critics of suburbia, like Lewis Mumford, called its cultural life dull, superficial, bland, and stultifyingly conformist. And yet, the stark newness of the suburban communities required the early inhabitants to devise new ways of doing things from scratch. Lacking established social services and governments, they formed an intricate network of voluntary associations entirely supported by private funds and energies. There were the new churches and synagogues, thousands of new chapters of political parties, garden clubs, literary societies, and bowling leagues. With small children so numerous, school districts had to be created and developed quickly. Extra scholastic programs revolving around children—ballet schools, Cub Scouts and Brownies, Little Leagues, community swimming pools—had few precedents in cities.

With everyone a stranger in town, the informal cocktail party and the stroll-in backyard barbecue were effective ways by which people could introduce themselves to one another. Unlike at a formal dinner, guests milled around at the stand-up socials, finding compatible friends efficiently. Alcohol lubricated conversation; statisticians noticed that suburbia effected a significant alteration of American drinking habits. Consumption of neutral spirits like gin and vodka, which could be disguised in sweet soda pop and fruit juices for people who did not particularly like the taste of liquor, soared. Whiskey, with its acquired taste, declined in popularity. In 1954, the Lipton Company created a foodstuff that was soon mandatory at suburban socials: "Festival California Dip." It could be made in thirty seconds by mixing a dehydrated onion soup powder with a pint of sour cream and opening a bag of potato chips.

Automobiles

The new suburbs would not have been possible had automobiles not been accessible to anyone with a decent job. Consumer (short-term) credit was easier than it had been before the war. It meant debt; suburbanites were typically saddled with "monthly payments." Between 1946 and 1970, short-term loans increased from $8 billion to $27 billion. But it put a car in every suburban garage.

Whereas suburbia expanded into land far from commuter railroads, the car became the only way between home and work. Automobile factories, devoted to military production during the war, were quick to reconvert to manufacturing cars. Even in 1945, the year the war ended, almost 70,000 new cars were sold. In 1950, sales of new cars reached 6.7 million, in 1955 8 million. Used-car sales increased in proportion. During the Eisenhower decade, car registrations leapt from 49 million to 74 million.

Indeed, the new suburbs created the new phenomenon of the modestly fixed "two-car family." While father drove to work, mother clocked dozens, even a hundred miles each day shunting among markets and shops (suburban developments were built without them) and chauffeuring children from school to doctor and dentist and from Little League to ballet lessons to, in the suburban sea of children, an unending series of birthday parties. By 1960, one suburban family in five owned two vehicles. In Philadelphia, there were 67 cars per each 100 people; in the Philadelphia suburbs, the ratio was 120:100.

Cars have always been status symbols. The street watcher of 1925 knew what it said about drivers' incomes that one owned a Model T, another a Stutz Bearcat. In the postwar suburbs, with homes identical, the automobile became the major means by which people displayed the fact that they had moved up an economic notch (or were pretending they had). Paychecks and bank accounts did not show; the family car did. Automobile manufacturers provided a finely tuned social scale beginning with "the low-priced three," Chevrolet, Ford, and Plymouth up a step to Pontiac, Mercury, and Dodge, another jump to DeSoto, Oldsmobile, and Buick, with Cadillac, Lincoln, and Chrysler at the pinnacle of automotive achievement. Independent manufacturers like Hudson, Nash, Studebaker, and Packard made cars as good as GM, Ford, and Chrysler but declined in sales and soon disappeared in part because they could not stake out a social niche of their own.

Automobiles were never gaudier, before or since. One disapproving designer called the cars of the Fifties "jukeboxes on wheels." The talisman of car design was the "tail fin," a restrained version of which first appeared on the 1948 Cadillac. At first, when designers grafted the entirely nonfunctional fins on their cars, the loudest response was ridicule and, in 1953, most cars dropped them. Sales drooped! Tail fins were almost universally restored. Even the cheapest cars were festooned with chrome. According to the head of styling for Chrysler Corporation in 1959, his designers did not like it. "But people have demanded it.... Every attempt that I know of to strip a car, to take off the chrome, has met with failure."

The Automobile Economy   In 1956, Congress passed the Interstate Highway Act which pumped $1 billion a year into highway construction. (By 1960, expenditures rose to $2.9 billion annually.) Most of the limited-access interstates ran cross-country, which enabled Republicans to justify them as integral to national defense, but 5,000 miles of them connected suburbs to big cities.

Not only did high-speed highways encourage further suburban sprawl, but they also made big cities less livable for all but the rich. Already being sapped of middle-class taxpayers, once vibrant urban neighborhoods were carved into ghettos walled off from one another by the massive concrete freeway abutments. In Boston, six-lane Storrow Drive cut off the Back Bay neighborhood from the Charles River. In

MAP 45.1 Interstate Highway System.

The original Interstate Highway System. The limited-access roads were numbered according to a rule first established by the National Highway Act of 1925. East–West routes ended in an even number; North–South highways with an odd number. Thus, in the West, I-40 paralleled and eventually replaced historic "Route 66." I-5 provided a much faster alternative to U.S. 101. On the East Coast, I-95 relegated old U.S. 1 to local traffic. Interstates authorized by the Act of 1956 and since were freeways. However, existing toll roads incorporated into the system, like the New Jersey, Pennsylvania, Ohio, and Indiana Turnpikes, continued to be pay-to-drive.

Philadelphia, the Schuylkill Expressway isolated the western third of the city from the Schuylkill river. Suburbanites' cars roared in on them daily, raising noise levels and fouling the air. Only the poor, who had no choice, would live in the road-walled neighborhoods, and they were soon run down. The progressively poorer (and blacker) cities deteriorated physically. During the 1960s, further reducing urban tax bases, department stores, offices, and light industries closed their doors in city centers and moved to the suburbs.

Universal car ownership in the suburbs stimulated the growth of businesses devoted to or dependent on automobiles. Service stations (gasoline consumption doubled during the 1950s), parts and accessories stores, car washes, and drive-in restaurants blossomed in the suburbs. The first drive-in theater dated to 1933, but few were built as long as car ownership was limited and gasoline was rationed. For the new suburbanites with multiple restless and noisy children, drive-ins were places where they could watch a movie without worrying about the tots disturbing others. By 1958, there were more than 4,000 drive-in movies in the United States.

Suburban "shopping malls" or "plazas" grew at a dizzying rate. In 1945 there were just eight automobile-oriented retail centers in America, that is, a large department store and a dozen specialty shops surrounded by a parking lot. In 1960, there were almost 4,000.

Motels, commonly called "tourist cabins" before World War II, had a reputation as being for the "hotsheet trade" (just as drive-in theaters were thought of as "passion pits"). They were redeemed by the automobile economy. Motel chains like Holiday Inn trumpeted the cleanliness of their rooms and the diversions they

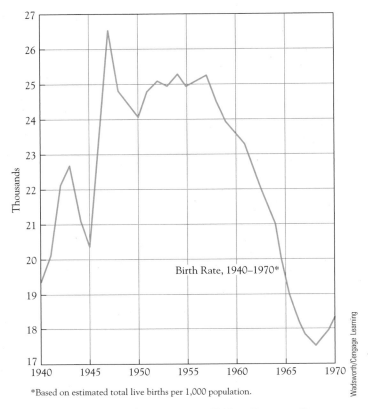

Birth Rate, 1940–1970*

*Based on estimated total live births per 1,000 population.

Wadsworth/Cengage Learning

CHART 45.1 The Baby Boom: The Fuel of Fifties Prosperity

During the 1920s, the American birth rate slowly declined. During the Great Depression of the 1930s, it dropped more sharply. World War II saw an increase until 1945 when so many men and more than a few women were overseas. Then came the boom when couples separated for as long as four years were reunited and wartime sweethearts kept clergymen and justices of the peace busy marrying them.

Experts said the spurt in births in 1946 was a fluke and that the birth rate would return to prewar levels. They were right that 1946 was the high point of the baby boom but dead wrong about how long the boom would last. Not until 1964 did the birth rate sink to below 1945 levels.

provided for children, especially swimming pools. Traveling families preferred them to downtown hotels. Women prized the informality of motels, saying they did not know how to dress at a "good hotel." More important, as at the drive-in, at motels children could be let loose. Excluding Las Vegas and Miami Beach—special cases—only eight new downtown hotels were built between 1945 and 1963. Motels, especially along the interstate highways, were built by the thousands.

Baby Boom   During the 1930s, about 2.5 million babies were born in the United States each year. In 1946, the total was 3.4 million. The jump surprised no one. The war had separated millions of couples. However, demographers said, after a few years of couples making up for lost time, the lower birth rate typical of the first half of the century would reassert itself. They were wrong. After a dip in 1946, annual births continued to increase until 1961 (4.2 million), and they did not drop to prebaby boom levels until the 1970s.

All races and social groups experienced the baby boom. However, the increase in the number of children was most noticeable in suburbia because all but a few of the adults in suburbia were couples in their 20s and 30s. Proportionately, kids were more numerous there than in cities and countryside and they were certainly more conspicuous. In Philadelphia, 65,000 children were born during the 1950s. In the Philadelphia suburbs there were 332,000—and more than a few of the city-born children emigrated out during the decade.

Beginning about 1952, when the first baby boomers started school, massive efforts were required to provide educational and recreational facilities for them. As the boomers matured, they attracted attention to the needs of each age group they swelled. By the end of the decade, economists observed that middle-class teenagers were a significant consumer group in their own right. They had $10 billion to spend each year, every cent of it discretionary; their parents took care of the necessities.

There had always been periodicals aimed at young people, most of them either moralistic and inspirational (the Boy Scouts' *Boy's Life* and church magazines) or semi-unrespectable to tasteless (comic books such as *Tales from the Crypt*).

The new and most successful magazines for teenagers reflected Fifties preoccupations: *Seventeen* (clothing and cosmetics for girls) and *Hot Rod* (automobiles for boys). Hollywood made movies about adolescent problems, the most famous, *Rebel Without a Cause,* about affluent, white, suburban teenagers (moviegoers, in other words) whose boorish or selfish parents misunderstood them. Adolescents claimed a new kind of popular music as peculiarly their own. Rock 'n' roll was derived from African American "rhythm and blues" with its earthy sexual references ("shake, rattle, and roll") sanitized so that white juveniles could play the records in the house.

Rock and roll could be seen as rebellious, something always attractive to adolescents. Elvis Presley, a truck driver from Memphis, might have been ignored had his career depended on his baritone, superb as it was. But he titillated teenagers and scandalized their parents with an act that included suggestive hip movements. Rebellion was just part of rock and roll's appeal, however. Producers of recorded music seized on juvenile themes for their songs: senior proms, fast cars, double-dating, teenage lovers bound by eternal love who were lost tragically to the world while racing to beat the Twentieth Century Limited to the crossing. A new kind of record, the compact nearly unbreakable 45-rpm disk that sold for 89¢ was flogged as the teenager's medium as opposed to old-fashioned 78-rpm platters.

Oddly, more than a few adults adopted adolescent fashions and idols rather than smiling indulgently about them. By the end of the decade, television's most popular afternoon program was *American Bandstand* on which Philadelphia teenagers solemnly evaluated just released songs and recently discovered singers ("I give him an eight, no, a nine."). *Bandstand* aired just after school hours for a teenage audience. Advertisers soon discovered, however, that a large proportion of the

© John Springer Collection/Corbis

Sloan Wilson's best-selling novel The Man in the Gray Flannel Suit *was made into a film in 1955. Tom Rath, portrayed by actor, Gregory Peck, was a rising young executive who, on his daily commute to work in New York City, mulls over the emptiness of his job and his home life in the suburbs where, instead of greeting him, his children watch television. He reminisces uselessly of a brief, exciting affair with an Italian girl during World War II. Wilson's book was an indictment of life in the 1950s for upwardly mobile Americans—and they read the book and saw the movie in droves.*

show's audience consisted of housewives who watched and hummed to themselves while at their ironing boards.

DISSENTERS

In 1960, sociologist Daniel Bell wrote in *The End of Ideology* that the anticapitalist critique of American society was dead. The ideologies of socialism and Communism were exhausted, "the old passions spent." Socialists and Communists had assailed capitalism for its material failures—the exploitation and impoverishment of working people while the rich grew richer. However, Bell argued, modern capitalists, unlike the greedy moneybags of yore, recognized that corporations had social responsibilities alongside their economic purposes, and that workers with enough money to be consumers were more profitable than workers whose wages were an expense to be kept at a minimum.

Critics of Abundance

Indeed, the Socialist and Communist parties withered away during the 1950s. Socialist party membership declined to 2,000–3,000. The Communists had about 5,000 members in 1960 but (it was revealed decades later) 1,500 of them were FBI informants.

There were still dissenters, and the commercial success of their books showed that they had a large audience. But the social critics of the Fifties did not make capitalist greed the villain. Their targets were the moral, social, and cultural consequences of abundance. They conceded that capitalism was meeting the material needs of the masses of people.

In 1950, David Riesman suggested in *The Lonely Crowd* that comfortable Americans were "other-directed." That is, they did not, as their forebears had, take their values from their heritage and upbringing, from within themselves; they thought and acted according to what was acceptable to those around them. In *White Collar* (1951), C. Wright Mills made a similar point. In return for generous paychecks, corporations insisted that their middle-class employees conform to corporate ideals. Curiously (for Mills was considered a radical of the left), he unfavorably contrasted dull suburbanites in white collars with the energetic and individualistic (and exploitative) entrepreneurs of the past. William H. Whyte made points similar to Mills's in *The Organization Man* (1956): Jobs in corporations and government bureaucracies placed a premium on anonymity, lack of enterprise, and suppression of imagination. Lewis Mumford execrated the suburbs as the hotbed of conformism.

Other best sellers elaborated on these themes: John Keats's *Insolent Chariots* (1958), on the tyranny of the automobile; Vance Packard's *Hidden Persuaders* (1957), on advertising; and *Status Seekers* (1961), on getting a symbolic leg up on others.

The most widely heard voice in this choir was that of a novelist, Sloan Wilson, in *The Man in the Gray Flannel Suit* (1955). Its principal characters were a suburban couple who were far better off than they had imagined ever being when the war ended. They had an active social life but found it unsatisfying. They needed a new car and new furniture but were already struggling with debt. The husband commuted to work by train, anonymously in a sea of men in white collars, neckties, and gray flannel suits. Grimly, he daydreamed nostalgically of his years as a soldier in Europe during World War II.

Beatniks and Squares

C. Wright Mills displayed his rebellion not only in books but in his personal life. A professor, he refused to wear the uniform of his profession: tweed jacket, starched shirt, bow tie. Even at prestigious Columbia University, he dressed in rumpled khaki trousers and plaid flannel shirts without a necktie (unknowingly pioneering what would be the uniform of the professors of the future).

Except for the fact that he drew a good salary from a large institution, Mills was a "beatnik," a gently mocking nickname given to young bohemians who shunned the rat race of regular jobs, family life, consumption, debt, and conformity. (The word *beatnik* was derived from *Beat,* a term the beatniks applied to themselves which, they said, was short for "beatific": They were "the blessed.")

The two best known beatniks (both out of Columbia University) were writers. Allen Ginsberg's long poem *Howl* (1956) was praised by established poets as notable as William Carlos Williams. Jack Kerouac's *On the Road* (1957), a novel about young men wandering in an old car around the country, was a best seller.

Most large cities had beatnik communities, the men dressing in the khakis and T-shirts, the women shunning cosmetics and the "perms" of the "squares," their name for conventional conformists. They romanticized African Americans for the "naturalness" of their lives, particularly jazz musicians, from whom they adopted marijuana. They rejected conventional sexual morality: Men and women lived together without marrying—a practice unacceptable in respectable society; a few were more-or-less open homosexuals. Their gathering place in beatnik centers like Greenwich Village in New York, Venice in Los Angeles, and North Beach in San Francisco was the coffee house, the chief activity there listening to other beatniks read their poetry.

Like other bohemian movements before and since, Beat was mostly style so that anyone could dabble in it. No sooner did newspaper reporters write articles about the beatnik scene in Greenwich Village or North Beach than, on weekends, the coffee houses were crowded with squares who had swapped their gray flannel suits and their wives their billowing dresses for beatnik accoutrements.

Fifties Women   A more significant rebellion against the popular culture of the Fifties was not recognized when it was first expressed. In 1956, a housewife named Grace Metalious published a novel *Peyton Place* that was promoted as lifting "the lid off a small New England town." The book was a melodramatic tale of greed, petty animosities, revenge taking, and illicit sex in a town that, on the surface, was idyllic and harmonious. Its target was hypocrisy. *Peyton Place* was sensationally successful, mostly because of its explicit sex scenes (although they were few and brief).

However, as feminists would point out a decade later, *Peyton Place* made a point quite at odds with the Fifties. Its three principal characters, a woman and two quite mature teenage girls, were strong characters who tried and largely succeeded in taking charge of their own lives—not just their sex lives—on their own terms. They were not quite the antitheses of the ideal Fifties woman, the fluttery, deferential housewife of TV's suburban families, but neither were they typical.

In 1957, the year *Peyton Place* sold its millions of copies, another woman began to write an explicit critique of what she called the "feminine mystique." Betty Friedan was an intelligent, well-educated woman who had given up a career in order to become a wife and mother in accepted "other-directed" fashion. In 1957, she attended a reunion of her alma mater, Smith College, with a commission to write an article about her generation for *McCall's* magazine.

McCall's expected a piece on the theme of "togetherness," the ideal of suburban domesticity, wife happily supporting husband, that the magazine promoted. Instead,

Friedan wrote of her middle-aged classmates' unhappiness with their lives. *McCall's* rejected the article; Friedan expanded it into a book, *The Feminine Mystique,* which was published in 1963, the last year of "the Fifties."

> The new mystique makes the housewife-mothers, who never had a chance to do anything else, the model for all women; it presupposes that history has reached a final and glorious end in the there and now, as far as women are concerned.

Friedan claimed that many women no longer accepted the role society prescribed for them. They wanted careers, independence, the same opportunities society offered to men.

Before the book was released in hardcover, Friedan's publisher sent an advance copy to a paperback company to sell the rights to the softbound edition. The head of the company was out of town. When he returned, every woman in the office had read it. They told him: "This is the book we've been waiting for. You've got to buy it." Friedan had tapped into a cauldron of dissent and resentment. In 1966, she helped to found the National Organization for Women (NOW) along with other women who were inspired by her book. The NOW was to lead the powerful revival of American feminism in the final decades of the twentieth century, a social movement second in importance only to the Civil Rights Movement.

46

COLD WAR STRATEGIES
The Eisenhower and Kennedy Years 1953–1963

*The middle of the road is all of the usable surface. The
extremes, right and left, are in the gutters.*

—Dwight D. Eisenhower

*We stand today on the edge of a new frontier—the frontier
of the 1960s—a frontier of unknown opportunities and
perils—a frontier of unfulfilled hopes and threats.*

—John F. Kennedy

Dwight D. Eisenhower was 21 in 1911 when he became a cadet at the military
academy at West Point. He was 62 when he became president. Except for two
years as the celebrity president of Columbia University, a job he hated, he had
spent his entire adult life in uniform, living on army bases, associating only with
other officers at work and play. Career officers like him—those uninterested in
party politics, in any case—lived insulated from mainstream America. So, the society Ike inherited from the Truman administration in 1953, a society remade by
twenty years of New Deal reforms and the war Eisenhower commanded abroad,
had as little to do with the America of turn-of-the-century Abilene, Kansas, where
Eisenhower was a boy, as General Motors had to do with horses and buggies.
Ike depended on advice, and he knew it, but he had a good deal of experience
commanding and he knew that he bore the responsibility for the acts that he
approved.

THE MIDDLE OF THE ROAD

Ike also inherited a war from Truman. The Korean Conflict was not quite a "hot
war" in 1953, but was more like simmering. Both sides had achieved their limited
objectives two years earlier: The U.S. "contained" Communism in North Korea;
China ensured that its borders were secure. The negotiations at Panmunjon to end
the fighting had dragged on fruitlessly because of disagreements over the fate of

Foreign Policy 1953–1963

1950	1955	1960	1965
			1953–1961 Dwight D. Eisenhower president
	John F. Kennedy president 1961–1963		
1954 CIA helps overthrow Guatemalan government			
	1956 Anti-Soviet uprising in Hungary		
U-2 spy plane shot down over Soviet Union 1960			
U.S.-sponsored invasion of Cuba at Bay of Pigs 1961			
	Cuban Missile Crisis 1962		

prisoners of war. China and North Korea insisted that all captured soldiers be returned. The United States and South Korea refused to return Chinese and North Korean soldiers who asked to remain, a substantial number.

Eisenhower broke the deadlock by refusing to rule out the use of nuclear weapons to end the war. He certainly did not intend to do so, but the threat prodded the Chinese and North Koreans to accept a face-saving solution of the POW problem. An armistice was signed in July 1953.

"Dynamic Conservatism"

As for post–New Deal America, Eisenhower was comfortable with it, as were most of the wealthy Republican businessmen who had sponsored his political career. They had pushed Ike to run because they regarded the right-wing Republicans who spoke of turning the clock back to 1929 as election losers. It was a stroke of luck for Ike that the ablest and most influential of them, Senator Taft, was sickened by cancer early in 1953 and died in July. Eisenhower neutralized the die-hard reactionaries in the party by paying lip service to their pieties but doing little for them except to slash federal expenditures, a program of which he heartily approved.

Party politics obligated Ike to name some Taft Republicans to his cabinet. However, calling on the charm and diplomatic skills he had honed as supreme commander in Europe, he prevented them from running amok. The most reckless of the right wingers in the cabinet was Secretary of Agriculture Ezra Taft Benson. Given his head, Benson would have rampaged through the federal bureaucracies like an avenging angel, destroying government regulatory agencies and wiping out New Deal social programs. He never got his sword unsheathed. When Benson proposed to eliminate government subsidies paid to farmers, a New Deal innovation, agricultural organizations, including Republican agribusinesses, howled. Eisenhower stalled Benson and, in 1956, an election year, he signed the Soil Bank Act that paid farmers for every acre they deposited in the "bank," that is, that they held out of cultivation. Poor Benson had no choice but to administer the program. Within ten years, one of every six dollars of farm income came not from sales of produce but from federal payments for crops that were never planted.

Eisenhower called his political philosophy "dynamic conservatism." The term had no more meaning in 1953 than it does today, which is very likely why Ike chose it. "Pragmatic moderation" would have been a perfect description of Eisenhower's policies, but the right-wing "conservatives" in the party would not have liked it.

**The Pragmatic
Moderate**

In 1955, a medical researcher, Jonas Salk, completed tests proving that his vaccine that provided immunity to poliomyelitis, also known as infantile paralysis, worked. Polio was the viral disease that had crippled Franklin D. Roosevelt. In the early 1950s, it was epidemic every summer among urban and suburban children with nearly 60,000 new cases each year. It was a devastating disease. Five percent of those stricken died; a third of those who contracted it were at least partly disabled for life, many severely paralyzed. The parents of young children—a significant group; this was the height of the baby boom—were understandably overjoyed to learn that a few injections would protect their children.

Secretary of Health, Education, and Welfare Oveta Culp Hobby certified the Salk vaccine as effective and safe. She thoughtlessly added that the decision to immunize one's children—and the costs of the shots—was an individual responsibility. When it was pointed out that, because of its contagiousness, polio was a public health problem that the government had a duty to address, she called the critics "socialists," a name almost as dirty as "communist." Public opinion was with the "socialists," and it was angry and vocal. Eisenhower quietly overruled Hobby and, after the usual decent interval, she resigned.

Several high-level officials in the administration advised President Eisenhower to award a contract to construct an atomic energy generating facility to a corporation, Dixon-Yates, rather than to the "socialistic" Tennessee Valley Authority, a government agency. Eisenhower agreed until he learned that Dixon-Yates was waist deep in collusion with officials of the Atomic Energy Commission in a mutually beneficial profiteering

Mothers with plenty of baby boom children line up at a Salk vaccine inoculation center for immunization shots. There would be plenty of howling and yowling inside when the kids got their needles, but their parents were glad to put up with it. A massive popular protest was beginning to take shape before President Eisenhower hastily reversed his Health Secretary's refusal to approve a federally funded immunization program. Note that only one woman in the photo is wearing slacks. Women wore them in 1955, but not all the time; shorts were for picnics or at a swimming pool.

Bettmann/CORBIS

scheme. He was being snookered just as President Harding had been in the Teapot Dome oil grab. Ike abruptly awarded the contract to neither Dixon-Yates nor the TVA but to a third party—in the public sector—that had not been in the running.

The president was embarrassed when, testifying before a congressional committee, Secretary of Defense Charles Wilson, formerly the head of General Motors, said that "what's good for the country is good for General Motors and vice versa." Wilson's phrasing was poor. He was not making the Coolidge-era-like point it sounded like. In any case, Eisenhower did not take orders from General Motors or any other corporation. In his farewell address in 1960, he warned against the ominous political power of the "military industrial complex" (of which General Motors was the most important single component), a stronger anti-big business statement than any president since has dared to make.

The Nuclear Arms Race Eisenhower was no war monger. His historical reputation as a great general was beyond question. His ambition as president was to be remembered as a man of peace. In his efforts to balance the federal budget, Eisenhower made his biggest spending cuts in the military sector. In the midst of a Cold War with the Soviet Union, he could not, of course, slight national security. However, his economy-minded Secretary of the Treasury, George Humphrey, pointed out that building up the nation's nuclear arsenal and developing planes and missiles capable of delivering the bombs cost a fraction of the money needed to maintain a huge conventional army and navy such as the Soviets had in Eastern Europe. Humphrey's (and Eisenhower's) policy was flippantly called "more bang for the buck."

No sooner had Eisenhower opted for nuclear buildup than he was given the results of a study that questioned the usefulness of an overwhelmingly larger nuclear arsenal as a deterrent if the Soviet Union determined on war with the United States. America had far more bombs and delivery systems than the Soviets did, but it did not matter.

It meant only that if a war broke out, the United States would flatten dozens of Soviet and Eastern European cities, killing tens of millions of people. Then the Soviets would successfully destroy a few American cities and a great many more cities of America's allies in Western Europe. The overwhelmingly superior conventional armies of the Warsaw Pact would steamroll NATO's weaker defense forces. Tactical nuclear weapons would not stop the enemy's armies. They were too widely dispersed and too mobile to be good targets.

FIFTIES FOREIGN POLICY

The chief consequence of Ike's nuclear buildup was to launch a nuclear arms race that Eisenhower and his presidential successors and Stalin's successors in the Kremlin found impossible, for thirty years, to slow down. The deterrent for both sides was the "balance of terror," the knowledge that war between the United States and USSR meant "mutually assured destruction." What conceivable national goal was more important than avoiding that?

Fortunately, Eisenhower could think of none because several of his top advisors missed the point. Saving money was not George Humphrey's only justification of "more bang for a buck" policy. He also growled that the United States had "no business getting into little wars. Let's intervene decisively with all we have got or stay out." Secretary of State John Foster Dulles seemed equally oblivious to the implications of his overly aggressive foreign policy.

| Dull, Duller, Dulles | John Foster Dulles was related to two secretaries of state. Fresh out of law school, he specialized in international law for Sullivan and Cromwell, the firm that engineered Congress's |

choice of the Panama route for the interocean canal. Dulles himself had represented a number of companies and banks with large investments abroad. His practice was a kind of diplomacy in that he dealt with both foreign governments and the American State Department.

Dulles was immensely successful as a lawyer, but his personality was unsuited to the world of striped trousers diplomacy in which sociability, charm, indirection, and patience were central. Had he ever been an ambassador, the limitations of his personality would have been found out early in his career, but he never was; he was a lawyer who dealt in specifics written down on papers to be signed. "Dull, Duller, Dulles," his Democratic party critics gibed about his inability to make small talk.

His lack of the diplomat's touch made him unpopular not only in neutral countries, but also with America's allies. To make matters worse, he insisted on representing the United States in person when he should have stayed home. He flew 500,000 miles on the job, demoralizing American ambassadors by treating them as mere ceremonial figures who greeted his plane in foreign capitals and then disappeared while he did the work.

Worse than his glum earnestness, Dulles was an anachronism in his deeply felt religion. He was a Calvinist whose belief that Satan was actively at work in the world was as real and as sincere as John Winthrop's. The manifestation of evil that obsessed Dulles was not the pope or fornication but godless international communism. With Satan its origin, Dulles saw communism as a monolithic force bent on conquering the world.

He ignored evidence that he might be mistaken. When Nikita Khrushchev, who emerged on top in the Soviet Union after the power struggle following Stalin's death, hinted that he wanted to ease Cold War tensions, Dulles dismissed the "peace feelers" as treacherous tricks. When, in 1955, the Soviets withdrew their troops from Austria, consenting to the creation of a non-Communist neutral democratic republic, Dulles refused to credit those who said that, perhaps, the Russians had no more territorial ambitions in Europe.

In the conflict between good and evil, there were only bonded brothers in the Lord and enemies, only friends and foes; It was "us versus them." If a nation was not unreservedly in the American camp, it was in the Communist camp, however surreptitiously. In Dulles's cosmos, there was no "third world" in which individual nations might refuse to do as the United States directed in every particular but wished to remain friendly.

| The CIA in Iran | A crisis in Iran, long underway when Dulles took over, provided him his first opportunity to overthrow what he |

defined as a hostile regime. He was able to work covertly—secretly, as the Communists did—because his brother, Allen Dulles, was director of the Central Intelligence Agency, a body that, in 1948, was authorized to take "executive action," that is, covert action without congressional approval, "against hostile foreign states or groups or in support of friendly foreign states or groups."

In oil-rich Iran, the nationalistic reform government of Mohammed Mossadegh had attempted to take over the British Anglo-Iranian Oil Company (AIOC), paying for the take-over with 25 percent of the profits from oil rather than the 60 percent the British had been pocketing. The AIOC retaliated by withdrawing its managerial and technical employees, which shut down Iranian oil production and threw the country into economic as well as political chaos. The United States had no financial interests in Iran and a minimal diplomatic presence. However, the British convinced Dulles that Mossadegh was, if not a Communist himself, a weak and unwitting tool of the Communists.

Mossadegh was no Communist, but he was erratic and foolishly broadened the front on which he was battling the British company and their Iranian allies. He split with Mohammed Reza Pahlavi, the shah (emperor) of Iran, a 34-year-old playboy more interested in ceremonies and the high life than in politics, and demanded that he abdicate. As the country eased toward civil war, the Shah fled to Italy. In the meantime, with a secret fund of $1 million to be used "in any way that would bring about the fall of Mossadegh," CIA operative Kermit Roosevelt Jr. (Teddy's grandson) had supervised a successful propaganda campaign in Iran depicting Mossadegh as a Soviet stooge and assembled a junta of Iranian generals to reinstate the Shah.

The operation was successful, thanks as much to Mossadegh's blunders as to Roosevelt's manipulations. After only three days in exile, the shah returned, assuming greater powers than he had before and beholden to the United States for being back on his "peacock throne." Anglo-Iranian's new share of the oil revenues was, ironically, less than Mossadegh had offered the company. American interests took part of the remainder.

It had not been oil, however, that set the Dulles brothers to interfering in Iranian affairs but the fear that Mossdegh's policies would lead to incursions in the country by the neighboring Soviet Union. The next and more cynical Dulles intervention in another country's internal politics was, indeed, carried out on behalf of American economic interests.

Coup d'État in Guatemala

The United Fruit Company was the child of the McKinley-Roosevelt age of American imperialism. It evolved from a railroad in Costa Rica built during the 1870s by an American entrepreneur, Minor Keith. Keith established large banana plantation along the line on 800,000 tax-free acres granted to him by his father-in-law, the president of Costa Rica, and found a ready market for his fruit in the United States. Bananas were an excellent export crop; they were harvested green and ripened during shipment.

During Theodore Roosevelt's presidency, United Fruit expanded its holdings throughout the Caribbean and Central America. Its headquarters and greatest holdings (generating a fourth of the company's revenues) were in Guatemala. Guatemalans

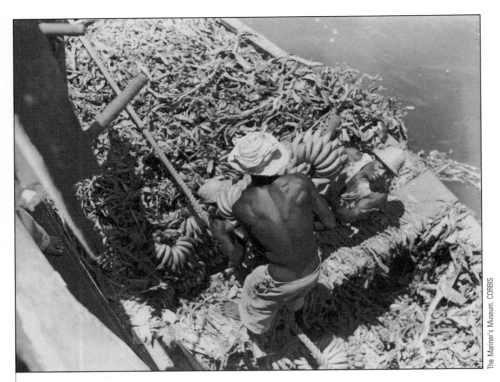

Two United Fruit Company employees in Honduras load bunches of bananas on a boat bound for the United States. United Fruit and one other American company virtually monopolized banana culture in Central America. Employees enjoyed generally better pay and conditions than the masses of poor Central Americans. But the price of United Fruit paternalism was domination of the government and economy through corrupt politicians and generals.

called the company *el pulpo,* the octopus, because its tentacles reached everywhere. United Fruit even ran the country's post office.

As Latin American employers went, United Fruit was a jewel. Its Indian and Afro-Caribbean workers earned higher wages than those on other plantations. The company built decent housing, schools, and hospitals for them and sponsored programs to combat yellow fever, malaria, and other tropical diseases. However, United Fruit insisted on the unquestioned authority of a feudal lord. If employees threatened to strike, the company turned to the Guatemalan armies, the commanders of which were on its payroll.

In 1951, in only the second democratic election in Guatemalan history, Jacobo Arbenz Guzmán was elected on his promises of land redistribution. In June 1952, he announced that the government would purchase uncultivated land on large plantations at the value the owners themselves had placed on it when paying taxes the previous month. United Fruit had valued its wastelands at $3 per acre. Faced with losing it, the company changed its estimate: Its unused land was worth $75 per acre. With broad popular support, Arbenz ignored the revision.

United Fruit turned to its former attorney, now Secretary of State John Foster Dulles. Company representatives knew what button to push; they claimed that Arbenz was a Communist who, if he was not promptly stopped, would establish a Soviet satellite state in Guatemala. Dulles turned to his brother Allen (who had sat on United Fruit's Board of Directors) who financed a military coup led by a Guatemalan general, Carlos Castillo Armas, who put a halt to Arbenz's land reforms.

Seeds of a Tragedy   Arbenz was no more a Communist than Mossadegh was, and he was a far more stable and constructive national leader. He was, in fact, a lifelong anti-Communist, seeing nothing in Marxist ideology for Central America. He was a moderate, democratic reformer who, with at least 60 percent of the people behind him, hoped to improve the lot of Guatemala's peasants while continuing to have cordial commercial relations with the United Fruit Company and friendly political relations with the United States.

By smearing him as a Communist and justifying the protection of a private corporation's assets on those grounds, Dulles pointed American foreign policy in a direction that inevitably led to disaster.

Also in 1954, Dulles refused to sign the Geneva Accords, an agreement that ended a long war between the French and a coalition of Vietnamese rebels, the Viet Minh by dividing the country into two zones. The leader of the Viet Minh, Ho Chih Minh, who withdrew to the north, really was a Communist but he was no Soviet agent. With the French defeated, Ho regarded neighboring Red China as the chief threat to Vietnamese independence, and he hoped to win financial assistance from the United States as well as from the Soviets, while aligning with neither power. Indeed, Ho had non-Communists in his coalition to whose views he had to pay attention.

All these things were well known in Washington. A flexible and opportunistic secretary of state would have exploited Ho's circumstances to establish a working relationship with Vietnam. Dulles was not that secretary of state. Even before the French had completed their evacuation of Vietnam, the CIA began secretly to prevent the democratic elections that the Geneva Accords called for in 1956 because, it was obvious to all, Ho Chih Minh would be elected president.

Brinkmanship: Theory and Practice   Eisenhower deferred to Dulles in the matters of Iran, Guatemala, and Vietnam. He knew little about those countries, and he was impressed by the breadth of Dulles's knowledge. The secretary's espousal of "brinkmanship"—"the ability to get to the verge without getting into war"—must have worried the cautious and compromising Eisenhower. However, he did not repudiate Dulles's occasionally bellicose rhetoric, assuming it was bluff and that, in the end—short of the end!—Dulles would act responsibly. His assumption led to a mortifying embarrassment in 1956.

For several years, the government's official radio network in Europe, Voice of America, and the CIA-funded Radio Free Europe broadly implied to Eastern Europeans that if they rebelled against Soviet domination, the United States would support them. Whether or not the State Department authorized this message, Dulles was on record as rejecting containment policy as passive. He called for an active campaign to reduce the area of Soviet domination.

Someone's at the Door, Honey

During the 1950s and 1960s, most Americans were introduced to the Jehovah's Witnesses for the first time. Their religion obligated them to "witness" their beliefs but, instead of preaching on streetcorners, they knocked on doors and doorbells. Always neatly dressed and in pairs and often racially mixed, highly unusual at the time, they clutched Bibles and handbags stuffed with copies of their two magazines, the *Watchtower* and *Awake!*

They were not selling them; the magazines were free. They smiled, but they did not gush; they were solemn. Their ice-breaking question was grimly cheerless: "Do you think everything is well with the world?" The Jehovah's Witnesses were not a new sect. They had been around for almost a century, but they had only recently become numerous enough to bring their message to what seemed to be every house in the United States. They were prepared to be cursed, have doors slammed in their faces, and even to have dogs sicced on them. Indeed, they welcomed hostile rejection because they read in St. Paul that it meant they were preaching the true word of God.

The Witnesses were fundamentalists who believed that the Bible was "inspired and historically accurate" and a reliable guide to every aspect of daily life. They were far more conversant with the Bible than members of any other self-styled fundamentalist denomination. The best of the doorbell ringers needed no more than five or ten seconds to find the biblical verse that answered any question asked of them.

They believed that "the end of the world" was right around the corner despite a number of disappointments. In 1876, their founder, Charles Taze Russell, predicted that Armageddon—the final battle

In the summer of 1956, thousands of Poles in Warsaw rioted in favor of Wadyslaw Gomulka. Gomulka was a Communist, but after he openly criticized the extent of Russia's domination of the country, he was ousted. After the riots, the Soviets relented and allowed Gomulka to assume power.

Tens of thousands of Hungarians then noisily protested in support of an even more strident critic of the Soviets, Imre Nagy. It appeared the Russians would again ease off when, within days, the demonstrations evolved into a full-scale violent rebellion. Spokesmen for the rebels appealed to the United States to send troops or, at least, assistance. Eisenhower was silent. Going to the brink was one thing; intervening in Hungary was leaping from it into war. When the Soviets realized that the United States was not moving, their troops invaded Hungary and harshly suppressed the rebels. Hundreds of thousands of Hungarians fled the country. They hated the Soviet Union, but few had kind words for John Foster Dulles.

Also in 1956, Egypt seized the Suez Canal. With what they believed was American approval, a combined British, French, and Israeli force invaded Egypt. In fact, whatever the three countries had been told by others, Eisenhower had opposed military action against Egypt from the start. When Khrushchev threatened to send Russian "volunteers" to assist the Egyptians, Eisenhower denounced the invasion publicly and forced the three allies into a humiliating withdrawal.

between good and evil—would occur in 1914. When the First World War erupted in that year, membership jumped. After New Year's day 1915, Russell's successor named 1918 as the date. It was set again at 1925, 1941, 1975, and 1984. In anxious times such as during the nuclear balance of terror, the warning at the front door that it could happen any minute was not preposterous. Tens of thousands of people without religious inclinations were building fallout shelters.

Jehovah's Witnesses differed from most other fundamentalists in being free of racial prejudice and in their refusal to cooperate with the military in any way. Their rejection of racism resulted in a large number of converts among African Americans. Their refusal to serve in the armed forces was unique in that they were not pacifists. Indeed, they looked forward zestfully to Armageddon when they would take up arms for Jehovah and exterminate those who had rejected God's message. Thousands of Witnesses

were imprisoned during World War II and the Korean conflict as conscientious objectors who would not even serve as medics. All governments but God's were evil, the United States no less so than the Soviet Union.

They did not believe in hell. When Jehovah's Kingdom was established, the "instruments of Satan" would simply cease to exist. Only 144,000 elect would reside in heaven with the Lord God Jehovah. Other Witnesses would live under Jehovah's rule on earth. The mark of Fifties America can be seen in the Witnesses's pictorial representation of Jehovah's earthly kingdom to this day. Drawn in a distinctively 1950s style, it shows lions lying down with lambs on a broad weedless lawn mowed as closely as a golf green surrounding a sprawling "ranch" house such as was the suburban beau ideal of the era. Often, the scene is of a suburban barbecue except that the beaming hosts and guests are black, brown, and Asian as well as white.

Peaceful Coexistence

While Dulles rattled his saber, Eisenhower cautiously responded to peaceful overtures by the rotund, homely, and very clever Ukrainian who was Stalin's successor in the Soviet Union. Nikita Khrushchev bewildered American Kremlinologists (experts on the Soviet Union) which was probably one of his intentions. At times he was a coarse buffoon who drank too much vodka at public functions and showed it. At the United Nations in New York, he stunned the General Assembly when, to protest a disagreeable speech, he took off his shoe and banged it on the desk in front of him. On other occasions, Khrushchev was witty, charming, and ingratiating; he was slick.

In 1956, at a closed Communist party Congress, Khrushchev denounced Stalin for his totalitarian rule and the crimes he had committed against other Communist leaders and whole populations of Russians. Statues of Stalin were pulled down everywhere in the Soviet Union except in Stalin's native Georgia. His embalmed corpse was removed from Lenin's tomb in Moscow (the Soviet Union's holy of holies), and Stalingrad was renamed Volgograd.

There were other indications that Khruschev was breaking cleanly with Stalinist tyranny. In 1958, the Russian writer Boris Pasternak was awarded the Nobel Prize in literature for his anti-Communist novel *Dr. Zhivago*. Khruschev condemned the Swedish prize committee for its political values, and Pasternak was forbidden to go the Stockholm to accept his award. But the writer was not jailed—or murdered as Stalin would have seen done.

Khruschev's destalinization policy did not include calling off the Cold War with the United States. He was still a believing Communist, convinced that the conflict with the capitalist world had to be resolved. However, acknowledging that nuclear war was unthinkable, he called for the "peaceful coexistence" of Communism and the West. Let the irreconcilable differences between the two systems be resolved not by war but by "historical forces."

Goodwill Tours and the U-2   This was a line with which Eisenhower was comfortable. No sooner had Dulles died in 1959 than he personally sponsored an accommodating Soviet policy. He sent Vice President Richard Nixon on a "goodwill tour" of Russia and agreed with Khruschev to exchange visits. When Khruschev arrived in the United States, Eisenhower saw to it that he was lavishly feted, and the clever premier turned his wit, humble background, and common touch to scoring a public relations triumph. Americans were presented not with a monster, but a good-humored, unpretentious guest with an unaffected interest in everyday things. Khrushchev drew nationwide laughter when, for security reasons, his request to visit California's Disneyland was denied. The real reason he was kept out, Khruschev explained to American reporters, was that the Magic Kingdom was a cover for intercontinental ballistic missiles aimed at the Soviet Union.

Eisenhower was scheduled to visit Russia in May 1960. He had good reason to expect to be as great a success as Khruschev's visit had been. Ike had been portrayed as a hero in the Soviet Union during the war, and he had remained as personally cordial as circumstances allowed with Marshall Georgyi Zhukov, a general who had been unafraid to contradict Stalin. Then, on May 5, Khrushchev announced that the Russians had shot down an American plane deep within their air space. It was a U-2, a top-secret high-altitude spy plane flying under the auspices of the CIA. Assuming that the pilot had been killed or had committed suicide (as U-2 pilots were provided the means to do), Eisenhower said that it was a weather-monitoring plane that had wandered off course.

Khrushchev pounced. The pilot was alive and had confessed to being a spy. Possibly in an attempt to salvage Eisenhower's visit, Khrushchev implied that the flight had been ordered by subordinates without Eisenhower's approval. Ike refused to shirk responsibility. The Democrats had been criticizing him roundly for allowing the reckless Dulles to make foreign policy. He acknowledged that he had personally approved the flight, and Khrushchev had no choice but to denounce Eisenhower as a warmonger and cancel his visit. The Cold War was quite chilly again.

1960: CHANGING OF THE GUARD

The chill in the Cold War suited the political strategy of a contender for the 1960 Democratic presidential nomination, John Fitzgerald Kennedy. A 42-year-old senator from Massachusetts, Kennedy claimed that the Eisenhower administration had, with its cuts in military spending, allowed the Russians to open a dangerous "missile gap," a gross disparity between the number of intercontinental ballistic missiles the Soviets had available to strike the United States, and the number of missiles in the American arsenal. This was nonsense and irresponsible. Nonsense because "more bang for a buck" policy had favored spending on missiles at the expense of conventional forces. Irresponsible because Kennedy ignored the obvious fact that there would be no winners after an exchange of nuclear bombs, no matter which side scored the most hits.

The Candidates After a brilliantly engineered campaign, Kennedy narrowly won the Democratic nomination on the first ballot. He quietly offered the vice presidential spot to his chief rival, Lyndon B. Johnson of Texas. Kennedy expected Johnson to decline. He was the majority leader in the Senate and a very powerful one. The vice presidency was without power. But Kennedy was not popular in the southern states. He hoped that Johnson would respond to his courtesy offer of the vice presidency by marshaling southern Democrats to work for Kennedy's election.

When Johnson accepted the invitation, Kennedy and his chief advisor, his brother Robert F. Kennedy, were shocked. They should not have been. For Johnson, to run for vice president was a "can't lose" opportunity. He was up for reelection to the Senate in Texas, but state law permitted him to run for both offices. If the Republicans won the presidential election, he would still be majority leader and, by virtue of helping Kennedy, the front-runner for the nomination in 1964. If Kennedy won, Johnson would be credited for the victory because winning southern electoral votes was essential to a Democratic victory. Texas, which Johnson knew he could carry, had voted Republican in 1952 and 1956.

The Republican nominee, Vice President Richard Nixon, had a touchy assignment. Although Eisenhower had never liked him, and Nixon resented several slighting remarks about him Ike had made, he had to defend the Eisenhower administration. At the same time, he had to offer something new to appeal to a mania for change, youth, and "vigor" that Kennedy's successes in the primary elections had revealed. ("Vigor" was Kennedy's "buzz word.") Nixon was only five years older than Kennedy, but he never did overcome the popular perception that he was the candidate of the old order. Nixon made a point of his experience, eight years as an active or, at least, conspicuous vice president. Then Eisenhower thoughtlessly embarrassed him by saying he could not recall a major decision to which Nixon had contributed.

A Close Election The Democrats revived the "Tricky Dicky" theme that had dogged Nixon since he had entered politics. He could not be trusted: "Would you buy a used car from this man?" was a favorite Democratic joke. But mostly the Kennedy brothers and a tight-knit coterie around them ran a superbly efficient campaign drawing on Kennedy's father's millions for funds. Kennedy had put to rest the dictum that a Catholic like him could not be elected president when he won the primary election in West Virginia, a Bible Belt state thought to be intensely anti-Catholic. During the campaign, he entered the lion's den, the Southern Baptist Convention that had taken the lead rejecting Catholic Al Smith in 1928. He gave a superb speech on the subject of religious tolerance. If he converted few of those present to his side, his speech was lauded nationally. And Lyndon Johnson crisscrossed Texas and the South as tirelessly as if he were himself the presidential candidate.

The popular vote was closer than in any election since 1888. Kennedy won by a wafer-thin margin of 118,574 votes out of almost 70 million cast. (An unreconstructed Dixiecrat won 500,000 votes and 15 electoral votes in the South.) Kennedy's comfortable 303 to 219 electoral vote margin concealed very close scrapes in several large states. Kennedy may have carried Illinois (27 electoral votes) because of extensive ballot box fraud in Chicago, governed by the last of the old time city bosses, Mayor Richard E. Daley.

Some pundits said that Kennedy won because his young high-society wife Jacquelyn was more glamorous than shy Pat Nixon, or because the Massachusetts senator looked better in the first of four televised debates with Nixon. Nixon was, in fact, extremely nervous at the debate. Beads of perspiration collected on his upper lip, and ineptly applied makeup failed to cover his heavy five-o'clock shadow.

But those explanations were fatuous. Nixon looked fine in the other three debates and performed well in all four. Neither man "won" them. Enfranchised Americans have often voted foolishly but it is difficult to believe that several hundred thousand people in four closely run states preferred Jackie Kennedy to Pat Nixon for First Lady. Had Eisenhower been able and willing to run—he was limited to two terms by the Twenty-Second Amendment—he would have won in a walk despite Kennedy's vigor, Jackie's attractiveness, and Kennedy's hackneyed theme of "it's time to get this country moving again."

Camelot

Kennedy was a masterful actor. He was no more an intellectual than Eisenhower was: His favorite writer was Ian Fleming, creator of the British super spy James Bond. (Eisenhower's was Louis Lamour who, critics said, wrote the same western potboiler over and over, changing only the name of the horse.) However, Kennedy won the hearts (and for his administration, the talents) of the intelligentsia by inviting venerable poet Robert Frost to a read a verse at his inauguration and cellist Pablo Casals to perform at the White House. Jacquelyn Kennedy, although only 32, proved to be a trouper, fashionable without snobbery and articulate on TV discussing her personal project recovering the history of the White House by assembling and refurbishing artifacts of past presidents that had been discarded.

Kennedy put the Washington press corps in his pocket with his good humor and ready wit. He even preempted criticism of his appointment of his brother Robert to be attorney general by stating that "Bobby" needed to get some experience before he had to practice law. With most newspaper publishers rock-solid Republicans, Kennedy's popularity with reporters won a more favorable press coverage than any other twentieth-century Democratic president.

The Kennedy family was large, athletic, and competitive. Kennedy appealed to young suburbanites by releasing films and photographs of his brothers, sisters, and in-laws playing rough-and-tumble touch football on the beach at the Kennedy family vacation compound in Hyannisport on Cape Cod—but few pictures of the

John F. and Jacquelyn Kennedy were young, attractive, and stylish. They made the most of it all in order to contrast themselves with the elderly, homespun Eisenhowers who preceded them in the White House. Spotlighting their "classiness" was politically risky, however. A good many working-class and farm people disliked and resented the sophisticated upper class of the Northeast. The Kennedy image might have worn thin had the era of "Camelot" not been so brief. But elegance came naturally to the Kennedys, and it worked until the president's assassination.

© 2UPI-Bettmann/Corbis

homes there that would have drawn attention to the Kennedy wealth and privilege. He and Jacquelyn were the parents of two small, photogenic children, an ingratiating asset absent in the White House since the days of the only president who was younger than Kennedy, Teddy Roosevelt.

There were plenty of Kennedy-haters, but in the glow of "Camelot," as Kennedy lovers called his brief presidency, they sounded sour and carping. *Camelot* was a blockbuster musical of the early 1960s, based on the idyllic, mythical reign of King Arthur in ancient Britain. Adultery destroyed Arthur's Camelot. Kennedy did not cease his all too numerous adulteries when he was elected president but his sexual irregularities were not widely known until years after his death.

KENNEDY FOREIGN POLICY

Kennedy was an unapologetic Cold Warrior. Neither John Foster Dulles nor, twenty years later, President Ronald Reagan, exceeded the belligerence of Kennedy's statement that "Freedom and Communism are in deadly embrace; the world cannot exist half-slave and half-free." Kennedy probably knew that the "missile gap" of which he had spoken was a fiction, but he sincerely believed that Dulles's "brinkmanship" and threats of "massive retaliation" had been counterproductive.

Flexible Response and the Third World Kennedy's foreign policy advisors, mostly from elite universities and "think tanks"—Secretary of State Dean Rusk and security advisors Walt W. Rostow and McGeorge Bundy—revived and updated containment policy with their doctrine of "flexible response." The United States would respond to Soviet and Chinese actions not with Dulles's bluster but in proportion to their seriousness.

If the Soviets or Chinese actively aided guerrilla movements fighting friendly regimes, the United States would fund the military forces of those regimes and send specialists to advise them; it was the Truman Doctrine plus on-site counselors. If the Soviets were suspected of subverting elections in the Third World, the United States would launch its own covert manipulative operations. Kennedy sponsored the development of elite antiguerrilla units in the army, notably the Special Forces called "Green Berets" after their distinctive headgear. He increased funding of the Central Intelligence Agency, which had 15,000 agents around the world.

Truman and Eisenhower had both thought in traditional terms, that wealthy Europe and Japan were the places that counted in the Cold War competition. Kennedy stated that "the great battleground for the defense and expansion of freedom today is the whole southern half of the globe—Asia, Latin America, Africa, and the Middle East—the lands of the rising peoples."

He preferred to back democratic reform movements in the "developing countries." Unlike Dulles, he was willing to cooperate with democratic socialists. Kennedy took the initiative in organizing the Alliance for Progress in the Western Hemisphere, a program that promised economic aid to Latin American nations in the hope that they would abandon military dictatorship and adopt free institutions. Unfortunately, the choice in the undeveloped countries was rarely between liberal reformers and Communists. Envy of American riches; resentment of the economic power and profiteering of American investors in their countries; the fact that the United States had supported many dictators as long as they were anti-Communist; Soviet opportunism; and the romantic zaniness that is common among middle- and upper-class revolutionaries meant that Third World liberation movements were inclined to be suspicious of American intentions and willing to overlook the Russian record in Eastern Europe. Consequently, Kennedy sometimes found the pro-American politicians in "the whole southern half of the globe" were reactionaries.

The Bay of Pigs "Flexible Response" proved to be a disaster in Cuba. Once a pliant American dependency, since 1959 Cuba had been governed by a revolutionary regime headed by Fidel Castro. In 1960, baiting the United States in interminable but effective speeches to huge crowds, Castro began to expropriate American-owned properties before negotiating compensation. Eisenhower approved a secret CIA project to arm and train 2,000 anti-Castro Cubans to invade the island. They were not ready to move until after Kennedy was in office. He had misgivings, but the CIA assured him that Castro was unpopular. At the sound of the first gunfire, anti-Castro rebellions would break out all over the island. The prospect of a major triumph at the beginning of his presidency was attractive. To dismiss the anti-Castro invasion force would have provided ammunition to Republicans ever ready to accuse Democrats of timidity. Kennedy gave the go-ahead.

On April 17, 1961, the invaders waded ashore at the Bahía de Cochinos, the Bay of Pigs, on Cuba's southern coast. Everything went wrong. There was no uprising. Castro's soldiers, seasoned by years of guerrilla warfare, made short work of the outnumbered liberators. Instead of ousting an anti-American but possibly still flexible regime, Kennedy had pushed Castro, who feared another invasion, into the arms of the Soviets.

Kennedy's Bay of Pigs fiasco heartened Nikita Khrushchev to take a harder line with the United States. When he met with Khruschev in Vienna in June, Kennedy found himself outwitted and upstaged at every turn. The Ukrainian tongue-tied him in private and, when they appeared together before reporters and cameras, patronized him as a nice boy who only needed experience. Kennedy returned home seething with anger. Khrushchev went back to Moscow encouraged to act aggressively. The Soviets resumed nuclear testing in the atmosphere and ordered the sealing of the border between East and West Berlin.

The Berlin Wall The Communist regime of East Germany had been plagued by the defections of trained technologists who could double and triple their incomes in West Germany's booming economy. The "brain drain" was crippling East German industry, and Western propagandists made hay of the fact that East Germans defectors were "voting with their feet." To put an end to the problem, Khrushchev ordered a wall built around West Berlin that was as ugly in appearance as it was symbolically.

Republicans urged Kennedy to bulldoze the wall. Kennedy let it stand. The wall was on East German soil; to knock it down meant trespassing—"invading," the Soviets might well call it and respond militarily. The wall did not threaten either the United States or the security of West Berlin—there was no blockade as in 1948. Kennedy reasoned that the Berlin Wall was a self-inflicted propaganda disaster for the Soviets. It was, particularly when East Germans continued to flee the country by crashing through gates, scaling the wall, or tunneling under it. East German border guards were ordered to shoot, and they did.

The Missile Crisis In October 1962, a U-2 flight over Cuba revealed that the Soviets were installing missiles. Such a threat a hundred miles from the United States could not be let to pass. Before he informed the public of the discovery, however, Kennedy assembled his most trusted advisors. He rejected a proposal by Dean Acheson that the sites be bombed and another that American troops invade Cuba. Although Kennedy did not know it at the time, he had decided correctly. The CIA—wrong again—had told him that there was only a handful of Russians in Cuba; in fact there were 40,000 Russian troops there. The CIA also grossly underestimated the size of the Cuban army, which numbered 270,000 men and women.

After hours of agonizing discussion, Kennedy adopted his brother's moderate and flexible approach to the crisis. Announcing the discovery of the missile sites on television, he proclaimed a naval blockade of Cuba and demanded that the Soviets dismantle the installations and remove all nuclear devices. Castro panicked. He fled to a bunker beneath the Soviet Embassy and demanded that Khrushchev launch a nuclear attack on the United States. Castro's hysteria gave Khrushchev pause. He too believed in flexible response and began to wonder about his Cuban ally's mental stability.

For four days, work on the sites continued and Soviet ships carrying twenty missiles continued on their way to Cuba. (Twenty missiles were already there; forty would represent a full third of the Russian arsenal at the time.) Americans gathered solemnly around their television sets, apprehensive that the nuclear holocaust would begin any minute. Secretary of State Dean Rusk summed it up when he told the small group of men in Kennedy's office, "We're eyeball to eyeball."

Rusk was able to add: "and I think the other fellow just blinked." The Cuba-bound Russian freighters stopped in midocean. After several hours, shadowed by American planes, they turned around. On October 26, Khrushchev sent a long conciliatory letter to Kennedy in which he said he would remove the missiles from Cuba if the United States pledged not to invade the island. The next day, he sent a second message saying that he would remove the weapons from Cuba if the United States removed its missiles from Turkey, which bordered the Soviet Union.

Kennedy could have accepted Khruschev's second offer as readily as the first. Before the crisis, he had been considering dismantling the Turkish missile sites as a conciliatory gesture. However, reasoning from the differences between the two Soviet notes that there were division and indecision in the Kremlin, he saw the chance for some diplomatic one-upmanship that might strengthen Khruschev's more accommodating advisors. He ignored the second note, as if it had been lost in the mail, and accepted the terms of the first letter. On October 28, Khrushchev accepted the bargain as if he had never mentioned Turkey.

Assassination   By the fall of 1963, Kennedy had regained the confidence he had exuded in 1960. Public opinion polls showed his popularity up well above the 50 percent mark in California and other western and midwestern states that Nixon had carried in 1960. Their electoral votes would more than compensate for southern states lost because of his support of civil rights legislation. Vice President Johnson assured him that more white southerners than Kennedy realized were moderate on racial questions.

Johnson invited Kennedy to make a speaking tour of Texas with him. Kennedy hesitated. He feared he would be booed and jeered on the streets. But Johnson persevered and Kennedy agreed.

They were met with cheering crowds, and Kennedy was reassured. Then, as the motorcade passed through a broad open space in downtown Dallas known as Dealey Plaza, the president's head was shattered by rifle fire. Within a few hours, Dallas police had arrested Lee Harvey Oswald, a ne'er-do-well former Marine and hanger-on of pro-Castro organizations who worked in a textbook clearinghouse overlooking Dealey Plaza.

Kennedy's death unleashed a storm of anxieties and conspiracy theories. Because extreme right-wing political organizations like the John Birch Society were prominent in Dallas, liberals were inclined to blame far right "kooks" for the assassination. They circulated stories of Dallas schoolchildren cheering when they heard Kennedy had been killed. (The rumors were false.) Others said that the CIA had killed Kennedy because, after the Bay and Pigs and the Missile Crisis, he had grown disgusted by the agency's bad advice.

Oswald's own political associations were with organizations of the left. Indeed, he had lived for a time in the Soviet Union and tried to renounce his American citizenship. Few thought the Soviet Union would engineer the murder. They had no reason to want Kennedy out of the way. Castro, on the other hand, bore a grudge and, as Khrushchev had learned, was capable of rash action.

Lee Harvey Oswald was unable to clear things up. Two days after his arrest, he was shot to death in the basement of the Dallas police headquarters by a nightclub operator named Jack Ruby. Ruby said he was distressed to the point of distraction by the death of the president whom he had idolized. Because Ruby had nebulous underworld connections, his appearance in the story added the theory that the Mafia had killed Kennedy.

A National Tragedy A commission headed by Chief Justice Earl Warren found that Oswald was not part of a conspiracy, that he acted alone. He was a solitary misfit much like Charles Guiteau and Leon Czolgosz. However, sloppiness in gathering evidence and soft spots in several of the Warren Commission's conclusions only increased belief in conspiracies. In later years, several more careful independent investigations confirmed the commission's findings (while faulting much of its work). But suspicions lived on. In 1988, a large majority of Americans said that they did not accept the official account of the murder. In 1991, a Hollywood film implicating government agencies in the killing, all allegedly coordinated by a homosexual aesthete from New Orleans, was a huge commercial success. In 2008, yet another book claiming that Oswald did not act alone was published to positive reviews from usually cautious critics.

John F. Kennedy was not a major president, not even a "near great," a term some historians, unfortunately, like to use. He accomplished little domestically. In foreign policy, his success in the Missile Crisis was to pale in significance when set beside Kennedy's then barely noticed military intervention in Vietnam, an involvement that was to escalate out of control and poison American life for decades.

Still, the assassination was a national tragedy like Lincoln's murder. Kennedy had inspired an idealism that, after his death, was to dissipate into disillusionment, cynicism, and mindless political and social turmoil. Daniel Patrick Moynihan, an official in his administration who was to become senator from New York, summed it up pretty well for his generation when he told of a conversation he had at Kennedy's funeral: Journalist "Mary McGrory said to me that we'll never laugh again. And I said, 'Heavens, Mary. We'll laugh again. It's just that we'll never be young again.'"

47

▼

RACE AND RIGHTS

The African American Struggle for Civil Equality
1953–1968

*The time has come for Americans of all races and creeds
and political beliefs to understand and to respect one
another. So let us put an end to the teaching and the
preaching of hate and evil and violence. Let us turn away
from the fanatics of the far left and the far right, from the
apostles of bitterness and bigotry, from those defiant of law,
and those who pour venom into our Nation's
bloodstream....*

—Lyndon Baines Johnson

"African American" and "Afro-American" were terms rarely heard in 1953. There was the African Methodist Episcopal Church, the largest black church, which dated back to 1787 when its founders were no more than a generation or so removed from their native lands. By the twentieth century, however, black organizations that wanted to honor their members' ancestry preferred "Abyssinian" or "Ethiopian."

"Black" was unacceptable to African Americans of mixed ancestry who regarded their lighter skin color as a mark of superior social status. African Americans' favored identifications of themselves were "Negro" (capitalized as the equivalent of "Caucasian") and "colored" as in the National Association for the Advancement of Colored People. Respectful whites said "Negro" or "colored." Others used one of dozens of slang terms, most of which were insulting. The name African Americans despised was, of course, *nigger.*

BEING BLACK IN AMERICA

In 1953, two of three Negroes still lived in the South: the former slave states plus Oklahoma. However, the black population of the Northeast had doubled since 1900 as southerners were driven north by poverty and harassment and drawn by

The Fight for Civil Rights 1947–1968

1945	1950	1955	1960	1965	1970

1947 Major League baseball integrated

1948 Segregation in armed forces ended

1950 NAACP wins two important civil rights cases

1954 *Brown v. School Board of Topeka*

1955 Martin Luther King leads Montgomery bus boycott

1957 National Guard enforces school integration in Little Rock

1964 Civil Rights Act

1965 Voting Rights Act

1965 Malcolm X assassinated

Martin Luther King assassinated 1968

better-paying jobs and relative tolerance. Five percent of the black population lived in the Midwest as compared to less than 2 percent in 1900. African Americans in the western states, numbered 600,000 by 1953, almost all of them recent arrivals lured by high-paying jobs in defense plants during World War II.

Wherever they lived, blacks were, at best, second-class citizens. They were reminded of their inferior social status everywhere except within large urban ghettos like New York's Harlem and Chicago's South Side. There, like the new immigrants half a century earlier, they could insulate themselves from constant reminders of the distaste, even the contempt, in which the white majority held them.

Jim Crow South and North   Social segregation was as thoroughgoing in the South as it had been in 1900. Schools, hospitals, buses and trolleys, waiting rooms, movie theaters, grandstands at baseball fields, parks, and libraries were segregated by race. Reminders of the color line were everywhere in the shape of "white only" and "colored only" signs enameled on drinking fountains in courthouses and scrawled in paint on privies behind service stations.

No signs were necessary to inform southern blacks that they would not be served in cafés where they saw white people coming and going. A typical local ordinance like this one from Montgomery, Alabama, made it

unlawful to conduct a restaurant of any other place for the serving of food … at which white and colored people are served in the same room unless such white and colored people are effectually separated by a solid partition extending from the floor upward to a distance of seven feet or higher and unless a separate entrance from the street is provided for each compartment.

Your dollar was good, but you ordered and paid for your egg-salad sandwich wrapped in waxed paper at the kitchen door.

A traveling African American caught at night in a strange town knew that if he did not bump into a local who could direct him to a hotel for the race, he was better advised to hunker down on a bench in the "colored" section of a railroad or bus station than to wander around looking for a room.

"Jim Crow" was not an exclusively southern institution. In 1953, interracial marriages were forbidden in thirty of the forty-eight states. Even Massachusetts forbade ministers and priests to marry a couple from one of the thirty states where they could not legally marry. There was one or another kind of racially discriminatory state law in thirty-two states, restrictive municipal ordinances in many of the other sixteen, and racial customs as rigorously enforced as laws almost everywhere.

Prejudice   Pennsylvania's state teachers' colleges were open to black students. However, African American high school graduates were encouraged to apply to all-black Cheyney State. They were told—truthfully enough—that they would feel more comfortable there.

In Philadelphia, municipal swimming pools were open to blacks only one day a week—when almost all white children stayed home. In Wildwood, New Jersey, a summer resort boasting five miles of ocean beach, African Americans knew to spread their blankets and picnic baskets on only one short stretch of sand. Blacks

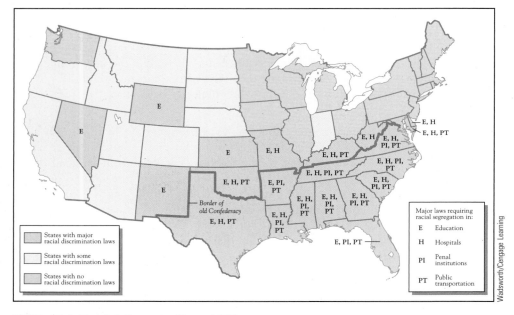

MAP 47.1 Racial Segregation, 1949.

State laws drew a "color line" through public institutions and most public accommodations in all the states where, a century earlier, slavery had been legal. More than ten states that had never known slavery had laws that discriminated against African Americans in one way or another. Even states with no discriminatory legislation on the books unofficially approved it. In Pennsylvania, for example, while blacks could attend any one of the state-supported teacher's colleges, one of them, Cheyney State, was all black. Rather than deal daily with prejudice, almost all African Americans who wanted to be teachers enrolled there.

could promenade on the boardwalk, take a spin on the Tilt-a-Whirl, and buy the kids a "sno-cone" on only one evening each week. Authorities justified these restrictions on the grounds that, if crowds of young whites and blacks mixed on the beach or on the boardwalk, there would be violence.

Residential restrictions were universal except in small towns where only a handful of blacks lived. In fact, few African Americans complained about residential segregation as long as it did not mean substandard housing. When they were at home, they wanted to feel "at home," just as they preferred their own churches and clubs. The wealthiest African Americans in New York City preferred to live in Harlem (on the best streets) rather than in apartments in white neighborhoods.

Unskilled African Americans were hired to work only the most menial, lowest paying jobs. Even where labor unions defended African Americans' rights to desirable employment such as in Detroit's automobile industry or on the docks in San Francisco, Philadelphia, and New York, black and white stevedores worked in segregated gangs. Black doctors employed by municipal hospitals were assigned to hospitals in African American neighborhoods, black teachers to largely black schools. Lawyers, dentists, and other professionals expected to have all-black clienteles.

The national capital was a Jim Crow town. Some government agencies hired African Americans only to sweep floors and work in cafeterias. When Adam Clayton Powell Jr. was elected to Congress from New York in 1944, he delighted in discomfiting his southern white colleagues by lunching with black constituents in the House dining room. In fact, African Americans were denied service in many up-scale restaurants in the North.

Winds of Change   By 1953, however, there were signs of change in the air. The lynch mob murdering with impunity was a thing of the past (although, in 1955, several Mississippians murdered a black boy from Chicago for being "uppity" and got away with it).

Americans' disgust with Nazi anti-Jewish laws in Germany led northern states, after the war, to repeal their own antimiscegenation laws. Laws prohibiting interracial marriage survived in the south until 1967 when, in *Loving* v. *Virginia*, the Supreme Court declared them unconstitutional in every state.

In many southern cities (although not in rural counties where blacks were more numerous), legal and extra-legal devices preventing African Americans from voting were falling into disuse. In 1940, only 3 percent of southern blacks constitutionally eligible to vote were actually registered; by 1953, 20 percent were.

In 1947, a star black baseball player, Jackie Roosevelt Robinson, cracked the most conspicuous segregated national institution, major league baseball, when he joined the Brooklyn Dodgers of the National League. By the end of his first season, several teams had signed black players. By 1953, only two or three major league teams still refused to recruit blacks.

In 1948, President Truman ordered an end to segregation in the armed forces. The generals and admirals dodged the order for three years. However, when high casualties during the Korean War reduced both black and white units by half and more, rendering them tactically useless, the army brass gave in, combining black and white regiments at half-strength into one that was combat ready. At the Democratic National Convention in 1948, Minneapolis mayor Hubert H. Humphrey successfully pushed through a resolution pledging the party to back full civil rights for African Americans.

THE BATTLE IN THE COURTS

The big breakthrough in ending institutionalized segregation came in 1954 when, in *Brown v. School Board of Topeka,* the Supreme Court ruled that racially separate schools violated the right of African Americans to the equal treatment guaranteed them by the Fourteenth Amendment. The announcement of the decision came as a shock to many people. However, *Brown* was the culmination of a long, expensive, incremental campaign in the courts led by the NAACP.

The legal foundation of racially segregated schools (and the Jim Crow laws) was the 1896 Supreme Court decision in the case of *Plessy* v. *Ferguson.* In 1896, with only one dissenter, the Court ruled that it did not violate Fourteenth Amendment protections if public facilities such as schools were segregated by race as long as the white and color facilities were equal in quality.

Separate and Unequal   Over the years, African American groups had periodically won court cases when they proved that a specific public facility for blacks was grossly unequal to the whites' facility. More often, when a local authority knew it was going to lose a separate but equal case, it headed off a judgment by appropriating enough money to improve the black facility in question. None of those little victories, however, had any bearing on segregation as an institution.

During the 1930s, the NAACP's chief attorney, Charles H. Houston, concluded that the racial discrimination most damaging to African Americans was in public education. There was little point, Houston reasoned, in challenging separate but equal as a doctrine. Supreme Courts rarely reverse the rulings of earlier Courts, especially when, as in the case of *Plessy,* the vote was an overwhelming 8–1.

Houston persuaded the NAACP leadership that, for the moment, they should accept "separate but equal" as a rule of the game and attack race-based discrimination in which educational opportunities were made available to whites but not to African Americans.

Thus, only a few southern states provided pharmacy, dentistry, medical, nursing, law, and other graduate schools for blacks. They could get away with it because there was little demand for such advanced training among the overwhelmingly poor, uneducated, rural African American population of the South, and, therefore, no legal challenges. When, in North Carolina, a qualified black college graduate applied to the state's whites-only pharmacy school, the state solved the problem by paying his expenses at a pharmacy school in a northern state.

Warming Up   Other states avoided lawsuits by adopting this practice. Houston won his first victory against it in 1935 when he represented Donald Murray, an African American who applied for admission to the University of Maryland law school and refused to take the state's money and study in the north, claiming that, as a citizen of Maryland, he had the his right to pursue his studies in his own state. The Maryland courts found in favor of Murray, presenting the state legislature with the options of admitting Murray to the university law school or paying to build and hire the faculty for a separate but equal black law school in the state. Murray was admitted, and Maryland quietly abandoned its whites-only policy in other graduate schools.

Because Maryland gave in at the state level, the Murray ruling applied only to that state. Houston needed a case that he or his adversary could and would fight all the way to the Supreme Court. He found his plaintiff in Lloyd Gaines, a black Missourian who, like Murray, was denied admission to the University of Missouri law school and refused to accept tuition and expenses to attend the law school in neighboring Iowa. *Gaines* v. *Canada* went to the Supreme Court which ruled, in a 6–2 decision, that Gaines had a right to attend law school in his home state. Missouri was ordered to admit Gaines to the white law school or create a separate but equal law school for blacks.

The Missouri legislature appropriated money to open a law school at Lincoln University, a tax-supported black school. Houston intended to sue that the slapped-together new law school was not the equal of the University of Missouri's. While visiting Chicago late in 1939, however, Gaines simply disappeared. Some believed he was murdered by white racists. Others, recalling Gaines's erratic personality, guessed that he had had his fill of litigation, was worn down by the stress of the case, and simply walked off. The case has never been solved.

McLaurin and Sweatt It took Houston's successor as the NAACP's legal strategist, Thurgood Marshall of Baltimore, several years before he could find solid lawsuits comparable to the *Gaines* case. Finally, on the same day in 1950, he won not one but two major decisions.

The first was *McLaurin* v. *Oklahoma*. In response to a court order, the whites-only University of Oklahoma admitted George McLaurin, an African American, to its graduate program in education. However, because state law mandated racially segregated education, McLaurin was required to sit in a roped-off "colored-only" row at the rear of lecture halls or even in the corridor outside classrooms. A "colored-only" desk in the library and a "colored-only" table in the cafeteria were set aside for him.

Neither the university president nor most students approved of McLaurin's humiliation. He usually had moral support at his table at lunchtime. But white students were deterred from denying the color line in classrooms by the threat of a $20 per day fine that the state legislature was prepared to enforce. Fortunately, the "Oklahoma solution" did not last. The Supreme Court unanimously ruled that the university was palpably denying McLaurin treatment equal to that of white students.

The state of Texas had hurriedly created a separate law school for African Americans. Represented by the NAACP, Heman Sweatt, who had been turned down by the University of Texas law school, maintained that the newly founded black law school could not provide an education equal to that at the University. In *Sweatt* v. *Painter*, the Court unanimously agreed. It held that the instructors at

Bettmann/Corbis

George McLaurin was admitted to the white University of Oklahoma's graduate school in education because there was no segregated equivalent in the state. Because of a state law forbidding interracial education, he was forced to sit in isolated rows in classes or, in this case, in the corridor outside a lecture. His humiliation did not last long. The Supreme Court found that such treatment violated the Fourteenth Amendment's equal treatment doctrine.

the new black law school were not the equals of the accomplished professors at the white university. Moreover, a degree from the jerry-built black law school would not carry with it the prestige of a University of Texas degree. Texas was ordered to admit Sweatt to its law school.

The *McLaurin* and *Sweatt* cases were significant; they had results. Within six months in 1950, about 1,000 African Americans were admitted to formerly all-white universities in Arkansas, Kentucky, Maryland, and Oklahoma—and they did not have to sit in the corridors. Delaware desegregated all of its graduate schools. Some NAACP lawyers thought they detected in Chief Justice Fred Vinson's opinion a hint that he suspected that racially separate educational facilities could never be equal. If so, the time was ripe to attempt to reverse *Plessy* as it applied to all levels of education.

Brown v. School Board of Topeka   Marshall and NAACP president Roy Wilkins were not so sure. Postgraduate education was an easier nut to crack than elementary and secondary schools. Few people, white or black, were interested in graduate school. Not so primary and secondary schools: All children attended them. Middle-class and especially lower-class whites—the political backbone of southern racism—were passionately interested in keeping the schools whites only. With good reason, Marshall and Wilkins worried that a majority of justices would grasp at any formula to avoid a social upheaval by justifying separate but equal public schools.

Their anxiety was justified. Although they did not know it, only one justice, William O. Douglass, had no reservations about ruling segregation unconstitutional. The equally liberal Hugo Black, who leaned in that direction, was troubled by distinctions between "reasonable segregation" and "unreasonable segregation," a bad sign. Felix Frankfurter despised racism, but he was also an outspoken critic of judges who allowed their personal values to distort their reading of what was obvious in the law. A straw vote in the Court's chambers had showed a one vote majority for finding segregation acceptable in primary and secondary schools. However, Chief Justice Vinson (who voted with the majority) did not want so important an issue decided by one vote. He ordered the Court to hear *Brown* v. *School Board* a second time in 1953.

Then, in September, an apparently healthy Vinson died. To succeed him as Chief Justice, President Eisenhower named former California governor Earl Warren. Warren was a don't-rock-the-boat moderate Republican. He had gone along with the internment of California's Japanese-Americans during the war. Eisenhower expected him to resolve *Brown* v. *School Board of Topeka* in favor of segregation or, at least, to delay action. At a White House social, the president quite improperly let Warren know his wishes. This angered Warren, who intended to vote to reverse *Plessy*. He went to work to persuade the four justices leaning against reversal to go along with the majority. So momentous a decision, he argued, would stir up less fuss if it had the prestige of a unanimous decision behind it. So effective a politician was Warren that he convinced even the one justice who firmly believed in the validity of *Plessy*. All nine signed Warren's opinion.

Resistance   Most cities and larger towns in the upper South integrated their schools without incident. Many whites were happy to be rid of segregation if for no other reason than the expense of supporting parallel school systems. In the deep South, however, white resistance was widespread. Demagogic politicians courted voters by pledging "segregation forever" and "the South shall rise again." A reincarnation of the Ku Klux Klan spread rapidly throughout the lower South. Black pupils in integrated schools were harassed, sometimes with the connivance of teachers, so that many withdrew back into the Jim Crow schools.

In Arkansas, where trouble was not expected, Little Rock exploded in September 1957. A mob of white adults greeted the first black pupils at Central High School with shouts, curses, and rocks. Claiming that the presence of the African American pupils was the cause of the disorder, Governor Orval Faubus called out the Arkansas National Guard to prevent desegregation.

President Eisenhower was furious. (Although still angrier with Earl Warren than with Faubus; he later said that naming Warren Chief Justice was the biggest mistake of his presidency.) Faubus was defying a federal court order being enforced by federal marshalls. That, Ike would not tolerate. He assumed command of the Arkansas National Guard and ordered it to enforce integration at Central High. Overnight, the perplexed guardsmen's orders were reversed.

DIRECT ACTION AND POLITICS

While the NAACP shepherded lawsuits through the courts, other civil rights organizations concentrated on direct action: demonstrations, strikes, boycotts, and nonviolent civil disobedience, peacefully violating discriminatory laws in order to draw attention to the injustice of them.

The master of direct action before 1953 was Adam Clayton Powell Jr., the pastor of the Abyssinian Baptist Church in Harlem. Powell was handsome, eloquent, brazen, colorful, worldly rather than pious. Before World War II he had organized rent strikes against Harlem slumlords, a successful demonstration demanding that the New York World's Fair of 1939 hire more African Americans, and a boycott to pressure shop owners on 125th Street, Harlem's business section, to hire African Americans. "Mass action is the most powerful force on earth," he said. Powell's arrogance annoyed whites but Harlemites loved it. They elected him to Congress in 1944 and sent him back every two years.

The blacks and whites who founded the Congress on Racial Equality (CORE) in Chicago in 1942, were anything but arrogant. They were members of the Fellowship

Greg Villet/Time & Life Pictures/Getty Images

A Montgomery, Alabama city bus during the great boycott of 1955. Normally, the bus would be filled, with blacks the majority of passengers. African Americans were required to give up seats close to the driver as the bus filled. It was this humiliation that launched the boycott.

for Reconciliation (FOR), a mostly Christian pacifist organization, who took as their inspiration Mohandas Gandhi, the Indian agitator who had shaken British imperial rule by espousing nonviolent mass disobedience of unjust laws. The FOR admonished members to submit passively to arrest after breaking the law. By their moral example, they would in time force the repeal of the unjust laws they violated. In 1947, sixteen members of CORE—eight white, eight black—openly violated southern state laws requiring the segregation of buses and trains by race. Four were convicted and sentenced to labor on chain gangs.

Martin Luther King Jr. The Montgomery Bus Boycott of 1955 was grounded on CORE's principles of nonviolent civil disobedience largely because of the leadership of a young Baptist preacher, Martin Luther King Jr., who had written his doctoral dissertation on Gandhi. In Montgomery, as in almost every other southern city, the law required African Americans to move to the back of bus if a white person wanted the seats they occupied nearer the front. The 1955 protest began when a woman named Rosa Parks, weary after a day's work, refused to give up her seat behind the driver to a white passenger. When she was arrested, Montgomery's African Americans responded by boycotting the city-owned bus system. They walked, hitchhiked, or carpooled to their jobs with such unanimity that the bus company faced bankruptcy.

Journalists and television reporters flocked to Montgomery as King emerged as the boycott's spokesman. The police harassed him, repeatedly arresting him and roughing him up. Terrorists bombed his home. Nevertheless, King pleaded with his followers to remain nonviolent. Not only was it the Christian way to turn the other cheek, he argued, but also peaceful submission was politically effective. If blacks resisted violently, onlookers would approve of forceful repression. However, if decent white people were confronted on their television sets with police officers brutalizing peaceful African Americans and their white supporters simply because they demanded to be treated decently, they would, King believed, force the authorities to change obnoxious laws.

King's technique worked. He became a national figure overnight. Prominent northern churchmen and important labor leaders like Walter Reuther of the United Automobile Workers came to Montgomery to march with the boycotters. They raised money to finance the Southern Christian Leadership Conference (SCLC), which King founded to spread his message. After 1960, when SCLC's youth organization, the Student Nonviolent Coordinating Committee (SNCC) peacefully violated laws that prohibited blacks from eating at lunch counters in the South, white university students in the North picketed and boycotted branches of chain stores like F. W. Woolworth in their hometowns. When a white mob burned an interstate bus on which white and black "freedom riders" from CORE were peaceably defying segregated seating, the federal government sent marshals south to identify and prosecute violent racists.

Ike, Kennedy, and Race Neither Dwight D. Eisenhower nor John F. Kennedy had thought of racial discrimination as a compelling issue. Both, for different reasons, were dismayed by the militance with which, after the *Brown* decision, civil rights movement leaders demanded equality for African Americans.

Ike had grown up in Abilene, Kansas, and Denison, Texas, both Jim Crow towns, in the early twentieth century. His proper, church-going family bore black people no animosity—his mother was a Jehovah's Witness—but they accepted the color line as a fact of life. The U.S. army, in which Eisenhower spent his entire adult life, was strictly segregated and not entirely happy about the four African American regiments it was required to maintain. Black draftees during the two world wars were assigned to segregated units, and few were combat soldiers, reflecting the common prejudice that blacks were unreliable. (Only 5 percent of black soldiers saw action in World War II compared to 27 percent of whites.) African Americans were assigned to transportation companies or the Quartermaster Corps (supply). Until World War II, there were few black officers, and most of them were chaplains with whom Officer's Club officers like Eisenhower had no contact.

Kennedy too had lived in an all-white world, within the rarefied upper class that educated its children at private schools and elite institutions like Harvard. Not even the Kennedys' political ambitions involved them in racial issues. Boston had the smallest African American population among large cities, and the Irish-Americans who dominated Massachusetts politics were as racist as Georgia cotton growers. The only blacks with whom John F. Kennedy had rubbed elbows were waiters serving canapés or, during World War II, cooks, dish washers, and hospital orderlies, the jobs to which the navy assigned African American recruits.

As president, Kennedy was more receptive than Eisenhower to civil rights demonstrators because the almost solid African American Democratic vote in large northern cities was essential to the party's electoral success. The catch was that the Democrats' once "solid South" counted on white segregationists. Franklin D. Roosevelt had held the unlikely alliance together by sidestepping the issue of Jim Crow laws and even refusing to support antilynching legislation. That was no longer possible after the emergence of Martin Luther King.

"Segregation Forever"   By the fall of 1962, hard-line segregationist southern politicians made it clear that they were determined to resist by direct action what they had lost in the courts. The governor of Mississippi, Ross Barnett, himself a former Klansman, ordered the state university at Oxford to refuse admission to a young African American, James Meredith. The president and his brother, Attorney-General Robert Kennedy, wrangled with Barnett by phone for hours. They had no choice, they told him, but to enforce Meredith's court-ordered admission. By continuing his rabble-rousing, Barnett was accomplishing nothing but fomenting a riot that would foul the reputation of Ol' Miss and savage the beautiful university town of Oxford.

Such appeals meant nothing to Barnett. When Meredith registered, Oxford was plunged into a riot as white students, Klansmen, and other racists attacked federal marshalls guarding Meredith in a makeshift citadel. The marshalls, whom the Kennedys had ordered not to use firearms until their backs were to the wall, were nearly overrun when troops arrived to lift the siege. Miraculously, only two people were killed; however, 166 marshals were wounded. It cost the federal government $4 million to ensure that one student was enrolled in the state university he paid taxes to support.

In January 1963, the battlefront moved east to Alabama. Governor George C. Wallace was a much cleverer politician than Barnett. Ironically, he had risen in Alabama politics as a populist Democrat who avoided the ravings of racist demagogues. Then, in 1958, he narrowly lost the gubernatorial election to one of them. "You know why I lost? ... ," he told a friend. "I was outniggered ... and I'll tell you here and now, I will never be outniggered again."

In 1962, Wallace "out-niggered" his rivals and won. He said in his inaugural address, "I draw the line in the dust and toss the gauntlet before the feet of tyranny, and I say segregation now, segregation tomorrow, segregation forever." In January 1963, he personally blocked the doorway of the University of Alabama registration hall to prevent two African Americans from entering. His defiance was symbolic—a "media event" staged for the cameras. Wallace stepped aside when he was confronted by an assistant attorney general, federal marshals, and national guardsmen. But it was enough to transform the obscure first-term governor into the undisputed leader of the South's "segregation forever" forces.

The March on Washington   Later in 1963, Kennedy faced a threat of social disruption from King's Southern Christian Leadership Conference. King, Bayard Rustin of CORE, labor leader A. Philip Randolph, and their white supporters were organizing a massive civil rights "March on Washington" in August. Kennedy feared there would be a riot that would dwarf Little Rock and Oxford. He and his brother Robert pleaded with King to let the segregationist turmoil subside before demonstrating. In return for canceling the march, Kennedy would send a comprehensive civil rights bill to Congress. He reminded King that, in 1941, Randolph had accommodated President Roosevelt's request that he cancel a protest march whence the president issued Executive Order 8802 prohibiting companies with government defense contracts to discriminate against blacks when hiring workers.

King wobbled but, in the end, he refused to budge. In part, he did not trust the Kennedys. More important, Roosevelt had been able to deliver an executive order in 1941. Kennedy was having trouble getting any legislation through Congress. His support could not guarantee passage of even a watered-down civil rights bill. In the meantime, the momentum generated by the march would be lost. King assured the president that the demonstration was aimed not at him but at winning the sympathy of the American people. It would be peaceful.

As many as 200,000 people, white and black, followed King through the streets of Washington to the Lincoln Memorial where he delivered what is considered his greatest sermon. "I have a dream today," he began,

> I have a dream today that one day ... little black boys and black girls will be able to join hands with little white boys and white girls and walk together as sisters and brothers. ... When we let freedom ring, when we let it ring from every village and every hamlet, from every state and every city, we will be able to speed up that day when all of God's children, black men and white men, Jews and Gentiles, Protestants and

Catholics, will be able to join hands and sing, in the words of that old Negro spiritual, "Free at last! Free at last! Thank God Almighty, we are free at last!"

The march was orderly and King made it clear that he considered the administration a friend of civil rights, not an adversary. Kennedy reciprocated by endorsing a sweeping civil rights bill to be debated in Congress in 1964.

THE CIVIL RIGHTS REVOLUTION

Even when southern racial hostilities were burning at their hottest, some sociologists, novelists, and other intellectuals suggested that once the Jim Crow laws were gone and racial terrorism quashed, human relationships between white and black southerners would be healthier than black-white relations in the North.

Southerners, they pointed out, had been living side by side for two and a half centuries. They had nowhere been equal, but they had dealt with one another daily on a personal, intimate level. Despite the twentieth-century color line, they continued to do so because few southerners lived in big cities. Of the twenty largest American cities in 1960, only New Orleans was in the South and, with its cosmopolitan heritage, was not truly southern. Most southerners lived in the country, in crossroads villages, railroad whistlestops, and in towns where strict residential segregation was impossible to enforce. Whites and blacks lived on the same streets, trundled in and out of the same shops, loitered on the same squares, courthouse steps, and at the same depots. Until puberty, children of both races played together; only in increments did they learn the meaning of race.

Race in the North   By way of contrast, few African Americans had lived in the North until after about 1910. When emigrants from the South arrived in large numbers, they clustered in the "colored sections" of big cities that were soon self-contained and impenetrable to whites. When black ghettos grew, sprawling into and absorbing formerly white neighborhoods, the result was chronic tension and ructions between white and black youths.

In Philadelphia, Pittsburgh, Cleveland, Detroit, Chicago, men and women of both races commuted to work in the same buses and subways; they punched the same time clocks; tended machines side by side; loaded and unloaded freight on trains and trucks; and competed for a variety of unskilled and semiskilled jobs. At the end of the day, however, they scattered to single-race neighborhoods where their personal associations were exclusively white or African American and their social and cultural lives were not merely segregated but hermetically sealed from the social and cultural lives of the other race.

The impersonality of big city life was redoubled when relationships involved people of different races. One observer suggested that a black teenager in a small southern town hesitated less about asking a white woman tending her tomato plants for a glass of cold water than a thirsty African American boy in a northern city would before asking a white man washing his car for a drink from his garden hose. Once civil inequality and Jim Crow were abolished in the South, the argument went, interracial relations would be vastly better in the South than between the "two nations" of the northern cities.

The Southerner Who Ended Segregation

President Kennedy did not live to see his civil rights bill enacted by Congress or, voted down. When he was murdered in 1963, the task of shepherding it through Congress fell to Lyndon B. Johnson who seized on the project with an ardor that stunned both his former southern colleagues in the Senate and civil rights movement leaders.

Not that Johnson had ever been a rabid segregationist. Like most Texas politicians, he was more westerner than southerner. He sported cowboy boots and broad-brimmed John B. Stetson hats, not the rumpled white linen suit of the stereotyped southern senator. Before he developed ambitions for national office, he "voted southern" on bills involving race—that was a prerequisite of being a politician in the South—but he never made segregation his issue.

Personally, Johnson had long disliked Jim Crow. "I'll tell you what's at the bottom of it," he said privately. "If you can convince the lowest white man he's better than the best colored man, he won't notice you're picking his pocket. Hell, give him somebody to look down on, and he'll empty his pockets for you." Again privately, he said of a militant racist Senator from Mississippi, "Jim Eastland could be standing right in the middle of the worst Mississippi flood ever known, and he'd say that the niggers caused it, helped out some by the Communists."

A Revolution in Civil Rights

The national outpouring of grief following Kennedy's murder provided Johnson a major boost in winning over congressmen and senators who had been sitting on the fence on civil rights. His years of deal making in the Senate with Republican leader Everett Dirksen enabled him to win the support of twenty-seven of thirty-five Republican senators for what became the Civil Rights Act of 1964. Industrious Democratic liberals like Hubert Humphrey of Minnesota and Mike Mansfield of Montana overcame a southern filibuster and other parliamentary obstacles to the bill.

The Civil Rights Act of 1964 definitively ended segregation in public schools and pulled down the "white" and "colored" signs that had been a part of southern life for more than half a century. It created a Fair Employment Practices Commission to end a yawning gap in joblessness between whites and blacks in the North as well as the South.

Johnson understood that, by passing the Civil Rights Act, the Democratic party was losing the votes of the South for, he said, "a generation." An entirely new southern Democratic party had to be pieced together by guaranteeing that southern blacks could vote. In some southern states, at least, a bloc Democratic vote by African Americans plus southern white moderates might salvage the party. However, a SNCC voter registration drive in Mississippi during the summer of 1964—"Freedom Summer"—was a complete flop when African American farmers told the northern college students who canvassed them that trying to vote was not worth risking their lives. White racists in the little town of Philadelphia, Mississippi, underscored their argument when they murdered three northern civil rights workers.

So, LBJ threw his influence behind the Voting Rights Act of 1965. It provided for federal supervision of voter registration and elections in congressional districts in which less than 50 percent of eligible voters were actually registered. The law eliminated decades-old techniques for disenfranchising blacks.

These acts were revolutionary. In just two years, they institutionalized every demand that civil rights agitators had been making for decades. They should have earned Johnson a central niche in any African American pantheon of benefactors.

But Johnson's achievement earned him nothing of the kind. By 1968 (after yet a third law aimed at improving life for African Americans the Fair Housing Act of 1968) LBJ had little mass support among blacks, and he was demonized by many of the white middle-class liberals whose programs he had helped make law as part of his "Great Society."

The big reason for his failure was a military conflict in Southeast Asia that Johnson transformed into a major war from which he could not extricate the United States. Even Martin Luther King abandoned the president on the issue of the Vietnam War. Moreover, beginning in 1968, Johnson's Democratic party began to lose the support of large numbers of northern white ethnic working-class men and women who had voted Democratic for half a century. They were alienated by what they saw as the party's coddling of African Americans while neglecting of their interests. The most stinging betrayal was the rejection of Martin Luther King's dream of a color-blind society by young urban blacks in the North and even African American university intellectuals.

BLACK SEPARATISM

Since slavery times, some African Americans had concluded that the two races could never live side by side as equals. The few thousand free blacks who sailed to Liberia before the Civil War believed that escaping the United States was their only hope of living full lives. During the 1910s and early 1920's, Marcus Garvey's United Negro Improvement Association (UNIA) had rallied tens of thousands of northern blacks around the slogan "Back to Africa" and "self-help" programs, founding black-owned businesses, patronizing them, and having as little to do with whites as was possible.

The Black Muslims   Garvey's UNIA was nonsectarian. Blacks of all religious faiths were welcomed as members. Garvey himself was a Roman Catholic. Contemporary with Garveyism, however, several smaller "separationist" movements claiming to be Muslim germinated in the ghettos of several northern cities and, in a modest way, flourished.

The Nation of Islam was proclaimed in Detroit in 1930 by Wallace D. Fard who had been a disciple of the "Noble Prophet" Drew Ali (Timothy Drew), whose Moorish Science Temples of America had been founded in 1913. Drew rejected the term "Negro"; African Americans, he said, were properly called "Moors." His followers wore fezzes and claimed to be Muslims, which was the black man's religion.

In 1929, Drew was arrested as an accomplice in the murder of a rival Moor. While out on bail awaiting trial, he died under suspicious circumstances. (His followers insisted that he too had been murdered.) The next year, Fard emerged from the wreckage of the Moors to proclaim the Nation of Islam (the Nation)—or

"Black Muslims." Of mysterious background—he concealed his past—Fard had a mind as fertile as that of Joseph Smith, the founder of Mormonism. He layered the Black Muslim credo with an unfounded but inspiring history of the races in which civilized and virtuous black people had been forced into subjection by "white devils." In 1934, Fard simply disappeared, very likely murdered. His successor as the head of the Black Muslims, Elijah Poole, who called himself Elijah Muhammed, said that Fard was God and had returned to his heavenly home.

Elijah Muhammed's religion was only selectively Muslim. He taught the subordination of women to men, forbade drinking alcohol and eating of pork, and so on. Other doctrines were at odds with Islamic orthodoxy. Elijah's teaching that Islam was exclusively for blacks contradicted the Muslim rejection of all racial distinctions. His claim to be God's prophet was blasphemous; Islam maintained that Mohammed was the final prophet, the last human being through whom God spoke.

Elijah cared nothing for what Islamic scholars said. (And few of them took notice of the Black Muslims.) The Nation of Islam, although small in numbers, was a going concern in Detroit and other northern cities.

Malcolm X

During World War II, Elijah Muhammed was imprisoned for telling blacks not to serve in the armed forces. He discovered

Malcolm X made more converts to the Black Muslims in a few years than Elijah Muhammed had made in two decades. He was also an excellent fund raiser, earning large fees for lectures at universities where he was popular among radical and liberal students for his message of defiance of whites (and even because he freely insulted his white audiences).

AP Photos

that penitentiaries were prime recruiting grounds for the Nation and, several years after the war, the Black Muslims made a jailhouse convert who transformed the organization from a tiny fringe group to a major force among northern blacks.

Malcolm Little—or "Malcolm X" as he began to call himself—was a powerful preacher. Rising quickly to be Elijah's chief aide, he won converts by the thousand. In the early 1960s, he enriched the Nation's treasury by collecting big speakers' fees and donations from romantic white university students who were thrilled by his militant condemnations of white America.

Malcolm rejected Martin Luther King's call for blacks to integrate into American society. Instead, they should separate from whites and glory in their blackness. Young African American northerners who took no interest in Malcolm's Islamic religion (in which he sincerely believed) were captivated by the pride and defiance he represented. One disciple was Stokely Carmichael of the Student Non-Violent Coordinating Committee who said in 1966, "If we are to proceed toward true liberation, we must cut ourselves off from white people."

In 1965, Elijah Muhammed and Malcolm X had a falling out. Malcolm had idolized the Prophet. When he discovered that Elijah was a racketeer and sexually exploiting Black Muslim women, he left the Nation. Not long after his departure, he was gunned down by Nation thugs.

Malcolm preached self-defense, never aggressive violence. However, his rhetoric glorying in conflict appealed to former civil rights workers who had been beaten by police. Hubert Geroid "H. Rap" Brown, from SNCC like Carmichael, proclaimed as his motto, "Burn, Baby, Burn." When, in 1966, James Meredith, who had integrated the University of Mississippi four years earlier, was shot during a one-man "march against fear" from Memphis to Jackson, Stokely Carmichael took charge of thousands of supporters whom he soon had shouting as they walked, "Black Power!"

THE END OF AN ERA

LBJ's "Great Society" and Martin Luther King Jr's "dream" were blueprints for a future in which a person's race was not a burden. "Black Power" was a slogan that, after it was shouted, led nowhere but to shouting it again. Nevertheless, its instantaneous popularity among young urban blacks marked an end to King's previously unchallenged status as black America's spokesman. The SCLC continued to politic and demonstrate. However, black powerites increasingly denounced him as an "Uncle Tom," a pious, deferential front man of "The Man," white America. King himself was mystified. Rather than criticizing Carmichael and Brown for their lack of a program and reckless encouragement of violence, he tried to accommodate them. So did Bayard Rustin who had been preaching pacifism and racial brotherhood before the black power generation was born.

Black Power   "Black Power" destroyed SNCC, the student wing of the SCLC. Carmichael and Brown expelled its white members. The organization disappeared when its treasury was depleted. Some civil rights leaders like the Rev. Jesse Jackson (an aide to King) and African American intellectuals like sociologist Charles Hamilton tried to give "black power" substance and respectability by saying that it meant nothing more than ethnic pressure politics in the time-honored American tradition: African Americans demanded concessions on issues important to them as the price of delivering a bloc vote on election day. But that, of course, was not what black powerites like Carmichael and Brown, who considered themselves revolutionaries, had in mind.

To a few black nationalists in the Marcus Garvey tradition, black power was a demand for a geographical separation of the races, setting aside part of the United States as a black nation. (One group specified Georgia, Alabama, and Mississippi.)

In Oakland, California, African American teenagers and college students formed the Black Panther Party for Self-Defense. The Panthers entered candidates in local elections, formed an alliance with the small Peace and Freedom party, and won favorable publicity by setting up a lunch program for black schoolchildren. The Black Panthers were best known for carrying shotguns and hunting rifles while, dressed in black shirts, trousers, berets, and boots, they "patrolled" Oakland's streets. The inevitable consequence of the adolescent posturing was the determination of the police to smash the organization.

To the great majority of African Americans who embraced the slogan, black power meant little more than dressing up in dashikis (colorful West African blouses), affecting a "natural" hair style called the "Afro," and shunning friendships and even casual social relationships with whites. In universities, the self-enforced segregation of African American students and faculty—choosing the isolation that Oklahoma had forced on George McLaurin—undoubtedly set back King's color-blind society by decades.

Riots   Some black powerites claimed responsibility for African American riots that rocked northern cities during the later 1960s. In fact, the violence began in Philadelphia and Rochester, New York, in 1964 before the slogan had been coined. Every summer, there was violence somewhere. In 1965, the black Watts area of Los Angeles was chaos for days, leaving 34 people dead, more than 1,000 seriously injured, and block after block of homes and businesses burned to the ground.

The summers of 1966 and 1967 were worse with uprisings in Cleveland, Detroit, Hunter's Point in San Francisco, Omaha, Newark, New York, Chicago, and Washington, where the smell of incinerated buildings hung over Capitol Hill for weeks.

The riots of the 1960s were not "race riots." They did not pit black mobs against white mobs. They were spontaneous outbursts of rage and opportunist that were contained in areas that were almost entirely African American in population. The most common immediate cause of the uprisings was an arrest on the streets—almost always by white policemen. One riot began with a heated argument between white and black drivers involved in an automobile accident. The Omaha riot began when teenagers—for whatever reason teenagers do such things—pelted racially mixed Jehovah's Witnesses with stones.

In almost every case, the rioters' first targets were stores and shops, which were looted and then set aflame. African American merchants rushed to their businesses and painted "black owned" or "soul brother" in the display windows. At first, the mobs seemed to pass them by, but many were destroyed by fires that firemen were unable to control when they were attacked by rioters.

The Kerner Commission, appointed by LBJ in 1968 to explain the violence, found that the riots were the result of inarticulate rage caused by the chronic poverty of the black ghettos (thus the looting), poor housing, the fact that so high a percentage of African American households were without male heads (most of the rioters were teenagers and young men), police arrogance and brutality in dealing with blacks, and criminal opportunism.

Finis   Early in 1968, 1,300 black employees of the Memphis Sanitation Department went on strike to protest the fact that, during a storm, most black workers but no whites were sent home without pay to wait the bad weather out. The strikers asked Martin Luther King for moral support. In March, he led a march which, much to his distress, turned violent. He agreed to return to Memphis in April on the condition that the leaders of the strike guarantee nonviolence.

There had been more than the usual death threats and in a speech he gave there, "I've Been to the Mountaintop," King seemed to have a premonition that the end was near. On April 4, while standing on the balcony of his motel room, he was killed instantly by a sniper. Riots erupted in more than a hundred cities. When they abated, the momentous era of a revolution in civil rights was over.

A ne'er-do-well drifter, James Earl Ray, was arrested and convicted of King's murder. But there were many more holes in the official account that King was killed by a "lone gunman" than there were in the Warren Commission's findings in the murder of President Kennedy. King's own family remained convinced that there was a conspiracy behind his assassination.

48

LYNDON JOHNSON'S GREAT SOCIETY
Reform, War, Disgrace 1961–1968

*We have a problem in making our power credible, and
Vietnam is the place.*

—John F. Kennedy

*The battle against Communism must be joined in Southeast
Asia with strength and determination.*

—Lyndon B. Johnson

Lyndon Baines Johnson (LBJ) rendered a greater service to African Americans
than any other president except Abraham Lincoln. In addition to the Civil
Rights Act of 1964, the Voting Rights Act of 1965, and the Fair Housing Act
of 1968, many of the programs of his "Great Society" (the name LBJ gave to his
program) benefited African Americans disproportionately because they were aimed
at helping the nation's poor and blacks were disproportionately poor.

And yet, at commemorations of the revolution in the lives of African Americans
in the twenty-first century, his name is rarely mentioned. Indeed, he was more often
assailed than honored by African Americans and their white supporters even before
he retired from the presidency in 1969. There was the rash of riots in black neighborhoods in 1967–1968. The Great Society was expensive and many of its programs were failures, hurriedly conceptualized and wastefully administered. And
most of all there was Johnson's prosecution of an increasingly unpopular war in
Vietnam, which turned against him the very people—white and black—to whom
the president had dedicated himself to helping.

LYNDON B. JOHNSON

John F. Kennedy's Washington, bustling with young intellectuals brimming with
ideas, was a different city than the somewhat torpid capital over which Ike presided. Vice President Lyndon B. Johnson would have been quite at home with the
action had JF Kennedy and his brother assigned him a greater role to play in it. But

Escalation and Frustration in Vietnam 1963–1969

▌1963	┌1964	┌1965	┌1966	┌1967	┌1968	1969┐

1963-1969 **Lyndon B. Johnson president; 16,000 "advisers" in Vietnam**

Aug 1964 **Gulf of Tonkin Resolution authorizes war**
Dec 1964 **23,000 soldiers in Vietnam**

Oct 1965 **Antiwar demonstrations in ninety cities**
Dec 1965 **200,000 troops in Vietnam**

Dec 1966 **400,000 troops in Vietnam**

Massive antiwar demonstrations in New York and San Francisco April 1967
500,000 troops in Vietnam Dec 1967

Tet Offensive Jan 1968

President Johnson announces his retirement Dec 1968

they did not, and Johnson was not comfortable mixing socially with the sophisticated easterners of the New Frontier when they condescended to chat with him at receptions and banquets. He knew that when his back was turned, they mocked his Texas drawl, unfashionably cut business suits, and hand-tooled cowboy boots.

Essence of Politician

Kennedy had grown up rich, privileged, and self-confident. He was a proper Bostonian despite his Catholic religion and the fact that the family fortune was new money amassed by dubious means. (JFK's father, Joseph Kennedy, made his money in not quite respectable Hollywood during the 1920s and from liquor bootlegged from Great Britain.) Nevertheless, the Kennedy brothers and sisters attended the best schools and were introduced when young to the elite in both Washington and London.

Johnson's family was not poor, as he sometimes pretended, but his father was unpretentious and provincial, a middling rancher and opportunist in the hill country of central Texas. LBJ went to public schools and had to pay his own way through teacher's college, dropping out for a year when he ran short of money. He taught school for several years but, by 1930, he was irresistibly drawn to Texas state politics, which were notoriously tumultuous. In 1931—the depths of the depression—he went to Washington as a congressman's aide and became a devotee of Franklin D. Roosevelt and the New Deal. His faith in the federal government's spending power as a means of shaping society for the better never wavered.

Johnson got lucky when fellow Texan Sam Rayburn, a major player in the House of Representatives, took a shine to him. With Rayburn's help, Johnson was elected to Congress in 1936. Except for a brief stint in the navy during World War II, he remained there until 1948 when he won a Senate seat by so narrow a margin of controversial votes that Texas Democrats, mostly in good humor, called him "Landslide Lyndon." Texas politicians had been called worse. Johnson shrugged and became the voice in the Senate for Sam Rayburn, who was now Speaker of the House. By 1955, Johnson was the Senate's majority leader.

The "Johnson Treatment"

He was as deft a herder of Democrats (and persuader of Republicans) as Rayburn was. He put together majorities in

Lyndon B. Johnson. He was pure politician. Aside from his wife and daughters, he was keenly interested in nothing else. Aside from riding on his ranch when he vacationed there, he had no hobbies. He had ideals. Personally, he was more sincerely concerned to improve life for the deprived than any other president. And he knew how to get things done when he had the power or, at least, he thought he did. But the pit he dug for himself in Vietnam and the blind thoughtlessness of many of those who owed him big ruined his presidency and his reputation since.

the Senate by administering large doses of homey Texas charm, cutting deals with senators who had pet projects designed to bring federal money to their states, and, when necessary, Johnson knew how to twist a colleague's arm without breaking it. Some said that Johnson "had something" on as many senators as FBI Director J. Edgar Hoover did. That was not true, but the fact that many believed it was an indication of Johnson's effectiveness.

The vice presidency declawed Johnson. Outside of the Senate, he had no bait to dangle in front of foot-dragging senators to persuade them to support Kennedy's New Frontier.

JFK's assassination empowered Johnson anew. As the president of a grief-stricken nation, he was able to push several of Kennedy's stalled initiatives on reluctant senators and congressmen as memorials to the dead president. The Economic Opportunity Act of 1964 created VISTA (Volunteers in Service to America), which sent amateur social workers into economically distressed rural and urban areas; "Head Start" programs to remedy educational deficiencies among poor, preschool children. The Wilderness Preservation Act closed 9.1 million acres of federal land to both economic exploitation and intensive recreational development. In valuing wilderness for its wildness, Johnson expanded the concept of preservation beyond Theodore Roosevelt's imaginings.

Johnson's greatest achievement before he stood for election in 1964 was the Civil Rights Act. It was Kennedy's bill but seemed hopelessly stalled in November 1963. Johnson himself had a tough time out-maneuvering southern segregationists and Republican conservatives like Senator Barry Goldwater of Arizona. But his years making deals in the Senate gave him leverage that Kennedy, never a Senate wheeler-dealer, lacked.

1964   In 1964, the Democratic convention met in Atlantic City, New Jersey. It was an unusual choice. Atlantic City was a decayed seashore resort. The surf had reclaimed most of a once broad beach; formerly fashionable hotels had declined into dingy obsolete hulks, some with toilets and bath tubs still "at the end the hall." The celebrated boardwalk was seedier, dirtier than most big city streets. Two blocks inland slum housing and a "high-crime zone" extended for 2 miles. By meeting there the Democrats were making a statement that Johnson's Great Society meant to attack poverty in America where it was worst. The extent of poverty had been dramatically revealed in a surprising best seller of 1962, *The Other America* by former socialist Michael Harrington.

The Atlantic City convention promised to be dull. There would be no surprises in the platform; Johnson would be nominated by acclamation. The only question for reporters to blather about endlessly was LBJ's choice of a running mate. Would he, despite well-founded gossip that he and Robert F. Kennedy despised one another, select "Bobby." He would not. Johnson did not need a Kennedy on the ticket to carry the Northeast. Johnson pleased the liberal wing of the party by picking Senator Hubert Humphrey of Minnesota who had been instrumental in pushing the Civil Rights Act through, and who, at the convention, tried to work out a compromise between two delegations claiming to represent the state of Mississippi: the regular white supremacy party and the racially integrated Freedom Democrats.

The Birthing of   Just about the only news that enlivened newspaper and
Women's Lib   television coverage of the convention was an apparently
frivolous demonstration that had little to do with Johnson or the party. On the boardwalk outside the convention hall, a group of women calling themselves the Women's Liberation Front staged an act of political theatre aimed at, they said, the dehumanization of women in American society.

Atlantic City—the convention hall—was home to the annual Miss America Pageant. Begun fifty years earlier as a promotional stunt to extend the resort's summer season into September, the annual selection and coronation of Miss America had evolved into a lavish show and, more remarkably, a respected national institution. Each year, a large television audience watched fifty young women in a swimsuit competition, an evening gown competition, and a demonstration of a talent which could be anything from singing a Puccini aria to folding origami birds.

The "Women's Libbers" (as they were immediately dubbed) said that the pageant demeaned women as a sex by elevating as society's ideal "Miss," an automaton with a forced, frozen smile who looked best in a prom gown and a swimsuit. Miss America was not a person, but a "sex object." To ensure that journalists gathered around to hear their message, the Libbers built a small bonfire in a barrel, removed their brassieres from under their blouses, and ceremonially burned them. Brassieres, they explained, were just one way men dehumanized women by making fetishes of their breasts.

The reasoning was murky. Miss America contestants were "beauty objects" surely enough, but they were also virtually nonsexual under the rules and according to the customs under which they presented themselves. (Contestants signed documents certifying that they were virgins.) Brassieres had been invented not to sexualize breasts but for the comfort of large-busted women. But the theatre was titillating; the boardwalk demonstration attracted plenty of attention. Few recognized it at the time but, along with the publication of Betty Friedan's *The Feminine Mystique* the previous year, the "bra burners" were launching a social-political movement expressing the discontent with the lives of a large proportion of middle- and upper-class women.

The John Birch Society   In 1964, however, the most dynamic political movement in the United States was the John Birch Society, founded six years earlier by a candy manufacturer, Robert Welch. "Bircher" politics were familiar enough. They were anti-Communist, anti-liberal, anti-big government, anti-taxes, anti-New Deal, and tacitly anti-civil rights. The society was unique in that its members' mentality was not political but apocalyptic. Birchers thought of themselves as recruiting sergeants for the army of righteousness that would very soon be confronting the forces of evil in the final struggle at Armageddon. Democrats (and many Republicans!) were not political rivals to be voted into obscurity. They were dupes—their leaders knowing agents—of international communism, which was directed by a "furtive conspiratorial cabal of internationalists, greedy bankers, and corrupt politicians" bent on a "one world government."

There was no time to lose. To Birchers, Communists already dominated most national governments. The society published graphs showing France as 85 percent Communist, Bolivia 92 percent Communist, and so on. The State Department and mainstream Protestant churches were arms of the conspiracy. President Eisenhower, Robert Welch wrote, had been "knowingly receiving and abiding by Communist orders, and consciously serving the Communist conspiracy, for all his adult life."

Political Missionaries   This kind of lunacy is usually associated with cultists in white robes holed up in the wilderness. After about 1960, however, the Birch Society grew rapidly, especially among lower-middle-class whites. The Birchers were tireless missionaries. They preached endlessly to friends until they made converts or were told to go away and not come back. They spoke to church groups and lodges. The society flooded the post office with mass mailings, erected billboards festooned with American flags, and sponsored dozens of radio programs.

Local chapters rented storefronts and failed roadhouses, turning them into "reading rooms" where the walls were papered with posters and the tables stacked with books and pamphlets. Curious visitors were cornered in easy chairs while reading room librarians hammered home their message until they had another signed membership card. By 1964, the Society claimed more than 600,000 members, about a quarter of them in southern California. A book by a Bircher, John A. Stormer, *None Dare Call It Treason*, published in 1964, sold 7 million copies.

The society was a tightly disciplined party within the Republican party and meant to capture it in 1964. The Birchers' candidate was Senator Barry Goldwater of Arizona, who had succeeded Robert A. Taft as the leader of Republican conservatives in Congress. Goldwater was not a member, but he concluded early on in his quest for the Republican nomination that the Birchers were his political storm troopers. He needed them to put him across.

A Choice, Not an Echo   Goldwater's weakness as a politician was his inclination, when he was excited, to shoot off his mouth recklessly about using nuclear weapons. Before 1963, few political analysts gave him a chance to be the Republican nominee. Then the frontrunner, the popular and successful governor of New York Nelson Rockefeller destroyed his career when he divorced his wife of thirty years to marry a younger woman. By the time the 1964 convention met, it was clear that Rockefeller's love life had cost him the support of the party's moderates. They tried to deny Goldwater the nomination by dragooning the drab Governor William Scranton of Pennsylvania into running but they were much too late.

The Birchers and less hysterical conservatives had a majority of the delegates and nominated Goldwater as "a choice, not an echo" of the Democrats. Unlike most nominees chosen by an extreme wing of a party, Goldwater refused to sidle toward the center so as to attract moderate voters. In his acceptance speech, he said that "extremism in the pursuit of liberty is no vice ... moderation in the pursuit of justice is no virtue"—good Bircher rhetoric. Rather than balancing the Republican ticket by choosing a moderate as his running mate, he chose a congressman who shared his views.

The Goldwater campaign was doomed from the start. Democratic party propagandists depicted him as a man who would push the red button launching a nuclear holocaust in a crisis or even if he woke up with a hangover.

President Johnson won 61 percent of the popular vote—still the record. The landslide swept Democrats into Congress from districts that had voted Republican for twenty years. The Democratic majority in the Senate was 68–32 and, in the House, 295–140.

THE GREAT SOCIETY

Johnson's Great Society was John F. Kennedy's New Frontier and more. LBJ wanted history to remember him as the president who completed the reforms his idol, Franklin D. Roosevelt, had begun before World War II. He envisioned an America in which "no child will go unfed and no youngster will go unschooled; where every child has a good teacher and every teacher has good pay, and both have good classrooms; where every human being has dignity and every worker has a job; where education is blind to color and employment is unaware of race; where decency appeals and courage abounds."

An Avalanche of Legislation   LBJ declared a "War on Poverty" by setting up VISTA and the "Job Corps," two programs directed by the Office of Economic Opportunity. VISTA was a domestic Peace Corps, volunteers bringing their skills to economically stricken areas, the Job Corps a combination training center and employment agency for the chronically unemployed. Medicare, created in 1965, provided subsidized health insurance for people over 65 years of age. It fell far short of the government health care programs in other wealthy countries but, Johnson calculated, it was the most he could wring out of Congress with powerful doctors' and insurance companies lobbying against him.

The Johnson Congress pumped money into education at every level. The government underwrote cheap student loans, making higher education available to hundreds of thousands of young people from working-class families who, otherwise, could not have afforded it. Traditionally, college professors were poorly paid. Those with families commonly worked second jobs in the evening or during summers to make ends meet. Suddenly, thanks to the Great Society—in just two years—they found themselves banking salaries that launched them into the upper middle class.

Johnson appealed to the artistic community that adored the Kennedys by establishing the National Arts and Humanities Act of 1965. It established the National Endowment for the Arts, which made grants to museums and paid stipends to artists and musicians so that they could devote themselves entirely to their art for a year or so. His National Endowment for the Humanities provided similar grants to scholars.

Tears in the Fabric   Conservatives, a helpless minority in Congress, howled that Johnson and his liberal supporters believed that they could solve any and all problems simply by throwing money at them. There was more than a little truth in the gibe. Johnson, Humphrey, and the older liberals in Congress had personally witnessed FDR's remaking of American society by massive infusions of federal money and federal supervision of economic and social engineering projects.

However, too many Great Society bureaucracies were created too quickly and funded too generously with too little federal supervision. There were simply not enough skilled administrators around to fill the top spots of all the new agencies. Indeed, the thousands of mid-level and low-level jobs in many programs were filled not by people capable of handling them but by political activists who needed a job.

The consequence was inefficiency and waste beyond the margin of tolerability allowed of every big bureaucracy. Petty corruption was common. VISTA offices were staffed with so many clerical workers that many had nothing to do. Officers in middle management treated their positions as political platforms. College deans, rolling in money after decades of paying for their own paper and pencils, ensured that the first beneficiaries of their suddenly bloated budgets were their own salaries and unnecessary administrative jobs for their friends.

The worst bureaucratic abuses were not obvious until after 1970. However, the African American riots of 1964–1968 dramatically illustrated that Johnson's numerous poverty programs failed in the cities from the start. The arrogant posturings of the Black Power agitators aroused the beginnings of an anti-Democratic "white backlash" among northern white working-class voters who prided themselves that they "pulled their own weight," supported their families, paid their taxes, and patriotically supported the government while government dished out "welfare" to idle, irresponsible African Americans. Members of labor unions that had controlled access to well-paid skilled jobs protested that Great Society nondiscrimination policies forbade them from giving their own sons preference when there were vacancies in their crafts. The government did not prevent multimillionaires from bequeathing their fortunes to their children. Was it fair that a Democratic government forbade a machinist or a member of the close-knit tug boat operators from bequeathing their jobs to their sons in favor of other applicants, other whites as well as blacks?

In the end, however, it was not rioting, bloated bureaucracies, and white resentment of Great Society "favoritism" toward blacks that turned the people who benefited most from Lyndon Johnson's programs, bringing him down, but his steady "escalation" of a small war in Vietnam into a major conflict which he could neither win nor extricate the country from.

VIETNAM! VIETNAM!

"Were there no outside world," Theodore H. White wrote in 1969, "Lyndon Johnson might conceivably have gone down as the greatest of twentieth-century presidents." Only five years after LBJ's landslide victory, White knew there was no longer a chance of that. Most of LBJ's most devoted aides also knew it—although they kept their disappointments to themselves.

What happened? Vietnam happened. President Johnson inherited an unnecessary CIA-recommended involvement in a minor Southeast Asian country which few Americans could have found on a globe and transformed it from a sideshow into a major war. The United States had no tangible interests in South Vietnam. The CIA instituted covert operations there during the later 1950s because, during Eisenhower's presidency, the CIA had free rein to meddle anywhere in the world with only self-serving and often dishonest reports to the president.

A Long Way from the LBJ Ranch   Indochina—Vietnam, Laos, Cambodia—had been part of France's colonial empire since 1887. There, as elsewhere, the French ruled through a friendly indigenous elite that was largely Roman Catholic in religion. During the twentieth century, however, a Vietnamese nationalist movement, including many members of the educated elite, slowly coalesced. During the 1920s, a Vietnamese living in Paris, Ho Chi Minh, emerged as the leader in exile of the movement. Ho also became a Communist and lived in Russia and China until 1940 when he returned to Vietnam to organize a guerrilla army, the Viet Minh, to fight the Japanese who had occupied the country.

Ho thought President Roosevelt was his friend. The anti-imperialist FDR was determined not to restore Indochina to the French. However, FDR was dead when, in 1945, the Japanese withdrew from Vietnam, Ho and the Viet Minh pro-claimed the Republic of Vietnam (patterning their statement on the Declaration of Independence), and French troops moved back in. Ho offered a compromise: a self-governing Vietnam within a French "imperial community" patterned on the rela-tionship of New Zealand, Australia, South Africa, and Canada to Great Britain.

This was not enough for the French imperialists. They set up a puppet regime whence Ho and the Viet Minh retreated to the jungles and rice paddies and re-sumed the guerrilla war they had fought against the Japanese. During the early 1950s, the CIA convinced President Truman and then President Eisenhower that Ho's war was not a war for independence, but a Communist uprising that had to be combated. The Eisenhower administration sent massive aid to the French but, after a decisive defeat in 1954, the French gave up and went home.

The conflict was settled—or so it seemed—by the Geneva Accords of that year. Vietnam was partitioned at the seventeenth parallel into two administrative zones. The Viet Minh, largely but not entirely Communist, would govern the northern half of the country from Hanoi; non-Communist nationalists headed by Ngo Dinh Diem, then in exile in the United States, would run the south from Saigon. In 1956—after two years of settling down—Vietnam would hold democratic elections to determine the united country's permanent government. The United States participated in the talks at Geneva. However, Secretary of State Dulles refused to sign the agreement. It was the year of the CIA's great successes in Iran and Guatemala. Dulles instructed his brother, Allen, head of the CIA, to institute covert operations to foil the accords.

An American Show

Ngo Dinh Diem was a CIA creation. Touted in the United States as "Vietnam's George Washington," Diem received $320 million in American aid just in 1955. He meant well. He stabilized South Vietnam but, by 1955, it was obvious to the CIA that he had no chance to defeat Ho Chi Minh in national elections. Diem's anti-French credentials were as good as Ho's, but he had not won the fame Ho had by fighting the Japanese and French. Moreover, he was Catholic and, therefore, associated by many Vietnamese with the French regime. Unwilling to "lose" Vietnam at the ballot box, Washington approved when Diem canceled the 1956 election and proclaimed South Vietnam an independent republic.

Had Diem not been corrupt, he might have succeeded in building an independent South Vietnam. The large Catholic minority in South Vietnam and many Buddhists feared Ho Chih Minh and the Communists. But Diem was blindered by his privileged past and the gushing praises of his influential American friends. He filled the top offices of his government with members of his large wealthy family. He squandered American aid intended for economic development, diverting more than a little to his family's purses; he increased taxes on the peasantry; jailed critics; and favored Roman Catholic Vietnamese more blatantly than the French had.

In 1960, opposition groups, including South Vietnamese Communists, formed the National Liberation Front (NLF) and began to attack isolated patrols of Diem's army, to murder village officials and tax collectors loyal to Diem, and to terrorize uncooperative peasants. In parts of the country the NLF controlled, it set up its own officials who collected taxes and enforced the law.

Diem knew what the magic word was in Cold War Washington. He called the NLF Viet Cong—Vietnamese Communists—which was only part of the truth in 1960. The South Vietnamese lobby in the United States was assigned to Diem's beautiful, intelligent, and articulate sister, "Madame Nhu." The newly elected Kennedy administration was not enchanted by her but, while trying to get a fix on the situation in Vietnam, continued financial aid.

Kennedy's Uncertainty The CIA urged Kennedy to send American troops to South Vietnam. Allen Dulles assured him that the Viet Cong was weak and unpopular. The guerrillas could easily be defeated and driven into the North. Kennedy hesitated. Since the CIA had stung him with its utterly bad advice at the Bay of Pigs, he rightfully distrusted the agency's integrity. He wondered why Diem's 250,000 strong ARVN (Army of the Republic of Vietnam) could not handle 15,000 poorly equipped NLF guerrillas. Nevertheless, he dispatched 3,000 Green Berets, specialists in counterinsurgency, to Vietnam, to advise and train the ARVN.

The situation did not improve. The NLF steadily increased its territorial base and began to launch raids deep within areas Diem controlled. Kennedy sent soldiers to defend the Green Beret bases and other American facilities. By the fall of 1963, there were 16,000 American soldiers in South Vietnam. Each time the CIA and army called for more, Kennedy refused. He told them that the intervention in Vietnam was like "taking a drink. The effect wears off, and you have to take another." He told his closest aides that he was going to signal his determination to get out of the country by bringing home 1,000 soldiers in December 1963 and, with luck, withdraw the entire American contingent after he was reelected in November 1964.

Kennedy still had hopes for an independent, pro-American South Vietnam, but he had given up on Diem because of the regime's military impotence and the widespread corruption in the government. When anti-Diem protests in Saigon threatened to throw the city into anarchy, he gave the go-ahead (through intermediaries) to several ARVN generals who wanted to depose Diem. Kennedy insisted that Diem not be harmed. He ordered a plane readied to fly Diem and his family to exile in the United States and ordered the generals to drive the Diems to it as soon as they were in custody. Instead, the rebels viciously slaughtered Diem's entire inner circle. Kennedy was visibly shaken when he heard the news. A month later, Kennedy was dead.

Mr. Johnson's War

Like Kennedy, Lyndon Johnson seemed to want out of the mess in Vietnam. He agreed to the modest increase in American military presence that Kennedy had turned down, but he quietly offered economic aid to North Vietnam in return for opening peace talks. The North Vietnamese replied that they could not speak for the NLF. This was partially but not entirely true. The NLF or Viet Cong was still a movement of *South* Vietnamese but, by 1964, it wholly depended on arms and other supplies from North Vietnam. Ho Chi Minh could have forced the NLF to the negotiations table by cutting off that aid. But he did not and, riding high in early 1964, the NLF refused to talk until after the United States had withdrawn all its troops from the country.

Dominoes and the Gulf of Tonkin Resolution This Johnson could not possibly do with an election pitting himself against the militaristic Goldwater looming. He believed that without the American military backup, the ARVN would collapse and the NLF, joined by North Vietnamese troops, would quickly overrun the South. He was determined not to be the first Cold War president to see "international Communism" expand.

Johnson subscribed to what President Eisenhower had called the "domino theory." Eisenhower said that if South Vietnam went Communist, the other nations of Southeast Asia—Vietnam, Cambodia, Laos, Thailand, Burma, even Malaysia and Indonesia—would topple like a row of dominoes standing on end. "You knock over the first one"—South Vietnam—"and what will happen to the last one is the certainty that it will go over very quickly." Why this was inevitable was never explained, but it became an axiom of American policy.

In August 1964, a few months before the election, LBJ was informed that North Vietnamese patrol boats had fired on American destroyers in the Gulf of Tonkin. It is not certain to this day if the incident actually occurred. In any case, Johnson had already prepared what came to be called the Gulf of Tonkin Resolution. It gave him congressional authority "to take all necessary measures to repel any armed attack against the forces of the United States and to prevent future aggression."

Only two senators voted against the resolution, Wayne Morse of Oregon, a lifelong maverick, and Ernest Gruening of Alaska. Gruening said that he would not vote for "a predated declaration of war." Indeed, Johnson used the Gulf of Tonkin Resolution to transform a still minor civil conflict in Vietnam into a major war. By the end of 1964, the American military contingent in South Vietnam increased to 23,000 men.

Escalation In February 1965, the Viet Cong attacked an American base near Pleiku. Johnson responded by sending over 3,500 marines, the first Americans in Vietnam identified as combat troops. In April, 20,000 more arrived and, in regular increments, more and more men. By the end of 1965 there were 200,000 American fighting men in South Vietnam, a huge army by any standard. And it doubled in size by the end of 1966 and reached 500,000 by the end of 1967.

Between 1965 and 1968, the air force bombed bridges, factories, and military installations in North Vietnam. To deprive the Viet Cong (and, by now, North Vietnamese soldiers) of cover in the jungle that covered much of the country, planes sprayed defoliants over tens of thousands of acres, killing trees, underbrush, and crops. The idea was to make it possible for American soldiers to carry out search-and-destroy missions against the no longer concealed enemy.

Johnson's policy of step-by-step increases in the scope of the war was called "escalation." The object was to demonstrate to the enemy that every aggression would be met by an increase in technologically superior American military power.

The Vietnam war up close: a platoon is pinned down in a rice paddy, one soldier is seriously wounded by an enemy he probably never saw. Superior American technology meant little when fighting an enemy that refused to be drawn into a battle in which well-trained soldiers and marines had the edge. Viet Cong guerrillas attacked isolated units like this one, killed or wounded several men, then disappeared into rice fields or jungles. When the Viet Cong and North Vietnamese calculated that they could win a big battle, as in the "Tet Offensive" of 1968, they were soundly defeated. By 1968, however, Americans were so frustrated by the years of military ineffectiveness and misinformation and disgusted by the ever-increasing casualties that they sneered at the army's claims that "Tet" was a victory.

Further resistance was hopeless. Twice, in 1965 and 1967, LBJ calculated that the Viet Cong and North Vietnamese had gotten the point. He suspended the bombing and offered to open peace talks.

Both proposals were rejected. North Vietnam was now deeply involved in the war and answered each American escalation with an escalation of its own. By 1966, by American count, 100,000 North Vietnamese soldiers were in action. China and the Soviet Union both escalated their contributions to the war, supplying North Vietnam with ground-to-air missiles as well as more conventional arms and equipment.

The Tet Offensive   Early in 1968, General William Westmoreland announced that victory was within reach. The timing of his optimistic statement could not have been worse. Within days, during celebrations of Tet, Vietnam's lunar New Year, 70,000 Viet Cong and North Vietnamese launched simultaneous attacks on thirty South Vietnamese cities. It was the first conventional military action in the war. For several days the NLF and Viet Cong controlled much of the city of Hue. In Saigon, commandos attacked the American embassy. The Viet Cong took back jungle areas the search-and-destroy missions had cleared with defoliants.

Stunned American forces regrouped quickly and counterattacked. When the smoke cleared, the enemy had suffered devastating casualties. Tet was an American victory and, in May, North Vietnam agreed to begin peace talks in Paris. However, the American people's confidence in the war had been badly eroded by the number of American boys dead and wounded, the weekly total of casualties reported weekly, sometimes daily, on the television news. In 1965, 26 Americans died in Vietnam each week, in 1966 96 a week, in 1967, 180. In 1968, during the Tet offensive, more than 280 Americans were killed each week. The cost of the war had risen to $25 billion a year, nearly $70,000,000 a day!

Despite the tremendous effort and loss of life, victory seemed as distant as ever. A few weeks after the Tet offensive, public approval of Johnson's handling of the war dropped from 40 percent to 26 percent. LBJ was stunned. Years later, two top aides remembered they were so worried about his state of mind that they secretly consulted psychiatrists.

TROUBLED YEARS

Johnson craved consensus. When he made his plea for the Civil Rights Act, he quoted the book of Isaiah—"let us come together" and he referred to a song nonviolent civil rights demonstrators sang, "We Shall Overcome." He earnestly hoped that Americans would rise above their racial hatreds. His overwhelming election victory in 1964 persuaded him that a consensus behind building the Great Society was a realistic possibility. He wanted a consensus behind his war in Vietnam too. What he got was a people more bitterly divided than they had been since the Civil War, a cleavage that remains with us in the twenty-first century.

Hawks and Doves

Before 1964, the chief critics of Johnson's Vietnam policy were conservative Republicans like Goldwater, a few retired generals, and John Birch types. People said that Johnson was making the same mistake President Truman had made in Korea. He was fighting a war for limited goals, holding the army back, rather than unleashing it to win total victory. By offering to negotiate a settlement, he encouraged the enemy.

Known as "Hawks" (because of their aggressiveness), they wanted to obliterate North Vietnam into an unconditional surrender. Former Air Force Chief Curtis LeMay called for bombing North Vietnam "back into the Stone Age." Former film actor Ronald Reagan said "we should declare war on North Vietnam. We could pave the whole place over by noon and be home by dinner."

When LBJ escalated the war (although never to anything like total war), most Hawks fell in behind him. "Doves"—those who wanted the war ended—became the president's chief critics. As the war dragged on and the casualty lists lengthened, the antiwar movement grew. Johnson was doubly distressed by it because most Doves were liberal Democrats who had been warm supporters and beneficiaries of the Great Society. Conspicuous in the antiwar demonstrations were university professors, ministers, priests and nuns, middle-class professionals, and African American civil rights leaders. Most numerous of all were college students, more than a few of them sustained by Great Society loans and exempt from the draft.

Drug Culture

Two "mind-bending" drugs were at the heart of the 1960s "counterculture": cannabis and LSD. Cannabis is hemp, a plant cultivated in America for its fiber since colonial times. George Washington grew it at Mount Vernon; in Kentucky it was a commercial crop second only to tobacco.

Some Indian tribes smoked the dried leaves of the plant with tobacco to dull pain. A few southern planters noticed that slaves smoked or chewed the leaves but took little interest. Before the Civil War, a few other people knew that inhaling the smoke from burning hemp leaves induced a mild euphoria. Some physicians prescribed cannabis in a tincture (dissolved in alcohol) to treat pain, poor appetite, hysteria, and depression.

Its use as a "recreational drug" has two origins. In the mid-nineteenth century there was a vogue for things Turkish among swells in Northeastern cities. They formed hashish clubs (hashish is concentrated, more powerful cannabis) where they enjoyed the euphoria they had read about in the novels of Alexandre Dumas and Honoré de Balzac. During the same years, settlers in Texas and New Mexico noticed Mexicans smoking "marijuana" for its intoxicating effects. The practice spread to New Orleans where patrons of the city's high-class brothels picked it up at the end of the century from African American musicians.

During the 1920s, white musicians were attracted to jazz when it spread north to Kansas City, St. Louis, and Chicago, and they adopted "weed," "reefers," and "pot" as badges of their subculture. Smoking marijuana remained pretty much a musicians' practice until, in the 1950s, beatniks picked up on it in the jazz clubs they frequented. The hippies of the 1960s inherited the practice from the beat generation and created a mass market for it among the millions of young people who adopted hippie fashions.

LSD—lysergic acid diethylamide—is a man-made drug with a shorter and simpler history. It was synthesized in 1938 by a Swiss researcher, Albert Hoffman, who was looking for a new headache medication. LSD was a dead end on that street but, in 1943, Hoffman ingested a larger dose than he had previously and reported that he fell into "a kind of drunkenness which was not unpleasant and which was characterized by extreme activity of imagination, ... an uninterrupted stream of fantastic images of extraordinary plasticity and vividness and accompanied by an intense, kaleidoscope-like play of colors."

In the late 1950s, the cerebral British writer Aldous Huxley "dropped acid" in an attempt to enhance his intellectual

---

Mass demonstrations made for good television news and put the antiwar movement at the center of public attention. In October 1965, 100,000 people attended demonstrations in ninety cities. In April 1967, about 300,000 Americans marched in opposition to the war in New York and San Francisco. Some young men burned their draft cards and went to jail rather than into the army. About 40,000 went into exile to avoid being drafted, most to Canada and Sweden. More than 500,000 soldiers deserted (almost all briefly) and there were some 250,000 "bad discharges," uncooperative soldiers the army preferred to get rid of rather than imprison.

Draft dodgers who had influential social and political connections flocked into the National Guard when it became unlikely guardsmen would be called up.

perceptions and wrote glowingly of LSD's potential to inspire artistic creativity. LSD was not then illegal. (Marijuana was, under federal laws of 1936, 1951, and 1956.) So, a young Harvard psychologist, Timothy Leary, began experimenting with it. Leary soon abandoned science for the joy of his mystical experiences during LSD "trips." When he began to preach the use of it, he lost his job but found thousands of enthusiastic young disciples in San Francisco during the "Summer of Love" in 1966 and in university auditoriums and rock concert halls throughout the country.

Jolyon West was a researcher who administered LSD to several species of animals: Siamese fighting fish swam up and down instead of forward and backward and an elephant expired. After interviewing humans who dropped acid frequently, he concluded that LSD was dangerous. One young man he studied reminded him "of teenagers I've examined who've had frontal lobotomies .... This boy likes himself better. You have to realize that lobotomies make people happy. They attenuate those inner struggles and conflicts that are characteristics of the human condition."

Such warnings did not influence the flower children. Their purpose, however poorly they articulated it, was, in Leary's words, to "tune in, turn on, and drop out," ostensibly from the materialistic mass culture of America, but also from the internal unhappiness that reality has

been known to cause. LSD and marijuana did the trick in the short run; few adolescents and young adults of any era think about the long run.

Where the beatniks saw marijuana as "fun," Leary and the hippies made sacraments of pot and LSD. New Leftists who wanted to span the gap between the political "movement" and the apolitical "counterculture" said that using drugs was a revolutionary act: "Drug consciousness is the key to it." Abbie Hoffman, a charter member of SNCC and prominent leader of the antiwar movement, found a new cause in drugs. He told of a girl who walked into his office. "We got to talking about civil rights, the South, and so on. She asked about drugs. I asked if she had ever taken LSD. When she responded that she hadn't, I threw her a white capsule."

The New Left's social revolution never got started, but the personal revolutions of the 1960s numbered in the tens of millions. LSD did not make the transition into the 1970s but cannabis did. Marijuana use, shorn of its religious significance, spread rapidly. In 1969, a country and western singer sold millions of copies of a record called "Okie from Muskogee." It was a super-patriotic, anti-"long haired hippie" song about salt of the earth Oklahomans that began: "We don't smoke marijuana in Muskogee." A newspaper reporter wondered about that. He drove to Muskogee and bought an ounce of pot within half an hour of parking his car.

George W. Bush, to be elected president in 2000 and 2004, pulled strings to find safety in the guard. His predecessor in the White House, William Jefferson Clinton, was frantically struggling to find a refuge in the National Guard when he stumbled on another way to avoid service.

The Arguments   The antiwar movement spoke with several voices expressing sometimes contrary principles. A few protestors in every demonstration were members of radical fringe groups like the Socialist Workers party, a "Trotskyist" Communist sect on its last legs during the 1960s and the even

Gino Beghe, Library of Congress, Prints & Photographs Division, [POS 6 - U.S. no. 1048]

A "peacenik" wall poster of the Vietnam era. It and dozens conveying the same message decorated dormitory rooms and student apartments. Principled pacifists were an important component of the antiwar movement. Other protesters regarded the Vietnam War as a bad war in a bad cause; a few were pro-Viet Cong for ideological or romantic reasons; yet other antiwar agitators said the war should be ended because it could not be won or because it was weakening the United States.

more marginal Progressive Labor party, which was devoted to the "teachings" of Chairman Mao Zedong. They were not really "Doves," of course, but partisans who hoped for the military defeat of the "imperialist capitalist" United States. Youthful romantics, who knew little about Communism and were many times more numerous than the Marxists, were enchanted by the romantic tableau of the outnumbered, poorly equipped Viet Cong resisting American power.

Genuine Doves like the famous pediatrician, Dr. Benjamin Spock, were anti-Communist. However, they believed that the United States was fighting against the wishes of a majority of the Vietnamese people and, therefore, was in the wrong. They disapproved of the fact that their powerful nation was showering terrible destruction on a small country in an unworthy cause.

Religious pacifists like the Quakers and members of the Fellowship for Reconciliation opposed the war because they opposed all wars. Other morally concerned people agreed that some wars were justified. However, they insisted that the war in Vietnam was not one of them. With no clearcut battle lines, American troops unavoidably warred on civilians as well as on enemy soldiers. Bombs and defoliants took innocent lives. And there were, as in all wars, atrocities. The most publicized occurred at the village of My Lai in March 1968 when American soldiers gone berserk killed 347 unarmed men, women, and children. The Viet Cong were guilty of similar crimes but that, Doves said, did not justify Americans stooping to the same level.

Some critics of the war were unconcerned with moral issues that, they believed, should play little or no role in power politics. They argued that the United States was exhausting its military fighting in a small, unimportant country while the power of China and the Soviet Union was untouched. George Kennan and Senator William Fulbright of Arkansas pointed out that the United States was neglecting its commitments elsewhere in the world in its fixation on Vietnam. Several retired generals, including the former commander of the Marine Corps, said the same. Senators Gaylord Nelson of Wisconsin and Wayne Morse were distressed that the war effort was alienating neutral nations and even allies.

The Student Movement

Not all discontent among university students was directed into the antiwar movement. Already by 1963, it was clear that the baby boomers were not as apolitical as the youth of the 1950s had been. Large numbers of students demonstrated against capital punishment, protested against violations of civil liberties by the House Un-American Activities Committee, and worked in the civil rights movement. In 1963, Students for a Democratic Society (SDS), issued the Port Huron Statement, a comprehensive critique of American society largely written by a graduate of the University of Michigan, Tom Hayden. SDS called for young people to take the lead in drafting a plan by which the United States could be a progressive force for peace and justice.

The New Left, or "the Movement," as SDS and similar groups were collectively labeled, was, like "black power," less a political phenomenon as an expression of anger and frustration. Hayden and a few others tried to channel student energies into real concerns like the problems of the poor and the power of large corporations. But many of the campus demonstrations and riots of the late 1960s were unfocused, antiwar but also reflecting trivial grievances such as student participation in defining curriculum and setting university rules of behavior.

The era of massive campus protests began at the University of California at Berkeley with the founding of the Free Speech Movement in 1964. By 1968, the demonstrations took a violent turn when students at Columbia University seized several buildings and refused to budge until their inchoate and shifting demands were met. (They were forcibly suppressed by police.)

The Counterculture

For many young people, the "Movement" was a rest stop on the way to a purely personal rebellion. In 1967, in the Haight-Ashbury district of San Francisco and in New York's "East Village," thousands of teenagers congregated to establish what they called a "counterculture," a new way of living based on "love," a word the wise do not try to define. To the "flower children" or "hippies," as they were later called, the counterculture boiled down to promiscuous sex, drugs, and extravagant colorful fashions that, like adolescent fashions since the 1920s, were designed to identify their wearers as a distinct group and to disturb those outside the group—"everyone" over 30" during the 1960s.

Conventional Americans were alternately disturbed by the apparent immorality of the "long-haired kids" and amused by them. "Far more interesting than the hippies themselves," sociologist Bennett Berger observed, "is America's inability to leave them alone." In San Francisco, Grey Line tour buses took curiosity seekers through the hippie neighborhood of Haight-Ashbury where tourists snapped photographs as they would have done at the sight of a snake charmer in Calcutta. Entrepreneurs found that commercializing the counterculture was easy. Advertisers used hippie themes to sell their wares. Musical groups created "acid rock," a din created by powerfully amplified musical instruments. Hippies embraced it; so did their cousins back home.

Some flower children retreated from the cities to communes that friendly intellectuals compared to the utopian communities of nineteenth-century America. However, individual self-gratification was the central principle of hippiedom and drugs played a large part in the counterculture. Few communal ventures lasted much beyond the visits of journalists and photographers recording the first moments of the new world a-borning. "Do your own thing," a hippie mantra borrowed from Ralph Waldo Emerson (who would have been a hand-clapping hanger-on had he been around) was a weak social foundation when it was time for someone to take out the garbage or disinfect the communal commode.

THE ELECTION OF 1968

In 1964, Lyndon Johnson had been able to shout gleefully while striding through the presidential airline, "I am the king! I am the king!" In 1968, he discovered that not even a monarch can survive a social, cultural, and moral crisis as grave as the war and the massive demonstrations had exposed. He did not even try. Early in the year, he announced that he would not stand for reelection. He was brought to this humiliating pass—for he had wanted to be reelected—by a quiet senator from Minnesota, Eugene McCarthy.

Eugene McCarthy McCarthy was a tall man with a gray solemnity about him. His record as a liberal Democratic workhorse was solid, but no one mistook him for a mover and shaker. Minnesota already had its walking dynamo in Hubert Humphrey. But the quiet, reflective McCarthy was anguished by the issue that Humphrey, vice president after 1965, had no choice but to dodge, the war. Late in 1967, McCarthy announced that he would challenge President Johnson for the Democratic presidential nomination the next year.

Pundits admired his dignity, reflective intellect, and principle. Some were enamored with his natural diffidence, a quality rare in politicians. McCarthy seemed sincerely to believe that a public servant should serve. But the experts gave him no chance of beating Johnson in the primaries. Low as the president's popularity had sunk, his hold on the party machinery was as firm as ever.

McCarthy's only political base was the amorphous antiwar movement. Professional politicians shunned him. Labor unions, still vital to Democratic success at the polls, begrudged him several votes he had cast against their legislative programs.

McCarthy had no support among blacks and very little among white ethnics, bulwarks of the party in the North. He was the candidate of the segment of the educated white middle class that opposed the war in Vietnam.

Johnson Retires   Time would prove the experts right about McCarthy's chances. In early 1968, however, antiwar activists were so aroused as to turn the Democratic party upside down. Thousands of university students dropped their studies and rushed to New Hampshire, site of the first presidential primary. They got "clean for Gene," shearing their long hair, shaving their beards, and donning neckties, brassieres, and jumpers so as not to distract the voters of the culturally conservative state from the issue at hand—the war. Sleeping on the floors of the McCarthy campaign's storefront headquarters, they rang door bells, handed out pamphlets at supermarkets, stuffed envelopes, and argued endlessly but nonconfrontationally with shoppers outside supermarkets.

Johnson's name was not on the ballot. New Hampshire's governor ran as his stand-in. He and McCarthy split the vote evenly but, in a traditionally cautious state with an obscure senator running against a sitting president, New Hampshire was a resounding rebuke of Johnson. He knew it and announced his retirement. McCarthy's supporters looked forward hungrily to primary elections elsewhere.

Who Will End   Johnson's announcement caught everyone by surprise, **the War?**   including Vice President Humphrey, who was in Mexico on a goodwill tour. He rushed back to Washington to announce his candidacy. He had an edge on McCarthy because of his long-standing ties with organized labor, African Americans, big city political machines, party professionals, and big money contributors.

Still, McCarthy's people believed they could beat Humphrey. To them, the sole issue was the war and, as vice president, Humphrey was—whatever his private feelings—in the prowar camp. What neither Humphrey nor McCarthy foresaw was that, with Johnson gone, Robert F. Kennedy, now senator from New York, jumped into the contest.

Kennedy was a threat to both McCarthy and Humphrey. LBJ had eased him out of the cabinet as soon as it was graceful to do, so he was not identified with the war. He had criticized it on several occasions. His connections with African Americans were as strong as Humphrey's, with Mexican Americans stronger for he was a close friend of Cesar Chavez, the leader of the mostly Hispanic farmworkers' union in California. When Martin Luther King Jr., was assassinated in April 1968, Bobby's expressions of grief seemed more sincere than any other Democrat's. Kennedy was also a threat to Humphrey because he had maintained connections with the party pros and labor leaders who had helped his brother win the presidential nomination in 1960. Among Democrats, he was anathema only to white southerners and to Doves who had mobilized to support McCarthy, and not to all of them. Some, like Richard Goodwin, switched their allegiance to Kennedy because they believed that he, but not McCarthy, could defeat the Republicans in the general election.

Kennedy ran well in the primaries, although not without setbacks. McCarthy won the next-to-last primary in Oregon. Then, on the night Kennedy won the final

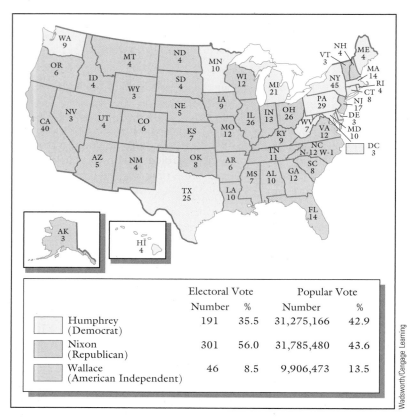

The following list shows states, their abbreviations and electoral votes as depicted on the map:

WA 9, MT 4, ND 4, MN 10, NH 4, VT 3, ME 4, OR 6, ID 4, WY 3, SD 4, WI 12, NY 45, MA 14, RI, CT 4, NV 3, UT 4, CO 6, NE 5, IA 9, IL 26, IN 13, OH 26, MI 21, PA 29, NJ 17, DE 3, CA 40, KS 7, MO 12, KY 9, WV 7, VA 12, MD 10, DC 3, AZ 5, NM 4, OK 8, AR 6, TN 11, NC N-12 W-1, SC 8, GA 12, MS 7, AL 10, TX 25, LA 10, FL 14, AK 3, HI 4

	Electoral Vote		Popular Vote	
	Number	%	Number	%
Humphrey (Democrat)	191	35.5	31,275,166	42.9
Nixon (Republican)	301	56.0	31,785,480	43.6
Wallace (American Independent)	46	8.5	9,906,473	13.5

Wadsworth/Cengage Learning

MAP 48.1 The Presidential Election, 1968.

George Wallace's strategy was to deny both Nixon and Humphrey a majority in the electoral college. Had he carried one large southern state and either Illinois or Ohio, where he was popular, he would have succeeded. LBJ's magic still worked in Texas, which Humphrey won. In the nine presidential elections since 1968, the Democratic candidate won only once.

important primary in California, he was shot point-blank in the head by a Jordanian who opposed Kennedy's support for the Jewish state of Israel.

The murder of a fourth prominent political leader in five years demoralized the antiwar Democrats and contributed to week-long riots in Chicago during the Democratic national convention. Most of Kennedy's delegates refused to unite behind McCarthy; they backed Senator George McGovern of South Dakota as an antiwar candidate. With the opposition divided, Humphrey won the Democratic nomination on the first ballot.

Nixon and Wallace   Richard M. Nixon easily won the Republican nomination. The former vice president had retired from politics—or so he had said—after failing to win the governorship of California in 1962. In reality, with the doggedness which characterized his entire career, he quietly firmed up support among moderate "Rockefeller Republicans" and won over conservatives by campaigning for Goldwater in 1964. Nixon attended every local Republican function to which he was invited, no matter how small the town, insignificant the occasion, or dubious the candidate he had to endorse. By making himself available to the party's grass-roots workers, he wove an unbreakable web of supporters.

The Democrats were divided. Many in the party's antiwar wing announced that they would vote for Benjamin Spock. Humphrey tried to woo them by hinting that he would end the war but, as Johnson's vice president, he could not repudiate administration policy. Humphrey's ambiguity enabled Nixon to waffle on the war issue. He espoused a hawkish policy at the same time that he reminded voters that it had been a Republican president, Dwight D. Eisenhower, who had ended the Democratic party's futile war in Korea.

The only obstacle to a Nixon victory seemed to be the American Independent party, founded as his personal vehicle by Governor George Wallace. Wallace had a large following among southern whites thanks to his dramatic opposition to the now lost cause of school segregation. He had won a large number of votes in Democratic primaries in midwestern industrial states by playing on working-class voters' frustration with antiwar demonstrations they considered unpatriotic. Many blue-collar ethnics who had liked Kennedy found Wallace more to their taste than civil rights pioneer Hubert Humphrey. Extreme right Goldwaterites preferred Wallace to Nixon.

A Close Call   Wallace knew he could not win. His goal was to collect just enough electoral votes that neither Humphrey nor Nixon had a majority. In that case, as in 1800 and 1824, the House of Representatives would select the next president, each state casting one vote. Wallace reckoned that anti-civil-rights congressmen were a majority in the delegations of as many as sixteen states—almost a third of the total. With such a prize his for the giving, Wallace thought Nixon would have to make a deal with him, a reversal of the Democratic party's civil rights policies in return for a majority in the electoral college.

There was nothing obscure about his intentions. Both the Humphrey and Nixon camps knew what he meant to do by running. Humphrey publicly called on Nixon to pledge jointly with him that, in the event neither had a majority in the electoral college, that neither would deal with Wallace. Whichever of them had fewer electoral votes would direct his supporters in the House to vote for the electoral vote leader.

Believing that Wallace would take more votes from Humphrey than from him, Nixon ignored the proposal. In the end, it did not matter. Although Wallace did better than any third-party candidate since 1924, winning 13.5 percent of the popular vote and 46 electoral votes, Nixon eked out a plurality of 500,000 votes and a majority in the electoral college. It was close. A rush of blue-collar workers from Wallace to Humphrey during the final week of the campaign indicated to some pollsters that, had the campaign lasted two weeks longer, Humphrey would have won.

49

PRESIDENTS ON THE GRIDDLE
The Nixon, Ford, and Carter Years 1968–1980

*In a country where there is no hereditary throne nor
hereditary aristocracy, an office raised far above all other
offices offers too great a stimulus to ambition. This
glittering prize, always dangling before the eyes of
prominent statesmen, has a power stronger than any dignity
under a European crown to lure them from the path of
straightforward consistency.*

—James Lord Bryce

*Americans expect their presidents to do what no monarch
by Divine Right could ever do—resolve for them all the
contradictions and complexities of life.*

—Robert T. Hartmann

That Richard M. Nixon made it to the top of the political the heap was a miracle. Few people particularly liked him; he was himself too suspicious to have a close friend. He came up short in the superficial qualities thought essential to success in American politics. He was not physically attractive; his manner was often furtive. He was shy—he disguised his discomfort in front of a crowd only by a mighty act of will—and suspicious; he did not like people in general or en masse.

Nixon was more changeable—"duplicitous," Democrats said—than most politicians could be and still get away with it. At several turns of his career, his supporters had to assure voters that the "Old Nixon" was no more; the Nixon that deserved their votes now was a "New Nixon." Democrats called him "Tricky Dicky." John F. Kennedy said that Nixon pretended to be so many different things that he had forgotten who he was. Robert Dole, Republican presidential candidate in 1996, was harshest of all. When he saw former presidents Jimmy Carter, Gerald Ford, and Nixon standing together at a ceremonial function, he remarked, "There they are: see no evil, hear no evil, and evil."

948

Revolution and Reaction in Foreign Policy 1969–1981

1969	1971	1973	1975	1977	1979	1981
			1969–1974 Richard M. Nixon president			

1969 Cambodia bombed

1970 Troops in Vietnam reduced to 335,000; U.S. troops in Cambodia

1971 Nixon visits China

1972 Troops in Vietnam reduced to 24,000; Nixon declares *détente* in USSR

1972–1974 Watergate scandal unfolds

1973 Paris Peace Accords; Kissinger mediates Arab–Israeli war

1974 Nixon resigns

Gerald Ford president; severe economic problems 1974–1977

1975 South Vietnam government collapses

Jimmy Carter president 1977–1981

USSR invades Afghanistan Dec 1979

Carter ends *détente*, resumes Cold War 1980

THE NIXON PRESIDENCY

Liberal Democrats hated Nixon. Many Republicans who accepted Nixon as their leader did so only when there was no alternative to him but losing an election. In 1952, Dwight D. Eisenhower wanted to dump Nixon as his vice presidential running mate when Nixon was accused of drawing on a secret "slush fund" set up by southern California businessmen. In a brilliantly conceived and executed television address, Nixon nimbly sidestepped the graft question and put Eisenhower in a position in which he would alienate more voters than would back him if he dropped Nixon from the ticket.

When President Nixon faced impeachment in 1973 and 1974, aides who owed their careers to him trampled one another in their haste to betray him. All was forgiven at his funeral in 1994. Eulogists focused on his diplomatic achievements, which were numerous, one momentous. Except for his daughters, however, no one at the memorial service spoke of him with affection.

Richard Nixon clawed his way to the top from stable but rather drab lower-middle-class origins in Whittier, California. Although he overstated them in his midcareer book *Six Crises,* he overcame formidable obstacles to succeed. Nixon had a little luck, but he was mostly pluck. Whatever else historians may say of Richard Nixon in the future, he earned everything he ever got.

Political Savvy As president, Nixon had little interest in domestic issues. He believed that "the country could run itself domestically without a president." He left all the most important domestic policy decisions to two young aides. Ironically, with Nixon himself unconvivial and distant, H. R. Haldeman and John Ehrlichman cultivated an arrogance that put people off. They were unpopular with congressmen, and they offended foreign diplomats with their rudeness. But they did the job Nixon wanted them to do. They insulated him from many of the ceremonials, courtesy conversations, and "photo-ops" that can devour a president's work day. Nixon was a worker.

Regarding most domestic issues as distractions, Nixon surprised and disturbed his right-wing Goldwater supporters by leaving Johnson's Great Society pretty much intact. Indeed, it was during his administration that "affirmative action" was first interpreted to mean preferential treatment for, at first, would-be government contractors owned by members of minority groups. Lyndon Johnson, who coined the term *affirmative action,* defined it as aggressively recruiting members of minority groups in colleges, graduate schools, and well-paid positions in business and government, but not as discriminatory.

Politicking, which Nixon had never enjoyed—cheerleading, beaming, waving, and handshaking—he assigned to Vice President Spiro T. Agnew. Agnew was the former governor of Maryland who, with his Greek ancestry, Nixon had named to the Republican ticket to attract blue-collar ethnic voters who were more likely to vote for Wallace or Humphrey.

Agnew enjoyed the crowds on the banquet and auditorium circuit. He came to relish the job of hatchet man that he was assigned so that Nixon, a former hatchet man himself, could play the statesman. He delighted Republican conservatives by flailing at students and weak-willed, overpaid educators who were the most conspicuous element in the antiwar movement. He excoriated liberal Supreme Court justices for coddling criminals and the "liberal news media"—the three network news organizations and influential newspapers like the Washington *Post* and New York *Times.* As an orator, Agnew was fond of alliteration. His masterpiece was "nattering nabobs of negativism," that is, journalists.

Agnew's relentless liberal-baiting provided Nixon with an effective smokescreen hiding the fact that he did not dismantle the Great Society. His only major modification of Johnson's welfare state was his "New Federalism." Instead of spending money directly on Great Society social programs, the Nixon administration distributed the funds among the states to administer them. The New Federalism actually increased the size of government bureaucracies. Nixon did not care. He (and later Republican presidents, including Ronald Reagan) learned that the numerous agencies the Democrats created were excellent targets when the Republicans were out of office, but they provided lots of high-salaried, do-nothing jobs for prominent Republicans when the party was in.

On some fronts, Nixon might as well have been a Democrat. His Family Assistance Plan provided a flat annual payment to poor households if their breadwinners registered with employment agencies. (It failed in Congress.) When, in 1971, a spurt in inflation seemed to threaten his upcoming reelection campaign, Nixon experimented with wage and price controls, a Republican party anathema, in order to halt it.

Nixon understood that, for all the anti-big government propaganda, the people who ran the Republican party had no complaint with big government as long as it was business friendly. As for the party's populist "conservatives"—southern whites, Goldwaterites, the remnants of the declining John Birch Society—Nixon understood that for all their caterwauling about Great Society spending, they would put up with annually larger deficits if the administration—here is where Spiro T. Agnew came in—denounced the social and cultural pieties that increasingly preoccupied

President Nixon in the Oval Office with his young aides H. R. Haldemann (foreground) and John Erlichman (seated, rear). Nixon secretly recorded conversations in the office. His decision to do so was curious if for no other reason than the fact that the tapes revealed him to be a foulmouth. Lyndon Johnson, Kennedy, and Ike used the "F" word now and then; it was a staple of Nixon's casual language.

Democratic liberals in the 1970s. Except for the fact that Nixon did not cozy up to fundamentalist evangelical groups—they were not then politically organized—he designed the successful formula for winning elections that Ronald Reagan and George W. Bush were to exploit into two-term presidencies.

The Warren Court

One of Agnew's favorite targets was the "Warren Court." Chief Justice Earl Warren had tried to resign when Lyndon Johnson was president so that Johnson could name a liberal successor. But Johnson's choice for chief justice, an old Texas crony already on the Court, Abe Fortas, was revealed to have accepted fees for giving speeches that, while hardly criminal, were improper. Warren stayed on and suffered the humiliation of swearing in his old enemy whence he resigned. Nixon had the satisfaction not only of naming the new chief justice, but Abe Fortas's successor as well.

During Warren's years as chief justice—1953–1969—there had been a steady trend in the Court's rulings toward what critics called "judicial activism." To Warren's liberal defenders, the Court was bringing the Constitution up to date on issues that the Founding Fathers had not confronted. Republican conservatives condemned Warren and the justices who voted with him because, they said, the Supreme Court was sending unconstitutional state and federal laws back to the legislatures and Congress for rewriting and the justices were themselves writing laws.

During the 1960s, several decisions concerning the constitutional rights of accused criminals and the authority of police officers aroused popular anger. In *Escobedo* v. *Illinois* (1964), by a vote of just 5–4, the Court freed Danny Escobedo, a petty criminal, because, when he asked the police to see a lawyer, the cops put him off until after they had extracted a confession from him; only then was Escobedo's lawyer summoned. The Court ruled that Escobedo had been denied his constitutional right to counsel. To ordinary people, an obviously guilty criminal was walking the streets because the police did not oblige him.

Far more controversial was *Miranda* v. *Arizona* (1968). In another 5–4 decision, the Court ruled that Ernesto Miranda's confession to charges of kidnapping and rape could not be used against him in court because the officer who arrested him did not inform him that he had a right to see a lawyer before answering questions. To ordinary people, taught since elementary school that "ignorance of the law is no excuse for breaking it"—a principle upheld by the courts—the *Miranda* decision was more troubling than *Escobedo*. Miranda was ignorant of his right to see a lawyer; the Court was saying that it was a police function to educate him and every other arrested suspect in that provision of the Constitution. *Miranda* was an extremely unpopular ruling. "What next?" people asked. The job of the police was to arrest suspects and gather evidence to put criminals away; it was not to show them ways to avoid conviction. Other Warren Court rulings threw out evidence of a crime collected in police searches when the evidence had not been specifically described in a search warrant or if it was not in a defendant's immediate proximity when it was confiscated.

The rulings were particularly obnoxious because most were 5–4—split—decisions. Chief Justice Warren had labored long and hard for a unanimous vote in *Brown* v. *School Board* because the decision was so revolutionary. Why, critics asked, was he willing to push on with bare majority votes in decisions regarding long-established and accepted procedures to control crime? The Warren Court's defenders replied that the rights of the individual trumped all.

Nixon's Vietnam

Doves had blamed Lyndon Johnson for failing to end the war in Vietnam, failing to acknowledge that the North Vietnamese were also responsible for the bloody stalemate. In 1969, it became Nixon's turn.

He wanted out of the war. He had watched the unwinnable conflict destroy Johnson's political career, and he took little interest in what he called a "sideshow." Nixon had bigger fish to fry. Simply to call it quits—to declare victory and bring the boys home, as Republican Senator George Aiken of Vermont proposed—might actually have worked. But Nixon did not want to alienate Republican Hawks, an important part of the coalition that had elected him.

Vietnamization   Nixon's solution was ingenious and, for a time, effective. He assigned Spiro Agnew the job of smearing the radical and pacifist antiwar protesters as anti-American. He reasoned that he could silence the mass movement that had coalesced around the "peacenik" hard core by reducing the long weekly casualty lists. He announced that he would "Vietnamize" the war, that he would bring American draftees home and replace them at its front lines with South Vietnamese soldiers.

The United States would continue to "participate in the defense and development of allies and friends," he said, but Americans would no longer "undertake all the defense of the free nations of the world.... In the previous administration, we Americanized the war in Vietnam. In this administration we are Vietnamizing the search for peace."

The army undertook a crash program to train the large ARVN, which had been neglected when Johnson thought that escalation of the American effort would force an end to the fighting. As South Vietnamese units were deemed ready for combat, American troops came home. At about the same rate that LBJ had increased the American presence in South Vietnam, Nixon reduced it. From a high of 541,000 American soldiers when Nixon took office, the American force declined to 335,000 in 1970 and 24,000 in 1972.

Nixon returned the American role in the war to where it had been in 1964. The difference was that, in 1964, there were few well-trained North Vietnamese troops in the fight. By 1970, the North Vietnamese were the chief enemy, the North Vietnamese army having absorbed the Viet Cong. As Nixon expected, antiwar demonstrations declined in size if not in ardor. However, Nixon failed to anticipate that Democratic congressmen who had supported Johnson's war were now in opposition, many of them demanding that the Republican president make more serious efforts to end it. And Democrats were still the majority in both House and Senate.

Expanding the War   Nixon and his foreign policy advisor, Henry A. Kissinger, believed that in order to save the nation's "credibility" abroad, they had to salvage the independence of South Vietnam out of the wreckage, even if temporarily. Having abandoned escalation, they tried to bludgeon North Vietnam into negotiations by expanding the scope of the war with low casualty air attacks. In the spring of 1969, shortly after he was inaugurated, Nixon sent bombers over neutral Cambodia to destroy sanctuaries where about 50,000 North Vietnamese troops rested between battles. For a year, the American people knew nothing of these attacks. However, when Nixon sent ground forces into Cambodia in 1970, mostly ARVN but Americans too, the expansion of the war into yet another country could not be concealed.

The result was renewed uproar. Critics condemned the president for attacking a neutral nation. Several hundred university presidents closed their campuses for fear of student violence. Events at two colleges proved their wisdom. At Kent State University in Ohio, the National Guard opened fire on demonstrators, killing four students and wounding eleven. Ten days later, two students demonstrating at Jackson State College in Mississippi were killed by police.

The now hostile Congress reacted by repealing the Tonkin Gulf Resolution. Nixon replied that repeal was irrelevant. As commander in chief, he had the right to take whatever military action he believed necessary. Nonetheless, when he expanded the war into Laos in February 1971, he made sure that ARVN troops carried the burden of the fighting.

Falling Dominos   Without American troops by its side, the ARVN was humiliated in Laos. The Communist organization in that country, the Pathet Lao, grew in strength until, in 1975, it seized effective control of the small, backward country. Tens of thousands of Laotian refugees fled into Thailand.

In Cambodia, the consequences were worse. Young Cambodians were so angered by the American bombing that they flocked to join the Communist Khmer Rouge, which increased in size from 3,000 in 1970 to 30,000 in a few years. In 1976, the commander, Pol Pot, came to power instituting a regime as criminal as the Nazi government of Germany. In three years, the Khmer Rouge murdered 3 million people in a population of 7.2 million!

Eisenhower's Southeast Asian dominoes had fallen not because the United States was weak in the face of a threat, but because the United States had expanded a war that, ten years earlier, had been little more than an armed brawl. Indochinese neutrals like Cambodia's Prince Sihanouk were undercut by the chaos American intervention created. The long war had transformed North Vietnam into a military dictatorship. Laos was an anarchy in which the single organized group was Communist. Cambodia was one big killing field run by a monster.

In South Vietnam, the fighting dragged on until the fall of 1972 when, after twelve days of earth-shaking bombing, the North Vietnamese finally agreed to meet with Kissinger in Paris and arrange a cease-fire. The Paris Accords that went into effect in January 1973 required the United States to withdraw all its troops from Vietnam within 60 days and the North Vietnamese to release all prisoners of war. Until elections were held, North Vietnamese soldiers would remain in those parts of South Vietnam they occupied, a substantial part of the country.

For two years, the country simmered. Then, in April 1975, the ARVN suddenly collapsed and the North Vietnamese army moved on a virtually undefended Saigon. North and South Vietnam were united. Saigon was renamed Ho Chi Minh City. Ironically, Cambodia's nightmare ended only when the North Vietnamese invaded the country, overthrew Pol Pot, and installed a puppet regime that, if dictatorial, was not built on a foundation of mass murder.

The Bottom   America's longest war ravaged a prosperous country. Once
Line   an exporter of rice, Vietnam was short of food through the
1980s. About a million ARVN soldiers lost their lives, the Viet Cong and North Vietnamese about the same. Estimates of civilian dead ran as high as 3.5 million. About 5.2 million acres of jungle and farmland were ruined by defoliation. The Viet Cong destroyed hundreds of villages, dozens of towns; American bombing wrecked bridges and highways. The Air Force dropped more bombs on Vietnam than had fallen on Europe during World War II.

The vengeance of the victors (and Pol Pot) caused a massive flight of refugees. About 10 percent of the people of Indochina fled their homes after the war. Some spent everything they owned to bribe North Vietnamese officials to let them go. Others piled into leaky boats and cast off into open waters; unknown numbers drowned. To the credit of the United States, some 600,000 Vietnamese, Laotians, Cambodians, and ethnic minorities like the Hmong (persecuted by every government in Indochina) were admitted to the United States.

The war cost the United States $150 billion, more than any other American conflict except World War II. Some 57,000 Americans were killed, 300,000 were wounded. Numbers of veterans came home alcoholic, addicted to heroin, or mentally disturbed. And yet, for ten years, veterans were ignored, even shunned. Politicians, not only antiwar liberals but super-patriotic Hawks who wanted to fight on indefinitely, would not vote money to address their problems. Only in 1982 was a monument to war dead erected in Washington.

NIXON-KISSINGER FOREIGN POLICY

For more than twenty years, American policy makers divided the world into two hostile camps competing for clients in a "Third World" of unaligned, mostly undeveloped states. Only John Foster Dulles considered a nuclear confrontation between the United States and the Soviet Union thinkable. The Kennedy and Johnson administrations were open to graduated disarmament and, except for responding to direct Soviet provocations, concentrated on competing with the Soviet Union for "friendlies" in the Third World.

Before he was elected, Nixon said nothing to indicate that he foresaw anything except more of the same. To what extent he imagined another kind of foreign policy before 1968, or whether he was persuaded to follow a new path by his National Security advisor, Henry Kissinger, is not clear. But the two worked harmoniously in harness to reshape geopolitics in just a few years.

Ping Pong   Henry Kissinger, 46 years old in 1969, was brilliant, witty,
Diplomacy   urbane, and so cheerfully conceited it was charming. He was
                       a refugee from Nazism who, after living in the United States
for thirty years, still spoke in so thick a German accent that his critics wondered it was an affectation. As a scholar at Harvard, he was a proponent of *Realpolitik*, an amoral, opportunistic approach to foreign policy untainted by ideological first principles like those that had crippled John Foster Dulles and even Kennedy's and Johnson's secretary of state, Dean Rusk.

He and Nixon recognized that the bipolar Soviet-American standoff of the Cold War was being displaced by a world in which there were five centers of military or economic power. Japan had no army but it was an economic powerhouse with interests at odds with American interests. Western Europe, led by France and Germany, regularly asserted significant dissents from America's wants in Europe. China was not, as American policy makers had held since 1950, a satellite of the Soviet Union, if it ever was. It was well known that there had been several large-scale military confrontations between China and the USSR on their 2,000 mile border.

Nixon and Kissinger welcomed the change. In 1971, Nixon said, "It will be a safer world and a better world, if we have a strong and healthy United States, Europe, Soviet Union, China, Japan—each balancing the other, not playing one against the other, an even balance." He was extending an invitation to one or the other of America's Cold War enemies to join with him in making some adjustments.

The Chinese responded with an invitation of their own. The Sports Ministry of the People's Republic invited an American table tennis team touring in Japan to fly on over for a few games with Chinese players. The coach was bewildered—understandably:

Americans were forbidden to go to China. He phoned home. Kissinger, astonished but not bewildered, told the team to pack its paddles and get going.

Rapprochement with China   The ice broken, Kissinger opened top-secret talks with Chinese diplomats. Unbeknownst to anyone, he flew to Beijing where he arranged for a goodwill tour of China by Nixon himself. Only then was the news released: The lifelong scourge of Red China would tour the Forbidden City, view the Great Wall, and sit down with chopsticks at a Mandarin banquet with Mao Zedong and Zhou Enlai, drinking toasts to Sino-American amity with fiery Chinese spirits.

Nixon's meeting with Mao was ceremonial; the chairman was quite senile. Zhou, however, who had long advocated establishing relations with the United States, was active and alert. Two of his protégés, Hua Guofeng (who would succeed Mao in 1976) and Deng Xiaoping (whom Mao had jailed), reassured Nixon that he had calculated correctly in making the trip.

Nixon invited Chinese students to study at American universities and China opened its doors to American tourists, who came by the tens of thousands within a few years, clambering up the Great Wall and buying red-ribboned trinkets by the ton. American businessmen involved in everything from oil exploration to bottling soft drinks flew in, anxious to sell American technology and consumer goods in the market that had long symbolized the traveling salesman's ultimate territory. The United States dropped its veto of Communist China's claim to China's seat in the United Nations without betraying Taiwan and established a legation in Beijing. In 1979, the two countries established full diplomatic relations.

Détente   While Chinese leaders, particularly Deng Xiaoping and his coterie, had high hopes for American help with economic modernization, their chief motive in courting the United States was China's uneasy relations with the Soviet Union. They were "playing the America card" in their Cold War.

That was fine with Nixon and Kissinger. By "playing the China card"—worrying the one country in the world capable of wreaking destruction on America—they expected the Soviets to seek their own détente—a relaxation of tensions—with the United States. The gambit worked. Leonid Brezhnev, a crusty and unimaginative old Bolshevik who had ousted Khruschev from power and reversed Khruschev's destalinization of the Soviet regime, was shocked into an untypical flexibility and openness. In June 1972, just months after the China trip, he welcomed Nixon to Moscow and agreed to open what came to be called the Strategic Arms Limitation Talks (SALT), the first step toward slowing down the arms race since the Kennedy administration.

The photos of Richard M. Nixon clinking champagne glasses with little Chinamen in Chairman Mao shirts and bear-hugging a grinning Brezhnev, who looked like a bear, threw conservative Republicans into a staggering confusion that they began to explain by blaming the sinister foreigner Kissinger. However, as Nixon understood, only a Republican with impeccable Cold Warrior credentials could have accomplished the constructive revolution in international affairs that he did. Had a Democratic president done the same thing, the entire Republican opposition, Nixon among them, would have denounced him as skating close to treason.

Shuttle Diplomacy

In 1973, Nixon named Kissinger what he already was in fact: secretary of state. For another year, his diplomatic successes piled up. His greatest triumph came in the Middle East after the Yom Kippur War of 1973, in which Egypt and Syria attacked Israel and, for the first time in the long Arab-Israeli conflict, fought the Israelis to a draw.

Knowing that the Israelis were not inclined to accept less than victory, and fearing the consequences of a prolonged war in the oil-rich Middle East, Kissinger shuttled frantically from Damascus to Cairo to Tel Aviv and back around the circle again, carrying proposals and counterproposals in his briefcase and head. Unlike Dulles, who had also represented the United States on the fly, Kissinger was a sly, flexible, realistic, and ingratiating diplomat. He ended the war, winning the gratitude of Egyptian President Anwar Sadat while not alienating the Israelis.

After 1974, Kissinger was less successful, in part because of revived tensions that were not his doing. Leonid Brezhnev may have wanted to reduce the chance of a nuclear conflict with the United States, but he continued to aid guerrillas in Africa and Latin America that, in Kissinger's view of détente, he should have terminated. Cuba's Fidel Castro, with a large army he needed to keep in trim, "loaned" combat troops to rebels in several countries, notably Angola in southwestern Africa.

Nixon and Kissinger had little choice but to respond by aiding anti-Soviet and anti-Cuban Angolans. Liberal Democrats, haunted by Vietnam, joined right-wing Republicans in excoriating Kissinger, albeit for different reasons. Liberal attacks on the secretary of state intensified when it was revealed that, in 1973, the CIA had covertly aided and may have instigated a military coup in Chile that deposed and murdered the democratically elected president Salvador Allende. As in Guatemala twenty years earlier, Allende's only crime was to threaten the financial interests of American corporations. Unlike in Guatemala, the strongman the CIA helped bring to power in Chile, Agostín Pinochet, instituted a brutal regime in which opponents were tortured and murdered by the thousands. Neither Kissinger nor Nixon expressed regret for the fruits of their intervention.

WATERGATE AND GERALD FORD

When news of the Pinochet connection broke, Kissinger was no longer serving Richard M. Nixon. In August 1974, Richard Nixon resigned the presidency in the face of certain impeachment and virtually certain conviction. His debacle had its beginnings in his campaign for reelection in 1972.

Redefining the Democratic Party

Between 1968 and 1972, representatives of what a conservative judge, Robert Bork, called a "New Class," acquired an influence in the Democratic party out of proportion to their numbers. The New Class consisted of white, educated, middle-class liberals—teachers, professors, a majority of college students, many lawyers, social workers, white-collar government employees—the same kinds of people who were progressives early in the twentieth century. They had little interest in the economic issues that, during the New Deal, had bound working people to the Democratic party. They were sympathetic to African Americans, but in a romantic, patronizing way.

Mostly, they were motivated by issues that could seem more psychological—self-therapeutic—than political. In a trice, they abandoned their hopes for a new age of racial harmony with the emergence of the black separatism preached by Malcolm X and others and idolized the Black Panthers who carried carbines around in a foolish adolescent tableau. It is difficult to come up with a better explanation of such a turnaround than that of those who mocked them: They felt agonizingly guilty for being born white.

The new class supported other groups that made a plausible claim that they were victims of oppression: Mexican Americans, Indians, feminist women, homosexuals. They were opposed to pretty much every aspect of American foreign policy.

In 1972, thanks to new party rules intended to take the party away from professional politicians and labor leaders and be more representative of the gender, race, and even the sexual orientation of the American population, they took virtual control of the party's nominating convention in Miami. Old-time party stalwarts who had been delegates at every convention because they got out the vote in November—big city political machine stalwarts, union leaders, those southern "good old boys" who had not already gone Republican—found themselves at home watching the convention on television because of the McGovern Rules, named after the liberal, antiwar senator from South Dakota, George McGovern.

The delegates nominated McGovern and adopted a platform calling for a negotiated end to the Southeast Asian war and supporting feminist demands that abortions be made freely available to women who wanted them. They would have voted to accept homosexuality as an "alternative life style" had not McGovern blanched at what that plank would do to drive religious, working-class voters to the Republicans and scheduled the debate for late at night when few people would be watching television.

The Election of 1972   George McGovern was a decent man who tried to distance himself from his lifestyle supporters without openly denouncing them. He emphasized his pledge to bring peace in Vietnam, to sponsor tax reforms benefiting middle- and lower-income people, and his record of personal integrity as contrasted to Nixon's deviousness.

He never had a chance. Vietnamization had reduced the appeal of the antiwar movement. There were no more long casualty lists to anger working people whose sons had been dying. Virtually no labor unions supported McGovern; most Democratic pros sat on their hands. He looked foolish when, after saying he stood "1000 percent" behind Senator Thomas Eagleton, his vice presidential running mate, it was revealed that Eagleton had been treated for depression with electroconvulsive therapy, and he changed his mind and dumped him.

Nixon won 60.8 percent of the popular vote, a swing of 20 million votes in eight years. He carried every state but Massachusetts (and the District of Columbia). The fact that he was a shoo-in from the beginning of the campaign makes the surreptitious activities of his Committee to Reelect the President (an unwisely selected name: It abbreviated as CREEP) and Nixon's approval of them, impossible to explain except as a reflection of a psychology far more abnormal that Thomas Eagleton's depressions.

Covering Up a Burglary

On June 17, 1972, early in the campaign, Washington police arrested five men who were trying to plant electronic eavesdropping devices in Democratic party headquarters in an upscale apartment and office complex called the Watergate. Three of the suspects were on CREEP's payroll. McGovern tried to exploit the incident but got nowhere when Nixon and his campaign manager, Attorney General John Mitchell, denied any knowledge of the incident and denounced the burglars as common criminals.

Nixon may not have known specifically about the break-in in advance. However, when he learned that the burglars had acted on orders from his aides, he did not consider turning them in or even disciplining them in-house. He instructed his staff to dig up money to hush up the men in jail. Two of them refused to take the fall. They informed Judge John Sirica that they had been working for highly placed officials of the administration.

Two reporters for the Washington *Post,* Robert Woodward and Carl Bernstein, made contact with an anonymous informant with the code name "Deep Throat" (the title of a popular pornographic movie). Now known to have been a disgruntled FBI executive, he fed them inside information that led, in increments, to Nixon's involvement in the cover-up. A Senate investigating committee headed by Sam Ervin of North Carolina picked away at the tangle from yet another direction, uncovering other illegal acts and "dirty tricks" authorized by the White House.

A President Run Amok

On Nixon's personal command, an "enemies list" had been compiled. On it were the names of journalists, politicians, intellectuals, and even movie stars who had criticized the president. Donald Segretti, a CREEP employee, was put in charge of spreading half-truths and lies to discredit the critics. G. Gordon Liddy, who was involved in the Watergate break-in, had proposed fantastic schemes involving yachts and prostitutes to entrap Nixon's "enemies" in career-ending scandals. The Watergate break-in proved to be just one of several White House approved burglaries. Nixon operatives stole the medical records of Daniel Ellsberg, a Defense Department employee who published confidential information about the prosecution of the war in Vietnam, from Ellsberg's psychiatrist's office. The White House and the Republican party were shot through with criminals. When fingers were pointed at the president himself, Nixon unwisely told an interviewer, "When the president does it, that means it is not illegal."

In the midst of the unfolding scandal, Vice President Agnew pleaded no-contest to income tax evasion and charges that he had accepted bribes when he was governor of Maryland. Agnew resigned in October 1973 and was replaced under the six-year-old Twenty-fifth Amendment by Congressman Gerald Ford of Michigan.

Resignation

Then came Nixon's turn. He had tape-recorded conversations in the Oval Office that, after long legal wrangles, he was ordered to surrender to the Courts. At least one had been tampered with, but others clearly implicated him in the cover-up. Probably just as destructive, the tapes revealed the president to be a foulmouth. The transcripts were regularly punctuated with "[Expletive Deleted]" the expletive being obvious enough to anyone who had ever been in a men's locker room.

Gerald Ford, the most accidental of presidents, was never elected to national office. Ford won widespread affection by not pretending to be anything but the plain-spoken and hard-working public servant that he had been in Congress. He was harshly criticized when he pardoned Richard Nixon in advance of any crimes he might have been guilty. But Ford was right to do so, his critics wrong. The country had had enough of Nixon, charges, investigations, exposures, and trials. The Watergate scandal was, in Ford's words, a "long national nightmare" best left in bed when the sun came up.

Official White House Photo

Why did Nixon not destroy the tapes early in the crisis before doing so was a criminal offense? Some insiders said he intended to profit by selling them after he retired. Others said that, like Lyndon Johnson, his mind cracked. For several years, Nixon had been medicating himself with large doses of illegally acquired Dilantin, a drug that alleviates anxiety. Secretary of State Kissinger was startled when Nixon asked him to kneel with him and pray. (Neither were religious men.) Secretary of Defense Schlesinger quietly informed the Joint Chiefs of Staff not to carry out any orders from the White House until they were cleared with him or Kissinger.

After the House of Representatives Judiciary Committee recommended impeaching Nixon, he threw in the towel. On August 9, 1974, on national television, he resigned the presidency and flew to his home in San Clemente, California.

A Ford, Not a Lincoln   Gerald Ford had a safe seat in the House from Michigan. He rose to be minority leader on the basis of seniority and reliable party loyalty. His only ambition, before events made him vice president, was to be Speaker.

Ford was easy to ridicule. He was clumsy and a sometimes blank expression made him look stupid. Lyndon Johnson said that Ford's problem was that he played center on the University of Michigan football team without a helmet. Photographers laid in wait to snap shots of him bumping his head on door frames, tumbling down the slopes of the Rockies on everything but his skis, and slicing golf balls into crowds of spectators.

But Ford's modesty and forthrightness were a relief after Nixon's deceit. In his first address as president, he told Americans that fate had given them "a Ford, not a Lincoln." Democrats howled "deal" when Ford pardoned Nixon of all crimes he may have committed. But Ford's justification for the pardon was plausible—the nation needed to put Watergate behind it even at great costs. Attempts by two deranged California women within a few days helped to win sympathy for the first president who had not been elected to any national office.

Despite his unusual route to the White House, Gerald Ford had no intention of being a caretaker president. But it was his misfortune to confront serious problems while an important segment of his party plotted against him. The Republican right, now led by former California Governor Ronald Reagan, disliked détente and Nixon's (now Ford's) failure to launch a frontal attack on government regulation and the liberal welfare state.

Running on Half-Empty

The most serious of the woes facing Ford struck at one of the basic assumptions of twentieth-century American life: Cheap energy was available in unlimited quantities to fuel the economy and support the freewheeling lifestyle of the middle class.

By the mid-1970s, 90 percent of the American economy was generated by burning fossil fuels: coal, natural gas, and especially petroleum. Fossil fuels are nonrenewable. Unlike food crops and lumber, once they are used, they are gone; they cannot be called on again. While experts disagreed about the extent of the world's reserves of coal, gas, and oil, no one challenged the obvious fact that one day they would be no more.

The United States was by far the world's biggest user of nonrenewable sources of energy. In 1975, while comprising 6 percent of the world's population, Americans consumed a third of the world's annual production of oil. Much of it was burned to less than basic ends. Americans overheated and overcooled their offices and homes. They pumped gasoline into a dizzying variety of recreational vehicles, some of which brought the roar of the freeway to the wilderness and scarred fragile land. American worship of the private automobile meant that little tax money was spent on public mass transit. Consumer goods were packaged in throwaway containers of glass, metal, paper, and petroleum-based plastics; supermarkets wrapped lemons individually and fast-food cheeseburgers were cradled in styrofoam caskets to be discarded within seconds of being handed over the counter. The bill of indictment, drawn up by environmentalists, went on, but, resisting criticism and satire alike, American consumption increased.

OPEC and the Energy Crisis

About 60 percent of the oil that Americans consumed in the 1970s was produced at home, and large reserves remained under native ground. But vast quantities of crude were imported, and in October 1973, Americans discovered how little control they had over the 40 percent of their oil that came from abroad.

The Organization of Petroleum Exporting Countries (OPEC) temporarily suspended oil shipments and announced the first of a series of big jumps in the price of their product. One of their justifications was that the irresponsible consumption habits of the advanced Western nations jeopardized their future. If countries like Saudi Arabia and Nigeria continued to supply oil cheaply, the consuming nations would continue to burn it profligately, thus hastening the day when the wells ran dry. On that day, if the oil-exporting countries had not laid the groundwork for another kind of economy, they would be destitute. Particularly in the Middle East, there were few alternative resources to support fast-growing populations. By raising prices, OPEC said, the oil producing nations would amass capital with which to build for a future without petroleum while encouraging the consuming nations to conserve, thus lengthening the era when oil would be available.

It was a good argument, but few Americans were impressed and few greedy dissolutes in the OPEC countries really believed it. Arab sheiks and Nigerian generals devoted more of their windfall profits to building personal palaces than to economic development. American motorists knew only that, suddenly, they had to wait in long lines to pay unprecedented prices for gasoline. In big cities and in Hawaii, gasoline for private cars was hardly to be had for weeks.

The price of gas did not climb to levels the Japanese and Europeans paid, but it was plenty shocking to people who remembered when "two dollars worth" was enough to get through the week. Moreover, the prices of goods that consumed oil in their production climbed too. Inflation, already 9 percent during Nixon's last year, rose to 12 percent under Ford.

Whip Inflation Now!   Nixon's experiment with wage and price controls had failed. Ford's alternative was a voluntary campaign called "WIN!" for "Whip Inflation Now!" He urged Americans to deter inflation by refusing to buy exorbitantly priced goods and by ceasing to demand higher wages. The campaign was ridiculed from the start; within a few weeks, Ford quietly retired the WIN! button he had been wearing.

He then tightened the money supply in order to slow down the economy. The result was the most serious recession since 1937, with unemployment increasing to 9 percent. Ford was stymied by a vicious circle: Slowing inflation meant throwing people out of work; fighting unemployment meant inflation; trying to steer a middle course meant "stagflation," recession plus inflation.

Early in 1976, polls showed Ford losing to most of the likely Democratic candidates. Capitalizing on the news, Ronald Reagan launched a well-financed campaign to replace him as the party's candidate. With his control of the party organization, Ford beat Reagan at the Republican convention, but the economic travails of his two years in office took their toll. In November 1976, he lost narrowly to an unlikely Democratic candidate, James Earl Carter of Georgia, who called himself "Jimmy." The Democrats were back, but the decline in the prestige of the presidency continued.

QUIET CRISIS

Since 1960, every president had been identified with Congress. The day of the governor as presidential candidate seemed to have ended with FDR. Governors did not get the national publicity that Senators did. Then one-term governor Jimmy Carter came out of nowhere to win the Democratic nomination and the presidency in part because of his lack of an association with the federal government (in larger part because, as a southerner, he carried southern states that had been drifting into the Republican column). Without a real animus for Gerald Ford, voters were attracted to the idea of an "outsider," which is how Carter presented himself. Once he started winning primaries, the media did the rest. When television commentators said that there was a bandwagon a-rolling, American voters knew they had a civic obligation to climb aboard.

Inauguration Day, when Carter and his shrewd but uningratiating wife, Rosalyn, walked the length of Pennsylvania Avenue, was very nearly the last entirely satisfactory day of the Carter presidency. Whether the perspective of time will attribute his failure as chief executive to his unsuitability to the office, or to the massiveness of the problems he faced, it is difficult to imagine historians of the future depicting the Carter era other than dolefully.

Peacemaking   Carter had his successes. He defused an explosive situation in Central America where Panamanians were protesting American sovereignty in the Panama Canal Zone. The narrow strip of U.S. territory bisected the small republic and seemed to be an insult in an age when nationalist sensibilities in small countries were as touchy as boils.

Most policy makers saw no need to hold on to the canal zone. The United States would be able to seize control of the canal within hours of an international crisis. In 1978 the Senate narrowly ratified an agreement with Panama to guarantee the permanent neutrality of the canal itself while gradually transferring sovereignty and operation of the canal to Panama. Ronald Reagan, who began to campaign for the presidency as soon as Carter was inaugurated, denounced the treaty, but a grass-roots protest never gelled.

Carter's greatest achievement was his single-handed salvaging of the rapprochement between Israel and Egypt that began to take shape in November 1977 when Egyptian President Anwar Sadat risked the enmity of the Arab world by calling for peace in the Middle East in a speech to the Israeli parliament. Rather than cooperate with Sadat, Israeli Prime Minister Menachem Begin, a former terrorist, refused to make concessions commensurate with the Egyptian president's high-stakes gamble.

In 1978, Carter brought Sadat and Begin to Camp David, the presidential retreat in the Maryland woods outside Washington. Sadat grew so angry with Begin's hostility that he actually packed his suitcases to depart. Although Carter could not persuade Begin to agree that the West Bank of the Jordan River, which Israel had occupied in 1967, must eventually be returned to Arab rule, he did bring the two men together. In March 1979, Israel and Egypt signed a treaty.

Jimmy Carter's finest hour. In 1978, he persuaded Egyptian president Anwar Sadat (left) to sign the Camp David Accords establishing a process leading to peace between Egypt and Israel. He had to threaten Israeli prime minister Menachem Begin (right) to get him to sign. Begin came to Camp David for the sake of appearances. He had no intention of making concessions. Carter should have been awarded the Nobel Peace Prize for his remarkable diplomacy at Camp David.

The End of Détente

While Carter preserved the possibility of peace in the Middle East, he scrapped the détente that Nixon, Kissinger, and Ford had nurtured. Like Nixon, Carter virtually ignored his first secretary of state and looked for guidance on foreign policy to a White House advisor, Zbigniew Brzezinski. He was a poor choice. Where Kissinger was a flexible, even cynical opportunist, Brzezinski was an anti-Soviet ideologue and unreconstructed Cold Warrior. A Polish refugee from Communism, Brzezinski's hatred of the Soviet Union blinded him to opportunities to improve relations between the nuclear superpowers. Moreover, where Kissinger had been a charmer, Brzezinski was tactless and crude. The foreign ministers of several allies discreetly informed the State Department that they would not deal with him.

Carter's hostility toward the Soviet Union had other origins. A deeply religious man, moralistic to the point of sanctimony, he denounced the Soviet Union for trampling on human rights. In March 1977, Carter set back the Strategic Arms Limitation Talks with completely new proposals. Eventually, a new SALT-II treaty was negotiated and signed, but Carter withdrew it from Senate consideration in December 1979 when the Soviet Union invaded Afghanistan to prop up a client government. He refused to allow American athletes to compete in the 1980 Olympics because they were held in Moscow. Détente was dead.

Plus C'est la Même Chose

Inflation continued to worsen, rising almost to 20 percent in 1980. By the end of the year, $1 bought what, in 1940, 15¢ took home. Half of the collapse in purchasing power had occurred during the 1970s.

Carter could not be faulted for the ongoing energy crisis. After the crunch of 1974, Americans became more energy conscious, replacing their big "gas guzzlers" with more-efficient smaller cars. Even this sensible turn contributed to the nation's economic woes, however. American automobile manufacturers had repeatedly refused to develop small cars except, briefly, during the 1960s when the German-made Volkswagen "Beetle" grabbed a big slice of the new car market. When gasoline prices soared during the 1970s, Ford, General Motors, and Chrysler had nothing to compete with Japanese imports: Toyotas, Datsuns, and Hondas. The automobile buyer's dollars sailed across the Pacific.

In 1979, oil consumption was higher than ever, and a higher proportion of it was imported than in 1976. American oil refiners actually cut back on domestic production, which led many people to wonder if the crisis was genuine or just a cover under which the refiners reaped bloated profits. They did; as prices soared, the oil companies paid huge dividends to stockholders.

The price of electricity rose by 200 percent. Utility companies called for the construction of more nuclear power plants in anticipation of even higher rate increases. But Americans had become apprehensive about nuclear energy following an accident and near-catastrophe at the Three Mile Island nuclear plant near Harrisburg, Pennsylvania, and the release, at about the same time, of *The China Syndrome*, a film that portrayed an unnervingly similar accident.

When It Rains, It Pours

Personally, Carter was embarrassed by his aides, his family, and his own miscues. He had surrounded himself with cronies from Georgia who did not or would not understand capital etiquette and ritual. Banker Bert Lance, whom Carter wanted as budget director, was tainted by irregular loan scams. Ambassador to the United Nations Andrew Young foolishly met with leaders of the terrorist Palestine Liberation Organization that the United States did not recognize. Carter had to fire him.

Journalists, stimulated by the role reporters had played in exposing the Watergate scandal, leapt on trivia—a Carter aide tipsy in a cocktail lounge; the president's "down-home" brother Billy's ignorant opinions—to embarrass the president. The religious Carter foolishly told an interviewer for *Playboy* magazine, "I've looked on a lot of women with lust. I've committed adultery in my heart many times." In 1980, with Carter's presidency on the line, his mother told a reporter, "Sometimes when I look at all my children, I say to myself, 'Lillian, you should have stayed a virgin.'"

50

MORNING IN AMERICA
The Age of Reagan 1980–1992

I have long believed there was a divine plan that placed this land here to be found by people of a special kind, that we have a rendezvous with destiny. Yes, there is a spirit moving in this land and a hunger in the people for a spiritual revival. If the task I seek should be given to me, I would pray only that I could perform it in a way that would serve God.

—Ronald Reagan

Jimmy Carter won the 1976 election because of regional pride. He was the first presidential candidate from the South since 1848 and carried every former Confederate state except Virginia. Even then, his majority in the electoral college was a narrow 297 to 240. Had the right wing Ronald Reagan been the Republican nominee instead of moderate Gerald Ford, Carter would probably have lost. Every southern state Carter won had voted Republican four years earlier and, except for Georgia, would do so again in 1980.

The Republican right wing could read the numbers. Although Reagan would be pushing 70 in 1980, they began to lay the foundations for his candidacy soon after Carter's inauguration. For four years, Reagan sniped at almost every Carter policy. In the end, his industrious promotion of himself was unnecessary. He had help in discrediting Carter from the least likely of places—Iran.

THE AYATOLLAH AND THE ACTOR

Iran was important to American oil companies, but it was not a country about which ordinary Americans thought very much. The shah of Iran, Mohammed Reza Pahlavi, had been a hot item in gossip columns late in the 1950s when he divorced his beautiful wife, Princess Soraya, because she could not bear children. Since then, about all Americans knew about him was what they were told, that he

966

Conservative Zenith 1979–1993

1979	1981	1983	1985	1987	1989	1991	1993

Oct 1979 Iranian students seize fifty American hostages

Jan 1981 Iran hostages released

1981–1989 Ronald Reagan president; taxes slashed, deficit soars, businesses deregulated

"Star Wars" arms program proposed 1985

1987 Reagan and Gorbachev revive *détente*

George H. W. Bush president 1989–1993

U.S. topples and arrests Panamanian dictator 1989

U.S. drives Iraqi army from Kuwait; Bush breaks "no new taxes" pledge 1991

Bush defeated in three-candidate presidential election 1992

was an effective and popular pro-American ruler. Jimmy Carter, in a moment he came to rue, called Iran an "island of stability" in the chaotic Middle East.

In fact, the shah was unpopular. His secular modernization policies enriched the Westernized middle and upper classes of Teheran, but they did little for the impoverished peasant population and made bitter enemies of the nation's imams, mullahs, and ayatollahs, Muslim clergy whose hold on the religious masses depended on their backwardness. Instead of combating their influence by improving the peasantry's lives, the shah used his secret police to harass and imprison the leaders of the clergy and everyone else who criticized his regime. He attempted to loosen the hold of the mullahs on the peasants by emphasizing Iran's pre-Islamic greatness as the empire of Persia. The campaign was a miserable failure among illiterate peasants who were interested in rainfall and the price they were paid for their wheat, not in ancient history.

The Iranian Tragedy   Late in 1978, Iran was thrown into turmoil by riots and strikes. The secret police were overwhelmed. When agents of the secret police were identified, they were murdered. In February 1979, the Ayatollah ("Sign of God") Ruhollah Khomeini, the leader of Iran's Muslim clergy, returned from a fourteen-year exile to take charge of a coalition of the shah's enemies. Khomeini was a scholar and a virtually medieval reactionary. He taught that God willed that Muslim states should be theocracies; that is, they should be governed by clerics like him according to sharia law, religious law as laid down in Islam's holy book, the Koran. He was anti-Christian, anti-Jewish, and anti-Ba'hai, a tiny sect elsewhere but with numerous believers in Iran. He banned everything from pornography to Hollywood films and rock and roll music.

The shah concluded that his day was done and fled the country, residing briefly in Egypt and Europe. Hoping to have friendly relations with the Ayatollah, President Carter refused to admit the shah to the United States as a political refugee. However, when the shah asked for permission to visit the United States for treatment of a cancer that was terminal, Carter granted him a visa on humanitarian grounds.

That was enough to infuriate rabidly militant Iranian university students who stormed and seized the American embassy in Teheran, taking fifty Americans hostage. For more than a year, they languished in isolation while Carter, through intermediaries, searched for a diplomatic solution that would win their release. He got nowhere. The kidnappers themselves were not particularly religious, but Khomeini, in the midst of his campaign to cleanse the country religiously, found the hostage issue valuable in maintaining power. Carter authorized a raid to rescue them that was probably doomed from the start to fail; as usual, the CIA's information of the captives' whereabouts was wrong. But the raid was a fiasco from the start when two American helicopters collided outside of the capital.

Not until January 20, 1981, the day he handed the presidency over to Ronald Reagan, were the hostages released. Not without reason, Khomeini believed that the new president was capable of dropping nuclear bombs on the country.

The Campaign of 1980   Carter easily beat back a challenge for the Democratic presidential nomination by Massachusetts Senator Edward Kennedy. Ronald Reagan defeated moderate Republicans George H. W. Bush and Congressman John Anderson in the primary elections. Anderson criticized Reagan as a reckless warmonger. Bush attacked Reagan's bizarre economic proposals—increased spending on the military plus reduced taxes plus a balanced budget—as "voodoo economics." When it became clear that Reagan would be nominated, Anderson announced that he would run as an independent. He hoped to attract moderate Republicans and Democrats disillusioned with the hapless Carter. His candidacy worried Reagan's political handlers enough that they named Bush, a moderate, as Reagan's running mate.

Rather than attack Carter's handling of the hostage crisis head-on—which might have aroused sympathy for the president—Reagan criticized his foreign policy in generalities. He hammered on America's low prestige abroad, attributing it to Carter's "softness." He condemned Carter's transfer of the Panama Canal Zone to Panama. He promised a massive military buildup and the will to use force in order to end the slide of American influence, prestige, and pride. Domestically, Reagan had a ready-made issue in the weak economy, shaky throughout Carter's presidency. He said he would strengthen it by reducing regulation of business which, he said, had destroyed initiative. And (now with George Bush's concurrence) he promised rich rewards from voodoo economics.

Fundamentalist preachers turned politician, like the Reverends Jerry Falwell and Pat Robertson, put together a loosely organized army of fundamentalist Christian "ward heelers" to get out the vote and PACs (Political Action Committees) to raise money. They assailed the liberal social and cultural policies that they blamed for a decline in morality. Falwell's PAC, the "Moral Majority" blamed the Democrats for everything from the high divorce rate to the increase of violent crime in big cities.

The Democrats Routed   Pollsters predicted a close election. Several speculated that the winner would be determined in California, the last big state to report returns. In fact, the election of 1980 was over two hours before the polls closed on the West Coast. Reagan won an electoral college landslide, 489 votes to just 49 for Carter. He won 43.9 million popular votes to Carter's 35.5 million, with 5.7 million going to John Anderson. Apparently, many voters simply lied to the pollsters, perhaps embarrassed to admit they were going to vote for a movie star.

Reagan had blown the half-century-old Democratic party coalition into smithereens. The white South had been gone since 1968. In 1980, the Irish-American and Italian-American vote in the northern states, always dependably Democratic, went to Reagan. In all but three states, slavic Americans voted Republican. Jews, 80 percent Democratic two decades earlier, split evenly, as did members of labor unions. Reagan won 60 percent of the elderly who were expected to vote Democratic in order to protect their social security. For liberals, the most painful wound was the fact that young voters—the "youth" that liberal intellectuals had ennobled as the nation's idealistic vanguard since the 1960s—cast 60 percent of their votes for the elderly Republican candidate.

The political earthquake extended beyond the presidential election. The Moral Majority's PACs defeated the half dozen liberal Democratic senators they had targeted, including 1972 presidential nominee George McGovern. For the first time in nearly thirty years, the Republicans had a majority in the Senate. The Democrats still held the House. However, several conservative Democrats, stunned by the results of the election, announced that they would support the president's program. A new era had begun.

THE REAGAN REVOLUTION

Reagan would be 78 in 1989 when he left the White House for his ranch in Santa Barbara. He was the oldest person ever to hold the post. A few years after his retirement, he was struck down by Alzheimer's disease. Looking back on his presidency, some pundits said they detected early signs of his mental decline even then. And yet, this elderly actor stamped his personality and his values on the 1980s as indelibly as Franklin D. Roosevelt had impressed his on the 1930s and 1940s.

Man of the Decade   "He has no dark side," an aide said of Reagan, "What you see is what you get." Americans had seen a lot of Ronald Reagan for more than forty years. He appeared in fifty-four films during the 1930s and 1940s, often as the lead. During the 1950s, he was the host of a popular television show. Long interested in politics—as a young man he was a New Deal liberal—Reagan was drawn to Goldwater conservatism. Funded by Republican businessmen, he became the most eloquent and popular speaker on the party's "rubber chicken" banquet circuit. He was governor of California between 1967 and 1975 and learned how to talk a more extreme game than he actually played.

Few people who knew Reagan personally disliked him. He may have been a zealot, but his manner was avuncular and good natured. Lobbyists for liberal causes like the wilderness preservation movement found a more congenial listener in Reagan than in the dour, suspicious Carter (although no better a friend).

He was a master of the uplifting sound bite: "The difference between an American and any other person is that the American lives in anticipation of the future because he knows what a great place it will be." He was a cheerful raconteur, a walking *People* magazine with his treasury of show-business stories. He conveyed his good nature to audiences of thousands, small groups gathered in a parlor, and television viewers. He won the affection of some of his critics when, shortly after his inauguration, he was shot in the chest by a unbalanced young man—narrowly escaping death—and cracked jokes as he was lifted to the operating table. Reagan was called "the Great Communicator" for his ability to sell himself and his policies. He was also known as "the Teflon president." He was so well liked personally that nothing messy or damaging stuck to him, neither his own poor decisions, nor an administration that was riddled with scandal, nor when former aides wrote books ridiculing him.

The criticisms that did not stick to Reagan were legion. After a lifetime comfortable in the moral Babylon of Hollywood, he presented himself as a born-again Christian to accommodate fundamentalist voters. And he got away with it. More than a hundred highly placed officials in his administration were accused of misconduct. Most resigned. Some went to jail. Reagan's popularity rating remained steady. An exasperated liberal pundit, Garry Wills, found the right word to describe what he saw when he said that Reagan had "bedazzled" the nation.

Sandra Day O'Connor, the first woman to sit on the Supreme Court, with President Reagan and Chief Justice Warren Burger. O'Connor was expected to be a dependable conservative vote on the Court. Most of the time, but not always, she was.

Reshaping the Supreme Court Like other conservatives, Reagan believed that the Supreme Court had betrayed its constitutional mandate by becoming result-oriented, that the Court ignored constitutional strictures in order to legislate a liberal political agenda. During his eight years in office, a series of vacancies allowed him to continue the slow transformation of the Court that Richard Nixon had begun. (Carter appointed no justices.)

Reagan's first appointee was Sandra Day O'Connor of Arizona, a protegée of Nixon's most conservative appointee, William Rehnquist. By naming the first woman on the Court, Reagan snookered feminists, all of them Democrats; they had no choice but to applaud O'Connor's victory over the gender gap while Reagan added a conservative to the Court. In 1986, Reagan promoted Rehnquist to chief justice and appointed Antonin Scalia, an archconservative with a biting writing style, to the Court. Only in 1988, at the end of his term, did a Reagan nominee fail confirmation by the Senate. The Senate found Robert Bork, a talented jurist and superior Constitutional scholar, too political in his judgments. A replacement nominee, a conservative mediocrity, was dumped for the rather trivial reason that he had smoked marijuana while in law school.

Reaganomics Reagan's steady increase in popularity owed partly to good luck. Some of the problems that had hobbled Ford and Carter resolved themselves after 1980. A vicious eight-year war between Iran and Iraq prevented the Ayatollah from vexing the United States. The senility of the corrupt and unimaginative Soviet premier Leonid Brezhnev and, after his death in 1982, three years of geriatric caretaker leadership, left the Soviet Union with little direction until 1985. OPEC, which had dictated world energy prices during the 1970s, fell apart, and the retail cost of gasoline declined.

But the keystone of Reagan's popularity was the fact that his presidency was a time of fitfully increasing prosperity. The good times, Reagan believed, were due to his economic policy, which critics called "Reaganomics."

Reaganomics was based on the "supply-side" theories of economist Arthur Laffer. Laffer advocated cuts in the taxes of the wealthy as the means of stimulating economic growth. The wealthy would invest their windfalls in productive businesses whereas middle-class and, even more so, working-class people would spend their tax savings on consumer goods. That was fine, but the key to economic recovery was the infusion of capital into the economy. Growth meant more jobs. The formerly unemployed would no longer need public assistance (enabling government to reduce spending on social programs) and they would begin to pay taxes, making up for reductions in the upper brackets. Greater tax revenues would enable Reagan to balance the budget while increasing military spending, both of which he had promised.

Prosperity in Practice Democratic politicians who had not slept through their college history courses pointed out that Reaganomics was the "trickle-down" economics of the Coolidge era with a new name. Reagan was not impressed and, at his behest, Congress reduced taxes by 25 percent over three years. The windfall, for those in the upper brackets, was substantial. An upper-middle-class family making $75,000 a year (about $173,000 today) paid federal income taxes of 52.9 percent during the 1950s and 39.3 percent during the 1970s. In 1985, after the Reagan tax cut, such a family was taxed only 29.6 percent of its income. The rich did even better. The average tax bill for an annual income of $500,000–$1 million in 1981 ($1.2–$2.4 million today) was $301,072. By the time Reagan left office it was $166,066, proportionately less than a waiter in Western Europe paid. People with multimillion dollar incomes saved multiple millions.

Government revenues dropped by $131 billion, which Reagan said he would make up by slashing expenditures on bureaucracy and social programs. He cut 37,000 jobs from the federal payroll and reduced spending on education, medical research, food stamps for the poor, and other programs instituted during the 1960s. Federal spending on low-income housing dropped from $32 billion in 1980 to $7 billion in 1988.

The Deficit Mushrooms

Reaganomics did not work quite as Arthur Laffer predicted. Much of the tax break went not into investment but into consumption. By 1986, investment in manufacturing was only 1 percent higher than it had been in the recession year of 1982 while sales of high-end homes boomed. Luxury imports such as Mercedes-Benz automobiles soared. Americans even imported drinking water; Perrier, a bottled French mineral water, became a mania. The image of a ship crossing the Atlantic burning tons of unrenewable fossil fuels with a hold full of water was mind-boggling although there is no evidence it intruded on the minds of many.

The money to feed the consumption binge and compensate for the failure of Americans to invest came from abroad. West German, Japanese, and Arab investors bought prime real estate, control of corporations, and U.S. Treasury bonds in huge blocks. The United States, the world's creditor nation when Reagan took office, became the world's biggest debtor. In 1981, foreigners owed Americans $2,500 for each American family of four. By 1989, the United States owed foreigners $7,000 for each family of four.

The greatest financial irony of the Reagan years was the growth in the federal deficit, the annual increase in the government's debt. Since the 1930s, the Republican party's conservatives, from Robert Taft through Barry Goldwater to Reagan, had said that big-spending Democrats would drive the government into bankruptcy. Reagan dramatized the issue by calling for a constitutional amendment mandating a balanced budget.

All the while, his administration borrowed and spent at levels that smashed all records. In 1981, the federal government owed $738 billion, about 26¢ on each dollar produced and earned in the United States that year. In 1989, the debt was $2.1 trillion, about 43¢ on each dollar produced and earned. Reagan borrowed more money in eight years than thirty-nine previous presidents had borrowed in two centuries.

Deregulation

Since the New Deal, the federal government had regulated important aspects of national economic life. This regulation, Reagan said, discouraged the spirit of enterprise. As president, he weakened the regulatory apparatus in several ways. He abolished some agencies and cut the budgets of others. To head other offices, he appointed officials who deliberately neglected to do what their jobs mandated. Airlines, trucking companies, banks, and stock brokers found there were fewer federal watchdogs apt to drop in and ask to see the books.

Profits increased. Airlines that had been required to maintain little-used routes as a public service closed them and raised fares on crowded air lanes. In 1981, a person could fly from San Francisco to Los Angeles for $36. In 1989, the same ticket cost $148. Getting from big cities to small ones by air became extremely expensive, when it was possible. By the hundreds, small towns that had boasted regularly scheduled flights to cities with major airports lost them. Consumer advocates claimed that the deregulated airlines routinely sent unsafe planes and unqualified pilots aloft. Similar criticisms were made of the condition of large trucks and the qualifications of truck drivers. Serious accidents involving monstrous "semis" increased during the decade.

Several of Reagan's appointees to environmental agencies openly despised "tree huggers," their name for conservation and environmentalist activists. The head of the Environmental Protection Agency (EPA), Ann Burford, was forced to resign in 1983 when it was revealed she had actively interfered with the enforcement of EPA regulations. Reagan's secretary of the interior, James Watt of Colorado, formerly the head of an anticonservation group known as "Sagebrush Rebels," opened wilderness areas to mining companies and tried to open protected scenic coastline to offshore oil drillers.

On the issue of the environment alone, anti-Reagan forces grew in influence. The Wilderness Society had 48,000 members in 1981, 240,000 in 1989. The Natural Resources Defense Council increased its membership from 85,000 to 170,000. The World Wildlife Fund had 60,000 members in 1982, 1 million in 1990. The Sierra Club and Audubon Society made similar gains. Reagan was nonplussed. He even vetoed a Clean Water Act aimed at stopping the dumping of toxic industrial wastes.

Finance Run Amok   Deregulation of financial institutions led to irresponsible and sometimes corrupt practices in "thrifts," better known as savings and loan associations. Formerly restricted to making loans on real estate, deregulation permitted them to function like savings banks, even offering checking accounts. Presented with opportunities to cash in on big profits that was impossible when they were restricted to home mortgages, savings and loans plunged into risky investments. In 1988 alone, 135 savings and loans had to be bailed out or closed by the Federal Savings and Loan Insurance Corporation (FSLIC) that insured them largely with tax money.

Before the Reagan deregulation, however, the FSLIC and the Federal Deposit Insurance Corporation (FDIC) (which insured savings accounts in banks) had been required to enforce strict management standards to qualify for the insurance. During the Reagan years, supervision was virtually nil and shoddy practices multiplied. One of the sons of vice president George H. W. Bush was the beneficiary of transactions that would not have been allowed before deregulation. An energy company paid him $120,000 during a year the company was losing $12 million. The company also loaned him $180,000 at low interest to buy stock in the company.

Then, one week before the huge losses were announced and the price of the company's stock dropped by 60 percent, Bush Jr. sold his shares for $850,000.

The champion financial wheeler-dealer of the 1980s was Michael Milken, who sold deregulated savings and loans billions of dollars in "junk bonds," loans that promised to pay extremely high interest because conservative investors would not touch them. Milken pocketed $550 million in commissions. He went too far and did not have a father who was vice president; he went to jail. So did several prominent Wall Street wheeler-dealers. Freed of close supervision by the Securities and Exchange Commission (SEC), more than a few stockbrokers turned to outright fraud. By paying bribes to executives of large corporations, they learned before the public of important decisions that would affect the value of stocks. Using this insider information, they bought and sold shares at immense profit.

The Reagan administration continued to approve corporate mergers and takeovers that did little but enrich a few individuals at the expense of middle-class shareholders. In 1970, there had been 10 corporate reshufflings (mergers, takeovers) paying fees of $1 million or more to those who arranged them. In 1980, there were 94. In 1986, there were 346. In 1988, the Reagan administration approved a deal between tobacco giant R. J. Reynolds and the Nabisco Company despite the fact that even the principals admitted, the consequences of the merger would be higher prices for consumers, fewer jobs, and personal profits of $10 million for a handful of top shareholders.

The Election of 1984   In 1984, Walter Mondale of Minnesota, vice president under Jimmy Carter, won the Democratic party presidential nomination by beating back challenges from Senator Gary Hart of Colorado and Reverend Jesse Jackson, a civil rights activist. Jackson was a mesmerizing orator in the tradition of the black churches in which he, like Martin Luther King, had been an ordained minister. Hart had managed George McGovern's presidential campaign and remained popular among the young, educated, and generally affluent Democrats who had voted for McGovern and continued to think more in terms of "soft" personal issues rather than the "hard" working-class issues of the old Democratic party.

Mondale, who was an old-line New Deal Democrat, hoped that labor union and African American support and his exploitation of the "sleaze factor," the corruption in the Reagan administration, would be enough to help him overcome the president's personal popularity. But he was unable to bring back the traditionally Democratic voters who had gone for Reagan in 1980. The Republicans depicted Mondale as a pork-barrel politician, promising something to every constituent group. His play to win over Hart's supporters by naming a congresswoman, Geraldine Ferraro, as his running mate, made little political sense. Feminists were not apt to vote Republican under any circumstances and Republican women were not moved by Mondale's ham-handed appeals to "sisterhood."

Reagan's popularity was at flood tide in 1984. He won by a landslide, carrying 59 percent of the vote and every state except Mondale's Minnesota and the District of Columbia. He announced that the theme of his second term was "Morning in America."

FOREIGN POLICY IN THE EIGHTIES

Reagan was a hard-line Cold Warrior. In 1982, he called Russia an "evil empire.... the focus of evil in the world." In 1985, he promulgated the Reagan Doctrine, warmed-over John Foster Dulles. The United States would support anti-Communist struggles everywhere in the world. Before he left office in 1989, however, Reagan scored a major breakthrough in nuclear arms reduction and set the stage for a rapprochement between the United States and the Soviet Union that went beyond the Nixon-Kissinger détente he had once criticized.

South Africa and the Middle East   Reagan criticized South African apartheid (strict segregation of races), but he resisted calls for economic sanctions that many believed would force a change in South Africa. He continued to support rebels in Angola who were fighting a Soviet-backed government defended by Cuban troops.

Reagan continued Jimmy Carter's policy of aiding anti-Russian guerrillas in Afghanistan despite the fact that they were Muslim fundamentalists similar to those who had swept Khomeini to power in Iran. In 1983, he sent marines to Lebanon, which was torn by a multisided civil war. When a suicide bomber driving an explosive-laden truck killed 241 sleeping marines, he withdrew the force. His Teflon worked as ever. Reagan was not widely criticized either for sending the marines to Lebanon or for withdrawing them in failure.

In 1986, Reagan won applause by bombing Libya. The Libyan leader, Muammar Qadaffi, had long been suspected of financing terrorists. When American intelligence claimed to have evidence of a direct link between Qadaffi and terrorists in West Germany, American bombers raided several Libyan cities. Public opinion was favorable.

Central America   In October 1983, the president ordered a surprise occupation of Grenada, a tiny Caribbean island republic of 110,000 people. Grenada was in chaos after the assassination of a Marxist president. Reagan justified the intervention on the grounds that about 1,000 Americans (many of them medical students) lived on Grenada and that there was a Cuban military presence left over from the Marxist regime. The Cuban soldiers turned out to be construction workers, but the American residents were real.

Nicaragua was under the control of leftists calling themselves "Sandinistas" after a national hero. Openly committed to overthrowing the regime, the Reagan administration subsidized a guerrilla army known as the *contras* (those against). Humanitarian groups and liberals, including a large number of Democratic congressmen, said that by keeping the *contras* alive, the United States was perpetuating turmoil and misery in a country that had known little prosperity since it lost the transoceanic canal to Panama. Other critics said that the *contras* were reactionary and anti-democratic. Still others feared that the United States would become involved in another quagmire like Vietnam. Beginning in October 1984, a worried Congress attached the Boland Amendments to several bills authorizing money for foreign aid. The Boland Amendment explicitly forbade U.S. aid to the *contras*.

The Iran-Contra   Reagan had no intention of abandoning the *contras*. As if he
Affair   had never heard about what Watergate had done to Nixon,
                   he told his aides "to figure out a way to take action." They
embarked on a bizarre adventure that mocked the president's depiction of
international affairs as a struggle between good and evil. Two National Security
Advisors, Robert McFarlane and John Poindexter, and a marine colonel, Oliver
North, secretly sold eighteen Hawk missiles to the Ayatollah Khomeini's Iran.
Some of the profits from the deal simply disappeared into someone's pocket. The
balance was given to the *contras*.

How deeply Defense Secretary Weinberger and the president were involved in
the affair was never clearly determined. Weinberger was indicted for withholding
information and Reagan changed the story of his involvement several times. He
had either sanctioned violation of the Boland law—an impeachable crime, like
Nixon's—or he did not know what was going on in his administration.

Liberals screamed bloody murder. But Ronald Reagan was no ordinary political target. Times were good; stocks and real estate values were rising; football
players were better than ever; and television entertainers brought tears and laughter
nightly into American living rooms. To the bewilderment of the Democrats, the
public took little interest in the issue. Indeed, after being convicted in 1989 on three
criminal counts, Oliver North went on in 1994 to lose an election to the Senate
from Virginia by a very narrow margin.

Changing   Even before the Iran-Contra affair made the news, Reagan's
Policies   foreign policy underwent some abrupt changes. Rather than
            defend an anti-Communist dictator in Haiti in 1986,
American agents played an important role in persuading him to go into exile.
The United States also played a key role in the ouster of the pro-American but
abysmally corrupt president of the Philippines, Ferdinand Marcos. When Marcos
declared himself the victor in a disputed election, riots broke out throughout the
country. Fearing a civil war, the United States supported his opponent, Corazon
Aquino. Marcos was given asylum in Hawai'i.

Reagan was unsuccessful in his attempt to eliminate Manuel Noriega, the
military dictator of Panama. Evidence indicated that Noriega was deeply involved
in smuggling cocaine and other drugs to the United States. He was indicted in the
United States, and Reagan cut off the flow of American dollars to Panama. However, Noriega's hold on the Panamanian army was strong, and he rallied public
support by baiting the United States, always a crowd-pleaser in Latin America.

Weapons   The most important of Reagan's foreign policy shifts was in
Buildup   his dealings with the Soviet Union. Calling the SALT-II treaty
           a "one-way street" with Americans making all the conces-
sions to the Soviets, he refused to submit it to the Senate for ratification. In 1986,
Reagan announced that the United States would no longer be bound by SALT-I.

In the meantime, the president had sponsored the greatest peacetime military
buildup in the nation's history, spending $2 trillion on both old and new weapons
systems. Battleships were taken out of mothballs and put to sea despite the fact that

they could be sunk by a cheap missile that was in the armories of a dozen nations. Reagan revived the MX missile, which he renamed the Peacekeeper. When it was announced that the Peacekeepers were to be installed in old Minuteman missile silos, critics said Reagan was just pumping money into the treasuries of defense contractors or he was planning a first strike against the Soviets. It was well known that the Russians had the Minuteman sites targeted. The Peacekeepers were useless unless they were fired in a surprise attack.

In 1983, Pershing II missiles were installed in West Germany from where they could hit Soviet targets in five minutes. The Russians responded by increasing their striking capability. A new arms race was underway. By 1985, the two superpowers had more than 50,000 nuclear warheads between them.

The most controversial of Reagan's weapons proposals was SDI, the Strategic Defense Initiative, known as "Star Wars" after a popular movie. In theory, SDI was a system by which satellites orbiting the earth would be equipped with lasers fired at missiles by computer. Reagan claimed that the system would create an umbrella preventing a successful missile attack on the United States.

Some critics of Star Wars said that SDI simply would not work: Low-flying missiles and planes would be unaffected by lasers from space. Financiers worried that the astronomical costs of the project would bankrupt the United States. Antiwar groups said that SDI was an offensive, not a defensive weapon. By making the United States safer from nuclear attack, it would encourage a first-strike attack on the Soviet Union. Others said that the Soviets would simply develop counter-measures, which had always been the case in military technology, and the insanity would go on and on.

Turning toward Disarmament Still, it was not criticism that led President Reagan to reverse direction in defense policies. During his second term, the hawkish Casper Weinberger resigned as secretary of defense and the more statesmanlike secretary of state, George Schultz, increased his influence on the president.

White House insiders said that Nancy Reagan played a major part in persuading the president to turn toward disarmament. Deeply devoted to her husband, she was concerned about his place in history, and she knew that presidents who furthered the chances for peace won better historical reputations than warmongers did.

The concerns of allies in Europe also influenced the president. Chancellor Helmut Kohl of West Germany, President François Mitterand of France, and Prime Minister Margaret Thatcher of Great Britain remained loyal to the NATO alliance. However, all made it clear that they were unnerved by some of Reagan's more reckless speeches. Most important, the Soviet Union underwent profound changes during the 1980s.

In 1985, Mikhail Gorbachev emerged as head of both the Soviet government and Communist party. At home, Gorbachev tried to institute far-reaching economic and political reforms. His policy of *perestroika* (restructuring) was designed to revive the Soviet economy, which had been moribund under strict government control. *Glasnost* (opening) promised political and intellectual freedoms previously unheard of in the Soviet Union.

If his reforms were to succeed, Gorbachev needed to divert Soviet resources from the military to the domestic economy. Doing that depended on American cooperation. At first, Reagan resisted Gorbachev's proposals to end the arms race. Then, in Washington in December 1987, the two men, all smiles and handshakes, signed a treaty eliminating many short-range and medium-range missiles. The Soviets destroyed 1,752 missiles and the Americans 867. These represented only 4 percent of the nuclear missiles in existence. Nevertheless, nuclear power 32,000 times the force of the Hiroshima bomb was wiped out.

THE BUSH PRESIDENCY

The Democrats approached the presidential campaign of 1988 with high hopes. They believed that the Reagan presidency was an aberration, the personal triumph of a single inexplicably beloved man. A majority of governors were Democrats. The Democratic party enjoyed a comfortable majority in the House and had regained control of the Senate in 1986. With Ronald Reagan disqualified from running, why should not the Democrats win the presidency, too?

1988: Dukakis versus Bush   The Democratic party was swamped with would-be presidential candidates. The front-runner in the early going was Gary Hart, the former senator from Colorado. Then, in a bizarre sequence of events, including publication of a photo showing the married Hart with a beautiful young model sitting on his lap aboard a yacht unfortunately called the *Monkey Business,* political analysts suggested that the candidate's judgment was, perhaps, a little less than what the presidency called for.

Hart withdrew from the race and someone ridiculed the remaining candidates as "the seven dwarfs" because of their deficiency in presidential stature. In fact, several of the dwarfs were able men, and Jesse Jackson remained, as he had been in 1976, one of the nation's most inspiring speakers. Because he was black, however, party professionals considered him unelectable. They hoped that Senator Sam Nunn of Georgia, a respected expert on national defense, would jump into the thirty-five primary election races; or that Governor Mario Cuomo of New York, another inspiring orator whose thoughtful humanism was tempered by a hard-headed political realism, would run.

But neither did, and the nomination went to Governor Michael Dukakis of Massachusetts. The son of Greek immigrants, Dukakis had been a successful governor. He balanced state budgets in Massachusetts while Reagan borrowed and spent at obscene levels. During his governorship, a state with serious economic difficulties became a prosperous center of finance and high-technology industry. For vice president, Dukakis chose a courtly Senator Lloyd Bentsen of Texas. He hoped the ticket would remind voters of the Massachusetts–Texas axis that had won the election of 1960.

The Republican nominee was Vice President George Bush, who handily defeated Senator Robert Dole of Kansas in the primaries. Bush was a wealthy oilman who had a varied political career. He had been a congressman, ambassador to China and the United Nations, and head of the CIA. He had changed his political orientation several times, beginning as a liberal Republican, then inviting John

Birchers into the Texas Republican party, challenging Reagan in 1980 as a moderate, and cheerleading for right-wing causes as vice president.

As his running mate, Bush chose Senator Dan Quayle of Indiana, a handsome, affable young man who had led the life of a playboy.

Negative Campaigning
The first polls showed Dukakis winning in a landslide, but the gap between the two candidates narrowed during the summer. Dukakis's record as governor proved his competence but in manner he was mechanical and dull, an unnerving contrast to the very ebullient Reagan. By way of contrast, finally reaching the top seemed to liberate Bush. As Dukakis grew drabber and duller, Bush exuded confidence, authority, and decisiveness, traits for which he had never been known. He promised both to continue the policies of what he now called the "Reagan–Bush administration" and also to usher in "a kinder, gentler America." Advised that he had to shore up support among the Republican party's right wing, which distrusted him, he emphatically promised, "read my lips; no new taxes."

While Bush took the high road, his handlers smeared Dukakis. They pointed out that Dukakis was a member of the American Civil Liberties Union, an almost 70-year-old legal aid organization originally dedicated to defending freedom of expression that had degenerated into a citadel of wackiness. In one case, the ACLU went to court to defend the right of elementary school pupils to wear T-shirts emblazoned with obscene slogans.

Much more damaging was the case of Willie Horton. Under Massachusetts law, some imprisoned felons were granted furloughs, brief releases from the penitentiary. While on furlough, a convicted murderer, Willie Horton, raped a woman and killed her husband. Horton was an African American. While never mentioning race, by televising photographs of Horton, the Republican campaign implicitly blamed Dukakis for the tragedy. In fact, Dukakis did not approve Horton's furlough. He did not have the legal authority to prevent it had he known of it. But the incident had occurred on his watch, and he could not shake the accusations that he was responsible. Bush won the election with 54 percent of the popular vote.

Dubious Legacy
A few months after the election, Ronald Reagan told a joke to a Republican audience. Two fellows, he said, were hiking in the woods when, down a hill, a grizzly bear came trotting toward them. One of the men pulled a pair of sneakers out of his pack and put them on. The other said, "You don't think you can outrun that bear, do you?" The first man said, "I don't have to outrun the bear. I just have to outrun you."

Ronald Reagan outran George Bush. He left him squatting on the mountainside. He retired to his California ranch in January 1989 leaving Bush to preside over a financial crisis that Reagan's cuts in taxes coupled with profligate spending that had to explode under the new president.

The Collapse of Communism
In May 1989, thousands of student demonstrators gathered in Tiananmen Square, a huge plaza in the center of Beijing. Soviet Premier Gorbachev was visiting China, and the students used

the occasion to demand *glasnost*-like reforms in their country. Within two days, there were a million people in the square; the drama played out "live" on American television because two television news bureaus were in Beijing to cover the Gorbachev visit. They had stumbled on a much bigger story than the visit of the Soviet premier. Americans even caught glimpses of the brutal suppression of the demonstration which resulted in at least 500 and, according to some sources, 7,000 deaths.

Meanwhile, in Eastern Europe, the countries that had been satellites of the Soviet Union since World War II exploited Gorbachev's relaxation of government controls to oust their Communist rulers. Poland elected a non-Communist government in mid-1989. By the end of the year, Czechoslovakia did the same. In October, Erich Honecker, the hard-line Communist chief of East Germany, resigned; the next month, a festive crowd of young people breached the Berlin Wall and one East German in a hundred poured through it in search of higher pay. In December, the dictator of Romania, Nicolae Ceausescu, was murdered by anti-Communist rebels. In April 1990, Hungary elected an anti-Communist government. In a few astonishing months, a European order almost half a century old was in chaos.

Gorbachev's position in the Soviet Union was shaken. His policy of *glasnost* had indeed opened up Soviet society but *perestroika*—structural reforms that needed time to work—had had little effect on the Soviet economy. Food shortages in cities led to protests. On May Day 1990, Communism's holiday, Gorbachev and his colleagues were roundly jeered as they reviewed the traditional parade. A few days later, Boris Yeltsin, a critic of Gorbachev, was elected president of the Russian Republic, the largest constituent of the Soviet Union. For the next year and a half, Yeltsin increased his following at Gorbachev's expense by calling for a free-market economy and supporting claims to independence in many of the other fourteen Soviet republics. At the end of 1991, the Soviet Union was formally dissolved.

**The President's
Finest Hour**   Bush acted with admirable restraint. He was convinced that Soviet-American friendship depended on Gorbachev remaining in power. He refused to gloat over the fall of The Berlin Wall. He tried to allay the fears of the Red Army generals and the Communist

The demolition of the Berlin Wall, begun by demonstrators brick by brick, later finished by bulldozers, was the dramatic symbol of the fall of the "Iron Curtain" and the end of the Soviet empire in Eastern Europe.

DPA/Camera Press London

hard-liners in the Kremlin who opposed Gorbachev by convincing the West German premier, Helmut Kohl, to delay any attempts to reunify Germany. In valuing the interests of peace and Soviet-American cooperation above winning propaganda victories abroad and making political hay at home, he rose, albeit briefly, according to one of his few sympathetic biographers, to presidential greatness.

In December 1989, Bush succeeded in toppling the vexatious Manuel Noriega from power in Panama. After an American military officer was shot in Panama City, Bush unleashed 24,000 troops in a superbly engineered military invasion. Within a few days, with little loss in American lives, Noriega was under arrest, and a friendly government installed in Panama City.

In February 1990, with Soviet and Cuban aid to Nicaragua drying up, the Sandinistas were voted out of office by a political alliance backed by the United States. A less desirable right-wing party took control of El Salvador but, pressured by the United States, eased up its repression of opponents and signed an armistice with leftist rebels, ending the long civil war in that country.

Crisis in the Middle East   Bush's greatest success was in the Middle East. The crisis there was precipitated in August 1990 when Iraq occupied Kuwait, a small sheikdom floating on oil. At first, Bush was indecisive. He considered accepting the Iraqi occupation and making the most of it. However, when Iraqi President Saddam Hussein moved his army to the Kuwaiti-Saudi Arabian border, Bush secured a unanimous vote in the United Nations Security Council (his friendliness with Gorbachev paid off) calling for a boycott of all foreign trade with Iraq. Although rich in oil, Iraq needed to import most of the materials needed to support a modern economy.

Bush's advisors were divided, but the president did not believe that economic sanctions were enough to force Saddam Hussein to withdraw from Kuwait. He feared, with plenty of precedents to back him up, that as time went on, the boycott would disintegrate. Apprehensions over the security of Saudi Arabia—the world's leading oil producer—prompted Bush to send a token American military force to Saudi Arabia on August 7. Saddam did not flinch but grew more defiant; he formally annexed Kuwait to Iraq. Bush then sent more than 400,000 troops to Arabia. Other nations, particularly Britain and France, sent large contingents.

The Hundred Hours War   In January, after Saddam Hussein ignored a United Nations ultimatum that he evacuate Kuwait, the American-led force launched a withering air attack that, in little more than a week, totaled 12,000 sorties. With an American television reporter in Baghdad, the world was presented with the media phenomenon of watching a war from both sides.

In the face of the onslaught, Saddam sent most of his air force to neighboring Iran, leaving the skies to American planes. Saddam, like some Americans, including General Colin Powell, believed that his huge army, dug in behind formidable defenses, could turn back any ground assault. He was wrong. The Iraqi army was large, but most soldiers were poorly trained and mistreated by their officers. The air war was chillingly effective, not only devastating the Iraqi communications and transportation system, but also terrifying front-line Iraqi troops. When the ground attack came on February 23, 1992, most units surrendered without resistance. In just a few days, the Iraqi army was routed by a daring flanking action designed by General Norman Schwarzkopf. Believing that Saddam could not survive the humiliating defeat—that his generals would oust him—Bush ordered a halt to the ground war when it was 100 hours old, leaving the Iraqi army's elite "Republican Guard" intact.

Mixed Results   A few months later, Bush's sudden termination of the advance looked like a blunder. The Republican Guard remained loyal; Saddam Hussein stayed in power. He rebuilt the rump of his army and brutally suppressed rebellions among Kurds in northern Iraq and Shi'ite Muslims in

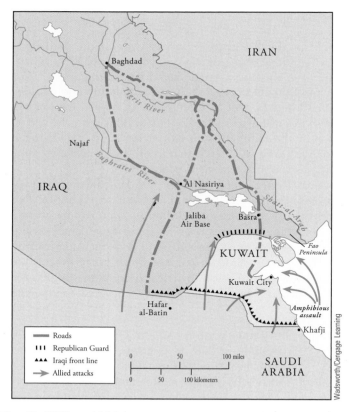

MAP 50.1 The Gulf War, 1991.

After weeks of bombardments that destroyed Iraqi communications and demoralized the highly touted Iraqi army, American and allied troops advanced through Kuwait and deep into Iraq. They crushed the Iraqi troops that did not retreat in a panic, but the elite "Republican Guards" withdrew on Saddam Hussein's orders and remained intact. The Guards' loyalty to Saddam ensured his survival.

A Statistical American

During the 1980s, the statistical American—an imaginary person constructed of majorities, medians, and means—was a Caucasian female, just over 30 years of age. She was married to the only husband she had ever had; she had one child and was about to have another. She was about 5 feet 4 inches tall and weighed 134 pounds. Statisticians said that she had tried marijuana when she was younger, but no longer used it, although she had friends who did. She did not smoke cigarettes; she did drink, but moderately, on "special occasions."

A study by a scientific management firm revealed she would spend seven of the seventy-five years she would live in the bathroom, six years eating, five years waiting in lines, four years cleaning house, three years in meetings, one year "looking for things," eight months opening junk mail, and six months waiting at red lights.

The statistical American adult female considered herself middle class. She had attended college and was likely to work outside the home, but shaky economic conditions during the first half of the decade made her career opportunities uncertain. Her household's income was about $20,000 a year. She and her husband had to watch their expenditures closely. By a tiny margin, she was more likely to be registered as a Democrat than as a Republican but, if she voted in 1984, she was more likely than not to have voted for Ronald Reagan than Walter Mondale. She had had a fling with the new feminism—"consciousness-raising" meetings with friends for a few months—but had lost interest, perhaps when her husband agreed to do a bigger share of the household chores. She thought that the Equal Rights Amendment (ERA) was a good idea but its failure did not particularly disturb her.

More than half of her women friends were married. Most of those who had been divorced married again within three years. She attached no stigma to divorce and experienced only a slight sense of unease around people who lived with members of the opposite sex without benefit of marriage. She did not believe that homosexuality was on a moral parity with heterosexuality. She was both amused and repelled by "gay culture" but by 1985 she was disturbed by the quantum leap in the spread of AIDS, which she regarded as a homosexual disease.

She almost certainly had sexual relations with her husband before they married, and almost as likely with at least one other man. There was a fair chance that she had a brief affair after marrying about which she may or may not have told her husband.

The statistical American was more likely to be Protestant than Catholic, but more likely to be Catholic than a member of any specific Protestant denomination. If she was a Catholic, she practiced birth control, usually the pill, despite the Church's prohibition of it. Catholic or Protestant, she attended church services far less frequently than her mother had.

The statistical American was in excellent health; she saw a dentist and a doctor more than once a year, and paid a little less than half the cost of her health care. She would outlive her husband by eight years and, with few children, the prospect was that her dotage would be economically difficult but not desperate.

The statistical American lived in a state with a population of about 3 million people—Colorado, Iowa, Oklahoma, Connecticut—and in a city of about 100,000 —Roanoke, Virginia; Reno, Nevada; Durham, North Carolina.

the South. Frustrating as the failure of Bush's hopes were, his wisdom in not advancing into Baghdad and occupying Iraq was demonstrated a decade later when his own son, President George W. Bush, did just that and mired the United States in bloody, daily combat with Saddam's supporters, Shi'ite militias aided by Iran, and terrorists attached to a fanatical Muslim, anti-Western, and well-financed organization known as Al Qaeda.

At first, Bush's and Schwarzkopf's textbook victory in the Gulf War seemed to guarantee the president's reelection in 1992. He proclaimed that Americans had put the "Vietnam Syndrome"—a demoralized army and defeatism at home—behind them. The president's ratings in public opinion polls soared in early 1991. Then the financial crisis caused by Reagan's reckless spending came home to roost. The 1991 budget was due and there was not enough money in the treasury even to pay the interest on the national debt. There was no easy way out of the crisis thanks to a Republican law, the Graham-Rudman Act, that provided for lopping 40 percent off the top of every government appropriation if the deficit was not reduced. In order to beat the deadline, Bush had no choice but to scrap the pledge that had been the core of his campaign promises in 1988: "read my lips; no more taxes." He agreed to an increase in taxes. Conservative Republicans who had endorsed Reaganomics and celebrated the Gulf War, denounced him. Bush saved the government's finances but at the cost of contributing to a stubborn recession in 1992. The economic crunch relegated Bush's achievements abroad to the realm of ancient history. It was if the American people asked him, "What have you done for me lately?" It was a sad end for a man who had his greatest achievements at the pinnacle of his career.

Primary Elections, 1992   Bush was challenged in the Republican primaries by a right-wing television commentator, Patrick Buchanan, who had vociferously opposed the Gulf War. Buchanan won no early primaries, but by taking almost 40 percent of the Republican votes in some states, he signaled that Bush was in trouble in his own party.

The Democratic party's primary campaign was unusual. Instead of one candidate pulling ahead early and, thanks to "momentum" generated by the "media," coasting to the nomination, several aspirants won convention delegates in at least one state. Senator Thomas Harkin of Iowa, a liberal with a populist tinge, won his own state. Paul Tsongas of Massachusetts won New Hampshire and Maryland. Senator Robert Kerrey of Nebraska won South Dakota. Most surprising of all, former California governor Jerry Brown, despite a nagging reputation for bizarre "New Age" beliefs—he had been called "Governor Moonbeam"—won most of the delegates from Colorado.

Then, however, young Governor William Clinton of Arkansas rushed to the head of what humorist Russell Baker called "the march of the Millard Fillmores." He rode out a past as a Vietnam War draft dodger, accusations of a reckless adultery habit when he was governor of Arkansas, and claims that he was too slick to be trusted. He sewed up the convention before it met. Clinton's strategy was to woo the New Age liberals who had supported Gary Hart by speaking for liberal lifestyle issues (he was pro-abortion, pro affirmative action, and called for an end to discrimination against homosexuals) while appealing to moderates with an economic policy that emphasized growth.

The Election
of 1992

Populist conservatives who had never liked the aristocratic Bush bolted to support the independent candidacy of H. Ross Perot, a Texas billionaire. Perot offered little in the way of a program, but hundreds of thousands of uneasy Americans formed local "Perot for President" organizations. The candidate himself pledged to spend millions of his own money in the cause. In July, polls showed him leading both Bush and Clinton.

On the day Clinton accepted the Democratic nomination, Perot was on the ballot in twenty-four states with no significant obstacles to winning a line on all fifty. Then, suddenly, he quit the race, claiming that he and his daughter had been threatened by assassins. Some of Perot's supporters condemned him, but others continued to gather signatures on petitions. Then Perot jumped back into the contest and outclassed both Bush and Clinton in the first of the candidates' televised debates. But his erratic behavior troubled too many people who had been prepared to vote for him. His 19 percent of the popular vote in the general election was more than any third-party presidential candidate had won since Theodore Roosevelt in 1912 but, analysts believed, it could have been much more.

Perot's name on the ballot helped Bill Clinton carry several mountain states that had not gone Democratic since 1964. Clinton also won California. In electoral votes, the entire Northeast and several southern states also went Democratic. Although Clinton won only 43 percent of the popular vote—one of the lowest for a winning candidate—he had 370 electoral votes to Bush's 168.

51

MILLENNIUM YEARS
Society and Culture in the Later Twentieth Century

*We are in great haste to construct a magnetic telegraph
from Maine to Texas; but Maine and Texas, it may be,
have nothing important to communicate. We are eager to
tunnel under the Atlantic and bring the Old World
somewhat nearer to the New; but, perchance, the first
news that will leak through into the broad, flapping
American ear will be that Princess Adelade has the
whooping cough.*

—Henry David Thoreau

*In my nightmare I could picture such a world ...
Everybody would be comfortable, but since there
could be no great demand for intellectual exertion
everybody would also be slightly idiotic. Their
shallow minds would be easily bored, and therefore
unstable. Their life would be largely a quest for
amusement. The raffish existence led today [1940] by
certain groups would have become the normal
existence of large sections of society.*

—John Buchan

Americans celebrated the arrival of the third millennium on New Year's Eve 1999. They were off by a year, spoilsports rushed to point out. December 31, 1999, was the final day of the 999th year since A.D. 1000; the second millennium would end on December 31, 2000. But there was no deterring people who, after lifetimes of dating their letters and mortgage checks "nineteen-something," would, the next morning, experience the novelty of writing "2000." The millennium parties went on as scheduled.

Not everyone donned a paper hat and drank too much. Nagging at some reflective men and women was the apprehension that morally, psychically, and politically, the United States was rotting. In 2000, an eminent scholar, 93-year-old Jacques Barzun,

Immigration 1965–2008

1960	1965	1970	1975	1980	1985	1990	1995	2000	2005 2010

1965 Immigration and Nationality Act

1973 *Roe v. Wade*

1975 Southeast Asian refugee crisis begins

1980 "Mariel Boatlift": 120,000 Cubans flee to U.S.

Congress authorizes immigration of 1.4 million southeast Asians 1990

Tens of thousands of refugees flee Haiti by boat 1993

Illegal Mexican immigration crisis 1990-2000

African American wins Democratic presidential primaries 2008

published a history of Western civilization in which he concluded that our culture was in the throes of decadence. Barzun waved away objections that Americans' energy, ingenuity, and openness to the new were as vibrant as ever. Those things did not mean cultural vitality, he wrote. A time of decadence is often "a very active time, full of deep concerns, but peculiarly restless, for it sees no clear lines of advance.... Institutions function painfully. Repetition and frustration are the intolerable result. Boredom and fatigue are great historical forces."

That long-accepted moral standards had decayed was obvious to all except those who did not believe in moral standards. As for the American psyche, Barzun pointed to "the search in all directions for a new faith or faiths, dozens of cults ..., the impulse to PRIMITIVISM." In politics he saw endless bickering and no direction but everywhere "a floating hostility to things as they are" and no constructive alternatives to them. "When people accept futility and the absurd as normal," he wrote, "the culture is decadent."

WE THE PEOPLE: WHO AND WHERE

No philosopher of the 1960s—when Barzun retired—could have written such words. It was a truism of the decade of student activism and the hippies' counterculture that the country was entering an era of beneficent social and cultural change. Intellectuals were celebrating the "generation gap" that, they said, yawned between the altruism, ideals, and values of youth and the materialism and timid conformism of their parents. This new generation was different. Young people were bored by consumer baubles and they scorned conformity. A revolution was underway.

In fact, the United States was at the beginning of a series of changes so considerable that it is reasonable, looking back, to call them revolutionary. But they were not the changes anticipated in the 1960s. No one predicted—no one could have foreseen—the changes in the very composition of the American population that the final decades of the millennium held in store.

Rust Belt and Sun Belt
In 1965, at the end of the baby boom, the population of the United States was 194,300,000; today it is about 304 million. Population growth was steady at 22 to 24 million each decade until the 1990s when it jumped to 32 million.

Growth was not uniform throughout the country. In the "snow belt"—the northern plains states and upper New England—and in the "rust belt," the one-time heartland of heavy industry bordering the Great Lakes—population growth lagged. In the "sun belt" that stretched from southern California through Texas to Florida, population soared.

For a century, the upper parts of the midwestern states plus much of Pennsylvania had been dedicated to "smokestack industry": iron manufacture, steelmaking, oil refining, the automobile industry, chemicals, rubber, glass, and the like. During the final decades of the century, however, one once mighty industrial corporation after another "downsized" or just shut down its plants, transforming the industrial heartland into the rust belt.

The Decline of Smokestack Industry

The decline of heavy industry had several causes. Where once the Carnegie Steels and Pennsylvania Railroads had embraced new technologies to keep their enterprises vital, by the 1960s, the factories in many industries had not been updated for decades. American companies could not compete with the modern facilities of their European and Japanese competitors. By 2000, Japan was losing markets to Taiwan, Korea, and Indonesia.

Conforming to new antipollution standards required reinvesting profits that would otherwise be dividends, a diversion of dollars that boards of directors were unwilling to approve. Employees were as short-sighted as shareholders. Their powerful industrial unions almost always rejected proposals that their members' wages be frozen for a few years in the interests of updating machinery. Unions fought against new technologies that would eliminate jobs. Frazzled executives could hardly fail to notice that there was more money to be made more easily in "clean" businesses—finance and high-tech—telecommunications and computers, than in dirty manufacturing.

The consequences for the inhabitants of the rust belt were dramatic. Factory workers who had assumed they were secure as employees of mammoth Chrysler Corporation, Bethlehem Steel, and Firestone Rubber were let go by the tens of thousands, sometimes with no warning. Even the Pennsylvania Railroad and New York Central, once the best-managed railways in the world, were crippled by the decline in freight from shippers. The two companies merged in an attempt to survive and, two years later, Penn-Central declared bankruptcy.

Bound for the Southland

Retailers on the Main Streets of one-company industrial towns—from grocers to barbers—and doctors and lawyers with offices on the side streets—padlocked their doors and joined their former customers, patients, and clients in an exodus to Florida, Texas, Arizona, and California. Devastated tax revenues in the rust belt crippled schools and municipal services, encouraging more emigration.

The Dakotas, eastern Montana, Nebraska, and Kansas stagnated as family farmers gave up trying to compete with finely integrated agribusiness corporations. They sold their acres to the big companies and joined the trek to the sunny south, but not to new farms. Each year of the 1970s and 1980s, America's farm population declined by 2.5 to 3 percent. As many as 240,000 farm folk abandoned agriculture each year.

College graduates in snow-belt Maine, New Hampshire, and Vermont went home after the ceremonies just long enough to say goodbye to parents and pack up mementos whence they took off for hi-tech or service industry jobs in the sun belt, some of which paid as much as the head of the class at Harvard Law was offered on Wall Street.

Demographics and Democrats The growth of the sunbelt states and the stagnation of population in the rust belt was a big part of the Democratic party's decline in the final decades of the millennium—and the growth of a small-minded Republican party.

Few could imagine such a reversal of fortune in 1965 when the Democratic party looked to be in for a very long run as the governing party. Lyndon B. Johnson had just been reelected president with 61 percent of the vote; his conservative opponent had dragged the Republicans down to the worst defeat in the party's history. Democratic congressmen outnumbered Republicans 295 to 140; there were 68 Democratic senators to 32 Republicans.

In fact, 1965 was the Democrats' apex. It was downhill for the party for the rest of the century. Beginning in 1966, slowly in Congress, emphatically in presidential elections, the Republican party rose to be the nation's majority party. The transfer of power was gradual but sufficiently traumatic for the Democrats that, virtually to date, their party has been paralyzed, with no alternatives to Republican policies to offer.

The causes of the rise and increased conservatism of the Republican party were several. Most important was the Republican capture, *in toto,* of the "Solid South" because of the Democrats' support of civil equality for African Americans. What had been a bloc of congressmen and electoral votes on which Democratic political strategists could build became the Republicans' starting line. The rise of the "religious right"—dozens of television preachers and thousands of ministers urging their

TABLE 51.1

The Ten Largest Cities 1880–2000

1880	1920	1960	2000
New York	New York	New York	New York
Philadelphia	Chicago	Chicago	Los Angeles
Brooklyn	Philadelphia	Los Angeles	Chicago
Chicago	Detroit	Philadelphia	Houston
Boston	Cleveland	Detroit	Philadelphia
St. Louis	St. Louis	Baltimore	Phoenix
Baltimore	Boston	Houston	San Antonio
Cincinnati	Baltimore	Cleveland	San Diego
San Francisco	Pittsburgh	Washington	Dallas
New Orleans	Los Angeles	St. Louis	San Jose

Aside from New York, a constant, the "standings" of American cities by size of population has been in constant flux. None has slipped in the last century as much as St. Louis, among the "top ten" as recently as 1960, now not in the "top fifty." Philadelphia, America's second city throughout the nineteenth century, and third through the first half of the twentieth, is projected not to be in the "top ten" in 2010.

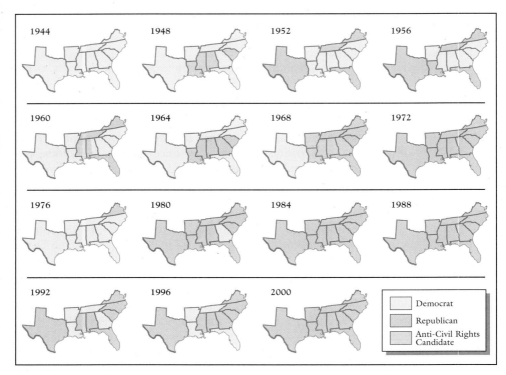

MAP 51.1 The South Changes Parties, 1944–2000

Between 1880 and 1944, the former Confederate states voted Democratic. Racism was the reason. Very few black southerners, who were Republican, voted. Aside from eastern Tennesseeans, an overwhelming majority of whites voted Democratic because it was the party of "white supremacy." With occasional exceptions (such as in 1928), electoral college maps of the southern states from 1880 to 1940 were the 1944 map shown here. The South was "solid."

Racism was also the chief reason why, beginning in 1948, the southern states began to drift away from the Democratic party and, by the end of the century, to line up unanimously in the Republican column. In 1948, the Democrats adopted a plank in their platform calling for legislation to protect the civil rights of African Americans. In protest, a majority of voters in four states of the deep South supported a "Dixiecrat" candidate. Never again, to date, have the former Confederate states voted solidly Democratic. Dwight D. Eisenhower's status as a hero probably had as much to do with his victories in the South as race. However, race alone accounted for George Wallace's successes in 1968. By 1972, the Republicans swept the South by wooing Wallace supporters with the party's tacit disapproval of the civil rights revolution.

In 1976, Democratic candidate Jimmy Carter came close to reviving the "Solid South" simply because he was the first born-and-bred southerner to run for president since Zachary Taylor in 1848. (But in 1980, he carried only his native Georgia.) In 1992 and 1996, when the Democrats nominated southerners for both president and vice president, they won just enough southern electoral votes to carry the elections. By 2000, however, the reversal of southern white political allegiances was complete, even as overt, unembarrassed racism was no longer acceptable in the former Confederacy.

followers to vote Republican as a sacred duty—added millions of former New Deal Democrats to the Republican column. The Democrats alienated many Catholic voters otherwise suspicious of locking arms with Protestant fundamentalists by the party's zealous support of in-your-face abortion rights and "gay rights" activists.

New Political Numbers   The votes of the northeastern states and the industrial Midwest, especially the big cities, were as important to the Democratic party as the Solid South. They usually vote Democratic to this day, but they do not carry the political weight they once did. In the 1960s, the Northeastern states (excluding Republican Vermont) and the industrial midwestern states cast 252 votes in the electoral college (269 elected the president). The southwestern states (excluding Democratic Texas) cast 74 electoral votes.

Since 2000, the Northeastern states (including a now Democratic Vermont) have had 166 electoral votes. Ohio, Indiana, and Illinois now lean Republican with Republican rural counties usually able to outvote the Democratic "rust belt" counties that border the Great Lakes. The southwestern states—Republican except California—now cast 137 electoral votes, and Florida, big as well as sunny, has added 29 electoral votes to the Republican column as often as not.

In 1965, five of the nation's ten largest cities were in the Northeast, three in the industrial Midwest. All of them were beginning to lose population while communities of middling size in Florida and the Southwest were beginning to sprawl into conurbations of suburbs that lacked a core but were nonetheless cities—some of them quite large. During the 1960s, only two of the ten largest cities were in the West and South: traditionally Republican Los Angeles and Houston, a Democratic stronghold then being republicanized by the civil rights issue and the energetic leadership of a young George H. W. Bush.

In 2009, only two of the top ten cities were Northeastern (New York and Philadelphia); only one is Midwestern (Chicago). The remaining seven were in California, Arizona, and Texas.

The most striking political illustration of the geographical reshuffling of population was in the changing apportionment of seats in the House of Representatives. Between 1965 and 2009, Democratic Pennsylvania's representation in the House declined from thirty seats to nineteen, New York's from forty-three to twenty-nine. In sharp contrast, California sent thirty representatives to Congress during the 1960s; today, California has fifty-three representatives. Texas's representation increased from twenty-two to thirty-two during the same period, Florida's from eight to twenty-five, more than Pennsylvania.

Newcomers

No one in 1965 could have foreseen the revived importance of immigration in American life. President John F. Kennedy was thinking history when he called the United States a "nation of immigrants" because it was no longer true. In 1963, when Kennedy was murdered, less than one American in twenty was foreign-born, the smallest proportion of immigrants in the population ever. In the 1960s, the United States was a nation of natives.

America
Americanized
Immigration to the United States was reduced to a trickle by, first, the Chinese Exclusion Act of 1882. The Immigration Act of 1924 dammed up the stream of new immigrants from Italy, Greece, Poland, and other Eastern European countries by establishing very small quotas as to how many people from each of those countries would be admitted each year.

During the 1930s, the Immigration and Naturalization Service (INS) recorded only 500,000 arrivals, fewer in ten years than in any single year between 1900 and 1920. During the 1940s, despite the repeal of the Chinese Exclusion Act and several congressional acts providing sanctuary for World War II refugees, just 1 million immigrants arrived.

With few new arrivals to refresh the cultures of the several "old countries," big city ethnic communities shrunk as second and third-generation ethnics assimilated, married out of their group, and moved away. By the 1960s, Americans speaking a language other than English as their first language could be found only on the borders of Quebec (French), Mexico (Spanish), and in the remnants of urban ethnic ghettos. Even the teenage children of Mexicans in Los Angeles prefered to speak English among themselves.

Immigration
Reform
President Johnson found the ethnic discrimination in immigration law embarrassing. While his Great Society was ending institutionalized discrimination against African Americans, the United States was turning immigrants away on the basis of their nationality. Johnson called immigration policy "a cruel and enduring wrong in the conduct of the American nation."

The Immigration and Nationality Act of 1965 was designed to right the wrong without returning to the unrestricted immigration of the nineteenth and early twentieth centuries. It set the number of immigrants admitted each year slightly higher than they were in 1964, 170,000 annually for the countries of the Eastern Hemisphere, 120,000 for the peoples of the Americas. But applicants were approved on a first-come, first-served basis with no reference to race or national origins. (Would-be immigrants who had family already residing in the United States were given special preference.)

Critics of the act—they were few—said that a swarm of impoverished nonwhites would take jobs away from Americans and upset the nation's ethnic balance. Senator Edward Kennedy of Massachusetts replied that the act "will not flood our cities with immigrants. It will not upset the ethnic mix of our society. It will not relax the standards of admission. It will not cause American workers to lose their jobs."

Desperate
Millions
Kennedy might have been right on target had it not been for the war in Vietnam that was being escalated as he spoke. In 1965, the Johnson administration and most Americans believed that the conflict would be over quickly. Instead, it dragged on and, under President Nixon, was expanded, engulfing the whole of Indochina: Laos, Cambodia, and Thailand as well as Vietnam.

When the South Vietnamese government collapsed in 1975, the havoc created the most serious refugee problem since World War II. Within ten years, 3 million

Indochinese fled their homes. In addition to Cambodians and Laotians already in camps in Thailand petitioning the United States for refuge, pro-American Vietnamese fled, many of them paying their life's savings to Communist officials to allow them to go. The Hmong, a tribal mountain people who had been American allies, fled from Vietnam, Laos, and Cambodia. Long persecuted by every other Indochinese people, they faced mass murder by the criminal Pol Pot regime and a scarcely better fate at the hands of the North Vietnamese.

The instability spread beyond Indochina. Malaysians attacked long-established communities of "overseas Chinese." Unpopular throughout Asia because of their clannishness and success in business—they were called the "Jews of Asia"—overseas Chinese in Indochina and Malaysia, mostly, petty capitalists, had little interest in emigrating to the China their grandparents had left.

Congress acknowledged America's share of responsibility for the plight of the refugees by enacting special legislation in 1980 and again in 1990. It authorized 1.4 million Indochinese to resettle in the United States and assisted them in getting here—which was essential; they were penniless. About 900,000 were Vietnamese. Today, there are about 270,000 Hmong (immigrants and their American-born children) in the United States, 200,000 Lao, and 200,000 Thais. (Philippine-Americans remain the largest Asian-American ethnic group.)

America's "ethnic balance" had been given a powerful jolt. In 1965, only 1 American in 100 was ethnically Asian. In 2009, 1 American in 20 was Asia born or of Asian descent. The anxiety of what a massive Asian immigration would mean to American culture, however, proved groundless. Indochinese immigrants avidly embraced American citizenship. By 2006, 72 percent of the foreign-born Vietnamese in the United States were naturalized citizens.

Cubanoamericanos   Before 1965, the only sizable Spanish speaking communities in the United States were the 800,000 or so Puerto Ricans in New York City and the more numerous, but constantly fluctuating Mexican-American population living throughout the southwestern states.

When Fidel Castro came to power in Cuba in 1959 and pointed the country toward socialism, a third large Hispanic community took shape. The first Cubans to flee were political refugees, friends of the regime Castro had overthrown. They settled in Miami, the traditional gathering place of Cuban exiles. Then came a wave of upper- and middle-class Cubans, educated professionals among them, fearful of losing their status and wealth if they stayed. Throughout the 1960s and 1970s, despite the difficulties of evading Cuban authorities, tens of thousands of Cubans made it to Florida each year. Because they were refugees from Communism, Congress welcomed them with generous financial assistance.

In 1980, with the Cuban economy struggling, Castro announced that anyone who wanted to leave, was free to do so. An estimated 120,000 fled via the so-called "Mariel Boatlift." Emigrants crowded daily into anything that floated, hoping to complete the 90-mile trip to Key West or, if they were lucky, to be plucked from sinking boats by the Coast Guard.

Today, about 1.25 million people are identified as *cubanoamericanos*. A large section of Miami is called "Little Havana" because its population is largely Cuban

"Vote for Me" placards in San Luis, Arizona. The Spanish names of the candidates seem to give the lie to the apprehensions of some Americans that the Mexican immigrants of the late twentieth century were not assimilating. Many of them clustered with other Mexicans, continued to speak Spanish, and picked up English only by accident. But so had the Italians, Yiddish-speaking Jews, Poles, Lithuanians, and other "new immigrant" groups of the late 1800s and early 1900s and, in three generations, the assimilation of their descendants was complete.

American. The earliest Cuban refugees considered their American sojourn temporary; they expected to return when Castro was overthrown. He was not, and with the anti-Castro zealots who are still alive few in number, not many Cuban Americans think about "going back." For the U.S.-born majority, Cuba is not their homeland. Cuban Americans, like the Vietnamese, have embraced American culture and, as a group, they have been remarkably successful economically and politically.

The Mexican Invasion   Mexicans, far and away the largest hispanic immigrant group in the United States, have been slower than Cubans to assimilate, largely because so many were single men who came to the United States, some illegally, to make money to send back to their families. Where ethnic communities were overwhelmingly male, individuals working as many hours as they could, and spending little, there was no incentive to learn English and little interest in American ways.

In cities with large Mexican populations and, therefore, families, assimilation was more likely. Parents of children born in the United States were more likely to apply for citizenship and to be inclined toward assimilation. When well-meaning but misguided California legislators mandated bilingual education in elementary schools with large numbers of Mexican pupils (some of their instruction in Spanish, some in English) a majority of Mexican parents protested. Their children spoke Spanish at home, they said; they wanted the schools to teach them English so they would be comfortable in the larger society of which they would be a part when they grew up.

**The Waning
of Racism**

The Mexican immigration caused more concern than any other because of the Mexicans' numbers, their extreme poverty, their lack of education and skills, and the illegal status of many. Racial differences, however, common in the 1960s when Mexicans were called "greasers" or "beaners," played virtually no part in the propaganda of groups advocating choking off the influx.

Nor was race an issue with the Asian immigration although, well into the 1960s, Chinese and Japanese had been objects of ridicule or contempt. It was difficult to think of Asians as incapable of being good Americans when, every year, Vietnamese and Chinese children were prominent in the finals of the National Spelling Bee, the National Geographic Society's annual geography quiz, and science fairs all over the country. Asians were proportionately more numerous in colleges and graduate schools than Caucasians.

Most significantly, white racism directed at African Americans, still institutionalized in the law in the 1960s, diminished so that, by 2000, it survived as acceptable only among marginal, uneducated whites.

Discrimination against blacks in employment, and housing was gone by 2000. Socially, whites and blacks mixed easily; interracial couples rarely drew stares. African American athletes were national heroes, black actors and actresses national favorites. In 2008, an African American senator capped it off when he was easily elected president. That anti-black racism, an American institution since the beginning, waned to insignificance in a few decades was the most encouraging social and cultural phenomenon of an era otherwise marked by troubling developments.

THE MOST RELIGIOUS COUNTRY

Americans are, by measurable standards, the Western world's most religious people. Far more Americans than Europeans say they believe in God; far more belong to a church and far more say that they attend religious services regularly. That is what they say. It is safe to conclude from the many polls and surveys that many more Americans than Europeans *believe* they are religious or want others to think that is so than is the fact.

**Catholicism:
Disguised
Decline**

In 2009, the Roman Catholic Church was, as it has been for a century, the largest denomination. Since 1965, Church membership has grown at the same rate as the nation's population. However, this was so only because many of the era's immigrants were Catholic: almost all the Mexicans, Central Americans, Cubans, Haitians, and Philippinos; and a large minority of the Vietnamese. The attachment of native-born Catholics to the Church declined sharply during the millennium years while respect for the Church's authority was shaken among those who did not depart.

In 1965, there were 58,000 priests and 180,000 nuns in the United States. At the end of the century there were just 45,000 priests and 75,000 nuns. Annual ordinations of priests were a third of what they had been. Fifteen percent of Catholic parishes were without a full-time priest compared to one in a hundred in the 1960s. In 1965, three of four Catholics heard mass weekly; in 2007, one in four did.

The collapse began with the Second Vatican Council of 1962–1965. The council scrapped practices to which ordinary Catholics had clung as comforting and as part of what made their faith unique: the Latin Mass, abstinence from meat on Fridays, and the like. Many felt betrayed by "Holy Mother Church" and left the Church in large numbers. Many of those who remained ceased to respect the Church's authority that they had believed was absolute. By 2000, Catholics were only slightly less likely to practice birth control as non-Catholics, to whom it was not forbidden.

Decay and Demoralization   Catholics were active in the divorce-remarriage mania of the late twentieth century. In this, the Church tried to accommodate them by freely granting annulments. Previously, every application for a Church annulment of a marriage had been rigorously reviewed. The procedure was lengthy and expensive. In 1965, the Church granted only 338 annulments in the United States. By 2000, bishops were handing them out as liberally as they distributed palm fronds on Palm Sunday, 50,000 a year.

In 2002, the Church was rocked by exposés of seminaries rife with homosexuality and of priests who, for decades, had sexually abused young boys and gone unpunished. It was revealed that the Cardinal Archbishop of Boston not only failed to punish child molesters among his priests but assigned them to positions where young boys would be exposed to them. This was unheard of before the 1960s when there was no shortage of priests and bishops had confidence in their authority. Then, priests with "problems" ranging from chronic drunkenness to keeping mistresses to pederasty were sent to remote, unpublicized Church rehabilitation centers.

Mainstream Protestantism   The millennium years were even harder on the mainstream Protestant churches. With few immigrants drawn to them, the traditionally most important American denominations declined in membership. The numbers of Disciples of Christ dropped by almost half between 1965 and 2000. Membership in the Episcopal Church declined by almost a third with a dispute over the consecration of an openly homosexual bishop threatening to split what was left in two. The United Church of Christ (the remnant of Congregationalism, of the Puritans) shrunk by 24 percent. Membership in the United Methodist Church declined by 20 percent, in the Presbyterian Church by 8 percent.

The mainstream denominations had in common their clergy's acceptance of scientific findings that contradicted the Bible read literally, a trend that began in the nineteenth century. Scripture was not, verbatim, the word of God and therefore not an inerrant revelation of truth and prescription of moral behavior. The Bible was a fount of inspiration and to some "liberal" Protestants, not even that.

The mainstream denominations abandoned doctrines once central to them, played down spirituality as superstition, and were embarassed by the emotionalism of those who claimed to have a personal relationship with God. They promoted their churches as providers of social services to the less fortunate. But with plenty of secular institutions serving those purposes, communicants abandoned the mainstream denominations by the tens of thousands, some to churchlessness, some to evangelical fundamentalist denominations that clung to "that old time religion" and offered emotional fulfillment.

Fundamentalism The one major denomination to grow during the post-1965 era was the Southern Baptist Convention which rejected the path taken by the mainstream churches. Indeed, liberal Baptist ministers and congregations were made to feel unwelcome after a fundamentalist takeover of church leadership in 1979. Most departed and the Southern Baptists shrugged off the defections. By clinging to the "fundamentals"—the literal truth of the Bible and the necessity of a personal relationship with God—they increased their membership by 60 percent in forty years.

The word *fundamentalism* was coined in 1910 by ministers troubled by the increasing acceptance of the geologists' calculations that the earth was millions of years old—a seventeenth-century bishop had dated the earth's creation in 4004 B.C.—and of Darwinian evolution, which contradicted the biblical account of the world's creation.

The early fundamentalists were enthusiastic in their support of Prohibition and in calling for state laws that forbade teaching evolution in public schools. But they were not part of a "religious right" doing the heavy lifting for the rich as fundamentalists were at the end of the century. On the contrary, their political hero was William Jennings Bryan, who was a lifelong foe of the power wielded by the rich and by big business. Bryan pioneered many of the reforms that, in the 1930s, were effected by Democratic party liberals, the "left." In the South and West, Franklin D. Roosevelt's New Deal depended on the votes of "poor white" fundamentalists.

The Lakewood Church in Houston, one of the very biggest of the "megachurches," at the grand opening in July 2005. Formerly the home of the Houston Rockets basketball team, Lakewood cost approximately $75 million to convert into a multistructure campus. The "chapel" can accommodate 16,000 people for Sunday services and often does.

Pentecostals   The fastest growing fundamentalist churches were the pentecostal denominations. The largest of them, the Assemblies of God, grew by 400 percent between 1960 and 1990. Membership in the Pentecostal Assemblies increased by 1000 percent. The Church of God in Christ had 393 churches in 1960, 5,500 in 1995; its membership had increased by 1300 percent.

The Pentecostals' name and distinctive beliefs are based on the New Testament account of the first pentecost (the fiftieth day after Easter). Christ's disciples were gathered in a room when the Holy Spirit descended on them in the form of tongues of fire. This "baptism of the Holy Spirit" gave those who were blessed with it the ability to "speak with new tongues."

Traditionally, this passage was interpreted to mean that the Holy Spirit enabled the early disciples to preach in languages they did not know in order to spread Christianity worldwide. The Pentecostals, who emerged in the first years of the twentieth century, believed that glossolalia (speaking in tongues) was sacred not as a missionary tool but because, however much it sounded like hysterical babbling to nonbelievers, it was miraculous evidence of the Holy Spirit's presence.

Pentecostals also believed in "faith healing," the ability of those full of the Holy Spirit to cure illness merely by laying their hands on the afflicted. Oral Roberts became a national celebrity in the 1950s when, on television, he healed supplicants who formed long lines to receive his touch. Roberts had been the first televangelist. Many of his most successful imitators were also pentecostals, notably Jimmy Swaggart and Pat Robertson although, because Roberts had been persuasively accused of fraud, they avoided faith healing and glossolalia on their telecasts.

The Religious Right   Jerry Falwell, a nonpentecostal televangelist, was a Baptist minister whose weekly program, the Old Time Gospel Hour, a mixture of gospel music, Falwell's preaching, and appeals for contributions, was very popular. In the late 1970s, Falwell took a political turn and founded the aggressively political Moral Majority. It was a coalition of political action committees that drew their support from people who were disturbed by social and cultural trends they regarded as immoral but which were reversible—if the moral majority of the population mobilized and voted as a bloc.

The Moral Majority's targets included the runaway increase in the number of divorces (which were undercutting the institutions of marriage and family); the sexual revolution (widespread acceptance of casual sexual intercourse); the Supreme Court's approval in *Roe* v. *Wade* (1973) of abortion on demand; and feminism generally (women had divinely ordained roles subordinate to men). Utterly beyond toleration was the just emerging "gay liberation movement," demands by homosexuals and their sympathizers that laws and practices discriminating against them be abolished and that homosexuality be accepted as an "alternate lifestyle."

The Moral Majority was effectively an arm of the Republican party. It was instrumental in Ronald Reagan's election victory in 1980 and the unexpected defeat of several veteran liberal Democratic senators. Republican party strategists whose chief interests were in cutting taxes for the wealthy and freeing big business and finance from government regulation recognized the value to them of the "religious right" and began actively to court fundamentalist and evangelical Protestants.

By 1990, there were thirty-six wholly religious cable channels and 1,300 radio stations. Most of the programming was strictly religious—Bible study, gospel singers—but many of them also featured right-wing political preachers. The most successful of the minister-politicians was Pat Robertson, whose *700 Club* on the Christian Broadcasting Network made him so famous that he was able to make a serious bid for the Republican presidential nomination in 1988.

OH BRAVE NEW AGE

Frances Trollope, the British author of a famous book in 1832 about the manners of Americans, was so nonplussed by the enthusiasm of Americans for outlandish religious beliefs that, she observed, if a Hindu holy man came to the United States, he would have a large following within months. Mrs. Trollope thought this was witty hyperbole. Had she been able to revisit the United States during the millennium years, she would have discovered that she had been a prophet. Americans by the tens of thousands were joining a mélange of cults, some with bona fide Hindu gurus.

Cults and Gurus   In the dictionary, a *cult* is a religious group, nothing more or less. In 1969, however, the word took on a sinister cast. Two grisly mass murders in Los Angeles were traced to the "Manson Family," a hippie commune headed by 35-year-old Charles Manson. Claiming to be the reincarnation of Jesus, Manson had something like total "mind control" over his followers. He ordered the killings, and they were carried out.

No other cult of the era was murderous but many, like the Manson Family, were spinoffs of the hippie episode. Most cult members were emotionally troubled teenagers, many of them runaways resentful of their parents and, they believed, rebels against society's materialistic values. With nothing of substance to substitute for the lives they rejected, they made "new values" of promiscuous sex and drugs and simply drifting. Manson had a sure eye for the type, boys and girls sitting listlessly on curbs or beaches, and he had a sweet, comforting, irresistible personality that any televangelist would have envied.

The cults of the era were "personality driven." They revolved around a compelling guru, an "enlightened teacher who brings light into darkness." Gifted gurus found drifting, dim adolescents easy prey to offers of a life of emotional security and fulfillment. They won control of their followers by similar methods. Recruits were isolated from the world outside the cult, especially from their families. In the midst of boys and girls like them who were already converted, gently and lovingly at first but then threateningly, through endless repetition, discussion of little else but their closed world, and peer pressure, they were instilled with an "us-versus-them" mentality and made to feel secure and psychologically at peace only in the commune or ashram.

Cults germinated like weeds in the millennium years. Some were lucrative enterprises for those who ran them.

The Family   The Children of God or Family of Love was founded in 1968
of Love   by a former minister of the Christian and Missionary Alliance, David Berg. He recruited his followers among religiously

inclined hippies—"Jesus Freaks"—by preaching biblical fundamentalism with a twist. Berg said that Jesus blessed sexual intercourse with anyone as long as a couple (or a writhing pile of Children of God) "did it" in his name. Girls were told to imagine that they were coupling with Christ.

Sometime after 1970, Berg introduced the evangelical technique of "flirty fishing." Female Children were sent out to trawl teenage hangouts and lure likely converts back to the commune by promising sex. Plenty of boys and young men came and some of them stayed. The Children of God continued to flourish even after two of Berg's daughters, his daughter-in-law, and several other former members accused him of sexually molesting them when they were prepubescent.

Deprogrammers Charges of that sort aroused already distraught parents of cultists to seek help in rescuing them. They turned to Ted Patrick, a well-known civil rights activist in southern California who called himself a deprogrammer. On television talk shows, he said that gurus like Berg brainwashed their members, systematically destroying their sense of self and transforming them into docile, obedient zombies. For a fee, Patrick and helpers "snatched" (Patrick's word) Children of God and other cultists off the street and even from their communes. They took them forcefully to a motel room where they subjected them to a deprogramming that was a mirror image of the cults' technique. Patrick's successes in restoring cult members to their families brought him more business than he could handle, and he soon had imitators.

The deprogrammers were on safe legal ground despite the snatching and forced detention if their subjects were younger than 18 and therefore legally subject to their parents' authority. Deprogrammers could work on cultists 18 and older if the parents could convince a judge that their children were mentally unfit to care for themselves and named the parents their legal conservators.

In the mid-1970s, when exposés of sordid cult practices were staples in newspapers and on television talk shows, it was not difficult to win conservatorships. By the end of the decade, however, when the American Civil Liberties Union and other organizations intervened on behalf of cult members, Patrick was successfully sued and, in one case, sentenced to a year in jail on criminal charges.

Rama, Rama, Ted Patrick specialized in Hare Krishnas, members of the
Hare, Hare Society for Krishna Consciousness. Unlike the Children of God, they practiced a strict sexual morality, shunned tobacco, alcohol, and coffee, and were vegetarians. They proselytized openly, walking the streets of cities in groups dressed in eye-catching orange robes, banging on tambourines and ceaselessly chanting the cult's mantra (sacred syllables) that, like an advertising jingle, planted itself in the heads of many who heard it.

Hare Krishna Hare Krishna,
Krishna Krishna Hare Hare,
Hare Rama Hare Rama,
Rama Rama, Hare Hare.

People found them amusing rather than worrisome. In fact, their religion was acceptable Hinduism, which encompasses a great variety of practices. Hare Krishnas attracted the interest of authorities only when defectors revealed that the cult used members as unpaid labor on the society's farms, at their vegetarian restaurants, and in other profit-making businesses. The Hare Krishnas were then accused of making slaves by brainwashing them. Nevertheless, deprogrammers backed off in 1983 when a California court awarded a snatched Hare Krishna $32 million for false imprisonment. (The Supreme Court upheld the decision but reduced the damages.)

Overreaching The Baghwan Shree Rajneesh was a retired professor who, some years before he came to the United States, had founded a lucrative ashram (a commune of believers) in India. He may or may not have used his disciples as unpaid labor. Most of his considerable income came from the gifts of the tens of thousands who, each year, visited the ashram.

In 1981, the Baghwan purchased 64,000 acres in thinly populated Wasco county, Oregon. He attracted several thousand mostly American disciples to Rajneeshpuram. They were generally older than the Children of God and certainly had more money. The hook that caught them was the Baghwan's encouragement of wild sex and plenty of it.

The Baghwan himself seemed to do little but take daily rides in one of the Rolls Royces his followers had given him, waving at them as they were doing what they did. (He owned 74 or 93 Rolls Royces—the sources differ. The Rajneeshis' goal was to increase his collection to 365, one for each day of the year.)

When, in a local election, the Rajneeshpuram faithful outvoted the more conventional residents of Antelope, Oregon, the trouble began. The Baghwan's second-in-command, Ma Anand Sheelah, an American *née* Sheila Silverman, went out of her way to antagonize and bully the ashram's neighbors and summarily expelled Rajneeshis who mildly questioned her commands. With evidence to back up their accusations, several of the exiles said that Ma had tried to murder the Baghwan's doctor and, in order to demonstrate to the locals that she "meant business," contaminated the salad bars of restaurants in The Dalles, the county seat, with salmonella bacteria. At least a dozen people were infected.

Ma fled abroad, but she was extradited and convicted of attempted murder and served three years of a twenty-year sentence in prison. The Baghwan pled guilty to immigration fraud and was deported. After twenty countries refused to admit him, he returned to India where, fifteen years after his death, his ashram is still going strong.

The Moonies The most successful cult of the era was the Unification Church, the creation of a Korean, Sun Myung Moon. In 2008, Moon claimed a worldwide following of 3 million. Outside observers said that the true figure was closer to 250,000, but even that dwarfed the membership rolls of any other cult. (Worldwide, most "Moonies," a name they did not like, were Korean and Japanese.)

Moon was a fundamentalist Christian who claimed that God had named him to complete the work of Jesus. In the United States, the Moonies first attracted attention in the 1970s when, indistinguishable from hippies in appearance, they raised money at large airports by blocking the way of hurrying travelers and offering them a flower— usually badly wilted—in return for a donation. It was the peak of the brainwashing scare and the Moonies fit the bill. They smiled robotically, their eyes glazed as if they were drugged. Many, perhaps most travelers they accosted, were so discomfited that they dug out their pocket change just to get away.

Moon's mind control of them was pretty well demonstrated by several mass weddings of thousands of brides and grooms in Seoul and at New York's Madison Square Garden. The couples—Moon did the pairings—were introduced only minutes before the ceremonies.

The Republican Party Cult Several writers investigated and wrote about Moon. None satisfactorily explained how he parlayed a cult of teenagers into a huge commercial and financial conglomerate. Surely he did not turn the trick with dimes and quarters extorted from air travelers. Nevertheless, by 1982, when Moon spent a year in federal prison for tax evasion, he owned farms, fishing fleets, and canneries in at least three states; companies manufacturing firearms and other products; banks, and real estate empires on three continents. He admitted to spending $830 million to found and develop the Washington *Times* to compete with the capital's liberal Washington *Post*.

Moon was a far right conservative who contributed generously to the Republican party. He hired prominent Republicans as lobbyists, paying one retired senator to be his congressional lobbyist for, Democrats alleged, $50,000 a month. The party embraced him, somehow taking him into the tent with the religious right to whom, as a blasphemer, Moon might have been seen as anathema. However, as someone has said, money talks.

New Age One expert on cults estimated that only about 30,000 mostly young Americans passed through cloistered cults like the Children of God and the Hare Krishnas. Much more numerous were those who embraced one or another manifestation of "New Age," self-styled as a "New Global Movement Toward Spiritual Development, Health and Healing, Higher Consciousness, and Related Subjects."

Although rooted in the counterculture of the 1960s, New Age peaked in influence in the 1980s and 1990s with outposts ranging from shops in strip malls to Sedona, a wealthy community in Arizona's red rock country where there was a concentration of spiritually energizing "vortexes" to which New Agers flocked. A more economical destination for New Agers was Marfa, Texas, which offered dancing lights in the nocturnal sky.

Alternative Lifestyle New Age meant "transformative experiences." It was "spiritual" not "religious," a word New Agers disliked, associating it with passé Western religions, Christianity and Judaism. New Agers rejected as much of convention and tradition and mainstream American lifestyle as it was convenient to discard while holding jobs and living within society.

New Agers embraced almost anything novel and non-Western, the primitive, anything that could be defined as "alternative." Rather than take a throbbing toe to a physician, New Agers sought out Holistic practitioners, Vedantic healers, counselors at vegetarian grocery stores, masseuses of a dozen schools, acupuncturists, aroma therapists, herbalists. Some pored over the works of (nonbiblical) prophets like the sixteenth-century Michel de Nostradumus and the twentieth-century Edgar Cayce. Others subscribed to supernatural or extraterrestrial explanations of flying saucers, plane crashes, puzzling noises in the cellar, and dreams they had of being tucked into bed with Marie Antoinette.

New Age needed no publicity department. With the proliferation of cable television, regiments of television reporters assigned to fill airtime with cheaply produced programming sought out New Agers for interviews and documentaries. New Age books were published by the hundreds of titles annually. New Age art (sunsets, misty mountains) adorned New Age calendars and tea cups. New Age music (twanging sitars, not much melody) was the Muzak of thousands of New Age shops selling the books and recordings along with Sixties drug paraphernalia, tarot cards, distilled scents, divination bones, and crystals possessing "powers."

New Age was not political. However, because it could be dabbled in by people who had jobs, lived within society, mated (in "new equalitarian relationships"), and raised children (with a "new openness"), the New Age mentality penetrated American culture as the cults did not. New Agers who were interested in public affairs inclined to be liberals and supported the causes that repulsed and mobilized the religious right.

CYBERAMERICA

In the early twentieth century, the automobile revolutionized Americans' daily lives. At midcentury, television worked social and cultural changes so far-reaching that, by 1965, few people could remember (or wanted to remember) what their days were like without it. In the 1990s, the home computer hooked up to the World Wide Web—the Internet—reshaped daily life in America as profoundly and quickly as cars and television had done.

From the Army to Alma Mater The basic principles of the computer, a device that crunches lots of big numbers very rapidly, were understood by mathematicians in the nineteenth century. During World War II, American and British scientists experimented with proto-computers for the military; for example, to calculate instantly the trajectory of an artillery projectile so that it returned to earth in an ammunition dump rather than a dairy farm. The breakthrough machine, ENIAC, was not finished until 1946, too late to go to war.

But not too late for government and business, which also dealt with big numbers and complex mathematics. In 1951, the developers of ENIAC perfected UNIVAC, which could be manufactured and sold. Within a few years, several companies, led by International Business Machines Corporation (IBM) were selling computers to corporations, government agencies, and universities. The "IBM card," the means by which data was fed into computers, became the symbol of new technology.

At first, many people were vaguely troubled by the new experience of blacking out boxes instead of writing words when they applied for jobs, dealt with government agencies, and chose their courses at college; then waiting for a machine to convert their work into holes in IBM cards of which they could make no sense;

Steve Jobs (left) and Steve Wozniak, co-founders of Apple Computer Inc. at the unveiling of the Apple II computer in 1977. They developed the Apple I in Wozniak's garage and were millionaires within a year. Wozniak was the technological genius. Jobs was the salesman and promoter extraordinaire. The Apple corporation almost went under because of some bad business decisions but held on to become the most innovative maker of computer "hardware."

Tom Munnecke/Hulton Archive/Getty Images

then carrying the cards to a clerk who could make no sense of them either. Only the machines understood them. Were computers going to rule the world? Science fiction writers churned out tales of societies in which they did. The masterpiece of the genre was a film of 1968, *2001: A Space Odyssey*, in which the villain was HAL, a computer on a space ship that spoke in a voice that was simultaneously soothing and sinister.

Bringing HAL Home

Despite *2001* (and the declaration in 1977 of the president of Digital Equipment Corporation that "there is no reason anyone would want a computer in their home"), Americans began to adopt little HALs. Two "techno-nerds" in California, Steve Wozniak and Steve Jobs, began to sell the affordable Apple computer, which they had invented in a garage.

Apples might have become the world standard except for bad business decisions and IBM's vast marketing network. In 1981, the company purchased Disk Operating System (DOS) from a nerd who had effectively stolen it, Bill Gates. IBM's consumer computers running DOS sold as soon as they were put on the market. In a trice there were 2 million desktop computers in American homes and innumerable nerds were churning out "software," programs to put home computers to work at practical jobs and running entertaining games.

The Internet

The Internet, the instantaneous linkage of computers worldwide over (at first) telephone lines, was, like the computer, developed for the military. However, it was turned over to the National Science Foundation for civilian use in 1990. With the runaway growth of the World Wide Web, anyone who was "online" could, by typing a "search" word, gain access to a new kind of communication and a world of mostly free information.

The Web also opened up what seemed to be infinite commercial possibilities. People could book airline tickets and hotel rooms or buy just about anything sold anywhere in the world from a corner of the kitchen. Internet companies called "dot-coms" after the suffix on most Web sites (.com) sprung up, their owners sanguine they would take over retailing from shops and mail-order catalog companies. More than 300 dot-coms issued stock in 1998 and 1999. Web sites that provided services or information free told investors they would reap huge dividends from advertisers paying to have their commercial messages flashed on millions of computer screens.

The Bubble   Nine percent of American households were on the Internet in 1996 when the Web began its commercial takeoff, 20 percent in 1998, 50 percent by 2001. How could investors lose? Capital rushed to any enterprise connected with the Web: "breathe the word 'Internet' around a stock, and anything can happen." In 1996, the value of stock in Yahoo! rose 153 percent in one day. Other "start-up" companies had similarly giddy experiences.

Nothing like it had happened since the Coolidge bull market. But in so heady an atmosphere, it was no more acceptable to mention 1929 than it was to discuss venereal disease at a college beer party. Bill Gates, whose "Windows" had made him "the world's richest man," wrote in 1995 that "Gold rushes … encourage impetuous investments. A few will pay off, but when the frenzy is behind us, we will look back incredulously at the wreckage of failed ventures and wonder, 'who founded these companies? What was going on in their minds?'"

He may have been thinking of www.doodoo.com, which, for $19.95, delivered a box of horse manure to any address in America. Others less ridiculous should also have given investors pause: Dot-coms that made restaurant reservations (why not the telephone?) and took orders for the week's milk, eggs, and Cheez-its (easier than ten minutes at the supermarket?). And there were simply too many heavily capitalized dot-coms competing in very limited markets, such as wine and cigar dealers, for example.

Bust   The prices of "old technology" stocks followed high-tech issues up the mountain (which also had its precedent in the 1920s). The New York Stock Exchange index, 2,365 in 1990, rose to more than 11,000 in ten years—400 percent. The market peaked in March 2000, tottered for a few months, then collapsed, led by the bursting of the Internet bubble. Dot-coms folded by the hundreds, some because they were absurd enterprises from their inception, some because their directors squandered capital on advertising and on their own grotesque salaries.

The Internet advertising bonanza did not materialize. "Web surfers" had learned years earlier that one went to the bathroom during television commercials. They had no trouble not noticing ads on their computers. Capitalized at $135 million, AllAdvantage.com assured advertisers their spiels would be seen because AllAdvantage would *pay* Internet users 50¢ for every hour that ads streamed across the bottom of their screens. Two million people signed up. In three months, AllAdvantage collected $10 million from advertisers and paid its members $40 million.

In 2000, less than 1 percent of American retail sales were made online. In early 2001, the shares of a third of dot-coms devoted to huckstering were valued at less than $10. An Internet company selling fine wines, in which suckers had invested $200 million, dismissed 235 of 310 employees in January 2001 and was foreclosed by creditors in April. Internet use continued to increase but, perhaps dismaying to those who had envisioned a noble cyber-America, the category of Web site getting the most hits was pornography.

BUSINESS CULTURE

Greed is what makes people rush into bubbles like the dot-com insanity instead of pausing to think. The millennium years—and the years since 2000—were an age of greed. Its prophets were several writers of the 1970s, including Robert Ringer, who published *Looking Out for Number One* in 1978. Its frankest proponent was *Wall Street's* Ivan Boesky who told university students in 1986 that "Greed is good. You can be greedy and still feel good about yourself."

The Age of Greed began in 1980 with the election to the presidency of Ronald Reagan. His administration slashed the taxes the wealthiest Americans paid and freed big corporations from much of the government oversight that the New Deal had instituted and rapacious exploiters of natural resources from conservation policies dating back to Theodore Roosevelt. None of Reagan's successors in the White House, least of all the one Democrat, Bill Clinton, entertained reversing the "Reagan Revolution."

Greed Is Good   The founders of dot-coms that never showed even the promise of profit nevertheless paid themselves annual salaries of $500,000 and more out of start-up capital up to the week the company cash reserve ran dry. The executives of pretty much every big corporation in the country increased their salaries repeatedly at the expense of the shareholders for whom they ostensibly worked. In 1980, the salaries of CEOs (the chief executive officers of corporations) were forty times the average salaries of their company's employees. In 2000, the ratio was 474:1. By way of comparison, British CEOs were paid twenty-four times the average employee's compensation, French CEOs fifteen times, and Swedish CEOs thirteen times.

John D. Rockefeller and the Vanderbilts were called "robber barons." Rockefeller was indeed ferocious with competitors. William Vanderbilt, when asked about the public's interest in how his New York Central was run, replied "The public be damned!" But neither dreamed of stealing from those who owned stock in their companies.

Stockholders were the favored prey of corporate executives of the millennium years. The more or less honest ones obscenely overpaid themselves. More than a few of the "giants of American business" whose photographs were run in magazines like *Forbes* and *Time* encouraged investment for the purpose of stealing it. The top executives of Enron, an energy broker, stole or destroyed $67 billion of its capital. Stockholders in WorldCom (telecommunications) lost $9 billion to theft and $140 billion in the value of their holdings, all covered up for five years by company accountants so more investors could be wooed.

Webvan squandered $1.2 billion in start-up capital, much of it going into the pockets of the company's executives. Two weeks before Webvan declared bankruptcy, wiping out other investors, its founder sold his shares at a personal profit of $2.7 million.

Feeling Good about Incompetence
There was no penalty for being an incompetent business executive. In April 2001, hours before the Pacific Gas and Electric Company filed for bankruptcy, the corporation paid all its top executives big bonuses as rewards for their splendid work. Coca Cola's CEO, after supervising the loss of $4 billion, was given a severance check for $18 million. American Telephone and Telegraph fired CEO John Walther after nine months because he "lacked intellectual leadership." Nevertheless, AT&T wrote him a final check for $26 million. Under the management of Jill Barron, a toy manufacturer, Mattel, lost $2.5 billion. She joined the line at the unemployment office with $40 million in severance pay and bonuses in her purse.

Academia in the Age of Greed
Reading about the astronomical salaries corporate executives drew, university administrators began to pay themselves very well too. The annual salary of President Mark G. Yudoff of the University of Texas was $787,000. John W. Shumaker of the University of Tennessee "earned" $735,000 a year. Manuel Esteban, president of California State University-Chico complained to a reporter that he was underpaid and due for a raise before he had put in a semester's work.

Education moguls prepared well at taxpayer expense for their golden years and so that they could build up the estates they would bequeath their children. In 1992, David Gardner retired from the presidency of the University of California after nine years service. His pension was to be $60,000 a year. However, his subordinates arranged with the state legislature—both political parties agreeing—to present Gardner with a parting check for $797,000 and annual payments of $126,000 of taxpayer money.

Gardner was 59; why did he retire so young? Because, he explained, he could not carry on with his wife recently deceased. She had always been by his side during his nearly annual trips to Hawai'i to check up on the university's astronomical observatory there.

Fortuitously, with only $345 in pension money coming in each day, Gardner found a retirement job with an $825 million foundation which, apparently, he could handle without his late wife's companionship.

52

ONLY YESTERDAY
Politics and the Economy 1993–2009

*Americans have no political ideas. They follow leaders
who attract them or know how to manage them. The
kind of political leaders they like are human circuses.*

—William Graham Sumner

*Some great and glorious day, the plain folks of this land
will reach their heart's desire at last and the White
House will be adorned by a downright moron.*

—H. L. Mencken

In 1994, when physicians confirmed that Ronald Reagan had been stricken by Alzheimer's disease, his wife shut him up away from the public. Nevertheless, during his long confinement and since his death, Reagan's person has continued to loom over American politics, just as the ghost of Franklin D. Roosevelt had for a generation after his death. Republican politicians invoked Reagan's name as reverently as liberal Democrats once traded on FDR's legacy.

Every Republican who sought the party's presidential nomination between 1988 and 2008 claimed to be the heir of the Great Communicator. They were highly selective in the principles of Reaganism they remembered. None paid much attention to Reagan's advocacy, at the end of his presidency, of nuclear disarmament and forbearance with the Soviet Union. But they all knew by heart the powerful spell: *lower taxes, lower taxes.*

THE CLINTONS

Many believed that George H. W. Bush lost his bid for reelection in 1992 because, having told voters, "read my lips: no new taxes," Reagan's irresponsible financial policies caught up with him and he had to ask Congress for an increase.

The Democrat who defeated Bush in 1992, William Jefferson "Bill" Clinton, needed no lessons about how Americans felt about taxes. During his first term as governor of Arkansas, he sponsored an increase in the state motor vehicle tax—the cost of license plates!—and he was not reelected. Clinton promptly remade himself.

Politics 1993–2009

1990	1995	2000	2005	2010

1993–2001 William J. Clinton president

George W. Bush president 2001–2009

1994 Clinton health care reform fails; Republicans win majorities in both houses of Congress

1995 Republican attempt to neutralize Clinton fails

1998 House of Representatives impeaches president

2000 Supreme Court resolves disputed election in Florida

2001 "9/11" terrorist attack saves Bush presidency

2003 Iraq war begins

Barack Obama wins hotly contested Democratic presidential nomination 2008

He was no longer a "liberal." He was a "New Democrat." Like President Reagan, he became a devoted friend of business and a sworn enemy of higher taxes. As a New Democrat, Clinton was elected governor for a decade.

High Achiever   He was born William Jefferson Blythe in 1946, a posthumous child; his father died in an automobile accident shortly before his appearance. When his mother remarried in 1950 and moved to Hot Springs, people naturally enough called him "Billy Clinton" after his stepfather. As a teenager, he legally adopted Clinton as his surname.

Not that he admired his stepfather. Roger Clinton was a drunk who regularly battered Bill's mother. But Clinton suffered none of the psychological traumas associated with growing up in a dysfunctional home. He was a model student, good-natured, and sociable. He was popular, the highest attainment of adolescence. Ever striving for recognition, able to wriggle out of embarrassments with ease, and snapping back resiliently from setbacks were to characterize his career.

Clinton graduated from Georgetown University and won a prestigious Rhodes Scholarship—a year's paid study at Oxford University with few demands beyond making the acquaintance of future members of the British elite. In England he participated in anti-Vietnam demonstrations but, with his political ambitions well-formed, he took care to be inconspicuous. Just as quietly in letters to the United States, he explored ways to dodge military service.

Hillary Rodham   At Yale University's School of Law, Clinton met and set up housekeeping with fellow student Hillary Rodham, who also had big ambitions. Her background was rather different than Clinton's although not one in which he was uncomfortable. She was a midwesterner from a family several social notches above the smoking, drinking, card-playing Clintons of Little Rock. She was a Republican—an active one—when she matriculated at Wellesley. There she was surrounded by girls talking civil rights, protesting the Vietnam war, and groping their way toward feminism. She was soon conflicted, she told an advisor; she was "a mind conservative and a heart liberal." By the time she got to Yale Law, she was a certified Democrat of the political correctness persuasion.

A year after Bill graduated, the two married and established their residence in Arkansas: Bill's political career was their first priority and it took off with a bang when he was elected governor when just 32 years of age. Hillary practiced law with Little Rock's most prestigious firm. The temptations to exploit their ties—hot-shot lawyer and governor—must have been numerous. Except for one slip, however—and that ambiguous—they managed for ten years to avoid even the appearance of insider influence peddling.

Pleasing the Crowd

"New Democrats" like the Clintons were ultra-liberal on cultural and social issues. They were feminists, supported "A Woman's Choice" (abortion on demand), "gay rights," and so on. Bill Clinton's sympathy for African American causes was unreserved and sincere. After 1980, however, he was as big business-friendly as the Reagan Republicans and of one mind with them about taxation and government spending. He avoided spendy social programs that traditionally Democrats proposed. "The age of big government is over," he proclaimed.

In an electoral democracy, a politician who wants to win elections must be an opportunist, embracing causes that will win voters over. Clinton lived to win elections, and he appeared to critical Arkansans to lack any principle at all. "He'll be what people want him to be," one Little Rocker said. "He'll do or say what it will take to be elected."

He won the dubious nickname "Slick Willie" because of the ease with which he changed positions. With the emergence of the religious right in the 1980s, Clinton reactivated his identification as a Southern Baptist. He abandoned his opposition to the death penalty when it looked to hurt him at the polls and, at the small cost of arousing the ire of Hillary's social circle, he refused to commute the death sentences of several convicted murderers in the Arkansas state prison. When, as president, he ordered the military to cease discharging homosexuals and there was a noisy national reaction, Clinton quickly backed off. He changed his position to "don't ask, don't tell"—homosexuals in the army and navy should keep their proclivities to themselves and their superiors should not actively seek out homosexuals in the ranks. Characteristically, he described as new and up-to-date what had been unofficial army policy since George Washington was a major.

The Happy Schmoozer

Democrats of an earlier generation called their hero Al Smith the "Happy Warrior" because of his zest for politicking. Clinton surpassed him. He so delighted in making speeches that he had difficulty concluding them. As president he set the record for public appearances, twenty-eight each year compared to John F. Kennedy's nineteen and Herbert Hoover's eight. No prominent politician enjoyed schmoozing with the party faithful at fund-raising parties a fraction as much as he did.

Clinton's sole political weakness was a goatish sex drive he found difficult to control. He had at least one extended sexual affair when he was governor, and he liked to top off banquets and fund-raisers with a one-night stand with one of the political groupies who were fixtures at such events. Two Arkansas state troopers who served as Clinton's bodyguards later admitted that among their duties was watching hotel room doors when the governor was entertaining guests. His hobby was risky because rumors of it were a staple of gossip in Little Rock political circles. In 1992, Gennifer Flowers, an Arkansas state employee who was Clinton's longtime mistress, threatened his presidential campaign when she publicized their relationship complete with recorded phone conversations.

An Up and Down Co-Presidency

During the 1992 campaign, Clinton said that by voting for him, Americans would get "two for the price of one"—two co-presidents, Hillary and himself. When the popular response to this extra-constitutional innovation was unfavorable, he abandoned the slogan but not his intentions. One of his first acts as president was to name Mrs. Clinton to manage a health care reform bill.

A National Shame

Americans with good medical insurance enjoyed excellent health care—although at greater cost than the people of other nations. In 1993, annual per capita expenditure on medical care in the United States was $3,700. In Switzerland (the second most expensive country for doctors, hospitals, and drugs), the price tag was $2,644. Americans paid up to five times what Canadians, Europeans, and Japanese paid for prescriptions, including drugs manufactured in the United States.

About 39 million Americans were uninsured. Consequently, by virtually every public health index (infant mortality, death of women in childbirth), the United States ranked lower than every other developed nation and some third world countries—thirty-seventh in the world overall. Only Haiti and Bolivia had lower immunization rates.

Greed in the medical profession and in health care businesses was at the bottom of the anomaly. Pharmaceutical companies took profits of a thousand percent on their pills (on sales within the United States); manufacturers of medical hardware ranging from wheelchairs to CAT (computed axial tomography) scanners charged far more in the United States than they did in other countries. Any federal health care reform would necessarily have reduced the scale of the profiteering.

As a group, American medical students were more interested in big incomes than in the science of medicine or the service to others of medical practice. Most aspired to be specialists—"procedure men"—who worked a fraction of the hours general practitioners put in but took home several times their incomes. In Britain and Germany, 70 percent of physicians were primary care doctors, in Canada 51 percent. In the United States, just 13 percent of physicians were.

The health care bureaucracy, like bureaucracies in government, education, and corporations, was bloated with overpaid paper shufflers. The number of American physicians increased by half between 1983 and 1998. The number of "health care managers" increased 683 percent.

Hillary's Project

Harry S. Truman and Lyndon Johnson both tried to remedy a health care crisis far less serious than the one Clinton faced. They were foiled by the American Medical Association (the doctors' lobby) and the pharmaceutical and insurance companies. Republicans successfully denounced the plans they proposed as "socialistic," a never-fail line in American politics. So the Clintons did not consider proposing a genuinely socialized national health scheme like some of those in Western Europe.

They also rejected the nonsocialist health care system in neighboring Canada. Most Canadians liked their recently introduced "single payer" health insurance: Everyone who could afford them paid premiums; a consortium of insurance companies paid everyone's medical expenses according to a scale of fees the government judged reasonable. However, there were just enough well-publicized complaints by Canadians about long waits for some operations to provide the Republicans ammunition with which to frighten American voters who were insured.

Clinton tried to appease the insurance companies by leaving their independence and immense profits intact. In his plan, the federal government would subsidize the insurance companies in return for their agreement to apportion responsibility for the 39 million uninsured among them. Unfortunately, in trying to please big business as well as resolving the health care problem (and to disguise, as the income tax code did, the extent to which the government sanctioned profiteering), the Clinton bill was impossibly contrived, complicated, and

President Clinton delivering his State of the Union address in 1995, the year his popularity hit bottom. To the left is Albert Gore who, as vice president, was president of the Senate. To the right is the new Speaker of the House, Newt Gingrich, who engineered the Republican party's capture of Congress in 1994. He was about to launch a campaign to destroy Clinton's presidency, but it taught him that, as a political engineer, he was not in the president's league.

AP Photo/Ron Edmonds

convoluted. Even the articulate president could never clearly explain how the system would work. Congressional Republicans exploited the public's mystification by tacking dozens of amendments on the Clinton bill, transforming it from mere incoherence into gibberish.

Managing such a bill called for a veteran arm-twister like Lyndon Johnson. Hillary Clinton had no contacts in Congress; she was out of her depth. And she was unpopular, having got off to a bumpy start as First Lady. In a television interview, she boasted that she was not the kind of woman who stayed home and baked chocolate chip cookies. She actually sneered when she quoted a country-and-western lyric that called on the women of the republic to "stand by your man." At a stroke she had heaped contempt on women who baked for their children and believed (at least in principle) in spousal loyalty.

When her blunder was pointed out to her, Mrs. Clinton good-humoredly whipped up a batch of cookies for a visiting troop of visiting girl scouts and the TV cameras that accompanied them, but it would take her years to put to rest the public image of her as an obnoxious rich girl.

Midterm Setback

Clinton foundered during his first two years as president, burning his fingers with foolish appointments. A personal friend of Hillary Clinton he named Assistant Attorney General turned out to have authored an inane essay proposing that African Americans be granted multiple votes in elections as compensation for the oppression of their ancestors. In a speech, Clinton's Surgeon General said that the public schools should start teaching their pupils about masturbation.

In 1994, the Republicans won control of the Senate and—for the first time since 1952—the House of Representatives. Within a year, worried that Clinton's indiscretions would drag them down with him, 137 Democratic officeholders became Republicans, among them the Native American trophy senator from Colorado, Ben Nighthorse Campbell.

The new Speaker of the House, Newt Gingrich of Georgia, thought he saw an opportunity to repeat the Reagan revolution of 1980 with himself in the role of Republican presidential nominee. He called on the Republican majority in Congress to honor the "Contract with America" that he had drawn up before the 1994 election. It called for a three-fifths majority in Congress to increase taxes, reducing the number of House committees and the size of committee staffs, limiting the terms of committee chairmen, and opening all committee meetings to the public.

The Giddy but Brief Reign of Gingrich the First

Republican congressmen backed Gingrich because he had engineered the party's victory in 1994. Lacking Reagan's personality, however, he had little following in the country and, when he began to believe his own press releases—that he was as powerful as Clinton—he overreached and wrote a quick end to his glory days.

Gingrich called for cuts in spending on Medicare and Social Security. That was a mistake Reagan never made. It was one thing to pare expenditures on social programs that served the poor. Few of the poor people voted. Threatening programs valued by the elderly, however, was playing Russian Roulette. Mobilized by a powerful lobby, the America Association of Retired Persons, old people took voting seriously. Florida retirement communities chartered buses to get them to the polls en masse. The political center had given the Republicans control of Congress in 1994. Gingrich made a gift of the center to Clinton when he talked about economizing with Social Security and Medicare.

Late in 1995, Gingrich destroyed himself. Thinking of something like a coup d'état, he persuaded Congress to withhold operating expenses from the administration. Clinton had no choice but to lay off tens of thousands of federal employees with Gingrich getting the blame; Clinton could not pay them. Some federal departments shut down entirely. Government services on which millions depended were suspended. Clinton closed down the National Park system. The parks were not essential, but they were extremely popular. Gingrich discovered that, as a political scatback, he was not in Clinton's league. He capitulated. The government reopened. Clinton, written off as a one-term president in 1994, rang in election year 1996 with his approval rating climbing.

1996: A Personal Victory   The Republican presidential candidate in 1996 was a quintessential midwesterner, Senator Robert Dole of Kansas. Dole was presidential caliber. To his credit—historically speaking—he despised the humiliations of late-twentieth-century political campaigns—the eternal toothy beaming and waving to crowds, the rock-star-like public appearances, the pandering after votes, the begging for contributions—all the things that Clinton loved. Worse, Dole was incapable of concealing his disgust with the personality and beauty show that politicking had become. Worse yet, he often responded to questions with a witty, self-deprecating frankness. American voters traded in slogans and insisted on celebrity smiles in their leaders. Wit was grounds for suspicion.

Dole revived a Clinton scandal that had surfaced briefly in 1992. Back in the 1970s, the Clintons had invested borrowed money in a vacation home development in Arkansas called Whitewater. The venture flopped; investors, the Clintons included, lost their money. Then, according to Republicans, Governor Clinton steered state money to Hillary's law firm where it was diverted to banker friends so that they could make up their Whitewater losses. In return, the bankers fed Hillary Clinton information that enabled her to parlay a small personal investment into a windfall profit.

Unfortunately for Dole, there was no solid proof of wrongdoing. Moreover, with the country at the beginning of the dot-com speculation, *how* anyone made money was of little interest.

When Whitewater fizzled as an issue, Dole turned to Clinton's practice of inviting rich Democrats to high-status "sleepovers" at the White House in return for big campaign contributions. That sort of thing was standard Clinton operating procedure but the voters shrugged. With Ross Perot in the running again, taking votes from Dole, Clinton was reelected with less than half the popular vote but easily in the electoral college. It was, however, a personal victory, not a Democratic party victory. The Republicans retained control of Congress and actually added two seats in the Senate.

FOREIGN POLICY IN THE 1990s

Clinton was the first president in fifty years who was not faced with the challenge of the Cold War: avoiding a nuclear showdown with the Soviet Union while exploiting opportunities to improve the geopolitical position of the United States. He did not have to ask "What will the Russians do?" when he was confronted by problems abroad that required attention. He was able to respond to them flexibly and he did. No doubt because he had been a "peacenik" during the 1960s, he was determined to avoid a real war. He always acted in concert with allies and with United Nations approval. He involved the United States in no bloody Vietnams or insoluble Iraqs.

Somalia   Clinton's first test came in Somalia, an impoverished godforsaken land in East Africa. Somalia qualified as a pawn during the Cold War only because its neighbor and traditional enemy was Ethiopia. The Soviets and Americans had taken turns buying Somalia's friendship by pumping money into the country. When the Cold War ended, so did the subsidies. Somalia was plunged into a vicious civil war among clans with a nomadic mentality.

In the capital, Mogadishu, the Somali warlords did not vie for control of the police and the water, electricity, and telephone systems. They destroyed them. The city, never much, was reduced to worse than chaos. Teenage thugs armed with sophisticated left-over Russian and American weapons terrorized the streets. In the countryside, mostly arid scrub suited only to browsing goats, much of the population was starving.

At the urging of humanitarian organizations and the United Nations, Clinton sent 26,000 soldiers and marines in. As a relief mission, the intervention was successful. The famine abated and, or so it seemed, Mogadishu was pacified. Then an American Blackhawk helicopter crashed in the city and the crew was literally torn to pieces by the people it was trying to protect. Clinton wanted no more of that. He had to negotiate a truce with the warlords in order to get the soldiers out of the country without further casualties, but he got them out.

Haiti   Haiti was close to a Somali-level chaos and its proximity to the United States gave the country's desperation an urgency that could not be ignored. Extreme poverty—the worst in the Western Hemisphere—no realistic hope of relief, a history of brutal, corrupt dictatorships, and terrorization by both the government and criminal gangs drove thousands of Haitians to flee. They crowded into boats incapable of making a landfall anywhere but, with luck, would stay afloat long enough that the refugees in them would be picked up by U.S. Coast Guard cutters patrolling Haitian waters.

With the massive immigration from Mexico arousing anxiety at home, Clinton could not allow the Haitian exodus to continue. But he was under pressure within the Democratic party by a "Haiti Lobby" that had made a hero of Haiti's deposed president, Jean-Bertrand Aristide and was keen about all humanitarian actions that had no consequences in their backyards, as the free admission of Haitian immigrants would not.

After an unsuccessful attempt to land marines in the Haitian capital of Port-au-Prince in October 1993, Clinton turned to diplomacy. He assembled a blue ribbon team headed by former president Jimmy Carter and General Colin Powell.

They negotiated an agreement with Haiti's military dictators under which the generals who had ousted Aristide would go into exile (with quite enough money to rent pleasant villas) and Aristide would return. In September 1994, the deposed president returned accompanied by 20,000 American troops who launched a program to train an army and constabulary.

The Balkans I: Bosnia   Somalia and Haiti were nations, countries with clear-cut borders and common languages and religions. Bosnia in the Balkans was a multiethnic former province of the Turkish and Austrian empires and Yugoslavia. Its three major ethnic groups—Orthodox Serbs, Catholic Croats, and slavic Muslims—had lived jumbled side by side for centuries, on the face of it a multicultural success story. In fact, the three groups had gotten along only when forced to do so by authoritarian governments. When Yugoslavia disintegrated after 1989, Bosnian Serbs attacked Bosnian Croats and Bosnian Muslims, who also savaged one another. The Croats and Serbs were well armed by independent Croatia and Serbia (officially still known as Yugoslavia). The Muslims, without a foreign patron, suffered most.

Some Americans demanded that Clinton end the slaughter. He hoped that as a European problem, the European Community or the European members of NATO would take the problem off his hands (as they should have). When they dithered, Clinton authorized a campaign of air strikes on Serbian positions. Combined with economic pressure on Yugoslavia, they forced the Serbian troops to withdraw whence the United States and several Western European nations moved in soldiers as peacekeepers—policemen preventing the three ethnic groups from killing one another.

The Balkans II: Kosovo   In 1996, in Kosovo, another Yugoslavian province, the Kosovo Liberation Army (KLA), made up of Albanian Kosovars, attacked the Serbian minority that enjoyed a privileged status. The Yugoslavian government of Slobodan Milosevic sent in troops, and a bitter stalemate ensued with both Serbs and Albanians perpetrating atrocities. Milosevic squandered whatever goodwill the Serbs had by calling for an "ethnic cleansing" of Kosovo, that is, clearing the province of Albanians.

Some 250,000 Albanians fled to neighboring countries, and scenes of their pitiable condition mobilized sympathy for their cause in the United States and Western Europe. The American media grimly reported Serbian atrocities and ignored KLA murders of Serbian Kosovars. In 1999, the United States and NATO intervened on behalf of the Albanians by bombing Serbia proper, including the capital, Belgrade. When a ceasefire was negotiated, 30,000 NATO troops took up positions in Kosovo as peacekeepers. The Clinton administration said that 10,000 Albanian civilians were missing and presumed killed. An international refugee organization on the scene placed the number at something less than 3,000, including Serbs.

"America First" Revived   The most vociferous critic of Clinton's interventions in Bosnia and Kosovo was a brilliant but counterproductively antagonistic television commentator, Pat Buchanan. He was a veteran far-right Republican war horse who, during the Cold War, had been a saber rattler, espousing an aggressive anti-Soviet policy.

With the end of the Cold War, Buchanan became an isolationist of the kind that, through the America First Committee, had tried to keep the United States from joining the British and Soviet Union in the war with Nazi Germany. Like the America Firsters, Buchanan said that Americans should not get involved in conflicts in which national interests were not threatened. That was certainly true in Bosnia and Kosovo (and Somalia) although not in Haiti.

Interestingly, the ultra-right-winger Buchanan took a position that, during the Vietnam era, liberal and radical antiwar protesters had held: The United States should not be the world's policeman. To Buchanan, policing Bosnia and Kosovo was particularly absurd because interethnic homicide was as integral a part of Balkan culture as growing cabbages and cooking lamb stew. Thinking that peace-keepers could end it was as futile as it was foolish.

Buchanan also opposed NAFTA, the North American Fair Trade Area Treaty, as a betrayal of American industrial workers whose jobs would be lost to Mexico.

NAFTA   NAFTA provided for the elimination over fifteen years of all trade barriers among Canada, the United States, and Mexico. Clinton hoped that by creating jobs in Mexico, NAFTA would reduce the huge illegal immigration of Mexicans into the United States.

Maquiladoras (Mexican factories that imported duty-free materials and parts from the United States, assembled them, and shipped back finished products) were constructed all along the Texas border. They hired tens of thousands of Mexicans and paid (by Mexican standards) excellent wages. American corporations built many of the *maquiladoras,* "outsourcing" their manufacturing to them.

But NAFTA had little effect on the illegal immigration. The Mexican states of Nuevo Leon and Coahuila, where the *maquiladoras* were built, enjoyed an unprecedented prosperity but impoverished rural Mexicans living farther south were untouched by the boom. They continued to cross the border surreptitiously in undiminished numbers.

THE END OF THE AFFAIR

Allegations about Clinton's irregular sex life hovered in the background throughout his second term. Gennifer Flowers refused to disappear. She posed nude for *Penthouse* magazine, played in several films, appeared on television shows where she commented derisively on the broadness of Hillary Clinton's behind, and published *Gennifer Flowers: Passion and Betrayal.* She was then replaced in the spotlight by another former Arkansas state employee, Paula Jones, who sued Clinton for sexual harassment, asking personal damages of $850,000.

Pretty Women   Jones claimed that, in 1991, a state trooper had escorted her to then Governor Clinton's hotel room where he propositioned her (without much finesse, in her telling; he exposed himself). Several other women came forward with similar stories; one said that Clinton physically assaulted her, drawing blood by biting her lip.

In 1997, when Clinton's lawyers were unable to postpone the trial until after he had left the presidency, he settled with Jones for $850,000 on the condition she drop the suit. Jones was happy with the money; the Republicans who had financed her case were not.

The Starr Commission (headed by a California lawyer, Kenneth Starr) was created to investigate Whitewater. Finding nothing, it latched on to Monica Lewinsky, whose interactions with the president were juicier than Jones's because they occurred in 1995, when Clinton was president. Lewinsky, a 22-year-old unpaid intern in the White House, had told a friend of ongoing sexual play with the president during off hours. When East Wing aides got wind of the hanky-panky, they fired Lewinsky. She complained to Clinton; he asked a friend, Vernon Jordan, to find her a job outside Washington. The generous salary she was paid for a job for which she had no particular qualifications looked very much like hush money.

Lewinsky was called before the Starr Commission and denied everything. Alas for her, a friend had recorded their phone conversations and given the tapes to Starr. He told Lewinsky that she would be prosecuted for perjury unless she cooperated with the commission. It was not an empty threat and she told all, including the fact that Clinton had instructed her to lie to the committee.

Clinton continued to stonewall. He swore indignantly and under oath that he had had no sexual relationship with "that woman." Starr sprung another trap; he had physical evidence. Lewinsky had set aside a dress stained with the president's semen. Clinton admitted to "inappropriate sexual contact" with Ms. Lewinsky.

A Sorry Bunch   The Starr Report of September 1998 described the Clinton-Lewinsky encounters in lubricious detail. Clinton's supporters denounced it as pornography. Starr, they said, should have listed the dates and circumstances of the alleged encounters—period.

They were right—Starr was a lawyer of the most unsavory kind—but Clinton's defenders were equally cynical. Democratic feminists who had recently run a Republican senator out of office because he kissed women at parties after he had had one drink too many, blamed Clinton's moments of weakness on Paula Jones ("trailer park trash") and Lewinsky ("a conniving slut"). University professors published solemn essays explaining that the president had not perjured himself when he denied having sex with Lewinsky because, to Southern Baptists like the president, sexual play and oral sex (the Lewinsky-Clinton favorites) were not sex in the sense that copulation was. It was not the American Republic's finest hour.

Impeachment   In December 1998, the House of Representatives impeached the president on several counts of perjury and obstruction of justice (Clinton's instructions to Lewinsky to lie to the Starr Commission). He was obviously guilty of the first and probably of the second. The debate in the Senate, the jury in federal impeachment trials, quite properly centered on the question of whether or not Clinton's crimes amounted to the "high crimes and misdemeanors" the Constitution established as grounds for impeachment.

There was never a chance Clinton would be convicted and removed from office. The Republicans had made the distasteful but hardly momentous business a partisan

one when he had a script. If he had to improvise, he often made a fool of himself. "One of the great things about books," he told a group of high school students, "is sometimes there are some fantastic pictures," and on another occasion, "it isn't pollution that's harming the environment, it's the impurities in our air and water." But his political handlers were usually able to keep him on script.

| Another Disputed Election | The election was closer than close. Gore won 500,000 more votes than Bush. However, with Florida's returns uncertain, he fell three votes short of a majority in the electoral college. It was close to a repeat of the famous disputed election of 1876. |

Florida's returns were a mess. Some counties counted absentee ballots that had arrived after the legal deadline. The voting machines in others misfunctioned. In Palm Beach County, which used punch-out ballots, there were disagreements as to whether ballots to which the "chads" (the tiny rectangular punch-outs) were clinging should be disqualified. In another county, poll watchers differed (according to their party) over whether a sloppy erasure should be considered valid erasure. In a heavily Jewish district where Gore won by a landslide, an unlikely 3,000 votes for Reform party candidate Pat Buchanan, widely accused of anti-Semitism, were recorded.

The dispute took a month to resolve. With Bush slightly ahead in the count, Democrats demanded a hand recount, which the Florida Supreme Court ordered. It was just underway when the Republicans asked the Supreme Court to stop it. On December 9, seven weeks before inauguration day, the Supreme Court said that the recount was unconstitutional, halted it, and gave Florida's electoral votes and the presidency to Bush.

| 9/11 | For nine months, the new president was regarded as not quite legitimate, much as Rutherford B. Hayes had been |

disdained in 1877. There was evidence his handlers were uneasy. They sent him to elementary schools and on other trivial assignments while Vice President Dick Cheney made a number of statements that were properly the president's job. Then, on September 11, 2001, Muslim fanatics simultaneously hijacked four airliners. They flew one into the Pentagon and two into the twin towers of New York's World Trade Center, bringing both to the ground. The fourth plane, probably intended for the White House, crashed in rural Pennsylvania when several passengers, having learned via cell phone that they were already dead men, heroically stormed the cockpit and foiled the terrorists, saving perhaps thousands of lives.

In New York, almost 3,000 were killed, including firemen and policemen who had rushed into the buildings within minutes of the first bombing. For months, dazed Americans watched retelecasts of the collapsing skyscrapers, the search for bodies in the rubble, and the funerals of dead policemen and firemen.

The perpetrators of the atrocity were members of Al Qaeda, a fanatical Islamic organization headed by a Saudi millionaire, Osama bin Laden. In 1998, he had proclaimed that "to kill the Americans and their allies ... is an individual duty for every Muslim ... in accordance with the words of Almighty Allah." After Al Qaeda bombed two American embassies in East Africa, President Clinton had ordered air strikes on what was believed to be Al Qaeda headquarters in Afghanistan.

911, the telephone number Americans dial in emergencies, took on an ominous new significance on September 11, 2001, when Muslim terrorists in hijacked jetliners leveled both of the 110-story towers of New York's World Trade Center, damaged the Pentagon, and would have destroyed the White House or Capitol if passengers on a fourth commandeered plane had not forced the aircraft down in rural Pennsylvania. The atrocity won the world's sympathy for the United States, which President Bush squandered when he invaded Iraq, falsely claiming the Iraqi dictator possessed weapons of mass destruction intended for use by terrorists.

Sean Adair/Reuters/CORBIS

Inexplicable Inaction In transitional meetings with the Clinton administration and after Bush's inauguration, intelligence officers informed the new president that Al Qaeda was capable of and apparently planning a major attack within the United States. That was the sort of thing that wafted over Bush's head. The reports were ignored.

Administration officials shrugged off reports from pilot training schools that young Arab men had paid them cash to learn how to control an airliner in flight but were uninterested in learning how to take off and land, pretty obvious stuff. The FBI failed to examine the personal computer of a suspected terrorist who was in custody.

In Florida, when an antagonistic young Arab man applied to the Agriculture Department for a grant so that he could train as a crop duster, the official who interviewed him did not report it despite the fact that crop dusting had long been red-flagged because it was a superb way to create epidemics of fatal diseases in builtup areas.

Afghanistan Although Bush was giving a talk when the news of the bombing was brought to him, he said nothing until he had rushed off to consult with advisors. Once coached, however, he performed admirably. His statements were eloquent, dignified, and restrained. Politically, the tragedy was his salvation. His "approval rating" soared as the nation united behind him.

For almost the last time, his diplomatic initiatives were skillful, measured, and productive. Diplomats quickly secured the cooperation of Afghanistan's neighbors (Iran excepted) for an invasion, allies' agreement to participate in the attack, and the tacit approval of Russia and China.

The United States rushed military aid to the Northern Alliance, the only military opposition to Afghanistan's Taliban, which sheltered Al Qaeda. Within a month, allied troops—mostly Americans—destroyed or defeated every large concentration of Taliban and Al Qaeda military. The remnants, including Osama bin Laden, escaped into the rugged Hindu Kush on the Pakistan border. It would be slow going, military analysts said, but given time and Pakistan's cooperation, they could be rooted out and finished off.

The Northern Alliance was ready to go. However, Pakistan's military rulers cooperated only enough to keep American dollars flowing in. Islamic fundamentalists were a powerful force in Pakistan too; even the army was shot through with Taliban and Al Qaeda sympathizers.

And Bush's chief foreign policy advisors, Vice President Cheney, Secretary of Defense Donald Rumsfeld, and Rumsfeld's top aides, Paul Wolfowitz and Richard Perle, had other plans for the bulk of American armed forces.

War on Terror   Bush proclaimed a "war on terror." Hundreds of suspected Islamic terrorists were rounded up in the United States, Europe, and elsewhere. Those thought to be leaders were imprisoned at Guantanamo Bay in Cuba so they could be questioned without the legal snarls their lawyers could create in American courts. Several very big fish were held secretly in third world countries where there were even fewer restraints.

The country faced an agonizing dilemma, how to respect its libertarian and humanitarian principles while at war with terrorists who were restrained by no such principles and capable, just twenty of them, of atrocities like 9/11. Alan Dershowitz, a respected Harvard Law School professor illustrated the profound difficulty of the problem with a hypothetical but eminently possible situation:

> The government knows for certain that an Al Qaeda-sponsored catastrophe is in the offing within a week, but, it has no specifics. It has in custody an Al Qaeda who, the government knows, is privy to the details of the imminent attack. Are the authorities justified, in subjecting their prisoner to the cruelest of tortures in order to avert the deaths of thousands of innocent people?

The Constitution said no. Had a national referendum been held on Dershowitz's hypothetical question, it is safe to say that a large majority of Americans would have voted yes.

Obsession   Bits of inconclusive evidence indicate that some of Bush's advisors were contemplating a war on Iraq before 9/11. Cheney and Rumsfeld had been high officials under Bush's father and had been astonished—angered—when Iraqi dictator Saddam Hussein survived the crushing defeat that was inflicted on his army.

Paul Wolfowitz and Richard Perle were neoconservatives, one time liberals and socialists who had first moved to the right because of their disgust with the moral relativism liberals embraced during the 1970s. Internationally, neoconservatives believed in American empire. As the sole surviving superpower, they said, the United States should use its might, or the threat of it, to force small, troublemaking countries to cooperate in maintaining order. Saddam Hussein obsessed them because he had survived 1991 when Bush the elder had halted the American army before it completely destroyed the Iraq army. If the American imperium was to be credible, the error of 1991 had to be corrected. Saddam Hussein had to be eliminated and Iraq remade into a prosperous democracy and rock of stability in the Middle East.

WMD   The "War on Terror" was Bush's first pretext for calling for an international invasion of Iraq but it was flimsy. Saddam Hussein had no connection with Al Qaeda. Indeed, they were hostile to one another. Saddam's Iraq was a secular state; Osama bin Laden was a religious fanatic. In Iraq, the only fundamentalists were Shi'ite Muslims whom Saddam persecuted. Osama bin Laden, a Sunni Muslim, despised Shi'ites as intensely as he despised Christians.

President Bush ignored these and other obvious facts, if he was capable of comprehending them. He insisted that Saddam Hussein was in league with Al Qaeda. And with no evidence, he said that Saddam possessed WMD, "weapons of mass destruction": chemical, biological, and possibly nuclear weapons far more threatening than high-jacked airliners.

In time, historians may be able to say if Bush, Cheney, and Rumsfeld simply lied about Iraq's WMD or if they were misinformed. To date, the evidence is inconclusive. It is known that military intelligence told the president that Saddam almost certainly did not have WMD. But an anti-Saddam Iraqi whom the administration looked on as a likely successor to Saddam insisted that the WMD were there.

When the CIA waffled on the question, Bush sent the agency's director, George Tenet, back to his office to rewrite his report so that it justified the administration's position. Bush also dismissed out of hand the provisional findings of a UN inspection team in Iraq that it could find no evidence of chemical, germ, and nuclear weapons or even evidence of development programs.

Probably, the Bush people confidently believed that the WMD were there. When the invasion force found them, the war would be justified.

Painted in a Corner   Great Britain backed Bush. France and Germany declined to participate because of the lack of evidence that Iraq was responsible for terrorism in the West. In addition to Britain and Australia, Bush's "Coalition of the Willing" consisted of small nations dependent on American aid. They contributed only token behind-the-lines units. (Iceland sent one major, a noncombatant woman.)

On March 19, 2003, the coalition invaded. As in 1991, the conventional war was over quickly. In Baghdad, television cameramen got the footage they believed would be history's symbol of the war, a crowd pulling down a statue of Saddam. President Bush helicoptered theatrically to an aircraft carrier where he proclaimed the end of the war to assembled soldiers and sailors and television cameras.

The war had only begun. Saddam loyalists, well prepared, launched mortar and rocket attacks on American positions and truck convoys. Soldiers and foreign civilians were kidnapped; several were beheaded on videotape that was distributed free of charge to TV channels worldwide. Prominent Iraqis who cooperated with the Americans were assassinated.

After the army scoured the country for months, Bush announced that there were no WMD after all. Nevertheless, the ongoing war was justified because a monstrous dictator had been removed. But what the United States had in his place was a country in anarchy with a breakaway Kurdish state in the north, a civil war between Shi'ites and Sunnis on the verge of erupting, and Al Qaeda suicide terrorists—for Al Qaeda sent hundreds of its agents into the country, blowing themselves up amid crowds of Shi'ites in marketplaces.

A President Repudiated
The disaster was not far enough along in 2004 to affect Bush's chances for reelection. His opponent, Senator John Kerry of Massachusetts, was a strong candidate. He was a Vietnam veteran who, while Bush was pulling strings to stay out of the fighting, earned two Purple Hearts and a Silver Star in combat. When Kerry left the navy in 1970, he became an articulate spokesman for Vietnam Veterans Against the War. He was so effective that an enraged President Nixon added his name to his "enemies list."

With the clever Karl Rove again in charge of Republican strategy, the party smeared Kerry where, because of Bush's draft dodging, he seemed to be strongest, his military service. Financed by wealthy Republicans, a group called the "Swift Boat Veterans for Truth"—Kerry had commanded a "swift boat," a shallow-draft patrol boat, on Vietnamese rivers—waged a saturation campaign claiming that Kerry had been a coward in Vietnam. Kerry probably erred when he refused to dignify the smear by addressing it. The Republicans depicted his silence as confirmation of their charges. Bush actually improved on his 2000 victory, winning 51.2 percent of the popular vote.

On the Homefront
Clinton's currying of big business was always done quietly. Bush reveled in his Reaganism while his spending wiped out the Clinton surpluses even before the invasion. The national debt resumed its annual increase. He raised farm subsidies. (Nevertheless, food costs increased sharply during his presidency.) In 2008, during a serious economic downturn, Bush's response was, despite the deficit, an Oprah Winfrey-type giveaway: He mailed tax refunds to every taxpayer. When, in 2008, a catastrophe in mortgage finance threatened to bring the entire financial down, Bush sponsored a bailout that doubled the national debt in one stroke—to patch up a crisis his own policies had encouraged.

On environmental issues, Bush made Clinton look like a Sierra Clubber. He increased logging in National Forests that had not yet recovered from the "cut and run" Reagan days. He withdrew the United States from the Kyoto Global Warming Treaty and eased pollution controls on industry. He scrapped limits on dumping coal mining wastes into streams, and rejected automobile fuel efficiency standards recommended by his own study group. When the price of gasoline soared to $4 a gallon in 2008, his response was to call for a resumption of offshore drilling that had long been prohibited. He reduced the fines the Environmental Protection Agency was authorized to impose by 60 percent.

None of these policies dented his approval rating. However, his reelection in 2004 was his last hurrah. The Iraq war ground on with no indications it could be ended. Bush's repetitive cheerleading wore thin with all but right-wing Republicans. Doubts of his competence and honesty increased. In August 2005, Hurricane Katrina, which had been heading directly at New Orleans for a week, smashed into and devastated the city. The Bush administration had made no preparations. Afterward, federal indifference to the destruction and mass misery caused by the storm aroused widespread anger.

In 2006, the Democrats regained control of Congress for the first time in ten years. In 2008, the president's approval rating dropped to 25 percent, lower than any president's since pollsters had been surveying approval.

THE LONGEST CAMPAIGN

In the spring of 2006, with almost three years of Bush's presidency remaining, one Republican and one Democrat announced that they were candidates to succeed him. By summer, still two years before the nominating conventions, half a dozen more would-bes were campaigning for delegates, delivering speeches, shaking hands, squeezing into booths in cafés to chat with yawning farmers in baseball caps advertising machinery.

By January 2007—a full year before the Iowa caucuses and the New Hampshire primary—nine Democrats and fifteen Republicans were running for president.

Politics as a Show The endless election campaign is uniquely American. No other democratic nation tolerates anything like it. Candidates for seats in Britain's House of Commons (which chooses the prime minister) have eighteen days to win over voters. Canada allows thirty-six days. In France, where the president is elected in a national election as in the United States, the vote is held no more than thirty-five days after the presidency is vacated.

Effectively perpetual electioneering is an unintended consequence of the primary as the means by which the parties choose their candidates. When the two parties chose their nominees at conventions in July or August of election years, all the prenomination politicking was carried out by party bigwigs behind closed doors. Hustling the popular vote began in September. An election was a two-month affair.

Early in the twentieth century, progressives introduced the primary in order to take the nominating process out of the hands of party bosses and give it to the people. Primaries did that but, in states that adopted the reform, they also extended the political huckstering and hoopla season from two months to ten.

Until the 1950s, only about a dozen states held primary elections. Except for Oregonians, Wisconsinites and a few others, primary elections did not intrude on people's lives. Then, in 1952, the New Hampshire primary attracted national attention when surprise winners became major contenders overnight. If the primary election in one small state could sway national parties, would-be presidential candidates could not afford to ignore it. They began to campaign in the state months before election year—and newspaper reporters followed them.

New Hampshire boosters were delighted with the attention (and the dollars that campaigners and journalists were spending in the state). A law was enacted to provide that whenever another state scheduled its primary earlier than New Hampshire's the New Hampshire primary was to be automatically rescheduled for one week earlier. The opening of the primary season crept forward from March of election years to January; the presidential election was extended by two months.

Television's Big Year
The nation's apparently insatiable appetite for political news helped ensure that every state adopted the primary or a caucus system. Thanks to television, they became "media events." Would-be nominees began to campaign widely earlier and earlier.

The costs of politicking soared. Facing long campaigns, candidates hired high-salaried election strategists, squadrons of advance men, producers of slick television ads, and paid for time on TV channels for more than a year. Campaigns spent a fortune in plane fares alone as their operatives flew from "key state" to "key state" as ward heelers had once rushed from polling place to polling place by trolley car. Dollars were as important as votes, more important early on. In January 2007, a year before New Hampshire, TV commentators were ranking the contenders' chances according to how much money they had raised.

The television networks and cable news channels "hyped" the elections as if they were sporting events: "Super Tuesday" was an unembarrassed derivative of the National Football League's "Super Bowl." Between December 2007 and June 2008, it was an unusual evening news program that did not devote up to half its time to videotapes of the major candidates beaming and shaking hands that day. Americans loved it. Late-night talk show hosts and even satirists like Jon Stewart and Stephen Colbert (of the "Comedy Channel"!) competed to have candidates as guests.

McCain and Obama
In 2000, John McCain lost the Republican nomination to George W. Bush because he ran as the candidate of the party's moderates while Bush's handlers sewed up the religious right and undercut McCain with sometimes dirty and dishonest smears. During Bush's presidency, McCain firmed up his image as a middle-of-the roader who appealed to Democrats; John Kerry tried to get him to run for vice president as a Democratic in 2004.

In the 2008 primaries, the Republican right was less a threat to McCain because it was split between two men, former governors Mitt Romney of Massachusetts and Mike Huckabee (himself a fundamentalist minister) of Arkansas. Moreover, McCain supported Bush's war in Iraq with more enthusiasm than any of his rivals, winning some administration support. By March, McCain had sewed up the nomination.

Democratic voters, in the meantime, had passed over several experienced and accomplished candidates and split down the middle between two inexperienced

Republican John McCain debates Democrat Barack Obama during the 2008 presidential campaign. Obama was by far the most articulate and effective debater. McCain had reversed his stand on too many issues to be persuasive.

Jim Bourg/AP Photo

"symbolic leaders," the one term senator from New York Hillary Clinton of New York and Barack Obama who had just been elected to the senate two years earlier. Neither had a record of achievement, but Clinton's sex excited many voters while Obama was an African American. (Indeed, his father was a Kenyan.)

Both were articulate speakers and debaters. Dividing primary victories from the start, both were careful not to take strong stands on any issue that might scare away voters leaning in their direction. For half a year they repeated their slogans, "Change" in the case of Obama, "Experience" for Clinton. The strategy of both was to wait for the novelty hungry media to come up with something that reflected poorly on their opponent. Clinton did not have to say anything when the pastor of Obama's church was videotaped in an anti-white, unpatriotic rant. Television compensated Obama for that with tape of Clinton, who had lived a life of privilege (which showed) pretending to be one of the boys, lifting a beer in a greasy glass at a gritty blue-collar bar in Pennsylvania.

The two split the primaries, with Obama unbeatable in southern states with large black populations and Clinton—perhaps demonstrating that "brewski" was not so bad an idea after all—winning states with a large white working-class vote. Because she won most of the larger states, she would have been nominated if, as had been traditional, the winner of a primary was awarded all of the state's delegates. However, in another well-meaning reform with unintended consequences, the Democratic party apportioned delegates from each state according to the percentage of voters each candidate won. When Clinton won the Pennsylvania primary, she was awarded 85 delegates to Obama's 73, a net gain on Obama of only twelve. Had Pennsylvania's primary been winner-take-all, Clinton would have gained on 158 delegates while Obama won none. The Democrats' proportional system guaranteed that the 2008 primary campaign (that began in 2006) and every future campaign in which there were at least two strong candidates, would drag on and on and on.

The State of the Union

Obama won the nomination in June 2008. He and McCain immediately commenced the general campaign. There was no breather.

Obama led in the polls from the start. By naming Senator Joseph Biden of Delaware to be his running mate, a long-time Democratic leader in both domestic and foreign policy, he undercut McCain's claim that his administration would be unprepared to grapple with difficult national issues. In his campaigning, he continued to cleave to the middle of the high road, the path that had won him the Democratic nomination. He stuck with his slogans and refused to respond in kind to McCain's unsavory and sometimes dishonest attacks during their televised debates. He held his ground as the dignified, responsible candidate.

McCain was unable to reclaim his former political base among middle-of-the-road Republicans (and Democrats). He had thrown away his maverick reputation by his all-out support for the Iraq war. The media cut him no slack in what seemed to be his numerous misrepresentations. He made a surprise play for American's weakness for novelty by picking a political unknown as his running mate. Sarah Palin, recently elected governor of Alaska, was attractive and "perky" in the manner of the morning talk show hostess and the press and the polls showed a flurry of interest in her.

But the favorable reaction evaporated quickly and Palin won over few undecided voters. She was a fundamentalist active in several right-wing groups, including the unpopular gun lobby. McCain already had their votes. Worse, interviews with Palin exposed her as shockingly ignorant of foreign and domestic issues beyond her own narrow interests. The idea that McCain might die in office, putting her into the White House, ended any chance the Republicans had of squeezing out another narrow victory. Obama won a comfortable victory with 52 percent of the popular vote.

The state of the Union he inherited in January 2009 was far from robust. The Iraq war seemed to be as mucky a morass as ever, inescapable without arousing to passionate anger a substantial part of the population. The financial collapse that President Bush had shrugged off with a smile and thumbs up seemed to be approaching free-fall. An epidemic of mortgage foreclosures was displacing from their homes not only imprudent working-class borrowers but well-heeled households that had been considered upper middle class. A treasury already bled dry from thirty years of irresponsible fiscal policies was being hit almost weekly by pleas for bailouts by irresponsibly managed financial firms and industries. Economists nervously feared a spiral of factory closures and rising unemployment such as in the Great Depression.

Pundits hoping to put a bright face on Obama's inauguration depicted him as a Franklin D. Roosevelt. He was popular and had a comfortable Democratic majority in Congress. But 2009's "Old Order" Republicans were not nearly so demoralized as the Old Order of Calvin Coolidge and Herbert Hoover had been. Nor were there many indications except Obama's natural leadership qualities that he was capable of sponsoring, let alone enacting the far reaching reforms such as those that, in the New Deal, remade the country.

Appendix A

The Declaration of Independence

The Unanimous Declaration of the Thirteen United States of America

When in the Course of human events it becomes necessary for one people to dissolve the political bands which have connected them with another, and to assume among the Powers of the earth, the separate and equal station to which the Laws of Nature and of Nature's God entitle them, a decent respect to the opinions of mankind requires that they should declare the causes which impel them to the separation.

We hold these truths to be self-evident, that all men are created equal, that they are endowed by their Creator with certain unalienable Rights, that among these are Life, Liberty and the pursuit of Happiness. That to secure these rights, Governments are instituted among Men, deriving their just Powers from the consent of the governed. That whenever any Form of Government becomes destructive of these ends, it is the Right of the People to alter or to abolish it, and to institute new Government, laying its foundation on such principles and organizing its Powers in such form, as to them shall seem most likely to effect their Safety and Happiness. Prudence, indeed, will dictate that Governments long established should not be changed for light and transient causes; and accordingly all experience hath shewn, that mankind are more disposed to suffer, while evils are sufferable, than to right themselves by abolishing the forms to which they are accustomed. But when a long train of abuses and usurpations, pursuing invariably the same Object evinces a design to reduce them under absolute Despotism, it is their right, it is their duty, to throw off such Government, and to provide new Guards for their future security. Such has been the patient sufferance of these Colonies; and such is now the necessity which constrains them to alter their former Systems of Government. The history of the present King of Great Britain is a history of repeated injuries and usurpations, all having in direct object the establishment of an absolute Tyranny over these States. To prove this, let Facts be submitted to a candid world.

Text is reprinted from the facsimile of the engrossed copy in the National Archives. The original spelling, capitalization, and punctuation have been retained. Paragraphing has been added.

He has refused his Assent to Laws, the most wholesome and necessary for the public good.

He has forbidden his Governors to pass Laws of immediate and pressing importance, unless suspended in their operation till his Assent should be obtained; and when so suspended, he has utterly neglected to attend to them.

He has refused to pass other Laws for the accommodation of large districts of people, unless those people would relinquish the right of Representation in the Legislature, a right inestimable to them and formidable to tyrants only.

He has called together legislative bodies at places unusual, uncomfortable, and distant from the depository of their Public Records, for the sole Purpose of fatiguing them into compliance with his measures.

He has dissolved Representative Houses repeatedly, for opposing with manly firmness his invasions on the rights of the People.

He has refused for a long time, after such dissolutions, to cause others to be elected; whereby the Legislative Powers, incapable of Annihilation, have returned to the People at large for their exercise; the State remaining in the mean time exposed to all the dangers of invasion from without, and convulsions within.

He has endeavoured to prevent the Population of these States; for that purpose obstructing the Laws for Naturalization of Foreigners; refusing to pass others to encourage their migrations hither, and raising the conditions of new Appropriations of Lands.

He has obstructed the Administration of Justice, by refusing his Assent to Laws for establishing Judiciary Powers.

He has made Judges dependent on his Will alone, for the tenure of their offices, and the amount and payment of their salaries.

He has erected a multitude of New Offices, and sent hither swarms of Officers to harass our People, and eat out their substance.

He has kept among us, in times of peace, Standing Armies without the Consent of our legislatures.

He has affected to render the Military independent of and superior to the Civil Power.

He has combined with others to subject us to a jurisdiction foreign to our constitution, and unacknowledged by our laws; giving his Assent to their Acts of pretended Legislation:

For Quartering large bodies of armed troops among us:

For protecting them, by a mock Trial, from Punishment for any Murders which they should commit on the Inhabitants of these States:

For cutting off our Trade with all parts of the world:

For imposing Taxes on us without our Consent:

For depriving us in many cases, of the benefits of Trial by Jury:

For transporting us beyond Seas to be tried for pretended offences:

For abolishing the free System of English Laws in a neighbouring Province, establishing therein an Arbitrary government, and enlarging its Boundaries so as to render it at once an example and fit instrument for introducing the same absolute rule into these Colonies:

For taking away our Charters, abolishing our most valuable Laws, and altering fundamentally the Forms of our Governments:

For suspending our own Legislatures, and declaring themselves invested with Power to legislate for us in all cases whatsoever.

He has abdicated Government here, by declaring us out of his Protection, and waging War against us.

He has plundered our seas, ravaged our Coasts, burnt our towns, and destroyed the lives of our people.

He is at this time transporting large Armies of foreign Mercenaries to compleat the works of death, desolation and tyranny, already begun with circumstances of Cruelty and perfidy scarcely paralleled in the most barbarous ages, and totally unworthy the Head of a civilized nation.

He has constrained our fellow Citizens taken Captive on the high Seas to bear Arms against their Country, to become the executioners of their friends and Brethren, or to fall themselves by their Hands.

He has excited domestic insurrections amongst us, and has endeavoured to bring on the inhabitants of our frontiers, the merciless Indian Savages, whose known rule of warfare, is an undistinguished destruction of all ages, sexes and conditions.

In every stage of these Oppressions We have Petitioned for Redress in the most humble terms: Our repeated Petitions have been answered only by repeated injury. A Prince, whose character is thus marked by every act which may define a Tyrant, is unfit to be the ruler of a free People.

Nor have We been wanting in attentions to our British brethren. We have warned them from time to time of attempts by their legislature to extend an unwarrantable jurisdiction over us. We have reminded them of the circumstances of our emigration and settlement here. We have appealed to their native justice and magnanimity, and we have conjured them by the ties of our common kindred to disavow the usurpations, which, would inevitably interrupt our connections and correspondence. They too have been deaf to the voice of justice and of consanguinity. We must, therefore, acquiesce in the necessity, which denounces our Separation, and hold them, as we hold the rest of mankind, Enemies in War, in Peace Friends.

We, therefore, the Representatives of the United States of America, in General Congress, Assembled, appealing to the Supreme Judge of the world for the rectitude of our intentions, do, in the Name, and by Authority of the good People of these Colonies, solemnly publish and declare, That these United Colonies are, and of Right ought to be Free and Independent States; that they are Absolved from all Allegiance to the British Crown, and that all political connection between them and the State of Great Britain, is and ought to be totally dissolved; and that, as Free and Independent States, they have full Power to levy War, conclude Peace, contract Alliances, establish Commerce, and to do all other Acts and Things which Independent States may of right do. And for the support of this Declaration, with a firm reliance on the protection of divine Providence, we mutually pledge to each other our Lives, our Fortunes and our sacred Honor.

Appendix B

THE CONSTITUTION OF THE UNITED STATES OF AMERICA

We the People of the United States, in Order to form a more perfect Union, establish Justice, insure domestic Tranquility, provide for the common defence, promote the general Welfare, and secure the Blessings of Liberty to ourselves and our Posterity, do ordain and establish this Constitution for the United States of America.

Article I

Section 1 All legislative Powers herein granted shall be vested in a Congress of the United States, which shall consist of a Senate and House of Representatives.

Section 2 The House of Representatives shall be composed of Members chosen every second Year by the People of the several States, and the Electors in each State shall have the Qualifications requisite for Electors of the most numerous Branch of the State Legislature.

No Person shall be a Representative who shall not have attained to the Age of twenty five Years, and been seven Years a Citizen of the United States, and who shall not, when elected, be an Inhabitant of that State in which he shall be chosen.

Representatives and direct Taxes[1] shall be apportioned among the several States which may be included within this Union, according to their respective Numbers, which shall be determined by adding to the whole Number of free Persons, including those bound to Service for a Term of Years, and excluding Indians not taxed, three fifths of all other Persons.[2] The actual Enumeration shall be made within three Years after the first Meeting of the Congress of the United States, and within every subsequent Term of ten Years, in such Manner as they shall by Law direct. The Number of Representatives shall not exceed one for every thirty Thousand, but each State shall have at Least one Representative; and until such enumeration shall be made, the State of New Hampshire shall be entitled to chuse three; Massachusetts eight; Rhode Island and Providence Plantations one; Connecticut five; New York six; New Jersey four; Pennsylvania eight; Delaware one; Maryland six; Virginia ten; North Carolina five; South Carolina five; and Georgia three.

Text is from the engrossed copy in the National Archives. Original spelling, capitalization, and punctuation have been retained.

When vacancies happen in the Representation from any State, the Executive Authority thereof shall issue Writs of Election to fill such Vacancies.

The House of Representatives shall chuse their Speaker and other Officers; and shall have the sole Power of Impeachment.

Section 3   The Senate of the United States shall be composed of two Senators from each State, chosen by the Legislature thereof, for six Years; and each Senator shall have one Vote.[3]

Immediately after they shall be assembled in Consequence of the first Election, they shall be divided as equally as may be into three Classes. The Seats of the Senators of the first Class shall be vacated at the Expiration of the second Year, of the second Class at the Expiration of the fourth Year, and of the third Class at the Expiration of the sixth Year, so that one third may be chosen every second Year; and if Vacancies happen by Resignation, or otherwise, during the Recess of the Legislature of any State, the Executive thereof may make temporary Appointments until the next Meeting of the Legislature, which shall then fill such Vacancies.[4]

No Person shall be a Senator who shall not have attained to the Age of thirty Years, and been nine Years a Citizen of the United States, and who shall not, when elected, be an Inhabitant of that State for which he shall be chosen.

The Vice President of the United States shall be President of the Senate, but shall have no Vote, unless they be equally divided.

The Senate shall chuse their other Officers, and also a President pro tempore, in the Absence of the Vice President, or when he shall exercise the Office of President of the United States.

The Senate shall have the sole Power to try all Impeachments. When sitting for that Purpose, they shall be on Oath or Affirmation. When the President of the United States is tried, the Chief Justice shall preside: And no Person shall be convicted without the Concurrence of two thirds of the Members present.

Judgment in Cases of Impeachment shall not extend further than to removal from Office, and disqualification to hold and enjoy any Office of honor, Trust or Profit under the United States: but the Party convicted shall nevertheless be liable and subject to Indictment, Trial, Judgment and Punishment, according to Law.

Section 4   The Times, Places and Manner of holding Elections for Senators and Representatives, shall be prescribed in each State by the Legislature thereof, but the Congress may at any time by Law make or alter such Regulation, except as to the Places of chusing Senators.

The Congress shall assemble at least once in every Year, and such Meeting shall be on the first Monday in December, unless they shall by Law appoint a different Day.[5]

Section 5   Each House shall be the Judge of the Elections, Returns and Qualifications of its own Members, and a Majority of each shall constitute a Quorum to do Business; but a smaller Number may adjourn from day to day, and may be authorized to compel the Attendance of absent Members, in such Manner, and under such Penalties as each House may provide.

Each House may determine the Rules of its Proceedings, punish its Members for disorderly Behaviour, and, with the Concurrence of two thirds, expel a Member.

Each House shall keep a Journal of its Proceedings, and from time to time publish the same, excepting such Parts as may in their Judgment require Secrecy; and the Yeas and Nays of the Members of either House on any question shall, at the Desire of one fifth of those Present, be entered on the Journal.

Neither House, during the Session of Congress, shall, without the Consent of the other, adjourn for more than three days, nor to any other Place than that in which the two Houses shall be sitting.

Section 6   The Senators and Representatives shall receive a Compensation for their Services, to be ascertained by Law, and paid out of the Treasury of the United States. They shall in all Cases, except Treason, Felony and Breach of the Peace, be privileged from Arrest during their Attendance at the Session of their respective Houses, and in going to and returning from the same; and for any Speech or Debate in either House, they shall not be questioned in any other Place.

No Senator or Representative shall, during the Time for which he was elected, be appointed to any civil Office under the Authority of the United States, which shall have been created, or the Emoluments whereof shall have been encreased during such time; and no Person holding any Office under the United States, shall be a Member of either House during his Continuance in Office.

Section 7   All Bills for raising Revenue shall originate in the House of Representatives; but the Senate may propose or concur with Amendments as on other Bills.

Every Bill which shall have passed the House of Representatives and the Senate shall, before it become a Law, be presented to the President of the United States; If he approve he shall sign it, but if not he shall return it, with his Objections to that House in which it shall have originated, who shall enter the Objections at large on their Journal, and proceed to reconsider it. If after such Reconsideration two thirds of that House shall agree to pass the Bill, it shall be sent, together with the Objections, to the other House, by which it shall likewise be reconsidered, and if approved by two thirds of that House, it shall become a Law. But in all such Cases the Votes of both Houses shall be determined by yeas and Nays, and the Names of the Persons voting for and against the Bill shall be entered on the Journal of each House respectively. If any Bill shall not be returned by the President within ten Days (Sundays excepted) after it shall have been presented to him, the Same shall be a Law, in like Manner as if he had signed it, unless the Congress by their Adjournment prevent its Return, in which Case it shall not be a Law.

Every Order, Resolution, or Vote to which the Concurrence of the Senate and House of Representatives may be necessary (except on a question of Adjournment) shall be presented to the President of the United States; and before the Same shall take Effect, shall be approved by him, or being disapproved by him shall be repassed by two thirds of the Senate and House of Representatives, according to the Rules and Limitations prescribed in the Case of a Bill.

Section 8   The Congress shall have power To lay and collect Taxes, Duties, Imposts and Excises, to pay the Debts and provide for the common Defence and general Welfare of the United States; but all Duties, Imposts and Excises shall be uniform throughout the United States;

To borrow Money on the credit of the United States;

To regulate Commerce with foreign Nations, and among the several States, and with the Indian Tribes;

To establish an uniform Rule of Naturalization, and uniform Laws on the subject of Bankruptcies throughout the United States;

To coin Money, regulate the Value thereof, and of foreign Coin, and fix the Standard of Weights and Measures;

To provide for the Punishment of counterfeiting the Securities and current Coin of the United States;

To establish Post Offices and post Roads;

To promote the Progress of Science and useful Arts, by securing for limited Times to Authors and Inventors the exclusive Right to their respective Writings and Discoveries;

To constitute Tribunals inferior to the supreme Court;

To define and punish Piracies and Felonies committed on the high Seas, and Offences against the Law of Nations;

To declare War, grant Letters of Marque and Reprisal, and make Rules concerning Captures on Land and Water;

To raise and support Armies, but no Appropriation of Money to that Use shall be for a longer Term than two Years;

To provide and maintain a Navy;

To make Rules for the Government and Regulation of the land and naval Forces;

To provide for calling forth the Militia to execute the Laws of the Union, suppress Insurrections and repel Invasions;

To provide for organizing, arming, and disciplining, the Militia, and for governing such Part of them as may be employed in the Service of the United States, reserving to the States respectively, the Appointment of the Officers, and the Authority of training the Militia according to the discipline prescribed by Congress;

To exercise exclusive Legislation in all Cases whatsoever, over such District (not exceeding ten Miles square) as may, by Cession of particular States, and the Acceptance of Congress, become the Seat of the Government of the United States, and to exercise like Authority over all Places purchased by the Consent of the Legislature of the State in which the Same shall be, for the Erection of Forts, Magazines, Arsenals, dock-Yards, and other needful Buildings;—And

To make all Laws which shall be necessary and proper for carrying into Execution the foregoing Powers, and all other Powers vested by this Constitution in the Government of the United States, or in any Department or Officer thereof.

Section 9   The Migration or Importation of such Persons as any of the States now existing shall think proper to admit, shall not be prohibited by the Congress prior to the Year one thousand eight hundred and eight, but a Tax or duty may be imposed on such Importation, not exceeding ten dollars for each Person.

The Privilege of the Writ of Habeas Corpus shall not be suspended, unless when in Cases of Rebellion or Invasion the public Safety may require it.

No Bill of Attainder or ex post facto Law shall be passed.

No Capitation, or other direct, Tax shall be laid, unless in Proportion to the Census or Enumeration herein before directed to be taken.

No Tax or Duty shall be laid on Articles exported from any State.

No Preference shall be given by any Regulation of Commerce or Revenue to the Ports of one State over those of another: nor shall Vessels bound to, or from, one State, be obliged to enter, clear, or pay Duties in another.

No Money shall be drawn from the Treasury, but in Consequence of Appropriations made by Law, and a regular Statement and Account of the Receipts and Expenditures of all public Money shall be published from time to time.

No Title of Nobility shall be granted by the United States: And no Person holding any Office of Profit or Trust under them, shall, without the Consent of the Congress, accept of any present, Emolument, Office, or Title, of any kind whatever, from any King, Prince, or foreign State.

Section 10   No State shall enter into any Treaty, Alliance, or Confederation; grant Letters of Marque and Reprisal; coin Money; emit Bills of Credit; make any Thing but gold and silver Coin a Tender in Payment of Debts; pass any Bill of Attainder, ex post facto Law, or Law impairing the Obligation of Contracts, or grant any Title of Nobility.

No State shall, without the Consent of the Congress, lay any Imposts or Duties on Imports or Exports, except what may be absolutely necessary for executing its inspection Laws: and the net Produce of all Duties and Imposts, laid by any State on Imports or Exports, shall be for the Use of the Treasury of the United States; and all such Laws shall be subject to the Revision and Controul of the Congress.

No State shall, without the Consent of Congress, lay any Duty of Tonnage, keep Troops, or Ships of War in time of Peace, enter into any Agreement or Compact with another State, or with a foreign Power, or engage in War, unless actually invaded, or in such imminent Danger as will not admit of delay.

Article II

Section 1   The executive Power shall be vested in a President of the United States of America. He shall hold his Office during the Term of four Years, and, together with the Vice President, chosen for the same Term, be elected, as follows:

Each State shall appoint, in such Manner as the Legislature thereof may direct, a Number of Electors, equal to the whole Number of Senators and Representatives to which the State may be entitled in the Congress: but no Senator or Representative, or Person holding an Office of Trust or Profit under the United States, shall be appointed an Elector.

The Electors shall meet in their respective States, and vote by Ballot for two Persons, of whom one at least shall not be an Inhabitant of the same State with themselves. And they shall make a List of all the Persons voted for, and of the Number of Votes for each; which List they shall sign and certify, and transmit sealed to the Seat of the Government of the United States, directed to the President of the Senate. The President of the Senate shall, in the Presence of the Senate and

House of Representatives, open all the Certificates, and the Votes shall then be counted. The Person having the greatest Number of Votes shall be the President, if such Number be a Majority of the whole Number of Electors appointed; and if there be more than one who have such Majority, and have an equal Number of Votes, then the House of Representatives shall immediately chuse by Ballot one of them for President; and if no Person have a Majority, then from the five highest on the List the said House shall in like Manner chuse the President. But in chusing the President, the Votes shall be taken by States, the Representation from each State having one Vote; A quorum for this Purpose shall consist of a Member or Members from two thirds of the States, and a Majority of all the States shall be necessary to a Choice. In every Case, after the Choice of the President, the Person having the greatest Number of Votes of the Electors shall be the Vice President. But if there should remain two or more who have equal Votes, the Senate shall chuse from them by Ballot the Vice President.[6]

The Congress may determine the Time of chusing the Electors, and the Day on which they shall give their Votes; which Day shall be the same throughout the United States.

No Person except a natural born Citizen, or a Citizen of the United States, at the time of the Adoption of this Constitution, shall be eligible to the Office of President, neither shall any Person be eligible to that Office who shall not have attained to the Age of thirty five Years, and been fourteen Years a Resident within the United States.

In Case of the Removal of the President from Office, or of his Death, Resignation, or Inability to discharge the Powers and Duties of the said Office, the Same shall devolve on the Vice President, and the Congress may by Law provide for the Case of Removal, Death, Resignation or Inability, both of the President and Vice President, declaring what Officer shall then act as President, and such Officer shall act accordingly, until the Disability be removed, or a President shall be elected.[7]

The President shall, at stated Times, receive for his Services, a Compensation, which shall neither be encreased nor diminished during the Period for which he shall have been elected, and he shall not receive within that Period any other Emolument from the United States, or any of them.

Before he enter on the Execution of his Office, he shall take the following Oath or Affirmation:—"I do solemnly swear (or affirm) that I will faithfully execute the Office of President of the United States, and will to the best of my Ability, preserve, protect and defend the Constitution of the United States."

Section 2   The President shall be Commander in Chief of the Army and Navy of the United States, and of the Militia of the several States, when called into the actual Service of the United States; he may require the Opinion, in writing, of the principal Officer in each of the executive Departments, upon any Subject relating to the Duties of their respective Offices, and he shall have Power to grant Reprieves and Pardons for Offences against the United States, except in Cases of Impeachment.

He shall have Power, by and with the Advice and Consent of the Senate, to make Treaties, provided two thirds of the Senators present concur; and he shall nominate, and by and with the Advice and Consent of the Senate, shall appoint Ambassadors, other public Ministers and Consuls, Judges of the supreme Court, and all other Officers of the United States, whose Appointments are not herein otherwise provided for, and which shall be established by Law; but the Congress may by Law vest the Appointment of such inferior Officers, as they think proper, in the President alone, in the Courts of Law, or in the Heads of Departments.

The President shall have Power to fill up all Vacancies that may happen during the Recess of the Senate, by granting Commissions which shall expire at the End of their next Session.

Section 3 He shall from time to time give the Congress Information of the State of the Union, and recommend to their Consideration such Measures as he shall judge necessary and expedient; he may, on extraordinary Occasions, convene both Houses, or either of them, and in Case of Disagreement between them, with Respect to the Time of Adjournment, he may adjourn them to such Time as he shall think proper; he shall receive Ambassadors and other public Ministers; he shall take Care that the Laws be faithfully executed, and shall Commission all the Officers of the United States.

Section 4 The President, Vice President and all civil Officers of the United States, shall be removed from Office on Impeachment for, and Conviction of, Treason, Bribery, or other high Crimes and Misdemeanors.

Article III

Section 1 The judicial Power of the United States, shall be vested in one supreme Court, and in such inferior Courts as the Congress may from time to time ordain and establish. The Judges, both of the supreme and inferior Courts, shall hold their Offices during good Behaviour, and shall, at stated Times, receive for their Services, a Compensation, which shall not be diminished during their Continuance in Office.

Section 2 The judicial Power shall extend to all Cases, in Law and Equity, arising under this Constitution, the Laws of the United States, and Treaties made, or which shall be made, under their Authority;—to all Cases affecting Ambassadors, other public Ministers and Consuls;—to all Cases of admiralty and maritime Jurisdiction;—to Controversies to which the United States shall be a Party;—to Controversies between two or more States;—between a State and Citizens of another State;[8]—between Citizens of different States,—between Citizens of the same State claiming Lands under Grants of different States, and between a State, or the Citizens thereof, and foreign States, Citizens or Subjects.

In all Cases affecting Ambassadors, other public Ministers and Consuls, and those in which a State shall be Party, the supreme Court shall have original Jurisdiction. In all the other Cases before mentioned, the supreme Court shall have appellate Jurisdiction, both as to Law and Fact, with such Exceptions, and under such Regulations as the Congress shall make.

The Trial of all Crimes, except in Cases of Impeachment, shall be by Jury; and such Trial shall be held in the State where the said Crimes shall have been committed; but when not committed within any State, the Trial shall be at such Place or Places as the Congress may by Law have directed.

Section 3 Treason against the United States, shall consist only in levying War against them, or in adhering to their Enemies, giving them Aid and Comfort. No Person shall be convicted of Treason unless on the Testimony of two Witnesses to the same overt Act, or on Confession in open Court.

The Congress shall have Power to declare the Punishment of Treason, but no Attainder of Treason shall work Corruption of Blood, or Forfeiture except during the Life of the Person attainted.

Article IV

Section 1 Full Faith and Credit shall be given in each State to the public Acts, Records, and judicial Proceedings of every other State. And the Congress may by general Laws prescribe the Manner in which such Acts, Records and Proceedings shall be proved, and the Effect thereof.

Section 2 The Citizens of each State shall be entitled to all Privileges and Immunities of Citizens in the several States.

A Person charged in any State with Treason, Felony, or other Crime, who shall flee from Justice, and be found in another State, shall on Demand of the executive Authority of the State from which he fled, be delivered up, to be removed to the State having Jurisdiction of the Crime.

No Person held to Service or Labour in one State, under the Laws thereof, escaping into another, shall, in Consequence of any Law or Regulation therein, be discharged from such Service or Labour, but shall be delivered up on Claim of the Party to whom such Service or Labour may be due.

Section 3 New States may be admitted by the Congress into this Union; but no new State shall be formed or erected within the Jurisdiction of any other State, nor any State be formed by the Junction of two or more States, or Parts of States, without the Consent of the Legislatures of the States concerned as well as of the Congress.

The Congress shall have Power to dispose of and make all needful Rules and Regulations respecting the Territory or other Property belonging to the United States; and nothing in this Constitution shall be so construed as to Prejudice any Claims of the United States, or of any particular State.

Section 4 The United States shall guarantee to every State in this Union a Republican Form of Government, and shall protect each of them against Invasion; and on Application of the Legislature, or of the Executive (when the Legislature cannot be convened) against domestic Violence.

Article V

The Congress, whenever two thirds of both Houses shall deem it necessary, shall propose Amendments to this Constitution, or, on the Application of the Legislatures of two thirds of the several States, shall call a Convention for proposing Amendments, which, in either Case, shall be valid to all Intents and Purposes, as Part of this Constitution, when ratified by the Legislatures of three fourths of the several States, or by Conventions in three fourths thereof, as the one or the other Mode of Ratification may be proposed by the Congress; Provided that no Amendment which may be made prior to the Year One thousand eight hundred and eight shall in any Manner affect the first and fourth Clauses in the Ninth Section of the first Article; and that no State, without its Consent, shall be deprived of its equal Suffrage in the Senate.

Article VI

All Debts contracted and Engagements entered into, before the Adoption of this Constitution, shall be as valid against the United States under this Constitution, as under the Confederation.

This Constitution, and the Laws of the United States which shall be made in Pursuance thereof; and all Treaties made, or which shall be made, under the Authority of the United States, shall be the supreme Law of the Land; and the Judges in every State shall be bound thereby, any Thing in the Constitution or Laws of any State to the Contrary notwithstanding.

The Senators and Representatives before mentioned, and the Members of the several State Legislatures, and all executive and judicial Officers, both of the United States and of the several States, shall be bound by Oath or Affirmation, to support this Constitution; but no religious Test shall ever be required as a Qualification to any Office or public Trust under the United States.

Article VII

The Ratification of the Conventions of nine States, shall be sufficient for the Establishment of this Constitution between the States so ratifying the Same.

Done in Convention by the Unanimous Consent of the States present the Seventeenth Day of September in the Year of our Lord one thousand seven hundred and Eighty seven and of the Independence of the United States of America the Twelfth. **In witness** whereof We have hereunto subscribed our Names,

Articles in Addition to, and Amendment of, the Constitution of the United States of America, Proposed by Congress, and Ratified by the Legislatures of the Several States, Pursuant to the Fifth Article of the Original Constitution.

Amendment I[9]

Congress shall make no law respecting an establishment of religion, or prohibiting the free exercise there-of; or abridging the freedom of speech, or of the press; or the right of the people peaceably to assemble, and to petition the Government for a redress of grievances.

Amendment II

A well regulated Militia, being necessary to the security of a free State, the right of the people to keep and bear Arms shall not be infringed.

Amendment III

No Soldier shall, in time of peace, be quartered in any house, without the consent of the Owner, nor in time of war, but in a manner to be prescribed by law.

Amendment IV

The right of the people to be secure in their persons, houses, papers, and effects, against unreasonable searches and seizures, shall not be violated, and no Warrants shall issue, but upon probable cause, supported by Oath or affirmation, and particularly describing the place to be searched, and the persons or things to be seized.

Amendment V

No person shall be held to answer for a capital or otherwise infamous crime, unless on a presentment or indictment of a Grand Jury, except in cases arising in the land or naval forces, or in the Militia, when in actual service in time of War or public danger; nor shall any person be subject for the same offence to be twice put in jeopardy of life or limb; nor shall be compelled in any criminal case to be a witness against himself, nor be deprived of life, liberty, or property, without due process of law; nor shall private property be taken for public use, without just compensation.

Amendment VI

In all criminal prosecutions, the accused shall enjoy the right to a speedy and public trial, by an impartial jury of the State and district wherein the crime shall have been committed, which district shall have been previously ascertained by law, and to be informed of the nature and cause of the accusation; to be confronted with the witnesses against him; to have compulsory process for obtaining witnesses in his favor, and to have the Assistance of Counsel for his defence.

Amendment VII

In suits at common law, where the value in controversy shall exceed twenty dollars, the right of trial by jury shall be preserved, and no fact tried by a jury, shall be otherwise reexamined in any Court of the United States, than according to the rules of the common law.

Amendment VIII

Excessive bail shall not be required, nor excessive fines imposed, nor cruel and unusual punishments inflicted.

Amendment IX

The enumeration in the Constitution, of certain rights, shall not be construed to deny or disparage others retained by the people.

Amendment X

The powers not delegated to the United States by the Constitution; nor prohibited by it to the States, are reserved to the States respectively, or to the people.

Amendment XI[10]

The Judicial power of the United States shall not be construed to extend to any suit in law or equity, commenced or prosecuted against one of the United States by Citizens of another State, or by Citizens or Subjects of any Foreign State.

Amendment XII[11]

The Electors shall meet in their respective States and vote by ballot for President and Vice-President, one of whom, at least, shall not be an inhabitant of the same State with themselves; they shall name in their ballots the person voted for as President, and in distinct ballots the person voted for as Vice-President, and they shall make distinct lists of all persons voted for as President, and of all persons voted for as Vice-President, and of the number of votes for each, which lists they shall sign and certify, and transmit sealed to the seat of the government of the United States, directed to the President of the Senate;—The President of the Senate shall, in the presence of the Senate and House of Representatives, open all the certificates and the votes shall then be counted;—The person having the greatest number of votes for President, shall be the President, if such number be a majority of the whole number of Electors appointed; and if no person have such majority, then from the persons having the highest numbers not exceeding three on the list of those voted for as President, the House of Representatives shall choose immediately, by ballot, the President. But in choosing the President, the votes shall be taken by states, the representation from each state having one vote; a quorum for this purpose shall consist of a member or members from two-thirds of the states, and a majority of all the states shall be necessary to a choice. And if the House of Representatives shall not choose a President whenever the right of choice shall devolve upon them, before the fourth day of March next following, then the Vice-President shall act as President, as in the case of the death or other constitutional disability of the President.—The person having the greatest number of votes as Vice-President, shall be the Vice-President, if such number be a majority of the whole number of Electors appointed, and if no person have a majority, then from the two highest numbers on the list, the Senate shall choose the Vice-President; a quorum for the purpose shall consist of two-thirds of the whole number of Senators, and a majority of the whole number shall be necessary to a choice. But no person constitutionally ineligible to the office of President shall be eligible to that of Vice-President of the United States.

Amendment XIII[12]

Section 1 Neither slavery nor involuntary servitude, except as a punishment for crime whereof the party shall have been duly convicted, shall exist within the United States, or any place subject to their jurisdiction.

Section 2 Congress shall have power to enforce this article by appropriate legislation.

Amendment XIV[13]

Section 1 All persons born or naturalized in the United States, and subject to the jurisdiction thereof, are citizens of the United States and of the State wherein they reside. No State shall make or enforce any law which shall abridge the privileges or immunities of citizens of the United States; nor shall any State deprive any person of life, liberty, or property, without due process of law; nor deny to any person within its jurisdiction the equal protection of the laws.

Section 2 Representatives shall be apportioned among the several States according to their respective numbers, counting the whole number of persons in each State, excluding Indians not taxed. But when the right to vote at any election for the choice of electors for President and Vice-President of the United States, Representatives in Congress, the Executive and Judicial officers of a State, or the members of the Legislature thereof, is denied to any of the male inhabitants of such State, being twenty-one years of age, and citizens of the United States, or in any way abridged, except for participation in rebellion, or other crime, the basis of representation therein shall be reduced in the proportion which the number of such male citizens shall bear to the whole number of male citizens twenty-one years of age in such State.

Section 3 No person shall be a Senator or Representative in Congress, or elector of President and Vice-President, or hold any office, civil or military, under the United States, or under any State, who, having previously taken an oath, as a member of Congress, or as an officer of the United States, or as a member of any State legislature, or as an executive or judicial officer of any State, to support the Constitution of the United States, shall have engaged in insurrection or rebellion against the same, or given aid or comfort to the enemies thereof. But Congress may by a vote of two-thirds of each House, remove such disability.

Section 4 The validity of the public debt of the United States, authorized by law, including debts incurred for payment of pensions and bounties for services in suppressing insurrection or rebellion, shall not be questioned. But neither the United States nor any State shall assume or pay any debt or obligation incurred in aid of insurrection or rebellion against the United States, or any claim for the loss or emancipation of any slave; but all such debts, obligations, and claims shall be held illegal and void.

Section 5 The Congress shall have the power to enforce, by appropriate legislation, the provisions of this article.

Amendment XV[14]

Section 1 The right of citizens of the United States to vote shall not be denied or abridged by the United States or by any State on account of race, color, or previous conditions of servitude—

Section 2 The Congress shall have power to enforce this article by appropriate legislation.

Amendment XVI[15]

The Congress shall have power to lay and collect taxes on incomes, from whatever source derived, without apportionment among the several States, and without regard to any census or enumeration.

Amendment XVII[16]

The Senate of the United States shall be composed of two Senators from each State, elected by the people thereof, for six years; and each Senator shall have one vote. The electors in each State shall have the qualifications requisite for electors of the most numerous branch of the State legislatures.

When vacancies happen in the representation of any State in the Senate, the executive authority of such State shall issue writs of election to fill such vacancies: Provided, That the legislature of any State may empower the executive thereof to make temporary appointments until the people fill the vacancies by election as the legislature may direct.

This amendment shall not be so construed as to affect the election or term of any Senator chosen before it becomes valid as part of the Constitution.

Amendment XVIII[17]

Section 1   After one year from the ratification of this article the manufacture, sale, or transportation of intoxicating liquors within, the importation thereof into, or the exportation thereof from the United States and all territory subject to the jurisdiction thereof for beverage purposes is hereby prohibited.

Section 2   The Congress and the several States shall have concurrent power to enforce this article by appropriate legislation.

Section 3   This article shall be inoperative unless it shall have been ratified as an amendment to the Constitution by the legislatures of the several States, as provided in the Constitution, within seven years from the date of the submission hereof to the States by the Congress.

Amendment XIX[18]

The right of citizens of the United States to vote shall not be denied or abridged by the United States or by any State on account of sex.

Congress shall have power to enforce this article by appropriate legislation.

Amendment XX[19]

Section 1   The terms of the President and Vice-President shall end at noon on the 20th day of January, and the terms of Senators and Representatives at noon on the 3rd day of January, of the years in which such terms would have ended if this article had not been ratified; and the terms of their successors shall then begin.

Section 2   The Congress shall assemble at least once in every year, and such meeting shall begin at noon on the 3rd day of January, unless they shall by law appoint a different day.

Section 3   If, at the time fixed for the beginning of the term of the President, the President elect shall have died, the Vice-President elect shall become President. If a President shall not have been chosen before the time fixed for the beginning of his term, or if the President elect shall have failed to qualify, then the Vice-President elect shall act as President until a President shall have qualified; and the Congress may by law provide for the case wherein neither a President elect nor a Vice-President elect shall have qualified, declaring who shall then act as President, or the manner in which one who is to act shall be selected, and such person shall act accordingly until a President or Vice-President shall have qualified.

Section 4   The Congress may by law provide for the case of the death of any of the persons from whom the House of Representatives may choose a President whenever the right of choice shall have devolved upon them, and for the case of the death of any of the persons from whom the Senate may choose a Vice-President whenever the right of choice shall have devolved upon them.

Section 5   Sections 1 and 2 shall take effect on the 15th day of October following the ratification of this article.

Section 6   This article shall be inoperative unless it shall have been ratified as an amendment to the Constitution by the legislatures of three-fourths of the several States within seven years from the date of its submission.

Amendment XXI[20]

Section 1   The eighteenth article of amendment to the Constitution of the United States is hereby repealed.

Section 2   The transportation or importation into any State, Territory, or possession of the United States for delivery or use therein of intoxicating liquors, in violation of the laws thereof, is hereby prohibited.

Section 3   This article shall be inoperative unless it shall have been ratified as an amendment to the Constitution by conventions in the several States, as provided in the Constitution, within seven years from the date of the submission hereof to the States by the Congress.

Amendment XXII[21]

No person shall be elected to the office of the President more than twice, and no person who has held the office of President, or acted as President, for more than two years of a term to which some other person was elected President shall be electesd to the office of the President more than once.

But this Article shall not apply to any person holding the office of President when this Article was proposed by the Congress, and shall not prevent any person who may be holding the office of President, or acting as President, during the term within which this Article becomes operative from holding the office of President or acting as President during the remainder of such term.

Amendment XXIII[22]

Section 1 The District constituting the seat of Government of the United States shall appoint in such manner as the Congress may direct:

A number of electors of President and Vice President equal to the whole number of Senators and Representatives in Congress to which the District would be entitled if it were a State, but in no event more than the least populous State; they shall be in addition to those appointed by the States, but they shall be considered, for the purposes of the election of President and Vice President, to be electors appointed by the State; and they shall meet in the District and perform such duties as provided by the twelfth article of amendment.

Section 2 The Congress shall have power to enforce this article by appropriate legislation.

Amendment XXIV[23]

Section 1 The right of citizens of the United States to vote in any primary or other election for President or Vice President, or for Senator or Representative in Congress, shall not be denied or abridged by the United States or any State by reason of failure to pay any poll tax or other tax.

Section 2 The Congress shall have power to enforce this article by appropriate legislation.

Amendment XXV[24]

Section 1 In case of the removal of the President from office or of his death or resignation, the Vice President shall become President.

Section 2 Whenever there is a vacancy in the office of the Vice President, the President shall nominate a Vice President who shall take office upon confirmation by a majority vote of both Houses of Congress.

Section 3 Whenever the President transmits to the President pro tempore of the Senate and the Speaker of the House of Representatives his written declaration that he is unable to discharge the powers and duties of his office, and until he transmits them a written declaration to the contrary, such powers and duties shall be discharged by the Vice President as Acting President.

Section 4 Whenever the Vice President and a majority of either the principal officers of the executive department or of such other body as Congress may by law provide, transmit to the President pro tempore of the Senate and the Speaker of the House of Representatives their written declaration that the President is unable to discharge the powers and duties of his office, the Vice President shall immediately assume the powers and duties of the office of Acting President.

Thereafter, when the President transmits to the President pro tempore of the Senate and the Speaker of the House of Representatives his written declaration that no inability exists, he shall resume the powers and duties of his office unless the Vice President and a majority of either the principal officers of the executive department or of such other body as Congress may by law provide, transmit within four days to the President pro tempore of the Senate and the Speaker of the House of Representatives their written declaration that the President is unable to discharge the powers and duties of his office. Thereupon Congress shall decide the issue, assembling within forty-eight hours for that purpose if not in session. If the Congress, within twenty-one days after receipt of the latter written declaration, or, if Congress is not in session, within twenty-one days after Congress is required to assemble, determines by two-thirds vote of both Houses that the President is unable to discharge the powers and duties of his office, the Vice President shall continue to discharge the same as Acting President; otherwise, the President shall resume the powers and duties of his office.

Amendment XXVI[25]

Section 1   The right of citizens of the United States, who are eighteen years of age or older, to vote shall not be denied or abridged by the United States or by any State on account of age.

Section 2   The Congress shall have power to enforce this article by appropriate legislation.

Amendment XXVII[26]

No law, varying the compensation for the service of the Senators and Representatives, shall take effect, until an election of Representatives shall have intervened.

NOTES

1. Modified by the Sixteenth Amendment.
2. Replaced by the Fourteenth Amendment.
3. Superseded by the Seventeenth Amendment.
4. Modified by the Seventeenth Amendment.
5. Superseded by the Twentieth Amendment.
6. Superseded by the Twelfth Amendment
7. Modified by the Twenty-fifth Amendment.
8. Modified by the Eleventh Amendment.
9. The first ten amendments were passed by Congress September 25, 1789. They were ratified by three-fourths of the states December 15, 1791.
10. Passed March 4, 1794. Ratified January 23, 1795.
11. Passed December 9, 1803. Ratified June 15, 1804.
12. Passed January 31, 1865. Ratified December 6, 1865.
13. Passed June 13, 1866. Ratified July 9, 1868.

14. Passed February 26, 1869. Ratified February 2, 1870.
15. Passed July 12, 1909. Ratified February 3, 1913.
16. Passed May 13, 1912. Ratified April 8, 1913.
17. Passed December 18, 1917. Ratified January 16, 1919.
18. Passed June 4, 1919. Ratified August 18, 1920.
19. Passed March 2, 1932. Ratified January 23, 1933.
20. Passed February 20, 1933. Ratified December 5, 1933.
21. Passed March 12, 1947. Ratified March 1, 1951.
22. Passed June 16, 1960. Ratified April 3, 1961.
23. Passed August 27, 1962. Ratified January 23, 1964.
24. Passed July 6, 1965. Ratified February 11, 1967.
25. Passed March 23, 1971. Ratified July 5, 1971.
26. Passed September 25, 1789. Ratified May 7, 1992.

Credits

These pages constitute an extension of the copyright page. We have made every effort to trace the ownership of all copyrighted material and to secure permission from copyright holders. In the event of any question arising as to the use of any material, we will be pleased to make the necessary corrections in future printings. Thanks are due to the following authors, publishers, and agents for permission to use the material indicated.

Text Credits

Chapter 47
919: Reprinted by arrangement with The Heirs to the Estate of Martin Luther King Jr., c/o Writer's House as agent for the proprietor New York, NY. Copyright 1963 Dr. Martin Luther King Jr; copyright renewed 1991 Coretta Scott King

Photo Credits

Chapter 24
474: National Archives; 476: Library of Congress, Prints and Photographs Division, Washington, D.C. [LC-BH83-171]; 487: The Granger Collection, New York.

Chapter 25
494: Harcourt Picture Collection; 504: Culver Pictures, Inc.

Chapter 26
513: Images courtesy Special Collections and University Archives, University of Oregon Libraries. #CN312.; 521: Southern Pacific Transportation Company.

Chapter 27
531: Collection of The New-York Historical Society. #50974; 540: Keystone-Mast Collection UCR/California Museum of Photography, UC Riverside.

Chapter 28
550: Culver Pictures, Inc.; 559: The Granger Collection, New York.

Chapter 29
565: Museum of the City of New York; 579: Library of Congress, Prints and Photographs Collection, Washington, D.C. [LC-USZ62-79046].

Chapter 30
584: Library of Congress, Prints and Photographs Division, Washington, D.C. [LC-USZ62-133890]; 595: The Granger Collection, New York.

Chapter 31
600: Bridgeman Art Library; 606: W.A. Raymond/Historical/Corbis; 616: The Kansas State Historical Society, Topeka, Kansas.

Chapter 32
621: Library of Congress; 628: AP Photo/Library of Congress.

Chapter 33
644: Underwood & Underwood, 1902. Reproduced from the Collections of the Library of Congress, Prints and Photographs Division Washington, D.C. [LC-USZ62-10313]; 651, Culver Pictuers, Inc.

Chapter 34
670: Bettmann/CORBIS; 680: The Granger Collection, NewYork.

Chapter 35
685: Library of Congress Prints and Photographs Division Washington, D.C. [LC-USZ62-48772]; 691: Bettmann/CORBIS; 697: Library of Congress Prints and Photographs Division Washington, D.C. [LC-USZ62-83207].

Chapter 36
706: Bettmann/Corbis; 715: Bettmann/Corbis; 719: Library of Congress.

Chapter 37
728: National Archives; 730: National Archives; 742: Brown Brothers.

Chapter 38
748: The Granger Collection, New York; 755: AP Photos; 758: AP Photos.

Chapter 39
764: Brown Brothers; 776: Bettmann/Corbis.

Chapter 40
783: Bettmann/Corbis; 792: Library of Congress, Prints and Photographs Division, Washington, D.C.

Chapter 41
798: AP Photos; 802: Bettmann/Corbis; 811: Bettmann/CORBIS.

Chapter 42
816: Hulton Archive/Getty Images; 826: AP Photos;

Chapter 43
839: Bettmann/CORBIS. 848: Library of Congress, Prints and Photographs Division Washington, D.C. [LC-USZ62-134192].

Chapter 44
852: Margaret Bourke-White/Time & Life Pictures/Getty Images; 858: Frank Cancellare/Bettmann/Corbis.

Chapter 45
880: AP Photos; 886: John Springer Collection/CORBIS.

Chapter 46
892: Bettmann/CORBIS; 896: The Mariners' Museum/CORBIS; 903: Bettmann/Corbis.

Chapter 47
914: Bettmann/CORBIS; 916: Grey Villet/Time & Life Pictures/Getty Images; 923: AP Photo.

Chapter 48
929: Library of Congress, Prints and Photographs Division, Washington, D.C. [LC-U91-242-2]; 938: Bettmann/CORBIS; 942: Gino Beghe, Library of Congress, Prints & Photographs Division, [POS 6 - U.S., no. 1048].

Chapter 49
951: Official White House Photo; 960: Official White House Photo; 964: AP Photo.

Chapter 50
970: AP Photos; 980: DPA/Camera Press London.

Chapter 51
994: HECTOR MATA/AFP/Getty Images; 997: AP Photo/Jessica Kourkounis; 1004: Tom Munnecke/Getty Images.

Chapter 52
1012: AP Photo/Ron Edmonds; 1020: AP Photo/Pablo Martinez Monsivais; 1022: Sean Adair/Reuters/CORBIS; 1028: Jim Bourg/AP Photo.

Index

"Greater fool" principle, 775
Great Northern Railroad, 519, 533, 558
Great Plains, 583–584, 602–609; arid agricultural land of, 602–605, *603;* barbed wire on, 605; bonanza farms and, 607; debt and, 608–609; deep plowing and, 604–605; fleeing to cities from, 608; irrigation methods, 605; life on, 607–608; machines on, 606–607; sod houses on, 604
Great Salt Lake, 582
Great Society, 922, 924, 927–947; anti-war movement and, 941–943; drug culture and, *940–941;* election of 1968 and, 944–947; Hawks vs. Doves in, 939–941; immigration reform and, 992; Johnson's political skill and, 927–930; legislation of, 929–930, 932–934; Nixon and, 950–951; Vietnam and, 934–939
Great White Fleet, 687
Greed, Age of, 1006–1007; medical profession and, 1011
Greeley, Horace: 1872 election and, 489
Greenback Labor party, 508
"Greenbacks," 507
Green Berets, 904
Greenwich Village, 564
Grenada, occupation of, 975
Gruening, Ernest, 937
Guadalcanal, in World War II, 846
Guam, 687
Guantanamo Bay, 688, 1023
Guatemala, coup d'état in, 895–896
Guggenheim mining syndicate, 597
Guiteau, Charles, 503–504
Gulf of Tonkin Resolution, 937; repeal of, 953
Gulf War (1991), 981–984, *982*
Gum Shan Hok (Guests of the Golden Mountain), 559–556
Gunsmoke (TV), 876
Guthrie, Woody, 789, 812

Habeas corpus, Lincoln and, 473
Haig, Douglas, 712
Haight-Ashbury, 943–944
Haiti: American intervention in, 693; Clinton and, 1015–1016; Reagan administration and, 976
Halderman, H. R., 949–950, *951*
Half-Breeds, Republican, 501
Hall, A. Oakley, 569
Hamilton, Charles, 924–925
Hammer v. Dagenhart (1918), 667
Hammett, Dashiell, 786
Hancock, Winfield Scott, 501
Hanna, Mark, 555, 620–621, 623, 625, 636, 640–641, 676
Hansen, Ole, 744
Harding, Warren G.: death of, 762; 1920 election and, 741–742, *742;* presidency of, 759–761
Hare Krishnas, 1000–1001
Harkin, Thomas, 984

Harlan, John Marshall, 630
Harlem, 911, 916
Harper, William Rainey, 660
Harper's, 654
Harriman, Edward H., 532, 677
Harrington, Michael, *The Other America,* 930
Harrison, Benjamin: election of 1892 and, 612; presidency of, 618, 682
Hart, Gary, 974, 978
Harvard University: elective system at, 650; football and, 661
Hawaii: acquisition of, 631; annexation of, 638. *See also* Pearl Harbor
"Hawai'i for the Hawai'ians," 638
Hawley-Smoot Tariff, 782
Hay, John, *634,* 677, 687–688
Haydon, Tom, 943
Hayes, "Lemonade Lucy," 499
Hayes, Rutherford B.: election of 1876 and, 490–491; presidency of, 492, 499, 501, 512, 616
Hay Herran Treaty, 690
Haymarket Square rally, 536–537
Hays, Arthur Garfield, 758–759
Hays, Will, 757
Hays Code, 757
Haywood, William D. "Big Bill," 733, 746
Hazard of New Fortunes, A (Howells), 564
Head Start, 929
Health and fitness, middle class, 655
Health care: bureaucracy, 1011; Clinton administration and, 1011–1013
Health insurance, 1011–1012; Canadian "single payer," 1012
Hearst, William Randolph, 633, *634,* 636, 836
Hellcats, in World War II, 834
Hellman, Lillian, 786
Henry Street Settlement, 567
Hepburn Act (1906), 679
Hickham Field, 828
Hickok, James Butler "Wild Bill," 594, *595,* 596–597
Hicks, Granville, 786
Hidden Persuaders (Packard), 887
Higginson, Thomas Wentworth, 655
High schools, 648–649
Hill, James J., 519, 558, 607, 677
Hillman, Sidney, 811
Hirohito, emperor of Japan, 849, 850, 861
Hiroshima, in World War II, 849
Hiss, Alger, 867–868
"History of the Standard Oil Company" (Tarbell), 669
Hitler, Adolph, 814, 818–820, 842; *Mein Kampf (My Struggle),* 820
Hmong immigrants, 993
Hoar, George F., 493–495, 639
Hobby, Oveta Culp, 892
Ho Chi Minh, 897, 934–937
Hoff, Maxie, 755
Hoffman, Abby, *940–941*

Hollywood: *Birth of a Nation* (film) and, 749–750; Great Depression and, 789–790; Hays Code and, 757; Jewish immigrants and, 756; World War I propaganda and, 734–735
Holmes, Oliver Wendell, Jr., 733–734, 797
Holocaust, 851, *852*
Homelessness in the Great Depression, 780
Home Owners' Loan Corporation, 799
Homestead Act, 601–602, 604
Homestead strike, 551
Honduras, American intervention in, 693
Honecker, Erich, 980
Hoover, Herbert: election of 1928 and, 768; election of 1932 and, 791–794; generosity of, 784; in Harding administration, 760; presidency of, 778, 781, 782–785; World War I and, 825; in World War I government, 725–726
Hoover, J. Edgar, 789, 929
Hoover Dam, 784
"Hoovervilles," 783, *783*
Hopkins, Harry, 799–800
"Horizontal integration," 526–527
Horses: cars drawn by, 577; Plains Indians and, 585; in World War I, 711
Horton, Willie, 979
Hot Rod (magazine), 885
Housing: assembly line, 879–880; fair, 879, 922
Houston, Charles H., 912–913
Howard, O.O., 480, 588
Howe, Edgar Watson, 647
Howells, William Dean, *639; A Hazard of New Fortunes,* 564
"Howl" (Ginsberg), 888
How the Other Half Lives (Riis), 572
Hua Guofeng, 956
Huckabee, Mike, 1027
Huerta, Victoriano, 705–706
Hughes, Charles Evans, 672–673, 716, 761
Hula hoops, 874
Hull, Cordell, 815, 817, 825
Hull House, 567
Humphrey, George, 893–895
Humphrey, Hubert, 859, 912, 930, 944–945, 947
Hungary: collapse of Communism and, 980; 1956 revolt in, 898
Hurricane Katrina, 1026
Hussein, Saddam: Gulf War and, 982; invasion of Iraq and, 1023–1024; invasion of Kuwait by, 981
Hutton, Barbara, *804–805*
Huxley, Aldous, *940–941*

"I" beam girder, 579
Illinois Central Railroad, 600
I Love Lucy (TV), 876
Immigration, late 19th century, 546, 556–562, *557;* assimilation and, 565–566; birth pains of world